On Stage: a history of theatre

On Stage

A HISTORY OF THEATRE

Vera Mowry Roberts

Department of Speech and Theatre

Hunter College of the City University of New York

Harper & Row, publishers

New York, Evanston and London

FOR CHRISTOPHER

who is just beginning to discover

the wonderful world of theatre

While this book was in the making, a scholarly acquaintance of mine expressed a polite interest.

"A book on theatre, eh? Garrick's perhaps?" (Garrick was an eighteenth-century actor and playwright.) "Or is it on arena staging?" He knew that I had been one of a small group which, some years ago, founded Arena Stage in the nation's capital.

"No, the whole thing," I said.

"From the Greeks to Broadway?" He was incredulous.

"From before the Greeks," I replied firmly.

But I was beginning to wonder. Was I about to produce another digest, another condensation—modern shortcuts which I abhor? "Read the play itself; read the whole book," I had always told my students who were given to plot outlines and condensed books. But my misgivings, fortunately, gave way to certainty. It is not reasonable to suppose that even the most devoted of college students would cover, for himself, all the original materials that went into the making of this book.

I am aware that specialists will deplore the necessary brevity of particular treatments, and I am aware that in trying to include all aspects of theatre I may be accused of superficiality in some. But I am convinced that any study of so significant a part of our cultural history must be placed in historical and social perspective if an initial understanding and appreciation is to be gained. The production of a play is not an isolated event. It grows out of the author's orientation to his world and is influenced by his potential audience and its tastes in subject matter and production styles. The author is bound by the theatrical means at his disposal. All of these aspects of theatre must be taken into account.

The plan of this book is the result of several years of study and teaching in the history of theatre. I know this plan will work. It allows for comparisons from period to period; it brings an almost incredible welter of information into comprehensible form. Each chapter considers the place of theatre in the social framework of its age, the producers, actors, and audience; the plays themselves; the location and design of the playhouse; the settings, including lighting and music; the costumes and makeup; and the actors and acting styles of the age. At the end of each chapter is a summary of the unique contributions to theatre in the period thus covered. However, the plan is predicated on the proposition that this presentation is a basic study guide for further exploration. It is assumed that the individual teacher, and the individual student, will find inspiration and the basic materials for additional study in the plays themselves and in other source works. No one can know theatre in any period without knowledge of the plays that were being performed; so appropriate lists are included. Neither can one's knowledge be adequate without some conception of how they were done and what it meant to the people who did them as well as to those who saw them. As a guide to further study, I have appended a play list and bibliography, as well as a suggested guide to further thought and inquiry.

Perhaps more than any other area of specialization, theatre avoids the worst connotations of the term and, by its very nature, takes the student into many areas of human knowledge—literature, art, music, politics, economics, philosophy, science, invention—exploring practically all of man's activities and ideas. The study of theatre can be and ideally *is* the most "liberalizing" of all the liberal arts. Certainly it is a most rewarding field of study for those insatiable people who desire to know "all about everything."

It would be a manifest error to contend that this is all that can be said about the history of theatre. Yet I submit that my experience as both teacher and student, and my fairly extensive labors in many fields of theatrical activity, have convinced me that this is a workable presentation. I trust that those who use the book will likewise find it so.

ACKNOWLEDGMENTS: No one writes of theatre history these days without being greatly indebted to the many scholars who have done significant research in the field, and I hereby make grateful acknowledgment to these many people. In the matter of illustrations, my debt is more specific. Some of the pictures I have used are from those I have collected through the years myself. The others come from sources which are acknowledged in their captions; each has my sincere thanks. For materials which have been hitherto published elsewhere, I am grateful to the following publishers for permission to use them in this book: Harvard University Press (Vitruvius, *The Ten Books of Architecture*, translated by Morris Hicky Freeman, 1914); The University of Chicago Press (Flickinger, *The Greek Theatre and Its Drama*, 1934); Coward-McCann, Inc. (Sayler, *Inside the Moscow Art Theatre*, 1925); David McKay Co., Inc. (Cheney, *The Theatre*, 1935), Edizione Radio Italiana, Torino (Bacchelli and Longhi, *Teatro e immagini del Settecento Italiano*, 1954); Harcourt, Brace & Company (Macgowan and Jones, *Continental Stagecraft*, 1922); The Macmillan Co. (Hotson, *Shakespeare's Wooden O*, copyright 1959 by Leslie Hotson); and Skira International, Switzerland. Finally, I must mention the following persons as having been particularly helpful in the long and arduous task of finding the right illustrations: Helen D. Willard, Harvard Theatre Collection; Richard Leacroft, Leicester, England; Mary Isabel Fry, Henry E. Huntington Library and Art Gallery; Robert Treat Paine, Jr., Boston Museum of Fine Arts; Prof. Dr. Jericke, Goethe-Nationalmuseum, Weimar, Germany; Dr. Vriesen, Theatermuseum, Munich, Germany; Prof. Alois Nagler, Yale University; Messrs. Tangen and Messing, Museum of Modern Art; George Freedley, Curator, Theatre Collection, New York Public Library; George M. Reid, Cleveland Museum of Art; Prof. Glenn Hughes, University of Washington; Prof. Paul Baker, Baylor University; Victor Jackson, New York City; Herbert B. Kennedy, Jr., Stanford University; and Mr. and Mrs. Warner Schreiner, New York City.

VERA MOWRY ROBERTS

New York City
April, 1962

CONTENTS

THE EVER-PRESENT BEGINNINGS

Theatre in human society has been a part of man's community existence since long before recorded history. From the dawn of time to the present moment, dramatic presentations have been concerned with inspiration, education, and entertainment—with the worship and propitiation of the gods, with the initiation and indoctrination of the young, and with thought-provoking or laughter-impelling ideas and situations. There is hardly a facet of man's existence which has not been touched by or absorbed in theatre.

Since its primitive beginnings, theatre has assumed many shapes and forms. People today are inclined to think of theatre in terms of Broadway openings and luxurious productions. But this narrow refinement is the end product of a long and complicated development. Just as all of man's other social institutions can be traced back to primitive beginnings, so too can theatre. Even the very new technique of using psychodrama in the treatment of mental illness is but a highly sophisticated application of one principle of primitive dance-drama. To trace the development of theatre from root to flower can enrich our understanding and appreciation of what is perhaps the oldest art form. It can show us further that even today's theatre permits no narrow definition, but has a breadth of influence and application which is truly astonishing.

Anyone who will observe a child's birth, growth, and development, may see in the process a microcosm of the development of man. He

1

may watch the slow process wherein the mind distinguishes between fact and fantasy, the flowering of imagination and its subsequent discipline, the dawn of social consciousness. If he is particularly interested in theatre, he sees its beginnings in the imitative propensity which is natural to all children, that faculty through which the child learns so much of the world around him. He watches the child assume myriad characters and act out innumerable life situations: the little girl plays mother, schoolteacher, nurse; the little boy plays father, doctor, cowboy. Upon occasion children even play dog, cat, tree, or bullfighter, creating situations and dialogue as the play progresses.

Making the analogy to the race of man, we see the beginnings of theatre in the imitative faculty of primitive man, who used his skill to show his fellow-tribesmen how he made the bow they so much admired, how he overcame the wily bear whose meat they enjoyed, how he obtained the scalp that dangles from his belt.

The theatre historian is fortunate in the uneven development of civilization, for he does not have to depend utterly upon speculation concerning prehistoric man. Within recorded history civilized man has come into contact with primitive man in practically all stages of development and has noted his characteristics and his activities. Human beings in remote areas of the world, who have long been the subject of study by ethnologists and anthropologists, have furnished us with a fairly complete record of the progressive growth of social institutions, including theatre. So we can suppose the steps which led in remote ages to the sudden flowering of the great age of classic Greek theatre, where, we generally contend, Western drama originated.

Necessity, magic, and pleasure

The rudiments of theatre seem to have developed in primitive society for three basic reasons: (1) the need to supplement the spoken language, (2) the need to insure and to increase food supply, and (3) the need to insure victory over human foes. The reasons could hardly be more fundamental. Other motivations for primitive drama were initiation rites and pleasure plays.

What chiefly distinguishes man from his fellow-animals is his power of articulate speech. In the very early eras of communication, however, even this power was not sufficiently developed to transmit from person to person all that was thought or desired. Even today we have observed that among the Arapaho Indians of the Plains and in some of the pygmy tribes of Africa language is in such a low state of development that talk is impossible in the dark, since communication relies so heavily on gesture. No doubt prehistoric man, impelled to

2

1 Navajo medicinal drama and initiation ceremony
In this detail from a Navajo group at The American Museum of Natural
History, a masked man representing a god is exorcising the evil
spirits from a patient. To the right, a boy is being initiated by a goddess
who is whipping him with yucca leaves. Close by stands the masked
figure of the Talking God ready to sprinkle the youth with
cornmeal to signify his holy condition.
(The American Museum of Natural History)

explain or describe or warn his fellow-tribesman, found the language
at his command inadequate and supplemented the spoken word with
appropriate gestures. Thus theatre, that unique combination of word
and action, was born. Today, people who "talk with their hands" are
hearkening back to these early beginnings.

In primitive tribes the chief activity is getting food. Most of the
primitive theatricals, observed and supposed, are dedicated to this
practical purpose. An example is the marathon Buffalo Dance of the
Mandan Indians of North America (figure 2), which may go on for
weeks without stopping until a buffalo herd is sighted. Another example is the Sun Dance of the Plains Indians, which recognized the
importance of sunshine for plant growth (figure 3). The Cherokees,
too, observed a seasonal succession of dance-dramas celebrating the
growth and maturation of corn, their staple food.

3

These ritual dramas were also presented as prelude or postlude to battles with other tribes. Much publicized by the movies and television, the typical firelit war dance has the dual purpose of securing the favor of the gods, and of exciting the warriors to the pitch of enthusiasm which might insure victory in the coming fight. Less publicized is another type of war dance, like that of the Sea Dyaks of Borneo. This dance is a very dramatic and elaborate presentation which enacts not only the motive for the coming battle, but also the departure of the warriors, the ambuscades, the surprise attack, the combat, the victory, the homecoming, the mourning of the dead, and the commemoration of their bravery. Here, indeed, is a complete and unified drama.

From the child's "Cowboy and Indians" to Amos 'n Andy's "Mystic Knights of the Sea" and the Ancient Order of the Scottish Rite, man creates drama. Circumcision, first communion, Bar Mitzvah, initiations of all sorts, have kinship with the various initiation exercises observed in primitive tribes. All imply a death to the old life, birth into a new life, education in its practices, and a pledge to follow them. All are accompanied by ceremonies which often involve special costumes, special settings, ritualized texts, prescribed actions, and sometimes music—in other words, the attributes of the drama. Practically everyone is acquainted with this manifestation of the drama, and to primitive man it was a most important function; by it the boys of the tribe were transformed into men, and the continuity of community life was insured.

But just as children seem often to "play pretend just for fun," so, too, primitive man has been seen to engage in what seem to be purely pleasure plays. The Canoe Dance of the Australian natives seems to be a play of this nature, as does the Baboon Dance of the African Bushmen. And certainly among the Omaha Indians, in whose vocabulary the same word means "to love" and "to dance," the love dances seem to be engaged in for purely pleasurable purposes. It is true, of course, that pleasure plays are in the minority when counted with the plays of purpose, but this fact can be explained by the greater amount of time early man necessarily spent in purposeful activity.

Drama a community activity

In the drama of savage peoples the production was a group effort. Depending upon the type and purpose of the play, the participants were the whole tribe (excepting, usually, the women, who were considered "unclean" and hence unfit to communicate with the gods), the warriors alone, the medicine man alone, a specially designated clan

2 *Buffalo Dance of the Mandan Indians*
Charles Bodmer's painting shows a dance designed to insure
the food supply of a hunting tribe. The dancers wearing buffalo
heads represent the quarry, others the hunters. As in all similar primitive
rituals, the object of the performance is to insure a successful hunt.
(The American Museum of Natural History)

or clans, or various combinations of these. Where women participated, they most frequently supplied the musical accompaniment,
though sometimes they were permitted to be actors (such as the Corn
Maidens in the Great Serpent Play of the Hopi Indians of northern
Arizona), and there is at least one play on record, from Samoa, where
women were the only participants.

Audiences generally included all those members of the tribe who
were not participants in the play, but frequently the audience was
limited to men, and sometimes to a very select group of the initiate.
However the plays were produced, acted, or viewed in primitive
society, they were an integral part of group activity, taken with great
seriousness and sometimes with great enjoyment by every member
of the social group.

Religious origins of dance-drama

Religion has everywhere been the source of the drama, no less with
primitive man than with the ancient Greeks or the medieval mystery

3 Dakota Sun Dance
A painting by Short Bull, Chief of the Ogala Dakota Sioux tribe,
illustrates the circular form maintained in the vegetation ritual
performance depicted. Here the object is to call down the power of the
sun to aid in making the crops grow and insuring the food supply. The
circle in the center represents the windbreak made of fresh green
cottonwood boughs forming a circular enclosure within which the
ceremonies are held. The figures within the circle are represented as
performing the famous torture feature of the sun dance in which
devotees are suspended by cords passing through their skin. The camp
of the assembled people is indicated by the tepees with their
typical tribal decorations. (The American Museum of Natural History)

players. It is not difficult for us to trace what must have happened.
In very early times, when the social group was exceedingly small,
the oldest and wisest of the group was looked upon with great reverence and respect by the other members, for he knew from experience
the best hunting grounds, the deepest water holes, the driest caves.
He was the helper and protector of the family group. When he died,
the family group needed to feel that he was still watching over them
and protecting them. They observed that death meant the cessation
of movement, the passage of something invisible (for the body as
they had known it was still there); therefore, they conceived an idea
of spirit as movement. Everything that moved was given personality
—animals, trees, and plants, though the latter two were moved only
by the wind. Early man reasoned that if spirit was everywhere in the
world about him, then the spirit of his deceased beloved kinsmen
must still be about as well. So arose ancestor worship, universally an
early form of religion. So, too, nature worship began, i.e., the propitiation of the spirits of natural phenomena. Somewhere along the line,

it was conceived that the spirits of men and of animals were interchangeable, and thus arose the whole gamut of totem cults.

Rites to solicit the aid of the great and wise of past times, ceremonies to propitiate natural forces, functions to honor the tribal totem, each developed as the spirit world grew. We have already remarked that war dances were performed, at least partly, to win the favor of the spirits, and the various rain dances and sun dances were aimed to control these natural elements through sympathetic magic. Rainmakers were important members of aboriginal societies. The beating together of stones to simulate thunder, the waving of forked sticks to represent lightning, the scattering of quartz crystals to represent the desired rain—all have appeared in the rain dances to show the spirits what the supplicants desired and needed. The races of men who cherished totems honored the symbol with ceremonies of propitiation so that the totem animal, and hence the tribe, might flourish, or so that, in cases where the totem animal was the main food supply, there might be plentiful numbers to fulfill the tribal needs. Some of the primitive love dances have the actors in animal or bird costume as an inducement to the animal or bird so represented to propagate and flourish.

Rituals sacred and inflexible

In all the early ceremonies, dance, music, and poetry were combined. The performance was generally called a dance even where there was a great deal of speaking. As rituals developed, their form became fixed, and not the slightest variation was permitted from performance to performance. Though there was no written language, the spoken word was sacred, and the plays were passed on from generation to generation by word of mouth. It is generally true that proficiency in these ceremonies became a part of the initiation exercises of all savage peoples.

The materials of the plays came from the daily lives of the people, just as the "let's pretend" games of modern children are derived from their experience. A ceremonial war dance originated in a particular happening at a specific time; then, through repetition, was generalized to symbolize all experience of this type as universally as the tribe could conceive. So meticulous was early man in the observance of a fixed ceremony that the slightest deviation was thought to portend disaster, and the culprit was, at least reportedly, sometimes put to death. It is said that on the island of Gaua in the New Hebrides the old men used to stand by with bows and arrows to shoot at any performer who made a mistake.

4 *War dance of the Apaches*
This drawing by George Catlin shows the Apaches preparing
for a war against the Navajos. It is typical of the round dances
found in all primitive societies. The performers, armed with spear and
shield, encircle the giant spear in the center to transfer its power to
themselves. The audience stands round about on all sides.
Here is one of the earliest forms of arena staging.
(The American Museum of Natural History)

Comic elements introduced

Since their plays were so intimately bound up with significant
matters, savage peoples had a drama which was almost always serious in tone and intent. Comic elements arrived late, but arrive they
did. Animal impersonations are inherently comic, and the slightest
"mugging" tendency on the part of the impersonator would no doubt
provoke laughter in the audience. We shall see that comedy was in-
sinuated into the serious Church drama of the Middle Ages; just so
it must have entered the serious ceremonials of primitive man. The
development of this tendency seems apparent in the burlesques of
more serious hunting rites of some Australian natives, such as the
Rock Wallaby Hunt where the hunter consistently misses his quarry

8

and is roundly abused by his companions. The natives of the Philippines have such a comic play, in which a searcher for honey suffers various indignities that are comic in the extreme. And so it goes. Man laughs, and as he becomes more at ease in his environment—or as he needs to find relief from a harsh environment—he finds things at which to laugh. When the environment fails to provide material, man invents it. In addition, as religious ceremonies begin to lose their deep significance, they tend more and more to metamorphose into the comic. We know what happened to the Feast of Fools in the medieval Church; primitive man no doubt had his own Feast of Fools.

Primitive man was thus both inventive and versatile in the creation of dramatic ceremonies. Transcriptions which have been made of some of the Polynesian songs and the Iroquois chants show a high order of poetic composition, and we can only suppose that the lack of a written language has prevented us in many instances from appreciating much of this creative ability.

Playing areas improvised

It is obvious that with a nomadic tribe of hunters there could be no fixed and designated playhouse or even a playing area. The ceremonials were held wherever the tribe encamped. Often this playing space was no more than an open area in the center of the camp. Sometimes, for special initiation rites, a particular location was arranged outside the camp proper. The Hopi Indians, for instance, had an elaborate arrangement for their drama of the Great Serpent, held during the March moon. They erected six or seven *kivas* (ceremonial chambers), each identically arranged, and in each of which was given the entire drama of six acts, the actors moving from the first to the second, and so on, as they completed each act. This arrangement, of course, called for a company of players for each act.

The Aztecs were the first to be known to have a rudimentary permanent theatre (figure 5), but they could hardly be called primitive. They evidently set up permanent platforms in the town market place, sometimes of wood, sometimes of stone and variously decorated, upon which were presented their dramatic performances. These platforms were always of generous size, and the audience stood around them to watch the shows.

Rudimentary settings developed

Primitive dance-dramas were almost always presented in what we today call arena staging. The oldest form of dance-drama is the round.

In times and places where the entire tribe participated in the performance, the form was that of the round. When only some participated
while some watched, as in the Dakota Sun Dance (figure 3) or the
Apache War Dance (figure 4), the form was still circular. Most often
the center of the circle held either a person or an object—a setting in
other words. A Paleolithic wall painting from Cogul in Spain shows a
group of nine women dancing around the figure of a man. A fire in the
center of the ring, a pit, or a post were customary props. The principle
of these ceremonies was the same everywhere: the participants
aimed to possess the qualities (usually life giving) of the person or
thing encircled. Supposedly, purification comes from fire, the fertility of Mother Earth from the pit, and the strength of growing things
from the post or its equivalent. A living tree, stacks of sugar cane,
bunches of fruit, bags of rice, a stack of spears, even a beribboned
maypole, can be the central object. The dancers who revolve around
the pole may carry flowers, fruit, branches of trees, spears, or colored
ribbons to identify themselves with the object of the dance. Thus,
almost universally, some idea of form and setting was apparent from
the first.

Sometimes these rudimentary settings were complicated and fairly
elaborate. In an initiation ceremony of New Guinea, the Duk-Duk
and his wife first appear from the sea, dancing on a raft, then they
land on the beach, where they continue the ritual. In one of their
hunting dances, the Indians of New Spain choose a large, smooth
stretch of ground for a stage, and erect poles with huge pieces of
bark, usually painted with totemic designs, fastened between them.
At the back and at each side of the stage huge fires serve as footlights.
In a large semicircle in front sit the women, who pound upon rolled
up opossum rugs and beat boomerangs together to form the orchestral accompaniment.

In one of the Australian initiation dramas, a large piece of ground
is cleared and laid out with banks of dirt and brakes of bushes to
form acting areas in which the women dance, the men perform, and
the novices participate. For the rain dance of the Dieri tribe a special
lodge is built which, at the climax of the presentation, is destroyed
by certain of the participants who knock it down with their heads
to signify the piercing of the clouds by rain. In the drama of the
Great Serpent, mentioned above, the Hopis light each *kiva* with a
fire, at which is stationed a prop man who smothers the fire at
appropriate intervals to cause a blackout while the scenes and actors
shift. The prop men also use blocks of clay into which cornstalks are
set and painted drops having circular holes through which are thrust

5 *Aztec temple complex at Tenochtitlan, Mexico*
This is a reconstruction by Ignacio Marquina from descriptions by Spanish
conquerors and remaining Aztec monuments. Its grandeur and
complexity are some indication of the degree of culture achieved by the
Aztecs. The decorated platform in the center of the picture is such
as might have been used for dramatic presentations.
(The American Museum of Natural History)

representations of the serpents which dance by virtue of a behind-
the-scenes operator. In various of the North American Indian ceremonials elaborate sand paintings are employed. These lend an effective picturesque quality to the performances.

Costumes universally in use

Though few of the primitive tribes had special theatres or settings,
none ever lacked costume and makeup. Masks or their equivalent
were universally used. Most interesting of these are the tortoiseshell
masks of the Torres Straits and the immense basketwork headpieces
of the Bismarck Archipelago. But whatever their materials, the masks
almost without exception covered the entire head of the wearer and
sometimes his shoulders and trunk as well. Sometimes the masks are
recognizable abstractions of the animals or birds to be hunted, sometimes they are totemic symbols, and sometimes they seem to be no
more than frightening caricatures. In all cases they function not only

11

6 *Costumed dancers of New Guinea*

These two figures show completely costumed performers in a presentation
representing the creation of the world as seen by the Latmul People,
Sepik River Region, New Guinea. The one on the left represents
the island which is conquered by the one on the right, who represents
the clan ancestor. The island figure is completely disguised by his
costume, while the face, hands, and feet of the ancestor figure are visible;
each, however, is changed by dress or makeup to disguise the
wearer and turn him into the character he represents.
(The American Museum of Natural History)

as a disguise, but also as an aid to the wearer in assuming the identity of the character he is impersonating.

In some hunting dramas, the participants don the heads and skins
of animals, as do the Plains Crees, who entice a buffalo herd by assuming the disguises of a buffalo calf and of a wolf who pretends to
attack the calf. Costume items frequently involve highly decorative
use of feathers, quills, and the teeth and skins of animals. Performers
may wear leg rattles of tortoiseshell, and use various hand props,
such as spears, wands, and—in the Booger Dance of the Cherokees
—a gourd representing a phallus. Body paint is often used; an interesting application of this technique has been observed among the
Australian natives who memorialized their first contacts with white
men in a dramatic play by simulating the appearance of the white
men. They painted their faces a brownish white and their bodies red

7 Primitive masks
The mask on the left, made and worn by the Indians of the Northwest
Coast, is intricately carved and articulated. When fully closed it
represents a fish; with top and bottom flaps open, it becomes a bird; with
all flaps open, it represents a human face. The masks on the right
are worn by men of the Fly River tribes in Papua, who assume
the character of oracles in their initiation ceremony, taboo to women.
Each man makes his own mask of tapa cloth stretched over a frame.
Its height indicates the position of the man wearing it.
(The American Museum of Natural History)

or blue, while they tied rushes onto their legs and covered their
heads with an imitation cabbage-tree hat.

Universally in these primitive dance-dramas, it is important that
the performer lose his own identity and assume that of the character
he is impersonating. Only thus can he project the qualities of his characterization to his audience. He must *be* what he is masked and costumed to represent. He is *possessed* by the spirit of the image. The
Javanese dancer who puts on a horse effigy is fed with stalks of grain;
the ancient Germanic tribesman assumes the spirit of an animal the
moment he dons its skin.

Acting becomes an art

As the social organization of primitive tribes increased in complexity, the performance of ritual dramas ceased to be a function of

13

the whole community and fell to the lot of special clans, a shaman, a medicine man, or a priest. These specialized performers were often highly trained and specially gifted. The Hopi Snake Dance, for instance, was performed by the Snake and Antelope clans, each consisting of ten highly trained men who performed for nine days.

Needless to say, the length of some of these performances made great demands on the actors, since stress was laid on correctness of action, speech, songs, and music. Endurance, if nothing else, was a prime requisite, and sometimes the participants had to undergo actual physical torture as part of the performance. Interestingly enough, among the Areoi of Polynesia and the natives of New Pomerania, groups of actors toured performances to other islands and villages. Such touring companies also existed among the Mayas of Yucatan, although here again, as with the Aztecs, their society could hardly be called primitive.

Summary

The beginnings of drama are everywhere in human activity. Primitive man dramatized, in deadly earnest, his major concerns: his success in his struggle to survive and his relationship to the spirit world. These concerns are still basic to drama, in highly diversified forms, no matter what the state of civilization. In acting out these concerns and thereby attempting to control his environment, primitive man assumed various characters with the help of costume and makeup, chiefly masks; he made use of special effects and settings of some sort; and he made music an almost universal accompaniment.

Comedy also appeared, though sparse and late. Man does not laugh at himself when he lives in fear. But as he becomes more at ease with his environment, he can—and does—laugh, and through laughter he develops an objectivity about himself and his world.

In primitive drama, then, the serious mood predominates, but there are also some elements of comedy. There is also the religious emphasis which was to recur in succeeding periods, the costumes, and the special effects and settings which have almost universally been parts of theatrical production. Without any strain on the imagination, it is possible to find in these primitive beginnings of drama the prototypes of many of the components of today's theatre.

DRAMA IN ANCIENT EGYPT

The oldest civilization that the Western world knows is that of ancient Egypt. Although comparatively little has been discovered of its dramatic activities, certainly Egypt had its influence (though there is but little factual evidence) on the ancient Greeks who were its near neighbors. It is profitable for us to learn what we can of that which passed for drama in the land of the Pharaohs and the pyramids.

Poorly developed theatre

We do not know why some civilizations of an apparently high order do not develop a drama which combines great plays with great productions as the classic Greeks did. The ancient Hebrews, for instance, had no drama to speak of, though certainly dance was a part of their culture; some, however, have seen indications in the Song of Solomon and The Book of Job that these were intended for dramatic presentation. The ancient Peruvians and the Aztecs of Mexico, on the other hand, seem to have had a regular and impressive drama. The Peruvians composed both tragedies and comedies to be played by noblemen and their sons before the court on festival occasions. The tragedies dealt with the splendor of former kings and heroes or commemorated military events of signal importance, while the comedies seem to have had for their subject matter things of domestic import or scenes of everyday life. The texts were evidently in blank

15

8 Egyptian temple
A model of the temple of Queen Hatshepsut, reconstructed as it was
in 1480 B.C. In just such a temple as this it is believed that scenes of the
Abydos Passion Play were presented in ancient Egypt.
(The Metropolitan Museum of Art)

verse. The Aztec scripts, also, seem to have been written in verse,
and comprise comedy as well as tragedy. As we have seen before,
they were usually presented in a special kind of theatre, although
sometimes they were given on the steps or terraces of temples by
actors carefully trained by the priests.

It is true, of course, that prehistoric Egyptians, as did all primitive
people, danced. Among the earliest records of very ancient Egypt
are ones which show dance-dramas similar to those we have discussed. Women dancers accompanying a coffin, as depicted in an Old
Kingdom tomb near Saggara (2500 B.C.), throw their legs high in a
step that might indicate life triumphing over death (figure 9). A wall
painting (1900 B.C.) from the Middle Kingdom shows three dancers
doing a pantomime which is entitled "The Wind." Some Old Kingdom

16

dance figures are adorned with grapevines and swing branches; others are shown with arms bent at the elbow, fingertips on shoulders, in representation of the cow-goddess with her horns. We may suppose, then, that the early development of Egyptian dance-drama followed the same lines as elsewhere.

However, so far as Egyptologists can ascertain, the ancient Egyptians never developed a high order of drama and their only dramatic presentations were connected with religious observance. They were usually accompanied by grand processionals and festivals, and often lasted several days. As in many later periods of the theatre, the presentations were generally seasonal, following the inundation pattern of the Nile as did so many of the institutions of Egyptian life. Some presentations were evidently dependent upon the funeral rites of prominent citizens. At any rate, with one exception, there seem to have been no regulated, repeated performances of given plays such as we are accustomed to in many later periods of theatre.

First recorded drama

The oldest evidences of the drama in Egypt are the fifty-five so-called Pyramid Texts which date back to about 3000 B.C. These were written on the inside walls of tombs, mastabas, and pyramids and dealt with the resurrection of the entombed. They are supposed to be dramas because they incorporate stage directions and indications of characters speaking separate lines. It has been estimated that over a period of time about four thousand such texts were produced. They are presumed to be a development from even more ancient rites celebrating the return of spring as symbolic of the return of life after the winter solstice, a deeply rooted primitive nature rite.

Another type of ancient Egyptian drama was the Coronation Festival Play, which was evidently performed to celebrate the crowning of a new monarch. The earliest of these to be discovered is a Memphite drama of about 3100 B.C., which had the god Ptah as one of its characters and was performed in the capital of the First Dynasty. Another of these plays dates from the Middle Kingdom (about 2000 B.C.) and commemorates the coronation of Senroset I. If a ruler lived long enough to mark the thirtieth anniversary of his coronation, this jubilee occasion was marked by a special drama called a Heb Sed, which seems to have enacted the events of his long reign.

There is also evidence that the priests occasionally presented a Medicinal Drama which celebrated their skill in the administration of medicine; it also memorialized the goddess Isis' cure of her child Horus from the bite of a scorpion by using herbs and magic. It is a

9 *Egyptian tomb painting and papyrus*
Above, from the Acropolis of Memphis at Saggarah, girls performing
acrobatic dances. Right, Funerary papyrus from the tomb of Queen
Meryet-Amun, at Thebes. These two illustrations give some idea of
dance movement, costume, and the use of masks in ancient Egypt.
(Schreiner; The Metropolitan Museum of Art)

pertinent speculation that these Medicinal Dramas were developments from the more primitive dances of the shaman or medicine
man whose ritual was supposed to cure or prevent disease.

The most interesting of these ancient plays is the Abydos Passion
Play, which was evidently celebrated yearly from 2500 B.C. down
to between 569 and 526 B.C. Our most accurate record of it comes
from an actor, I-kher-nefert, who, in 1868 B.C., wrote of his commission to produce the drama at Abydos and to play the leading role.
The production involved a processional pageant, a series of dramatic
scenes, and a triumphant festival. This elaborate production seems to
have moved from place to place, culminating in the Temple of Osiris
at Abydos. It detailed the suffering and death of Osiris, the passion of
his sister-wife Isis, the birth of their son Horus, and the final resurrection of Osiris and his establishment as ruler of the Land of the
Dead. It was essentially a fertility drama concerned with the annual
inundation of the Nile.

18

All of these texts are serious in intent and presentation, and there is no evidence of any comical elements present in any of them. The ancient Egyptians took their drama seriously; they never looked upon it as pure entertainment. It is for this reason, perhaps, that ancient Egyptian drama was held at a comparatively primitive level and its theatre never developed into a separate identifiable institution.

Priesthood controls production

In ancient Egypt there seem to have been no playhouses or specialized playing areas. The Coronation Festival Plays, the Heb Seds, and the Pyramid Texts were played in the mortuary temples which accompanied the tombs of the kings. The Medicinal Dramas and the Passion Plays were done in the temples erected for the worship of the deities. All dramatic activities seem to have been under the direction of the priests, who were very powerful members of society. All presentations were evidently given by daylight. Characters were costumed in accordance with their roles, and where they were impersonating one of the animal-headed deities they wore head masks. Makeup was in an advanced stage of development in ancient Egypt, even for ordinary purposes, so it is reasonable to suppose that makeup was likewise used extensively in the dramatic presentations. Actors were generally recruited from the priesthood, though when large casts were needed, these were supplemented by chosen laymen.

19

Performances, even when dealing with mythological materials, tended to be as realistic as possible, and there is some evidence that in the long Abydos Passion Play, the battle scenes were so realistic as to entail the actual combat and death-in-battle of some of the participants.

Although there is no actual evidence, it is supposed that all performances were in some way accompanied by music, for the ancient Egyptians were very fond of music and had a special deity, Bes, to preside over it.

Summary

Theatre in ancient Egypt, in common with many other institutions and practices of that society, was inextricably bound up with the cult of the dead. The Pyramid Texts bear a relationship to the more primitive cult of ancestor worship; the Medicinal Dramas are extensions of the feats of medicine men and shamans. Even the most truly dramatic presentation, the Abydos Passion Play, might be said to derive from plays of primitive nature worship. Even the most outstanding characteristic of Egyptian drama, the emphasis upon spectacle, derives from the primitive propensity for putting on a good show. But this emphasis upon spectacle also points forward to a continuing characteristic of theatre for many centuries to come.

The elements present in primitive dance-drama and in the drama of ancient Egypt recur again and again in later periods of theatre, most notably in the period of the Greeks—our first acquaintance with real theatre.

THE GOLDEN AGE OF GREECE

It is obvious that the great triumvirate of Greek tragedy—Aeschylus, Sophocles, and Euripides—did not, like Minerva, spring full-armed from the head of Zeus, but were the end products of a long line of development. Several reputable scholars have pointed out that Egyptian culture was greatly admired by the Greeks, among other reasons for its religious development. Even Herodotus, Greek historian living in the fifth century B.C., held that the Greek Dionysus was but a slightly disguised Egyptian Osiris, whose suffering, death, and resurrection made him the symbol of the renewal of life and the yearly round of the seasons. It has been suggested that the acceptance of the Egyptian deity and his "naturalization" into Greek legend brought ceremonies to Greece which, for the first time, can truly be called dramatic.

Festival origins of tragedy and comedy

Dionysus was the god of fertility whose powers applied especially to wine, the wealth of Greece. Four festivals were held throughout the year in his honor. The first of these was the Festival of Vintage, sometimes called the Country or Rural Dionysia; it was held in late December and early January. The second was the Festival of the Winepress, the Lenaea, held in late January and early February. The third was the Festival of Tasting, the Anthesteria, held in late February and early March. The fourth and last was the great

21

10 *Ancient Theatre of Dionysus at Athens*
This model shows the theatre as it was in about 400 B.C. At this time, the
orchestra was a full circle, with the *skene* on the perimeter opposite
the seats. The altar in the center of the orchestra is not apparent in this
model, but the *paradoi, proskenion,* and *episkenion* are
clearly visible. Also apparent is the fact that the arrangement of the
seats was dictated by topography. (The Cleveland Museum of Art,
Collection of the Educational Department)

Festival of Celebration, or the City Dionysia, held in late March and
early April. Greek drama came to flower in this last Festival.

The pattern of the Dionysiac feast is described by Aristophanes
in *The Acharnians;* Aristophanes uses this peasant celebration as
part of a comic action. He tells of a processional, led by the daughter of a peasant as a Canephorus bearing the sacrificial offering, followed by a slave bearing the phallus, symbol of fertility, who in turn
is followed by the master of the house singing the usual spicy phallic
song, while the mistress of the house watches from the rooftop. Here
is the essence of all Dionysiac festivals—sacrifice, symbol, and song.
Festivals involving more than one family were correspondingly elaborated, but these essentials were always present. In the earliest
times the sacrifice was a human one; later a goat, an ox, or a bull,
representative of the god, was substituted. This was a dedicated
offering, without blemish, and the worshippers partook of the un-
cooked flesh to acquire the characteristics of the god. They pretended
the animal was resurrected, sometimes immediately substituting
the animal selected for the next festival's sacrifice, sometimes pre-

tending that the sacrificed animal was actually drawing a plow. (In this latter case the sacrifice tended to be an ox, rather than a goat.) A statue of Dionysus was a part of the procession, or, later, a young man impersonated the god. Designated participants intoned a chant called a dithyramb, detailing the exploits of the god. In the god's honor, some of the participants were dressed as satyrs or goatmen, and some were attired to represent the dead, thus indicating that Dionysus was the lord of life and could resurrect the dead. After the sacrifice, there was dancing, singing, and much drinking of wine.

Aristotle tells us in his *Poetics:*

> Tragedy, indeed, originated from those who led the dithyramb, but comedy from those who sung the Phallic verses, which even now in many cities remain in use; and it gradually increased as obvious improvements became known. And tragedy, having experienced many changes, rested when it had arrived at its proper nature (Sec. 1449a, ll. 10–15, Theodore Buckley translation).

Dithyramb and phallic song were at first extemporaneous, becoming conventional in the course of time. Participants at first were any who cared to join in the celebration, often the whole population of a village. Later, the performers were specialized, just as in the primitive dramas elsewhere. The cithara player, Arion, is credited with regularizing the dithyramb in song and dance. As time went on, its subject matter came to include not only the exploits of Dionysus, but also those of other gods and heroes. Sometime near the middle of the sixth century B.C., a leader of a rural Icarian dithyrambic chorus, Thespis by name, is said to have instituted the revolutionary innovation of separating himself from the chorus by ascending the sacrificial table and posing questions which the chorus answered in song and dance. Thus dialogue was born, and from this early rite dramatic tragedy grew, though the dithyramb, in its purer form, also continued on a separate course. The innovation of dialogue was so popular that it developed despite the adverse criticism of many, including the lawgiver Solon who accused Thespis of telling lies.

Comedy, on the other hand, was the outgrowth of another part of the festival. At the time when specified participants were performing in the processional and sacrificial festivities, it became the custom for the young men about town to dress themselves in special costumes and to participate, quite unofficially, in the rites. The townspeople, who were the spectators, engaged in badinage with these self-appointed performers, and the interchanges developed into a customary part of the celebration. This type of interchange grew from

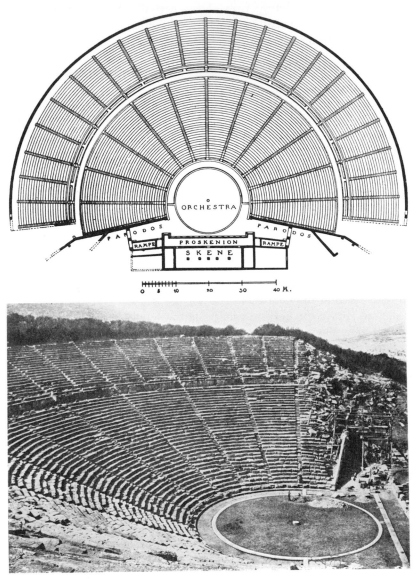

11 *The Greek theatre at Epidaurus*
Above, a plan showing the perfectly symmetrical arrangement of the
seating area, and the full *orchestra* circle of the Classic period (Dörpfeld
and Reich, *Das Greichishe Theater*). Below, the present ruins,
showing the lintel over the passageways which integrated *skene* and
seats, the *orchestra* of hard-packed earth, and the altar in the center
of the *orchestra*. (Theatre Collection, New York Public Library)

24

komos (a revel, or a band of revellers) into comedy, which originally used two choruses instead of the one used in tragedy; tragedy, in turn, is so named from *tragos* (goat) or *tragodia* (goat song), performed to honor the Dionysiac symbol.

The festival contests

In 534 B.C., the tyrant Pisistratus, whom the citizens of Athens had invested with power, brought the actor-director Thespis to Athens and instituted as a part of the City Dionysia the drama contests which remained a part of that celebration throughout the Golden Age of Greece. The plays which Thespis presented won the first prize.

For more than two centuries, the pattern of Attic drama remained fairly constant. Of the four great festivals of Dionysus, three included drama. Only the Anthesteria had no plays. At the Country Dionysia in December and January, both tragedies and comedies were presented. In some cases the works of playwrights who later competed in the great City Dionysia were presented; in other cases these rural celebrations were graced with performances of plays and companies hitherto seen at the larger celebration. At the Lenaea both comedies and tragedies were also presented, but the accent was on comedy; the attendant procession was not splendid but riotous. The Lenaea record for 419 and 418 B.C. at Athens shows that two trilogies of tragedies and five comedies were given. Earlier the comedies had numbered three.

The greatest festival of ancient Greece, the City Dionysia, took place in late March and early April, when Athens was crowded with foreign dignitaries, businessmen, and tourists. It lasted for five or six days, and even prisoners were released so that they might attend. It was the high point of the Attic year, the greatest of all the religious festivals. (It must be remembered that the production of plays in the Greek theatre remained a part of religious observance from first to last.) The festival began on the first day with a procession in which the figure of Dionysus was carried from his temple on the Acropolis to his grove where the sacrifice was offered. At nightfall, a procession returned the figure by torchlight to the theatre which was named in his honor, situated under the Acropolis. There it stood for the succeeding days of the festival. The second day and often the third was taken up with a contest between dithyrambic choruses representing the various Attic tribes. On the third or fourth day the presentation of tragedies began. Three poets participated, each presenting three tragedies and a satyr play. These began at dawn and ended by noon on each of the three days. The afternoons were devoted to

25

12 *Present ruins of the Theatre of Dionysus at Athens*
The present ruins, of course, are of the theatre as it was remodeled by
the Romans during the reign of Nero. The *orchestra* is reduced to a
semicircle, paved, and surrounded by a wall. See figure 13.
(Theatre Collection, New York Public Library)

comedy; sometimes three were given at a festival, sometimes five.
Some scholars have said that the six-day festival was characteristic
of earlier times, with the third day devoted to five comedies and the
last three to the tragedies and satyr plays. The five-day festival, pres-
sured by the economies of the Peloponnesian War (431–404 B.C.),
caused a change in schedule, with three tragedies, a satyr play, and
a comedy being given on each of the last three days. At the end of
the festival prizes were awarded to the best poet in each form—
traditionally a goat for tragedy and a basket of figs and a bottle of
wine for comedy, as well as varying sums of money appropriated by
the state. It was for this theatre that Aeschylus, Sophocles, Euripides,
and Aristophanes wrote.

Poets were permitted to compete as soon as they were citizens, at
age twenty. Aeschylus presented his first play at twenty-five,
Sophocles at twenty-eight, and Euripides at twenty-six. All poets
submitted their plays to a public official (called the *archon*) who
chose the plays to be presented and designated the leading actor for

each. This actor was paid by the state, and in the days when the number of actors in each play rose to three, all three were paid by the state. All other expenses were borne by a citizen (called the *choregus*) who either volunteered or was drafted for the job. This first of all theatrical patrons was usually a wealthy resident who hired and paid the chorus and its leader, as well as any supporting actors necessary, and who bore all costs of production. Great competition arose among these citizen-patrons and it is reported that some of them were led, into bankruptcy as a result of their prodigal spending. Often there were lavish productions which included not only refreshments for the entire audience of seventeen to twenty thousand people, but an extravagant party for the actors as well. As a reward for his participation, a winning patron had a tripod erected in his honor on the avenue leading to the theatre. Rivalry was destroyed about 308 B.C., when the functions of the patrons were designated to a public official known as the judge or *agonothetes*.

Provisions for awarding the prizes were elaborate. To select the judges one name from each of the ten Attic tribes was drawn from ten sealed jars. From the votes of these ten judges, five were drawn from a covered jar to decide the prize. Originally prizes were awarded only to participating poets and patrons, but by 446 B.C. prizes were also awarded to the outstanding tragic actors, and somewhat later to the outstanding comic actors. These prizes were always limited to the principal actor in each trilogy or comic play.

In the early days the playwright was frequently his own chief actor and director, as Aeschylus was. Sophocles is said to have refrained from taking leading male roles because of the lightness of his voice, although he won critical praise for his playing of women's parts, chiefly that of Nausicaa, and he always directed the plays that he had written. Euripides seems to have been content with the role of director and left acting chores to others.

The audience was tremendous, and critical. Since the productions were part of a great religious festival, all the citizens of Athens as well as visitors were in attendance. In the early days admission was free, but when the state began to bear the costs of production as well as the chief actors' salaries, an admission fee was charged. Provision was made, however, for subsidizing admissions for those unable to pay; every citizen of Athens was entitled to his "theoric money." There were no reserved seats except for the priests of Dionysus, who sat in special chairs near the front, and for state guests. Tickets in the form of coins were issued, lead ones for general admission, ivory ones for reserved seats.

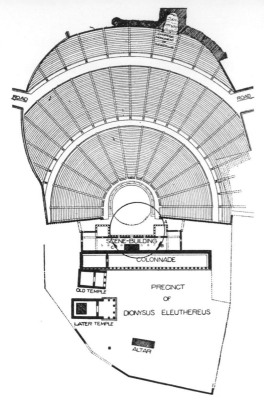

**13 Plan of the Theatre
of Dionysus at Athens**
This is the plan of the theatre as
remodeled by Lycurgus in the
fourth century B.C., when stone
benches were installed for the
audience, and the original *skene*
transformed into a colonnade. The
superimposed circle shows the
position of the old *orchestra* which
was used in the days when there
was no scene building at all.
(Flickinger, *The Greek Theatre
and Its Drama*)

Performances began at dawn, and wealthy citizens often sent their
slaves ahead of them to hold seats. The less wealthy members of the
audience came themselves, often in the hours of darkness before
dawn, and milled about the entrances for vantage points from which
to get the seats they wished when they were allowed to enter the
theatre. Everyone was in a festive mood, and there was much quarreling over particularly advantageous locations. The spectators wore
garlands on their heads, and brought along lunch and sometimes
sunhats and cushions, for it would be a long day. The audience
was critical and was not slow in letting its opinion be known. Unpopular plays were often hooted from the theatre, and unpopular actors
pelted with figs, olives, nuts, or even stones. The actor Aeschines
nearly lost his life in such a stone barrage, it is said, and thereafter
retired from the theatre permanently. Applause was as much in order
then as now, and it is difficult to conceive that the judges were not
influenced by the public reception of the various presentations.

All preparations for the productions were conducted in secret, and
though the stories of the tragedies were generally well known to the
audiences, the trappings of production and the interpretations of the
individual poets were always eagerly anticipated. Sometimes the
results were unexpected; it is said that children died and women

miscarried when the horribly costumed Furies appeared in the last play of Aeschylus' *Oresteia* trilogy. Public interest in the production had been aroused, as was usual, by the presentation a few days before the event of a preview, or *proagon*, in a place adjoining the theatre. This preview used the playwright and performers in an announcement of the forthcoming production, and is perhaps the earliest publicity device known. For such a preview, Sophocles is said to have startled his audience by dressing his chorus in mourning to mark the death of Euripides.

The Attic citizen took his drama seriously, not only because it was a part of a great religious festival, but because he loved talk and display and the tales the poets told. This first great theatre audience was composed of spectators widely distributed in social station and in personal propensities, but united in their love of good theatre. It was an audience in many ways comparable to that of Shakespeare's day. In these two periods (as perhaps in no other) great and diverse audiences witnessed great plays combined with great productions and acting to make unsurpassed theatre.

Playwriting develops to unequaled heights

In the dramatic presentations of the City Dionysia, there were three types of plays presented: tragedy, satyr play, and comedy. Early presentations were governed by the rule that the tragic poets must present a tetrology consisting of three tragedies on a single theme, plus a satyr play which treated the personages or the situations of the preceding trilogy in burlesque fashion. A chorus of satyrs was always present, and this comic afterpiece with its special style is thought to have been included in the festival primarily to perpetuate the satyrs who had traditionally been a part of the Dionysiac celebration. No doubt, also, its comic and lascivious complexion had tremendous popular appeal, being designed to relieve the heaviness of the tragedies. All three of the great classic dramatists wrote satyr plays. Aeschylus is said to have been a master in this type, but of the many which he must have written, only a few fragments survive. The not-very-entertaining fragment of *The Trackers* of Sophocles, which is all that we have of his satyr plays, is surely not representative of his skill. Our only adequate idea of the type comes from Euripides, whose *Cyclops* survives in its highly entertaining entirety.

The early standard of a tragic trilogy on a single theme was changed as time went on, as evidenced by the existence of Aeschylus' independent play, *The Persians*, which had no connection with its two companion pieces, and by the practice of Sophocles and subsequent playwrights of presenting three separate tragedies. But whether the tragedies were connected in theme or separate entities, they remained the work of a single dramatist. After the fifth century, the satyr play was relegated to a comparatively unimportant place in the festival; only one seems to have been given from that time forward, and that preceding the revival of an old tragedy.

We have seen how Thespis transformed the chorus leader into an actor, but in the early days of Aeschylus there was still only one actor. Aeschylus is credited with being the first, in his later plays, to add a second actor. Sophocles added another to make three. Throughout the entire period of Greek drama there were never more than three participants designated as "actors," although in addition to the chorus there seem to have been various non-speaking extras.

In the early plays, the chorus was large and was an integral part of the drama. In *The Suppliants* of Aeschylus, the chief characters are the fifty women who represent the daughters of Danaus, and the Argive king to whom they appeal for succor is of secondary importance. Aeschylus is generally credited with reducing this unwieldy chorus to twelve for each part of the trilogy; Sophocles raised it again to fifteen, a figure which seems to have remained fairly constant thereafter. In comedy, the traditional size of the chorus was twenty-four.

As playwrights discovered the advantages of enlarging the parts of the actors as opposed to that of the chorus, the function of the chorus became less important. In contrast to *The Suppliants,* which opens with the appearance of the chorus, *Agamemnon* opens with a single dramatic figure and the effective monologue of the Watchman. In Aeschylus' works, however, the chorus is an essential part of the mood and the action of the plays. Sophocles' chorus plays a lesser, though relevant, part in the action and is more often than not employed to give lyrical emphasis to a climax or to prepare for a shift in mood. With Euripides, the actors gain still more ground at the expense of the chorus. The number of characters is increased (in *The Phoenician Women* there are eleven), and the lines of the chorus are fewer in number and mostly explanatory of the action. Aristotle comments that it was the playwright Agathon, who won the first of his two victories in 416 B.C., who first wrote choral odes which were unconnected with the plot and served only as interludes. Though its functions thus deteriorated, the chorus seems always to have been a part of tragedy; in the later comedies it disappeared entirely.

From the first appearance of Thespis at Athens to the first plays of Aeschylus, and indeed contemporary with him, many poet-play-

14 A Greek theatre in Hellenistic times
Detail of a model of Delphi in about 160 A.D., showing the Temple of
Apollo and the Theatre. Here the stage house is different from that
of the Classic period. The stage is raised and approached by an inclined
plane; the *skene*, on the stage level, is backed by panels, which may,
upon occasion, have been scenically painted.
(The Metropolitan Museum of Art)

wrights were being produced at the Theatre of Dionysus. We have
the names of some of these but not much more. Of Pratinus (who
flourished in 496 B.C.), we know simply that he was one of the three
competing poets when Aeschylus first participated in the festival, and
that he was especially successful in his satyr plays. Of Choerilus
(523–482 B.C.), we know that he wrote one hundred sixty plays and
won thirteen victories, but none of his plays are extant. Of Phrynichus,
who won his first poetic victory in 511 B.C., a few scattered fragments
remain; it is recorded that he incurred a fine for his *Capture of
Miletus*, which celebrated a disaster of political import, and the
play was never imitated. Our knowledge of Greek drama is based

upon only thirty-three tragedies and eleven comedies, three sizeable fragments, and one satyr play. This is all that has been preserved of the hundreds that must have been written. We assume, with some reason, that Aeschylus, Sophocles, Euripides, and Aristophanes were the best of all those who wrote for the Greek theatre, both because these alone have survived and because what can be garnered of the critical opinion of their contemporaries seems to verify such a judgment. In any event, it was not until Shakespeare that playwriting achieved so great a peak, and then it was considerably different in kind.

Aeschylus (525–456 B.C.) is the first of the three great tragedians, and is considered by some critics to be the greatest tragic poet of all time. Of the ninety plays for which we have titles, only seven are extant. He won the prize for tragedy at Athens thirteen times, taking his first award when he was forty-one years old. The most famous of his works is the *Oresteia* trilogy, in which is told the story of the house of Atreus; the three plays are separately entitled *Agamemnon, The Libation Bearers, The Furies.* It opens with the return of Agamemnon from the Trojan Wars; he is murdered by his wife, Clytemnestra; she, in turn, perishes at the hands of Orestes, their son; Orestes is persecuted by the Furies, and is at the end pardoned by the goddess Athena. In addition to *The Suppliants,* generally conceded to be the earliest of his extant plays, and *The Persians* we also have *Prometheus Bound* and *The Seven Against Thebes,* two single plays of what were originally trilogies. We know the subject matter of four more of his trilogies, but of the rest nothing beyond the titles is known.

Fortunately, the extant plays cover a large part of his career so that we can see in their progression an illustration of the development of dramatic art. The earliest have a close formal affinity with the narratives from which they are taken. The chorus of young women in *The Suppliants,* or the Elders in *The Persians,* really constitute chief characters, and the plays themselves are not so much representations of dramatic conflicts as delineations of the effects of past events on sympathetic onlookers. The single element of dramatic conflict acted out in view of the audience (the essence of drama today) is the attempt of the Herald in *The Suppliants* to drive the daughters of Danaus to the waiting ship of the sons of Aegyptus. The chorus has more than two-thirds of the lines of the play. In each of these plays the hero and the antagonist are not developed as individuals; the emphasis is on the results of past actions. Aeschylus further develops this rudimentary dramatic form, however, in *The Seven Against*

Thebes, in which Eteocles, as the hero, holds the stage most of the time, though the antagonist Polynices is not represented, and the chorus is prominent and important. By the time he arrived at his final great trilogy, the dramatic element—as opposed to the lyric, elegiac, or narrative—is paramount. Agamemnon and Clytemnestra are real, complex embodiments of hero and antagonist; our interest lies in present action, in the represented dramatic conflict, rather than in past events. Dramatic art thus came of age.

Aeschylus grew to artistic maturity as the democracy of Athens was rising to the peak of its greatness, and he' is a masterful interpreter of that society. The chief interest of his plays lies not primarily in the isolated, individual character, but in that character placed in the total scheme of things; he presents his central theme with piercing insight and great dramatic power. Yet—and here is the measure of his skill as a dramatist—his people are individually characterized to the degree that the audience becomes intensely interested in what happens to them. Aeschylus presupposed a superhuman factor in the universe; at the same time, he believed in the fundamental dignity and worth of man, his possession of free will, and his responsibility in the exercise of that will. His poetry is often impassioned, full of images, irresistible in movement.

Sophocles (496–406 B.C.) was but sixteen years older than Euripides (480–406 B.C.), and they died within a few months of each other. But the subject matter and the treatment in Sophocles' plays make him older in the art of the drama than Euripides. He was nearly ninety when he died, and had written about 125 plays. Seven of these are extant. It is recorded that he won twenty-nine prizes, eighteen of them at the City Dionysia. He used much of the same subject matter as Aeschylus, but was more interested than the older dramatist in the tragic interplay between characters or in the inner conflicts of an individual character. His three best-known plays are *Antigone, Electra,* and *Oedipus Rex;* the others still extant are *The Women of Trachis, Ajax, Philoctetes,* and *Oedipus at Colonus.* A comparison of his *Electra* with Aeschylus' *Libation Bearers* reveals that Sophocles used the legend of Electra to inquire into human character and its motivations, whereas the older dramatist was concerned with the rightness of the blood feud.

Building upon the advances in dramatic structure evident in the plays of Aeschylus, Sophocles brought dramaturgy to a state of perfection. In *Antigone,* for instance, he opened immediately with a scene of conflict between two of the major characters, Ismene and Antigone, and continued with a series of incidents which form an effective plot with elements of suspense and alternating scenes of reassurance and despair. By the time he wrote *Oedipus Rex,* his tools had been perfected, and the balance between plot and character was firmly established. Though the essence of this play is the withdrawal of veils from the past, Sophocles unfolded his plot with a careful selection of scenes, each revelation being not merely exposition, but dramatic motivation for the next action of the hero. The characters are always present on stage when they are needed, and their delineation is unerring. Even the choral odes are germane and not mere interludes.

From *Oedipus Rex,* a play of faultless construction in which the leading character is driven to his doom by the ineluctable series of his own choices, Aristotle chiefly draws his definition of the tragic hero: "a man who is highly renowned and prosperous, but one who is not pre-eminently virtuous and just, whose misfortune, however, is not brought upon him by vice and depravity, but by some error of judgment or frailty." (*Poetics,* sec. 1453a, ll. 5–10) Edith Hamilton, the renowned Greek scholar, calls Sophocles "the quintessential Greek" (*The Greek Way,* 1930), a dramatist who displays an unerring skill in balanced construction, who handles complex dramatic situations with clarity and symmetry, who writes verse that is lucid, fluent, and grand. He is the essence of everything that we mean when we speak of the glory that was Greece, the consummate artist in everything that he did.

Although Euripides was a contemporary of Sophocles, Euripides is the much more modern of the two. Euripides never attained the artistic perfection of Sophocles, but he probed more deeply into the psychological motivations of his characters. He was a dramatist in conflict. He was at war with the accepted theology of his day, though he bowed to it in ritual observances; he inveighed against imperialism and military aggression; he saw the legends of heroes as the glorification of tyrants, schemers, cowards; he was a passionate critic of his times, who fought against the passing of Periclean Athens through the long life-and-death struggle with militaristic Sparta when things intellectual were being smothered in things practical and freedom of speech and action was continually being curtailed. He died a short while before Athens fell to Sparta, a political and military event which rendered the resurrection of an Attic Golden Age impossible. He had been a friend of Protagoras, Socrates, and Alcibiades, and only the fact that his criticisms were never voiced directly, but only through the characters in his plays, saved him from the unhappy fate that awaited the others. He did, however, become

15 *A modern example of the classic Greek theatre*
The Hearst Greek Theatre was presented to the University of
California at Berkeley in 1903 by the late William Randolph Hearst.
Modeled after its Athenian predecessors, it seats about 8,500 persons. In
addition to dramatic productions, it is used for University meetings,
concerts, and student rallies. (The University of California at Berkeley)

a voluntary exile from Athens in a kind of personal protest against
the abuses he abhorred. He suffered the disapproval of his contemporaries in another way, for of the ninety-odd plays which he
wrote only five took the prize for tragedy. Interestingly enough, we
have more plays of his than of any other classic dramatist; eighteen
are still extant.

His modernity is seen in his treatment of the Electra myth, for his
title character is presented as a sexually frustrated, neurotic young
woman, and her brother as a weak-willed boy motivated by his sister.
His *Medea* shows a woman being driven mad by jealousy, and his
Phaedra in *Hippolytus* is overpowered by a guilty passion. Euripides
engages in psychological analysis centuries before the term was

invented; hence he is called by some the father of modern drama. He was highly critical of militarism, giving the world its greatest pacifist play, *The Trojan Women,* as well as the anti-war play, *Hecuba.* He was also constantly questioning the power and authority of the gods, as he does in *Heracles, Ion,* and *Iphigenia Among the Tauri.*

His dramatic skill was not so well balanced as that of Sophocles; his interest in character generally outweighed his attention to plot construction. His aim seems to have been the representation of complex characters in as many emotional and theatrical scenes as possible, and he allows the unity of his plays to depend largely on the revelation of character. His plays contain a wealth of realistic detail and thus seem closer to us than do the more artistically balanced productions of Sophocles. Euripides also enlarged the types of possible plays by writing what we would call tragi-comedy or romantic drama (*Iphigenia Among the Tauri, Alcestis*), and a most delightful high comedy (*Helen*). These new genres pointed forward to the comedies of Menander. In point of view, Euripides was an iconoclast; in treatment, however, he often tried to adhere to the traditional and the accepted. He, like many another dramatist after him, conformed to the extent that would gain him a hearing while he attempted to say that which was revolutionary.

Of tragic playwrights after Euripides there is little record and there are no literary remains. It is recorded that a play of Philocles actually defeated Sophocles' *Oedipus Rex* in the contest, and it is said that the playwright Agathon wrote plays for which he invented the characters instead of borrowing them from legend or history. Euphorion, son of Aeschylus, Iophon, son of Sophocles, and Euripides, nephew of his namesake, also wrote tragedies in addition to reviving the plays of their great ancestors. But no new names arose to rival their greatness.

Though the glory of Greek drama was the tragedy, comedy had a parallel development. As we have seen, it, too, grew out of the early festivals of Dionysus, though from the secular aspect. Comedy was more improvisational than tragedy in its origins and dealt with current ideas of interest rather than with traditional materials. For these reasons it remained more episodic than tragedy. A multiplicity of characters developed with less and less emphasis upon the importance of the chorus as an integral part of the action. The traditional twenty-four members of the comic chorus were generally divided into two equal groups, one for each side of the argument comprising the central issue of the play. But, as we have said, the functions of the chorus were gradually assumed by individualized characters.

There were supposedly some 252 writers of comic plays. These comedies used caricature, lampoon, invective, sarcasm, irony, parody, and satire to make their point. They were more important than tragedy at the Lenaea, and though less important at the City Dionysia, prizes were awarded the comic writers.

The entire production of classic comedy is generally divided into three periods: Old, ending with the fifth century B.C.; Middle, to about 340 B.C.; and New, in which the best work dates from about 300 B.C. Aristophanes (*ca.,* 448–*ca.,* 380 B.C.) is the best representative of Old Comedy, and the only writer of that comedy whose plays are still extant. Of his forty known plays, eleven texts have come down to us, some of which were first performed at the Lenaea and some at the City Dionysia. We know the names of some of his predecessors—Cratinus,, Eupolis, Epicharmus—but only scattered fragments of their works remain.

If Sophocles "drew men as they ought to be and Euripides drew men as they are" (a statement ascribed to Sophocles by Aristotle), then Aristophanes drew them as they should not be. Aristotle said that "Comedy tends to represent the agents as worse than the men of the present day" (*Poetics,* sec. 1448a., l. 20). The examples we have seem to bear out this statement. In them public figures are rendered ridiculous—rulers, thinkers, warriors, lawyers, politicians, writers. As always with satiric writers, the aim of Aristophanes was to expose truth by exploding pretension, and though many of his plays today could not be performed without considerable censorship, they were hailed with delight by his more expansive contemporaries. Six of his plays are classed as political satires: *The Acharnians,* *The Knights, The Wasps, The Peace, Lysistrata,* and *The Women in Parliament.* Five are called philosophical and literary satires: *The Clouds, The Women at the Festival, The Frogs, The Birds,* and *Wealth,* his last play.

Tradition has it that in *The Knights* the playwright's attack on the militaristic demagogue, Cleon, who had succeeded Pericles, was so incisive that no actor would undertake the part and no mask maker would produce the character mask. Aristophanes himself is said to have played the part, smearing his face with winelees to indicate the alcoholic propensities of his model. Another tradition is that Socrates, impaled in *The Clouds,* was so diverted by his comic counterpart that he rose from his place in the audience so that the spectators might see and appreciate the cleverness of the dramatic takeoff. Euripides came in for his share of ridicule in *The Acharnians, The Women at the Festival,* and *The Frogs.* Aeschylus, as well, is a

16 Greek vases showing costumed figures
The vase on the left depicts a scene with Dionysus, a Maenad, and two
satyrs. The long lines of the costumes, the long sleeves of the figure
of Dionysus, and the masks, tails, and phalli of the satyrs are clearly
visible. The vase at the right, from the fifth century B.C.,
depicting satyrs dancing, shows similar characteristics. (Boston
Museum of Fine Arts, The Metropolitan Museum of Art)

character in the last of these. Scholars are fond of pointing out the
original of a famous college yell in the chorus of this play, when they
simulate their namesakes with a "brekekekex, ko-ax, ko-ax." Situations as well as persons are satirized in the plays of Aristophanes. In
The Acharnians, for instance, an Athenian citizen, tired of war, makes
a private treaty with the enemy, and enjoys the advantage of trading
with them. Aristophanes departs from topical satire in his later plays
and becomes more diffuse. This tendency coincides with the decline
of democracy in Athens and marks the death of Old Comedy.

There are only fragmentary remains of Middle Comedy, though
thirty-seven names are listed as its writers. Alexis and Antiphanes
were evidently the most eminent in this period, although we possess
not a single play of either. Anaxandrides of Rhodes, who wrote sixty-
five comedies in the fourth century B.C., is said to have destroyed or
sold for waste paper his unsuccessful plays. From the extant fragments, scholars have deduced that Middle Comedy was less ribald,

less personal, less fantastic than Old Comedy. Its plays had more plot, more dramatic illusion. The chorus decreased in dramatic importance and the material was more social than political.

Menander (*ca.*, 342–292 B.C.) is the outstanding representative of New Comedy; contemporary critical comment names him the most able of all his fellows. Certainly he was the most revived and most copied of them all. He is supposed to have written about 105 comedies of which only scattered fragments remained until four much more complete texts were recovered early in this century. They were found in an old Egyptian papyrus which had been torn up to protect various legal documents, and they were complete enough so that they could be more or less satisfactorily reconstructed. They are comedies of errors called *Hero, The Girl from Samos, The Shearing of Glycera* (sometimes translated as *The Rape of the Locks*), and *The Arbitration*. Within the last few years there was discovered in Switzerland another Menander play, *The Curmudgeon*, which is the only complete text of a Menander play now extant. It is a delightfully lively comedy which gives modern readers an insight into Menander's great comic genius. By this time (the second half of the fourth century), the chorus had entirely disappeared from comedy, and the possible cast of characters had expanded to include twenty-seven types. Among these were irascible and good-natured old fathers, light-minded and honest sons, cunning servants, greedy parasites, swaggering soldiers, dishonest matchmakers, obliging companions, parasitic relatives, and impudent prostitutes. These types reappeared in later epochs of the theatre. Situations were domestic in character, and generally farcical in presentation. Plots usually turned on such things as an ill-used maiden or a foundling who turned out to be well born. The background was that of middle-class city life, and the dramatist's observation of this milieu was exact. His graceful composition, urbanity, wit, and apt characterization caused his plays to be widely admired and mightily copied.

Presumably Menander's sixty or more fellow-writers of comedy, including Philemon and Apollodorus of Gela, followed the same pattern, writing of the same subjects in the same way. What we have of Plautus, the Roman comic writer, gives us an excellent sample of what late Greek comedy must have been. The plots and characters are stereotyped, yet in the best of the plays there is presented a vast panorama of human weakness and charm, an interplay of character upon character in basic relationships, transcending time and place.

So, for more than two and one-half centuries the Greek drama developed into perhaps the greatest theatre the world has ever known, and then, first in tragedy and later in comedy, declined to ineffectualness. The course of the drama paralleled and reflected the rise and decline of the great Greek democratic society.

The theatre of Dionysus

There are no contemporary descriptions of the playhouse in which the great Attic plays were produced. Aristotle, writing in the fourth century, says little or nothing of the physical aspects of the drama. For many years all that was known of playing space and production in the ancient Greek theatre was derived from *The Ten Books on Architecture* of the Roman architect, Vitruvius, which was written about 15 B.C., and from the *Onomastikon* of Pollux, which appeared in the second century A.D. Pollux's work was based, in part, upon the seventeen-book *Theatrike Historia* of King Juba II of Mauretania, who began his compilation at the time of Augustus, but whose total work was subsequently lost. Both Pollux and Vitruvius are obscure and contradictory, and their information obviously includes developments much later in point of time than the sixth and fifth centuries. More authoritative reconstructions have been possible through archaeological research, and through production indications in the plays themselves. In the former field, a great debt is owed to Wilhelm Dörpfeld, whose excavations in the late nineteenth century led to an interesting study published in 1896. So far as the plays themselves are concerned, the perspicacious reader may still today see rudimentary production guides in them. We will not enter into the scholarly dispute which has raged and indeed still rages concerning the production aspects of the great plays, but will present in the following pages what seems a reasonable, and reasonably authenticated, exposition.

In the Golden Age of Greece, each major city erected a theatre as one of the edifices dedicated to religion. This theatre was an evolution from the circular dancing place of the early Dionysiac festivals around which the spectators sat or stood. There was an obvious advantage in having this dancing place, or *orchestra,* in a hollow since a large crowd of spectators could have vantage points on surrounding hillsides. The Theatre of Dionysus at Athens, the most famous of them all, began in just such a simple fashion, with the original *theatron,* or seeing-place, on the hillslope under the Acropolis, and the original *orchestra* at the foot of the hill. It was merely a circle of hard-stamped earth, and there were no seats for the spectators except perhaps some removable chairs near the circle for the dignitaries. The first plays of Aeschylus were evidently given in this spot, with

40

no scenic background except the wide blue Grecian sky and the Attic countryside.

Various archaeological and literary researches have traced the evolution of this playhouse through the Classic era, the Hellenistic period, and the Roman Empire. The relation of audience to actors changed as the years passed. As the fifth century B.C. progressed, wooden benches were provided for the spectators. The increase in the number of actors and the number of speaking parts in the dramas dictated an arrangement for the expeditious entrances of these actors and a place for their changing of masks. About 465 B.C., the *orchestra* circle was moved closer to the hillside to allow for the construction of a long, wooden building between the *orchestra* circle and the old Temple of Dionysus. In this building, also, the wooden seats were stored when a production was not in progress. At the same time the hillside was somewhat hollowed out at the center and built up on the lower ends, so that the rows of seats in the bottom section could be carried around three-quarters of the *orchestra* circle. The second and third tiers of seats did not form complete semicircles, but were limited at the sides and top by topography and by other construction. The seats faced toward the circle where both actors and chorus performed. The wall of the scene building, or *skene,* served as the background for the plays, and at this time probably had a single door facing the *orchestra* circle. A massive, T-shaped stone foundation, extending beyond this single door, seems to have been the base for the erection of whatever temporary altar, temple, porch, or stairway was called for by a particular play.

Toward the end of the fifth century B.C., foundations were laid for a stone *skene* with projecting side wings to be erected in front of the old one. When this building was completed, the T-shaped foundation lay within it, and may have been used as a base for the erection of superstructures. The building had three doors, and was probably two stories high (figure 10). It no doubt followed the basic plan which had proved practical in the temporary wooden structures used before this time.

In the fourth century the theatre was remodeled by Lycurgus, with fine stone benches for the audience, a throne in the center of the first row of seats for the priest of Dionysus, and other special seats of honor; a new *skene* was erected, and the original one was transformed into a colonnade. This was the final form of the Greek theatre.

The remains of the theatre at Epidaurus give us a good idea of the Classic Greek theatre (figure 11). It is perfectly symmetrical, with twenty-two sections of seats in the outer circle, and twelve in the inner circle. This theatre, attributed by Pausanias to Polyclitus, had lintels over the passageways between *theatron* and *skene,* thus achieving a unity which most Greek theatres did not possess.

Playhouses change to suit the plays

The development of dramatic literature in the succeeding Hellenistic period deemphasized the importance of the chorus, and placed the burden of the performance on the actors; this change was reflected in the theatre proper by the development of a raised stage for the actors. Theatres built in this period, such as those at Priene, Assos, Ephesus, and Delos, among others, retained the *theatron, orchestra,* and *skene,* but the *skene* now encroached somewhat on the *orchestra* circle, and was different in construction from the Classic *skene.* It invariably had at least two stories, and the chief acting level was the *proskenion,* or roof of the first story. This acting area was approached on either side by ramps and was ten to twelve feet high. Theatres which had been built in Classic times, such as those at Athens, Eretria, and other places, were refurbished with the new Hellenistic stage building, just as in the time of the Roman Empire most Greek theatres were once more remodeled with the Roman stage design and semi-circular *orchestra.* The present remains at Athens belong to the period of Nero (figure 12).

Fundamental to the Greek idea of a theatre was the open-air playing space; Greek skies were almost always sunny and spectators could protect themselves from too much sun by wearing hats. Tiered seats, sectioned off by walkways (much in the manner of a modern football stadium) were standard, and these seats encircled the *orchestra* about three-quarters of the way around. Sight lines were generally good from every seat and, in spite of the fact that these theatres seated from fifteen to twenty thousand people, the acoustics were remarkable. All seats except those in the front row were backless benches, again like most football stadiums today. The front row held stone chairs with backs, the center one usually more ornate than the others and reserved for the priest of Dionysus. Often there was an open space behind this row where additional chairs could be placed if the list of dignitaries in attendance exceeded the special seating area. The *orchestra* circle was of packed earth; its size varied, but generally was quite large. The diameter of the circle at the Theatre of Dionysus at Athens was in its early days about eighty-five feet, and later about sixty-five. When the Roman engineers began remodeling Greek theatres, they paved the *orchestra* with stone, as

17 *Menander with masks*
This bas-relief of Menander holding a comic mask shows the relative size
of the mask as compared with the actual human head. The standing figure
may represent an actor. The masks on the table are two of those common to
New Comedy—the courtesan and the comic slave. (Lateran Museum)

they did at Athens. In the center of the *orchestra* circle in the Classic
theatre was an altar. In dramatic productions it was variously used:
in *The Persians* it was a monument; in *Prometheus Bound,* the rock to
which the god was lashed. In the theatre at Eretria in Magnesia, there
was an underground passage leading from the altar to the interior
of the *skene,* and scholars have speculated that these are the
"Charon's steps" mentioned by Pollux.

As we have observed, the *skene* was originally made of wood, then
of stone, and was over one hundred feet long, with wings projecting
about fifteen feet to either side. It faced the tiers of seats on the
opposite side of the *orchestra.* The front wall of the *skene* was
pierced by doors—one, then three, then five. In the Classic period,
the actors entered directly to the *orchestra* from the *skene;* in the
Hellenistic period the *skene* was fronted by a *proskenion,* higher
than the level of the *orchestra* and forming a kind of stage. There
was a second story to the *skene*—the *episkenion,* evidently even in
the days when the building was made of wood. The passageways
(*paradoi*) between the extending wings of the *skene* and the near

43

rows of seats were used sometimes for the entrances of actors, for chorus entrances, and for the entrance of the audiences. In performance, it was the convention, founded on fact in the theatre at Athens, that the right-hand passageway marked entrances from the city and places near at hand, the left those from the country and other places farther away.

This was the functional structure of the Greek theatre; it was sometimes elaborated, often decorated, but fairly constant in its basic design.

Greeks, too, knew the art of illusion

Knowing something of the basic design of the theatre, scholars long supposed that the scenic decoration of the Attic drama was austere in the extreme and the production eminently simple. But compilations of scattered references in recent years have revised this opinion: Greek dramatists were as interested as any in the long history of the theatre, in the invention and use of whatever trappings would enhance the scenic illusion. There seems to be general agreement now about the nature of at least some of these.

Even in the days before any kind of *skene* was erected at Athens and the only background for a given play was the natural open topography, effective dramatic use was made of the retaining wall of the *orchestra* circle opposite the audience. It seems probable that the ghost of Darius in *The Persians*, for instance, would rise from below this six-foot wall, or that Prometheus could descend over it. It also seems likely that even at this early period necessary properties, like tombs and altars, were set up at the edge of the terrace formed by this wall.

With the coming of the *skene* as a regular part of the theatre, further developments were possible. One of the earliest and most universally used was the *mechane,* which was evidently a kind of crane affixed to the roof of the *skene* and equipped with pulleys and ropes. It was used for ascents and descents of various kinds, as in the *Orestes* of Euripides where Apollo soars with Helena in the air above the palace roof; as in *The Mad Hercules* where Iris and Lyssa appear and one descends while the other flies away (this would presuppose a double operation of some sort); as in *The Clouds* where Socrates is ridiculed by suspending him in a basket midway between heaven and earth; as in *The Peace*, where, parodying Pegasus, Trygaeus ascends to heaven on a beetle. The *mechane* was needed primarily for the appearance of a god in a play, who usually interfered to effect dramatic resolutions of one sort or another; the term *deus ex machina* ("god from a machine") has come to stand for any contrivance which inorganically effects the resolution of a dramatic dilemma. The *mechane* seems to have raised actors from *orchestra* or stage level to the roof of the *proskenion;* this area, where action could also take place, is what is apparently meant by another often-mentioned contrivance of the Greek theatre—the *theologeion,* or speaking place of the gods.

Another mechanical aid to the dramatic illusion was a platform on wheels or rollers, the *eccyclema,* which could be shoved out from one of the doors of the *skene* as the action demanded, and pulled back in again. It was used for reveals, so that offstage action could be made visible to the spectators. The convention of Greek theatre disallowed murders on the stage itself, but it was often necessary or desirable that the audience see the results of such action. Creon's dead wife is wheeled out in *Antigone,* and for comic effect Euripides is wheeled round in *The Acharnians* because he is too busy to come out himself.

Several ancient writers speak of the thunder tub whose use is obvious. Some speak of hides filled with stones beaten against brass plates, others of the pouring of stones into brass tubs. In any event, this contrivance was the ancient ancestor of our present-day thunder sheet. Also mentioned are traps of various kinds; perhaps the "Charon's steps" at Eretria are a form of these. A beacon tower is also mentioned, and some writers speculate that this may have been nothing more than a specialized use of the roof over the *proskenion* or, in the earlier days of temporary settings, a structure especially erected.

Aristotle credits Sophocles with the introduction of the art of painting or decorating the *skene.* The earlier wooden *skene,* as we have seen, was very probably supplemented by additional front structures; slots in the wall of the *skene* have been interpreted as anchoring spots for such additional structures. Sophocles, in his role of producer-director, might well have embellished these temporary structures, as well as the walls of the permanent *skene,* with paintings. There were also movable painted scenes (*scaena ductilis*) set up one behind the other, a device probably dating back to the Classical period. Pollux and Vitruvius both mention three-sided prisms, or *periaktoi,* rotating on beams set into holes near the extremities of the stage area, with each side painted differently. These may also go back to Classical times, and were certainly used in the Hellenistic period; perhaps they are the "lightning machines" to which we find references.

There were also removable screens of wood or hide (*pinakes*) which, in the Hellenistic theatre, were placed between the columns

18 Greek masks
Left, a tragic mask of terracotta, from about 400 B.C.; center, a comic
mask from Smyrna; right, a tragic mask of terracotta, from
Myrino in the Hellenistic period. In the two tragic masks, the dome-shaped
top and the open mouth are clearly apparent. Note the eye holes for
the convenience of the actor in the mask at the right.
(Boston Museum of Fine Arts)

fronting the *skene*. Cross-sections of several of these columns seem to
verify, by their evident construction, that they were built to take
screens which could be inserted between them. Whether these screens
were painted abstractly or literally is not known, but the illusion they
afforded must have been welcome to the dramatists. They were used
both between the columns of the lower story and in the large openings (*thyromata*) on the second story, the stage level in Hellenistic
times.

Vitruvius says that the Greek theatre had three types of painted
scenes: tragic, comic, and satyric. He may have been simply con-
jecturing from the known types of plays, or he may have had reference to various styles of painting the screens and set pieces. No doubt
the decoration of these movable pieces would be done in subject matter and style to suit the play being produced. We shall see later how
this statement of Vitruvius affected scenic design in the Renaissance.

There is also mention of something called a semicircle, which is
supposed to have been a painted set piece placed in the *orchestra*
whenever sea battles and sea scenes were called for. There is no
doubt, too, that actual chariots were used when demanded, being
driven through the passageways into the *orchestra* circle, and that
other literal props were employed as needed. Attic dramatists were

46

no less interested in scenic investiture than those of later periods. However, since the plays were always given by daylight, special lighting effects were nonexistent; night and storms were played in bright sunshine, being announced in the dialogue and aided only by such devices as the thunder tub and the lightning machine. Audiences then, as now, accepted theatrical conventions readily.

All performances were enhanced, however, with musical accompaniment. Just as dance was an integral part of the drama, so too was music. Originally playwrights scored their own scripts and choreographed them as well. Both Aeschylus and Sophocles were proficient in these skills. Later the labor was divided, and separate artists supplied music and choreography. The chief musician was the flute player who preceded the entrance of the chorus, and who generally established himself on the altar for the duration of the play, accompanying both song and dance from that position. Every patron, or *choregus,* was anxious to secure the most accomplished flute player for his performances, and there was much competition to obtain the best. The competition was resolved when, in later times, the flutists were chosen by lot for the various performances. The flute was often accompanied by a harp, though we have little idea of what the melodies were like. We know only that Greek modes in music differed materially from our own, and that the ancients had little or no idea of polyphony.

The scenic illusion was further enhanced by costume and makeup, which was in no way realistic, but highly conventional with different conventions for the three types of plays.

The costume for tragedy was reputedly invented by Aeschylus. The effect aimed for was that of figures larger than life-size, who would be impressive, dignified, and easily seen and heard in the very large theatres in which they played. In the earliest days of Greek theatre, actors in the tragedies were garbed in the long, rich, Asiatic robes of the priests of Dionysus and wore Asiatic leg boots. This gave way to highly decorated Ionian dress. Then, as the fifth century progressed, costumes for tragedy became standardized, with a traditional dress for each role.

While the Athenian citizen never covered his arms in the ordinary business of life, the tragic actor wore an ornamented dress with long sleeves. It was generally striped or embroidered perpendicularly, and an ornamented belt was worn not at the normal waistline, as the Greeks usually belted their clothes, but high up in the style we know as Empire. The colors of these robes were standardized for the various characters: olive green, for instance, signified mourning; queens

47

wore white with purple borders. Additional barbaric jewelry was added for such a character as Medea. Overgarments, or mantles of saffron, frog-green, gold, or purple were frequently added. No one wore hats except for travelers. Members of the chorus were uniformly dressed to represent the characters they were impersonating in the drama—old men, maidens, women of the city, and so forth. (Mention has already been made of the effect on the audience of a most special costuming of a chorus of Furies.) Because they had to dance, members of the chorus wore their ordinary footgear or went barefoot, whereas the tragic actor wore a thick-soled boot, the *kothurnos,* a development from the earlier Asiatic leg boot. These boots, with the long lines of his costume plus the mask and body padding to give horizontal compensation, made the tragic actor about seven and a half feet tall, a truly awesome size. A probably apocryphal story is told of how an audience in Spain fled in fear and panic when a traveling company of Greek tragedians first appeared before them.

Much of the impressiveness of the Greek theatre lay in the masks of the performers, an interesting holdover from more primitive times. They were made of linen, cork, or wood, and fitted over the entire head, as primitive masks almost invariably do. The tragic mask was considerably larger than life-size, and typically rose in a dome-shaped fashion at the crown of the head. This protuberance, the *onkos,* effectively precluded the wearing of hats. Female characters sometimes drew their mantles over their heads, but, as noted above, only travelers wore hats, and in these cases special masks or none at all were worn. Since no more than three actors appeared in the speaking roles of a given play, the masks, which could be changed as many times as necessary, made doubling possible. The actor simply retired within the *skene* and changed his mask. Sometimes more than one mask was provided for a single character, as was the case for Helen in Euripides' play of that name when she reappears pale and with her hair shorn, or for the Oedipus of Sophocles, who appears besmeared with blood after he has put out his eyes. Sometimes compensation is made in the script for the fact that the actor had no time to change a mask, as when Electra is bid make no sign of joy at her brother's return. In time the features of these masks became conventional; Pollux lists twenty-eight varieties of tragic masks: six old men, eight young men, eleven women, three servants, in addition to necessary exceptions like Argus, the horned Acteon, the Gorgon, and so forth. The masks of tragedy and comedy which are so familiar to the modern world are two-dimensional representations of the old Greek masks. In every case, the mouth was opened wide to allow the

19 Comedy masks and figures
Left, terracotta masks of the Hellenistic period used in the presentation
of comedy. The woman is no doubt the courtesan, the man the young
man. Right, terracotta statues from the period of Old Comedy.
The man is an old slave; both have padded figures.
(Boston Museum of Fine Arts)

voice of the actor to emerge, and a convincing case has been built up
through investigation and experiment to prove that the mask included some sort of megaphonic arrangement to increase the carrying power of the wearer's voice.

Taken as a whole, the costume for tragedy was colorful and impressive. The weight and thickness of the actor's outfit forced him to
move slowly, but he was trained to move gracefully. The result was
well suited to the mood of the plays. And certainly the members of
the audience had little difficulty identifying the various characters
immediately, even from the farthest seats.

The costume for comedy differed considerably. The tunic was
short and worn over long, tight undergarments. The body was
grotesquely padded before and behind, and graced with a phallus
made of red leather. This phallus, a carryover from the Dionysiac
revels, served the double purpose of being a charm against evil and
a sign of fertility. The wearing of the phallus disappeared during the
time of Middle Comedy in the fourth century. On his feet the comic
actor wore short, soft boots, *socci*, and on his head a mask. These
masks lacked the dome-like protuberances of tragic masks; they
tended to be grotesque, and were made in a wide variety of characters.
Since satire and invective were so much a part of Greek comedy,
portrait masks were common and, as mentioned, both Socrates and
Euripides were thus represented in the plays of Aristophanes. These

49

masks were an early manifestation of the art we now call caricature.

The choruses of comedies were usually in fantastic dress, intended to represent their characters—wasps, Furies, birds. Many vase paintings give us a good idea of the wide variety that was achieved in these costumes. Here, too, color was significant: the procuress, for instance, invariably wore scarlet—perhaps the theatre's first "scarlet woman."

In the satyr plays, the actors wore uniform masks and uniform costumes which included hip fur, a phallus, and a tail—the traditional satyr representation (figure 16).

Acting highly specialized

As in that other great period of the theatre, the Elizabethan, women were never seen on the stage. Acting companies were made up solely of men, and infrequently included a boy or two. There may have been social or religious reasons for this, but the chief consideration was a practical one: the light voices of women could hardly carry in those huge theatres, nor could women sustain the weighty costumes and the arduous demands of performance.

Members of the acting profession were carefully selected and most arduously trained. Demosthenes once remarked that actors should be judged by their voices, politicians by their wisdom. Indeed, voice training formed a large part of the actor's education. There were specialized voice teachers, and voice production was practiced in all postures. Not only was the speaking voice assiduously cultivated, but the Attic performer practiced proficiency in song as well. In the ordinary course of a performance he was called upon to use three types of voice production: the iambic trimeter parts were done in a declamatory style, with particular emphasis upon enunciation; the recitative was intoned to musical accompaniment; the song proper was used for the lyrical passages. Songs were written for solo, duet, trio, or chorus, though never in harmony.

In addition to his vocal accomplishments, the actor was obliged to have at his command a whole catalogue of conventionalized gesture —a complete technical system of gesticulation. The styles differed for tragedy and for comedy; it is no wonder that actors specialized in one or the other of these two types, rarely performing in both.

Furthermore, the actor was a finished dancer, with complete command of the art of movement. Members of the chorus, no less than the actors, were accomplished dancers, singers, and speakers as well. Each type of play had its own dance movement. In tragedy it was the *emmeleia,* a slow and graceful movement which involved not just the feet, but the whole body. In comedy it was the *kordax*, a swift-moving and bawdy dance. The dance of the satyr play, the *sikinnis*, was a parody of the tragic dance in riotous and licentious form.

Those designated "actors" were highly specialized performers. The three actors of the theatre of Sophocles later came to be called the protagonist, the deuteragonist, and the tritagonist. They had special personal attributes and performed special functions in the plays. All were called *hypokrites*, in contradistinction to the *choreuti*, or members of the chorus, and the *choryphaeus*, or leader of the chorus. The protagonist was the chief actor; a play was said to be "done by" him. He possessed a penetrating tenor voice and played all the leading roles—Antigone, Electra, Medea, Oedipus, and so on. The deuteragonist was next in importance. He was a baritone and played the chief supporting roles, such as Creon in *Antigone*. The tritagonist was the least important of the three. He had a bass voice, and played the passionate heralds, dignified kings, and so on. All three of these doubled in other roles where necessary.

There were other actors who, as today, assumed the nonspeaking roles to round out the performance. Needless to say, this area was a training ground for the higher ranks.

The chorus leader was frequently assigned lines in the play as were also individual members of the chorus. For example, the chorus of old men in *Oedipus Rex* speak singly as well as together, and the leader is a special part. Through the passageways, the chorus entered the *orchestra* circle where they remained throughout the perform-ance, moving and speaking as the script demanded and the play-wright directed. The actors evidently moved from *orchestra* to *skene* and back again as was necessary, now with and among the chorus, now apart from them. The whole effect was one of carefully syn-chronized movement and utter discipline. We can suppose that all performers were carefully trained, and well rehearsed for each production.

Acting was a highly esteemed profession in ancient Greece, and people from all walks of life joined its ranks. Its members joined together in an actors' guild which they called the Artists of Dionysus, and on the basis of their fundamental religious employment (remem-ber that the Attic theatre was a part of the worship of Dionysus), they were, by action of the Amphictyonic Council, exempted from military service. This was, of course, after the time of Aeschylus, who did his military duty until he was sixty and was a widely renowned soldier as well as playwright. The Artists of Dionysus set up a system of rules governing employment and working conditions, much in the

20 *Comic actors*
This collection of terracotta statuettes, probably dating from the
fourth century B.C., represent various characters in Old Comedy.
Note the variety of expressions in the masks, the ludicrously padded bodies,
and the decisive gestures. (The Metropolitan Museum of Art)

manner of today's Actors' Equity, even extending their concern to
traveling companies. Being, in a sense, priests, actors were sometimes
used as special emissaries of the government, and no doubt this increased their stature in the eyes of ordinary citizens. In many succeeding centuries, actors never again enjoyed such prestige and
social standing; not until nearly our own day would they overcome
the disrepute in which they lived for centuries.

There was wide variation in the income of actors; leading members of the profession commanded very high salaries. There is a
record which shows that Polus, a leading protagonist, received the
equivalent of twelve hundred dollars for two days' performances—
a sum which would be considered generous even today. Sometimes
the protagonist served as a contractor, supplying all the parts and
paying his company as he saw fit. Lesser actors received smaller
sums, with the non-speaking actors getting least of all. It is easy to
imagine that the lesser members of provincial companies were likely
to fare as poorly as similar actors do today.

The Greek theatre operated on the star system, that much abused attribute of the modern theatre. Particular performers were idolized in much the same way as they are today, and some of them were just as foolish offstage as current ones are. Callipides, a much admired actor in the theatre, made himself ridiculous in many ways evidently, receiving his comeuppance from King Agesilaus from whom he demanded praise because he "sang like a nightingale." Replied the King, "I have heard the bird itself." But then, as now, this kind of actor was in the minority. Most of them were fine people as well as fine actors: witness Aeschylus himself who was his own protagonist. There was Nicostratus, who is said to have been so perfect an actor that the highest praise a provincial performer could receive was to have it said, "He does it like Nicostratus!" Other players of note included Aristodemus, Neoptolemus, Athenodorus, and Phrynichus, for all of whom high praise is on record. It was the same Polus we have mentioned above as being particularly well paid, who is said to have used an urn containing the ashes of his son to induce the proper emotion when he was playing Electra mourning over her supposedly dead brother's ashes. How modern in spirit that sounds!

At first, particular actors were associated with individual poets, as were Mynniscus and Cleander with Aeschylus, Tlepolemus and Cleidimides with Sophocles. Later, actors like musicians were assigned to the plays by lot—a practice which must have proved upsetting to the playwright-director.

As the art of playwriting declined, the prominence of the actors increased. As with all star systems, however, this one fell upon evil days, and it is written that by Aristotle's time it had become vicious.

Summary

When we say that Western theatre as we know it began with the Greeks, we have perhaps said all. Our conception of that shining and miraculous age is largely derived from the great Greek dramatic literature. Never before or since has man achieved so perfect a balance between the visible and the invisible, the material and the spiritual, the image and the imageless. As Edith Hamilton has pointed out, this balance is possible only when the mind and spirit are in harmony as they were with the Greeks, the mind seeing everything as related to the whole, the spirit seeing everything as highly individual, and the combination of mind and spirit seeing beauty in everything. Thus the magnificent simplicity of the Parthenon is related to the Greek landscape, making both more beautiful by their juxtaposition; thus the figures of Greek tragedy, though highly individual, illuminate man in his human, material, and divine relationships. The complete individual seen at the same time as completely universal is the heritage and the greatness of Greek tragedy. The immense influence of the Greek dramatic concept is apparent through the ages to our own day.

Hardly less influential is the final form of Greek comedy, with its universal character types, whose voices reecho and whose images are seen in many times and places.

The productions of these plays were a part of religious observances, with widespread participation among many classes of society. The actors were specialized, highly trained, and highly regarded as citizens and artists. The presentation of the plays was elaborate and ritualistic, with music, song, and dance being integral parts. Theatre was one of the greatest elements of the glory that was Greece.

It is true that without the theatre of Greece we would undoubtedly still have theatre of some sort today. But it is likewise certain that a theatre without the Greek tradition would be a very different one from that which we know and admire.

4

IMITATIONS AND INNOVATIONS
OF THE ROMANS

About fifteen years after the death of Aristophanes, and almost twenty-five years before the birth of Menander, the city of Rome saw its
first dramatic performance. The historian Livy tells us that in 364
B.C., in order to "disarm the wrath of the gods" who had visited the
city with a pestilence, the consuls "amongst other efforts . . . instituted scenic entertainments." How much like the reasons for drama
among primitive men this is! The "scenic entertainments," Livy goes
on to say, were mimetic dances by natives of Etruria "imported from
abroad." The music, dance, and verse of these Etruscan players became very popular in Rome, and were much imitated by young
Romans.

Thus, Etruria, or more particularly Fescennium in South Etruria,
is credited with being the first source of Roman drama. What the traveling company brought was evidently the essence of a harvest festival
to their rustic and sylvan deities such as we have met with before in
primitive man and in the very ancient Greeks. This particular festival stressed marriage songs of a rather wanton nature; these Fescennine Verses, as they came to be called, remained a popular style with
the Roman public down to the time of the Empire.

There were other imported entertainments. The mimes came from
Magna Graecia, although this form and the type of performer were
almost everywhere in the ancient world. Jugglers, acrobats, dancers

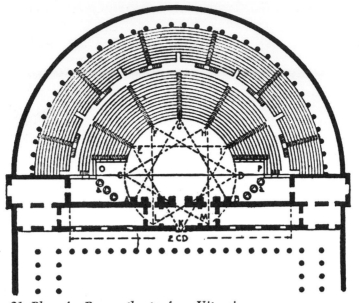

21 Plan of a Roman theatre from Vitruvius
This symmetrical arrangement, worked out on geometrical principles,
is typical of the plans not only for the theatres which the Romans built,
but also for those extant Greek structures which they remodeled.
(Vitruvius, *The Ten Books on Architecture*)

—both male and female—presented improvised parodies of myths
designed to excite laughter. The so-called *atellanae* from Atella in
Campania, were short, improvised comedies of practical jokes and
witty attacks on local matters. These latter were performed in masks.
Subsequent to the importation of these forms, there grew up in Rome
a form which Livy called the *satura*, or "medley," perhaps analogous
to a variety show with music, dancing and short, comic sketches.

The beginnings of drama in Rome were in some respects similar
to the beginnings in Greece: a rural religious festival was invited to
perform in the capital city. The similarity, however, ends there,
for the subsequent development was quite different from that of the
Greek theatre.

Roman theatre an instrument of government

Aside from the early effort of two frightened consuls to propitiate
the gods, Roman drama—more accurately, theatricals—had no connection with religion. The Romans were not a philosophic people, but

a practical one. They had many deities to whom they paid lip service, but true religious fervor was absent from their way of life. They were early and widely skeptical, and preferred to put their trust in arms, tools, and politics. In any event, whatever the intricate reasons, the theatre in Rome never achieved even a modicum of the greatness of Greece; however, some of its manifestations and practices are historically important.

One of the earliest entertainments offered the Roman public was the frequent Roman Games (*Ludi Romani*). In the early days of the Republic the people of Rome were an abstemious, courageous race of citizen-soldiers who possessed, above all, personal integrity and love of the state. At the end of the second Punic War (201 B.C.) there were less than fifty holidays in the year. The austere senators looked down on the frivolity of dramatic performances, and permitted no permanent theatres to be built. The succeeding centuries of conquest and civil war which led to the establishment of the Empire in 31 B.C. saw a breakdown in the stern asceticism of the Roman populace, and the corresponding lengthening of the time devoted to entertainment; by the last days of the Republic there were seventy-six holidays in the year, fifty-five of which were devoted to theatrical productions. The Empire committed itself to a policy of "bread and circuses" as a palliative for civic abuses, and by the fourth century the yearly calendar included 175 official holidays; more than one hundred of these were given over to plays and theatrical entertainments, sixty-four to chariot races, and ten to gladiatorial combats.

The officials in charge of the games hired the acting companies, which were composed of slaves under the control of a manager who was himself often a slave but who possessed the power of life and death over his company. In an interesting contradistinction to the policy at Athens, the Senate early declared that no Roman citizen could be an actor; if he joined the abased profession, he summarily lost all his civil rights. This stand probably resulted from a combination of republican resistance to the theatre on the grounds that it did not contribute to the austere existence deemed best for the citizen-soldier, and the fact that, as the Roman conquests spread and many captives were brought home to Rome, many Greek or Greek-trained performers became Roman slaves. In any event, actors were *infami* in the later Roman Republic and the Empire—an onus that has attached to them through many centuries, in many ways, and which is not entirely dissipated even today.

Needless to say, the audiences for dramatic performances in Rome were invariably festive and gay. In the early days of the Republic when there were few holidays, they were looked forward to as a pleasant release from the workaday world; in the later Empire, when half the year was a holiday, theatre was a diversion consuming time which otherwise would hang heavy. Simulated sea battles, wild-animal fights, contests between man and beast and between man and man variously armed, as well as the spectacular chariot races, vied with tragic spectacle, comedy, mime, and pantomime for the attention of the populace. Lavish display was everywhere, subsidized by the wealthy to impress and divert the poor.

Occasionally the government decreed games and theatrical productions, paying for them out of the public funds. More usually a wealthy man volunteered, or was appointed, to pay for productions which were free to the public. He volunteered in order to display his wealth, or to support his candidacy for office. Anything from a triumph to a funeral might be an excuse for a display.

In the theatres—temporary or permanent—seating was strictly according to social class. The Emperor and the donor of the play occupied the special boxes on either side of the stage; the senators sat in the semicircular orchestra on special chairs brought in for them; the first fourteen rows of seats were reserved for the knights; the rest of the seats were allotted to the various social classes, with the most unimportant and poorest citizens occupying the seats farthest from the stage. Each spectator entered the theatre with a ticket in the form of a coin, on which was a picture, a name, and a number to indicate the section of the house in which he was to sit. Here is the first recorded use of the reserved-seat house. At various spots throughout the house were persons paid by the donor, or the playwright, or one or more of the actors, to applaud vigorously; they were the theatre's first *claqueurs*. The rowdy audience was kept in check by specially assigned theatre police, who sat with their staves at either side of the stage where the entire audience was in view.

The mad effort to please the public, to attract and hold their attention, was everywhere evident in the production; the increasing need for more and more thrills to titillate a jaded public taste brought on ever-increasing spectaculars that descended finally to vulgarity and licentiousness and led to the eclipse of the drama which had been the glory of Greece.

Use and abuse of the Greeks

There was no indigenous tragedy in the Roman theatre. Whatever tragedy existed was sparse and poor, copied or adapted from the

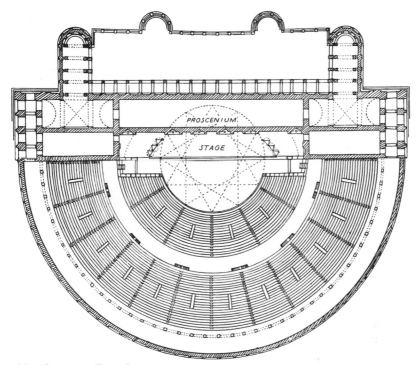

22 *The Marcellus Theatre at Rome*
The plan of the theatre, showing once more the precisely
symmetrical arrangement of the seats, the integration of stage house and
auditorium, and the semicircular *orchestra*. (Streit, *Das Theater*)

Greeks. At best we know of but thirty-six authors of tragedy in
Roman times, with a total output of about 150 plays—not many more
than Sophocles alone wrote during his lifetime. None of these are
extant save in meager fragments except the plays of Seneca (3 B.C.–
65 A.D.), preserved perhaps because of his great fame.

Tragedy was introduced to Roman audiences by Livius Andronicus in 240 B.C., when he was thirty years old. He is said to have been
a manumitted Greek slave, largely responsible for bringing Greek
literature to Rome. Until his death in 204 B.C., he continued to trans-
late, adapt, or copy the Greek plays. (He was also an actor, and is
credited with a unique innovation. Finding that his voice gave out
when he attempted to do lines, songs, and dance movement simultaneously, he assigned the voice parts to a speaker who stood at the
side of the stage while he, voiceless, pantomimed and danced the
part.) The chorus never functioned as it did in the original Greek

dramas, since the stage was raised and the orchestra space was used for seating the senators.

From the introduction of tragedy to the middle of the first century B.C., when new plays or adaptations largely ceased to be written for theatrical presentation, there were but few tragic dramatists, and all of them freely used Greek materials. One of the earliest and most popular dramatists of Rome was a specialist in tragedy, Marcus Pacuvius (220–130 B.C.). Of his work we possess about four hundred lines and twelve titles. Though he used Greek subject matter in his plays, his treatment reflects the Roman point of view: Cicero commends him for improving on Sophocles by having one of his heroes die with Stoic self-control rather than with the Sophoclean expression of agony. Naevius (*ca.*, 270–*ca.*, 199 B.C.) also followed Greek models, but on at least one occasion produced a play with Roman subject matter, *The Rape of the Sabine Women.* It is written that he died in exile, because his propensity for satire brought him into conflict with a wealthy and powerful family. Ennius (239–169 B.C.) seems to have attempted to improve his Greek originals with a rhetorical style that was typical of the Roman adaptors; but the fragments which still exist of twenty of his plays show some sign of dramatic power. The last important writer of tragedy for the Roman stage was Lucius Accius (*ca.*, 170–86 B.C.). Some fragments and titles of about forty of his plays have survived. Like Ennius, he capitalizes on the rhetorical possibilities of his originals, and concentrates on the violent, melodramatic elements. Pacuvius, Ennius, and Accius are also credited with writing one or more *praetextae* (from the *toga praetexta,* or purple bordered mantle which Roman magistrates wore) which used subject matter from Roman history.

As time went on, the public taste for the spectacular grew, and great displays became a necessary ingredient of any performance. Cicero, in 55 B.C., complains of "the sight of six hundred mules in *Clytemnestra* [and] three thousand bowls in *The Trojan Horse.*" (*Clytemnestra* was one of the plays of Accius.) If the performance was being given to mark a triumph, like as not the victor would parade over the stage his line of captive kings and soldiers, his chariots, and his plunder. Since the dialogue of the plays was solemn, bombastic, and exaggerated, the performances no doubt needed such visual distractions.

Though our only complete texts of Roman tragedy, those of Seneca, do not indicate these lavish visual displays, it is almost certain that the Senecan dramas were never actually performed. By this time, as we mentioned above, there was an almost complete divorce between theatre and drama; plays were now written to be read, not performed. The theatres themselves were occupied chiefly by mime and pantomime. Of Seneca's nine plays the most famous are *Medea, Phaedra, Agamemnon, Oedipus,* and *Thyestes.* Although these may be our first examples of "closet" drama, their influence on Renaissance playwrights and critics is inestimable.

It is difficult to conceive of these tedious, bombastic, and bloody plays as descendants of classic Greek tragedy. What the Roman author seems to have done is to take from the Greek stories all those instances which allowed him to write extended descriptions, high-flown oratory, and tedious debates, and which emphasized horror for its own sake. In the first act of his *Hercules Oetaeus* the hero speaks a long passage describing his labors; his Medea pours forth her emotions in an avalanche of words; his principal characters almost invariably speak one after the other in the oratorical style of debate rather than in conversation; Thyestes dines from the limbs of his children and recognizes their severed heads in full view of the audience. Seneca makes revenge the chief motive of many of his plays: his *Agamemnon* opens with the ghost of Thyestes swearing vengeance on the House of Atreus. The revenge motive, the ghost, the scenes of bloody horror, were adopted by Renaissance dramatists, who thus corrupted the Greek concern with fate, the death of heroes, and the emotional impact of rash deeds. Seneca emphasized all the wrong things in his adaptation of the Greeks, making melodrama rather than true tragedy.

Roman comedy also used two types of subject matter: one which concentrated on Greek materials, and one which used Roman materials. Writers of Roman comedy were no less dependent on their Greek masters than were the writers of tragedy. They used the Greek plays in a somewhat different way, however, cannibalizing scenes and characters from several plays and combining them in an attempt to form something new. Often the borrowed situations were dressed in Roman locales and characters, but the sources are unmistakable. A consistent plot line is often lacking, and where it does exist it is so overlaid with instances, subplots, and counterplots as to be exceedingly hard to follow. Secondary characters, likely to be more important in the staging than the nominal principals, developed as a whole company of stock personages. This is the tradition which descended to the avid copiers of the Renaissance.

We have the titles of seventy pieces from the Roman-based comedies and some four hundred-odd lines written by Titanius, Atta, and Afranius. But only two writers of Roman comedy are worth noting;

23 *The Marcellus Theatre in the eighteenth century*
A Piranesi etching of the Marcellus Theatre in the eighteenth century,
when other structures were built inside it. These are the outside
walls, and show how the Romans built free-standing theatres where the
natural topography could not support the tiers of seats. These thick
masonry walls were pierced by passageways leading to the
rows of seats in the auditorium.

both wrote from Greek material. Titus Maccius Plautus (*ca.*, 254–
184 B.C.), whom we know as Plautus, had had a colorful career as
provincial actor, soldier, businessman, and itinerant miller before he
took to writing comedies about the year 200 B.C.; in the time that was
left him, he turned out 130 pieces, of which twenty-one are extant—
the largest number of plays still in existence of any of the classic
playwrights. He based his plays on those of Greek New Comedy,
borrowing both plots and characters from the earlier masters. Frequently he Romanized situation, locale, and dialogue. He wrote with

far more exuberance than did his Greek prototypes; a quick appraiser of his audience, he wrote into his plays, with robust humor, situations which were native and topical. Thus he continued the tradition, though in paler form, of the great Aristophanic comedy. His production is exceedingly varied in worth, for he wrote with great speed.

He was firmly entrenched in the convention of type characters such as are found in the Greek New Comedy, and these types, often with the same names, appear over and over in his plays. *Miles Gloriosus* is the braggart soldier who is the prototype of Falstaff; the leading character in *The Crock of Gold* is Molière's model for *The Miser;* his *Amphitryon* had many copiers down to modern times, when Giraudoux produced his *Amphitryon 38; Persa* is the ancient version of *The Beggar's Opera; The Twin Menaechmi* is the source of *The Comedy of Errors.*

Titillating situations, rollicksome dialogue, and vivid characters mark the best of Plautus; at his worst he may be accused of lacking verisimilitude and abounding in bad taste. His plays, however, were received enthusiastically by the Roman audiences; he recouped his arid fortunes and, though a foreigner and an actor, he was granted the privilege of Roman citizenship.

Quite different in atmosphere were the plays of Publius Terentius Afer (*ca.*, 190–159 B.C.), whom we know as Terence. He was born a slave in Carthage, brought to Rome, and educated by his master who recognized his talent and set him free. He became the darling of Roman society, and frankly wrote for their aristocratic tastes. Taking Menander for his model, he attempted to develop his own style to the polished precision he saw in his master, and indeed there is a refinement apparent from his first play, *Andria*, to his last, *Adelphi.* (In the former of these he added a second lover, and introduced a situation unparalleled in Greek drama: a young man in love with a girl of his own station. Thus, because Roman women enjoyed a freedom not available in the Greek society which enforced an oriental seclusion of its young women, Terence was able to develop a love interest along modern lines.) The other four of his plays which are extant are *The Mother-in-Law, The Self-Avenger, The Eunuch,* and *Phormio*. Terence frankly scorned the popular taste, but the last mentioned of these plays (adapted from Apollodorus rather than Menander) presents us with a very delightful characterization of a parasite, who has had much progeny in succeeding literary periods. Legend has it that Terence died of heartbreak on a pilgrimage to Athens when his manuscripts were lost; actually he was lost at sea when he was about thirty years old. But his highly polished plays became

24 *The Roman theatre at Orange*
These ruins in the south of France are among the best preserved of the
ruins of many theatres built by the Romans all over the Empire.
They give a good idea of the height and massiveness of the Roman stage
house. Typical of the Roman theatre was the raised stage and the
high, intricately decorated front wall of the *skene*. The stage
itself was covered over with a wooden roof, also highly decorated.
(Theatre Collection, New York Public Library)

models for many future writers, including the learned nun Hroswitha, who wrote six plays "after Terence" in the tenth century.

Pantomime—an original contribution

Though the plays as we know them were scant and inferior, there
was no lack of theatrical fare. The mime and pantomime which had
shared the scene with the writers of tragedy and comedy in the Republic, became the darlings of the public from the time of the Empire, successfully precluding the writing of new plays, and almost
curtailing the revival of old ones.

The pantomime stands as the only original contribution of the
Romans to the art of theatre. It had its beginning when Livius
Andronicus, as mentioned above, separated the singing and speaking
from the dancing and gesticulation in his presentation of Greek tragedy. By the first century the pantomimes had become elaborate displays quite distinct from the drama. All the resources of the theatre
were used in the service of these performances, the stage pictures and
movement being supplemented by orchestral music and choral singing. The pantomimes employed extensive scenery and expensive costuming, and their wonders were extolled by many writers. They were
a favorite form of theatrical diversion for the Emperor Nero, who
delighted to play in them. The performers were exceedingly popular
with members of high society, and it is said that in the later Empire
the female dancers often performed on the tables at extravagant

banquets of the wealthy. Well-known poets sometimes enriched themselves by writing libretti for the pantomimes, and these libretti were, during performance, sung by the chorus. The choral singing was accompanied by an orchestra of flutes, pipes, cymbals, and trumpets. The subject matter might be anything from mythology or past history, primarily in the tragic vein, with the emphasis on love stories. From all accounts, however, neither music nor libretti were of particular artistic merit. The great popularity of the form was due to the skill of the dancer, or *pantomimus,* and the lavish staging. Relying solely upon an intricate system of gesticulation and movement, and dressed in rich costume and mask, the performer acted out the story being sung. So all-encompassing did this form become that the old word for actor, *histrio,* came to mean, in the later Empire, "performer of pantomime."

Vulgarity succeeds comedy

The mime, which replaced comedy in the Roman theatre, had a long history before its adoption by the Romans. It had originated in the ancient world with public entertainers of all kinds who performed in marketplaces, private houses, or wherever there was an audience. The performers were marked by their skill in mimicry, song, dance, and improvisation. Jesting, buffoonery, and an unfailing aura of indecency were constant elements from first to last. The characters were types, usually drawn from the lower orders of society, the situations titillating, the endings often abrupt. Needless to say, the plays were short. So popular did the form become in Rome that the literary dilettantes of the Empire amused themselves by writing mimes to be read aloud to their friends. But the mime which drove all other forms of spoken drama from the theatre was largely subliterary and improvised. Records of its performance may be found up to the beginning of the sixth century A.D.

The only vigorous rival of the mime was the persistent *atellana,* which eventually, however, also succumbed to the mime. The *atellanae* were rustic farces, originating, as we have seen, in Campania, and early imported into Rome. They were played in masks, and used traditional figures in ridiculous situations. The emphasis was on horseplay and obscene jest. Originally completely improvisational in nature, they assumed literary form some time in the first century A.D., when Pomponius and Novius began composing them. Fragments amounting to more than two hundred lines and one hundred titles are extant. Something of the character types and subject matter is evident from these titles: *Maccus the Soldier, Maccus the Inn-Keeper,*

25 *Tragic masks of the Roman theatre*
Left, a tragic mask of terracotta, showing a similar expression and
the same dome-shaped protrusion found in many Greek tragic masks.
Right, masks of the Roman theatre of about 100 B.C., as depicted
on a bas-relief. Again, these are the same as were in earlier use in the
Greek theatre. (Boston Museum of Fine Arts; Vatican Museum)

*Maccus the Maiden, Pappus the Farmer, Bucco the Gladiator, The
Two Dosseni, The She-Ass, The Candidate, The Pimp.* It is an interesting speculation that the character masks of these actors persisted
into the Renaissance *commedia dell'arte.* Maccus, the flat-nosed,
stupid country lad might well be the prototype of Pulcinella; Bucco,
the jabbering parasite, the forerunner of that line; Pappus, the silly
old man, the ancestor of Pantalone. There seems to be some evidence
for the persistence of mime through the Dark Ages, and it may well
be that this form, generally played without masks, absorbed the
masked *attellanae* and emerged in the Renaissance as the *commedia.*

Bread and circuses

It is no wonder that literary drama was of a low order and small
quantity in Roman times. Not only did the dramatists compete with
mimes and pantomimes, but with other "circuses" as well. The bloody
encounters of the gladiatorial combats and the animal games in the
huge Circus Maximus and the Colosseum drew crowds of eighty
thousand and upwards. Sometimes the Colosseum was flooded for
that peculiar institution of the *naumachia,* where slave-manned ships
fought each other to the death. The chariot races of the Circus Maximus have become legendary. When the visual capacities of an audience were thus sated, how could it be expected to meet the auditory

66

challenge of real theatre? Splendor was the word for Roman theatre; a rather tawdry splendor it became, but nonetheless lavish. Horace bemoaned the materialism of his contemporaries which prevented them from writing dramas as great as the Greek genius had produced. What if he had lived to see the excesses of the later Empire?

But though the Roman theatre never produced great drama, it contributed much of a more material and practical nature to the heritage of the theatre.

Theatre architecture masterful

The Romans were great engineers. Myriad roads, aqueducts, monuments, and buildings attest to the fact. It is natural, then, that their most significant contribution to theatre history is in this field.

The building of theatres occurred late in the history of Rome. Prior to 55 B.C. there were no permanent theatres. When dramatic performances were to be played, a temporary wooden *skene* fronted by a raised platform for the actors was built, but this was torn down after the performance. No seats were provided for the spectators, who had either to stand or bring their own chairs for the occasion. As late as 194 B.C., the citizens were outraged to find that special seats were provided and reserved for the senators apart from the general audience. In 174 B.C., the first *skene* of stone was built, but the spectators still brought their own seats. In fact, a law had been passed in 185 B.C. forbidding anyone to sit at dramatic performances. As time went on, this law seems to have been observed chiefly in the breach. The democratic Roman Republic thus showed its scorn of the effete Greeks whom they had conquered, and continued the tradition which looked down on theatricals as debilitating to the stronger virtues of the Roman citizen.

Even in 55 B.C., when Pompey succeeded in building the first stone theatre in Rome, he disguised it as a temple to Venus Victrix by incorporating in it, at the top of the rows of seats, a temple. He explained that the rows of seats were steps leading to the shrine. The ruse was flimsy, and no one was deceived, but at least lip service had been paid to the Republican tradition of austerity. His was the last gesture to the outworn idea, however, and with the coming of the Empire, two more stone theatres were erected in Rome, both finished in 13 B.C. One was built by Cornelius Balbus and seated eleven thousand five hundred; the other, finished by Augustus and named for his nephew Marcellus, seated twenty thousand five hundred. The Theatre of Marcellus is the only classic theatrical structure still extant in Rome, though only the outer walls of the original structure remain (figures 22 and 23). The Theatre of Pompey, as reported by the Elder Pliny, seated forty thousand. These three theatres were the only permanent ones built at Rome up to the time of its fall.

Many temporary structures, however, continued to be built. The most magnificent of these was, by all accounts, that erected by M. Aemilius Scaurus in 58 B.C. The Elder Pliny describes it as having three stories, supported by 360 columns. The lower level was made of marble; the second of glass; and the third was gilded wood. Between each of the thirty-eight foot lower columns were thirty-eight bronze statues. The theatre, according to Pliny, accommodated eighty thousand spectators. After a few days' use the whole thing was torn down.

Another of these temporary structures was a unique swivel theatre erected a few years later by C. Curio. This actually consisted of two wooden structures whose curving seats were built back to back with each unit on a pivot. After the presentation of plays, the seats were swung round, spectators and all, to form an amphitheatre for athletics and gladiatorial combats. Such was the grandeur of Rome.

About the same time as the Balbus and Marcellus theatres opened, Marcus Vitruvius Pollio completed his ten-volume book, *De Architectura*, the fifth volume of which takes up theatre architecture. With exposition and illustration, and with the skill of a professional engineer, he describes in detail the plans for an ideal theatre. From this, and from the ruins of actual structures, we have an accurate idea of the Roman theatre building.

The basic design was a modification of the Greek theatre, with some significant differences. Most importantly, the seats of the spectators (*cavea*) formed an integral structure with the *skene*; from this design the modern theatre was born. While the Romans sometimes built on a natural slope, as the Greeks invariably did, their structures more usually were free standing, with the outside walls highly decorated. A system of arched passageways (*vomitorii*) was included for audience dispersal.

What was the circular *orchestra* in the Greek theatre was here reduced to an exact semicircle, and it was paved. It was not used by any of the performers, but special chairs were placed there to seat the senators watching the performance.

The stage was always elevated, usually to a height of five feet. It was a tremendous area, often more than twenty feet deep and a hundred feet wide. The old *skene* was now an elaborate stage building, much higher than formerly because of its integration with the *cavea*. The front of this stage building (*frons scaenae*) formed an architectural background for the stage, and was highly elaborate. An ornate center door was flanked on either side by two smaller doors, and the whole area was a symmetrical mass of columns, pediments, niches, and statues. A roof extended over the stage, also highly ornamented. Around the top of the semicircular seating area was a roofed portico, from the top of which sailors manipulated awnings to protect the spectators from the sun.

This ideal theatre, as described by Vitruvius and built by Augustus and by Balbus, was a development from earlier Roman theatres built elsewhere, at Pompeii, Segasta, and Tyndaris. The latter two were converted from late Hellenistic theatres. At Tyndaris, and in the large theatre at Pompeii, both erected about 200 B.C., the auditorium is in the form of a horseshoe built against a natural hill slope. Open passageways lead into the *orchestra*. Both these theatres were subsequently remodeled; the passageways were vaulted over and special boxes for seating were erected over them. The small theatre at Pompeii, built about 75 B.C. (the same time as the large theatre was remodeled), is the oldest purely Roman theatre still preserved. It has the semicircular plan later described by Vitruvius, but the side tiers are cut short to make the building rectangular. A wooden roof was erected over the entire structure. It had a capacity of about fifteen hundred. On theatres of this comparatively small size wooden roofs were evidently usual, as on those at Taormina, Epidaurus, and Naples. Thus the Roman theatre reached a complete architectural unity such as the Greeks never attained. In the larger Roman theatres, the semicircular plan of seats was complete and uninterrupted, and the awnings mentioned above, invented by Catullus about 80 B.C., were used as roofs upon occasion. In later years, permanent corbels fastened this linen roof into place, so that sailors needed no longer to man it.

The avid builders of the Roman Empire erected more than 125 of these theatres, from England to North Africa and from Portugal to Asia Minor. Where the theatre was a new structure, the form developed at Rome was used. In the eastern provinces, where Greek and Hellenistic structures already stood, these were rebuilt according to the new specifications. Sometimes, as at Aizonoi and Pessimus, the theatre was an architectural unit with the circus of which the Romans were so fond. In the Greek colonies, where the Roman amphitheatre was not popular, extant structures were remodeled by cutting down the *orchestra circle,* paving it with stone, and building a wall around its perimeter. Thus the theatre could be used for animal fights, gladiatorial combats, and even the simulated sea battles.

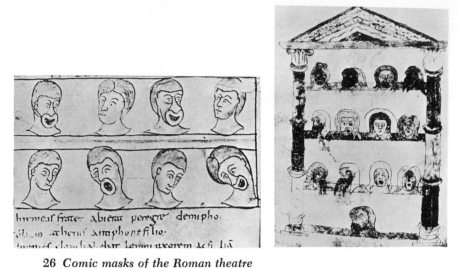

26 Comic masks of the Roman theatre
Left, masks for the *Phormio* of Terence, Ambrosianus manuscript.
Right, masks for the *Andria* of Terence, Basilicanus manuscript.
As in the Greek theatre, the masks for comedy lack the domed top, and
their expressions are dictated by the stock characters for whom
they were intended. (Vatican Museum)

In this fashion, as we indicated above, the Theatre of Dionysus at
Athens was reconstructed under Nero (figures 12 and 13). The backless stone benches for the audience were retained here, however, as
they were elsewhere in Roman theatre construction. Along with the
marvelous Colosseum at Rome, the ruins of many of these theatres
remain as monuments to Roman engineering skill. The best preserved
may be found today at Orange in the south of France (figure 24)
and at Aspendos in Asia Minor.

Innovations in settings

One of the most unusual innovations of the Romans was the use
of a front curtain. This curtain, often richly embroidered, was housed
in a sort of trough at the edge of the stage area, being dropped at the
beginning of a performance and raised at the end of it. Steps sometimes led from the stage to the orchestra; the front of the stage
elevation (*hyposcenium*) was ornamentally decorated, and sometimes had doors presumably to admit the creatures used in the animal
fights.

Vitruvius refers to the use of painted scenery, for which provision
was made in the *skene*. He particularly mentions *periaktoi*, the

painted pieces which revolved to indicate change of scene. He also quite elliptically refers to the three types of scenes: the tragic scene with its "columns, pediments, statues, and other objects suited to kings"; the comic scene with its "private dwellings, with balconies and views representing rows of windows, after the manner of ordinary dwellings"; and the satyric scene with its "trees, mountains, and other rustic objects delineated in landscape style." (*The. Ten Books on Architecture*, Cambridge, 1926, p. 150.) Just how these effects were achieved is not certain, but we know that there must have been more than rudimentary stage machinery because we have contemporary descriptions of pantomimes with disappearing mountains of wood, spouting fountains, running streams, and growing trees. It is true that the Romans were clever in controlling water, and it is not hard to believe that some of their theatres (as we read) were air conditioned by means of special passages of running water to cool the air. We also know that at least in some instances, fine sprays of water mingled with perfume were blown over the audience, to make the spectators comfortable.

The front of the stage building, in its fully developed form of actual columns, niches, and statuary, was a development from a much simpler beginning. The earlier wooden *scaenae* evidently had flat walls with painted decorations, although the traditional five doors were practical. Under the probable influence of the *thyromata* panels of the Hellenistic stages, these painted decorations became more extensive and rich in the first century B.C. Pliny tells the story of birds being lured by the realism of the paintings on the stage wall erected by Claudius Pulcher in 99 B.C. Many other such anecdotes attest to the realism striven for and apparently attained. The remains of the small theatre at Pompeii indicate the use of a painted *frons scaenae*. But the Roman love of pomp, luxury, and display made the splendidly intricate architectural design of the stage wall the one most typical and most universal. The earlier flat walls became broken and elaborated into series of niches, arches, entablatures, and columns, all wrought of stone and marble. The first tier alone of Pompey's theatre is said to have had fifty columns. Though the permanent decoration of the Roman stage was most elaborate, special decorations in the form of bronzes, paintings, and garlands were evidently added for festival performances. The stage roof, peculiar to the Roman theatre building, was not only an acoustical achievement, but served to protect this rich decoration as well. The linen roof over the audience was also decoratively painted on occasion, as Pliny reports of the splendidly painted roof stretched over the Theatre of Pompey in 66 A.D. for the visit of the king of Armenia. In design, form, and decoration, the theatres were among the most masterful creations of Roman architecture.

There were no lighting problems in the ordinary course of the performance, since productions were given in the daytime. The roofed-in theatres were no doubt illuminated equally on stage and in the seating area by lamps and torches. Occasionally, and as a curiosity, torchlit night performances were given.

Music was an important part of Roman theatricals, especially in the mimes and pantomimes. Songs were for solo voices or chorus, and dancing was usually accompanied by singing as well as by instrumental music. The flute, the lyre, the pipe, cymbals, trumpets, and the harp were the instruments most frequently used, and dancers sometimes used taps, called *scabilla*, attached to wooden soles. Musicians were ordinarily seated on the stage, though occasionally they were performers in the show.

Costumes follow the Greeks

We have seen that masks from the first had been a convention of Greek production, and it is likely that they were adopted by the Romans, along with the plays, costuming, and staging. In the *atellanae*, of course, the record is clear: masks were always a part of their production. That the use of the mask in tragedy and comedy might not have been firmly established in the Roman Republic is plausible when we read that the actor Roscius (*ca.*, 126–62 B.C.) is credited with making the mask mandatory for both tragedy and comedy, supposedly because he wished to mask his natural squint. Whatever the reason, his influence was evidently powerful enough to authenticate and perpetuate their use. They were much the same as those that had been in use in the Greek theatre: old men, young men, old women, young women, rustics, and slaves. They were usually made of terracotta. As the quantity of melodrama and thrill increased in the stage presentations of the Empire, the masks became more startling and horrible (figures 25, 26).

The costumes for comedy and tragedy also followed Greek models: long tragic gowns, short comic tunics, elevated tragic boots, and short comic shoes. In the early presentations of tragedy and comedy the two types were separate and consistent. In the Empire, however, several illustrations have shown that the grotesque comic costumes often appeared in the same productions with the traditional costume of tragedy, the juxtaposition being ludicrous in the extreme.

In the mimes the actors were barefoot and wore no masks. They

27 Roman comedy
Left, a bronze statuette of a Roman comic actor. The grotesque mask,
the padded body, the short tunic, the vigorous gesture are all
typical of his Greek predecessors. Right, a cast for making a comic mask,
found at Tarentum in southern Italy. The mask is for the stock
character of the comic slave. (Boston Museum of Fine Arts)

did use makeup, however, and sometimes wore wigs. The typical
costume of the mime was a hood which could be drawn over the
head or thrown back. One clown-type character whose head was
shaven seems to have worn a patchwork jacket, tights, and the phallus. Other characters, both men and women, seem to have worn costumes appropriate to their characters, with increasing emphasis on
elaborate display as the mime ascended in popularity with widespread audiences. The mime dancers became notable for the filmi-
ness of their attire, particularly the women, and sometimes they wore
nothing at all.

However far the pantomime diverged from its inspiration in the
tragedy, it did maintain the use of masks. Sometimes as many as five
were used by one performer during a single presentation. But since
there was no need for his voice to be heard, the mouths of these
masks were closed, not open as in the Greek originals. The panto-
mimist also wore a long tragic gown, now supple and made of silk.
As the pantomimes of the Empire became more elaborate, and
women joined the troupes, costumes came to be symbolic and generally scant. Mercury is described as wearing nothing but a short mantle over his left shoulder and a tiny pair of golden wings; a host of
Cupids wore nothing but wings and tiny arrows. Beautiful bodies

were much admired in pantomime actors, and they were not con-
cealed or camouflaged.

Acting a despised profession

So far did the Romans follow the Greek tradition that women did
not appear in the regular comedies and tragedies, men taking all the
parts. But in the mimes from the beginning and in the pantomimes
as time went on, women, as we have seen, were assigned the female
parts.

Though the Roman audience expected a high degree of skill from
theatrical performers, the demands on the individual artist were not
so great as in the Greek theatre. Those parts of the plays which were
sung were generally performed by specially trained singers (*cantores*),
while the actor pantomimed the action. We have already mentioned
that the player in the pantomimes was relieved of all vocalization.
Though all actors were expected to have some dancing skill, this was
especially stressed in the mimes and pantomimes. There was no lim-
itation in the Roman theatre to three actors as there was in the Greek.
Hence there was no doubling of parts except in the early traveling
companies of masked players. Actors were cheap and plentiful in the
Empire, and an acting company could be as large as it needed to be.
Often, indeed, it was even larger.

Actors were classified as tragedians, comedians, mimes, or pantomimists. Even within these classifications, actors specialized in particular roles. Quintilian tells us of the comedian Demetrius, who
specialized in gods, young men, good fathers, slaves, matrons, and
respectable old women, while his fellow-comedian Stratocles won his
success in the roles of sharp-tempered old men, cunning slaves, parasites, pimps, and other such lively figures. Aesopus, the great tragedian of the first century B.C., evidently played his best roles as
Agamemnon in the *Iphigenia* of Ennius, as Atreus in the *Clytemnestra* of Accius, and as the title character in Ennius' *Andromacha*.

The most famous of Roman actors was the comedian Roscius (d.
62 B.C.) who won fame and fortune through his acting. Before Roscius, the accepted style of acting was exaggerated and bombastic.
He introduced moderation and a kind of verisimilitude which, in his
skillful hands, became quite popular. Both he and Aesopus founded
schools of acting, and even today the fame of the former lives in the
compliment applied to a good actor: that he is "a veritable Roscius."
The early nineteenth century was particularly fond of the designation, and actors were billed as "The Young American Roscius"
(Samuel Cowell, 1820–64), "The Hibernian Roscius" (G. V. Brooke,

28 Wall painting from Pompeii
Paintings such as this, from the first century B.C., are found on the walls of private dwellings in Pompeii. Some have the tragic mask above them, some the comic mask. They seem to indicate that the Romans were interested in the differentiation of stage setting, and bear out Vitruvius' prescription of set scenes for the various types of plays. (The Metropolitan Museum of Art)

1818–66), "The Scottish Roscius" (H. E. Johnston, 1777–1845), "The Young Roscius" (William Betty, 1791–1874), "The American Roscius" (Ira Aldridge, 1804–1867), and—rather provincial and somewhat late—"The Ohio Roscius" (Louis Aldrich, 1843–1901).

Among the pantomimists, the most famous were the tragic dancer Pylades and the comic dancer Bathyllus; both gained great personal popularity as well as succeeding in establishing the new art form most firmly. The mime dancer Paris was said to have been the favorite of both Nero and his Empress. He suffered for the excellence of his art, for it is said that Nero, himself an actor, had him put to death in a fit of professional jealousy.

The income of Roman actors varied widely from nothing at all to a reported equivalent of twenty thousand dollars, the annual income of Roscius. So independently wealthy did Roscius become that for some years before his death he could afford to act without compensation—and did. Favorite performers, of course, were also the recipients of lavish gifts from wealthy admirers. It is said that Sulla had a golden ring bestowed upon Roscius, thus raising him to the rank of knight, while Cicero conducted a lawsuit for him against a wealthy citizen whose slave Roscius had instructed.

In spite of the honors and gifts given individual members of the profession, Roman actors as a whole were classed as *infami*. They had no civil rights, and, as we have mentioned, no Roman citizen could earn his livelihood in the theatre without losing all his civil

29 Roman comedy scenes

Left, a vase from Campania in southern Italy, showing two comic actors dancing. Here the costumes are similar to those found in Greek Old Comedy, with grotesque masks and body padding, long nether garments, and long sleeves. Right, a painting from Pompeii showing a scene from a comedy, with a slave, a courtesan, and another male figure. (Boston Museum of Fine Arts; Mauiri, *Roman Painting*)

privileges. Actors were, for the most part, slaves trained and supported to add prestige to their wealthy masters or to be hired out to the state or to other individuals as a total acting unit. The marriage of an actor to the child, grandchild, or great-grandchild of a senator was likely to be declared invalid, and any soldier appearing on the stage was instantly punished by death.

Having no basis in religion, acting was admired as an art by the Romans, but despised as a profession. Individual performers were patronized by the wealthy and many were intimate with the great and the near-great. Some of the more fascinating female mimes and pantomimists became the mistresses of prominent men. Seneca speaks of the pampered lives led by the slavewomen performers of the pantomimes who were owned by wealthy Romans, and it is said that when Antonius was traveling about Italy campaigning for Caesar, his traveling companion was the mime-dancer Cytheris. In the Empire the attempt to titillate jaded appetites produced shocking scenes in the theatre which were meant to rival the cruel games of the arena. On the day that Caligula was murdered the Theatre of Marcellus offered as part of a mime the actual crucifixion of a captured robber, and Heliogabalus is said to have ordered the realistic performance of adultery on the mime stage.

Thus it was that in the Empire actors as a class acquired a very dissolute reputation, and the early Christian Church declared against them. No Christian was permitted to witness a theatrical performance, much less become a part of it. For centuries the ban persisted and until after the time of Molière actors were not even permitted to be buried in holy ground. It is one of the ironies of history that in spite of this violent stand against the theatre, it was in the Church that the drama was reborn long after the fall of Rome.

Summary

We can find in Roman drama no evidence of great originality or creative genius. It exhibits no development from native and indigenous sources. Every part of Roman theatrical activity was an adoption or an adaptation of foreign models. Playwriting consisted almost entirely in copying from the Greeks. The great Roman theatre buildings were adapted from earlier Greek models. Staging practice was an extension of the Greek. Even the sole theatrical presentation which might be said to have originated with the Romans—the art of the pantomime—derived its materials from Greek legends. Roman theatre was an exotic and foreign growth pampered or reviled as the political atmosphere of the moment dictated. Yet its practices did have a great effect on the theatre of succeeding ages.

Through the critical dictates of Horace and the aping of Senecan forms, the Roman theatre delivered to posterity the idea of set forms in drama. Through its love of display, it established spectacle as a part of theatre.

Among the physical aspects of theatre, Rome initiated the use of the front curtain, established the integral theatre building where stage house and auditorium were a single unit, at least introduced the idea of an indoor theatre by roofing over some of its structures, and began the plan of a reserved-seat house.

On the debit side, we owe to the Romans the disrepute under which the acting profession suffered for centuries (and still does, to some extent, even today), as well as the shameful institution of hired *claques,* whose antics have since annoyed theatre patrons in more than one period of theatrical history.

For both good and bad, we owe the Romans much. Theatre never had with them, and never would again, the importance it had achieved with the Greeks. But many of the things they did have had a recurring influence through the years.

5

THEATRE

IN THE MIDDLE AGES

Theatre did not die with Rome. The seeds of drama were long underground and the quickening was slow, but the flowering did come, and even through the long winter of the Dark Ages there were sporadic and weak growths, the evidences of which we can now trace.

It had not been the early Christians alone who had deplored Roman theatre in the time of the Empire, for it is said that the Emperor Marcus Aurelius averted his eyes from the stage when public functions required his presence, and that he complained of the low state to which theatre in his day had sunk. But it was the Christians who were most violently opposed to this pagan activity. The newly converted were most violent of all (see Tertullian's *De Spectaculis*). The Christian Church early declared war on the theatre, and waged it vigorously for almost a millennium. Council followed council, edict followed edict, yet the love of many professed Christians for their spectacles was not killed. Even the Christian emperors went no further than to legislate against performances on Sundays and holy days. And in the sixth century, the eastern Emperor, Justinian, married Theodora, who was said to have been a mime dancer (although it must be recorded that he continued to oppose theatre). The Roman Popes and the Church hierarchy were implacably hostile; the ecclesiastical writer, Orosius, lays a large share of the blame for the sack of Rome by the Ostrogoths on the decay engendered by theatre. The invading barbarians, however, despised spectacles, though Sidonius, writing in 467, speaks of a theatre still in operation in Rome. In the next century, Cassiodorus suggests that the tastes of the new rulers were more debilitating to theatre than the ethics of Christianity. There is no further mention of theatre by Roman writers after the invasions of the Lombards in 568. In the Eastern Empire, a final reference in 692 seems to indicate the existence of theatre there, as does a reference from Barcelona somewhat earlier in the seventh century. In the eighth century, John of Damascus condemned secular performances as rivals of the Mass, and early in the ninth century the Church issued a decree forbidding members of the clergy to watch actors at plays given on the stage or at marriages, while Charlemagne forbade actors to don priests' robes. In the tenth century, the erudite nun, Hroswitha of Gandersheim, wrote six moral plays "after Terence," the texts of which are still extant. After this the information becomes more extensive and more definite.

The theatre, then, never really died. Evidently the performers of the Roman theatre continued to ply their craft in some form, their status no doubt the lowest of the low: jugglers, acrobats, dancers, rope walkers, animal trainers, mimes, and musicians continued to amuse and amaze their public wherever opportunity afforded. They performed at fairs, in marketplaces, at crossroads, and—if they were lucky—in the great halls of castles. Often they were beaten, jailed, and driven from town to town. As time went on their repertoires included the stock in trade of the Teutonic gleeman and scop, those wandering tellers of tales, as well as the accomplishments of the earlier theatre. The horizontally stratified medieval society was exceedingly fond of minstrelsy, and the jongleurs were welcomed by peasants, clergy, and nobility, not only because they provided entertainment but also because they brought news of other places. Most socially acceptable of these traveling entertainers were the minstrels who sang the *gestes*.

While these professionals, however debased, were managing to carry on the ragged tradition of theatre, the same evolution of folk festivals which we have witnessed in primitive man and in the very ancient Greeks was going on throughout what is now Europe. Seasonal festivities and fertility rites—issuing from earliest pagan times —were developing into festival plays and May games, sword dances, and mummers' plays. The Church first opposed, then compromised with all of these; and some they finally adopted and adapted to Christian practice. (Many of our Christmas, New Year's, and Easter customs are of pagan origin.) It was in the Church itself that the most significant drama of medieval times had its birth and development. Thus, ironically, the great opponent of theatre over many centuries became its progenitor; once more a wondrous theatre found its beginning in religious ceremony, just as it had with the Greeks.

Church influence preeminent

Medieval society was stratified on three levels: nobility, clergy, and peasants. Community of interests existed within these classes, but there was no such thing as nationalism. The nobility were the great landowners, the possessors of wealth. The clergy were the aristocracy of intellect, and, while its individual members supposedly possessed no wealth, the Church itself was rich and powerful. The peasants did the work of the world, and owed allegiance to these two masters—first to the Church for spiritual welfare, and second to the feudal lords for material welfare. The feudal lords, too, were subject to the Church, and medieval history offers a long series of power struggles between nobility and Church officials. The Church presided over every aspect of existence; it was universally accepted that life in this world was simply a preparation for life in the next and that no one could be admitted to the afterlife except through the Church. The individual man counted for little except as he joined the community effort to glorify God and the Church. Hence the Middle Ages is a great period of anonymity in art and accomplishment. Who designed the miraculous cathedrals which are the work of this period? Who wrote the plays, composed the music, painted the pictures? The names we have are few indeed, but the wonderful selfless products still endure.

Often the emphasis upon the life to come made existence in this vale of tears incredibly difficult. (Perhaps because life *was* so hard in feudal times the people *had* to look forward to Paradise to make earth bearable.) Few were the pleasures of either peasant or lord; wars were frequent, and the Crusades sapped the wealth and strength of all Europe. In this atmosphere, minstrels were welcomed, and the colorful ritual of the Catholic Church was looked upon with delight as well as reverence. Into this world the new drama was born.

Drama included in the Mass

By the sixth century the Mass, with its celebration of the Eucharist, was the most important service of the Church. The service was conducted in Latin and its ritual was fixed and rigid. The pattern of prayer, reading, chant, and song, while invariable in its main outline,

30 *The Christmas Play of St. George*
The great hall of a medieval castle, with its tall windows, vaulted
ceiling, and gallery over the entrance doors, was well suited to the
presentation of plays. The far end of the room, with its two great doors
and the gallery above them, has curious similarities to the stage
backing shown in the DeWitt drawing of the Swan theatre
(figure 56). Notice that here the audience surrounds the costumed
players. (Richard Leacroft Theatre Collection)

took cognizance of special events in the Church calendar as well.
It was in the Easter Mass that drama began.

One part of the Mass was the singing of "Alleluia" by the choir
at various intervals. Some time about the turn of the ninth century,
an anonymous monk-musician, thinking to add more beauty to the
service (or simply to relieve the monotony), hit upon the idea of
holding the last syllable of the "Alleluia," and singing it to more
music. These wordless sequences, called *sequentiae,* developed in

81

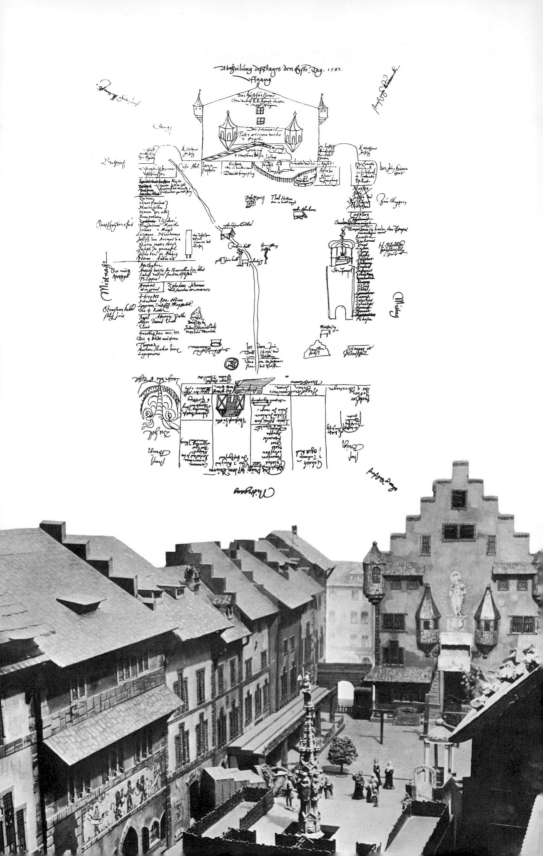

time into elaborate, beautiful, and melodious tunes for each particular feast day. They were immensely popular, particularly in the court of Charlemagne. They were also very long, very numerous, and had to be memorized by the monks because there were no hymnbooks.

There is a story, probably apocryphal, that a famous musician, Notker Balbulus of St. Gall, in what is now Switzerland, first wrote words to these wordless sequences because he had had a hard time learning them as a choir boy. He himself says that he got the idea from an unknown monk of Jumièges who arrived at St. Gall in flight from the Normans; but he was quite taken with the idea and immediately developed it. He used passages from the Bible suited to the special significance of the particular Mass, and for the first time music and words were paralleled on the basis of one note to a syllable. These worded sequences or tropes did indeed make the music easier to remember. Needless to say, the innovation proved immensely popular, was much copied throughout the Church, and literally hundreds of tropes were written. Many of these were antiphonal: the choir divided the lines and sang them back and forth. Much of the material was already in dialogue form, e.g. the colloquy of the shepherds and the angels at the birth of Christ, or the questions and answers of the angel at Christ's tomb with the visiting three Marys. Here was one of the elements of drama.

Another element was scenic representation. This was already present in the Mass, for in order to teach its parishioners the important aspects of the faith the Church had pictures and statuary as well as pantomime by the priests conducting the services. The Christmas story was made real by showing Mary and the Christ Child in the manger, the visits of the shepherds and the wise men, and the appearance of the star. In the Good Friday service preceding Easter, the cross was taken down from the high altar, wrapped in grave clothes, and deposited in a representational sepulchre. At the Easter service the priests went to the tomb, brought out the cross, and replaced it on the altar. This was a type of dumb show, presented without words, but it certainly and very graphically made the event clear

31 *The cycle plays at Luzerne*
Above left, a sketch of the setting for the first day from the prompt book of Renward Cysat, city clerk of Luzerne and twice director of the play. Below left, a model of the setting for the second day by Professor Albert Koester. The mansions were erected in the marketplace, with spectators viewing the performance from windows or from specially constructed stands. (Luzerne Zeatrobibliothek; Theater-Museum, Munich)

to the illiterate parishioners, who were listening to a service in a language they did not understand and to whom the Bible was a closed book.

The only element lacking was impersonation, and it soon followed. One of the most popular of the tropes was that sung at the Easter Mass, the so-called *Quem Quaeritis* trope, the earliest manuscript of which comes from Limoges and dates back to about 923. This is essentially a drama having three parts: the question by the angels, the answer of the three Marys, and the reply to the Marys' answer. The trope was sung antiphonally by the choir, and because of its hint of dialogue, was very popular. So long as it remained in the Mass, it could be nothing more than a lyrical embellishment. But some time in the tenth century it was transferred to the Matin service (theoretically at sunrise to begin the day with prayer, but actually at seven o'clock), because supposedly this corresponded with the actual time when Christ arose, and also because the plain Matin service needed beautifying. The new order of the Matin service at Easter then included the *Elevation of the Cross* in dumb show; the traditional first, second, and third readings and responses; the *Quem Quaeritis* trope; and the *Te Deum Laudamus*. As we see, there were now two dramatic elements in the same service; because of the comparative informality of the Matin service the trope could be unhampered in its development.

Because of its essentially dramatic character, the trope was soon taken out of the choir stalls and sung before the altar by two boy singers, representing angels, and three men singers as the three Marys. Thus the element of impersonation entered. After the *Elevation of the Cross*, a most dramatic event in itself, the empty sepulchre was left, so it was suggested that the singers sing the trope by the tomb. The boys sat on a rock by the tomb and the men stood near. It was not long until the participants began to dress in costume for the parts, and then true drama was born, even though the parts were still sung.

This dramatic presentation was, of course, under the careful supervision of the clergy. In the tenth century we find in the *Concordia Regularis* of Ethelwold, Bishop of Winchester, most specific and detailed instructions for the staging of the trope. No doubt the dramatic presentation was warmly welcomed by the worshipers, for it was soon expanded. Two new episodes found in the Biblical narrative were added: John and Peter at the tomb, and Christ's appearance to Mary Magdalene. The total presentation now required twenty to thirty minutes and constituted a small play.

Imitation of the Easter play for other occasions led to the adoption of a Christmas trope dealing with the visit of the shepherds to the manger. The action of the play was almost identical with the earlier one. It began, in song, *"Quem quaeritis in praesepe, pastores, dicite,"* ("Whom seek ye in the manger, shepherds, tell us") and used a manger instead of a sepulchre. The Easter play was known technically as the *Sepulchrum,* the Christmas play as the *Praesepe.* The Christmas play was also expanded by three scenes. They were the Annunciation, the birth of John the Baptist, and a scene depicting Joseph's doubts about the Virgin Mary—a most popular theme in medieval times.

In the Twelfth Day Matin service there was a dumb show in which a large tin star, hung on a wire extending the length of the church, was pulled along the wire from the entrance to the chancel. Some time in the eleventh century, a Twelfth Day, or Epiphany, play was built around this stage property. Three monks representing the three wise men entered the main door during the singing of the trope and followed the star up the aisle. After presenting their gifts, they sang the *Alleluia* and the *Te Deum Laudamus.* Text and dramatic occasions were expanded by the appearance of angels telling the wise men to go a different way, and by a scene in which Herod boasts of his qualities and asks where the Child is. Herod was the first villain introduced into medieval drama, and what a popular character he turned out to be!

These, and the play of the walk to Emmaus (given the Monday after Easter), as well as the play of the Slaughter of the Innocents (given on December 28), were finally consolidated into two series in chronological order given on Twelfth Day, the greatest feast day of the Church calendar, and on Easter. These two plays told the whole story of Christ's life, putting emphasis on the main Biblical events; each occupied the time between the Matin service and the Mass on the day when it was given.

The incorporation of the Christmas material with the Twelfth Day play left the earlier holiday without dramatic representation. But soon St. Augustine's famous *Sermon against Jews, Pagans, and Arians* began to take on dramatic qualities for the Christmas Matins. In this exceedingly rhetorical sermon, various prophets are called upon to give their testimony of Christ's coming, as are various Gentile sages, all in direct address; the listeners are called upon to mend their ways and do good. Drama entered with the designation of monks to portray the parts of the prophets, each of them in characteristic costumes designed by themselves. Rivalry begot richness, and the people desired to see these costumes more fully. So the *Procession of Prophets* was instituted. Soon more monks were put into the procession than the sermon called for; Adam and Noah were added, then Balaam, who rode an ass (another monk) with beating and braying—a humorous incident which became even more so because an angel followed after the ass and threw Balaam. As others sought prominence in the procession and strove to build up their parts into small plays, the *Procession of Prophets* became a series of little plays attached to the Christmas Matins.

Thus there was a series of plays portraying the whole plan of salvation, from the original sin to the birth, death, resurrection, and ascension of Christ. The plays were very effective in teaching the people the history of their religion and the churches were crowded on these great feast days. Gradually another element was added. The dialogue, sung in Latin, was supplemented by an immediate translation into the spoken vernacular. As the incidents multiplied and expanded, singing disappeared, characters not called for in the Biblical narrative were added, the casts grew larger, and the clergy called upon the laity for help. The increased complexity of the staging forced the performances out of the church into the churchyard since there was not room enough inside. This expansion caused further additions to be made; the plays were finally removed from consecrated ground, the clerics withdrew from the performances, and the dramas were secularized. This secularization is significant; from this point on the plays took on a definitely national growth and character.

Thus developed the most typical of the medieval dramas as a direct outgrowth of medieval society and as one of its most representative art forms. There were also other kinds of dramatic presentations in the latter part of the Middle Ages, and these we will consider as we discuss the plays themselves.

Mystery, morality, miracle: sacred drama develops

The dramatic literature of the Middle Ages may be divided into two main types: the cycle plays and the noncycle plays. The first type includes the many series of Biblical plays which developed along the line we have just discussed; the second includes saint plays, moralities, folk plays, serious plays, and comedies.

At the height of the vogue of the cycle play, each town of any consequence presented its own series. After 1264, when Pope Urban IV decreed the celebration of Corpus Christi Day on the Thursday after Trinity Sunday (two months after Easter), it became customary—particularly in England—to give the whole cycle of plays from

32 *Title page of a medieval book*
The scene above is from the farce
of *Master Pierre Pathelin,* the lower
from *The Morality of the Evil Rich
and the Leper.* As customary in plays
of these types, the costumes are
contemporary with the time
of performance.

creation to the day of Last Judgment on this day. That is why these
plays are sometimes called Corpus Christi plays. (The festival was
instituted to celebrate the decision that the bread and wine of the
communion actually became the body and blood of Christ.) A few
of these complete cycles are still in existence, as well as many single
plays which seem to have belonged to a cycle.

Among the earliest texts extant today are a few from the eleventh
century, such as *The Pastoral Office* (*Officium Pastorum*) and *The
Star* (*Stella*) from Rouen, two similar ones from Nevers, and a Herod
play from Compiègne. All of these are written entirely in Latin, and
are obviously for production in the church sanctuary itself. From the
next century we have the *Play of the Anti-Christ* (*Ludos de Anti-
christo*) from Tegernsee, *The Promise* (*Sponsus*) from Limoges,
and the famous Fleury Play-Book at Orleans containing five plays on
Biblical themes. This is the century also of three innovations: the
first signed pieces by Hilarius of both French and English background (a *Lazarus* and a *Daniel*), the first play in the vernacular
(the Beauvais *Daniel*), and the first play directed to be played out-

doors (the Anglo-Norman *Mystery of Adam* (*Mystère d'Adam*) whose stage directions indicate production on the church porch).

The thirteenth and fourteenth centuries are the years of the great cycles, sometimes called mystery plays, covering the whole plan of salvation, and the so-called passion plays confined to the death and resurrection of Christ. Four complete cycles survive: one of forty-eight plays from York, one of twenty-five plays from Chester, one of thirty-two plays from Wakefield (sometimes called the Towneley cycle), and one of forty-two plays from Coventry. There are also separate plays from Newcastle, from Northampton, from Norwich, from Tours, and from Origny; and we have evidence that cycles were given also at London, Worcester, Beverley, Lancaster, Leicester, Canterbury, Rouen, Padua, Friuli, Ravenna, and many other places. Of the extant plays, the Brome *Abraham and Isaac* (which may be a single survival of the London cycle) has been highly praised for its dramatic qualities; the Townley cycle has been called the most notable for its literary style, and its *Second Shepherd's Play* has been performed most successfully in recent times. Indeed, the whole York cycle has been enthusiastically and beautifully revived by E. Martin Browne, an English actor-producer.

The popularity of the cycle plays continued through the fifteenth century; additional ones originated in that time, most notably the *Mysteries and Moralities* especially adapted for production by the sisters of S. Michel at Huy near Liège, and the famous *Mystery of the Passion* written by Arnoul Greban, which is supposed to have taken forty days in performance.

After 1550, these plays generally ceased to be produced. The last attempt to produce the Coventry cycle was in 1591; a revival in Chester in 1607 was looked upon as an antiquarian curiosity. They had been immensely popular throughout all of western Europe, not only in France and England, but also in Italy and Spain. In both Italy and Spain the presentation of these Biblical plays endured longer than in England and France. Italian scene designers of the Renaissance used them for spectacular scenic effects, and in Spain they did not finally disappear until about midway into the eighteenth century. In modern times, the passion plays at Oberammergau, in Brittany, and at several other places give us a good idea of the survival of this form. Like the Gothic cathedral, added to over many centuries by different artists in differing styles, the medieval cycle play was an accretion over a long period of various dramatic elements —serious and comic, tragic and grotesque—all blending into a unique whole which ran the gamut of human emotions. Thus medieval

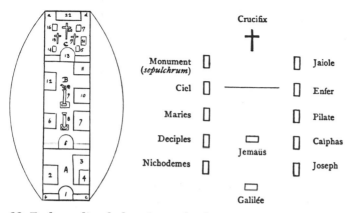

33 Early medieval plans for cycle plays
Right, a plan for the mansions in the Play of the Resurrection; left,
a plan for the mansions in the Donauschingen plays. The cycle
plays were presented within the churches with just such plans. Each
episode had its own platform, and all were related to the high altar.
(Chambers, *Medieval Stage;* Karlsruhe, *Schauspiele des Mittealters*)

architecture and medieval drama differed basically from their Greek
predecessors, in which unity of tone, purpose, and detail were paramount. The medieval heritage is most notable in the varied scenes
of Shakespeare's plays, the Greek in the unity of those of Racine.

Deriving from the cycle plays were the saint plays, or miracle
plays which had their start in the twelfth century; these, for the most
part, used non-Biblical materials. Myriads of saints were celebrated
in this fashion, the texts varying in length from what we consider a
normal playing time to several days. The two most popular figures
in these saint plays are St. Nicholas and the Virgin Mary (who indeed
was derived from the Bible, but to whom innumerable apocryphal
events are ascribed). More than forty plays of the *Miracles of Our
Lady* are preserved in two manuscripts at the Bibliothèque Nationale,
and these are evidences of the great cult of the Virgin Mary which
was so widespread in the Middle Ages. She seems not to have been
so popular, however, in England, where the Reformation no doubt
early eliminated traces of Mariolatry. The Fleury Play-Book, mentioned above, contains four St. Nicholas plays, and Hilarius, whom
we have also mentioned, wrote a famous St. Nicholas play. In England, St. George was the subject of many of these plays, notably at
Lydd, Bassingbourne, and Windsor. The patron saints of city, town,
and village all over Europe were honored with plays, and the
hagiology of the Church was combed for suitable subjects.

A third type of medieval play, the morality, seems to have begun about the middle of the fourteenth century, flourished through the fifteenth century, and lasted well into the sixteenth. The morality was an allegory which originated in the Lord's Prayer; it was regarded as the ideal prayer, and to make it more effective the clergy divided it into seven parts to combat the seven deadly sins. This exposition became a play of sorts, called *Paternoster*, with a list of characters including the hero, Man, the seven deadly sins, and the seven moral virtues. Like the cycle play, it originally appeared only in the church, then moved outdoors, being given by lay persons rather than priests. In various places, a special group of persons was chosen to perform the play. Only one of these plays, that of Beverley, survives. But there are several texts which use a similar theme and characters, the most important of which is the play called *Everyman*. This is an English play which may be a translation of the Dutch *Elckerlijk*, or the two may be from a common source. It is a very moving exposition of the salvation of Everyman through the offices of Good Deeds, who accompanies him to his judgment. A similar pattern is followed in other moralities—the fragmentary *Pride of Life; Purity and the Young Child; Mind, Will and Understanding; Mankind;* and the *Castle of Perseverance*. As the morality developed it became more particularized in its formation and use. It was adapted for production in the schools; education was then made the theme, as in *Wit and Science* and *The Nature of the Four Elements*. Sometimes the play became a propaganda instrument; sometimes it was used as political satire, as in Skelton's *Magnificence* and David Lyndsay's *Satire of the Three Estates*. As in the cycle plays, the character of the devil was a most popular one, and his page or attendant, usually called "the Vice," became the chief funster. His name soon developed into a type name, and became the prototype for many Falstaffian characters. The morality play as a type was transmuted into full-fledged and significant drama in the plays of Ben Jonson.

All of these plays had the moral purpose of edification. Before great drama could flourish this didactic element had to be disposed of. Such a step would not be likely to come from the clergy, but from the common people; the germ of it is found in another type of medieval drama, the folk play. We have already mentioned the development of this type of presentation from rural festivals; it is important because it took the drama out of its religious atmosphere and created pleasure for its own sake. The fusion of the May Day festivities and the legend of Robin Hood—a national hero as far as the peasants were concerned—produced in England such a play as

Robin Hood and the Sheriff of Nottingham, and in France the pretty pastoral of Adam de la Hale, *Game of Robin and Marion.* The *St. George Play,* which developed from the Anglo-Saxon sword dance, included impersonations of heroes, burlesques of these heroes, the killing of a fool who intervenes in the fight, and his resuscitation by a doctor variously named in different localities. The significance of these folk plays is that they introduced drama as pure entertainment, and the pastoral comedy elements were continued into a later age in such plays as Shakespeare's *A Winter's Tale* and *As You Like It.*

Other kinds of noncycle plays found in the Middle Ages were such history plays as the fifteenth century *Mystery of the Siege of Orleans,* which treated the almost-contemporary story of Joan of Arc, and Jacques Milet's *The History of the Destruction of Troy,* dealing with an earlier period. A unique manifestation of another kind of history was the late fourteenth century *The History of Griseldis,* dramatized from Boccaccio's tale for presentation at a French nuptial festivity.

The comedy accretions in the cycle plays were reflected in the presentation of various farces, *soties,* and humorous monologues as separate entities. Adam de la Hale is responsible for an early farce, *Play of the List,* written about 1267 to amuse a group of his friends. But the most famous, and justly so, of this type is the anonymous *Master Pierre Pathelin* (figure 32), which is usually dated about 1465. Numerous performances in our own day bear witness to its dramatic vitality. The *sotie* was essentially a comedy played by fools in their characteristic costume, and was marked by clever repartée and a tendency to satirize, such as in Gringore's *Play of the Prince of Fools.* In Germany, numerous farces featuring a *Narr,* or fool, were played by lively amateurs. The humorous monologue, while not truly a play, evidently had an important place in dramatic activity, and one of the most interesting of these is Rutebeuf's *Speech of the Herb Peddler* dating from the thirteenth century. An elaboration of the monologue is evident in *The Foure PP,* a dialogue between a palmer, a pardoner, a 'potecary, and a pedlar, written by John Heywood (d. 1580). These short pieces are sometimes called "interludes," and in Italy at least they were sometimes given between the scenes of the more solemn sacred plays. For the most part, however, the occasions upon which they were presented were very numerous and varied— fairs, festivals, banquets, visits, school functions, and so forth. It has been suggested that the mime tradition fostered the production of these secular performances, and that in them the professional actor chiefly appeared.

It seems to be true that in the Middle Ages the lines between types

34 *Hans Sachs*
Left, in these illustrations for a morality by Hans Sachs several of
the characters seem to be wearing masks. Particularly interesting is the
head mask in the form of a donkey in the upper picture. Right,
a contemporary portrait of this prolific writer.
(The Metropolitan Museum of Art)

of drama, and between drama and narrative, were very loosely drawn
so that no hard and fast distinctions can be made. We have simply
indicated here the most outstanding of the kinds of dramatic performances of the Middle Ages, and we shall discover how these
various beginnings were consummated in the periods that followed.

Performances abandon church

Occasionally it has been suggested that the magnificent theatre
buildings erected by the Romans all over Europe and the Near East
must have continued into the Middle Ages the tradition of the dramatic performances of Greece and Rome. But the truth of the matter
is that the majority of these structures, long unused after the fall of
Rome, fell into decay, were dismantled for their materials, or were
put to other uses. It was not until late in the medieval period that we
read of an elaborate production of a cycle play in the old Roman
theatre at Orange, and of another in the ancient Colosseum at Rome.
But in both cases the playhouse was only incidental to the type of

production, which had been developed quite independently of Roman theatre.

It seems likely that no permanent playhouses of any kind were built during the Middle Ages, although a dubious reference describes a playhouse at Autun in 1516 as having boxes and a pit with a moat separating the stage from the eighty thousand seats. Actually, the playing place was chosen and arranged for the occasion of the individual performance and varied with the type of play presented.

Heaven to the right, Hell to the left

The great cycle plays had two main methods of presentation: one on fixed stages and the other on movable platform stages. Both had a similar origin. We have seen that the church altar was the place where the first rudimentary dramas were given. As the embryonic drama expanded in incident and dramatis personae, the chancel became too small to be adequate. So the drama expanded into the nave of the church. But here visibility became a problem and platforms were erected so that the action could be seen by the spectators. At first there seem to have been but two of these, with the altar comprising a third. Then the number gradually grew as the scripts grew, progressing to the very complicated arrangement of the Donaueschingen Passion Play of the sixteenth century (figure 33), which used the plan of nave, choir, and sanctuary, and had twenty-two locations or "mansions."

The platform arrangement was maintained when the dramas moved out of the sanctuary. A platform was erected for each locality involved in the action, Heaven being to the left of the spectator, Hell to the right, or, if viewed from the vantage point of the high altar, Heaven was on the right, Hell on the left—an orientation strongly rooted in medieval tradition. Sometimes the church itself figured in the action, as in the *Mystery of Adam*, where it is directed that a character enter or emerge from the church, and as in the Benedictbeuern Christmas Play, where it is directed that the chair of Augustine be set in front of the church, from which position Heaven would be on the occupant's right, Hell on his left. The rectangular arrangement of mansions which was originally dictated by the shape of the church was at first maintained in the outdoor productions, with the platforms facing each other and the actors moving from one to another as the action demanded.

When the plays abandoned church property and were presented in the market square, as at Lucerne, the same rectangular plan prevailed. In other places variations were worked out. In Cornwall the

93

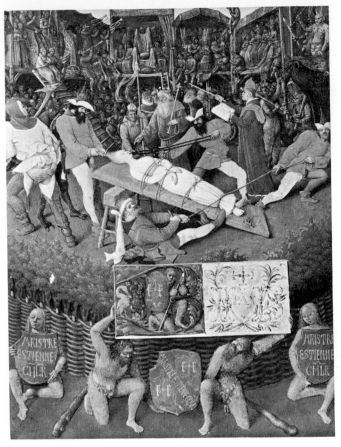

35 *The Martyrdom of St. Apollonia*
This famous Foquet miniature shows the use of raised mansion stages
with the angels to the right of the throne, the devil to the left, and the
climactic action of the saint play taking place on the *platea*, where
the priestly *régisseur*, book and baculus in hand, directs the
action. The figures in the foreground are merely the artist's decoration.
(Photographie Giraudon)

mansions were arranged in a circle, and in the famous Jean Fouquet
miniature of *The Martyrdom of St. Apollonia* (figure 35), the mansions do not quite encircle the playing area, with much of the action
taking place in the open area. The use of this open area, or *platea*, for
unlocalized action was fairly universal, whatever the arrangement of
the mansions.

In many places on the Continent the playing area became a long,
raised stage on which were erected the various mansions; here also

Heaven was to the left and Hell to the right of the spectator, but in reverse if seen from the traditional center stage point of view. The mansions were erected in a line along the stage, often extending for a hundred feet or more. The downstage area was then the *platea,* and actors emerged from or entered into the various structures upstage. The stage was provided with such trapdoors, underground passages, and overhead structures as were necessary. Such were the stages at Valenciennes (figure 36), at Mons, at Bourges. The audience sat on scaffolded seats, on the ground, or on the balconies or at windows of nearby houses.

Touring pageant wagons

In England, when the cycle plays became secularized they moved to stagewagons, or "pageants," rather than to stationary settings. Each separate play of the cycle had its separate wagon; these generally consisted of a lower and an upper deck, the lower curtained off for use primarily as a dressing and offstage area, the upper as the playing area (figure 37). Stations were set up—as many as were necessary to take care of the people—in the town square, at the town gates, on the green, at the crossroads, and so forth. The procession, headed by the clergy, proceeded in a predetermined order from one station to the next: Mass was celebrated, the first pageant wagon arrived as the church group moved to the next station, the first play was given; then the wagon moved on to the next station while the second pageant arrived and presented its play. Thus, although the plays had to be repeated, all the people could see them adequately. The stations were chosen by the town council and posted a month in advance. There were flags as markers at each station and grandstands for the spectators. Standing room was also sold on housetops. About a thousand people saw the play at each station; the number of stations varied from four to seven, to fourteen, and as many as sixteen. At York the ceremonies began at four-thirty in the morning; in Coventry, at six; in Newcastle, at noon. At Chester there were three days of plays beginning at noon each day. The pageants were stored in pageant houses from year to year, and were refurbished as necessary or desirable.

There are some records of pageant wagons being drawn up in a circle on the village green for the presentation of the cycle, but for the most part the plays in England were "traveling shows." This phenomenon marks the great difference between Continental and English productions, although it was no hard and fast rule. There is also some indication that wagons were occasionally used in France as well, and certainly in Spain the *fiestos de los carros* (festivals of the cars) was the well-established rule.

Effects lavish and literal

The arrangements for playing dictated the type of settings to be used, although whether the plays were stationary or perambulatory a verisimilitude in the staging was attempted. The earliest setting utilized the construction of the church, often placing Hell down the crypt stairs, and Heaven up the rood-loft stairs. Frequently a sepulchre was erected near the altar for the Easter play.

When platforms came into use they were beautifully curtained in silk and velvet and as lavishly furnished as possible. Because of their size (six to eight feet wide and eight to ten feet long), there could not be a great number of set pieces, but even here as much richness as possible was the rule. For the *Mystery of Adam,* for instance, we find it is directed that the Paradise shall be hung with curtains of silk, that there shall be many different fruit trees hung with fruit, and there shall be fragrant flowers and leaves. The extant sketches for the two days of the Lucerne play seem to indicate the building of rather elaborate structures with cupolas and a monster-like edifice for Hellmouth (figure 38). Where the plays were given on wagons the settings perforce remained comparatively simple; even so, however, there are accounts of flaming swords and altars, of leaves opening, and of hell fire.

It was in the horizontal simultaneous settings of France and the elaborate productions of the cycle plays in Italy that very complicated settings and effects were developed. Italian writers speak of monuments opening, of earthquakes, of heavenly beings descending from on high surrounded by the lights of stars, of trapdoors opening to swallow up buildings and persons, and of spotlights, which were evidently highly polished basins reflecting the sunlight. The famous architect, Brunelleschi, designed many of these settings. The elaborate and most minute directions for stage effects at Mons, at Valenciennes, and at Bourges, show us that a great deal of time, ingenuity, and money were expended to achieve them.

Contemporary accounts of the 1536 production of *The Acts of the Apostles* describe the rich colors of the canopy spread over the ancient Roman amphitheatre where the performance was given, and speak of the mechanical contrivances used to produce thunder and to simulate dragons spouting flames; of lions, camels, and flying owls; of devices used to raise and lower persons and beasts or to hide them in clouds; of ships sailing; of fountains spouting; of the burning or

36 *The cycle play at Valenciennes*
Model of the setting for the play given in France, from a miniature
painting by Hubert Calleau, 1547. Though here the platea is evidently
raised, the throne is still at the center, with Heaven to its right
and Hell to its left, other locations distributed between. Actors emerged
from the appropriate mansion and used the platea as undifferentiated
playing area. (The Cleveland Museum of Art, Collection
of the Educational Department)

decapitation of saints. At Mons, the playbook for the 1501 performance calls for highly complicated technical effects and describes how
they are to be achieved. According to its notations, trees and flowers
spring from the earth for the creation of the world; Noah's grapevines bear ripe fruit a moment after planting; water for the Deluge
is to be piped over the rooftops of the surrounding marketplace, and
fall in a downpour; the Hellmouth is to be alive with flame, gunpowder, and thunder; the Crucifixion is to seem meticulously real;
clouds are to descend during Christ's transfiguration and then he is
to ascend into Paradise. At Valenciennes, a spectator of 1547 speaks
of the verisimilitude of the miracle of the loaves and fishes; of the
turning of water into wine; of Lucifer coming up from Hell on a
dragon; of the souls of Herod and Judas being carried through the
air by devils. All these effects were under the supervision of a *maître
des feyntes,* who employed workmen to construct and operate them,
and who often went to great lengths to secure some little-seen or
spectacular wonder. There is a 1510 record in Vienna of the employment of eight "masters of machines" for a production there. Thus
the Middle Ages cared little for symbolic representation, but strove
for realism even in supernatural happenings; the spectators were no

37 *An English pageant wagon*
Model made from a drawing of an English pageant wagon at Coventry.
On the two-story movable wagon, drawn up in one of the town
squares, the actors perform the Trial of Jesus before Pilate. The curtained
area below the stage proper was used as a dressing and retiring room
for the actors not on stage. The audience stood all about the
pageant, or watched from the windows of surrounding houses. (The
Cleveland Museum of Art, Collection of the Educational Department)

doubt amazed and delighted, and certainly proud of the unique
achievements of their townsmen.

Noncycle plays, as a rule, had a much simpler production, although some of the saint plays were handled in the same way as the
cycle plays. Frequently, however, these saint plays were given in
schools, as were the moralities and the interludes. Here a simple platform sufficed, as it did for performances in town halls, in the banquet
rooms of manor houses (figure 30), and at court. Sometimes there
was not even a platform. The folk plays were usually given on village
greens without any particularized setting.

Most typical of the period, however, were the cycle plays, and we
shall see how the simultaneous setting and the unparticularized playing area were utilized in later designs for the theatre.

Costuming symbolic and stylized

The passion of the medieval populace for seeming truth and reality made costuming a necessity, although such costuming as there

was made no attempt at historical accuracy. We might say that costuming was treated symbolically rather than realistically. Typically, gloves were a sign of high rank. They were worn by God and his angels, by the prophets, by Pilate, and by Herod. The angels wore sheepskins overlaid with gold leaf, had gilded wings and diadems; their faces were often gilded. The fallen angels wore horrible masks, black clothes bristling with hair, cloven feet, and forked tails. Satan typically wore a horrible mask, hose, a hairy coat, and carried a staff and a leather club stuffed with wool with which to beat actors and spectators. Saved souls were dressed in white, damned souls in black. Judas wore a red wig and a yellow robe; Pilate and Herod had splendid clothes and carried clubs. Humble characters often wore the simple medieval peasant dress.

Several manuscripts and account books give specific descriptions of specialized costumes. Mezières' *Presentation of the Virgin* directs that Mary shall be clothed all in white and gold, the tunic very white and pleated, the mantle also of white in sendal or silk. Lucifer is to have horns, menacing teeth, a horrible expression, and to carry a bright iron chain with which to bind the archangel Michael. Michael himself is to be garbed "in a most fair fashion," and to brandish aloft a flashing sword. In the *Mystery of Adam,* whose rubrics, or production notes, are justly famous, God is to wear a dalmatic, Adam a red tunic, Eve a dress of white silk. For one of the Cornish plays, Adam and Eve wore white leather and had two costume changes—one to garments of fig leaves, the other to costumes made of skins. The devil often appeared in the guise of a serpent, and the animals, when they were not of domesticated variety like sheep and donkeys which could be used live, were simulated by having men wear appropriate skins. Wigs and beards were prepared for characters who would need them, as a listing at Twicksbury indicates in calling for "8 heads of hair for the Apostles, and 10 beards, and a face or vizard for the devil."

In the folk plays, the participants were usually costumed and had appropriate props, the clown invariably having a bladder on a stick to beat the spectators. The character of "The Vice" in the moralities carried a similar instrument, a device which was later used by the Elizabethan fool. In the French *soties,* the dress of all participants was that of the medieval fool, including the cap with long ears. Interludes were evidently played in the dress of the day.

In the early days of the cycle plays, costumes and properties were supplied by the Church. Even when the plays were secularized and moved out of the church proper, the clergy often provided robes, crosses, thuribles, and other items which were in their stores.

38 A favorite stage setting of medieval times
Left, a psalter of Henry of Blois showing an angel locking the damned
in Hell; right, an illustration showing Hellmouth, with the damned
souls and the attendant devils. Hell was a very literal place to the medieval
spectator, and was literally represented, not only in the plays,
but in other illustrations as well. The above representations, although
not primarily stage sets, are quite similar to what did appear
on medieval stages. (British Museum; Munich National Museum)

Otherwise, it seems to have been the general rule, particularly in
France, that each actor supplied his own costume. Special items were
generally paid for by the general fund, and much of our information
concerning costuming comes from inventories and expense accounts.

Though the costuming of the medieval plays would not satisfy a
modern audience, and though no attempt was made at historical
accuracy, the described results were almost invariably beautiful (or
horrifying) and effective. Medieval producers, no less than modern
ones, were aware of the aid which costume could give to characterization, and of the satisfaction effective costuming could provide an
audience.

Acting largely nonprofessional

The Middle Ages was the heyday of the amateur. By far the greatest number of parts, all through the entire period, fell to those whose

100

means of earning a living was not acting, although various elusive records indicate that professionals were also performing.

In their early stages the cycle plays were entirely in the hands of the clergy; they not only prepared the scripts but acted in them, taking the women's parts as well as the men's (a female character was indicated by the simple expedient of wearing a kerchief over the head and donning a cloak). There was also a clerical master of ceremonies, who held the prompt book and carried a short baton-like staff which was his badge of office.

As the plays expanded in text and the dramatis personae increased in number, laymen were invited to participate. Direction, however, remained in the hands of the clerical *régisseur,* who moved about in full view of the audience, prompt book and staff in hand. In some localities, this responsible position never devolved upon a lay member, but remained the prerogative of the Church. However, as the presentation of the plays became increasingly secular, the clergy withdrew from the acting assignments and often from that of director as well, so that the entire production was managed by the laity.

In England, production of the cycle plays was taken over by the guilds, which were powerfully functioning units by the twelfth century. The town council usually assigned the episodes to the guilds; the assignments often exhibited a piquant justice: to the plasterers and carpenters went the Creation; to the shipwrights, the Noah episode; to the goldsmiths, the Magi; to the cooks, the Harrowing of Hell; to the bakers, the Feeding of the Five Thousand or the Last Supper; to the scriveners, the Disputation in the Temple. The assignments, of course, varied from town to town, but ordinarily remained traditional in each place. Occasionally the craft guilds did not function, but the corporation of the town or a specially appointed body took care of the entire event.

The guild prepared its pageant with its setting, secured the costumes, hired and trained the actors, and presented its play in the sequence. The actors were paid with funds from special levies, guild treasuries, or town funds; the authorities demanded that the acting be good. Actors might be members of the producing guild or not, depending upon the demands of the parts and the available supply of potential actors. In 1476 in York, for instance, the Mayor appointed a committee of three or four actors at the beginning of Lent to interview aspirants for playing honors on Corpus Christi Day. In the same town, in 1446 and 1447, an expense account shows payments for acting to some minstrels and singers. It would appear that the amateur ranks were swelled by professionals when it seemed feasible and necessary. Some records indicate that actors were paid according to the dignity of the part: God in one instance was paid three shillings sixpence; Noah, one shilling; saved souls in Hell Wagon, twenty pence; damned souls, ten pence. But in other accounts, the length of the acting part determined the payment: for playing God, ten pence; Noah, one shilling; Noah's wife, eight pence. It is easy to imagine that the recruited professionals demanded and got whatever the traffic would bear.

There were frequent rehearsals—three or four times a week for two or three weeks before the play. When the plays were ready, the town council sent out vexillators, or standard bearers, to surrounding towns to read the notice of the play. They were usually three in number and were accompanied by two trumpeters.

In England, the production of religious plays was sometimes in the hands of a special religious guild, as at Sleaford, where the Guild of the Holy Trinity performed the play of the Ascension in 1480. Guilds of the same nature seemed to operate in London, and in 1378 we find a petition from the clerks of St. Paul's to Richard II complaining of the rivalry of certain "unexpert people" in the playing of an Old Testament drama. Even here there was rivalry between professional and amateur. In the small towns of the English countryside, Biblical plays sometimes toured from town to town, each vicinity bearing a part of the expense. Generally this type of production was an occasional rather than an annual affair.

In France and Italy, on the other hand, the production of plays was, after its relinquishment by the clergy, primarily in the hands of specially constituted organizations rather than the craft guilds. The *Confrèrie de la Passion*, chartered by Charles VI in Paris in 1402, was one of the most famous of these. It was licensed to perform in the Hôpital de la Trinité, and thus became the first permanently established playing company in a permanent playing place in the Middle Ages. It was the model for many another pious brotherhood in many another French town. Usually these were formed to do honor to a saint; at their annual observance (usually held in the summertime) they presented a dramatic performance, either from Biblical materials or from the lives of the saints. They sometimes recruited actors by means of processions or through the town crier.

Side by side with the brotherhoods were other more secular bodies of performers, the *Sociétés Joyeuse*, or mirthful fellowships. Those of a literary bent no doubt had their origin in the schools and presented *soties* and farces as well as religious plays. Another type were the fool companies, the most famous of which is that of *L'Infanterie*

39 Two scenes from Terence
Left, this scene, as presented at Venice, 1467, shows a *theatrum*, with the
audience surrounding the playing area and the actors emerging
from opposite mansions to the neutral *platea* between. Right, only the
stage area is represented in this scene, as presented at Ulm,
1486. The costumes are medieval; note particularly the long-toed
shoes worn by two of the actors. (Venice *Terence*, 1499)

Dijonnaise. These seem to have been inspired by the semiclerical
Feast of Fools, which earlier had allowed the minor clergy to burlesque the offices of the Church; the festival was marked by wearing
foolscaps instead of cowls. The *Enfants-sans-Souci* of Paris and the
Connards of Rouen are other famous fool companies. Their chief concern seems to have been with the various forms of contemporary
comedy. Allied in spirit was the unique *Basoche*, which, beginning in
1303, united the law clerks of Paris for mutual benefit and entertainment. All these were amateur organizations, although professionals
were by no means excluded from their ranks.

In Italy, the dramas were acted by companies of young boys.
Modena had its company of *San Pietro Martre*, Rome its *Gonfalone*,
Florence its *del Vangelista*. Each company was headed by a person
who was at the same time director, head actor, and prompter.

The professional minstrels and mimes evidently had a sort of
organization of their own; they even came under regulation by
Edward IV of England who, in 1469, placed his own household
minstrels in charge of regulating professional activity throughout
England. But it was no doubt the amalgamation of these professionals

103

with the various amateur fellowships which produced the traveling companies of the Middle Ages and the beginning of the Renaissance. Companies of this nature, either attached to a noble household and traveling under its protection or independent of any patronage, played the interludes and moralities in courts, manor houses, town halls, and at fairs. No doubt their repertoires were spiced with the tradition of the Goliards, those satiric wandering scholars of medieval times who so frequently came into conflict with authority.

But whatever the type of producing organization—professional or amateur, religious or secular—a high degree of skill was expected from the performers. In the huge cycle plays endurance was often a necessity, for stage effects such as the crucifixion of Christ and the hanging of Judas were frighteningly real; it was not unusual for the actor portraying one of these actually to faint from the strain. The number of lines assigned the various characters was often stupendous, and it is easy to understand why the *régisseur* with his prompt book was so universally necessary. Often more than one actor was assigned to a single part, taking the various age levels in sequence; and once at least, at Mons, the voice of God was assigned to three persons who spoke simultaneously. The number of speaking parts grew to tremendous proportions. In the twelfth and thirteenth centuries, casts comprised from twenty to thirty persons, but in the next two or three centuries the dramatis personae rose to two hundred or three hundred, in addition to extras and musicians. In the Bourges performance of the *Acts of the Apostles* there were 494 speaking parts, including five Marys. The deportment of the actors was strictly regulated: they were not to drink before, after, or during a performance; to eat only what was provided; not to leave the theatre during the rehearsal or the performances; to pay fines for any infringement of the rules. Indeed, there is record in England of fines imposed on actors who "spoiled the performance."

The style of delivery was declamatory. Often songs were required, so the actors had to be able to sing. That a high degree of skill in pantomime was necessary can be taken for granted, and what we today call overacting was looked upon with delight in such a character as Herod, who was a ranter always. Not without reason does Hamlet speak of out-Heroding Herod. Although, as we have mentioned above, most of the acting chores fell to men, women seem to have been included in the casts at both Metz and Valenciennes, perhaps because the number of men available was not adequate for the number of parts.

In the comedies, the emphasis was upon sparkling dialogue and farcical situations, requiring a great deal of skill from the performers. It was from such a tradition that the acting companies of the succeeding period developed.

Summary

Having no conscious roots in preceding centuries, the great popular theatre of the Middle Ages developed out of Church liturgy with accretions from indigenous materials. It was not imitative but original, and this originality was the main source of its vitality. Performances, as in ancient Greece, were linked to religious observance and given only at stated times in the Church calendar. From simple beginnings the production techniques developed into marvelously complicated affairs, engrossing the energies of wide portions of the population. Theatre was a great amateur endeavor.

The various and minor forms of noncycle productions were sporadic in presentation and covered a wide variety of materials and forms of presentation. They introduced secular materials, although many were frankly didactic in intent. The lines of distinction between literary forms were lightly drawn in this period, though the beginnings of subsequent emphases were apparent.

The noncycle plays contributed to the further development of clearcut plot structure, particularly in the moralities. In these and in the interludes, characters were created instead of adapted; the emphasis came to be placed on pure entertainment rather than upon edification—a most important step forward for the drama. The noncycle plays were chiefly played indoors, and this fact had significance for future production techniques.

From the cycle plays came an emphasis upon realism in stage effects and upon spectacle. More importantly, the cycle play initiated that mixture of comedy and tragedy which became the hallmark of the Elizabethan playwright. And finally, through them drama achieved widespread popular appeal. Audiences were heterogeneous and enthusiastic, often rising before dawn to see a performance and staying with it for days on end. So important were these performances to the people that businesses were closed during the showing, much as the usual activities had been suspended during the Dionysiac contests of ancient Greece. This involvement of the entire population in dramatic activity, as participant or as spectator, created fertile ground for the development of one of the world's greatest theatres—that of Shakespeare. We shall see how many of the ideas and practices of the Middle Ages bore flower and fruit in that later, more expansive, era.

6

RENAISSANCE THEATRE

IN ITALY, FRANCE,

AND GERMANY

Because the pageant of history is so vast and heterogeneous we are inclined, in our zeal to comprehend it, to compartmentalize and divide its wide panorama into neat little packages for easy consumption. We fix upon the date of 1453, the fall of Constantinople, and say it marks the beginning of the Renaissance. And, in a way, there is some truth in this, for that cataclysmic event drove eastern scholars to the West, and they brought with them many Greek manuscripts heretofore unknown to Western scholars. But if we define the Renaissance, and we can, to be the period of the triumph of Humanism over medieval scholasticism, when the rebirth of interest in the classics revolutionized man's attitude toward this world and the next, then we shall have to agree that 1453 is an arbitrary point indeed.

Petrarch, the father of Humanism, had written the first humanist play more than a century before that date, and a knowledge of the Roman classics, at least, had never died. Latin was the mother tongue not only of the Church, but of scholars and educated people everywhere throughout the Middle Ages. Seneca and Terence were a part of the literary treasure of the time, and other Roman writers were not unknown—in their native Latin, that is. But the Greek dramatists were known only as the Latins spoke of them, and those Latins were misinterpreted in the light of medieval scholasticism, not as they truly spoke. Even the Renaissance itself was somewhat guilty of monstrous misinterpretations of the ancient masters. But more of that later.

About the time that the great cycle plays were turning to the use of the vernacular, Dante wrote his masterpiece in his native Italian. Shortly thereafter Petrarch and Boccaccio wrote their great works in the same tongue. And, as we mentioned above, by 1349 Petrarch had produced the first humanist play, now lost, his *Philologia*. By the end of the century, another humanist play had been produced, the *Paulus* of Pier Paolo Vergerio, which bore certain resemblances to Terence but was wholly of the fourteenth century in sentiment, spirit, and manner. Several similar plays appeared in the first half of the fifteenth century; then came the influx of eastern scholars at the mid-century mark.

As early as the thirteenth century, an abridged Latin translation of Aristotle's *Poetics* had been made by a German scholar, and in the next century, Mantinus of Tortosa in Spain had done the same. But the full text in a new Latin translation did not appear until 1498 when Georgio Valla published it in Venice. The first Greek text appeared in 1508. By that time the Renaissance in Italy was well under way. In France, in Germany, in the Netherlands, in Spain, and in England, the Renaissance spirit spread, delayed over the years somewhat in proportion to the geographic distance from its source in Italy.

Though we are primarily concerned with its manifestations in drama, we must remember that the great revival of learning touched many areas of human activity. The growing conviction that life here and now was of more importance than the hereafter, that the rewards of this world were preferable to those of the next, had its good side as well as its bad; both are reflected in the drama. The spreading belief that all things are possible to man led to the great voyages and great discoveries, to the great music, the great art, and the great literature of this era. The subsiding fear of punishment in the next world led to libertinism, exploitation, political chicanery, and murder. It was the best and the worst of all possible worlds. And the drama, as the true mirror of its age, reflected these often contrary images. We can be exalted by Shakespeare and revolted by Machiavelli—but both are of the age.

Drama secular, not sacred

The early Renaissance theatre was of two distinct types: the select and formal theatre fostered by the Humanists, and the popular theatre which, in Italy, came to be called the *commedia dell'arte*. Both types were secular.

40 *Early Renaissance platform stages*
Left, a model of the simple platform stage erected in the converted
Marthakirke in Nuremburg, where many of the moralities of Hans Sachs
were presented. A trestle stage in the nave of the church, with a
backdrop and side curtains, sufficed for these presentations. Right,
stage and players of the fifteenth century, as reproduced in a volume
of Terence published by Johannes Trechsel in 1493. Here the backdrop
has become a series of curtained archways bearing the names
of the various characters. In this way the presentation of the classical
plays was related to the medieval ideas of mansions. (The Cleveland
Museum of Art, Collection of the Educational Department; The Henry E.
Huntington Library and Art Gallery)

We have seen that the great drama of the Middle Ages was Church
drama—universal, religious in subject matter, and under direction of
the Church. We have also seen how secular elements entered and
became a part of this drama, how there was a steady, but perhaps
weaker parallel development of nonreligious theatre with different
origins and themes. Though the presentation of mysteries and miracles was to continue through many years of the Renaissance period,
the animating spirit of the time was secular rather than religious. It
gave impetus to secular forms of the drama; the triumph of the
Renaissance submerged Church drama and favored secular themes.
Grotesque and comic elements had been increasingly incorporated
into the Church drama, and by 1548 the *Confrèrie de la Passion*
in Paris was forbidden by decree to give anything but secular pieces;

from that time on French drama developed secularly in both formal and popular types. In Germany, the grotesque and comic elements of the popular Shrovetide Play, as well as the pageantry of the Church dramas, were put to the use of the Reformation, which engaged the major vitalities of the German people throughout the sixteenth century.

Two theatres develop

It is in Italy, however, that the force of the Renaissance was earliest and most strongly felt. It is here that the literary and dramatic forms developed which had widespread and continuing influence far beyond their native soil. Here, too, the division between formal and popular theatre was most strongly marked.

It is easy to see in the popular theatre, though a definite connection has not yet been established, the continuation of the mime tradition reaching far back into the earliest days of theatrical history. For the vigor, art, and vulgarity of the *commedia* are certainly reminiscent of the early Greek comedies and the Atellan farces, with overtones of Menander, Plautus, and Terence. Its robustness, sincerity, originality, and theatrical zest infused theatre as a whole with irreplaceable benefits. It was a widespread popular comedy originating in Italy and spreading to Spain and to France, where it left the most lasting impression. It was produced by companies of highly specialized professional actor-managers who generally grouped together on family lines, with both men and women participating. The *commedia* itself, and the playing of specific roles, often became a family tradition. These highly skilled and sometimes very learned performers played before popular as well as select audiences, and so formed the most universal theatre of the day.

The more formal theatre, on the other hand, was the darling of the new intellectual elite who have been called Humanists. Its dramatic performances were generally given as special entertainments, or to mark special events. It was patronized and supported by the noble and the wealthy, such as the family of the Medici, the Duke of Urbino, the Popes, and their confreres. Its performers were both professional and amateur depending on the occasion, the purpose, and the producer. Its audiences, however, were almost always select. It was, indeed, a minority theatre which nevertheless made significant and lasting contributions to the general stream of theatrical history.

It was from these two types of Renaissance theatre, distinct and yet overlapping, that modern theatre as we know it evolved. Though the period itself produced no important dramatic literature, the modern stage was born in the Renaissance theatre.

Few plays of lasting value

With a few minor exceptions, the dramatic literature of this theatre is now the concern of only antiquarians and scholars. Scant indeed are the scripts which have lived beyond their first audiences. Yet to know this theatre we must know the materials with which it worked, and we must know how these materials were handled.

As a matter of fact, there are no complete playscripts from the *commedia*. It was an improvisational theatre using type characters and stock situations. The plays were simply scenarios freely stolen from novels, old plays, or any source at all, or ingeniously invented on the basis of current happenings, remembered incidents, or spicy gossip. The scenarios, of which about eight hundred are extant, were provided by the head of the company who was, in a sense, the author. They indicated the cast of characters and the line of action from situation to situation. Then the performers improvised the dialogue according to the inspiration of the moment.

The characters were stock figures, with specialized characteristics of attitude and appearance and particularized names. Often an actor assumed one of these characters for a lifetime. The men's parts were several: there was Arlecchino, or Harlequin, who was the clever servant (figure 42); Pantalone, a ridiculous older man who played duped husbands, old lovers, irate fathers, Venetian merchants (figure 43); The Doctor (of laws, not of medicine), who served as foil for Pantalone; The Captain, who was the braggart in direct line of descent from Plautus' *Miles Gloriosus* (figure 42); then a whole list of servant characters, each with his special characteristics—Pedrolino, Mezzetino, Burrattino, Brighella or Scapino, and Pulcinella, the prototype of Punch. Finally there was the lover, or the juvenile lead as we would call him, who was never dignified with a type name, but invariably was known by his own—Flavio, Ottavio, and so forth. His vis-à-vis was the feminine lover, or ingénue, who also bore her own name—Isabella (figure 43), Flaminia, Lucinda. The other women bore type names: Pasquella, the old woman; Columbina or Corallina, the soubrette—a very clever maid; and the other servant and confidante types, Harlequina and Pierrette.

The scenarios comprised chiefly comedies, but included also are tragedies, tragicomedies, pastorals, and—as the type developed—operas. Flaminio Scala's famous collection of fifty of these scenarios contains forty comedies, one tragedy, and nine operas. Though dia-

41 *Late Renaissance* commedia *stage*
In this painting by Marco Marcola, the *commedia* stage, which was
earlier the simple trestle platform (figure 40), has been elaborated to
contain a front curtain, scenery, and boxes. It is still, however, an outdoor
arrangement, and the performers maintain the traditional characters.
(The Art Institute of Chicago)

logue was not set down and memorized by the actors, they did have
certain speeches and bits of business which were standard and which
were used over and over again. The bits of business were called *lazzi*,
and these corresponded to the stock farce situations with which our
modern stage is familiar. There was the recognition lazzo, the food
lazzo, the jealousy lazzo, for instance. The set speeches were of two
kinds: one, the *chiusetti*, was a type of lyrical outburst on subjects
such as hope, parting, and friendship; the other, the *repertorio*, was
more prosaic, and took the form of advice, tirade, and various greet-
ings—to a lady, to a gentleman, and so forth. Each actor had at his
command the *lazzi* and speeches appropriate to his character and
used them as the scenario demanded. Connecting dialogue and action
were always improvised.

111

42 Commedia *characters*
Left, an unusual print of the character of The Captain with his oversize
wooden sword and, here, a somewhat Arabic headdress. This
character is often considered the direct descendent of the Miles
Gloriosus. Right, an old print of the juvenile, of Arlecchino, and of
Columbina, showing the lack of mask on the first figure, and the masked
figures of the other two. This practice was universal in the
commedia presentations. (Harvard Theatre Collection; Paris, Coll. Worms)

The formal theatre, however, used standard scripts of various
types: translations of the Greek and Latin masters, native models of
classic comedy and tragedy, original comedies, tragedies, pastorals,
and operas.

In 1429 Cusano discovered in Germany twelve hitherto unknown
plays of Plautus; after the invention of the printing press by a group
of German mechanics working with Gutenberg, they received wide
dissemination. Terence's comedies were first printed in 1473. Printed
translations of both Roman writers soon followed and were widely

read. Staged readings, as well as private readings, were held and the plays were performed before numerous cultured audiences. In 1502 the Venetian printer, Aldus, published the seven extant plays of Sophocles. A year later he published Euripides, and, in 1518, Aeschylus. Now the theatre was equipped with most of the classic masters, and the humanist writers aped them sedulously.

Even before the vogue of the Greek dramatists, Mussato had produced his *Eccerinis* (1315) on the Senecan model and Petrarch had followed Terence in his *Philologia*. After the printing of the Greeks early in the sixteenth century, Rucellai (1475–1525) produced his own *Orestes;* Dolce (1508–68), a *Giocasta* using the conflict between the sons of Oedipus; and Speroni (1500–88), wrote his notorious *Canace*. By and large, these imitators of classic tragedy, though using primarily Greek subject matter, worked in the Senecan technique of stressing the horrible; their plays swam in pools of blood.

Assiduous aping of the ancients was fostered by schools and scholars. The first neoclassic tragedy in France, *Cleopatra Captive* (1552) was written by Étienne Jodelle more to sustain his position as a member of the literary group which called itself the *Pléiade* than as an actable play. It was, however, performed at the court of Henry II, with the young author playing the title role to the great acclaim of his fellow-scholars who awarded him an ivy-crowned goat as a prize. He subsequently wrote an *Antigone* and a *Medea*. The poet Vondel (1587–1679) led the movement of classic revival in the Netherlands at a somewhat later date, choosing Terence as his model; in Germany Hans Sachs (1494–1576) wrote an original *Alcestis*, a strange companion to his two hundred-odd farces and comedies. Beginning in 1551 the schools and colleges founded by the Jesuits presented plays, chiefly in Latin, drawn from the repertoire of the classics, and written by such extramural scholars as Jodelle, Garnier and Grévin, or by faculty members or students. Various regulations promulgated by the order from time to time concerning these performances stressed their educational value and limited their subject matter to serious materials in the tragic tradition. These school productions took place in Italy, Germany, Spain, and France with varying degrees of frequency and elaborateness until the suppression of the order in 1773; they thus perpetuated a combination of entertainment and moral purpose, classic in pattern and elaborate in execution, over a very long period of time. So popular were the Latin and Greek plays in Germany that even Martin Luther encouraged Paul Rebhun to write his *Susanna* (1535) in the classic mode.

113

Both native comedy and native tragedy served theatre, and there were many practitioners. Chief among the Italian writers of comedy were Ariosto and Aretino, though no lesser persons than Machiavelli and Lorenzo de Medici were also writing. Additional names include those of Della Porta, Grazzini, Cecchi, Cini, Caro, and Bruno. From Ariosto's *The Supposes*, first produced at Ferrara in 1502, came Gascoigne's *The Supposes* and the plot of Shakespeare's *The Taming of the Shrew*. Ariosto's *Lena* has interesting situations and is noteworthy for its study of character. Pietro Aretino's comedies—*The Courtier, Marescalio, The Hypocrite, Talanta,* and *The Philosopher*—were produced between 1525 and 1542. They introduced the element of satire, and centered the interest on the principal character who is dominated by some single characteristic—misogyny, hypocrisy, theorizing, and so forth. This type of presentation is a natural development of the stock character, and will be evidenced again in the later and greater plays of Ben Jonson. Of the three plays of Machiavelli—*Clizia*, an untitled comedy in prose, and *Mandragola*—the last is by far the best and most famous. Some writers have called it the best Italian play produced in the sixteenth century. And it has interest quite apart from the personality of the writer. It is one of the few plays of the period in which we witness a real development of character during the course of the play: the heroine changes from a virtuous, chaste wife into a cynical and disillusioned mistress. Its unprincipled clergy, its precipitous and crafty hero, its cynical morality, all effectively reflect the tenor of the age. Like Lorenzo de Medici's *Aridosia*, performed at the marriage of Duke Alessandro in 1536, the *Mandragola* and the comedies of the other writers use stock characters and familiar situations, yet invest these with a native flavor. Marital infidelity is a favorite theme, and the plots abound with young wives married to old and cold husbands; with ardent suitors who go to any lengths to achieve the object of their desires; with cunning priests; with dissolute students; with clever servants, both loyal and disloyal. The picture they give of contemporary life is not a pleasant one by our standards, but it is bustling, vigorous, sensational, sometimes crude, and sometimes over-refined—in short, a rather accurate mirror of the age which produced the plays.

The level of native comedy is low by any dramatic standard, but that of native tragedy is even lower. It is almost completely derivative, tedious, and weltering in blood; early and late examples adhere to the pattern of Seneca. No one now remembers the names of the plays or the playwrights; Tebaldeo, Cammelli, Cinthio, Zinano, Groto, are the dust of scholarship.

43 *More* commedia *characters*
Above, an oil painting, artist unknown, at the Musée Carnavalet, of
the late sixteenth century. It purports to show Isabella Andreini and
other members of the famed I Gelosi. Isabella, playing the ingénue,
wears no mask. Below, a print of the popular water-gun scene in a
commedia performance, with a masked Arlecchino attacking
Pantalone, while The Captain loses his sword in fright.
(Musée Carnavalet; Harvard Theatre Collection)

Cinthio was perhaps more influential through his *Discourse on
Comedy and Tragedy* (1543) than through any of his plays. In this
critical work he insisted on the superiority of Senecan over Greek
tragedy because of its sententious maxims, its gravity, its "majesty."
And, indeed, play after play of the period illustrates the preoccupation of the playwrights with the revenge motive, the appearance of
ghosts, oratorical prologues and long declamatory passages, the substitution of horror for tragedy, of narration for action. Cinthio defended Horace's division of plays into five acts, each with a specific

purpose—a convention not completely inactive until well into the nineteenth century. He was also responsible for the initial emphasis on the arbitrary unity of time; this, coupled with Castelvetro's unity of place, and the subordination of the Aristotelian principle of unity of action, set a standard of dramatic construction which lasted almost as long as the five-act division.

Trissino lives because his *Sofonisba,* finished in 1515, was widely copied in many places; the type was finally and delightfully travestied in Fielding's *Tom Thumb.* Tasso, now praised in other fields of literature, was lauded by his contemporaries because his *Torrismondo* was so excellent an example of adherence to classic models. Were it not for the sumptuous settings these tragedies commanded, they would not be worth our notice.

Sumptuous also were the settings of that peculiar child of the Renaissance, the pastoral play. This was the escapist drama of the period; its time was always set in The Golden Age, its place was Arcadia, and its characters were shepherds and nymphs. Triggered, no doubt, by the Renaissance affectation for simple and placid country life, the pastorals proved immensely popular in highly sophisticated society and were presented upon numerous special occasions. Though examples of this kind of spectacle were numerous before 1573, it was not until that year, with the performance of Tasso's *Aminta,* that it was dignified with the name of "art." The triumph of Tasso's graceful gesture was so complete that there followed numerous imitations. Guarino's *The Faithful Shepherd* is the most famous of these. The pastoral had many manifestations all over the Continent, and Shakespeare did not scorn to use the form in such a play as *As You Like It.*

Related to the pastoral drama by reason of its luxuriant production was the one other form of theatrical presentation cultivated in the Renaissance—the opera. Though the chanting of lines and actual singing had been a part of the medieval cycle plays, and though the Humanist Poliziano had written, in 1422, a dramatic poem set to music and called *The Fable of Orpheus,* it remained for the little circle of musicians and poets gathered at the *palazzo* of Giovanni Bardi in Florence and dedicated to a study of the classics, to produce something new. In their study of the Greek plays they first discovered their musical characteristics, assuming that the dialogue of Greek tragedy had been declaimed or sung. In their zeal to recreate this aspect of the revered art, they created a new form of music-drama. It was *Dafne* (first performed in 1597), with words by Rinuccini and music by Peri, that thus became the first significant opera.

44 *Spectacular staging for classical drama and* commedia
Above, the design by Gaspar Am. Ort for P. P. Bissari's *Medea*
presented in Munich in 1662. Sea effects, fireworks, and flyings are all
a part of the presentation of this play. Below, a seventeenth
century *commedia* performance as engraved for the camera obscura.
Commedia performers did not scorn to use elaborate settings when and if
they were available. Notice the use of angle wings and linear
perspective. But the costumes and masks are typically *commedia*.
(Harvard Theatre Collection)

Dafne was followed by *Euridice*, by the same composers; and then,
in 1607 and 1608, by the first productions of one of the most highly
acclaimed Renaissance musicians, Monteverdi—a *Dafne*, an *Arianna*,
and an *Orfeo*. Thus, by accident almost, the Humanists produced
their only original contribution to theatrical literature, and so popular
did it become that from the building of the first public opera house
anywhere—that in Vienna in 1637—opera captured the imagination
of the public. In Italy, and for a long time in Germany, it effectively

117

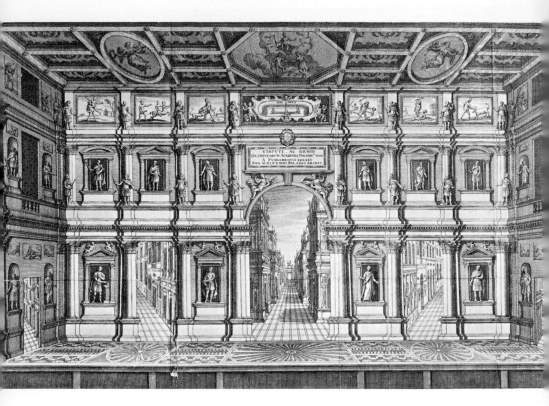

absorbed practically all of the interest to be exhibited in theatre, and left a heritage to aftertimes that is tremendous.

Simple staging in commedia theatre

Being primarily an actor's theatre, the *commedia dell'arte* placed little reliance upon playhouses or settings, though it did not scorn these physical enhancements when they were offered. The typical background of a *commedia* performance, however, was a simple platform and a backdrop, sometimes painted, sometimes not. The platform was always of a temporary nature, being erected in marketplaces, squares, open fields, or halls, and remaining only for the duration of the performance. If the platform were high enough, it was curtained off and the understage area used as a dressing room. If not, the area behind the backdrop served the purpose. When the backdrop was painted, the scene was either a street or a forest. Only the most rudimentary of stage props were used—a table, a chair, a basket—and since the performances were mostly outdoors, abso-

45 The Teatro Olimpico, Vicenza
Above, the floor plan of the building with its elliptical seating
arrangement, its five doors on the stage, and the vistas in forced
perspective behind them. Also, an interior view of the Olimpico,
showing the integration of stage and seats, the open orchestra, the raised
stage, the colonnade, and the statues of the members of the Academy who
commissioned the building. Left, the stage of the Olimpico as
completed by Scamozzi, showing the perspective vistas and the highly
decorated walls. (Walker, *Italian Drama*; Victoria and Albert Museum)

lutely no lighting effects were necessary. For music, one of the actors
with a guitar played during the performance, or sang the entr'acte.
The focus was on the actor and there it remained, whether he was
attempting by his skill to catch the attention of a noisy crowd at the
Parisian *théâtres de la foire,* or whether he had the undivided attention customary at command performances at courts and royal houses.

Court amateurs have elaborate accoutrements

But this simplicity was never practiced in the formal and elite
theatre of the day, for which special houses were built and increasingly complicated and magnificent settings invented. It all began
simply enough. The early Humanists combined what they found of
staging suggestions in the texts of Plautus and Terence with what
they knew of the medieval custom of mansions, and presented their
plays on platforms with backings which indicated three or more
individual doorways for the various characters, which grew to be
ornamented and elaborated, with suggestions of rooms behind them.

119

With the rediscovery of Vitruvius in 1484, attention began to be paid to the accommodations of the audience. The *cavea* which Vitruvius mentions caused much speculation, as well as various designs purporting to recreate a classic theatre. Until 1580, however, theatre buildings remained wholly on paper, or were simply temporary structures (converted halls and so forth). A more permanent kind of conversion was accomplished by Hans Sachs in 1550, when he transformed a disused Catholic church—the Marthakirche in Nuremberg, Germany—into a theatre with a simple, curtained stage (figure 40).

In 1580, the Olympic Academy of Vicenza commissioned Andrea Palladio to design and build a theatre according to the best classical ideas of the time, and this Teatro Olimpico (figure 45), as it came to be called, is the first permanent theatre building of the Italian Renaissance. It escaped the ravages of World War II and occasionally still houses a production. The theatre designed by Palladio has thirteen tiers of seats arranged in semi-elliptical fashion around an open floor area called the orchestra, abutting at the ends on a stage which is seventy feet long and eighteen feet deep. The banked tiers of seats are topped by a series of columns. Eighty stucco statues of the Academicians decorated the edifice, and the overall impression, according to the contemporary description by Filippo Pigafetta, was one of an incredible loveliness.

Palladio died before the building was completed, and Vicenzo Scamozzi, to whom the task fell, evidently altered the original plans for the stage proper. Behind the five doors originally planned for the stage (a "royal" door, designed like a Roman triumphal arch, and four lesser doors, two flanking the royal door on each side) he added perspective vistas. Influenced by the preoccupation of artists with the newly discovered principles of perspective, his vistas—three down the center arch and one each behind the other portals—he said represented the seven streets of Thebes. They were constructed of lath and plaster in full relief and in forced perspective. The rest was an elaborte mélange of statues, columns, architraves, and niches, after the manner of the Roman theatre. In this building was presented, on March 3, 1585, a production of *Oedipus Rex* which purported to be a faithful rendition of the Sophocles masterpiece, though what with four hundred chairs in the orchestra to accommodate the ladies, with a front curtain which dropped, with the spraying of perfume and the serving of wine and fruit before the performance, the whole thing sounds more like the kind of performance against which Marcus Aurelius railed.

120

This same Scamozzi, at the behest of Duke Vespasiano Gonzago of Mantua, designed and supervised the construction of a theatre at Sabionetta, which opened in 1588. The commission specified that the theatre be "in miniature" as were the palace, mint, and printing plant with which the Duke had already supplied the town. So Scamozzi designed a single vista for the stage, permanent, like the one at the Olimpico, but beginning almost at the edge of the stage on either side. The tiers of seats were arranged in horseshoe fashion, with a wide space between the front of the stage and the first row of seats; the seating capacity was about three hundred. This building, too, is still standing.

In 1618, in the little town of Parma, about twenty miles from Sabionetta, the Prince commissioned Aleotti, the Ferrarese, to build a theatre. This Teatro Farnese (figure 46), as it was called, used the same horseshoe arrangement for the tiers of seats, although there were a great many more of them; the theatre seated about thirty-five hundred spectators. It also retained the distance between seats and stage, but included innovations on the stage itself: the first permanent, sculptured proscenium arch, and behind it, a flat-wing system for change of scenes. The proscenium arch and modifications of the flat-wing system persist even in today's theatre. Sometimes the audience occupied the open floor space, but often this was used as a part of the spectacular performances, sometimes even being flooded to make a sea for boats. (Shades of the Roman *naumachia!*) The wooden interior of this building was destroyed in the bombings of World War II, but it is gradually being restored.

By the time the Olimpico celebrated its grandiose opening, Madrid had two permanent theatres, London three, and Paris at least one. This last was a direct line of development from the medieval cycle plays, having been built by the *Confrèrie de la Passion* in 1548, and called the Hôtel de Bourgogne. It seems to have been the first public playhouse built since the fall of Rome; though the *Confrèrie* ceased to produce its own plays there after 1578, they leased the house to other companies and it continued to be an active, producing theatre until 1783. Of the theatres in Madrid and London we shall speak later.

Another innovation of the Renaissance was a theatre of sorts, built outdoors, with walls and stage wings of clipped cypress and a floor of turf. Such garden theatres were eighty to a hundred feet long, twenty to eighty feet wide, and were built—grown, rather—at such places as the Villa Maria, the Villa Gori, the Villa Serraglio in Italy, and the Schloss Mirabell gardens in Salzburg, Germany. Immensely popular

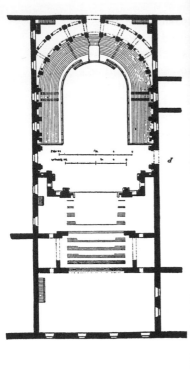

46 *The Teatro Farnese, Parma*
Above left, the floor plan of the Farnese, showing the horseshoe
arrangement of the seats, the wide and deep orchestra, the proscenium-
arch stage, and the wing-flat system for stage decoration. Above right,
interior view toward the seats, with one of the two great doors through
which performers could enter to the orchestra space. Below right, interior
view toward the stage, showing the highly decorated permanent
proscenium arch, and the front curtain. (Schreiner)

for the playing of pastorals, they were an affectation of the wealthy
which was mightily copied throughout Europe.

Stagecraft highly skilled

In addition to the building of impressive theatres, the formal
theatre of the Renaissance saw stage design carried to increasing

complexity and magnificence. The mansion stage of the early classic revival, as seen in the illustrations of the Trechsel edition of Terence (Lyons, 1493), was, as we have mentioned, simple enough (figure 40), but forces were at work which soon rendered it more elaborate. This stage itself was soon highly decorated with curtains of gold cloth and with tapestries and intricate columns. The early sixteenth-century stage of the *Rederykers* of the Netherlands is an illustration of the elaboration of the simple doorways into an intricately pedimented, two-level edifice (figure 52).

Just as the simple mansion settings of the cycle plays became complex enough to require as many as eight "masters of machines," so the stages of the classic revival developed from simplicity to elaboration. To them was added the wonders of perspective representation with which the artists of the Renaissance were so concerned. We read of a production at Ferrara in 1508 of Ariosto's *Cassaria* with its landscape in perspective of "houses, churches, towers, and gardens." By 1513, the scene was further elaborated. For in that year we find Castiglione, author of *The Courtier*, describing the production of Cardinal Bibbiena's comedy *La Calandria* (1508) at the court of the Duke of Urbino. He says, "The streets looked as if they were real, and everything was done in relief, and made even more striking through the art of painting and well-conceived perspective" (quoted in Alessandro d'Ancono, *Origini del Teatro Italiano*, Torini, 1891, II, 102). Pillars, statues, altars, and highly decorated stucco temples were a part of this design. The next year the same play was produced for Pope Leo X, with Peruzzi designing a set with "palaces and curious temples, loggias and cornices, all made to make them appear to be what they represented." (Giorgio Vasari, *The Lives of the Painters, Sculptors and Architects*, New York, 1927, II, 297.) This continuing emphasis upon realism is a curious echo of the realistic effects constantly striven for in the medieval plays. And, like the earlier plays, these, too, were performed on temporary stages, now erected in great banqueting halls or in courtyards. Often great artists worked in theatre; Raphael, for instance, designed the setting for a production of Ariosto's *The Supposes* in 1519.

When Sebastiano Serlio, who had been a pupil of Peruzzi, published in Paris the second book of his *Architettura* in 1545, he incorporated in it a principle he had used some ten years earlier in designing a setting at Vicenza. This principle was a further application of the idea of perspective; the floor of the rear stage was sloped upward to emphasize the forced perspective which had become so popular. Thus was born the raked stage which continued in use even into the

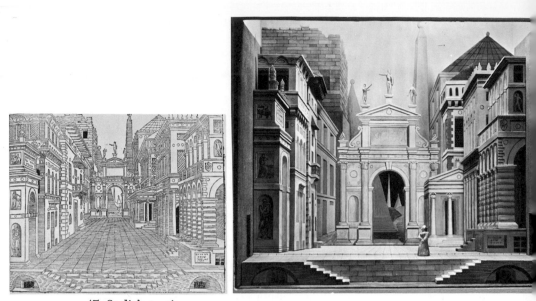

47 *Serlio's tragic scene*
Left, a print from the Paris edition of Jehan Martin of Serlio's *De Architettura*, 1545; right, a model of the same scene. Classical architecture was considered, in the Renaissance, to be proper to the dignity of tragedy, while the more decorated Gothic architecture of the immediate past was relegated to comedy. The tragic effect is achieved by the use of angle wings set in linear perspective, which stage designers adopted from fifteenth-century painters. This was a permanent setting, not changed during the performance.
(The Metropolitan Museum of Art; The Cleveland Museum of Art, Collection of the Educational Department)

twentieth century. In his further descriptions of stage effects, Serlio particularized the reference in Vitruvius to the three types of classic settings—comic, tragic, and satyric—and solidified a convention which was slavishly followed for many years in many places (figure 47).

For the comic scene he prescribed houses "for Citizens, but specially there must not want a brawthell or bawdy house, and a great Inne, and a Church." He prescribed galleries, windows, levels, some to be in relief and some to be painted. For the tragic scene he planned "none but stately houses . . . Chimneyes, Towers, Piramides, Oblisces, and other such like things or Images . . . cut out round, and well colloured." The satyric scene, he said, "should be made with Trees, Rootes, Herbs, Hils and Flowers, and with some countrey houses."

124

(*The First Book of Architecture*, London, 1611, II, 3, pp. 25ff.) He accompanied his descriptions with drawings, and it is these visualizations which were so influential with succeeding artisans.

As we have seen, the principle of the permanent perspective setting in relief was incorporated in the building of the Teatro Olimpico. But the desirability—or necessity—of sets which could be changed during the course of the production led to the development of nested angle wings and flat wings, such as are found·in the Farnese Theatre at Parma. When Sabbatini finally published his *The Practice of Making Scenes and Machines* in 1637, he described in detail the various wing systems and methods of changing them.

Serlio, Sabbatini, and Di Somi (whose *Dialogues* on playwriting and stagecraft appeared about 1556) also discuss in their works various stage machines and lighting effects. Since all changes were made in full view of the audience, great care was taken to make the operation smooth and interesting. In addition to the wing system, Sabbatini describes a scene change using an adaptation of the Greek three-sided prism, and cautions that this method requires great care in selecting reliable workers. He tells, with description and diagram, "How to Make Dolphins and Other Sea Monsters Appear to Spout Water While Swimming," "How to Produce a Constantly Flowing River," "How to Divide the Sky into Sections," "How Gradually to Cover Part of the Sky with Clouds," "How to Make a Cloud Descend Perpendicularly with Persons on It," and how to make it descend at an angle (descents and sky effects were exceedingly popular—perhaps an inheritance from the medieval cycles). He discusses how the lights should be arranged on the stage, and how to light them. He recommends oil lamps with strong wicks as most reliable and durable. Serlio describes how colored lighting effects may be achieved by using colored water or wine in glass vessels with lamps and reflectors behind them, and tells of the effects of various ingredients; Di Somi recommends that the auditorium be darkened so that the stage lights would appear brighter—a practice which did not become universal until more than a century later. Angelo Ingegneri, in 1598, went a step further by urging that the auditorium be completely darkened during the presentation of a play, and that none of the stage lights spill over into the auditorium. His system would wait much longer for acceptance. Methods for moving stars and suns, for making flashing lightning and the sound of thunder, for dimming the lights, and many more are detailed in these technical discussions.

Our most detailed accounts of lighting practices come from the writings of Joseph Furttenbach the Elder (1591–1667), who after spending ten years in Italy returned to his native Germany to develop there the wonders of the Italian Renaissance. His three treatises describe in detail many intricate lighting effects and methods for achieving them. He also describes and illustrates how to set up a theatre in which the seating arrangement is on parallel rows of benches rather than in the elliptical or semicircular tiers common in Italy. Finally he gives a great deal of attention to material concerning the construction and use of the rear stage behind the back shutters which, he says, may be used as a room or interior, or, with floor boards removed, as a pit for sea scenes (figure 48). What a far cry from the technically uncomplicated, open-air productions of Aeschylus' theatre!

These intricate stages, whether temporary or permanent, used a front curtain, and there were three ways in which it might operate. A curtain might be arranged to descend into a trough at the front of the stage when the play began; it might be raised; or it might be drawn in what we today call a festoon drape. Among Furttenbach's works are designs for special front curtains particularly related to the plays presented. In any event, once the curtain was withdrawn it remained so until the performance was over, with all integral scene changes being a part of the performance. Scene changes were cued to the music which always accompanied the performance. This essentially curtainless method of presentation remained up to the nineteenth century.

Thus Renaissance stagecraft, profiting from the inventions of medieval artisans and the development of suggestions found in classic sources, and encouraged by the Renaissance love of opulent display such as was exhibited in the sumptuous *tableaux vivants* of entries and festivities, developed into a highly complicated and skilled art.

Commedia *costumes stereotyped*

In both the formal and popular theatres, costume and makeup played an important part in creating the scenic illusion. In the popular theatre of the *commedia* they served to identify the characters, as well as to add to the stage decoration. For this reason, they tended to become stereotyped.

Perhaps a proof of the *commedia*'s ancient heritage may be found in the masks which were worn by almost all of the actors. Some scholars see in the black mask of Arlecchino a descendant of the Negro slaves of the Roman mime; in the mask of Pulcinella another hook-nosed descendant of a Roman mime mask; in the dark mask and red beard of Pantalone, the Dossennus of the *atellanae*. The speculation is highly probable, but whatever their ancestry the *commedia* masks served to emphasize, along with the costumes, the particular characteristics of the various performers.

Pantalone, an avaricious Venetian merchant with a large curved nose, white hair, and a beard, originally appeared in a long red cloak with a red cap and Turkish slippers. Soon the color of the cloak was changed to black, but the red cap and the slippers remained. His foil, the Doctor, also wore black, fashioned in the likeness of a professor's gown, with a black hat. His dark mask had red cheeks and a short beard. The Captain, originally an Italian fighting man, early changed to a Spanish type of braggart. He wore a long-nosed mask with a fierce moustache and carried a wooden sword. Arlecchino, with his black half mask, began in beggarly fashion with a patched costume which later evolved into the formal checked design which we know, particularly in his more famous French identity, Harlequin. His companion, Brighella, wore a full mask of grotesque and evil design and he was dressed in wide trousers with a short jacket laced with green braid. Mezzetino's colors were red and white, eventually striped. Pedrolino wore no mask, but had a white powdered face and wore a loose white costume. His French counterpart, Pierrot, became one of the most famous of all these figures. Pulcinella's mask was exceedingly ugly, with a wart, and he generally wore a huge cock's feather in his hat.

Among the women, Pasquella was likely to be masked, with an ugly countenance as befitted the evil old woman that she was; sometimes Columbina wore a half mask as the feminine counterpart to her partner, Arlecchino. The *inamorate* (juvenile and ingénue) rarely, if ever, were masked, and ordinarily wore contemporary dress as rich as the treasury of the company would allow.

As the popularity of the *commedia* grew and then waned, the dress of the various characters evolved and changed somewhat; but the basic patterns remained the same, always embodying the attitudes and actions of the type characters they dressed.

Classical adaptations and contemporary dress in formal theatre

In the plays of the formal Renaissance theatre the costumes became a part of stage decoration; the richer the production, the richer the costuming. Classical adaptations were used for the Greek and Roman plays. For native comedy and tragedy contemporary dress was the rule. But even here, as Di Somi says, richness was mandatory. Servants were not dressed in torn or mean garments, but in silks and velvets to improve the picture, so long as their masters were clothed more richly with embroidery, laces, and jewels. The aim was to make

48 *Typical seventeenth-century settings*
Left, the design by Lodovico Burnacini for *La Zenobia di Rodamisto*
produced in Vienna in 1662. This print includes the very ornate
proscenium arch designed for the production showing the incorporation
of a pit for the musicians. The stage setting includes angle wings
set in linear perspective. Right, the design by the same artist for
Il Fuoco Eterno produced in Vienna in 1674. Particularly apparent in
this print is the use of borders for ceiling pieces, and the upstage
area, or inner room of which Furttenbach speaks. (Harvard
Theatre Collection; Theater-Museum, Munich)

every actor as unique as possible in style and color, with an emphasis
on light and definite colors which would enhance the stage picture.
Costuming had another purpose, too. In a production where the players were likely to be drawn from the same social circle as the audience, Di Somi says, "Not only do I try to vary the actors' costumes,
but I strive as much as I can to transform each one from his usual
appearance, so that he will not readily be recognized by the audience,
which sees him daily" (as translated from the MS in the Biblioteca
Palatina, Parma, and quoted by Alois Nagler, *Sources of Theatrical
History*, p. 105).

In the pastorals, the shepherds wore white silk sleeveless shirts
covered over with the skins of animals. Unless they were young and
handsome, they also wore a type of fleshings over arms and legs and
always some kind of soft shoes. The nymphs were clothed in long-
sleeved ladies' shirts, with embroidery and colored ribbons, over
which went a long, rich mantle falling from one shoulder and forming the skirt. The animal skins, the mantles, and the ribbons were
varied in color and arrangement so that interest would be maintained

in the stage picture. Variety in coiffures, some curly, some smooth, some ivy-crowned, was prescribed for the shepherds. The nymphs were uniformly blond (wigs, of course), and golden fillets or colored ribbons and flimsy, floating veils adorned their heads. These visions carried golden darts and bows, while the shepherds bore leafy branches or sticks.

In other specialized types of performances, such as interludes and spectacles, the dramatis personae were garbed as befitted their characters, be they angels, deities, or princes. The only aim was to make the costumes as sumptuous and eye filling as possible. Expense was never an item for consideration, since these performances in the formal Renaissance theatre were always subsidized by wealthy patrons who vied with each other in lavish display. Furttenbach speaks enviously of the tons of gold the Italian princes were wont to expend on their theatricals while, in the poorer German court theatres which he served, he felt his creative energies shackled by necessary economies.

Titled dilettantes and scholars in amateur ranks

If we are to make an arbitrary division we might say that the formal theatre of the Renaissance was a theatre of amateurs, while that of the *commedia* was a theatre of professionals. We must be careful, however, to confine these labels to acting only, for certainly in other respects the professionalism of the formal theatre is obvious.

The corps of actors in the formal theatre was comprised largely of dilettantes and scholars. The classic revivals were often presented by members of the academies, and these, as well as the other types of formal theatre presentations, were the diversion of the wealthy and the titled. There is record, for instance, of Cesare Borgia being one of the actors in a complicated allegory of Virtue and Fortune in dispute, which preceded the *Menaechmi* given at the marriage of Lucrezia Borgia with Alfonso d'Este in 1502. In the pastorals sported the lords and their ladies, much as the ladies and courtiers of Jacobean England participated in the masques at a somewhat later date. For just such titled but inexperienced actors Di Somi wrote what must surely be one of the first handbooks for actors, when he devoted a section of his *Dialogues* to the art of acting. In it he gives most specific directions about gestures, movement, and speech, urging that the total effect should be one of naturalness. No doubt these amateur groups also profited from working with the professionals from the *commedia* with whom their casts were sometimes augmented. Often the skillful and beautiful *commedia* actresses became the favorites of the lords of the land. More generally, however, the *commedia*

49 *Spectacular stage effects*

Above, the design by Bernardo Buontalenti for *Six Interludes* presented
at Florence in 1589. This scene shows the continuing popularity of
the medieval hellfire, as well as the Renaissance innovation of cloud
machines descending from above. The fire, of course, is painted on
the flats—angle wings in the foreground, a backdrop upstage.
Below, the design by Alfonso Parigi for *Le Nozzi Degli Dei* presented
early in the seventeenth century. Again note the flames, the
cloud machines, the angle wings. The satyrs were a particularly popular
Renaissance concoction, so constructed as to allow the performer to
move in quite realistic fashion. (Stockholm Nationalmuseum,
Harvard Theatre Collection)

SCENA QVINTA D' INFERNO.

companies were invited—or commanded—to present a performance at a marriage, a visit, or at some other special event. Then the entire company performed, using the technical resources which the richer private theatre placed at its disposal.

Commedia *acting a family tradition*

The most famous of the acting companies was I Gelosi (The Jealous of Pleasing Ones), but there were many others: I Confidente (The Confident Ones), I Fideli (The Faithful Ones), I Accessi (The Brilliant Ones), I Desiosi (The Desirous of Pleasing Ones). Generally, as we have mentioned previously, the core of the company was a single family, as the Andreini family was in I Gelosi, and the scenarios and reputation of the group descended from one generation to the next. The members were closely knit, with the children being trained to take the place of their elders or to augment the troupe. The training was rigorous. *Commedia* players were expected to be proficient in song, dance, and acrobatics as well as in the more usual spoken dialogue. They had to have nimble wits as well as nimble heels, for the improvisational nature of the performance demanded it. Sometimes these performers were among the most cultured people of the age. The celebrated Isabella Andreini, a star of the latter half of the sixteenth century, was said to speak four languages and to hold intelligent conversations with the most learned men of her day. In addition, she was accomplished in song and dance, exceptionally beautiful—and renowned for her virtue. No less a person than Prince Vincenzo of Mantua acted as godfather at the christening of her child. Her husband, Francisco, was also an accomplished linguist, having five languages at his command. He was a musician and a writer—and an exceptionally popular Captain. Isabella herself played the *inamorata*, and lent her name to a succession of them. Favorite of the King of Poland was Constantini, who played Mezzetino; and Biancolleli was famous for his Arlecchino. Something of the skill of these performers is evident in the fame of Visentini, who could turn a somersault with a wineglass and not spill a drop; of Fiorilli, who as Scaramouche could still, at eighty-three, box his ear with his toe.

The most famous of the troupes played in the courts of the nobles and traveled from city to city. To the *commedia* performer Marie Fairet goes the honor of being the first woman performer on the professional stage in France, when her company visited Paris about the middle of the sixteenth century. In 1568 a *commedia* company traveled in Austria, delighting the court at Vienna. In 1571 a troupe was summoned to Paris to play at the marriage of Charles IX. They are reported to have taken Paris by storm, and, indeed, for many decades to come, the Italian Comedians were an integral part of the French theatrical scene, where they had a longer and more significant influence than in their native land. A *commedia* troupe performed before Elizabeth of England in 1577, and Philip II of Spain was greatly pleased with the troupe which he had invited to play at his court.

The less accomplished troupes traveled to the small towns, and played in the villages. All carried with them costumes, props, and what scenery they needed. The Spanish writer, Augustin de Rojas Villandrando, wrote amusingly in 1603 of the various classifications of traveling Spanish companies, from the *bululu* which is a single player, poor and mendicant, to the grandiose *compañía* with its thirty members, its carriages and carts, and its sixty plays. While Rojas was not writing specifically of *commedia* players, his descriptions no doubt were applicable to many of these.

But however famous or sought-after performers or companies might become, the implacable Church was still opposed to these professional theatre people, and many municipal edicts as well as Church pronouncements were issued against them. It is recorded that even so famous a player as Isabella Andreini, who died in 1601 soon after she had been newly honored by Queen Marie, was refused burial in hallowed ground in conformance with the law of the Church.

The *commedia* flourished during the sixteenth, seventeenth, and early eighteenth centuries; the boundaries of its influence were very wide. Perhaps never before or since has there been a form of theatre which so focused attention upon the individual performer, or expected so much skill from him.

Summary

Renaissance theatre, while continuing the production of sacred plays, was predominantly a secular activity. The leading strings of the Church were largely severed, and pagan literary influences had widespread effect. The combination of the persisting medieval traditions and the newly found classical materials gave Renaissance theatre a different aim and direction from its immediate predecessor.

It is true that the bustle of the Renaissance renewed interest in theatre, and that the people of the Renaissance probably enjoyed more forms of theatrical activity than those of many another period in history. But it is equally true that no great dramatic literature came out of the Renaissance on the Continent. Perhaps the insistence of the literary men on an adherence to classical models stifled the spirit of originality from which great drama arises. Certainly the informal theatre of the *commedia,* far less dependent on copying preexisting materials, was more vital and indigenous than the literary theatre of the day. But the Renaissance in Italy, France, and Germany did produce some theatrical manifestations which meant much to later times.

Its early and constant preoccupation with the classical writers set a pattern which was widely followed for many years in many places. The critical dictates of Cinthio and Castelvetro, and the mistaken application of Aristotelian principles put into practice by many playwrights, affected dramatic writing for many generations to come and in many areas of Continental Europe. The period also, of course, developed the opera and the pastoral as distinct theatrical forms.

In theatre architecture it invented the horseshoe type of seating arrangement, which persists even to our own day. It developed the proscenium arch, the painted set, indoor lighting, spectacular effects, and sumptuous costuming—all attributes of what many people today call "modern theatre." Through the *commedia* it also achieved a high degree of professionalism in the art of acting.

In Italy, especially, the drama of the theatre was played out against a background of almost incessant strife between families and city states, and under foreign invasions and dominations covering wide areas and long periods of time. In Germany, the involvements of the Reformation tended to turn the populace to interests other than theatre. In the face of these adverse conditions, it is a wonder that so much was accomplished. In the next chapters we shall see what the spirit of the Renaissance could accomplish in more united and comparatively more peaceful countries—the rising nations of England and Spain.

7

SHAKESPEARE

AND THE ELIZABETHANS

While internal strife and foreign invasion effectively prevented the building of great nation-states in France, Germany, and Italy, Spain and England each succeeded in developing a political and spiritual unity which fostered the development of unique and virile drama. Great dramatic literature and great theatre reached a peak almost simultaneously in these two countries.

The marriage of Ferdinand and Isabella in 1467 and their subsequent defeat of the Moors marked the beginning of Spain's greatness, just as the end of the War of the Roses and the accession of Henry VII in 1485 marked the beginning of England's influence and prosperity. These two great powers were briefly united in 1554 by the uneasy marriage of Mary of England and Philip of Spain. But the increasingly nationalistic Englishmen refused to crown Philip, and he left England the next year. By 1558 Mary was dead, Philip was King of Spain, and Elizabeth was on the throne of England. Thenceforth the destinies of these two powers were divided and in conflict. The conflict culminated in the invasion of the Spanish Armada and its defeat at the hands of the English in 1588. England was preserved, Spain looked elsewhere for conquest, and the great age of the drama in both countries was shortly to get under way.

Lope de Vega was born in 1562, Shakespeare in 1564. Both, though exposed to the classical conventions that had made so much headway in Italy and France, blithely ignored them, and produced a peculiarly national, unique drama which operated by its own conventions and was greater than any pale imitation of the ancients could possibly have been.

The Renaissance comes to England

For Englishmen of that day, the period we now call the Renaissance was a bewilderingly diverse phenomenon. Early in the century the study of Greek began at Oxford under William Grocyn and Thomas Linacre, and John Colet founded St. Paul's, a school devoted to the new humanist learning. Erasmus visited England and was a familiar of Sir Thomas More, the great English Humanist. Though More's *Utopia* (1516) was written in Latin, the language of international scholarship, the precedent of the vernacular established by the great works of Chaucer gained strength, and an increasing number of literary productions appeared in the native tongue.

The individuality of England was emphasized by the quarrel of Henry VIII with the Church of Rome and by the subsequent separation of England from the Papacy in 1533. Though the ties were nominally resumed under Mary (1553–1558), the schism was definite and irrevocable and resulted in the creation of a freer intellectual atmosphere and a sharpening of individual differences such as was not possible, for instance, in Catholic Spain. Indeed, the spirit of the Renaissance itself—with its emphasis upon the things of this world and the infinite capacity of the individual man to determine his own destiny, which contributed to the Lutheran revolt on the Continent — in itself undermined the power of the Roman Church.

The intrinsically political English separation had far-reaching economic, social, and intellectual repercussions. Though Tyndale could be persecuted for his English translation of the Bible in the first quarter of the century, by 1539 Henry VIII could authorize for use in churches an English Bible which incorporated as much of Tyndale's translation as he had been able to carry out.

Henry's court was the center of the new learning in England. Here the tentative Renaissance leanings of John Skelton flowered into the literature of two of the most important early English Renaissance writers, the sonneteers Sir Thomas Wyatt and Henry Howard, Earl of Surrey. The court was also the center of very lavish performances of interludes, masques, costume balls, and tournaments, under the supervision of a Master of the Revels, whose office was permanently

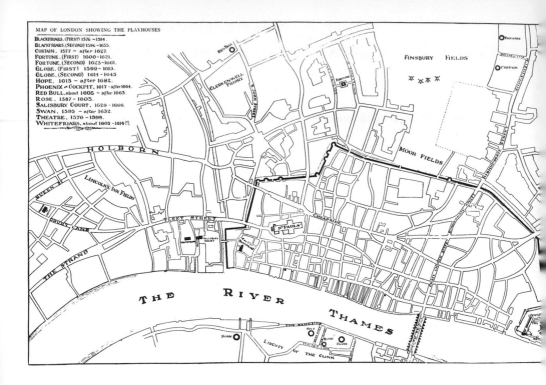

MAP OF LONDON SHOWING THE PLAYHOUSES
BLACKFRIARS, (FIRST) 1576 ~1584.
BLACKFRIARS,(SECOND) 1596 ~1655.
CURTAIN, 1577 ~ after 1627.
FORTUNE, (FIRST) 1600 ~1621.
FORTUNE, (SECOND) 1623~1661.
GLOBE, (FIRST) 1599~ 1613.
GLOBE, (SECOND) 1614 ~1645.
HOPE, 1613 ~ after 1682.
PHOENIX or COCKPIT, 1617 ~after 1664.
RED BULL, about 1605 ~ after 1663.
ROSE, 1587~1605.
SALISBURY COURT, 1629 ~1666.
SWAN, 1595 ~ after 1632.
THEATRE, 1576 ~1598.
WHITEFRIARS, about 1605 ~1614 (?).

instituted by Henry in 1544, although it had been sporadically in existence for several years before that time.

Drama begins to flourish

The schools, encouraged by the example of the court's dramatic productions, began to stage the classic plays which had for some time been used as reading exercises; so Terence, Plautus, and Seneca came to be produced in England. Latin plays for school productions began to be written; then the first school play in English appeared, Nicholas Udall's *Ralph Roister Doister* (*ca.*, 1540).

Productions of this kind continued after the accession of Elizabeth in 1558: *Gammer Gurton's Needle* at Cambridge (*ca.*, 1562) and the plays at the Inns of Court in London, notably Sackville and Norton's *Gorboduc* (1562). But the accession of Elizabeth caused a significant change in court drama. She did not care, as Henry did, for extravagant spectacle; she was not only more penurious but also of a more intellectual turn of mind. Elizabeth abolished spectacle and established legitimate drama in its stead. The acting chores were given to the boys of the Chapel Royal under the direction of Richard Edwards. These boys, chosen from all over the kingdom for their looks and their voices, had been primarily responsible for the musical por-

136

50 *London playhouses and their locations*
Left, a map of London showing the playhouses erected before
1640. The Theatre and The Curtain are in the northeast corner, The
Globe, The Rose, The Hope, and The Swan are south of the
Thames River. All except Blackfriars lay outside the walls of the old city.
Right, Merian's view of London in 1638, showing The Swan (39),
The Hope (38), and The Globe (37), with St. Paul's Cathedral
to the north, across the Thames. People usually took ferry boats across
the river to reach these theatres. (Folger Shakespeare Library)

tions of the court's worship services, receiving both upkeep and education for their work. Edwards, whom Elizabeth appointed to be
their master, was a musician, a good lyric poet, and a good dramatist. He wrote plays for the boys and coached them in the parts. Light
romantic comedy was his forte; by the time of his death in 1566, he
had established a new court drama that was the delight of critics.
The production resources of the Office of the Revels were available
to him, and the plays were beautifully set and costumed. William
Hunnis succeeded Edwards as master at the Chapel Royal. Elizabeth also established boys' troupes at St. Paul's Cathedral under Se-
bastian Westcott and at her summer palace at Windsor under Richard Farrant.

Farrant conceived the idea of having his boys give their plays before select audiences after the Queen had seen them, advancing the
argument that such an arrangement would give the boys more practice in public and would also be profitable financially, thus stimulat-
ing both master and boys to give more and better plays. Elizabeth
approved, and in September, 1575, Farrant took a lease on the great

137

hall in Blackfriars, which had formerly been a Church holding but was now under jurisdiction of the Crown and was the most aristocratic section of London. When the Windsor boys had a play ready, the Master of the Revels built the set and made costumes, then brought them to Blackfriars. A selected group of nobility was invited to a preview at very high prices. The production was then taken to play before the Queen, after which it returned to Blackfriars for a month's run. This scheme was very successful. Hunnis and the Chapel Royal boys joined Farrant in giving their plays at Blackfriars, and one or the other of the troupes gave plays every day. By 1583 John Lyly was writing for the children of St. Paul's to play there; with some intermissions because of litigation over the property, the boys' companies performed at Blackfriars for many years.

Meanwhile, the adult professional companies were also performing at London inns, and the best plays of the best troupes were presented before the court after having been chosen for that honor by the Master of the Revels. Elizabeth told her nobles that she liked these troupes, and many of them thereafter tried to acquire troupes to please the Queen. Thus, influenced by court appearances and the competition of the boy companies to improve both their plays and their performances, the professional troupes increased in number and in quality.

The theatre of Shakespeare and his contemporaries—the direct descendant of the popular drama of the medieval period—was significantly influenced by both the court drama and the school plays, both of which existed concurrently with the professional theatre.

The theatrical climate of Shakespeare

The theatre of Shakespeare's day was the culmination of a long development and the amalgamation of many disparate influences. It was also an accurate mirror of the diversity of Elizabethan life. In it was reflected conscious national pride in the achievements of Englishmen. This newly emerging national pride had manifestations in such works as Hakluyt's *The Principal Navigations, Voyages, and Discoveries of the English Nation,* which appeared first in 1559, and Raphael Holinshed's *Chronicle* (1578), that marvelous compendium which was the principal source not only of Shakespeare's historical plays but of other Elizabethan plays dealing with England's past.

The defeat of the Spanish Armada, the voyages of Frobisher, Davis, and Drake, and the consolidation of England's importance in world trade strengthened not only the Englishman's national pride but also his belief in the Renaissance ideal of the heroic proportions of the individual man and his infinite possibilities for a good life here and now.

The characteristics of the Renaissance on the Continent were anglicized in such a figure as Sir Philip Sidney, the courtier-soldier-poet, who was no less renowned for his poetry than for his exploits in battle. The art of living and the art of writing were inextricably combined; conduct and expression marched together in an expanding national consciousness.

The Renaissance Englishman became increasingly acquainted with the literature of other times and places by a swelling tide of translations from Latin, Greek, Italian, and French; if he was wealthy enough, he finished his education with a sojourn on the Continent. Accomplishment was not limited to the noble and the wealthy, however; individual enterprise and ability counted for much. A rising merchant class was changing the face of England. Feudalism was dead; a new world was being born.

As is true everywhere and at all times, the stage in its various forms mirrored the age and the people for which it existed. It reproduced the life of its contemporaries—their beliefs, traditions, emotions, aspirations, aims, and tastes. The Elizabethan theatre was so thoroughly national, so spontaneous and popular, in addition to possessing the more universal and essential qualities of human sympathy, artistic beauty, variety of presentation, and fertility of motive, that no age before or since has produced its equal. The period was one in which, as it were, men stood between two dreams of the past and the future, both colored by imagination, and both shedding glory on the present.

Vigor and pride were combined with a love of learning and elaborate art. Thought and action were no longer fettered; instead of tradition and prescription, instinct and passion ruled the hour. Instead of curbing passions and concealing appetites, the Elizabethans gloried in the outward manifestations of a passionate virility. They were coarse but not vicious, pleasure loving but not licentious, luxurious but not effeminate, violent but not cruel. They were, in the main, law abiding and contemptuous of treachery and baseness; they had an intolerance of political and ecclesiastical despotism, and a fervent love of their country.

For the theatre—which in Elizabeth's day, took the place now filled by the novel, the short story, the drama, the newspaper, motion pictures, radio, and television—these conditions were ideal. The demand of the Elizabethans for plays was insatiable, and theatre was a lucrative profession for those who could please the popular taste.

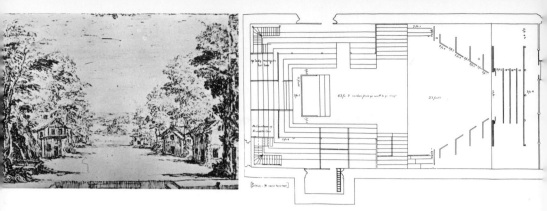

51 *Inigo Jones's production of* Florimene, *1635*
The plan of the set design, and a sketch of the border and
standing scene, the isle of Delos. In the court productions, the
Italianate system of flat wings behind a proscenium arch was much the
vogue. Here Inigo Jones is faithful to the Serlio prescription for the
satyric scene with its trees, flowers, and cottages. For such productions,
transformations or scene changes were made in full view of the audience.
(Reyher, *Les Masques Anglais;* Devonshire Collection, Chatsworth)

Secular fiction and history were ransacked in the search for plots—
the legends of Greece and Rome, Italian novels, English history,
even contemporary London. It is interesting to note that whatever
the locale of the play, the characters and development were essentially English: Romeo and Juliet are English youngsters with Italianate names; Hieronimo is a grief-stricken English father who seeks
revenge; Hamlet, Prince of Denmark, is a moody Englishman. Someone has said that an Englishman sees little fun in Molière's Alceste,
while a Frenchman sees in Falstaff only a needlessly fat man. It is
this quality of intrinsic nationalism that distinguishes the Elizabethan drama from that which had preceded it and that which followed in the Restoration. This quality, dictated by the tenor of the
times, contributes to its greatness.

The expanding intellectual horizons of the Elizabethans were evident in the materials of the playwrights. Geography, history, mechanics, recent inventions, popular science, legislation, preventive
medicine, astronomy, natural history, civic affairs, and gossip all
found their way into the theatre, to be consumed with avid interest
by the audiences. In addition to its capacity for welcoming all kinds
of information, the Elizabethan audience—like perhaps no other—
was marked by its devotion to the spoken word. Listening was easier
than reading, and the audience was quick to respond to oratory or
repartée. It liked sonorous declamation, and it liked slangy billings-
gate. It liked new words and phrases. It even liked classical allusions

which it did not understand. It responded to verse, to accent, to the march of the measure. It loved the music and the sentiment of the balcony scene of *Romeo and Juliet* no less than the thunderous rantings of *Tamburlaine*. Because of the tastes, capabilities, and aspirations of this audience, which were accurately gauged by many playwrights, we may say that never before or since has the theatre so fully engaged the affections and loyalties of so large a proportion of the population.

Some idea of the immense popularity of the theatre may be gained from the fact that in a population of about two hundred thousand, no less than twenty-three professional acting companies were performing in London at the height of the period of theatrical activity. In addition eight boy companies, the Inns of Court, other schools, and the court itself gave performances. Theatrical fare in the provinces was not as generous, but there were many provincial companies and many of the London companies traveled to the provinces in the off-seasons. English schools and colleges also fostered the production of plays, stressing classic forms and making participation mandatory. Even after the initial strength of classicism had spent itself, school productions of the classics—and especially those of the Inns of Court—remained a significant part of theatrical activity.

The thriving court drama was supervised by an especially appointed official, the Master of the Revels, whose office, as we have seen, became permanent under Henry VIII in 1544. It reached the height of its powers under Charles I; the Office of the Revels had then about one hundred employees. During Elizabeth's long reign it concerned itself mainly with legitimate drama. The Office of the Revels selected suitable plays for presentation, drilled the professional troupe selected to act in the plays, provided them with proper costumes, prepared the stage scenery and properties, saw that the players reached their destination, and managed the stage. It also supervised the activities of the various boy companies. With the accession of James I in 1603 the emphasis at court turned to the production of beautiful and elaborate masques, in which form Inigo Jones and Ben Jonson had a long and fruitful association.

For the majority of Londoners—and indeed for all Englishmen— the public theatre with its professional acting companies was not only the most accessible but the most popular form of theatre fare. Because of the tradition behind them, and because of the protection from oppressors thus afforded, these professional companies were nominally a part of noble households. They were the Earl of Leicester's Men, the Lord Admiral's Men, Lord Hunsdon's Men, the Earl of Pembroke's Men, the Lord Chamberlain's Men, and so on. The members of the nobility named (no one less than a baron was accorded the privilege) were the patrons of the various acting companies. The tradition had originated late in the Middle Ages; when the bands of strolling players were multiplying and ordinances were passed against them, the most competent sought and found the protection of a noble house. They were then at the call of their patron for special occasions but otherwise were quite at liberty to make their own way. The less competent companies were forced out of existence. This principle of patronage lasted through the Shakespearean period and was revived by the royal patents at the Restoration.

The companies of Shakespeare's London were really quite autonomous organizations, looking to the patron simply for the protection of his name and for whatever occasional financial or production aid he might be able to give. For instance, he sometimes gave his cast-off clothing to his company, to be used as costumes. Thus the theatre was, in actuality, a great popular institution operating as a free enterprise. The theatres of Shakespeare's day were controlled by corporations which included housekeepers, actor-sharers, and a business manager; such corporations chose the plays, ran the house, and divided the profits among themselves. They also hired and paid certain classes of actors and other employees.

Performances were usually given in the afternoons. The theatre was considered fashionable and was patronized by all classes of society. In the summertime performances generally began at three, in the wintertime at two o'clock. Advertising was done through three principal media: the next day's production was announced after the epilogue of a given performance; on the day of the play a flag was set on top of the theatre—white if a comedy were being given, black if a tragedy; and handbills, six by twelve inches, were posted all over London. In addition, parades and criers were often used. Admission prices were so graded that everyone, from apprentice to noble, found a price to his liking. Standing room in the pit cost a penny; seating in the galleries, depending upon location, from two pence to a shilling; and the stools on the stage for the gallants, a half crown plus six pence for the stool itself. There were no reserved seats as we know them, and at very popular plays people had to come early for advantageous locations. The rich sent their servants to reserve seats; the poor sent their wives. The admissions charged made legitimate drama one of the least expensive of entertainments for the average Londoner: admission to the tower of St. Paul's for a view of London cost a penny; the tilt-yard tournaments of the nobles—to which the general populace was admitted—eighteen pence. A book cost, for comparison's sake, sixpence or a shilling; a broadside (a single sheet of paper containing a ballad and a woodcut) cost a penny. No wonder the apprentices of London spent so much time at the theatre.

In fact so many people spent so many hours at the theatre that the city fathers, devoted to the ideal of hard and constant work, and the Puritans, to whom the theatre was anathema, were constantly at war with the players. This dark thread of disapproval runs all through the glory of Shakespeare's day. When the moral opposition joined forces with political expediency the Puritans closed the theatres.

Magnificent drama produced

The plays produced by the Elizabethans comprise the greatest body of dramatic literature in the English language, if not, indeed, in any language. It is easy to identify Shakespeare as the consummate flower of the English Renaissance, but we must also recognize that he was surrounded by a veritable bouquet.

The great stream of professional, popular drama which had developed from the Bible plays, the moralities, and the interludes was augmented by the school plays and the court productions to make a dramatic literature that is the wonder of all who know it. It was the culmination of development in dramatic art, as Shakespeare's plays were the culmination and harmonization of the various disparate elements which preceded him. The nature of the classic Greek play as embodied in Sophocles was a beautiful balance between plot and character. The Romans and their early Renaissance copiers had stressed incident over character, as had the episodic cycle plays and the short interludes, farces, and miracle plays of medieval times. In much of early Renaissance playwriting plot itself was lacking, and the characters were mere stereotypes. Shakespeare's immediate predecessors worked out the problems of plot and character. Thomas Kyd developed a comparatively well-knit plot line, including obligatory scenes and motivations as well as climax and dénouement. Marlowe built his plays upon character; what plot there is remained subservient to the title characters. The plays of John Lyly added the element of romance. Shakespeare's nearer contemporary, Robert Greene, worked out a balance between plot and character, and was more skillful than Kyd or Marlowe in reconciling and integrating subplots.

Shakespeare, taking into account all that had preceded him, produced plays as marvelous in their way as those of Sophocles had been: he balanced plot and character; he integrated main and

52 *Influences on Shakespearean playhouse design*
Left, an innyard, not only the forerunner of playhouses, but converted
for use as a theatre throughout the period. Spectators paid their
admission fee at the carriage entrance and stood about in the yard. The
stage was erected in the yard close to one of the four sides.
The galleries also held spectators, either as guests of the inn, or as
those who paid a higher admission to the players. (Folger Shakespeare
Library) Right, Rederyker stage, Antwerp, 1561. On such a stage
the academicians of Antwerp presented their plays, and some
scholars have seen in this design an influence on the Elizabethan
stage house. It is, of course, a development from the early Renaissance
platform stage shown above. See figure 40. (Brussels Bibliotheque Royale)

subplots; he used elements of romance; and he reconciled comedy
and tragedy by using comedy to heighten the tragic effect. He is our
greatest dramatic genius, not only for the characters he created and
his magnificent poetry, but also for his consummate skill in dramaturgy, and his most explicit and effective use of the theatre for which
he wrote. In his plays the classic tradition and the medieval heritage
are wonderfully combined and blended. His followers were not able
to maintain this balance of elements, and the decline of the dramatic
art was inevitable.

The rise, apogee, and fall of Elizabethan theatre is clearly traceable. Its development covered the period from the accession of Elizabeth to 1594; it reached its climax in the twenty years which followed,
and then declined to its eclipse in 1642. It would be impossible
just to mention all the names of plays and playwrights of that
burgeoning period, so we shall attempt to present here a more digest-
ible survey by considering the various types of plays which were

popular and successful, with some outstanding examples of each.

We may conveniently make four major divisions: tragedy, comedy, chronicle plays, and masques. Even as we make these major divisions, however, we must recognize that there are various types in each, and the school plays must be another consideration. Tragedy, then, was of two types, the classical and the native. Comedy had myriad types: the pastoral, the magical, the bourgeois, the allegorical and satirical—and combinations of them all. The chronicle plays were historical-legendary, factual-historical, biographical, and popular-legendary. The masques might be anything from the disguisings of the court of Henry VIII to the poetic effulgence of Milton's *Comus*. It was a diverse and prolific age. Often the same materials were treated over and over again by different playwrights, and frequently more than one playwright contributed to a particular script. All the widening horizons of the Renaissance were sources for the dramatists—any incident of human activity from ancient Greece to contemporary London. It was as Thomas Heywood said in his statement of the playwright's function:

> To give content to this most curious age,
> The gods themselves we've brought down to the stage,
> And figured them in planets, made even Hell
> Deliver up the furies, by no spell
> Saving the Muse's rapture. Further we
> Have trafficked by their help; no history
> We've left unrifled: our pens have been dipped
> As well in each hid manuscript,
> As tracts more vulgar, whether read or sung
> In our domestic or more foreign tongue.
> Of fairy elves, nymphs of the sea and land,
> The lawns and groves, no number can be scanned
> Which we've not given feet to; nay 'tis known
> That when our chronicles have barren grown
> Of story, we have all invention stretched,
> Dived low as to the centre, and then reached
> Unto the Primum Mobile above,
> Nor 'scaped things intermediate, for your love.

A noble boast, and nobly was it fulfilled.

The classical tragedy on the Elizabethan and Jacobean stage of the professional companies was an adaptation of Seneca. The most famous of these blood and thunder plays is Thomas Kyd's *The Spanish Tragedy*. Its leading character, Hieronimo, was a favorite bravura part of the renowned actor, Edward Alleyn, as well as of Richard Burbage of Shakespeare's company. The play is an unrelievedly dark revenge tragedy which strewed the stage with bloody corpses, to the great delight of its lusty audiences. It was first played in 1586 and remained popular for many years. The next year saw Marlowe's *Tamburlaine,* and again Alleyn played the title role, that of a Machiavellian hero, who spoke thrillingly in English blank verse. The revenge tragedy with its ghostly visitations and its welter of blood continued through the period. Marston's *Antonio's Revenge* (1599), Chapman's *The Revenge of Bussy D'Ambois* (ca., 1600), Massinger's *The Roman Actor* (1626), Webster's *The Duchess of Malfi* (1614) are but a few examples. Even Shakespeare tried his hand at the type in such a play as *Titus Andronicus* (ca., 1594).

The usual classical tragedy, as written and performed at the schools and universities, followed the Continental Renaissance ideal, and was attended by the unities of time, place, and action. In this form, violent events took place off stage and were related by messengers. But the love of the Elizabethan popular audience for action viewed rather than related, led in the public theatres to the wholesale slaughter which takes place in full view of the audience in many of these plays. No wonder that the universities—those keepers and producers of classical plays and their slavish imitations—had no use for professional actors and writers. They were destroying a sacred image by pandering to the public taste.

The classical tragedies written in Shakespeare's day did, however, at least pay lip service to the ancients, and did maintain an unrelievedly dark tone with a single line of action. Not so the native tragedy, which scorned the classical conventions, mixed in comic scenes, and often had subplots to counterpoint or underline the main plot. Many of Shakespeare's plays will illustrate this principle: the porter's scene in *Macbeth*, the gravediggers in *Hamlet*, the Gloucester story in *King Lear*. But even here, as we have said, the genius of Shakespeare transmuted what might have been mere comic interludes into integral parts of the tragedies, serving to heighten their tragic effect; some of his contemporaries were not so successful in handling their comic elements. The native tragedy was a curious amalgamation of Renaissance dramaturgy in main theme, and of medieval holdovers in subplots, clowns, and stage action. Shakespeare and many of his contemporaries, much to Ben Jonson's disgust, gave the people what they wanted. Some other contributors to the native tragic drama were Marlowe, Nashe, Lodge, Beaumont, Fletcher, Ford, Massinger, Heywood, Middleton, Tourneur, and Shirley. If we were not so overwhelmed by the pre-eminence of Shakespeare's genius, the plays of many of these would stand higher in our esteem than they do today.

Another union of Continental Renaissance and native English ideals was evident in the pastoral romance, a type of comedy in which is to be found a combination of the Italian pastoral play and the native English love of country life. These qualities combined were greatly in evidence in *The Pinner of Wakefield,* written by Robert Greene (d. 1592), and flowered in such plays as Shakespeare's *As You Like It* (ca. 1599).

The magical comedy is illustrated notably by Shakespeare's *A Midsummer's Night's Dream* (ca., 1595), by Greene's *Friar Bacon and Friar Bungay* (1594), by Marlowe's *Dr. Faustus* (1588), which is indeed not a comedy but illustrates the Elizabethan propensity for magical happenings on the stage. In these plays potions, spells, apparitions, and tricks of magic exhibit both medieval superstition and Renaissance love of curious learning.

In the bourgeois drama—to which Shakespeare notably did not contribute—we have Dekker's *The Shoemakers' Holiday* (1600) and *The Roaring Girl* (1611), Peele's *Old Wives' Tale* (1595), Jonson's *Bartholomew Fair* (1614), Greene's *Looking Glass for London* (ca., 1594), Kyd's *Arden of Faversham* (1592), the anonymous *A Yorkshire Tragedy* (ca., 1606, the title page credits Shakespeare), and *A Warning for Fair Women* (ca., 1599). *The Shoemakers' Holiday,* one of the most delightful of Elizabethan comedies, is concerned with the wonderful feats of Simon Eyre, an actual master shoemaker who became Lord Mayor of London. The others are also founded upon real characters and contemporary or recent happenings. These plays are a sort of tabloid newspaper of the times.

In contrast to the bourgeois drama and its real characters was the allegorical comedy, whose type-named characters recall the old moralities. But the playwrights of this new age added another dimension to allegory, and produced satires that are apt, biting, and often applicable to the universal shortcomings of mankind. Ben Jonson is the most notable dramatist of this type; Shakespeare played a leading role in Jonson's *Every Man in His Humour* (1598). Jonson's *Volpone* (1607) is one of the most noteworthy of the type; one of the most sensational was Nashe's *Isle of Dogs* (1597), which satire aroused official ire and caused the closing of the London theatres for a short time in that year.

The chronicle plays, whose plots are based on factual history, are easy to trace in Shakespeare: the Richards, the Henrys, and the Roman plays. The first English play of this sort appeared in 1550,

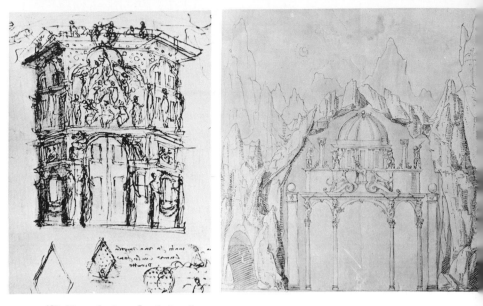

53 *Two designs by Inigo Jones*
Left, The House of Fame for Ben Jonson's *Masque of Queens,* 1609;
right, Oberon's palace for Ben Jonson's *Oberon,* 1611. The latter
sketch indicates that this scene is a transformation of a mountain into a
palace—only one of the many wonders wrought in these
elaborate productions. (Devonshire Collection, Chatsworth)

when John Bale wrote his *King Johan;* from that time on there were
many anonymous scripts, as well as chronicle plays by Peele, Greene,
and Marlowe; Rowley's treatment of the reigns of Henry VIII and
Elizabeth in the two curiously named plays, *When You See Me You
Know Me* (*ca.,* 1604), and *If You Know Not Me You Know Nobody*
(*ca.,* 1604), were both written after the death of Elizabeth. All of
these plays are basically factual, but in practically all of them, historical truth is stretched to fit the thesis that Queen Elizabeth was a
true, lawful, and strong sovereign of an illustrious house. It was this
category of play that the Master of the Revels scrutinized most carefully for possibly seditious material.

The historical-legendary plays may be traced from the first regular English tragedy of *Gorboduc* (1561) by Sackville and Norton,
through *Appius and Virginia* (*ca.,* 1609), *Cambyses* (1569), *Locrine*
(1591), *The History of King Leir and his Three Daughters* (*ca.,*
1590), and two plays about King Arthur, *The Misfortunes of Arthur*
(*ca.,* 1569), and *The Birth of Merlin* (*ca.,* 1608). Of the popular-
legendary plays we may note Munday's *John à Kent and John à*

Cumber (1594), and his two ventures into the Robin Hood legend with Chettle. The biographical plays treated Sir Thomas More, Thomas Lord Cromwell, Sir John Oldcastle, Sir Thomas Wyatt, Perkin Warbeck, and less noble figures like Jack Straw.

All people, places, and things were the stuff of the Elizabethan popular drama; and vital were the characters and events that set the lusty heartstrings of its spectators vibrating.

Concomitant with the variety of the popular drama were the continuing productions, chiefly of the classics, at the schools and universities. The chief products of the schools were tragedies and comedies on classic models, written by students and by faculty. Along with these were continuing productions of Aeschylus, of Euripides, of Sophocles, of Aristophanes, of Plautus, and of Terence. The universities, frowning on professional actors and professional playwrights, passed successive ordinances forbidding their performances within a five-mile limit of school precincts. But the students of the Inns of Court in London, while producing their own neoclassical plays, were ardent supporters of the popular theatre. And when those university men Marlowe, Greene, Peele, Nashe, and Lodge arrived in London, they quickly turned to writing for the popular stage, ignoring the prescriptions of their academic training.

In addition to all this activity, the Elizabethan court was the scene of much theatre. Besides the productions of the professional companies which were often given command performances at court, and the activities of the boy companies for which several of the leading dramatists wrote, the court originated a type of pseudodrama of its own—the masque. Its history goes back to William Cornish in 1512; his *The Golden Arbour of Pleasure* called for thirty courtiers, eight musicians, and eight boys "to sing like birds." Two years later he produced *Love and Duty,* and the elaborately staged, musically accompanied gracefulness of the court masque was under way. As we have seen, these spectacular and generally undramatic entertainments were out of favor in Elizabeth's court, fortunately for the legitimate drama. But they returned once again with the accession of the Stuarts. Ben Jonson wrote thirty-two masques for court production, and many other writers produced them in lesser numbers. William Davenant, later to be of some importance in the Restoration theatre, began by writing and producing court masques, and we have already mentioned the contribution of John Milton to this type.

The proliferating theatre of the English Renaissance produced all kinds of dramatic literature in various combinations. Polonius' "tragedy, comedy, history, pastoral, pastoral-comical, historical-pastoral, tragical-historical, tragical-comical-historical-pastoral" (*Hamlet*, Act II, Scene II, ll. 16–18) is not far from an accurate description of the kinds of things playwrights were producing for the avid theatre-going public. So few of the scripts have come down to us that we do not realize the numbers that were written. Thomas Heywood tells us that he "had a finger in" more than two hundred playscripts; and of Thomas Dekker's seventy, fifty are lost. So the list goes on—myriads of plays are mentioned of which no trace can be found, and doubtless there were many others of which we know not even the names. Who can say that the thirty-eight plays we now ascribe to Shakespeare represent his total output? The fact that these plays were written for acting companies, and, for the most part, jealously guarded from publication, no doubt meant that many would inevitably be lost to succeeding generations. Were it not, indeed, for the loving com-memorative labors of two of his fellow-actors, Heminge and Condell, even the Shakespeare canon as we know it would be considerably reduced. Of the feverish theatrical activity of Shakespeare's day we have today little conception. Suffice it to say, as we have said before, that never before or since were so many writing so much of so many different kinds for so enthusiastic an audience.

London becomes the center

The sixteenth-century Englishman could see dramatic perform-ances throughout the kingdom, but playhouses were built only in London. Traveling companies of players, either the London compa-nies in the summer months or provincial companies played in towns and villages and manor houses either upon invitation or their own advertisement. The titled patron might present his troupe with a letter of introduction to another noble, or to a town corporation. If the traveling company was to play for the household of a noble, a stage was set up in the great hall of the castle. In the towns, the com-pany would be met by the mayor, who offered them the hospitality of the town and gave a dinner in their honor. Afterwards they per-formed a play for this select audience. This performance was paid for by town funds, then a subsequent performance was generally given in the town hall and admission was charged for this second one. Records of such traveling companies are to be found at Bristol, Bath, Dover, Coventry, Nottingham, and at many other places. Shakespeare himself is presumed to have seen such a performance in the Guild Hall at Stratford, when the Earl of Leicester's troupe visited that town.

Sometimes the playing space would be the courtyard of the local inn; in London the innyards were the usual places of playing. The medieval innyard could easily be adapted (figure 52). It almost invariably had one wide arched entrance for horses and carriages, and was surrounded by a gallery of as many stories as the building was high, behind which were the guest rooms. The company of players stationed one of their number at the entrance to collect admissions from people who stood about in the yard to watch the performance. The performance was given on a platform of boards set upon barrels at some convenient spot in the yard. Guests at the inn sat or stood in the galleries. Depending upon the arrangements of the company with the proprietor of the inn, these privileged spectators were either guests of the house, or they paid to the company a fee which was more than that paid by the standees in the yard. This essential arrangement was retained by the permanent theatres built in London beginning in the fourth quarter of the century.

The passing of laws by Parliament prohibiting tours by masterless men and the requiring of licenses for patronized groups tended to concentrate the playing companies in London, where they played during the greater part of the year, traveling to the provinces only during the summer months. In Shakespeare's day there were six or seven hundred inns in London. The betters inns did not allow plays because of the brawls they caused, but others permitted them for a flat rate, or on a percentage basis. To advertise the plays, which were usually given at two or three o'clock in the afternoon, the actors, in the morning, put on their costumes and paraded the streets with trumpets and drums. As time went on, these temporary playhouses proved unsatisfactory, because the landlords of the inns changed their minds so often, because the actors were not the masters of their fate but at the mercy of the innkeepers, and because these performances naturally were interfered with by the regular commerce of the inn.

Some nameless business man of vision, aware of the growing popularity of the plays, rented a few of the large inns in London, and made them permanent playing places, erecting permanent stages in the innyards. This development permitted very much better staging, the use of more properties, and a measure of security for the acting companies. Benches were put in the galleries for the ladies and gentlemen, and the companies of players, who rented the inns thus arranged, were masters of the situation. They began to advertise by handbills, and they stationed a man at the gate with an iron box slotted at the top to admit a penny, the price of the general admission. Such resident companies were known to have operated at The Bull,

54 *Two contemporary drawings of Elizabethan playhouses*
Left, the title page of William Alabaster's *Roxana*, 1630, showing, in the
middle of the lower panel, a play being presented. Spectators seem
to be seated in the gallery above the stage, while others stand in the pit
below the stage. Right, a sketch from Kirkman's *Wits*, 1640, showing a
similar stage to that at the left, with a curtained inner stage and, here,
curtains masking the upper gallery. (Folger Shakespeare Library)

The Bell, The Cross-Keys, The Bel Sauvage, The Boar's Head, and
the Saracen's Head before any permanent theatres were built.

The Elizabethan playhouse—famous and infamous

London now had real playhouses, and the drama was even more
the national amusement. There were two forces working against the
drama, however: the Puritans who morally objected and the city
officials who opposed the drama because it spread the plague and
caused quarrels, fights, and riots. Since the players were at least
nominally the servants of nobles and hence wards of the Privy Council, the city officials could not molest them. As long as these foes
were kept separate, the actors were safe. But in 1573, when the
Puritans elected one of themselves Lord Mayor and dominated the
Board of Aldermen and Town Council, the Town Council put a ban
on all plays saying there was danger of plague. The ban was not
removed when the danger was over, so the players complained to

152

their patrons who, in turn, appealed to the Privy Council, who had the ban lifted. But the Town Council was not to be defeated. It met on December 6, 1574, and passed such stringent restrictions that it was hard to keep going at all. The Town Council's rules stated that plays could be given on only three days of the week; they had to be censored before being presented; the inns had to be licensed for plays by the Lord Mayor and the Aldermen, and the proprietors had to give a bond that there would be no disorder or immorality in connection with the performances; no plays could be given during the "sickness" or when prohibited by the Mayor; no plays could be given during the time of divine service; the proprietors must pay a poor tax.

Again the players asked their patrons to appeal to the Privy Council, which now felt that it could give little help except to define the plague clause to read that plays could not be given on the day after fifty or more had died of the plague. Elizabeth, who loved the plays but who was an excellent politician and careful of her money, went no further than to designate her own Master of the Revels as the censor and the source of licenses. The bond and the tax clauses remained and were serious hindrances.

Finally, James Burbage, ex-carpenter, ex-actor, and utterly devoted theatreman, conceived a good idea—he would build a theatre in one of the "liberties" in London where city officials had no jurisdiction. These liberties were the sites of former Roman Catholic Church holdings; by special law they were free of civil authority, being subject only to the Crown. In one of them, Burbage built a theatre for the Earl of Leicester's troupe, of which he was the manager. He was obliged to forgo the liberties of Blackfriars and Whitefriars because, even though they were nearest to St. Paul's and the center of population, they were too expensive. He eliminated the Clink because its moral reputation was very bad. So only Holywell near the Bishopsgate was left. Actually, though somewhat far from the center of population, this was a rather good choice, for it adjoined the city park and playground, Finnsbury Field. Not being able to get a right of way from the road, he cut a hole in the brick wall separating Holywell from Finnsbury Field and having obtained a twenty-one year lease from Gyles Allen, who owned the plot of ground he wanted, he drew up plans for the first theatre of Renaissance England. The lease was obtained on April 13, 1576, and The Theatre (for so he called it) was opened in the fall of that year. It was the sensation of the season, and influenced all succeeding theatre construction of the period.

The next year, Henry Lanman leased a plot of ground close to

Burbage's, and built a theatre on it which he called The Curtain, probably because the land upon which it was built was called Curten Close. In 1585 Burbage obtained control of The Curtain, thus becoming the first theatre monopolist in history.

While this was going on, a very shrewd servant of one Mr. Woodward of the Bankside, Philip Henslowe by name, succeeded to Woodward's extensive property by marrying his master's widow. He was variously in the lumber business, a tavern keeper, a farmer, a pawnbroker, and a real-estate operator, continuing to live on the Bankside. In 1585 he bought a piece of land on the Bankside from the Church and built a very fine theatre on it, copying the plan from Burbage. He opened it in 1587 as The Rose. It is from the careful records of his operations as theatre owner and manager that we have a great deal of our knowledge concerning the theatre of Shakespeare's day.

In the next twenty-five years, five more theatres were to be built in London, among them the famous Globe built by Burbage on the Bankside in 1599 from materials salvaged from The Theatre, the rights to which he had wisely kept in his original lease with Gyles Allen. Although there were individual variations—of what extent we do not know—the basic plan for all of these theatres was the same.

Burbage conceived an adaptation of the innyard playhouse, making The Theatre, however, octagonal in form to improve the sight lines over those possible in the rectangular innyard. He provided for about fifteen hundred spectators in three roofed galleries and a standing pit with an open top so that daylight could provide the chief illumination and ventilation could be improved (no small consideration in those bathless days). The building was made of timber and stucco and the roof over the galleries was thatched. In the galleries he installed wooden benches, leaving standing room behind them. Four special rooms, provided with locks and keys, were put in the galleries nearest the stage; these were "the lords' rooms." There were no seats in the open yard or pit; there the spectators stood.

Thus much of the outside structure of the Elizabethan public theatre has been authenticated upon evidence practically conclusive. Various extant views of London show the outside structure of several of the theatres (figure 50), and the famous contract for Henslowe's Fortune Theatre (the chief cornerstone of all subsequent imagined reconstructions) is fairly specific with regard to this portion of the house. But when we turn to the stage, the case is altered. The few contemporary illustrations of the stage are contradictory (figures 54, 56, 78), and the literary references are difficult to interpret. That

154

55 *Another interpretation of Shakespeare's stage*
Leslie Hotson maintains that the stage house of Shakespeare's theatre
was a separate structure, with dressing rooms below the stage,
and houses for the scenes erected with poles and curtains on the transverse
axis of the stage. Spectators, he says, surrounded the stage. These two
sketches from his book, *Shakespeare's Wooden O,* illustrate
his conception.

there was no front curtain seems certain, although curtains of some
kind were used, since several references speak of them. That there
was limited seating on the stage is also authenticated. The plays indicate that arrangements were provided for an "above" and a "within";
hence Shakespearean scholars have assumed that the stage projected
out into the pit, with the audience on three sides, while the house behind the stage was used as a kind of permanent setting. It is supposed
to have had practical doors and windows, a curtained recess at stage
level which could be used to reveal set scenes, and a gallery over the
recess at the second floor level. The third floor above the stage is
presumed to have been reserved for the musicians, since "music
above" is a fairly constant reference. Over the stage house and a part
of the stage itself extended a roof supported by pillars from the stage
floor. This roof was a partial shielding from the elements and allowed
for ascents and descents of props and actors as necessary; it was
called "the Heavens." "Hell" was the area under the stage; access to
it was through trapdoors and from behind scenes. The stage house
itself was the actors' domain, with dressing rooms, prop rooms, and
any necessary machinery; it could be entered through a stage door.
Atop the stage house was a small turret-like structure from which a
trumpeter signaled the beginning of the play, and from which a flag
was flown to indicate the type of play being given. Roof and turret

are authenticated in extant drawings, and the columns to support the roof are indispensible concomitants.

The stage façade and the arrangements for the actors remain something of a mystery, although many theories have been advanced. In recent years the Shakespearean scholar Leslie Hotson has pointed out (in his *Shakespeare's Wooden O*, 1960) that heretofore generally accepted reconstructions of the Globe have presupposed that the Elizabethans were too quickly conversant with Italian stage practice, or that they have been predicated on a system which worked backwards from the proscenium stage to the platform stage, attempting to reconcile these two forms. He maintains that Shakespeare's stage can only be approached from the English medieval stage, the pageant wagon, and calls attention once more to the Fortune contract, which provides for a *second* house to be erected *inside the yard of the first*. After diligent research in many contemporary references, he assumes that the below-stage area comprised the dressing rooms for the actors, and that they emerged through trapdoors at each corner of the stage. The audience completely surrounded the stage, with the "lords' rooms"—the galleries over the stage—entered through the stage door. At stage level one or more great doors permitted large movable properties to be brought on, and before these sat the dandies who payed so exhorbitantly for seating on the stage itself (figure 55). Only thus does Dekker's statement make sense: "The Throne of the Stage . . . on the very Rushes where the Comedy is to daunce, yea and under the state of *Cambises* himself . . . beating down the mews and hisses of the opposed rascality" (*The Gull's Hornbook*, London, 1609). If this conception is correct, assumptions about settings and their use must be revised as well; the conflicting views will be presented in their proper place. All authorities, however, do agree that the many theatres built in London at this time followed essentially the same form; they might be octagonal, round, or square, but their general plan was similar, and was useful for the presentation of almost any conceivable type of play, just as Burbage had planned.

The fiscal arrangement Burbage conceived for The Theatre was also more or less followed by other theatre operators, and was, of course, a refinement of the policies followed by the innyard players. He leased the theatre to Leicester's Men on these terms: the actors were to get all the pennies paid for general admission; Burbage and his brother-in-law John Brayne, who had invested his entire fortune in the project, were to get the extra shillings and sixpence paid for seats in the galleries. It was a profitable arrangement on both sides. The actors, under ordinary conditions, spent about a third of their

156

income for fixed expenses, then divided the rest among themselves. Their income was always assured, since everyone, whatever his location in the house, paid the general admission. And there were sufficient spectators in the galleries to insure the proprietors a good return on their money. Theatre had become a business enterprise as well as an art form.

In addition to these public playhouses, which were most typical of the period, there were sundry roofed-in theatres called, for no clear reason, "private." Such was Blackfriars, where Farrant's boy company had originally performed. James Burbage leased and remodeled the building in 1597, but was restrained from using it as a public theatre. After his death, his sons, Richard and Cuthbert, leased it to Henry Evans for the Children of the Chapel Royal. Shakespeare's troupe finally installed a "men's company" in the house in 1608. Blackfriars had been converted from the original "great hall," and was rectangular in shape, with a stage assumed to be across one end of the narrow dimension, since by this time Italinate scenery was in use in court theatricals. It had benches for the whole audience.

Other private theatres were Whitefriars, Salisbury Court, the Phoenix in Drury Lane, and the Cockpit-in-Court; the latter, designed by Inigo Jones, used a permanent architectural setting in the Italian mode. There were no standees in these private theatres, the capacity of which was very much smaller than that of public houses, and the admission prices were correspondingly higher. Their resources allowed for considerable ingenuity in staging.

Dramatic performances were also given in the great halls of palaces which were converted into theatres for these special occasions, and in specially prepared rooms in the schools and universities. Such a conversion, evidently usual when the students were performing themselves in plays of their own making, prevailed for the performance recorded as one by Shakespeare's company at Gray's Inn (one of the most dramatically-minded of the Inns of Court) on December 28, 1594. In its seventy-foot hall a scaffolded stage was erected, but whether in the middle or at one end is uncertain. Professor Hotson points out that as late as 1615, the University Registrary at Trinity College, Cambridge, bears record of a dramatic performance there stating that the area reserved for the king was at the upper end of the hall, *beyond* the stage. Thus a variety of arrangements was available for the performance of plays in the Elizabethan Renaissance.

Though the exact physical nature of the Elizabethan playhouses is not known to us, we do know that they were the colorful scene of

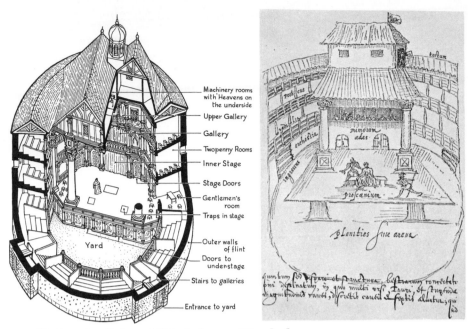

56 *Interior design of Elizabethan public playhouses*

Right, a sketch of the interior of the Swan playhouse, made by Arend von Buchell (1565–1641) in his commonplace book, to illustrate the "observations" of his friend Johnnes DeWitt, who visited the Swan in 1596. If this observation is correctly rendered, the stage backing at the Swan differed from those shown in figure 54, although here again spectators seem to be in the gallery above the stage. The only other early print extant is that of the Red Bull, 1672. See figure 78.
Left, a reconstruction of the Globe by Richard Leacroft for Methuen's outline, *The Theatre*. In this reconstruction, the axis of the stage is more nearly transverse than in the model of John Cranford Adams shown in figure 57, with the so-called lords' rooms actually being on the stage to left and right, and the stools for the "gulls" placed immediately in front of them. (Folger Shakespeare Library, Richard Leacroft Theatre Collection)

often boisterous entertainment, and probably the most popular amusement for Englishmen of all social classes. Famous in our day as the background of the great plays of Shakespeare, they, in their own day, were both greatly loved and greatly reviled.

"Piece out our imperfections . . ."

The public theatres lacked extensive settings and depended upon the audience, as the Prologue to Shakespeare's *Henry V* requests, to "piece out our imperfections with your thoughts." As we have mentioned above, the stage house is presumed to have had various doors, windows, and balconies or galleries. Some scholars have suggested that this architectural setting was an attempt by the popular theatre to adopt the Palladian setting of the Teatro Olimpico, but since the Olimpico dates almost ten years after England's first public theatre, this supposition is hardly tenable. In similar manner, the curtained recess, which has been presumed a part of stage architecture in England, is identified with the central arch of the Roman theatre and of the Olimpico, but no proof is at hand and it is equally tenable to say that this inner stage might have been a convenience invented and utilized for reveals, or set scenes. Professor Hotson dismisses the plausibility of the inner stage, saying that it is unlikely that a dramatist would allow his intimate scenes to be played so far from his audience, or that he would have them completely inaccessible to the gentry seated in the galleries above the stage. Professor Hotson advances the theory that the stage axis was transverse, and that the right and left ends of the stage were provided with holes for the insertion of posts and lintels so that "rooms" or "scenes" could be erected and hung about with curtains. Stagehands set the scenes at the beginning of the play, and, presumably invisible, drew the curtains as the performance required, removing the temporary structures and striking the set at the end of the performance. The terminology of setting and striking, he suggests, comes from the likeness of the curtains to the sails of a ship, and the similarity of the stage house itself to a ship with hold and deck. The "within" of the manuscripts means within one of these scenes; the "above" is the second story of these temporary structures. Since each of the four corner trapdoors emerged into one of these scenes, both small set pieces and actors could appear either in full sight of the audience or screened from them.

The other interpretation of the stage facilities would have us suppose that the gallery above the inner stage was used for a particularized location, as were the windows of the stage house and the inner stage itself. The walls of a besieged city, for instance, were represented by the first gallery; Romeo wooed Juliet as she appeared at a second-level stage window. The forestage was used for unlocalized action, or for action which became localized by reason of the actors indicating the place. We have also been asked to suppose that edifices were wheeled out from the inner stage, such as Cleopatra's monument in Shakespeare's play. Other students of the theatre say that such a scene as this was played on the gallery above the inner stage.

Various references can be cited to show that in addition to the practice of putting up place names to indicate locations, Shakespeare's contemporaries also utilized set pieces of linen and lath. Evidence can also be mustered for the fact that the stage roof was painted on its inner side to represent the heavens, and that a type of crane was integrated into it for ascents and descents. We also know that effects for thunder were available, that fireworks were employed, that torches augmented daylight, and that the firing of a very real cannon ignited the thatch of the Globe and burned it to the ground during a performance of *Henry VIII* in 1613. Many of the effects called for are reminiscent of the elaborations of the medieval mysteries: angels and prophets descending from Heaven, a serpent devouring a vine, a hand clutching a burning sword emerging from a cloud, Jonah being cast out of the whale's belly, bleeding heads, headless trunks, and many like wonders. Great care was taken to make these effects as realistic as possible, and these tricks were no doubt as highly regarded as had been those of the earlier plays. A trapdoor is indicated for the gravedigger's scene in *Hamlet,* and it was undoubtedly useful upon other occasions.

The versatility of the setting in the public playhouses, in any event, allowed for multiple scenes moving rapidly, such as many of the plays of the period include. Sir Philip Sidney, writing in the early 1580's, protested this lack of unity:

> You shall have Asia on the one side and Affrick on the other, and so many other under-kingdoms that the player, when he cometh on, must ever begin by telling where he is, or else the tale will not be conceived. Now we shall have three ladies walk to gather flowers, and then we must believe the stage to be a garden. By and by we hear news of shipwreck in the same place, and then we are to blame if we accept it not for a rock. Upon the back of that, comes out a hideous monster, with fire and smoke, and then the miserable beholders are bound to take it for a cave.

But Sidney's protest was a minority report. The imagination of the audience was equal to the agility demanded of it. The public theatres most definitely had no front curtain—a fact amply attested to by the endings of plays which provide for the clearing of the stage, even when dead bodies were lying around. In any event, the stage pillars and the entire interior of the house were as elaborately carved and painted as the treasury of the company allowed and each theatre prided itself on the beauty of its curtains. Contemporary descriptions often mention the sumptuous appearance of the theatres, and this extravagance was one of the great points of criticism employed by the

Puritans. We may be fairly sure, then, that within the limits of finances and a daily change of bill, the public theatres attempted to make their scenes as elaborate as possible.

In the court-subsidized theatres, where the performances were occasional and expenditures far more liberal, the settings were more extravagant. Indications are that these temporary playhouses first employed multiple settings without regard to perspective, after the fashion of the French medieval mysteries. Perhaps they used the transverse axis of the stage, with stage houses to either side and the audience below and above the stage. Gradually the Italian Renaissance innovation of single-setting in perspective came into vogue, followed by "painty" settings which could be changed at will. These "painty" settings followed the Italian inventions of wing flats and shutters and their use of three-sided prisms as Sabbatini describes them. Various records of the Office of the Revels show expenditures for "apt houses, made of canvas, framed, fashioned and painted," for gilding lions' heads, for making realistic fishes, and for innumerable costume items. Designers for the court theatres became increasingly well acquainted with the Continental stagecraft of the formal theatres, and adapted them to English uses. Many of the plans of Inigo Jones, court designer to James I and Charles I, are still extant to show us the use he made of elaborate proscenium arches, front curtains, scene dissolves, and cloud effects (figures 51, 53). He also seems to have utilized Serlio settings upon occasion as well as a raked stage. In fact, so important did scenic investiture become in the increasingly elaborate Stuart masques, for which Jones designed and Ben Jonson wrote, that these two artists quarreled violently about precedence and Jonson lost the argument.

Elaborate settings were often devised for the performances of the boy companies; the workshops of the Office of the Revels were responsible for dressing these shows and for mounting the productions. Frequent entries in the books of the Revels Office show sums paid out for transporting costumes and scenery to various locations, both for the use of the boy companies and for performances of the adult professional companies before the Queen and her court. Though the professional companies performed the plays of their repertoire on such an occasion, each play was newly costumed, sometimes given "painty" settings suitable to the court theatre, and rerehearsed. They were almost invariably given in the evening, so lighting was important. The theatrical effectiveness of such performances no doubt influenced both the private playhouses and the public theatres to use as much of their details as possible. By 1639 we find a special

57 *Reconstruction of the Globe Theatre*
Left, a sketch of a model of the Globe by John Cranford Adams as he
reconstructed it. His model shows the apron stage, the upper stage
levels, the inner stage, the doors and windows of the stage house, the pit,
the galleries, the heavens over the stage, and the music hut.
Right, the model shown at the left as constructed within the modern
playhouse at Hofstra College, New York, where Dr. Adams was
President. This stage is used for the annual Shakespeare Festival at
the College. (Folger Shakespeare Library; Hofstra College)

patent being issued to William Davenant to build a theatre especially for the use of scenes. He never built it, however, for the theatres
were closed by the Puritans three years later.

In these indoor playhouses, whether of the temporary type or of
the private kind, lighting, as we have mentioned, assumed great
importance, and the effects achieved by the Italians were assiduously
copied. The wonders of the Italian theatre were known to the audience of the private theatres and were looked for in these more select
playhouses of their native land. These innovations were increasingly
adopted.

Music, too, was an important part of theatre, both public and
select. There were interludes and postludes as well as integral songs
and dances. Performances of the boy companies were frequently
preceded by an hour's "musick" in the private theatres where they
played. Even the briefest acquaintance with Shakespeare's plays will
show the frequent use of songs. So far as the acting companies could
afford them, the musicians were of the best and every adequate actor
was also a competent musician. At court the musicians were very

good indeed. Thomas Campion composed for the court masques, as did Ferrabasco. A variety of instruments were available, including recorders, flutes, trumpets, violins, violas da gamba, and harpsichords, as well as drums. Cornets, hautboys (ancestor of the oboe), and the lute were the instruments most frequently used by the performers themselves. Much of the music composed for Elizabethan theatricals is still delightful to the modern ear.

Though early Shakespearean scholars tended to stress the simplicity of the Elizabethan theatre, and magnified the dramatists' greatness in triumphing over the crudity of their production facilities, it has since become apparent that, as in the Greek theatre, the playwrights used every device that could be invented to add to the scenic investiture of their plays. As the period advanced, you may be sure, these became ever more complicated and elaborate.

Costumes inaccurate, but elaborate

For many years it was assumed that scant attention was paid to costuming in the popular theatre of the English Renaissance; the actors wore contemporary dress, and that was that. But a careful study of the available sources, and the discovery of new ones, demonstrates that even the popular playhouses seem to have paid a great deal of attention to costuming. We may conveniently divide the types of costuming in Shakespeare's day as follows: classical, allegorical, professional, foreign, and historical.

It is true that many characters in the tragedies, and many more in the comedies, appeared in contemporary dress. But it is equally true that not a few of the cast of characters evidently wore "character" costumes. Just as in the theatre of the present day the presumably authentic costume is in reality a modern adaptation of a bygone mode, so in that day noncontemporary costumes were Elizabethan adaptations of other times and places (figure 59). Of course, our resources for historical accuracy are ever so much greater, and our antiquarian zest more fervent; our theatrical costume, on the whole, is likely to be ever so much more true to the character, the time, and the place. But the Elizabethans, no less than the moderns, realized the theatrical effectiveness of specialized costuming and used it so far as their resources allowed.

Inventories revealing such items as "senatores cloaks," and some extant sketches, show that the Elizabethans sought a flavor of antiquity in the costuming of classical plays, though the Roman legionary was likely to have the full sleeves and plumed hat of an Elizabethan courtier. The many deities of classical mythology are

163

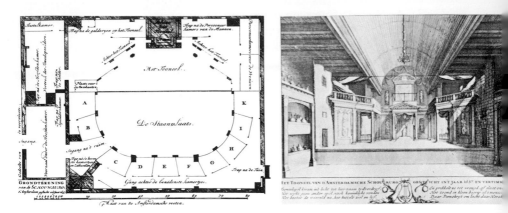

listed in Henslowe's records as having special costumes: "Junoes cotte," "sewtte for Nepton," "Dido's robe," and many others, along with appropriate properties. Some idea of how these, and others, appeared are available in the invaluable sketches of Inigo Jones.

Inventories and sketches also reveal that allegorical figures wore distinctive costumes. Ghosts and witches, fools and fairies, each had distinguishing items of costume in robes and headdresses, in capes and wigs; and the "robe to go invisible in," which Henslowe mentions, must have been a particular convention of the Elizabethan stage. Many are the mentions of bears and lions, of horses, dragons, and dogs, who evidently were costumed entire. Other items mention boar's heads, lion's heads, and, of course, the ass's head that Bottom wore.

Aside from these obviously required costumes, other types were also quite evidently in use. Lawyers, doctors, churchmen, and civil authorities wore distinguishing dress. Portia's disguise is a lawyer's gown. Friars, popes, and cardinals wear their typical dress. The figure of "Prologue," who appears in many of the plays, seems to have been particularized with a long black velvet robe, a flowing beard and wig, and a poet's laurel on his head.

Turks, Danes, and Spaniards received particular attention as well. The Turkish costume invariably included a scimitar, a turban, special slippers, and long, loose breeches. Danes and Spaniards are mentioned as having specialized costumes, and we know that the Dutchman on the Elizabethan stage always wore wide breeches which were called "slops." He might wear an Elizabethan doublet above them, but the nether coverings displayed his character.

Though the average Elizabethan playgoer could have little knowledge of how his ancestors must have looked, he was certainly aware

164

58 *The Schouwberg,*
Amsterdam, 1637
The floor plan (left); the house,
looking toward the stage (center);
looking toward the boxes (right).
These detailed plans and sketches
show an interesting similarity
to what Shakespeare's theatre
must have been. The
standing pit, the two galleries
divided into boxes,
the architectural stage setting
have definite counterparts
in England. A unique feature
of this house is the interesting
roof treatment, and the top gallery
of steeply raked benches.
(Harvard Theatre Collection)

that Henry V dressed differently from the courtiers of his day, and he must have expected a different costume for such a character. Accordingly, we find Henslowe mentioning "Harrye the V satten dublet," and "harey the fiftes vellet gowne." Various other mentions of robes and crowns, armor and swords, would indicate a like attention to historical flavor. The Egerton manuscript of *Richard II* even mentions the toe-chained shoes of that day, which must have been a curiosity to an Elizabethan audience.

In the main, the actors appeared in contemporary dress, as rich as they could manage. Critics of the theatre were not slow to point out the gorgeous apparel of the playhouse, where even servants were dressed in satin and lace. It would appear, as we have mentioned, that one of the functions of the patron was to present to his acting company his own cast-off apparel and that of his friends. Sometimes new clothes were provided by the Crown for command performances at court, these then becoming the property of the acting companies. We may suppose, as well, that specialized costumes designed and made for the single performances of court masques were sometimes bequeathed to deserving professional companies. These costumes were made of the finest materials available, and were a considerable item of expense to the Office of the Revels.

It seems fairly certain that makeup, except where necessary for disguises, was not used. If a character required heightened color on his cheeks, he merely rubbed them before going on stage. But if he needed a red nose like Bardolph, or a beard, then he attached them.

165

Ghosts whitened their faces with white lead, and Negro characters blackened theirs with burnt cork. In the open daylight of the public theatres, no other makeup was deemed necessary.

In the popular theatre, the elaborate and colorful costumes filled the eyes of the beholder, since the settings were generally simple. In the lavish court masques of the Stuart reign, the costumes were as intricate and elaborate as the settings themselves.

Acting demands versatility

Of all the theatre arts, acting is perhaps the most ephemeral. Not until the comparatively recent advent of sound recording and motion pictures has it been possible to make a record of practicing actors. Before the twentieth century we must rely on the recorded opinions of contemporaries and upon the evidences of the dramatic literature itself. What we have to say here of acting itself, then, cannot be entirely accurate; but it is reasonable.

The position of the actor in Shakespeare's day was, in many ways, anomalous. Condemned and maligned by some and strictly regulated by various civil ordinances, he was, nevertheless, often a most highly respected member of society and frequently moved in the best of social circles.

The professional actor had, however, one great advantage: he was a member of a repertory company, which gave a variety of plays over great lengths of time, and he thus had opportunity to grow as an artist. The competent actor of Shakespeare's day was specialized and capable. The demands of performance were arduous. The proximity of the audience demanded concentration from the performer, as well as skill in engaging and holding the attention of the sometimes boisterous crowd. The frequent change of bill, a different play every performance, meant that several parts must be kept in mind at once and that the actor be quick in memorizing lines. The intricacy of the lines in many of the scripts that have come down to us indicates an exceptional skill in the vocal arts. Contemporary records more often speak of "hearing" than of "seeing" a play, and thus show where the Elizabethan placed his emphasis. The integral songs and dances indicate the actors' proficiency also in these skills. Actors are often listed as musicians and instrumentalists in contemporary writings, and when the actor Augustine Phillips died, he willed his musical instruments to his apprentices as a natural and necessary part of their equipment as actors. We know that performances often closed with an impromptu entertainment by one or more of the company, called a *giggue;* that Tarlton, the comedian, was so adept at this improvisa-

166

tion, which he did in verse, that the type of skill has come to be known as "tarltonizing." Since many of the scripts called for some kind of fighting, the actor also had to be an expert fencer, able to make the scene realistic without inflicting harm on his fellow-actors. Fencing was a very popular sport in Shakespeare's London; schools of fencing and public matches were numerous. This same Richard Tarlton, the first great popular star of the days of Elizabeth, was honored by being made "Master of the Fence" the year before he died. A pleasing appearance, grace of movement, a good voice, a ready wit, a lively sympathy, a keen awareness, adaptability, and the capacity for feeling and projecting a variety of emotions were then, as now, essential attributes of the successful actor.

Probably then, as now, an occasional acting genius appeared upon the stage full blown as it were. But for the most part, the chief members of any acting company had survived a rigorous training. Sometimes recruits for the professional theatre came from the boy companies, those carefully selected wards of the Crown who were schooled in rhetoric and song. Sometimes, as was apparently true in Shakespeare's case, aspirants were apprenticed to one of the members of an extant company and received individual tutoring from him. When and if his training was judged to be completed, he was made a journeyman shareholder and could then himself take on an apprentice. The apprentice in the theatre, as in the other vocations, lived in the household of his master, receiving complete training and education from him.

The mature actors tended to specialize either in tragedy or comedy. Richard Burbage, son of James and a member of Shakespeare's company, was famous for his tragic roles, having created Macbeth, Hamlet, Lear, and Othello. His great rival and equal in fame was Edward Alleyn, Henslowe's partner and son-in-law, whose greatest parts were Hieronimo, Tamburlaine, and the Jew of Malta. Among the comedians we may remember Richard Tarlton of the Queen's Company, and her favorite, William Kempe (for whom Shakespeare evidently wrote Falstaff and Bottom), and his successor, Robert Arnim, who played the Fool in *Lear*. We might mention many other names, for writers of the Commonwealth and Restoration periods speak nostalgically of the great performances of the bygone day, and laud the skill of them.

We may suppose that with the comparatively small size of the theatres, and with the close and immediate contact of the audience (some of whom, indeed, sat on the stage), the acting style was what we would call today "natural." Hamlet's famous advice to the players

59 *Costume designs by Inigo Jones*
Left, a masker for Thomas Campion's *Lords' Maske*, 1613, and a
Naiad for Samuel Daniel's *Tethys Festival*, 1610. Right, Queen Henrietta
Maria as Chloris in Ben Jonson's *Chloridia*, 1631, and a Knight masker
in *Oberon*, 1611. In all of these, it is apparent that the basic
Elizabethan dress was used, with an overlay of decoration in a design
intended to convey the atmosphere and special nature of the character.
(Devonshire Collection, Chatsworth; Victoria and Albert Museum)

supports a natural acting style, and comments on the performances of
various actors by contemporaries also seem to support it. Edmund Gay-
ton, writing somewhat *post factum,* remembers an actor who could not
be shaken out of his character until, in the best Stanislavski tradition,
the performance was utterly over. Actors were schooled in rhetoric, a
popular subject of the day, which included not only voice production,
but innumerable and meticulous postures of hands, body, and face.
In the class-conscious society of Shakespeare's day, an actor playing
a king must move and speak like a king, and so on by degrees to the
lowest member of society. A great degree of skill was demanded,
and evidently was available. Although some actors obviously acquired great individual fame, this fame was evidently not as a "personality" actor who transformed every role to his own image, but as
a protean creature who could transform himself into many roles.

The actor's life was not an easy one. He rehearsed in the mornings, performed in the public theatres in the afternoons, and spent his evenings either learning new lines or giving performances in the private theatres or at court. In times of plague, or during the summer seasons, the London actor toured the provinces, traveling by horse and cart to the various towns, and carrying set pieces and costumes with him.

New scripts were often prepared under the eye of the dramatist who might be a member of the company, as was Shakespeare. If the dramatist were not a member of the company but had been paid a flat fee for his script, as was the custom, then the performance was prepared by the stage manager, or bookholder, who also acted as the prompter. When a company was commanded to court, then, as we have said, the Master of the Revels held special rehearsals, censoring and changing script and business where he thought it advisable and often re-outfitting the entire cast.

The professional company included various types of members. In the acting fraternity were the actor-playwrights, who received a flat sum in payment for writing as well as a proportionate share of the profits for acting; the actor-shareholders; and the hirelings who were paid a designated salary. The apprentices, as noted above, were also paid, but the payment went to the master, not the man. The "housekeepers" were the producers, and the owners or renters of theatre property. The paid employees, in addition to the hired actors, were the stage manager, the tireman (or wardrobe master), the money takers (or "gatherers"), and the caretakers (who sometimes also functioned as extras in the performances), as well as the musicians. Generally, as we have said of the Earl of Leicester's Men, the acting company got the general admissions, while the housekeepers collected the additional payments for gallery seats. The actors tolerated the seating of a few well-paying customers on the stage itself since all the money they paid went to the actors. After the set expenses were paid, the profits were divided among the shareholders. On opening nights the admission was generally doubled; the third performance of a given play was often designated author's night and he collected all the profits. Command performances were paid as flat sums to the company, and these sums were divided proportionately. Varied but typical arrangements were in force for performances in the private theatres and on the road. Sometimes the patrons were called upon for subsidies and loans though for the most part the major companies were completely self-sustaining.

Though actors worked hard they often made a great deal of

169

money. Edward Alleyn retired at thirty-nine, and spent the equivalent of eighty thousand dollars in our money every year for the twenty-two years left him. He endowed Dulwich College, which is one of the richest in England, in addition to supporting almshouses and other philanthropic ventures. Richard Burbage is said to have had a yearly income of about twenty thousand dollars (again in our money) from his country estates alone. And "that house in Stratford" of Shakespeare's needs no additional comment. In his day the theatre was a burgeoning and profitable business as well as a stupendous art form.

Women never appeared on the professional stage in England; the women's parts were taken by boys. It was an immensely practical arrangement, particularly when the company was on tour. These boys were highly skilled performers, and evidently quite satisfactory in their parts. It is to be noted in the playscripts that physical contact is at a minimum between Shakespearean lovers, the most famous of love scenes being played from balcony to garden.

Perhaps it was the Puritan influence no less than medieval tradition which kept women off the stage in England, and the appearance of a French actress on an English stage in 1629 and again in 1632 called down malediction. Only in the court masques did titled women make their dilettante appearance. When the moralist, William Prynne, inveighing against the performance of a French actress in England, said that women players were "notorious whores," he had his ears cut off and was imprisoned for life—at that moment Queen Henrietta Maria was rehearsing for a court performance!

Summary

The theatre of England might be said to have begun its decline with the accession of James I in 1603, although many great and good plays were written after that date. The common people did not like James because he was a foreigner, and because he built up a foreign court which was much more frivolous and unhealthy than the people at large. In the first year of his reign, Parliament passed an ordinance forbidding the nobles to patronize the acting companies, so the King took over half a dozen of the best, Shakespeare's among them. When the first military operations of the Great Rebellion began in 1642, one of the first acts of the Puritan Parliament was to close all the playhouses and forbid all play-acting. Many of the houses were torn down or burned and the actors scattered. Many of them fought with the Cavaliers, earning considerable military distinction. After Charles was beheaded in 1649, some of them fled with the court to France, some companies toured in Europe, and some individuals remained in England to ply their trade surreptitiously and await the turn of the tide.

But their heyday had been a glorious one. Though vestiges of medieval practices had perhaps a more profound influence on the English Renaissance stage than on that of the Continent, purely religious performances disappeared in England long before they did in other parts of Europe. Though the ferment of the Renaissance greatly affected subject matter and many details of production, there was not so close an adherence to classical forms in England as was evident in both France and Italy. The greatness of the English theatre of the period lay in its assimilation of foreign influences to produce a purely native theatre. By the time the period came to a close, it had contributed to the theatre a superb dramatic literature, completed the popularization of the theatre, marked its emergence as "show business," witnessed the development of the proscenium arch and painted settings and the establishment of indoor playhouses.

Theatre in Shakespeare's day was a great popular institution frequented by all classes of society from carter to nobleman. Even the Queen was an avid supporter and admirer of theatre. The insatiable curiosity of this large audience made for a wide variety of theatrical presentation and contributed to the greatness of Elizabethan dramatic writing. Artistic satisfaction—and an adequate living—attracted many good writers to the theatre, and held them there. The most important literature of the period is dramatic.

Elizabethan theatre developed an architecture and a stage design eminently suited to the plays and the conditions of production. Multiple and quick-changing scenes could be handled expeditiously on the platform stage, whether by inner recess, galleries, doors and windows, or by temporarily erected, curtained rooms. The construction of the playhouse itself brought the action and the marvelous lines close to every spectator. No fetters were placed on creative imagination by the exigencies of setting; the atmosphere was an utterly free one.

This freedom also challenged the skill of the actor, who rose to great heights of powerful and effective expression. It was the greatest of all ages for playwright, actor, and audience; its enduring fame continues to the present day.

8

SPANISH THEATRE

IN THE RENAISSANCE

The medieval history of Spain is marked by violent clashes not only between Moors and Christians, but also between the rulers of the various Christian kingdoms who occupied non-Moorish territories on the Spanish peninsula. Cities and their surrounding countryside changed hands with alarming frequency; wars were constant and bloody. Towards the end of the fifteenth century the alignment of powers centered around the two crowns of Aragon and Castile, with the Moorish possessions lying outside both. The marriage of Castilian Isabella and Aragonese Ferdinand in 1467 united the two leading Catholic powers. When, ten years later, Isabella succeeded to the throne of Castile, and Ferdinand to the throne of Aragon, the stage was set for Spanish national unity. By a series of astute moves these rulers reinstituted the Inquisition as a purely Spanish office, expelled the Moors from the peninsula, exiled the Jews, and emerged with a unified kingdom which rapidly enriched itself through New World conquests. By the time of Philip II (1556–1598), Spanish possessions and power in Europe and the New World had reached their apogee. The long decline throughout the whole of the next century reached its end in 1700, when the War of the Spanish Succession put the Bourbon Philip d'Anjou on the throne of Spain.

The greatest age of Spanish theatre parallels this political stream. Secular drama, tentative and rudimentary at the beginning of the sixteenth century, grew in strength and brilliance in the last half of that period and was most glorious during the first half of the seventeenth century. By 1650 all that is best in Spanish drama had been produced. After the death of Calderón, in 1681, no playwright of note appeared in Spain for many generations.

The union of Ferdinand and Isabella had the further effect of making the Spanish tongue as spoken in Castile the predominant language of the Spanish peninsula. From this point on, as elsewhere in the Renaissance, the development of the language became a powerful factor in strengthening national consciousness.

The progress of the Renaissance in Spain also was marked, as in England, by a developing awareness of national history and legend, and by a concern with national characteristics, customs, and ideas. Significant literary works in both prose and poetry treated the drama of history. Many more concerned themselves with travel and adventure, spurred by the expanding activities of Spaniards in all parts of the world. Ballads on heroic themes flourished, perpetuating the medieval conception of heroism, but also becoming infused with the Renaissance ideal of the infinite possibilities of the individual man. The novel also flourished; this is the period of Cervantes' *Don Quixote,* one of the great novels of all time. Many mystical works, notably the poems of St. John of the Cross, emerged from the Counter-Reformation, which was felt very strongly in Spain through the disciplinary influence of the pious Cardinal Ximenes (d. 1517).

The combination of strength afforded by the Office of the Spanish Inquisition, and the reforms wrought within the Church itself by the powerful Spanish Counter-Reformation, effectively strangled Protestantism in Spain. This strength, coupled with the necessity of the union of Christian forces against the Moors, assured a firm and irrevocably Catholic regime, thus setting Spain apart from the rest of the Continent. The authority of the Church was largely unquestioned, and the infection of individual judgment did not spread. Consequently the literature of the Spanish Renaissance, and notably its drama, while using the themes and materials current in the enlarged knowledge of the day, tended not to stress individual character traits and development, but rather to emphasize situation, romance, and honor.

The Golden Age flowers

The intensity of Spanish theatrical activity coincides with the production of great dramatic literature. Lope de Rueda, who became so influential that he is said to have founded Spanish national theatre,

60 Entry festival
Festival given for the entry of the Prince de Galles in Madrid, 1623. At
the left is a temporary stage fitted out for the presentation of
plays, with a curtained backdrop and musicians and actors performing.
Entry processions were popular diversions all over the Continent.

is first heard of in 1554. He is the first head of a company of players
of whom we have any knowledge, and he dominated Spanish theatre
until 1565. His activities paved the way for the flowering of the next
fifty years.

The Spanish popular theatre, like the Elizabethan, was a direct
descendant of the Middle Ages. The medieval pageant wagon had
developed in Spain as in England and here, too, performances were
often under the auspices of craft guilds. The entire festival was almost
invariably under the supervision of the officers of the city; it is from
city records that we get most of our information concerning the
Corpus Christi Day celebrations. The festivities began with the celebration of Mass in the cathedral, followed by a presentation of the
sacred drama within the choir of the church itself. The play was
ordinarily followed by a dance in the same location; then a procession, including Church and city officials, moved out of the cathedral
to specially designated places in the city where the cars of the players
stopped and the performance was given for the people gathered
there. Thus Corpus Christi Day came to be known as the Festival of
the Cars. The subject matter of the plays themselves included both

174

Biblical material and the lives of the saints, as well as moral, allegorical presentations.

In 1554, the corporation of the city of Seville took over the expense of presentation of the Corpus Christi Day drama from the various guilds, and in the same year we find the first mention, in Benavente, of the presentation of a sacred play by a professional acting company—that of Lope de Rueda. This particular performance was a special one honoring Philip II on his passage through Benavente. The Spanish evidently quite often gave sacred plays on special occasions of this kind, as well as at weddings, and so forth (figure 60). That Lope de Rueda and his company subsequently performed in the Festival of the Cars as well, is substantiated by the Seville city records. These Church-inspired performances continued unabated throughout the entire period of the Renaissance, as enthusiastically presented in 1679 as they had been two centuries earlier. All of the great names of Spanish drama are of those who wrote both sacred and secular plays, Lope de Vega himself producing something in the neighborhood of four hundred religious plays for the Church, along with his phenomenal output for the secular theatre. At the beginning of the seventeenth century the sacred plays seem to have been given in the public playhouses for a limited run after the festival day itself.

The secular drama developed out of the medieval Church play, through the *entremeses*, originally of a quasireligious character, which were short pieces accompanying the longer presentations. As time went on, they lost all religious significance. Though this transition from religious to secular themes in the *entremeses* led to the development of long secular drama, the shorter form maintained its identity as well. At the height of the Spanish theatre the public performance began with a ballad (*jácara*), played and sung by the company musicians. Then followed an introductory piece which was either a monologue or a short dramatic sketch (*loa*), not necessarily connected with what followed but designed to catch the attention of the audience and to put it in good humor. The three acts of the main fare for the day, the long drama (*comedia*), were interspersed with two *entremeses*, sometimes supplemented with a ballad or two set to music as requested by the audience; the afternoon's entertainment concluded with a dance.

Theatre atmosphere festive

Performances began at two or three o'clock in the afternoon (depending on the season of the year), and at first were limited to Sundays and feast days. To accommodate the growing demand,

175

Tuesdays and Thursdays were added to the schedule; then, finally, plays were being given in the larger cities on every day of the week except Saturday. Theatres were officially closed, however, during Lent, often during the summer months, and always during epidemics or national disasters like the death of a member of the royal family. Plays were advertised by public crier and by placards. Actors themselves often performed the office of crier, and seem to have been acting in this capacity as late as 1638, the year in which a well-known actor, Iñigo de Loaysa, was murdered in the streets of Valencia while announcing the play for the following day. The placards were about twelve by eighteen inches and were usually done by hand. They were posted some days before the performance in prominent places in the city or town.

Every member of the audience paid a single admission price which was quite low when compared with the prices of other commodities. At a time when the general admission was a half-real, for instance, board and lodging for a single person cost about six reals a week. The general admission entitled the person who paid it to standing room in the theatre. If he wished a seat he paid extra, some seats costing a sum equal to that which he had already paid; some, in the exclusive boxes, cost as much as twelve to twenty times the general admission price. The boxes were frequently rented for the year by the nobility and the rich; and city officials often reserved one for their exclusive use. Possession of particular boxes often descended to the heirs of a given family.

Theatrical performances were licensed by a city official, a license being necessary for each performance. Sometimes, before the original license was given, the official insisted upon a performance for his perusal (figure 61). The same system prevailed in all towns and cities; traveling companies had first to obtain a license, and then perform for the public.

The same public official also controlled the leasing of theatres to companies for performances, and the remodeling or building of them as well. Theatre buildings were almost invariably owned or erected by charitable organizations formed to care for the ill and the poor. A portion of every admission went to the proprietary organization, under the supervision of the official, as well as the money from the leases for buildings they owned outright. The acting companies were generally paid a flat sum for each performance, the distribution of sums within the company depending upon the company organization.

The audiences were boisterous and demanding. Hardest to please were the *mosqueteros*, the standing audience in the pit, who were all

61 *Spanish actor*
A member of a traveling company presenting his performance before
the town officials in order to secure a license for public performance.
(Blanco y Negro)

men. Many of these had made a game of getting into the theatre
without paying—a trick which, if successful, gave the perpetrator
high standing in the eyes of his fellows. Two peace officers were
stationed at the doors of the theatres to prevent riots and bloodshed,
but they were often unsuccessful. Women sat in a separate section
of the theatre, and the sellers of fruit and drink often acted as
messengers between the women's gallery and the men in the pit. In
the boxes the spectators were mixed, with the women there generally
going masked.

The success of a play often depended on the reaction of the people
in the pit; if they applauded and shouted *Victor!*, the play was a hit;
if they whistled and hissed, it was a failure. Their approval was
often courted by the playwright in the sketch before the play. There
was much eating and drinking during the performance, and unpopular actors and plays were sometimes pelted with orange skins and
fruit pits. So the popular theatre, as in Shakespeare's England, reflected the tastes of its audiences who were sharp in their judgments

and quick to respond. The popular Spanish stage thus developed types of plays which varied widely, as did those in England, from the more formal types of drama such as were being produced in Italy and France.

But the classic revival in Spain, as elsewhere, was the darling of the schools. The production of classic plays in the Spanish Jesuit schools was a definite part of the curriculum. Classic plays were also sometimes given in the court, Philip II bringing, in the first year of his reign, an Italian academician to produce Italian comedies at his court. Italian *commedia* companies also performed at court, as well as at some of the public theatres. So well received were they that one critic, in 1581, waxed indignant over the quantities of ducats these foreigners removed from Spain every year. Lavish court productions of specially prepared materials were also given, as in the Stuart court of England. But the professional acting companies were more often commanded to noble and royal households to perform the plays of their repertoire. The monarchs of Spain, like those of England, were intensely theatre-minded.

Critics were also vocal. There were objections to the use of women as performers, to the use of boys in women's parts, to the immorality of players in general, to the rowdiness of the audiences, to the lure of theatre which took craftsmen and merchants from their work, to the subject matter of the plays themselves. Succeeding decrees, from 1598 to 1682, attempted to correct these abuses. But until theatre itself reached a state of senescence, none of the decrees had a deterrent effect on the robust and burgeoning phenomenon that was characteristic of the Spanish Golden Age.

Prolific playwrights produce secular and sacred drama

No English writer has to his credit the phenomenal output of Lope de Vega, who is supposed to have written some eighteen hundred secular plays and about four hundred sacred plays. There are 431 of his plays still on record. It is obvious that in so prodigious a literary output there would be much that is superficial and inconsequential. Lope de Vega himself unashamedly said that he was interested only in pleasing his public and in giving them what they wanted. That he was successful in doing this there is little doubt, for he was almost sensationally renowned, and he most truly represents the national character.

Lope de Vega was preceded by a line of playwrights who had set the style and the subject matter which he was later to use. Spanish native drama grew and developed in the first fifty years of the sixteenth century. Its inheritance from the preceding period was a tradition of secular pieces performed by traveling *juglares*, or jugglers, and a tradition of religious plays as separate entities. These elements were united in the work of Juan del Encina, the first name of note in Spanish dramatic literature, who in 1497 produced a nativity drama in the vernacular in which the shepherds were easily recognizable local types. Thus he set a style which was followed by succeeding writers.

The most talented of his immediate disciples was the Portuguese Gil Vicente; of his forty-four plays eleven were written entirely in Spanish and seventeen more partly in Spanish. His dialogue was natural, his situations humorous, but he was generally ineffectual in plotting. It was Bartolomé de Torres Naharro, in the first quarter of the sixteenth century, who showed an awareness of dramatic theory and gave some care to plot structure. His long residence in Naples no doubt brought him into direct contact with the ideas of the Italian academicians, but he did not produce pseudo-classic plays. He divided the six plays published in his *Propalladia* (1517) into two kinds: realistic and romantic. In the latter classification are two, *Comedia Serafina* and *Himenea,* that are particularly interesting in that they foreshadow the later Spanish preoccupation with the so-called "cloak and sword" dramas, and thematically emphasize the *pundonor*, or point of honor.

Up to this time these secular plays, when performed, were chiefly the delectation of noble houses. Then came Lope de Rueda. From 1554 on he toured Spain with his company of players and as we have said, became so influential that he is called the founder of Spanish national theatre; he dominated that theatre until 1565. He was author, manager, and actor, and it is one of his productions that Cervantes describes with so much insight in the Prologue to his *Comedias*. Though Lope de Rueda's comedies often followed Italian plots, the characters and dialogue were completely Spanish. He is credited with inventing the *paso*, a kind of one-act play given as an interlude between the acts of a longer work. The most famous of these is *The Olives*, in which a peasant and his wife develop a violent argument over the selling price of the fruit from a tree which has not yet been planted.

Cervantes himself was greatly interested in the theatre, and like many a subsequent novelist, turned his hand to the making of plays. He is said to have written some thirty of them. But his was essentially a narrative genius, and his plays were never so successful as his great novel.

62 *Presentation of a sacred play*
The wagon is drawn up before a great house, and the play is being presented while both the gentry and the general populace watch. (Cheney, *The Theatre*)

Further progress in the divorce of native Spanish drama from classic models was made by Juan de la Cueva, a contemporary of Cervantes, who belonged to the next generation after Lope de Rueda. Though eleven of his fourteen plays were taken from the classics and aped Seneca, the other three used the materials of the ballads which sang of Spain's heroic past, and they were written in a style free of classic imitation.

Thus the way was paved for Lope de Vega, the flower of Spanish drama, whose long and amazingly successful career was marked by widespread adulation and imitation. He codified his technique and explained his theory in *New Art of Making Plays in This Epoch* (1609), at which time he had been writing plays for about twenty years. In this famous document he claims that he is not ignorant of classic models, having received a good classical education, but that he is perfectly aware that the division of playwriting into tragedy and comedy does not meet the tastes of the Spanish public. He writes plays, he says, that will please his audiences, plays written "in defiance of art," plays which mix tragedy and comedy and ignore the unities.

A few years before (1605), Cervantes, much in the manner of Sir Philip Sidney, had bemoaned plays which were not "more observant of place than of time," as in a comedy, where, "the first act of which was laid in Europe, the second in Asia, and the third in Africa; and had there been four acts, the fourth would doubtless have been in America" (*Don Quixote*, Part I, Chap. 48). He was a voice crying in the wilderness. The nature of the Spanish popular drama was essentially opposed to the classic ideal, and though Lope de Vega says that he actually wrote six plays on the classic model, the tremendous bulk of his hundreds of plays is in another vein.

The Spanish secular drama, called the *comedia*, was a three-act play where comedy and tragedy were interfused, drawing subject matter from heroic legend, from recent history, from current social problems, from chivalric tradition. The stress was almost universally on incident and plot; characters were stereotyped with very little development during the action of the play. The social milieu, as we have said, was not conducive to an emphasis on individual will and capacity; the interest of the play is chiefly in its multiplicity of incident and swift movement. Ordinarily written in verse, the best representatives exhibit great ingenuity in verse forms. There have been many attempts to classify these plays, but the form is so diverse as to defy any definite classification. One type of play which Lope de Vega and others wrote with great dash and vigor were the light "cloak and sword" plays founded upon intrigue, mistaken identities, love affairs, and the doings of a flamboyant aristocracy. Though presumably plays of contemporary manners, the picture they give of Spanish society is by no means accurate. But the disguisings, alarums, confusions, and obsession with the point of honor are generally rendered in such sparkling dialogue and dextrous plot that the plays are charming in the presentation. Lope de Vega's most famous of this kind is probably *Madrid Steel,* from which Molière took the idea for *The Physician in Spite of Himself*. It is a complicated love intrigue in which Lisardo masquerades as a physician to court Belisa, while her chaperone is distracted by Lisardo's bosom friend. After many trials, all ends happily. Many of Lope de Vega's contemporaries and followers were expert in the "cloak and sword." Tirso de Molina, in his *Deceiver of Seville,* created the character of Don Juan, who appears with such amazing frequency in other literature. Calderón himself, the last great star of Spain's Golden Age, wrote an ingenious comedy of love in *The Fairy Lady*.

Other types of plays might be classified in one category which includes historical or mythological dramas and those based upon legends. Lope de Vega's *Rome in Ashes,* a melodrama based on the character of Nero, is one example. Another is Guillén de Castro's *The*

Young Manhood of the Cid, based on the life of Spain's great national hero, and forming the basis of Corneille's more famous *The Cid.* Calderón's *The Wonder-Working Magician,* with its echoes of Faustus, takes its subject matter from Roman times, the passion of the pagan philosopher Cipriano for the Christian beauty Justina.

Harder to classify are such plays as Lope de Vega's *The Sheep-Well,* Calderón's *The Mayor of Zalamea,* and his *Life is a Dream.* The first narrates the struggle of the peasantry against feudal overlords. It is ostensibly from historical record, but emerges as a rather powerful social drama wherein the villagers of Fuente Ovejuna rise and kill their unjust Commander and then, in spite of torture, refuse to divulge the murderer. Their heroic conduct finally earns a pardon from King Ferdinand. Of a similar pattern is *The Mayor of Zalamea,* in which the courage of the low-born mayor against the injustices of the military earns him a lifetime appointment from the King. *Life is a Dream,* one of Calderón's most famous plays, is more philosophical in its consideration of the nature of reality, and is, in many ways, a curious precursor of the modern Italian playwright, Pirandello.

In addition to the three-act secular plays, the many playwrights of Spain were also writing *loas* and *entremeses,* the shorter accompaniments to the longer performances. Most of them were also writing religious plays. As we have mentioned, a large part of Lope de Vega's output was in sacred dramas, and of Calderón's 120 surviving pieces, about eighty are of the same kind.

A very large number of playwrights produced a staggering total of plays, one estimate being thirty thousand works by 1700. The death of Lope de Vega in 1635 marks the beginning of the decline in both quantity and quality, and by the time the eighty-one-year-old Calderón died in 1681, almost all of the practicing playwrights who had been Lope de Vega's contemporaries had disappeared.

Courtyards converted to playhouses

In Renaissance Spain, as in England, public playhouses developed from space originally intended for other purposes. In the south of Spain, where buildings were usually erected with an open courtyard in the center, traveling companies of players set up their stages in the courtyards, much as did their English counterparts in the innyards. Some of these buildings were used, in time, only for theatrical performances, and the records of some of the *cofradias* who profited from the incomes of these theatres, indicate that at least six public playhouses were opened in as many cities between 1520 and 1568, the first being that at Malaga.

63 *Restored corral theatre at Almagro, Spain*
This old theatre, restored in recent years, is in the same form as the
more famous corrals of Madrid; the stage is at one end, and galleries are
along the sides. Not visible here are the side benches which were on
the ground floor. (Otero Pedrayo, *Geographia de Espana*)

In the cities of the north, where courtyards were not the rule, theatres of a sort were made out of the courtyards, called *corrales,*
formed by the backs of houses built roughly in a square. Theatres
were made of them by erecting a broad stage from one side of the
courtyard to the other, with standing room for some spectators occupying the rest of the space and the windows of surrounding houses
serving as privileged spaces for others. Valladolid had such a theatre
by 1554, Barcelona by 1560, Cordoba by 1565, and Madrid had three
by 1569.

When the first permanent theatres were built in the capital and
theatrical center, the city of Madrid, in 1579 and 1582, they followed
the design set up by the converted *corrales* (figure 63). The old
theatres had been wholly open to the sky, so that performances had
to be suspended in bad weather. But in 1574 the Italian manager,
Ganassa, put a roof over the stage and the edges of the courtyard of
the *Corral de la Pacheca* in Madrid, and stretched an awning over
the rest of the open space. A description of the second famous permanent theatre of Madrid, the *Corral del Príncipe,* will illustrate the
design of the typical Spanish public theatre of the time.

The space to the sides and the space under the raised stage constituted the dressing rooms of the actors. The open space on the floor
of the theatre was paved and provided with raised benches along the

183

sides and several rows of benches immediately in front of the stage, both of which areas were reserved for men only. The rest of the space was left open for standees, also for men only. The area opposite the stage was supplied with a balcony, partitioned off and with a separate entrance; this was the *cazuela*, literally "stew pan," and was reserved for women. The side walls of the theatre were supplied with boxes or stalls, called *aposentos*, covered with an iron grating; these were the equivalents of the windows from the rooms of the surrounding houses of the old *corrales*, and were reserved for both men and women of noble and wealthy houses and for public officials. Just as the owner of a house whose rear wall became a part of a *corral* might reserve a room for himself and his family, or put in additional windows for others, the boxes of the permanent theatre retained their exclusive character. Stairways led to the women's gallery, the boxes and the benches; with the stage, these were roofed over. An awning was stretched over the remaining open space to shield spectators from the weather.

This basic design of specialized seating areas, standing pit, separate entrances for men and women to the pit and the balcony, and often to the boxes, and all of the audience forward of the stage area, remained fairly constant throughout the great period of Spanish theatre. This was the design of the other famous early theatre of Madrid, the *Corral de la Cruz,* and of the *corrales* of Seville—*Las Atarazanas, La Alcoba, San Pedro, Corral de Doña Elvira, Coliseo,* and *La Monteria.* The *Corral de Doña Elvira* seems to have been completely covered over with a permanent roof in 1617. *El Coliseo,* finished in 1607 and open to the sky, seems to have been refurbished seven years later and also covered over by a roof with a painted ceiling inside. Light was supplied to the interior by a row of wide windows over the boxes and just under the roof. Some idea of the size of this theatre may be gathered from the specification of twenty Doric columns ten feet high to support the first gallery, and a like number, seven feet high, to support the second. Though all six of these Seville theatres were in operation at various times, the most popular, and the most enduring, were the *Doña Elvira* and the *Coliseo.*

Even more than in England, the Spanish popular theatre seems to have been created almost solely by and for the general public, for there is little record of royal activity in theatre-building until the accession of Philip IV in 1621. It is possible that Philip II witnessed the presentation of sacred plays in the Escorial, as well as at their public performances. Philip III, who ascended the throne in 1598,

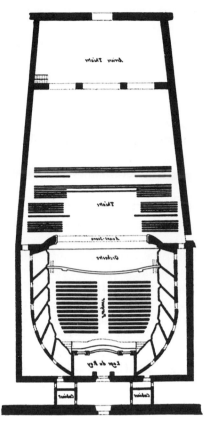

64 Spanish court theatre
The plan of the theatre of Philip IV
at El Buen Retiro. The space allotted
to the stage was greater than that
for the audience; the rear of the stage
could be opened to a garden;
the appointments were lavish.
(Dumont, *Parallele de Plan des Plus
Belles Salle de Spectacle, Etc.*)

is said to have commissioned a theatre in the Alcázar for the presentation of secular and sacred plays. This appears to have been a stage
erected in one of the royal ballrooms. He seems also to have caused
a theatre to be built in the Houses of the Treasury, near the palace.
His Queen was vigorously interested in theatre, and often had companies of players appear before her in her private apartments. Temporary stages were also constructed in various royal and noble
gardens for festival presentations upon special occasions. But when
Philip IV, who had a passion for theatre and more particularly for
actresses, built his new palace, El Buen Retiro, in 1632 he included
a sumptuous theatre (figures 64 and 65), built in the Italian manner
with the unique arrangement of having the back of the stage open on
the gardens. The theatre was in rather constant use, and by 1640
seems to have been open to the public quite as were those houses of
La Cruz and *El Príncipe*. The horseshoe-type auditorium had a special

185

loge opposite the stage for the King, boxes around its perimeter, an orchestra pit fronting the stage, and benches in the remaining area of the auditorium. The stage was equipped with a wing and back-shutter arrangement of flats.

Several standards for settings

Renaissance Spain had somewhat the same pattern of stage settings as did early seventeenth century England. Elaborate, Italianate settings were the rule in the occasional court productions; simplified settings in the public theatres. In Spain, of course, the custom of intricate settings for the sacred plays continued; contracts of the period usually show a certain number of days set aside for the preparation of the public theatres to set up the stage effects for the religious plays which, as we have mentioned, were shown in them after the ceremonial productions of Corpus Christi Day.

One of Ariosto's comedies was given in the royal palace at Valladolid as early as 1548, at a wedding celebration, and it was produced with such wonders of scenic display that Caluette de Estrella (*Felicissimo Viage del Principe Phelippe*, 1552), the person through whose writings we know about it, was too overwhelmed by the visual splendor to mention the name of the play. Philip II and his successor both imported Italian academicians to produce plays at court, and Philip IV hired the Italian architect, Cosme Lotti, to design and stage the elaborate spectacles which he loved. One of the most lavish of these was a production of *Circe*, given about 1634, on three stages built over the lake at El Buen Retiro (figure 65). This and similar ones following were open-air productions. Performances in gardens were evidently an affectation of the rich and powerful, for there are many such recorded. But the productions given indoors were equally elaborate. The stage of the theatre at El Buen Retiro was larger than the auditorium itself. and was equipped with a wing and back-shutter arrangement in the best Italian mode.

Stage machinery, as elaborate as could be devised, was the custom, as well, for the sacred plays. Trapdoors were an early device, and seem always to have been necessary to the performances. The cars upon which the actors rode in the procession, beautifully decorated and painted as they were, arrived at the point of presentation and were backed up against a temporary stage for the actual presentation. Here the stage axis was transverse. Each of the two cars bore an edifice of some sort on one end; the actors entered from below and up through these edifices. The honored members of the audience sat on one side of the transverse axis, the majority stood on the other.

Great sums of money were expended on these cars and stages; for a production at Plasencia in 1578, the stage in the square of the city was provided with a tank sixty by twenty feet, filled with water, floating a ship completely rigged, and carrying sailors and passengers. That the artifices, contrivances, appearances, tricks—as stage machinery was variously called—were elaborate and expensive is attested to by many financial records and descriptions of festival presentations in several Spanish towns. Typical is the description of the settings for four sacred plays of Lope de Vega, produced at Madrid in 1609; the settings included a sky with stars, dragon heads spouting flames of fire, a palace with a chapel, a table set with disappearing plates, and many other wonders, including sumptuous costumes.

The school productions also used intricate scenery, such as an interesting performance described as being given by the students of the college of San Hermengildo. It was a multiple setting, one tower representing a prison, another a great hall, with a large door between them representing the city of Seville. This 1570 description mentions the use of canvas for the painted set.

The public theatres, however, showed no such reliance on painted sets and wondrous effects. Stages of the early theatres were hardly more than the "four trestles, four boards, two actors, and a passion," of which Lope de Vega speaks. This simple platform stage, for most plays, was hung about on three sides with green baize curtains. The curtains on the sides of the stage led directly to the dressing rooms; since there was no front curtain, a person wounded or killed during the course of the action was disposed of by the simple stage direction that he "falls within the dressing room." At the back of the stage the curtain could be drawn to reveal doors, and the scene was often changed by the simple expedient of having actors exit through one door and come in the other. The second-story level of the rear stage wall was a gallery which sometimes did service for windows and balconies. As in Elizabethan plays, the actors frequently announced the locale of the action and described the surroundings; the audience then simply imagined the scene. Sometimes simple set pieces of linen or pasteboard appeared on the stage, remaining unchanged throughout the course of the action. Sometimes these set pieces were revealed by drawing a curtain aside. Though no attempt was made at effective illusion, painted canvas set pieces were frequently used to indicate that the stage represented a garden, or was dressed with a fountain, or rocks, or a mountain, or a fort. By the second quarter of the seventeenth century these painted canvases for scenery were more numerous

187

and more frequently used. Of this practice, Lope de Vega complains, saying that,

> Because there are no good actors, or because the poets are bad, or because the auditors lack understanding . . . the managers avail themselves of machinery, the poets of carpenters, and the auditors of their eyes (*Prologo Dialogistico*, 1623, prefixed to Part XVI of his *Comedias*).

He evidently never attempted to conceal his contempt for the scene painter and machinist.

Costumes provide the clues

If the stage of the public theatre was lacking in scenic effect, if the audience was asked to imagine what the locale of the play was, costuming was gorgeous and no little help to the audience in imagining locale. Characters dressed in hunting costume could be expected to indicate that the almost bare stage was a forest; sumptuous ball gowns indicated festivities at a palace, and so forth. There was, of course, no pretense at historical accuracy. As in England, playwrights had a tendency to transform past occurrences into current national usages and customs; and audiences, having little sense of the historic past, were not critical of what would seem to us glaring anachronisms. As Ticknor, the great historian of Spanish literature says, "Coriolanus was dressed like Don John of Austria, and Aristotle came on the stage with a curled periwig and buckles on his shoes, like a Spanish Abbé" (*History of Spanish Literature*, II, 539).

Some obvious distinctions, however, were made. These audiences would have been aware that Moors dressed differently from Christians, so stage Moors appeared in turbans and long mantles; but the Roman, who lay outside their immediate consciousness, was dressed in cloak and sword. Lope de Vega complained of the Roman costume in his *New Art*, saying that it was obviously not right. He also was disturbed by such "barbarous things" as a Turk wearing a Christian ruff. In the last decade of the sixteenth century, the learned Alonso Lopez Pinciano urged that actors study history in order to dress themselves properly when playing historical characters, and that due attention be paid to the rank and social class of the characters being represented. This latter admonition was more closely followed than the former. The Spanish were no less class conscious than the English, and did not expect that peasants should dress like princes. Besides, since the scenery was rudimentary, differentiation in contemporary dress was an aid to characterization and to locale.

But everywhere, richness was the rule. A description of the sacred

65 *More Spanish court theatre*
A print of the great lake at El Buen Retiro, scene of grandiose spectacles
on floating barges. (Hispanic Society of America)

plays of *Job* and *Saint Catalina* presented in Madrid in 1592, is
reminiscent of descriptions of medieval English mysteries. Job is to
be dressed in a long coat of purple damask and a hat of taffeta, and
buskins. God is to be dressed in a tunic of sateen or taffeta in gold and
purple with a white taffeta cloak. The three gallants in *Saint Catalina*
are to have coats of mail in the Roman fashion, and so forth. The
specifications for a 1624 production indicate that the costumes are to
be of brocatel and velvet and damask and sateen, trimmed with gold
passementerie.

Costumes for the sacred plays were supplied by the municipality,
which, as we have seen, underwrote all expenses for these presentations. For the performers of secular drama at the public theatres,
however, different arrangements prevailed. Principal players supplied their own costumes, while the head of the company provided
them for the lesser members. Costuming accounted for a large part
of the expenses of actors and managers. In 1589, the manager Sebas-
tian de Montemayor paid eleven hundred reals for a rich skirt and
jacket; in 1602, Melchor de Leon paid three hundred thirty reals for

189

a skirt of straw-colored satin; in 1619, the actors Juan Batista Muñiz and his wife paid twenty-four hundred reals for a costume of greenish-gold sateen with gold lace and fringe, red sateen edging, and a red taffeta silk lining. Compare these prices with the top price of five hundred reals paid to Lope de Vega for writing a secular play, and some idea of the extravagance of costuming is possible.

Managers who owned a sizable wardrobe often increased their revenues by hiring out costumes for special performances and for festivals. Actors in financial straits frequently pawned their expensive wardrobes to raise money.

In the poorer traveling companies, of course, the costuming was much more rudimentary and inexpensive. Cervantes, in the Prologue to the volume of his *Comedias* published in 1615, reminisces about Lope de Rueda's little company, and says of its accoutrements that they were all contained in a sack, and consisted of "four white pelices trimmed with gilded leather, and four beards and wigs, with four staffs, more or less." The *Amusing Journey* of Augustin de Rojas (1603), in listing the types and sizes of traveling companies, mentions the costumes typical of each, from just such a rudimentary supply as Cervantes describes to companies which required two chests to transport their costumes.

But whether actors and managers were a part of an impecunious provincial touring company or of one of the most prosperous organizations in one of the great cities, costumes were an integral and valued part of their possessions, and an indispensable aid to production.

Women on stage

The most significant difference between Elizabethan and Spanish acting companies is that in England no woman appeared on the professional stage, whereas in Spain they were important members of the company, and, for the most part, exceedingly popular. Spanish companies, however, from first to last, must sometimes have used boys in women's parts, as is evident from a series of edicts regulating theatrical entertainment. Allowing women in Spanish companies may have been the result of their popularity in the Italian *commedia* companies who visited frequently and were highly popular. It may also have been influenced by the undoubted sentiment on the part of many that having a boy act women's parts was somehow immoral. But it probably was the result of the tastes of the audiences who enjoyed seeing women on the stage. Though no licenses were issued for women to act on the public stages of Madrid until 1587, it is very likely that women did act there before that date.

66 *Augustin de Rojas rehearsing a Spanish play*
An old print after an original painting by A. Fabier. Of special interest here is the elaborate costume so typical of Spanish players.

The presence of women made the life of the theatre more complicated than it would otherwise have been, and many are the edicts requiring that any such female member be either married to an actor of the company, or be the daughter of an acting couple. Married male actors were required to have their wives with them, even though these wives were not actresses. These various rules were no doubt honored as much in the breach as in the observance, for many a Spanish noble took an actress as mistress, and Philip IV himself was the father of Don John of Austria, whose mother was La Calderona, a famous actress. Women seem to have been particularly popular in the various dances, and in "breeches parts," for there are frequent proscriptions against "licentious dances" and the wearing of male attire by females.

There is no record of a female head of a company, but as members of the acting companies they were as well paid as the men; prominent actresses sometimes made considerably more than the male members of the company. Allowances and privileges were extended equally to them as to the men.

Companies of one or many

Acting companies varied widely in composition and quality. The famous *Viage Entretenido* of Augustin de Rojas Villandrando (figure 66) lists the various types: a *bululu*, the lone player traveling on foot; a *ñaque*, two men; a *gangarilla*, three or four men and a boy to play the women's parts; a *cambaleo*, five men and a woman; a *garnacha*, five or six men, a woman to play the first lady's roles, and a boy to play the second; a *boxiganga*, six or seven men, two women, and a

191

boy; a *farándula*, three women besides the men; and the largest, a *compañia*, "sixteen persons who act, thirty who eat, one who takes the money at the door." Costumes, properties, and modes of transportation increase in complexity and cost as the company advances.

The more prosperous and well-known companies were organized on two basic principles: those in which the head of the company was the proprietor, paying a fixed salary to the members of the company, and those which operated on shares. In either case definite contracts were drawn to govern the operation of the company. These contracts set hours of rehearsal, with fines for tardiness; payments to each member of the company; traveling and maintenance allowances; and, in the case of sharing companies, a provision for the distribution of parts by mutual agreement. Actors were hired for periods of one or two years, the beginning of the period being marked by Shrovetide. Companies were not resident at a particular theatre, as Shakespeare's company was, but traveled from city to city, generally spending about a month in any given theatre. Various arrangements were made with the owners of theatre properties, generally entailing either a flat sum as rent or a portion of the receipts. For engagements to play the sacred plays on Corpus Christi Day, or for special performances at various other festivities, the companies were paid flat sums agreed upon in advance.

The life of the Spanish actor was strenuous. Rojas describes the daily program:

> Actors are up at dawn and write and study from five o'clock till nine, and from nine till twelve they are constantly rehearsing. They dine and then go to the *comedia*; leave the theatre at seven, and when they want rest they are called by the President of the Council, or the city fathers, whom they must serve whenever it pleases them (*Viage Entretenid*, Madrid, 1603, pp. 368-9).

Early morning performances were often required in the sacred plays, beginning at six even though there had been a festival performance the previous day from two in the afternoon until twelve at night. The Corpus Christi performances normally lasted two days, with a flat fee as payment for both days. The municipalities evidently got their money's worth!

Actors, of course, were paid only when they were working. The total number of days in which a constantly busy actor could give performances was something less than two hundred a year, because of all the times in which performances were prohibited and the theatres closed. No wonder that the records of litigation and imprisonment for debt include the names of so many actors and managers. The average wage for respected members of the profession seems to have been in the neighborhood of three thousand reals a year, plus board and traveling expenses while the company was playing. Adequate but not luxurious living could be had for about two and a half reals a day in those times, so the competent performers were not extravagantly paid. The less competent and the apprentices received considerably less. The apprentices received no wages at all, or only a slight sum at the end of the season, but did receive all expenses. Stars were paid, as they have always been, rather extravagantly. There is record of La Calderona being paid 1,050 reals for two days' performance in the Corpus Christi plays at Pinto in 1632; Maria de Cordoba received eight hundred reals for two performances in secular plays the next year, plus expenses for herself and her maid. Pedro Manuel de Castilla, one of the most celebrated leading men of his time, received twenty reals a day, ten reals for maintenance, and five hundred reals for Corpus performances. But there is no record that any of these Spanish players were ever wealthy enough to buy "that house in Stratford." They were generally considered, and may have been, an improvident lot. But certainly the expenses of costumes, which leading players were expected to bear out of their own pockets, must have taken up much of their income.

History records the names of over two thousand players of the Golden Age in Spain, and by far the majority of these were recruited from the lower and middle classes. There are, however, several outstanding examples of noble gentlemen who were so enamored of the theatre that they became actors or managers. Such a one was Alonso de Olmedo, who was both a distinguished actor and manager, and was, by special authorization of the King, allowed to retain privileges of his rank although he belonged to a generally despised profession. Throughout this entire period all actors were declared without civil rights, and any actor who died in his profession could not be buried in soil consecrated by the Church. How paradoxical this sounds when we read of the thousands of Church performances that these pariahs gave during the same period! Of course, many of them were highly respected and honored in their lifetimes. In addition, it is interesting to note that both Lope de Vega and Calderón, Spain's two greatest playwrights, both died after many years of service as priests of the Church. It was not unusual for actresses, particularly, to renounce the stage to enter a convent, as did the famous Maria de Riquèlme. It must have been a comfort for an actress past her prime to know that she had this refuge open to her.

67 Spanish audiences

These two old prints show, above, the entrance to the *cazuela* of a public theatre, where only women were seated, and, below, a view inside the theatre with the ticket taker vainly trying to make more room in the already overcrowded *cazuela*. (Blanco y Negro)

A high degree of skill was demanded of performers in the public theatres. The secular plays were almost invariably written in verse form, and the audiences expected a most felicitous performance. In addition, all actors and actresses had to be proficient in singing, dancing, and playing a musical instrument, for every public performance

194

included these forms of entertainment. A contemporary describes the famous Damian Arias de Peñafiel thus:

> Arias possesses a clear, pure voice, a tenacious memory, and vivacious manner, and in whatever he said it seemed that the Graces were revealed in every movement of his tongue and Apollo in every gesture. The most famous orators came to hear him in order to acquire perfection of diction and gesture (Caramuel, *Rythmica*, Campaniae, 1668, p. 706).

Actors tended to specialize in particular types. Arias played the first leading man; Carlos Vallego was a well-known second leading man; Cosme Perez was a peerless comic actor. There were also comic actresses; other actresses were designated simply as first, second, or third. Actors also were classified first, second, or third in their particular lines. If the company were large, there might also be a fourth or a fifth. A final classification was that of musician, which might be either a man or a woman. If a playwright were attached to a company, he might function also as an actor or as the manager. Many of the secular dramas of the period were produced by playwright-managers, but the great playwrights were primarily neither actors nor managers, nor, indeed, attached to any acting company at all.

Just as there was constant criticism from the Puritans in England, in Spain there was also a constant stream of criticism, chiefly from the Church. There are frequent complaints of the impropriety of certain actors and actresses playing in the sacred plays because of their immoral lives. Down through the years every form of theatrical entertainment came in for its share of criticism and regulation. Women were successively banned from the stages of public theatres, but the banishment never really took place. Subject matter was censored, costuming supervised, even methods of playing dictated. But all of these successive regulations had no lasting effect until theatre reached a point where it was itself no longer a vital institution. As we have said, from the middle of the seventeenth century almost to our own day, Spanish theatre was in eclipse.

Summary

Almost concurrent with the great age of Shakespeare, the theatre of Spain rose to its apogee. It welcomed a veritable flood of playwrights and plays, and saw a host of performers on its stages. The plays differed considerably in kind from those written in England, being chiefly either religious or romantic dramas. But they were indigenous and not copies of Italian neoclassicism; hence they were greater than their Continental contemporaries.

The public playhouses of Spain developed, much as England's did, from space not originally intended for theatre use. In Spain, the audience remained in front of the actors, but did consist in part of standees and in part of persons seated in galleries or boxes. Here, too, theatre was the greatest of popular amusements. An avid public combined with a fertile theatre produced Spain's greatest period of drama.

Plots and character types produced here were used again in the next period by French playwrights, and it may have been the example of the Spanish stage which made women the rule rather than the exception in French theatre after the middle of the seventeenth century. From there, of course, the custom traveled to England in the Restoration.

This period in Spain saw the complete professionalization of theatre, the establishment of permanent playhouses, and more or less permanent repertory companies. Stagecraft was progressively refined, and costuming expensive and brilliant. The major achievement of the period, however, was that it produced the greatest plays of Spanish literature, notably those of Lope de Vega and Calderón.

Never again would Spanish theatre be so vital and so meaningful either to its contemporaries or to the general stream of theatrical development.

9

THE GOLDEN DAYS IN FRANCE

In 1600, when Shakespeare and Lope de Vega were reaching the height of their powers and there were six permanent theatres in London and more than that in Spain, Paris had but one theatre and no dramatist of note. The Renaissance had sparked some little dramatic activity it is true. We have seen that Jodelet produced the first native tragedy, *Cleopatra Captive*, in 1552 and an *Antigone* and a *Medea* later; that the Italian *commedia* players were performing in Paris and elsewhere; and that there were some bands of native players. But the brilliant staging of the Italian formal theatre, the adroit acting of the popular *commedia*, or the powerful dramatic literature of the English had no counterpart in France.

The reason for this notable absence of flourishing theatre is twofold. For one, France in the sixteenth century was consumed by the Wars of Religion which ended only in 1594 when Henry IV, the first Bourbon king, entered Paris. The short span of his reign (he was assassinated in 1610), was devoted to consolidating his rule over the whole of France, and to the restoration of order, industry, and trade. It was not until the seventeenth century, then, that France possessed the elements of nationalism and an atmosphere ripe for the development of a national theatre.

A second factor inhibiting the growth of theatre was that since 1402, the Confrèrie de la Passion had held a theatrical monopoly in Paris. It had built its first permanent theatre in 1548; although by that

68 *Molière the actor*
Right, Molière as Arnolphe in *The School for Wives*. In this comedy of
his own, in which he was exceedingly popular, Molière wears
contemporary dress and wig. Left, in this portrait by his friend Mignard,
Molière is dressed for his role as Julius Caesar in *The Death of Pompey*
by Corneille. He wears an approximation of Roman dress, so far
as we can tell, but retains the full-bottomed wig (here crowned with
laurel) which was customary in tragedy. (Harvard Theatre Collection)

year it was forbidden to present passion plays and mysteries, the
Confrèrie turned to the successful performance of farces, *soties*,
and comedies. By 1578 it had ceased to produce its own plays, but its
theatrical monopoly was still in force and it leased its playhouse to
touring companies—a situation which still prevailed in 1600. In spite
of growing dramatic activity, the Confrèrie effectively prevented
any theatrical performances from being held in Paris and its environs,
except for those which it permitted and supervised in its own house.
There were only two loopholes: the Confrèrie had, naturally, no
jurisdiction over court performances; and in 1595 Henry IV, who was
exceedingly fond of visiting the fairs, granted a special license for
the performance of plays there. Again, it was not until the seventeenth century that a beachhead was established. From then on,
however, dramatic activity soon spread, and though the Confrèrie

did not actually lose its prerogative until 1677, it had ceased to be observed many years earlier.

Theatre awaits its patron

The short reign of Henry IV (he was assassinated in 1610) was marked by increasing dramatic activity in the capital. Two companies were evidently performing there in 1596, since there is extant a record of an official complaint of the Confrèrie against its rivals. In 1598 a company of English actors came to Paris, and in the same year also Valleran le Conte (sometimes written "Lecomte" although his signature on legal documents is "le Conte") arrived, the most influential of the early French professional actors. He had had a long and evidently successful career in the provinces, playing comedies as well as Biblical tragedies and the plays of Jodelle. He joined forces with the company of Benoit Petit, then occupying the Hôtel de Bourgogne, and in 1599 that house was leased to him. It was about this time that Alexandre Hardy evidently became the paid furnisher of plays to the company. But the Paris public was evidently not yet to be interested in the new tragedies and pastorals of Hardy, and this company, ousted by the farces of Robert Guérin and his troupe, left Paris for several years. By the year 1610, when Louis XIII succeeded to the throne, le Conte was back again, this time in association with the farce players. After 1613 there is no further mention of him.

Theatrical appetite in Paris was also satisfied by the appearances there of Italian *commedia* companies who pleased not only court circles but the general public as well with their performances. The mother of Louis XIII, Marie de Medici, was exceedingly fond of this native Italian entertainment, and with her benediction several companies of *commedia* actors, including that of the famed Isabella Andreini, appeared in the French capital. Though they played in Italian, their skill in pantomime and acrobatics made them very popular with the general public. Their influence was to be a potent one for more than a century.

Regular tragedy and comedy made little headway against the farce players and the *commedia* until the advent of that intrepid statesman and man of letters, Cardinal Richelieu. He reentered the government in 1624, becoming chief minister in 1629. In the latter year the actor Montdory and his company arrived in Paris after enjoying tremendous success in the provinces, chiefly as a result of their production of Pierre Corneille's first play, *Mélite* (1628). Montdory had much earlier been one of the younger members of Valleran le Conte's company, and on several occasions appeared in Paris at the

Hôtel de Bourgogne; he had become an actor of great renown. Cardinal Richelieu looked with favor upon his company, and despite the protests of the Confrèrie permitted them to perform in Paris outside the Hôtel de Bourgogne, which was then occupied by the Royal Company headed by the actor Bellerose. Montdory and his actors performed in a variety of locations, chiefly converted tennis courts, finally settling in 1634 in a converted tennis court in La Veille Rue du Temple in the Marais quarter, then a very fashionable section of Paris. From its location, the house was named the Théâtre du Marais. Now Paris had two permanent theatres; the long-standing theatrical monopoly of the Confrèrie was effectively broken, and the way paved for the development of a great national theatre.

In the same year that Louis XIV came to the throne, and a year after the death of Richelieu, Molière's Illustre Théâtre was formed and opened in a tennis court near the Tour de Nesle (now the location of the Institut de France, which houses the French Academy). It was New Year's Day, 1644. After slightly more than a year, however, the little company retired to the provinces, where a fruitful sojourn of some twelve years' duration enabled them to return in triumph to the capital to help develop the greatest period of French theatre. This era reached its peak in 1680 with the establishment of the first national theatre in existence—the Comédie Française.

Drama reflects the light of the Roi Soleil

In a country where the Roi Soleil declared "L'etat, c'est moi" (I am the state), and where his absolutism was without question, theatre was, necessarily, an adjunct or a reflection of the court. Unlike the public institution which the English had maintained a generation earlier, French theatre at the height of its development was the diversion of the aristocrats and the wealthy. Even the nominally public playhouses were patronized and supported by the King, by Richelieu, by Mazarin, by the Duc d'Anjou. France's major playwrights wrote equally for these houses and for the elaborate court productions, often upon demand by royalty, with exacting prescriptions of character, plot, and type of production. Even the not insignificant academic drama of the Jesuit schools was a reflection of the throne, the graduation plays being patronized by both Louis XIII and Louis XIV; Racine, at the request of Madame de Maintenon, wrote his two Biblical plays, Esther and Athalie, for her girls' school at St. Cyr.

The court often actively intervened in theatrical affairs. We have seen how Henry IV legalized the presentation of farces at the fairs

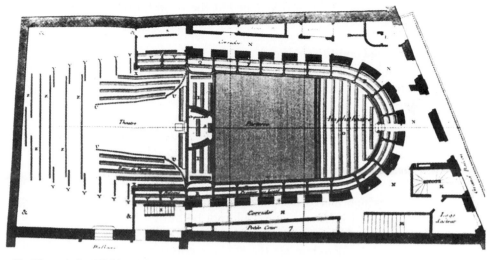

69 *Plan of the Théâtre Français*
This is the plan of the first theatre built for the Comédie Française.
The part of the auditorium nearest the stage is provided with backless
benches; part of the auditorium floor is reserved for standees. The boxes
encircle the pit, and space for seating on the stage is provided.
(Yale Theatrical Prints Collection)

in spite of the long-standing monopoly of the Confrèrie, and how
Richelieu sponsored the Thèâtre du Marais. Perhaps, as some suggest, it was to spite Richelieu that the King ordered six actors transferred from the Marais company to the Hôtel de Bourgogne in 1634.
There are many examples of the King or his ministers initiating or
directing theatrical activity during this period. The next year, for
instance, Richelieu conceived the somewhat absurd idea of having
plays written by a committee of five poets writing simultaneously,
each of whom was to produce one act of a drama. Over a period of
two years this unique drama factory wrote three productions and
then was dissolved. In 1641 the King, by a notable decree, barred
low comedy from the stage and gave impetus to the rising regular-
ized drama. Theatres were given or taken away from companies upon
royal whim; troupes were formed, reformed, or eliminated. Upon
Molière's death, in 1673, his company was merged by royal decree
with that of the Marais; and in 1680 the decree forming the Comèdie
Française merged this troupe with the Hôtel de Bourgogne players.
Throughout the great period of French drama, plays, playwrights,

201

players, and theatres functioned at the behest, and the whim, of the crown.

Social conditions discouraging

Outside of the schools, and excepting the court dilettantes who danced and sang in the court productions, acting was a full-time profession. Often the actors were playwrights as well, as was Molière (figure 68). Often they were actor-managers, like Bellerose. With minor exceptions, the women's roles were played by women, and, again with minor exceptions, there were no companies of child actors. Sometimes the actors earned personal fame and fortune; sometimes members of the nobility joined the profession. But, barring a repentance which included a renunciation of their profession, actors were considered infamous, and could not be buried in holy ground under the rites of the Church. Not infrequently they were despised and abused. Molière himself, though he seems not to have resented them, was often subjected to insults from titled patrons.

The chief spectators at the plays were, of course, members of court circles and tradesmen connected with court circles. Courtiers and hangers-on often behaved with an arrogance beyond belief. Many a doorkeeper was wounded or even killed in his effort to extract the admission price from one who thought he should be admitted free by reason of his position. Scuffles in the theatre, even riots, were not unusual. Rostand has immortalized one of these in his play, *Cyrano de Bergerac* (1898), which gives a fairly accurate idea of the conditions under which players performed in seventeenth-century France. Riotous members of the audience frequently interrupted the plays and sometimes made it impossible for the performance to continue. Members of the nobility demanded—and got—seats on the stage to which they strolled at their convenience, sometimes long after the play had begun. There they conversed audibly, frequently not about the play, and exhibited their finery and lace. Their sworn enemies were the men standing in the pit, the cheapest of admissions, and frequently word battles between these two groups ended in a free-for-all that had to be put down by civil authorities.

For such an audience Molière, Corneille, and Racine wrote. It is perhaps in no little measure due to the fact that the playwrights had to please two such opposite extremes as the spectators on the stage and those in the pit that they produced the strong and virile drama which they did.

Even the more exclusive court performances were thought of more as purely social events than anything else, and there was a great deal of talk and inattention. In the public theatres, performances were advertised to begin at two o'clock, but since it was extremely unfashionable to arrive on time, they frequently never got underway until nearly five, and this latter hour became the customary one. Not until the establishment of the Comédie Française in 1680 were performances given every day of the week—three or four was the customary number. In the days when Molière's troupe shared the Petit Bourbon with the Comédie Italienne, they played on Mondays, Wednesdays, Thursdays, Fridays, and Saturdays, with the Italians performing on Tuesdays and Sundays, the most lucrative days. Even those companies with exclusive occupancy of a theatre did not play every day of the week.

In spite of these conditions, and perhaps partly because of them, the seventeenth century produced the best dramatic literature which France has ever known.

Unity of time, place, and action

France had been stirred by the classically-oriented ferment of the Renaissance in somewhat lesser degree than Italy, although as early as 1537 Lazare de Baïf had written his *Electra,* and eleven years later the influence of Aristotle's *Poetics* is to be found in the critical work of Tomas Sebillet, *The Poetic Art,* in which he traces a parallel between the old French moralities and the classic tragedies. By the time that Jean de la Taille wrote his *Saul the Mad* (1572), Aristotle was the authority, and Taille's preface to this play enunciated the principle of the three unities of time, place, and action. From that time on, many French playwrights, whose names are entirely without significance today, wrote in the new classical pattern of the unities.

Though presumably true to Aristotelian precepts, the French writers of tragedy accepted these conventions as they were enunciated by Horace and practiced by Seneca. They rarely went back even to these sources, but followed the practice of Italian interpreters and copiers of Horace and Seneca. Thus their plays are narrative, oratorical, elegiac. Most of them were derivative literary exercises produced, if at all, in the schools and at court.

In the last few decades of the sixteenth century these literary men falteringly learned to include more action in their plays; to bring their chief characters on stage and face to face; to work out a plot line. When Alexandre Hardy began writing early in the next century for Valleran le Conte's company at the Hôtel de Bourgogne, the carefully worked out theories came to grips with the practice of a professional playwright producing for a paying audience. Though Hardy

70 A Jean Berain design
This highly ornate design, with its cupids and cloud machine, was made
by the talented Jean Berain for a production of *Hesione* at the Paris
Opera in 1701. It is typical of the lavishness of French taste in scene
design. (Stockholm Nationalmuseum)

was in sympathy with the new classical movement in dramatic art,
he had to cope with a medieval theatre where events, not rhetoric,
held the stage. So, good theatre man that he was, he made the best of
both worlds. He followed the classical conventions of five acts, the
Alexandrine line (six iambics with the caesura after the third), messengers, a ghost in the first act, and the sufferings, vengeances, and
horrors of the Greek and Roman prototypes. But he banished the
chorus and ignored the unities; he placed a series of varied scenes
on the stage which told a recognizable story from beginning to end.
Essentially he was more of a Romantic than a Classicist.

It is said that he wrote more than six hundred plays, of which
thirty-four survive. If he had been as skillful in character delineation
as he was in plot construction; if he had been able to strike the necessary balance between the two; if, in other words, he had possessed
something of the genius of Shakespeare, he might have effectively
turned the tide of French playwriting away from the classical unities
to a more native, less prescribed drama. But though his plays were
full of action and were highly theatrical, they lacked the full measure

of genius; and eventually they fell into disrepute because of their Romanticism.

Corneille concedes to Classicism

By the time we arrive at France's first authentic playwriting genius, Pierre Corneille, conflict between the Romanticists and the Classicists was reaching a climax. The Classicists had become a tremendously powerful group, basking under the benediction of Cardinal Richelieu. Corneille's first play, *Mélite,* written for Montdory's acting company while they were visiting his native Rouen and presented by them in Paris in 1629, turned him from the profession of the law to the theatre. *Mélite* was written after the free-ranging style of the Spaniards and Hardy, rather than the style of the classical unities. Corneille was not by instinct a Classicist, and neither his second play, *Clitandra* (1631) nor his highly successful *The Cid* (1636), completely observed the unities.

In *The Cid* (derived from Castro's *The Young Manhood of the Cid*), Corneille succeeded in proving his genius by producing a play in which the dramatic conflict was that interplay of character on event and event on character from which the plot moves forward. It was deservedly popular, and controversial. Its very popularity called down upon his head the ire of the French Academy founded by Richelieu in 1635 for the regularization of the conventions of French literature.

One of the pamphleteers who participated in the literary battle over *The Cid* was the playwright, Jean Mairet; his *Sophonisbe,* written the year before, had observed all the Classical unities but had at the same time added a real love interest derived from the pastoral, an innovation which thenceforth added another dimension to tragedy.

Although Corneille was defended by Rotrou (who had himself made much use of Spanish materials and ideas in his plays), and although Richelieu himself remained friendly, Corneille capitulated to the inevitable; he turned out in succession *Horace* (1640), *Cinna* (1641), *Polyeucte* (1642), and *The Death of Pompey* (1643), all in the style approved by the Academy. In all of these plays his grandly conceived heroes, speaking in ringing Alexandrine verse, dominate the action of the plot. While this dominance made possible the contribution of an impressive gallery of characters to dramatic literature, the resulting necessity of subordinating plot to character made little contribution to the advance of dramaturgy. Corneille was elected to the precious Academy in 1647; thereby he became the foremost writer of Classical tragedy in France. He observed all the unities of time, place, and action; he debarred all violent events from his stage and related them by messenger as the Greek playwrights had done; he wrote in the accepted high moral tone with impassioned affirmations of the heroic spirit. Called "the great Corneille," and much honored throughout his long life (he died in 1684), he wrote many more tragedies which do not today add to his stature. It is thus ironic that he seems never to have been completely at home with the classical conventions; under other circumstances, he might have produced a freer, richer drama.

Racine at home with the unities

Jean Racine, on the other hand, had a genius peculiarly suited to the classical restrictions, and rose to great eminence in the brilliant world of the *Roi Soleil*. His many successful plays were almost entirely on classical subjects, in wonderfully refined verse, with emphasis upon the inner conflicts of his characters. These plays demonstrate the possibility of perfection within the discipline of the classical precepts. His plots were not complex; but his characters, with their conflict of passion and will power, were very human in their weaknesses and strengths. His expositions were simple and dramatic, his situations real, his materials eminently suited to his technique. The most famous of his plays, today, is *Phaedra* (1677), though it lacks the serenity of the later *Esther* (1689) and *Athalie* (1691). *Bérénice* (1670), *Iphigenia* (1674), and *Andromeda* (1667); *Britannicus* (1669), *Bajazet* (1672), and *Mithridates* (1673)—his best and most well-known plays—illustrate both his subject matter and his concern with heroic characters. The continuing popularity of his plays on the French stage, even though styles of playwriting have changed phenomenally since his day, attests to their intrinsic vitality and dramatic effectiveness.

Corneille and Racine were the greatest writers of tragedy in the seventeenth century; only Corneille's younger brother, Thomas, and Georges de Scudéry deserve to be mentioned with them.

Molière—consummate comedian

Of the writers of comedy only one name is of real importance— that of Molière: writer, actor, producer, manager, director. He himself was a frustrated tragedian. In fact, his Paris début before the King was almost a fiasco because he presented a poor production of an early tragedy of Corneille—*Nicomède*; the day was saved by appending one of Molière's own little farces, *The Love-Sick Physician*.

Molière once tried to write a tragedy, a grand heroic drama called *Don Garcia of Navarre* (1661), which failed miserably after seven performances; Racine's one venture into comedy, *The Litigants* (1661), was not so bad as this. (Corneille, too, had written several successful comedies for Montdory's company, including *Mélite*, as well as a somewhat later one, *The Liar* in 1643.)

Molière's consummate skill in comedy was the end product of the development which had refined the medieval farce, added a love interest from the pastorals, incorporated the incidents and tricks of Italian comedy, and used the Spanish technique of developing plot complications within the play itself. Molière's plays perfectly amalgamate all these elements; the ingredient that proves him a genius, however, was his ability to create dramatic action by the effect of events on character which in turn causes other events to occur. He proved that tricks and intrigue are not necessarily, as Corneille once said, the mainsprings of comedy; but that in comedy, no less than in tragedy, human psychology can be the mainspring. In addition, he had an intense and sympathetic awareness of human character and of society; he drew from life, as it were, and so produced the highest form of comedy.

Molière was essentially a satirist and like all real satirists he was devoted to truth; his satire was an attempt to explode the pretensions of the world as it was with the hope that it might thereby develop into what it should be. This attempt is a perilous adventure for a dramatist, for he must raise a cleansing laughter without driving his audience from the theatre, and without raising a lasting resentment. Sometimes Molière did not succeed. One of his most telling satires, that on religious hypocrisy (*Tartuffe*, 1664), was debarred from the stage for five years after its initial performance.

The society which fostered Molière was a fertile field for his probe, and many were the absurdities which he punctured. One of his earliest efforts after his return to Paris pointed up the pretensions of a set of ultra-refined ladies and gentlemen of the court. That was *The Precious Ladies* in 1659. Discretion prompted him to make the silly young ladies of the play provincials and not members of the court, but the point of the satire was not lost on his audience. The immediate objects of his satire were discomfited, but everyone else laughed so heartily that some reform was effected.

Molière had always been a great admirer of the Italian *commedia*; he had, indeed, taken lessons in acting from Tiberio Fiorillo, the famous Scaramouche. He evidently saw cosmic comic types in the *commedia* characters, for he adapted them time and again for use

71 *Court presentations*
Above, Jacques Callot's etching of an elaborate entertainment given at
the court, *Combat at the Barrier*. The spectators are arranged on
temporary bleachers around three sides of the great hall. See figure 30.
Below, a court performance at Versailles of Molière's *The Imaginary
Invalid* in 1674. The King is seated down front center, and the
orchestra, which played chiefly for the elaborate interludes accompanying
the performance, is placed just below the stage.
(Boston Museum of Fine Arts, Harvard Theatre Collection)

in his own dramatis personae. Many of his characters are echoes of
the *commedia*. He learned to know the *commedia* well during his
travels in the provinces and during the years when Italian comedians
shared the theatres of the Petit-Bourbon and the Palais Royal with
him. The Arnolphe of his *The School for Wives* (1662) is redolent
of Pantalone, and his many physicians reminiscent of The Doctor
of the *commedia*. With this foundation, or inspiration, Molière's
characters emerge as fully rounded, interesting people, lovable or de-
testable as they reveal themselves. Molière is a master of comic char-

acterization, and this is the measure of his genius. The gallery of his memorable characters is a long one, from one Mascarille of his first important work, *The Blunderer* (1655), to the affected ladies, Magdélon and Cathos; the various Sganarelles; Ariste in *The School for Husbands* (1666); Alceste of *The Misanthrope* (1666); the ladies of *The Learned Ladies* (1672); and Argan of *The Imaginary Invalid* (1673), which role Molière was playing at the time of his death.

Molière's greatest achievement—had he accomplished nothing else, he might stand foremost in French letters for this alone—was that he raised comedy to the stature of tragedy. Finding a formless and raucous mass of farce, street entertainment, and acrobatics, he developed a supple and effective social satire which pleased men of good taste everywhere. Though he laughed at human nature with its frailties and stupidities, he also knew people thoroughly and loved them well. Keen observation coupled with love and insight, made him perhaps the greatest writer in the comic vein that the world has ever seen.

Command performances at court

Molière wrote for the court as well as for the public theatre. Plays given as parts of the elaborate court productions also included his satire and social criticism; however, they almost invariably incorporated much singing and dancing into the performance. These plays were written upon the demand of the King. Noteworthy in this genre are Molière's *The Bores* (1661), *Monsieur de Pourceaugnac* (1669), and *The Would-Be Gentleman* (1670), in which the inimitable M. Jourdain discovers that he has been speaking prose all his life. *Tartuffe* itself had been a part of the court entertainment, *The Pleasures of the Enchanted Island*, given at Versailles in 1664.

Molière was not alone in producing these court performances; both Corneille and Racine, as well as many of lesser note, contributed. Often playwrights collaborated in these productions: Corneille, Rotrou, and three others, upon command of Richelieu, wrote *The Comedy of the Tuilleries* in 1638; Molière, at a somewhat later date, collaborated with Corneille, Quinault, and various musicians. Even the major playwrights of the French seventeenth century were at the beck and call of royalty. The drama was an adjunct of the court.

Playhouses expeditious or elaborate

The court was exceedingly important, also, in providing places for playing; as we have observed, almost all of the playhouses were built and operated by royal permission or upon royal command.

There were three general categories of French theatres in the seventeenth century: the temporary ones, those converted from tennis courts, and the permanent ones built for continuing dramatic performances. Of temporary theatres, there were two types: those erected at fairs, and those built for court performances.

The stages of the fair theatres varied from primitive platforms on trestles to rather elaborate platforms and sets constructed by the wealthier mountebanks for the performances of their hired companies. These mountebanks were the traveling salesmen of the seventeenth century, peddling medicines and cures of one kind and another much in the manner of the medicine-show pitchmen of our own American pioneer days. They traveled from town to town, setting up their platforms in squares, marketplaces, or, in Paris, at the great fairs of St. Laurent and St. Germain (figure 72). The dramatic performances were come-ons for their pitch. The lesser entrepreneurs were content to present jugglers, tumblers, and dancers; the wealthier ones often presented complete dramatic performances. Even as important a *commedia* company as I Gelosi was brought into France by a mountebank. The acting was often of a high order of excellence; the fair actors frequently graduated to the regular theatres, or alternated between them.

The acting spaces these presentations utilized were all open-air arrangements, with the audience standing around three sides. The ruder sort of platform was backed only by a curtain; the more ornate might use a roofed superstructure with a pictorial backing. In any event, the platform served not only for the dramatic performance, but also for the sales platform of the producing quack.

The other type of temporary playhouse current in the seventeenth century was that used for court performances. These were built from time to time, at great expense, to house the single performances of court spectacles. This sort of temporary playhouse was the French counterpart of the court playing spaces designed by the Englishman Inigo Jones, and of many similar production places in the great houses of Italy.

More permanent were the tennis-court theatres, some of which housed dramatic performances through most of the century. By the end of the sixteenth century, it is estimated that there were several hundred halls of this sort constructed for the *jeu de paume*, or "game of the palm" in Paris alone. This game, unlike today's lawn tennis, was played with a short-handled racquet on an indoor court with galleries for the spectators. It had enjoyed a long and feverish popularity with many segments of the population, particularly the court.

210

The Valois monarchs had been exceedingly fond of the game, and the first Bourbon king, Henry IV, was a devoted player. But he was the last of the French kings to be really an expert at the game, and it declined in popularity after his death. Thus the long, narrow, roofed over courts with their side galleries were left available for other purposes (figure 73). Acting companies seeking shelter found the tennis courts expedient. They would erect a simple "shelf for acting" at one end, use the galleries for spectators, and put benches around the sides and down the length of the floor. Such converted tennis courts in the Rue Michel-le-Comte and the Quartier Saint-Martin were the early homes of Montdory's company. Montdory's final refuge in the Marais was just such a converted tennis court; this house continued in use until 1673, when the company was merged with that of the Palais Royal. Such also was the house near the Tour de Nesle in which Molière's company first opened on New Year's Day of 1644. Functional but not elaborate, these tennis-court playhouses served a real need in the growing French theatre.

A few permanent theatres also housed plays in Molière's day. The earliest of these was, of course, the Hôtel de Bourgogne, built by the Confrèrie de la Passion in 1548 and used throughout the next century. Its construction did not differ materially from that of the tennis-court theatres. The auditorium was long and narrow, with two galleries running along the walls and the stage across one end. The fact that it was more than twice as long as it was wide must have made the sightline problem acute.

This rectangular construction was used also in the King's private theatre in the Petit Bourbon Palace attached to the Louvre. A proscenium-arched stage stretched across one end of the long, finely proportioned ballroom, and the sides each had two galleries for spectators. When the room was appropriated for theatrical performances about the year 1577, when the visiting I Gelosi played there, the floor was left free for the accommodation of the King and his party. This arrangement became the custom for succeeding theatrical performances, although additional seats could be and on occasion were set up on the floor. This was the theatre which Louis XIII gave to the Italian comedians, and which Molière later shared with them. It was pulled down in 1660, on the sudden order of the Superintendent of Royal Buildings, and Molière, after two years' residence, was ousted without warning. He was able to salvage the boxes and fittings, but not the scenes and machines which the famous Torelli had designed at the instigation of Cardinal Mazarin in 1645. (Torelli's successor, Vigarani, claimed these for the Hall of Machines which he was then

72 *Open-air theatres*

Above, Tabarin's street show in the Place Dauphine. He performed to
draw an audience for his brother, the quack doctor Mondor; he was
an exceedingly popular entertainer, and the Place Dauphine was
his favorite place of playing. The particular kind of hat he wore became his
trademark. Below, an elevated outdoor stage in the Fair of St. Germain,
evidently built atop the stalls of the market at a particular vantage
point. Note the two practical doors on the stage. The actors seem to be
wearing masks as in the *commedia*. (Bibliothèque Nationale; Harvard
Theatre Collection)

building at the Tuileries, and was awarded them, but instead of using them he had them burned. This, apparently, was done out of jealousy, in the hope of destroying all trace of his predecessor.)

Louis XIV gave the homeless Molière and his troupe the theatre in the Palais Royal. This magnificent building was erected by Richelieu as his own residence, and had been called the Palais Cardinal before it reverted to the Crown upon Richelieu's death. The original private theatre it contained had been extensively remodeled at great expense, and the Cardinal had inaugurated the new house with a spectacular performance of *Miramé* in January, 1641. It seated about six hundred people. At one end of the long rectangle was the stage, with a proscenium arch topped by Richelieu's coat-of-arms; there were six broad steps leading down to the floor of the auditorium. At the opposite end of the hall was a kind of lobby formed by three large arcades. The floor of the hall rose from the stage to the opposite end by means of twenty-seven low, broad stone steps on which wooden seats were placed. Along each of the two sides of the hall were two decorated galleries. The rich appointments and the stage machinery were of Italian inspiration. After the property reverted to the King upon the death of Richelieu in 1642, it was used intermittently for court entertainments until Molière and his company moved into it in 1660. It had been hastily repaired and redecorated to receive the Molière company, then was extensively rebuilt and enlarged in 1670 to house the complicated stage machinery similar to that which Vigarani had destroyed ten years before. *Psyche* was the first spectacular production with the new machines, Molière having moved the play to his theatre after its initial production for the court at the Tuileries. When Molière died in 1673, the composer Lully claimed and received the Palais Royal for his new Academy of Music, and Molière's troupe was ousted. The building burned down in 1763.

When the master designer, Torelli, returned to Italy, Cardinal Mazarin had Vigarani appointed court decorator, and it was he, as we have mentioned, who, in 1660, constructed the aptly named Hall of Machines at the Tuileries. Its great stage was thirty-two feet wide at the proscenium, and 132 feet deep. It was equipped with the most intricate and expensive of machinery for producing the elaborate court spectacles which were then in vogue.

After Molière's death his company moved to a theatre in the Rue Guénégaud. This playhouse had been built by the eccentric Marquis de Sourdéac in 1670 to house opera. It had a large and fully equipped stage with a plethora of machinery. The Molière company, under the astute actor LaGrange, and with the financial support of Molière's widow, arranged to purchase from the Marquis his then new but currently unused theatre. It was this well-equipped house which sheltered the first national theatre in the Western world, formed when Louis XIV united the two then remaining Parisian companies (the Italians excepted) into the Comédie Francaise in October of 1680, giving to them the sole right to perform French plays in the capital.

Thus the playhouse of France in the seventeenth century, begun with the simple stage of the medieval period, developed to the elaborate opera-type house which became standard in theatre construction even to our own day.

Designers seek complex settings

French settings in the seventeenth century ranged from the simplest to the most complex. Yet we must remember that the tendency was toward complexity because of the pervasive influence of the court's love for spectacle and because of the ascendency of the opera. Some of what seem to us today the simplest of Molière's staging problems were often most intricate in their day.

The fair theatres and the provincial companies used, as we have seen, a minimum of setting and properties. Often an undecorated back curtain sufficed for the simple platform stage, though many extant prints show curious elaborations of this after the manner of the medieval doorways in the production of classical plays. Sometimes the back curtains were painted in landscapes, street scenes, or other pictorial representations. The necessity of portability, however, always limited the possibilities of elaboration on these temporary stages.

Another curious remnant of the Middle Ages was the early seventeenth-century stage of the Hôtel de Bourgogne. Sketches preserved in *Notes for the Decoration of the Plays Presented by the King's Comedians, Reported to His Majesty* show how the chief designer of the house and author of the *Notes*, Laurent Mahelot, produced multiple settings curiously reminiscent of the religious plays of the preceding century (figure 74). Many of these were for the multiple settings of plays by Alexandre Hardy, wherein four or five different localities were placed upstage and at the sides, with the central open area being used, as it was in the Middle Ages, as the general acting area. For *Hercules,* a tragedy by Rotrou produced in 1634, the stage showed a practical temple of Jupiter, a practical mountain with a full-grown tree, a funeral chamber, and a tomb. Like the medieval *mâitre des feyntes*, the stage manager of this house was charged with all kinds of effects: lightning, wind, thunder, flames, fireworks, simulated deaths, ascents, and descents, as well as an occasional hellfire.

214

To have achieved all of these effects on a stage as small as that which is estimated for the Hôtel de Bourgogne (about twenty-five feet wide by twenty-three feet deep), required most careful use of space. Recent researches reveal that the earliest stage settings of this house were of the simplest sort—a backdrop and a line of curtained enclosures down each of the two sides through which the actors emerged to the central acting area. This arrangement must have been similar to the curtained doorways of the old Terence engravings. The early stage also had an upper level after the manner of the old mysteries. This balcony stage could be used to increase the number of mansions, or to provide an operating platform for special effects. It was also supplied with a railing and with traps. The stage floor itself also had traps. A similar arrangement at the Marais, though with measurements somewhat larger than those of the Hôtel de Bourgogne, made the increasing complexity of production feasible there as well. In its latter days the Marais became famous for its machine plays, while the Hôtel de Bourgogne, swept up in the neo-classic tide, concentrated on building a reputation for the production of tragedy. In this period the multiple setting was replaced by an unlocalized set scene featuring painted representations of temples and palaces.

The early plays of Molière, given on a public stage which was also used to seat some privileged members of the audience, had the most conventional of settings. Folding screens, painted to represent stylized houses, were grouped to show a street or square in perspective. The actors issued from the houses to center stage and performed all scenes, whether domestic quarrels, lovemaking, or consultations with doctors, in this simulated out-of-doors. The street scene in comedy had a long tradition behind it. It had been a convention from Menander and Plautus to Machiavelli and the *commedia*. This particular arrangement of folding screens may have been influenced by the frame cubicles used earlier at the Hôtel de Bourgogne, which were, in turn, outgrowths of the medieval mysteries. It also, no doubt, served a very practical purpose in a theatre shared by Molière and the Italian comedians.

When Richelieu opened his newly redecorated theatre in 1641, the stage setting was an elaborated architectural structure in perspective, after the Italian style. It was criticized for its elaborateness as detracting from the play, but the criticism affected Richelieu not at all; he added to the performance, on subsequent occasions, extravagant ballet interludes.

This interpolation of what would seem to us extraneous material

73 *Tennis court to theatre*
Left, the interior of a *jeu de paume*,
an engraving from a book
on the rules of the game, printed
in 1632. Note the high windows,
the long narrow shape, and the side
galleries—all of which easily
could be adapted for theatre use.
Right, the interior
of a seventeenth-century
public theatre, from an engraving
attributed to Abraham Bosse.
Here is the narrow shelf for acting,
the side galleries, the standing pit
universally typical of the converted
tennis-court theatres.
(Bibliothèque Nationale)

—the more so because of the period's insistence upon the Classical unities—became more and more fashionable and sought after. When Molière was ordered, in 1661, to produce a play for Fouquet, the minister of finance, to honor the King, he wrote *The Bores*. The play began with the spouting of twenty natural fountains, during which a large shell opened and an actress, dressed as a naiad, emerged to speak the prologue. *The Would-Be Gentleman* was regularly concluded with an elaborate Turkish ballet in which the King himself danced; *The Imaginary Invalid* concluded with an equally elaborate burlesque ballet; *The Misanthrope* was presented with ballet interludes for which the scene was changed. Far from objecting to these interpolations, Molière attempted to preserve the elaborateness of the court presentations when he moved the productions to his own theatre.

Indeed, not only Molière, but others of his contemporaries, wrote many machine plays designed to exhibit the wonders of the intricately equipped stages which had been designed by Torelli, Vigarani, and their copyists. One of the most elaborate of these was Mo-

216

lière's *Psyche,* designed by Vigarani, and presented first at the Hall of Machines. Among its many wonders was Venus descending from the heavens in a great machine, a magnificent courtyard with a resplendent palace and a sea of fire. It was to produce this play that Molière spent a great deal of money reequipping the Palais Royal. Though the script seems thin stuff to us today, it was extremely successful in its own day.

Machines and chariots were an integral part, also, of Molière's *Amphitryon,* and the elaborate staging of Corneille's *Andromeda,* as designed by Torelli, was almost incredible. Mountains appeared and disappeared; gardens sprouted and died; waves engulfed the scene and receded to reveal a palace, which in turn dissolved into a temple. All of these changes were wrought in full view of the audience, being a part of the show. Extensive substage and overhead machinery was necessary for these effects; and the complexity of their operation needs not even to be mentioned. The stage designers were accomplished engineers as well as artists.

Lighting, of course, took advantage of all of the skill developed by the Italians, as well as all the ingenuity that was mustered locally. Footlights as well as overhead lighting were employed; both candles

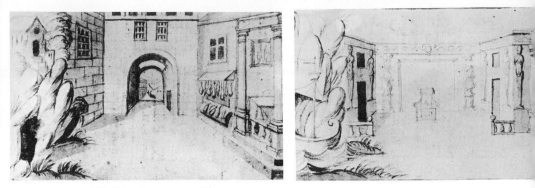

74 *Simultaneous settings*
Left, Mahelot's drawing of the set for Du Ryer's *Lisandre et Caliste*,
presented at the Hôtel de Bourgogne. Right, his drawing of the set
for Hardy's *Folie de Clidamant*. These simultaneous settings are the direct
descendants of medieval staging practice, and were Mahelot's
practical answer to the demands of the multiple-scene romantic drama
in a theatre which had no machinery for transformations and no
front curtain. (Bibliothèque Nationale)

and oil lamps were used. It is no wonder that Torelli earned for himself the title of The Great Sorcerer.

It is true that the poorer theatrical companies had to forego much
of this decoration, but we cannot think that their plays suffered
thereby. Indeed, we are rather sure that the satiric point of such a
play as Molière's *The Bores* must have been blunted by such display.
But such were the tastes of the times.

With the presence of so much spectacle and dancing there was, of
course, much music attached to the performances, and most of it was
specially composed for each event. The astute Lully, who enjoyed
an almost complete monopoly on music in the court of Louis XIV,
composed practically everything for court performances, including
the music for many of Molière's comedy ballets. At one point Molière
incurred his enmity by having Charpentier compose the music for
The Imaginary Invalid, with the consequence that this play was not
first performed at Versailles as had been intended, but at the Palais
Royal instead. At one time it seems that the orchestra was installed
at the back of the house, but the impracticality of such an arrangement later led to its being seated immediately in front of the stage,
our present arrangement for musical shows.

Thus, stage decoration in the seventeenth century was of all types
and kinds, but the ultimate aim of actors, producers, and audience

218

was always to arrive at the most elaborate and spectacular effects which could possibly be achieved.

Costumes marked by contemporary styles

Costuming on the French stage of the seventeenth century was not dissimilar in type to that of the Elizabethan period. For the most part contemporary costume was worn, save for the kinds of characters to whom this would be completely unsuitable—historical, fantastic, and allegorical figures.

Since actors supplied the costumes they wore from their individual purses, the richness of the dress depended on the affluence of the wearer. Some relief from this expense was afforded through the intrepidity of a M. Bourgeois, a Parisian merchant, who about the middle of the century set up what must certainly have been the first of all costume rental agencies. In addition, there was a lively business in secondhand clothes in the market district of Les Halles near the Hôtel de Bourgogne, and it is likely that many an actor acquired cast-off finery from these merchants.

In 1682, the learned Jesuit Claude-François Menestrier wrote a treatise on ballet, *On the Production of Music Ancient and Modern,* in which he advocated historical accuracy in costuming, keeping always in mind that for dances, not only the ensemble effect must be carefully observed, but also the individual costume must be functional. His careful descriptions of allegorical costuming are reminiscent of the Inigo Jones designs for the Stuart masques. An examination of costume and stage sketches of the period show that, in actuality, costuming on the opera and court stages was an adaptation of contemporary dress with a flavor of period and place. Appended comment often reveals that these costumes tended to be made of the richest possible materials with a maximum amount of ornamentation. Particularly lavish are the costumes designed by Jean Bérain for the Paris Opera in the last quarter of the century.

The popular theatres carried over, so far as their finances permitted, the splendid costuming of court spectacle and opera to dazzle the eyes of their public.

The Italian *commedia,* of course, preserved much of the original *commedia* costuming, although as time went on these costumes, too, bowed to contemporary taste and took on contemporary touches. It is interesting to note that in the staging of his early comedies (those written for production in the provinces, and now largely lost) Molière retained the masks of the *commedia* parts from which his characters were derived.

219

75 A Vigarani design
This imposing series of wing flats and borders, with an architecturally
designed backdrop is the work of Carlo Vigarani, son of Gaspare, whom
Mazarin brought to France as Torelli's successor. It was made for a
production of *Alcestis* at court in about 1675. (Stockholm Nationalmuseum)

Since long, full wigs were much the fashion for men, they were
generally worn on the stage, whatever the character. There is a curiously amusing portrait of Molière himself as Caesar, in a full-bottomed wig crowned by copious laurel leaves—no doubt artificial.
The portrait was painted by his friend, Mignard, and is one of the
few truly authentic pictures of the master (figure 68).

Since makeup was a prized and devious weapon of at least the
feminine half of the society who witnessed the plays, there is little
question that it was used on the stage as well. It is probable, however,
that actors used it only when required by their parts to alter their
appearances materially. They were no doubt schooled in the art of
makeup by the Italians, who had perfected its use some years earlier.

Thus, though there were some indications of at least an interest
in historical accuracy, the predominant costume of Molière's theatre
mirrored the dress of the times which was in itself widely varied,

generally richly decorated, and highly colored—theatrical without being itself of theatre.

Actors indebted to the Italians

It is of special interest to note that the greatest playwrights in both France and England were first of all actors. Both Molière and Shakespeare began in the theatre as actors. Indeed, Molière ended his days as an actor, and most of his contemporary fame rested upon this facet of his ability. Though Shakespeare eventually gave up acting, he spent all of his working life in the theatre. No doubt, for both Shakespeare and Molière this close and practical knowledge of what would work on the stage and what would not enabled them to achieve a pinnacle of greatness that might not otherwise have been possible. They were different, it is true, in their views of life—the Englishman's genius was larger, more comprehensive, more sympathetic; he did not have the satiric bent that is evident in all of Molière's work. But, then, their respective societies were different, and the theatre is in large measure a reflection of the society which produces it. To both of them, however, the art of acting was at least as important as that of writing plays—if not more important. As always, the conjunction of great acting with great drama made great theatre.

French actors, however, were subject to a constant influence that was not available to those in England: Italian *commedia* players were almost continuously performing in Paris and other parts of France. We have seen that with these players acting was a highly skilled and professional calling; and Molière had a part of his training with Fiorilli, one of the best of the *commedia* actors. A great deal of the credit for transforming native French actors from mere jugglers and rope dancers to performers skilled in characterization and projection belongs to the Italian companies that toured in France.

Actors of the early French companies in Paris assumed characters taken from the *commedia* repertoire. In the company at the Hôtel de Bourgogne Gros-Guillaume played Pantalone parts; Gaultier-Garguille, those of The Doctor; and Turlupin, the Harlequin roles (figure 77). The Players of the Prince of Orange, whose leading player was Montdory, had Jadot as their Doctor, and Jodelet as a Harlequin. Throughout the century, the *commedia* influence was to be a potent one.

Another great difference between French and English acting companies was that in France, from the first, women played the women's parts, and there was no particular prejudice against the practice. There was one exception, however. It was the custom for men, using

76 Torelli design showing scene change
This interesting pair of prints shows a basic principle for transforming
scenes. Notice that the downstage décor, consisting of wing flats
and borders, remains constant; compare the doorways and urns in the two
sketches. The upstage flats forming the perspective, and the backdrop,
are removed, so that a new backdrop, a sea effect, and a cloud
machine can appear. The costumes are also interesting, especially
the animated satyr in the first scene. See figure 49.
(Harvard Theatre Collection)

a falsetto voice, to play the roles of character women; Alizon early
played these parts with Montdory; Beauval was hired by Molière
for the same kind of parts. It is said that the practice was instituted
because French actresses, whatever their age or personal appearance,
assumed themselves to be young and beautiful and would play only
leading roles. But whatever the reason, we can judge of the effectiveness of the practice in the delight with which modern audiences greet
Charley's Aunt, though this is frankly a masquerade which the spectators share,. and so cannot have quite the same effect as serious
female impersonation. The women were almost without exception
married to actors who were also members of the company. Usually
the couple was hired as a unit. Sometimes it was the woman who
was sought, and the husband came along as a necessary adjunct;
sometimes it was the other way around. Though most of the women
on the stage were married, they were invariably called "Mademoi-
selle," using sometimes their own surnames, sometimes those of their
husbands.

The men usually assumed stage names. Molière was legally J. B.
Poquelin; Duparc was René Berthelot; Montfleury was Zacharie
Jacob; and the long list of actors whose stage names began with
"Belle" or "Beau" (beautiful)—Bellerose, Beauchâteau, for example
—evidences the belief that there was much in a name. Sometimes,

but rarely, the men used their own names, as did Joseph Béjart and LaGrange.

Companies of shareholders

The acting companies were closely knit and hard-working units. All persons designated as "actors" were shareholders in the enterprise; other functionaries received fixed salaries. Each company started with a fixed number of shares; the youngest and least efficient members were awarded a fourth of a share; the intermediate class had half a share; the mature and leading actors had each a full share. In addition to his share, or part thereof, each actor received a small remittance to pay for the expense of lighting and heating his dressing room. The division of the income to the shareholders was made after each performance, every player having the right to be present. Three of these were designated treasurer, secretary, and controller. To them fell the actual work. The first administered the reserve fund which paid fees, expenses, and debts; the second kept the records of payments to actors who held shares; the third, as we would say, audited the accounts of the other two.

The paid functionaries, whose salaries were by the day, the week, or the month, and the monies for which were subtracted from income before the shares were divided, included several people. There was the porter, the ticket seller, the box openers, and the door keepers. Outside employees included a tallow chandler, a printer, and a bill sticker. Non-acting employees for the stage proper included a copyist who wrote out the parts and acted as prompter and archivist for the company; a stage manager who might also, on occasion, play small parts; and a designer, who sometimes worked with a mechanic and who not only produced all the scenery for the plays but decorated the auditorium as well. He had to provide his own candle snuffers, and could claim all the candle ends as a supplement to his income.

The playwright was sometimes a shareholding actor, as was Molière. When the playwright was not an actor or a regular member of the company, he was sometimes awarded a share for the run of his play; sometimes he was given a flat payment. He usually helped to cast and direct his play; after it had been accepted by the company, they assembled to hear him read it. The distribution of parts was by mutual agreement, although we may be sure that in many instances the final decision was far from mutual.

Rehearsals began after the actors felt sure of their lines; the playwright, along with the more skilled members of the company, worked out the stage business and the interpretation of parts.

77 *Early actors at the Hôtel de Bourgogne*
Above, Agnan Sarat appears here in a farce with a milkmaid and
Harlequin. He was a very popular farce player. The Italian *commedia*
characters were a continuing influence throughout this period.
Below, the most famous of all the French farce players were this trio:
Turlupin, Gautier Garguille, and Gros Guillame. Each essayed roles in
serious drama as well, the first being Henri le Grand (or Belleville,
as he called himself when playing serious plays), the second Hugues
Guéru (Fléchelles), the third Robert Guérin. It was in their farce roles
that they were most popular. Turlupin wore the mask and costume of
the Italian *commedia* Brighella; the trademark of Gautier Garguille
was a pointed beard and a black cap; Gros Guillame made the most of
his portliness by wearing two belts, one low and one high, and
powdered his round face. When he died in 1648 it was said that "farce came
down with him." (Bibliothèque Nationale; Harvard Theatre Collection)

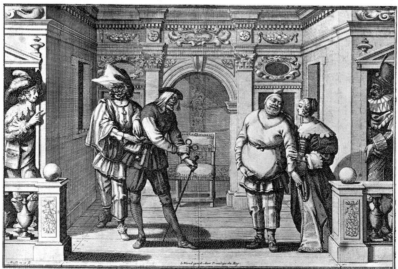

A final, and very important office in the company, was that of the "orator," who was essentially the company manager. He called the meetings of the company, composed the poster for the coming attractions, and addressed the audience at each performance, attempting by his cleverly worded epilogue speech to entice the spectators back for the next offering of the company.

Players were trained within the company itself, or new players were recruited from the provincial companies or other Parisian troupes. It was the custom, upon the retirement of one of the older actors, that the recruit taking his place pay him a pension. The company at the Hôtel de Bourgogne had a specially established pension plan; Molière's troupe eventually set up one also. Another interesting custom was that upon the death of one of the troupe the remaining members made a sizable payment to the nearest living relative as a token of appreciation.

Though there was no great vogue for companies of child actors, as there had been in England, at least one of these had some small success—The Little Actors of the Dauphin under the enterprising direction of an ex-organist from Troyes, one Raisin by name. From its ranks came one of the great actors of the century, Michel Boyron, called Baron. Early an orphan of two Hôtel de Bourgogne players, he grew to effect a stylistic change in the acting of tragedy which Molière worked in comedy but could not achieve in tragedy. Floridor, as well, who acted first with the Marais and then at the Hôtel de Bourgogne, seems also to have had a quiet, authoritative style in tragedy which won the admiration of Molière.

But the approved style of tragic acting—Baron and Floridor excepted—was a kind of chanting declamation, with great bravura exhibitions at the "tirades" or important passages. Such was the acting of Montfleury, of Bellerose, of Montdory, of Mlle. Champmeslé, and of practically all the tragedians of the Hôtel de Bourgogne where tragedy was most famous and most successful. Molière was naturally and artistically opposed to this style of playing. He sponsored and trained his company in a more natural delivery. He abjured attitudinizing and exaggerated delivery, and had his comedies played in an unaffected and lively way. This more natural style worked well in comedy; but when Molière tried it in tragedy, he was completely without success in unseating the prevailing heroic style. Perhaps his own lack of skill in the writing and playing of tragedy foreordained the defeat, for when Baron, who had at one time been a member of Molière's troupe, applied Molière's method to tragedy—some years after the playwright's death—he was forceful enough and skillful enough as a tragic actor to make it acceptable.

By the close of the century the economic position of actors was secure. Many of them had gained wealth and fame; their social position was often enviable, though anomalous. Honors were frequently their lot; they received money grants, special annuities, and such distinctions as the King himself standing godfather to the firstborn son of Molière and Armande Béjart. Often their professional association had a life-time's duration, as Molière and the Béjart family: Madeleine, Joseph, Geneviève, Louis, and the young Armande. Many of them lived most circumspectly; yet, as we have said, the Church classed them as infamous, and the priest sent for at Molière's death refused him the last rites of the Church because he was an actor. His scant and secret burial was in Church grounds only because the King himself interposed.

Summary

The greatest period of French theatre coincided, as did those of England and Spain, with a period of great national consciousness. It was, however, more influenced by Greek and Roman models than its neighbors to the north and to the south. It did succeed, nevertheless, in domesticating both classic tragedy and Italian comedy to a degree that made the former, if not equally great with its ancient predecessor, at least of an intrinsic Frenchness that had widespread subsequent influence. French comedy, eclipsing its Italian model, has, in Molière, a model of perfection for the world.

Its theatre, however, did not become the great popular institution which it was in England and in Spain, for theatre in France in the seventeenth century was, for the most part, the diversion of nobles and the well-to-do. But it did produce the most significant dramatic literature in French theatrical history; its comedy is the best in the world's dramatic literature, and its tragedy—carefully controlled in form and material—is the finest achievement in neoclassical drama. Many subsequent generations of French playwrights were to live in the shadow of this greatness.

Seventeenth century French theatre established women as professional actresses on an equal footing with men. It initiated revolutionary acting styles. It developed a system for the protection of retired actors.

In the field of production, it brought the proscenium arch with its picture-frame stage into general use, and popularized the conception of a separated audience viewing a series of scenes which changed as they watched. By the end of the seventeenth century, French theatre exhibited practically all the attributes of modern theatre, in essence at least; surely, it set a production style which would not be unseated for almost two centuries. It developed elaborate staging effects and multitudinous quantities of machinery to operate them. It emphasized extravagant costuming, and an integration of song and dance into the performance. Finally, of course, it saw the beginning of the first national theatre in the Western world, the Comédie Française. The effulgence of the *Roi Soleil* created a brilliant society; theatre, which was so much a part of that society, reflected its brilliance.

10

THE RESTORATION IN ENGLAND

The Puritan Revolution was fought not only against the King, but also against theatre; but the theatre was never so finally and roundly defeated as the King. The skirmishes and battles were equally protracted and bitter, but the growth of the Elizabethan–Jacobean drama was so hardy and so dear to so many Englishmen that it never completely died. Ordinance after ordinance was passed against stage plays, but there was hardly a year in London from 1642 to 1660 when plays were not being given. The records are full of recurrent raids by the soldiers of Parliament, the seizure of players and their goods, the ransacking of playhouses and their forcible demolition, and the jailing of theatre people. But these very records show that the Puritans had not succeeded in destroying theatrical activity.

It is true that dramatic activities were illegal; players were once more branded rogues and vagabonds, as well as suffering the much more serious charge of infamy. But incarcerations, floggings, and brandings had no lasting effects. There were always those of the King's party to be played for, always a sizable segment of the population willing to risk inconvenience and prosecution to enjoy theatre. The King's Players had gone with the King to Oxford; other English actors formed the English Company for the Prince of Wales in Paris; others played the English provinces; still others toured the Continent, particularly in Germany and the Netherlands. Some remained in London, to play when and where they could. Parliament was constantly being petitioned in their behalf: Why should these honest artists be deprived of their means of making a living? Why should their families—honest citizens, all—suffer deprivation by governmental action? This is the general tenor of all of these petitions. But they were of little avail.

Still, at least one of the playhouses seems to have survived the depredations of soldiers intact. The Red Bull evidently escaped all the military wrecking parties, may have been roofed over, and continued in sporadic operation throughout the period of the Commonwealth. In 1661, after the throne had been reestablished, Samuel Pepys writes of attending performances at the Red Bull. The private theatres of Salisbury Court and the Cockpit in Drury Lane, dismantled by the soldiers in 1649, were quickly rehabilitated and continued in use after the Restoration. But the other great playhouses of Jacobean London were effectively destroyed. The Globe and the Blackfriars were both torn down, one in 1644 and the other in 1655, to make way for tenements; the Fortune did not survive the wreckings of 1649. The Hope reverted to bear baiting, and both bears and house were destroyed in 1655. The great wooden masque house at Whitehall, designed and built by Inigo Jones, was torn down in 1645; the other Jones-designed theatre at court, the Cockpit, survived but housed no performances until the court was reinstalled.

The theatrical fare presented during the Commonwealth was most likely to be rewritten scenes from the older plays, which were called "drolls," and which were sandwiched in between rope dancing, sword tricks, and like secondary fare. Frequently enough, however, whole plays were given, sometimes even new ones, as was the performance of Killigrew's *Claracilla* in 1652 in Gibbon's Tennis Court near Lincoln's Inn Fields. This was, of course, raided, and the performers brought to justice.

During the Commonwealth Gibbon's Tennis Court also housed a performance presented by the devoted adventurer Sir William Davenant. He was responsible for the first legal performance under the Commonwealth, and it is he who figures so largely in Restoration theatre. This thrice-married ex-Poet Laureate, who in 1639 had been given a patent to build a theatre in London, had fought with the Royalist forces. He had been imprisoned in the Tower but was released in 1652. He lost no time in recouping his fortunes by a marriage of convenience, and in making friends with the government in power. By the time he returned from a trip to France late in 1655, he was married to his third wife, and had a sizable theatrical enterprise operating. Taking up residence in Rutland House, he publicly

78 *The Elizabethan playhouse*
      in the Restoration
Sketch from Kirkman's *Drolls,*
published in 1672, illustrating
the inside of the Red Bull playhouse
and the leading actor in each droll,
with Robert Coxe playing
the Simpleton. Here again is the
persistent platform stage,
with some of the audience standing
in the pit, some seated in a gallery.
The candelabra would seem
to indicate that the house was
roofed over. (Henry E. Huntington
Library and Art Gallery)

invited, in May, 1656, a paying audience to see *The First Day's Entertainment,* a "representation" with music and oratory "after the manner of the Ancients." It included a eulogy of the Lord Protector. By September, he was offering, in the hall at Rutland House, the first English opera, *The Siege of Rhodes,* with a minimum of music, no dancing at all, and none of the spectacular mechanical effects that marked Continental operatic presentations. He spent the next year in a series of moves to effect official sanction of public presentations, and by July of 1658, his opera was established in the Cockpit in Drury Lane, with new scenes, costumes, and machines—the theatre was legally open again in London. He continued with other similar presentations, and when it became apparent that the Restoration was inevitable he hurried to Paris to consolidate his position with Charles

II, thus becoming one of the two patentees for the London theatres of the Restoration.

Theatre an exclusive entertainment

The theatre of Restoration England was but distantly related to its great predecessor, even though one of its most prominent operators, this same Sir William Davenant, had been a theatre figure prior to the days of the Commonwealth. So agile was he in trimming his bark to the prevailing winds that he became the herald of the new rather than the preserver of the old. Through a series of Machiavellian moves, he effectively killed off all competition and with the courtier Thomas Killigrew established a complete monopoly of London theatrical activity. This Restoration theatre was by no means the great popular institution which Shakespeare's contemporaries loved, but rather was the exclusive activity of an exclusive society, pandering to the tastes and mirroring the activities of a highly artificial court society.

Owing their very existence to his Majesty, King Charles II, Davenant with his Duke's Company, and Killigrew with his King's Company, conducted their operations with a view to pleasing the court. If the public were also pleased, well and good. But they were not the main consideration. Restoration audiences were chiefly aristocrats and those pretending to be their associates. Theatre was one of the social activities of a circle brilliantly delineated in Pepys' famous *Diary*—a pleasure-loving, amoral people, contemptuous of what they conceived to be a narrow Puritan view of the world, and determined to enjoy all the sensual aspects of existence. Like children at a perpetual recess they thumbed their noses at the disciplinarians, exaggerated the manners and habits they had acquired in their French exile—and eventually were submerged by a newly developing society.

Charles II was very fond of theatre. As we have noted, he maintained, for a time, a company of English players while he was in exile, and he was a frequent spectator at theatrical performances in France, the Netherlands, and Germany. Upon his return to England, he did not confine his attendance to court performances, as his predecessors had done, but went with his favorites to performances at the public theatres where he had a royal box. Such attendance was frequent, and as may be imagined was a significant drawing card for the great and the near-great. Even when the King was not in attendance, the spectators were chiefly of the court party, both ladies and gentlemen in the extravagant dress of the time. People went to be seen quite as much as to see, and a great deal of socializing went on before, after, and during the performance.

Advertising was done by playbills which were posted, thrown into carriages, and delivered at the houses of the gentry. The theatres were opened at one o'clock for performances which began generally at three-thirty, servants being sent to hold seats for their masters since there was no reserved-seat policy. By 1699, performance time had advanced to five o'clock, by 1705 it was five-thirty. The play was always preceded by a series of three "Musicks"; there was music between the acts; and the performance was followed by an afterpiece with music.

The cheapest seats were in the upper gallery (quite the opposite of Shakespeare's house); the most expensive in the first gallery, or row of boxes. The pit, now provided with backless benches, was the resort of the gallants, the critics, and the poets, and was often the scene of brawls and duels. Theatre police, reminiscent of the Roman custom, were sometimes installed to prevent frays. The royal box was directly opposite the stage, with others on its level being used by court ladies and gentlemen. The more conservative playgoers occupied the middle gallery, which was also in the middle price range.

Tickets were sold in advance, the usual type being a brass check which indicated the part of the house for which it was issued. For special performances printed paper tickets were occasionally used. Actors and playwrights were given bone passes for which there was no charge. Gallants attempted, as a matter of sport, to evade the admission price and they often succeeded. It was the custom to make no charge for people who came merely to hear the music and to see the first act of the play; footmen were also admitted to the upper gallery for the fifth act, and were not charged. These privileges were widely abused, and toward the end of the century a "numberer" was installed in one of the boxes, whose duty it was to see that all those who saw the whole play had paid their admission. New plays usually rated double admission prices for their first nights; operas often charged three times as much.

The French custom of seating a selected portion of the audience on the stage itself did not become a practice in England until the century was almost over, chiefly because Charles II opposed it; once it became entrenched, however, it lasted quite as long as it did in France. The English fops had a special corner of the pit, near the stage, where they behaved quite as odiously as their French counterparts and as their Elizabethan forbears had behaved on Shakespeare's stage.

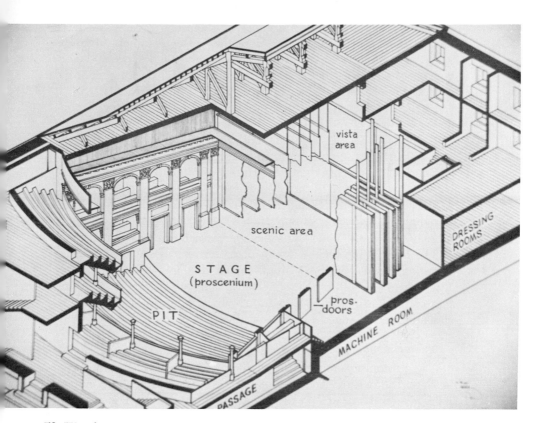

79 Wren's Drury Lane
This reconstruction by Richard Leacroft, of the second Drury Lane
opened in 1674, clearly shows the broad and deep apron stage
(proscenium here) which was the most typical characteristic of
Restoration and later English theatres. Actors entered from one of the
four proscenium doors. The wing-flat system behind the proscenium arch
functioned largely as a scenic background for the action. The pit
has backless benches; there is a double row of boxes and a gallery on the
third level opposite the stage. The decoration is simple and
classical in line. (Richard Leacroft Theatre Collection)

Refreshments, in the form of oranges, apples, and sweetmeats,
were sold in the theatres by persons holding concessions from the
management. Orange Moll at the Theatre Royal was the most famous
of these—the actress Nell Gwynn had once been her employee.
   Gentlemen of the audience frequented the backstage areas, visiting in the dressing rooms of the actors and actresses, and—one must

suppose—generally made nuisances of themselves. Actresses were new to the English stage, and were the center of much attention. They were greatly sought after by the young blades, were the recipients of numerous and costly gifts, and moved in the highest social circles; one of them became mistress to the King.

English audiences saw performances of several visiting French acting companies and Italian *commedia* players (the famous Fiorilli was a member of one of these), both at the Cockpit in Drury Lane and at court. These performances were generally much admired.

Charles II fitted out the Great Hall at Whitehall as a theatre, and there, as well as at the Cockpit-in-Court, he invited a chosen few to see the command performances of native and foreign players. More frequently, however, as we have noted, he went in person to the public playhouses; the court activities were chiefly balls and maskings.

The Restoration theatre was a place of business, of gossip, of assignation, of style, and, as it often seemed, only incidentally of drama. It was an effete culture that spawned this exotic growth, an importation of foreign modes and attitudes which would inevitably be assimilated and changed by native habits.

Neoclassical conventions preside

The Restoration marks the beginning of the neoclassical period in English literature, and as in France the main Greek and Roman influence on the drama was in the writing of tragedy. The works of Shakespeare and his contemporaries were considered to be reprehensible, at the least, for their lack of the classical unities; their plays, when presented in Restoration theatres, were considerably revised and rewritten. The Fool was excised from *Lear*, the Gravediggers from *Hamlet*; *Macbeth* was embellished with singing and dancing; *Romeo and Juliet* was given a happy ending. Passages from *Henry IV, Henry V, Henry VI* and *Richard II* were cannibalized and transformed into a new *Richard III*. How far this revision extended has been the study of modern scholars, and several curiously "rational" scripts have been published.

Sometimes the Restoration writers of tragedy took old stories and retold them in the new style, as Dryden did in *All for Love, or the World Well Lost* (1677), in which he rewrote the story of Antony and Cleopatra to the taste of his times. Although Dryden's play suffers greatly from comparison with that of Shakespeare, it is perhaps the best of the tragedies of the Restoration, illustrating how a playwright of real genius can overcome the most unseemly of obstacles. Probably the most popular of the Poet Laureate's tragedies was the *Conquest of Granada* (1670) which appeared in two parts of five acts each; his heavily heroic play of five years later, *Aureng-Zebe,* was also quite popular. Dryden wrote operas and comedies as well as tragedies, but the tragedies are his best work. Except for *All for Love,* which is written in blank verse, his tragedies are in the heroic couplet, a somewhat less than supple instrument for dramatic dialogue. Nevertheless, they achieved a kind of nobility which, although not on a level with Racine and Corneille, are still touched with genius.

Rant, bluster, and hyperbole characterized the typical heroic tragedy, with an emphasis upon the juxtaposition of love and honor between which the hero must painfully choose. Nathaniel Lee (*ca.,* 1653–1692) and John Banks (*ca.,* 1650–1706) were popular in this form in their own day; Banks perhaps deserves some permanent notice for his use of recent history as subject matter in *Virtue Betrayed* (based on the life of Anne Boleyn) and *The Island Queens* (about Mary of Scotland). The most popular writer of tragedy, next to Dryden, was Thomas Otway, whose many plays on classical subjects were produced between 1675 and 1682. Two of his plays, *The Orphan* (1680) and *Venice Preserved* (1682), continued to be popular with acting companies and with audiences until well into the nineteenth century.

Restoration tragedy, however, was almost no more than an intellectual exercise and a fashionable obeisance to the neoclassical spirit. It is not often read today, and less often produced.

Restoration comedy noteworthy

The best achievement of Restoration dramatists was in the field of comedy. Nowhere else in English literature (if we except, perhaps, Noël Coward), are there plays like these—hard, brilliant, infinitely accomplished, and infinitely remote from the life of the entire population except for that of a very narrow social circle. These are not the penetrating, satirical comedies of Molière, with their telling portraits of familiar social types. Nor are they the warmly human characterizations of Dekker or Greene, not to mention Shakespeare himself. The dramatis personae are drawn from a very limited social circle, the dialogue has a witty brilliance, and the plots are chiefly boudoir intrigues.

There are echoes of Ben Jonson in the names of the characters: Sir Frederick Frolick, Sir Fopling Flutter, Lady Flippant, Lady Wishfort, Mrs. Fainall, Millamant. But the dramatists' treatment of these characters has none of the undertone of criticism that the older dramatist uses. If we may suppose a single attitude on the part of the

80 *The Duke's Theatre, Dorset Garden*
Left, exterior view; right, interior, looking toward the stage. These two
prints, from Settle's *Empress of Morocco,* show the much more
elaborate Dorset Garden theatre. The music room is above the stage,
flanked by full relief statues of Thalia and Melpomene, and there is a
suggestion of proscenium doors to either side. The stage is raked,
and the decoration is rich and intricate.
(Henry E. Huntington Library and Art Gallery)

Restoration dramatists, it is one of objectivity in the presentation of
social types drawn quite unapologetically from their surrounding
society. The best of these plays are our best examples of the comedy
of manners—the clash of character on character in highly selected
situations. Perhaps no other society than that of the Restoration could
have produced such playwrights as George Etherege, William Wycherley, and William Congreve. At least no other society has. Others

were writing, of course. There was a prodigious amount of dramatic writing going on. But these three are the epitome of what we mean when we speak of the unique quality of Restoration comedy.

George Etherege, fast-living gallant and man-about-town who spent his retirement in Paris, preceded that retirement by a series of plays which took London by storm. The earliest appeared in 1664, *The Comical Revenge, or Love in a Tub*. The best of those that followed were *She Would If She Could* (1668), and *The Man of Mode, or Sir Fopling Flutter* (1676).

The second of the three, William Wycherley, had been educated in Paris, and was renowned there as a wit in the circle of the bluestocking daughter of Madame de Rambouillet, the group which Molière had so neatly pilloried. His first London production was *Love in a Wood* in 1671, which he followed a year later with *The Gentleman Dancing Master*. The most famous of his plays is *The Country Wife* (1675), in which he contrasts the provincialism of Margery Pinchwife with the London society into which she marries; neither milieu comes off very admirably. In his last play, *The Plain Dealer* (1676), he exhibits some impatience with the frivolity of his fashionable world, an apt prelude to his own imprisonment for debt and an endless series of lawsuits.

The best of the Restoration writers was William Congreve, whose plays today, in capable hands, are sheer delight. He belongs to the last decade of the century, and marks the culmination of this type of comedy. Not only does he exhibit supreme genius in the writing of comic dialogue, but he also achieves subtle and interesting characterization. Few heroines are so completely delightful as the Millamant of *The Way of the World* (1700), Congreve's last and best play. Millamant and Mirabell are the Restoration descendants of the delightful Shakespearean couple, Beatrice and Benedick (*Much Ado About Nothing*). Only a shade less successful are Prue and Ben, Valentine and Angelica of *Love for Love* (1695). Congreve's two other plays of note, *The Old Bachelor* (1693) and *The Double Dealer* (1693), are hardly less scintillating. Completely without any obvious intention to reform the society or the people whom he observed and used in his plays, Congreve's work is the epitome of the uninhibited, completely infectious gaiety that pervades Restoration comedy.

Surrounding these luminaries of Restoration comedy were many other writers, such as the versatile John Dryden whose most successful comedy was a froth entitled *Marriage à la Mode* (1672); Sir John Vanbrugh whose *The Relapse* (1696) was quite successfully revived in the twentieth century; Charles Sedley, Thomas Shadwell,

Mrs. Aphra Behn (our first successful female playwright), and finally, George Farquhar, writing at the turn of the century. While Farquhar belongs to the same tradition as Wycherley and Congreve, he marks the end of the type, and points forward to the next period and the sentimentality of the eighteenth century. His most enduringly interesting plays are *The Recruiting Officer* (1706) and *The Beaux Stratagem* (1707). Forces had been at work which doomed the society of Charles II, and never again would its amoral glitter light the English theatrical sky.

Beginnings of modern theatre architecture

The Restoration witnessed the final passing of the Elizabethan playhouse, and the establishment of an essentially modern theatre building. Even the few Elizabethan theatres that had not been ravaged during the Commonwealth met their end during the Restoration.

We have seen that the Red Bull (figure 78), reaching far back (in name at least) into the Elizabethan period as a playhouse converted from an inn, was still in operation during the early years of the Restoration. It had been built in 1607, and although some scholars are inclined to believe that it was roofed over in its later days, the weight of evidence seems to indicate its continuance as an open-roofed, standing-pit theatre such as Shakespeare knew. After Davenant and Killigrew succeeded in enforcing their monopoly, it ceased to be used as a playhouse.

The Phoenix or the Cockpit-in-Drury Lane, one of the private pre-Commonwealth houses, was in litigation during most of the Commonwealth period, and at the Restoration in 1660 was in lease to John Rhodes whose company of young players were taken over by Davenant to form The Duke's Company. Though the house had been dismantled by the Puritans in 1649, it had been refurbished, and had been used by Davenant for his *Siege of Rhodes* in 1658, with its scenes and machines presumably after the French fashion in stage settings. It was later used by troupes of visiting French and Italian comedians.

Another surviving Elizabethan private theatre was Salisbury Court in Fleet Street. Its interior also had been razed in 1649, but on the eve of the Restoration it had been fitted up once more and was sporadically in use by Davenant, George Jolly, and William Beeston until it was utterly destroyed in the Great Fire of London in 1666.

The Red Bull, the Phoenix, Salisbury Court—what echoes of a greater age must have resounded in those old walls as they housed a newer day! But newer walls soon took their places.

The patents obtained by Davenant and Killigrew in July of 1660 empowered each to build a theatre and raise a company of actors. The actors they took from the extant companies. Killigrew chose the company that was then performing at the Red Bull under Major Mohun, who had been an actor of note in Jacobean times and an officer in the Royalist army. Davenant, as noted above, took a group of younger actors from John Rhodes' Phoenix. Davenant occupied Salisbury Court, and Killigrew took his company to Gibbons' Tennis Court which had, during the preceding decade, been converted into a theatre.

As French actors had earlier discovered, a tennis court could be made into quite a presentable theatre; Gibbons', built on a plot of ground about 230 feet long by about 160 feet wide, had been provided with a stage equipped with an architectural setting similar to that of the Elizabethan theatres. It is an interesting speculation (though probably impossible to prove) that this so-called Elizabethan manner entailed the seating of the audience on two sides of the stage, with mansions or doors at either end of the transverse axis of the playing area. Killigrew occupied this house until he moved into the first Theatre Royal, between Bridges Street and Drury Lane, in 1663—the first new theatre of the Restoration.

Davenant, meanwhile, took lease on a somewhat smaller, unconverted tennis court near Lincoln's Inn Fields, called Lisle's; while his company was performing at Salisbury Court, he fitted it out with scenes and machines in the best modern manner, moving his company there in June, 1661, and calling it the Duke's Playhouse. It was approximately thirty by seventy-five feet, and, in order to provide for the scenes he wished, Davenant had to take over some adjoining property for use as a scene house. Davenant's company remained in this remodeled house until some years after his death in 1668, not moving into their sumptuous new building in Dorset Garden until November of 1671.

It was primarily because Davenant's newly converted theatre in Lisle's Tennis Court was a formidable rival to his old-style playhouse at Gibbons' that Killigrew rushed completion of the first Theatre Royal, into which his company moved in May of 1663. This house, popularly called the first Drury Lane, was fifty-eight by 112 feet, and was built at an approximate cost of twenty-four hundred pounds. We know very little of the design of the house, except that Pepys speaks disparagingly of the fact that the music was "below," by which he perhaps means some sort of an arrangement approximating our present-day orchestra pit.

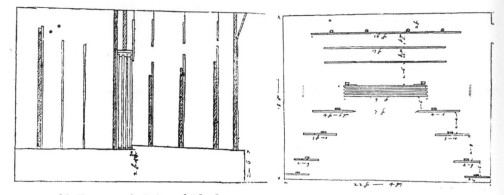

81 *Davenant's* **Seige of Rhodes**
Left, a cross-section of the set; right, the floor plan. These two
sketches show the elements and disposition of the "scenes" which
Davenant carried over into the Restoration from the pre-Commonwealth
practice of Inigo Jones. Flat wings in perspective and a backdrop were
to remain standard in stage setting for a very long period of time.
(British Museum)

Killigrew's theatre was burned to the ground in a disastrous fire on
January 25, 1672, and a new house, designed by Sir Christopher
Wren, was built on the same plot and opened in 1674 (figure 79). If
we accept the ingenious suggestion of Allardyce Nicoll (*History of
Restoration Drama,* 1923) that an unmarked plan for a theatre, discovered at Oxford, is indeed the first Drury Lane, then it, too, was
designed by Wren and was a very distinctive house. The plan shows
a rapidly sloping pit with rows of seats arranged in a semicircle,
ending in a gallery about midway in the auditorium, which again
ascends rapidly to a second gallery. A continuation of the circle
formed by the last row of pit seats forms a wide proscenium with
what appear to be four doors on each side. The deep apron is backed
by a raked stage whose total depth, from the front of the apron to the
back wall is slightly less than half the total length of the building. If
this is, indeed, the design for the first Drury Lane, it is radically different from the house built in 1674, into which the company moved
after a temporary sojourn in Lisle's Tennis Court.

The second Drury Lane, built at an approximate cost of four
thousand pounds, was fifty-eight by 140 feet. Again the stage area
covered about half the length of the building, with an apron as deep
as the stage behind the proscenium. Both apron and stage are slightly
raked, and a wing system is indicated for the stage furnishings. There
are two proscenium doors on either side of the apron, with a box

above each. The sloping pit is supplied with backless benches and is surrounded by two tiers of boxes, with an additional upper gallery at the end opposite the stage. The decoration indicated is not ornate, and, indeed, contemporary writers are one in declaring that the second Drury Lane was much plainer than the theatre at Dorset Garden. Three floors of dressing rooms are provided behind the stage. When the then-manager Christopher Rich remodeled the inside of the building in 1696, he shortened the apron by four feet, converted the downstage proscenium doors into boxes, and installed additional benches in the pit.

The Duke's Theatre in Dorset Garden (figure 80), opened in 1671, was evidently much more elaborate. It was 140 by 57 feet, and cost nearly nine thousand pounds. Though no floor plan has been discovered, contemporary references indicate a house arrangement similar to that at the second Drury Lane. A series of engravings published in 1673, with the text of Settle's *Empress of Morocco*, tells us much of the stage design. From the elaborately decorated proscenium, a half-roof extends out over the apron; above this is a pair of windows flanked by full relief figures of Thalia and Melpomene. The windows open into a room behind, which was evidently the music room—Pepys' "music above" is further evidence. The stage seems to be raked and supplied with grooved wings and shutters as was the Drury Lane. Again, there are proscenium doors with boxes above them, evidently two on each side. The house is decorated with statues and busts in relief and much more gorgeous ornamentation.

These were the theatres of the Restoration, influenced in their decoration and use by those of France, but also incorporating traditionally and peculiarly English characteristics, the deep apron and the proscenium doors and boxes. The characteristics of this stage shaped the kind of acting seen upon it as well as the plays written for it.

Staging flexible and effective

Some continuity of Restoration stage design with that of pre-Commonwealth times is evidenced in the person of John Webb, who had been assistant to Inigo Jones; Webb designed the settings for the *Siege of Rhodes* when Davenant presented it (figure 81). He also redesigned the two court theatres, The Cockpit and the Great Hall, laying out both the stage plans and the house. Plans and sketches for the *Siege of Rhodes* and for a court performance of Orrery's *Mustapha* reveal that he was following the ideas of Inigo Jones in court presentations. The designs show a highly decorated proscenium arch, backed by a series of wing flats and shutters. The *Mustapha* plan indicates a sky cloth from the top of the proscenium to a lower point in the back wall; the musicians were placed in an elevated gallery behind the back wall. In both designs the stage is raked to increase the illusion of forced perspective.

This plan, in essence, is the one followed throughout the period in practically all theatrical productions. As we have seen, the stages of the public theatres built during the Restoration were provided with grooves to receive the wing flats and shutters which formed the staple set. Both the patent houses had stock sets, one for tragedy and one for comedy. That for tragedy included a grove, a temple, a palace hall; for comedy there was a bedroom, a boudoir, a park. These were painted on flats, and in the comedies the pictured representations of places in London aspired to be as accurate as possible.

The operation of this set was easy and quick. After the "Third Musick" the actor speaking the prologue emerged from one of the proscenium doors onto the apron, spoke his lines, exited, and the front curtain rose. It was generally the festoon kind of curtain. Entrances and exits of the actors were usually to the apron from the proscenium doors, the upstage area serving as a kind of background. Sometimes the actors went within the scene by moving upstage and having the side flats click together to cover them. Sometimes scenes and players were revealed by an opposite arrangement. When the play was over, the epilogue was spoken while the curtain was still up. If the play was a tragedy, then it would be followed by a jig or comic afterpiece. Then the curtain would fall. Many stage directions in scripts of the time indicate that the scene "draws off," or "draws over," thus showing the method of operation. There were no waits between scenes; the action was continuous as on Shakespeare's stage.

Sometimes this flat- and back-shutter system included relieves, or set pieces in three dimensions. Sometimes the flats themselves were cut out to form trees, temples, and so forth, revealing the backing behind them. Sometimes they were transparencies, through which a back scene was dimly shown. Moonlight effects were generally achieved in this manner. For special performances, new scenes were sometimes prepared, and, by 1690, an act-drop curtain made its appearance in cases where the element of surprise was important in revealing a scene, or when there was a particularly difficult change to be made. These act-drop curtains were not popular in the public theatres, and their use was generally confined to the opera. An interesting and peculiar convention of the Restoration theatre was the green baize carpet of tragedy. For the presentation of tragic plays the floor of the stage was covered with green baize—a very useful convention in preserving the costumes of the actors who expired in the course of the performance.

Though most plays were given with a minimum of emphasis upon elaborate settings, stage effects were as popular as they have always been with theatre audiences. Stages were equipped with traps for graves and for the emergence and disappearance of ghosts and the like. Flying arrangements were made for such characters as the witches in *Macbeth*. Lifelike dummies of bodies and heads were made for tortures and dismemberments. Blood effects were eagerly worked over to achieve a sense of realism. The fires painted on the scenes were augmented by fireworks and smoke. Lightning and thunder were manufactured. Ascents and descents were arranged on movable platforms. Cloud effects were popular. Restoration staging was a curious mixture of the real and the conventional. Chairs, tables, and books were often painted on the flats; but when a character was stabbed, he had to bleed what looked like real blood.

Since Restoration theatres were entirely roofed in, lighting presented a problem. The general practice was to have both stage and house well lit by many chandeliers throughout the performance. Pepys complains of the glare of these lights when he was sitting in the gallery. The stage sometimes had a short strip of footlights down center, most frequently candles but sometimes oil lamps. One ingenious arrangement for lowering the lights was the substitution of "floats" for the footlights. These were wicks in cork floating in oil, the whole tank of which could be lowered into a trap. Candles and oil lamps lit the area behind the proscenium. Few changes in lighting were attempted in the course of a performance.

The preferred position for the musicians was backstage or above stage, although at Whitehall there seems to have been some rather clever arrangement to seat them in a pit to one side of the stage on occasion, at its front, or in the end of the gallery nearest the stage, as seemed to suit a particular performance. The prelude, entr'acte, and postlude were played from the designated spot; music called for in the play itself was generally furnished by musicians who came on to the stage in the course of the action.

Restoration staging was a curious compendium of preceding practices both native and foreign. The raked stage, the wing and shutter system in perspective, the flyings, and the front curtain were all imported from Continental practice. Trapdoors had been a part of Elizabethan staging, and the ubiquitous and unique proscenium doors and deep apron were, no doubt, remnants of the forward-

82 *Betterton's Hamlet*
What appears here to be a box set is no doubt an angle-wing flat, its
decoration contemporary with the production and not with the supposed
time of the play. The costumes of Hamlet and his mother are also
of Restoration times; note particularly the wig that Betterton is wearing.
His stance and forceful gesture lend credence to his reputation
as one of the best actors of his time. (Harvard Theatre Collection)

thrusting platform of Shakespeare's day and the doors of his stage house. Or perhaps the doors were derived from the mansions on a transverse stage axis which Shakespeare's stage may have inherited from medieval practice. In any event, the realistic stage effects went back beyond Shakespeare to medieval practices. Thus the Restoration stage was the descendant of differing traditions, all of which were combined to produce a flexible and effective instrument for the plays which were written for it.

Costumes blend many traditions

Restoration practice in costuming descended from the Elizabethans, with a curious admixture of what had been customary in both the public and private theatres and in the court masques.

The Restoration theatre had a costume "à la Turque," which always included a turban and wide trousers, and a costume "à la Romaine," which nodded in the direction of breastplate and short tunic but always included a Restoration wig. In historical plays, the leading characters were apt to be dressed in a reproduction of a known painting of the figure, as Henry VIII was dressed after Holbein's famous portrait, but other characters in the piece would wear the dress of a Restoration courtier.

These slight attempts at accurate costuming were confined to the men; women wore contemporary dress whatever the period of the play. Head feathers were always the sign of heroism and dignity, worn by men and women alike. The tragic actresses were almost universally garbed in black velvet. They had a special appurtenance in the long trains of their gowns which was cared for by a page boy, presumably invisible, who followed the actress about the stage, arranging the folds of the skirt and seeing that the train was well disposed when, as often happened, the action of the play required that the wearer die.

In the comedies, contemporary dress, enriched as much as possible, was usual. The leading characters wore the richest costumes; those less important might be rather indifferently dressed. Often the feminine stars blazed with jewels either borrowed for the occasion, or received as gifts from admirers. Because these costumes were exceedingly expensive they were limited, in the ordinary course of events, to only the most important performers. Where expense was no object, or where costumes were subsidized by a wealthy patron of the court, even the blacksmiths might be clothed in satin. The men almost invariably wore the usual Restoration wig, whatever the part, with the villain wearing a black one. A curious convention of disguise, similar to the Elizabethan "cloak to go invisible in," was the use of an eye patch, which presumably completely disguised the wearer, although he otherwise looked exactly as he had before donning the patch.

A great deal of makeup was employed. False noses, beards, and mustaches were widely used by the men. Powder, rouge, pencil, lip rouge, and the ever-present beauty patch were standard with the women. Colley Cibber once complained that the actresses would use no facial expression because they were afraid they would crack their heavy and stiff makeup. The outstanding exception to this seems to have been the beautiful Elizabeth Barry who evidently customarily wore little or no makeup and thus could use a full measure of facial expression.

However incongruous to modern eyes much of this costuming must seem, it cannot be denied that the general effect was quite a gorgeous one, well fitted to the brilliance of the plays being acted.

Innovations in acting styles

The greatest difference, of course, between acting companies of the Restoration and those before the Commonwealth is that the newer groups included women. The impetus for this came from the Continent, but Restoration managers justified it by the rather specious argument that it was immoral to have men in women's parts. Certainly the inclusion of women in the acting companies allowed dramatists to expand the female roles, and to write in them some of the most brilliant characterizations ever to adorn the English-speaking stage. For here again, as always, playwrights wrote with particular performers in mind, as Araminta, Angelica, and Millamant were created by Congreve for Anne Bracegirdle.

Early in the period, some women's parts were still being played by boys, and throughout the period, children were popular for the prologues and epilogues. One of the most noted of these was a seven-year-old girl who was evidently very effective, even though she could have had little conception of the meaning of the sentences she spoke. The most outstanding of the boy players were Edward Kynaston, whom Pepys praises, and Charles Hart, said to be a grandson of Shakespeare's sister Joan. As these boys outgrew their parts, they were replaced by women. Some performers specialized in tragedy, as did Elizabeth Barry. Some played only comedy roles, as did Anne Bracegirdle, Nell Gwynn, and Cave Underhill. More frequently, however, performers played both tragedy and comedy.

At first the actors who had survived the Commonwealth continued in prominence in the Restoration. Major Michael Mohun was one of these; he had his own company at the reopening of the theatres, and later was chosen by Killigrew to head the King's Company. It was to this company that Nell Gwynn (figure 83) belonged, along with Mistress Knepp (Pepys' friend), and Rebecca Marshall, whose feud with Orange Moll was one of the scandals of the age.

Davenant's rival Duke's Company began with a group of much younger actors, the best of whom was Thomas Betterton (figure 82). His is the greatest name of the period. His Hamlet, played in wig and frock coat, was famous; he supposedly played it as Shakespeare had instructed, having been coached by Davenant, who had the role from Taylor, himself instructed by Shakespeare. In any event, contemporary comments agree that it was a great Hamlet. Practically all the Shakespearean heroes fell within Betterton's compass, and he played the leading roles in the new comedy as well. His style is reputed to have been free of rant and exaggeration and to have been in character throughout. At one point he was sent by Charles II to study French theatre; he returned with some interesting ideas of picturesque and plastic grouping for ensemble playing, no doubt observed at the French opera, and formulated some rules for acting. These are reminiscent of the Elizabethan "rhetoricks" in the careful attention given to the disposition of every part of the body for the achieving of certain emotional effects: eyes uplifted for one effect, downcast for another; head turned left with right hand extended to signify rejection, and so forth. Whatever his technique, and it seems to have been most carefully thought out, the total effect was evidently one of naturalness and rightness. He won great fame in spite of an unprepossessing appearance and a total inability to dance or sing.

His partner in comedy, Anne Bracegirdle (figure 83), was a pleasant singer and a charming dancer, exceedingly comely, and very popular in "breeches parts." She seems to have had that indefinable charm without which no performer rises to greatness.

Actors were trained not only by being taken as apprentices in an established company, but by being enrolled in that peculiar institution of the Restoration, the Nursery, which maintained classes and gave student performances. The history of its establishment leads one to suppose that it was simply Davenant's invention to get rid of a formidable rival in the person of George Jolly, an itinerant English actor who had received permission from Charles II, in the first days of the Restoration, to form an acting company and to present plays in London. How Davenant scotched the plan is a story too long for

247

83 *Two Restoration actresses*
Left, Nell Gwynn as Epilogue to *Sir Patient Fancy;* right, Anne
Bracegirdle as the Indian Queen. In both these costumes, the basic
Restoration silhouette is maintained, an Elizabethan ruff being added to
the first, a feather headdress and fan transforming the second into an
Indian costume. There is also a page, in a curious version of an Indian
headdress, to bear the train of the Queen. (Harvard Theatre Collection)

telling here, but George Jolly ended up as mentor to the fledgling
actors of the Nursery. These students graduated into the established
companies in London, or into touring companies of the provinces,
some, perhaps, as far afield as the Irish Theatre at Dublin (which,
for once, Davenant was unable to control, the managership being
awarded to one John Ogilby).

The companies were run by royal patentees who, under the issued
patents, had great powers. As in the French companies, a specific
number of shares were divided among the actors, but in England the
manager retained as many shares as he could justify. English actresses, unlike the French, were not awarded shares; Davenant main-

tained the actresses in his company from seven shares allotted to him for the purpose; Killigrew paid his actresses as hirelings. Managers were permitted to sell their shares to nontheatrical people—thus beginning the domination of the theatre by businessmen and the subsequent abuse of the managerial system. These nontheatrical participants were called "the adventurers," and often they were all that the name implies. Such an adventurer was the Christopher Rich who took over the management of the United Company in 1693. His sharp practices drove a company of actors headed by Betterton to revolt; they seceded and formed their own theatre under special royal permission, performing once more at the old Lisle's Tennis Court. Abuse of his position as manager had indeed caused the demise of Killigrew's King's Company, and the amalgamation of the two patent houses in 1682.

Since the basis for payment of actors was the division of shares, their incomes were exceedingly variable. These were often augmented by tutoring and by the receipt of gifts. The best of the actors fared well; the others rather poorly. Fixed and occasional expenses, as well as the salaries of nonacting employees, were either paid from the manager's shares, or were deducted before the income was divided among the shareholders. It is interesting to note in some of the documents of the period that the patentee-manager was sometimes called the "Orator," as was the manager of French companies.

We have already spoken of the conviviality between performers and spectators, fostered by the freedom of the playhouses and the narrowness of the social circle from which spectators came. Companies made frequent appearances at court, and the court appeared frequently at the theatres. No such assiduous participation by court amateurs in court performances was evident in the Restoration as had been the case in pre-Commonwealth court circles. Some, indeed, there was, but little in comparison with the older times. Actors approved by a benign court were beginning their climb to the social acceptability that was to lead, almost two hundred years later, to the knighting of Henry Irving.

Summary

Though the Restoration theatre began its decline in 1688, when the Glorious Revolution exiled James II and established William and Mary on the throne, it still had many more brilliant moments. A more telling blow was delivered ten years later when Jeremy Collier launched his indignant diatribe called *A Short View of the Immorality and Profaneness of the English Stage*, which began a series of persecutions that eventually changed the whole character of English theatre. The end of the period may well be marked by the accession of Queen Anne in 1702. She was completely disinterested in the arts, literature, and theatre. That special darling of the court and court society would henceforth have to find a new audience. From this point on we are in a new era, with the middle classes and sentimentality replacing aristocratic flippancy.

But the unique period of the Restoration had, in its short and brilliant career, theatre of no little significance. Though the inspiration for its comedy had come from France, the comedies seen on its stages were not replicas of the French, but rather were imbued with a peculiarly native quality that made them the ultimate achievement in the comedy of manners, never equaled before or since in English dramatic writing. Tragedy, more nearly slavish to foreign models, was less successful, and, save for the genius of Dryden, produced little of note.

Other areas of theatrical activity initiated features that became characteristic of later theatres. Restoration theatre achieved the modernization of audience accommodation with a seated pit, galleries, and boxes. It introduced a new kind of managerial system involving people primarily nontheatrical. It initiated and popularized on the English-speaking stage the innovation of feminine stars. It advanced the complexity of stage design, with emphasis upon a wing-flat system of painted scenes. It standardized the roofed-in theatre building. It established, in the amalgamation of painted settings with the old Elizabethan platform stage, the peculiarly English construction of forestage and proscenium doors which was to remain for many decades the English and American tradition.

Never again would English theatre hold so special a position as it did in the Restoration, but vestiges of Restoration practices were to live on for generations to follow.

DEVELOPMENTS IN ENGLAND
AND AMERICA

We have seen how the English theatre, so vital an expression of English national life in Shakespeare's day, became powdered and perfumed after the French fashion as a result of its long exile during the Commonwealth. Yet even Restoration theatre was not a slavish imitation of its French predecessor. The tragedy of the period, it is true, was more closely akin to Continental ideals and dictums and carried the heroic French genre to a bombastic extreme. But Restoration comedy, while paying lip service to the French, was not the comedy of Molière, the great French master, but a thing apart. In English Restoration comedy, as we have seen, there is none of the satiric import of the French writer. Only its brilliance, its frivolity, its decorativeness is French; it possessed none of the implicit criticism of society which gave the necessary dimension and magnitude to the greatest of French comic dramatists. Indeed, its very amorality, its thoughtlessness, was the cause of its demise, for, as we have also seen, as early as 1698 it was severely taken to task by Jeremy Collier, whose criticism excited irate answers from Congreve, Vanbrugh, and the others. But Collier's criticism was the beginning of the end for the wits of the Restoration.

From the time of the Glorious Revolution which brought in the "bourgeois King" William, a de-emphasis upon the importance of court, nobility, and aristocracy in things theatrical was initiated;

84 *Old Drury Lane*
Left, a 1775 print of the Old Drury Lane, during Garrick's term as
manager; the rear boxes have been converted to galleries on the first and
second levels. See figure 79. Right, Richard Leacroft's redrawing
of the above, amended in accordance with scale drawings of ceiling and
proscenium opening in the Soane Museum. This corrected drawing
gives more reason to believe the designation of Old Drury Lane
as an intimate house where the features of the actors were clearly
visible from the farthest gallery. (Richard Leacroft Theatre Collection)

with this came a corresponding rise in the importance of the middle
classes. As we have noted, the beginning of the reign of Queen
Anne in 1702 marked the final withdrawal of court interest in drama.
Henceforth English theatre was no longer to be the plaything of the
wealthy and the court, but once more the property of the citizens.
The English national spirit was beginning to reassert itself.

So self-assured was this development that during the course of the
eighteenth century, literary England became a creditor nation rather
than a debtor nation, as it had largely been before. The Age of Reason, the neoclassic period, the Augustan Age, all terms applied to the
greater portion of the century, though ostensibly drawing its inspiration from the French, really went back to the ancients themselves,
and was sanguine enough to believe that it was doing for England
what the writers of the Augustan period had done for Rome. Not
only were the rules and order of the ancients to be applied to English literature, but they were to be improved upon, for obviously
their practice had violated their precepts—and there would be none
of that in England! The literary arbiters of the day—Pope, then Johnson—were confirmed neoclassicists, and their influence spanned the

century. Respect for science and logic, rationality, an ordered society, a pleasing style that never descended to dullness—these were the characteristics of the time. Anti-emotionalism was the creed. Yet, paradoxically enough, the very period saw a rise in sentimentality, and a slow but certain undercurrent of real feeling which gathered strength throughout the century and burst into the glory of the Romantic revolution just at its end. The contradictions of the age—its serenity, its tempestuousness; its logic, its inspiration; its doctrine of deism, its Wesleyan doctrine of personal salvation—made it a seed-bed of ideas and practices which spread throughout Europe, often with startling manifestations.

It is a fascinating century in many areas of human thought and action. Science, government, economics, and philosophy were seething with discovery and change. John Locke (1632–1704), originally a student of chemistry and medicine and a practicing physician, became the outstanding political philosopher of the Age of Reason. In his political doctrines the American colonists found justification for their War of Independence. As an empiricist he was confident that adequate observation and discussion could sift truth from error. His *Essay Concerning the Human Understanding* (1690), one of his most significant writings, examined the origin of ideas and predicated the new concept that the mind at birth is a *tabula rasa* upon which experience writes. Hence came the various manifestations, in the century to follow, of the theory that environment, the conditions of society, contained the roots of good and evil—that man was the product of his environment. George Berkeley (1685–1753), David Hume (1711–1776), and William Godwin (1756–1836), all speculated concerning Lockean principles, engendering considerable philosophical activity which had political and social repercussions in both Europe and America.

Political events, also, engendered closer contact with other European nations. Queen Anne's War, concluded in 1714, caused England to be more politically involved with the Continent; the Seven Years' War (1756–1763) won an empire in America; and the campaigns of Clive in India (1756–1760) won that jewel for the English crown. Then came the American War of Independence and the establishment of a new nation.

In literary circles, authors were declaring their independence of patrons, and, for the first time in many generations not only making a living but sometimes even earning a fortune solely through their pens. Alexander Pope, for instance, received his generous support solely from the general public, and Samuel Johnson wrote his famous

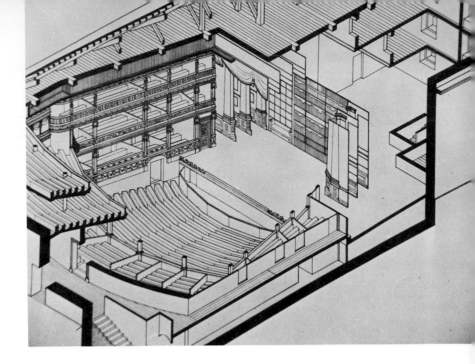

letter to Lord Chesterfield, stating his success independent of patronage. Essay, poem, novel, pamphlet proliferated. There were more avenues for literary expression than ever before. In the rush of experiment in new literary forms playwriting was often neglected; in the press of concern for philosophical, economic, and social ideas theatre was often an unimportant consideration. It was, nevertheless, an effectual mirror of the times, and had an interesting life of its own.

Theatre a middle-class amusement

During the eighteenth century, the English theatre was in the process of broadening its base. It was no longer the darling of the court; Queen Anne seldom went to the theatre, the successive Georges practically never. Though there were still devotees among court circles, theatregoing lacked the royal social sanction it had once enjoyed. The new audiences were increasingly of a new social class. London was the seething center of an expanding Empire, the economic and social hub of far-flung mercantile ventures, the Athens toward which the outlanders yearned. Very early in the century John Dennis, critic and playwright, was complaining of three categories of people who patronized the eighteenth-century theatre, who, he says, had no education at all: younger brothers suffering under the laws of primogeniture, merchants, and foreigners. All, he says, contributed to the debility of theatre. In any event, wealthy tradesmen

Internal View of the Old THEATRE ROYAL DRURY LANE, as it appeared in 1792.

85 *Old Drury Lane, continued*
Left, Richard Leacroft's reconstruction of the Drury Lane of Garrick's
time, with a single set of proscenium doors, an orchestra pit, and
three galleries opposite the stage. Again, see figure 79. Above, the
interior of Drury Lane in 1792, after more seats had been added
in the boxes and new candelabra installed. (Richard Leacroft Theatre
Collection, Henry E. Huntington Library and Art Gallery)

had evidently replaced the gallants and the men of letters in the pit,
though the front and side boxes were still occupied by the *beau
monde.*

The new playgoers, the tired businessmen of the age, demanded
and got plays which were not mentally taxing, but were interesting
and entertaining. At least this was the aim. And when the two patent
houses, very largely dedicated to pure drama, did not pander to their
tastes (Garrick over and over again tried to elevate English taste in
theatre), audiences resorted to the five or six other theatres of London for opera, pantomime, and puppet shows.

The rise of other forms of entertainment was not solely due to
public demand, but was, in some measure, a dodge to circumvent
authority. During most of the century only two theatres were licensed for dramatic performances—Drury Lane and Covent Garden.
But many another theatre presented plays, both long and short, under
the guise of concerts, much as, in our own Boston, plays for many
years were advertised as "moral discourses." Also the enterprising
John Rich (*ca.*, 1682–1761), son of Christopher Rich of Drury Lane
fame, made a very good thing of the pantomime originated by one
John Weaver, dancing master at Drury Lane. These pantomimes were
spectacular presentations in dumb show with music, and used as plot
the standard texts; one of the most famous of these was Marlowe's
Dr. Faustus. The pantomime had a lasting popularity, enduring even
today in the celebrated English Christmas pantomimes.

255

John Rich, under the name of Lun, was his own performer in the pantomimes, just as, quite universally, the chief managers of the day were also actors. Drury Lane (figures 84 and 85) was long under such management: first the trio of Cibber, Wilks, and Doggett beginning in 1710, then, after a slight interval, for thirty years under The Great Garrick, and again toward the end of the century under John Philip Kemble. Kemble also managed at Covent Garden; Rich had been its first actor-manager. And both William and Lewis Hallam, proprietor and manager, respectively, of the company which gave the first professional performances in America, were actors. Most famous of these, of course, is David Garrick who in many ways symbolizes this Age of Great Acting, as it has been called. In addition to his innovations in the art of acting, he introduced many improvements in staging, design, and theatre management, of which we shall speak in due time. For a time, at least, these men succeeded in warding off the complete domination of theatre management by nontheatre people. How completely the theatre was later taken over by businessmen is easily seen in the paucity of actor-managers today.

Though the theatre of the period was essentially that of the upper middle class, in many ways the audience was heterogeneous. Its composition dictated a later opening hour, with performances beginning at six so that those who worked might attend. Those of the working classes, whose day invariably extended from six in the morning to six at night and often to nine, were admitted late, with reduced prices if they came only to see the afterpiece. (The main performance of the evening was always followed by a musical farce or a condensed comedy which was advertised with the main piece, and which closed the evening about ten o'clock.)

For the first time in the history of theatre, advertising could now be done through the newspapers, which got their start in 1706, as well as through the use of playbills (figure 86). Programs and printed tickets were in use, although we will see that no individually reserved seats were customary until the nineteenth century. Admission was generally by brass checks to a particular part of the house, with the *beau monde* in the front and side boxes, the wealthy tradesmen in the pit and first gallery, and the mob in the upper gallery. Prices were higher than today, and considerably higher than under Elizabeth I. In the two major houses the upper gallery would cost about $4.50 in our money; the first gallery about $9.00; the pit, $13.50. Comparable prices in Shakespeare's theatre were thirty-one cents, sixty-two cents, and ninety-three cents, although it is true that other commodities were much higher in Shakespeare's day than they were in Garrick's.

The usual custom was to allow half-price admission after the third act, and all actors, managers, and playwrights were on the "free list."

As can be imagined, the upper gallery was a rowdy place, although serious disturbances were surprisingly few. Prostitutes were presumably confined to the upper boxes, but pickpockets were rife. To combat the deplorable practice of some dandies and poetasters who took it into their heads, often, to damn a play by hisses and catcalls, managements often employed claques, who were instructed to applaud and cheer at the right moments. It would appear that though this eighteenth-century audience was by no means as boisterous as Shakespeare's, nor as quick with the sword as the somewhat later "dandies," it was certainly not the quiet and well-behaved crowd to which we are accustomed in the theatre today. By its likes and dislikes, made vocal and visual, it determined the types of plays, their physical production to a large extent, and the style of acting. Great talent on the other side of the footlights sometimes dictated public taste, then as now, but as always the audience was the supreme arbiter.

English theatre in America

Opposition to theatre continued to be felt throughout the century, with more than fifty diatribes against it being published during that time. In America, dramatic performances were almost completely prohibited by the religious scruples of the New England colonies and the middle colonies; Virginia, that Cavalier settlement, was the one to which Hallam's company journeyed. Virginia had been the scene of the first recorded English production in the New World, that of a lost play entitled *Ye Beare and Ye Cubbe*, for which presentation the author and actors were brought into court in 1665. This inauspicious beginning of theatre in America was typical of conditions throughout the colonies. In 1709 the Province of New York forbade play acting along with cock fighting and other "disreputable" forms of entertainment, and both the New England colonies and Pennsylvania—the one basically Puritan, the other Quaker—were deeply opposed to any kind of theatrical entertainment.

By 1716, however, there was a small native company performing in Williamsburg, Virginia. In 1723, there is record of performances by strolling players outside of Philadelphia, and, by 1749 the company of Walter Murray and Thomas Kean was performing in a warehouse within the city limits. The next year they performed in New York and in Williamsburg, and in 1752 the Hallam Company came to Virginia. They made significant progress during the next

86 *Two eighteenth-century playbills*
These two playbills, from the middle of the century, show a typical
evening's entertainment: A tragedy followed by a farce. Notice that
dancing is added to *All For Love* at Covent Garden, and a Funeral
Procession to *Romeo and Juliet* at Drury Lane, while the masquerade
dance of Act I, "proper to the Play" is also advertised.
(Henry E. Huntington Library and Art Gallery)

twenty years all up and down the coast, but dispersed in 1774 when
the First Continental Congress passed a resolution, which, among
other things, discouraged all "expensive diversions and entertainments." During the Revolutionary War, British soldiers presented
plays in Boston, New York, and Philadelphia, and even the American
soldiers, though having both less leisure and less inclination for theatre, presented Addison's *Cato* at Valley Forge. When the war was
over, the self-exiled Hallam company returned and professional dramatic activity resumed.

The nascent theatre in Scotland suffered similar difficulties. Glas-
gow's first theatre was burned by a mob in 1752 at the instigation of
the militant Methodist, George Whitfield (1714–1770). The Presby-
tery of Edinburgh suppressed plays and outlawed playwrights for
several decades; when the Reverend John Home had his patriotic

Douglas (1756) produced, he was asked to resign from the ministry. But there was a flourishing theatre in Dublin which sent many performers to the stages of London, and smaller theatres were establishing firm hold in the English provinces.

Age undistinguished by its plays

The eighteenth century is universally known as The Age of Great Acting; the plays of the age were largely undistinguished. Altered versions of the classics were given and were immensely popular. Shakespeare, too, suffered at the hands of producers. *Romeo and Juliet*, in Garrick's version, had 142 performances in twenty-five seasons. Of the total Shakespeare canon, Garrick produced twenty-four at Drury Lane, most of them changed. *The Tempest, A Winter's Tale, A Midsummer Night's Dream, The Taming of the Shrew* were made into opera-like plays with music and dancing. The Gravediggers were cut out of *Hamlet*. Macbeth made a dying speech. When the American Company presented *Othello* in Newport in 1761, Desdemona was smothered "in an adjoining room." The tragedies of Racine were offered in translations by Ambrose Philips and Charles Johnson, and those of Voltaire by Aaron Hill. When comedies of the Restoration period were revived (as they frequently were), they were often bowdlerized. Public taste favored comedy; tragedy was usually propped up with the presentation of a comic afterpiece as liberally advertised as the main play.

The original dramatic writing of the period may be conveniently divided into seven types: classical tragedy (or, more exactly, pseudo-classic tragedy), domestic tragedy, comedy of manners, sentimental comedy, farce, ballad-opera, and pantomime; the last two are decidedly less literary than the first five, and worthy of notice only because they occupied so large a portion of the theatrical scene.

Firmly adhering to the accepted pattern of classical tragedy as interpreted by the French, English tragic dramatists of the eighteenth century dipped once more into the traditional materials, producing verse plays of almost startling stiffness. The general worthlessness of this genre is illustrated by the fact that the best of them was the *Cato* of Joseph Addison (1713), which owed its immediate popularity to its seeming application to the then-rife speculation over Queen Anne's successor and was thus widely translated, produced, and imitated on the Continent (figure 87). There was a *Siege of Damascus* by one John Hughes, a *Miriamne* by Elijah Fenton, and a *Sophonisba* by James Thomson, who belongs, not to the tradition of classical tragedy, but to the beginnings of romantic poetry. Delicious fun is

87 *Eighteenth-century stage settings*
Left, a model of the screen scene in Sheridan's *School for Scandal*, as
presented in the Drury Lane Theatre, 1777. The bookcases and window
are painted on the backdrop; the actors are playing on the apron.
Right, Addison's *Cato* as presented in the Niewe Hofzaal, Amsterdam,
1766. The stage decoration consists of wing flats, borders, and
backdrops; the doors are in the proscenium. The actresses are in
contemporary dress. (The Cleveland Museum of Art, Collection of
the Educational Department; Harvard Theatrical Collection)

poked at the sonorous inanities of this play, along with many other
things, by Henry Fielding in *The Tragedy of Tragedies, or The Life
and Death of Tom Thumb the Great.*

Using the form, though not the materials of classical tragedy,
James Young, another preromantic poet, wrote three plays, *Busiris*
(1719), *The Revenge* (1721) using the Othello theme, and *The
Brothers* (1735). The first American play to be produced by professional actors, Thomas Godfrey's *The Prince of Parthia* (1767), was
another of this kind, as were Arthur Murphy's two plays, *The Grecian Daughter* (1772) and *Alzuma* (1773). The one play of Samuel
Johnson (*Irene*, 1736), with which he came armed to London, is little
more than a series of dialogues on moral themes between Mahomet,
Emperor of the Turks, and various Greek captives. It was not produced until 1749 when Garrick performed this act of kindness for his
old friend and mentor.

Heroic drama was almost alien to the taste of eighteenth-century
theatregoers; dramatists met those tastes by the development of a
comparatively new genre, the domestic tragedy, or pathetic tragedy,
which used materials closer to the understanding and sympathy of
its audiences, while retaining the rudiments of classical form. Some

starts had been made in this direction during the Elizabethan period, when Thomas Heywood wrote *A Woman Killed With Kindness;* but the writers of the eighteenth century, in taking up domestic materials for tragedy once more, handled them with a sentimentality foreign to the Elizabethans. Such were the plays of Nicholas Rowe, Poet Laureate at his death in 1718—notably *Jane Shore* and *The Fair Penitent,* in which Mrs. Siddons starred for many years. The *Douglas* of the Reverend John Home, which we have already mentioned, was a combination of classical and domestic models, using materials from a Scottish ballad, and providing in Young Norval, the hero, one of the most popular acting parts of the century. The most famous of the genre, however, and the most influential, was George Lillo's *The London Merchant, or the History of George Barnwell,* first produced in 1731. It was epoch-making in that it was written in prose rather than verse (except for the prologue). Lillo's play supplied Diderot, the great French critic, with his theme that plays should be serious, bourgeois dramas of real life. The same theme was then successfully expounded by Lessing and long had a great effect on German stage literature.

The shallowness that marked much of the domestic tragedy of the period was evident also in the comedy of sentiment, begun in reaction to the amorality of Restoration comedy. An early example of the type is Colley Cibber's *Love's Last Shift* (1696) in which the roving husband completely reforms. Sir Richard Steele, of *Tatler* and *Spectator* fame, produced his first comedy of this kind in 1701. It was called *The Funeral, or, Grief à la Mode,* in which he said he intended to present virtue and vice in their true form. This was followed by *The Lying Lover* (1703), and *The Tender Husband* (1705); he did not return to playwriting until 1722 with his final play, *The Conscious Lovers.* Here the conscious morality and sentimentality of the chief characters are delightfully relieved by the realistic comedy of the servants.

Among the many sentimental comedies of Richard Cumberland, the best and most often played were *The Brothers* (1769) and *The West Indian* (1771); ruses, mistaken identities, and trials of character were Cumberland's favorite themes. Mrs. Elizabeth Inchbald, actress-playwright, had a successful comedy in 1785 with *I'll Tell You What.* She also wrote *Every One Has His Faults,* and *Wives as They Were and Maids as They Are,* which have some moments as sprightly as their titles. Thomas Holcroft, friend of Tom Paine and William Godwin, wrote many sentimental plays, the best known of which is *The Road to Ruin* (1792). Thomas Morton introduced the

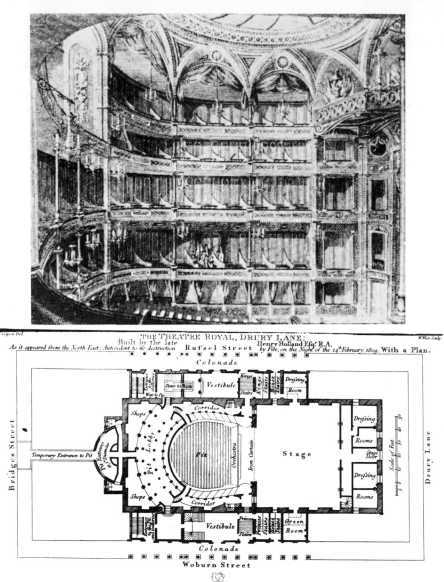

88 *New Drury Lane*

Above, the interior of the New Drury Lane, opened in 1794, as the
"largest theatre in all Europe." Below, the plan of the 1794 Drury Lane.
Note the abbreviated apron stage and the increased stage area for
scenes and machines. The actors are now performing largely "within the
scene," i.e., behind the proscenium arch. (Yale Theatrical Prints
Collection, Henry E. Huntington Library and Art Gallery)

name of "Mrs. Grundy" in his *Speed the Plough* (1798); this play had been preceded by *The Way to Get Married* (1796) and *A Cure for Heartache* (1797). Additional representatives of the type are Arthur Murphy's *Three Weeks After Marriage* (1764), and *The Way to Keep Him* (1760), whose subject matter is obvious.

The most prolific of these dramatists was John O'Keefe, among whose fifty-odd productions were *Tony Lumpkin in Town* (1778—obviously derived from Goldsmith's famous *She Stoops to Conquer*), *Wild Oats* (1791), and *The Castle of Andalusia* (1782). Almost equally prolific were the George Colmans, Senior and Junior. The elder Colman, erstwhile manager of Covent Garden and the Haymarket Theatres, wrote and adapted some thirty dramatic pieces, notably including *The Jealous Wife* (1761), and, with his good friend David Garrick, *The Clandestine Marriage* (1766). The younger Colman, among many less important pieces, immortalized the famous British character in his *John Bull* (1803).

Some reaction to the sentimental comedy is evident in the truly comic scenes of Oliver Goldsmith's *The Good Natured Man* as early as 1768, and again in Samuel Foote's *The Handsome Housemaid* (1773) which is, indeed, a burlesque of the sentimental comedy. But representatives of the true comedy of manners are very few and somewhat late in the century's development. The rash and protean Richard Brinsley Sheridan recovered something of the brilliance of Restoration comedy without its obscenity in two of his most celebrated plays, *The Rivals* (1775) and *School for Scandal* (1777), whose characters and situations continue to delight widespread audiences today (figure 87). The former is not without its passages of high-flown sentiment, and the way in which Charles Surface, in the latter, wins his uncle's heart by cherishing the old man's portrait is also purely sentimental. But the total tenor of both plays is sharp, incisive, and refreshing. Still very popular, too, is Goldsmith's *She Stoops to Conquer* (1773), which, while not so incisive as the plays of Sheridan, is still in the comedy of manners tradition. And the first native American comedy, Royall Tyler's *The Contrast* (1787), was of this genre, pointing up the superiority of the homegrown American to the Anglophile society in which he is deposited.

Criticism is implicit also in the many satirical portraits in the plays of Samuel Foote, and in the dramatic pieces written during the American Revolution by Mercy Otis Warren and John Leacock. As literary satires, Sheridan's *The Critic* (1779) and Fielding's *Tom Thumb* (1731) are unparalleled.

Farce, with its total emphasis upon amusing situations, was

89 Other eighteenth-century theatres
Above, the theatre built at Sadler's Wells in 1765. Note the dark little
boxes in the first tier and the curtained boxes over the single set of
proscenium doors in this small theatre. Below, the interior of Covent
Garden in 1794, its final remodeling before it burned down in 1808. Note
the chandeliers and the candelabra suspended from the tiers.
(Henry E. Huntington Library and Art Gallery)

domesticated to a thoroughly English species during the eighteenth
century, with such lively pieces as *The Lying Valet* (1741), *Miss In
Her Teens* (1747), *The Irish Widow* (1772), and *High Life Below
Stairs* (1759). Garrick was its chief protagonist.

The ballad-opera, in which the text of a burlesque farce was interspersed with songs written to popular tunes, was an eighteenth-century English growth. The most notable of the type, and certainly

good theatre in any age, is John Gay's *The Beggar's Opera* (1728), with its immortal characters, whom nobody any longer thinks of as being satiric. Sheridan also wrote in this genre; his delightful *The Duenna* (1777) is also good theatre even today.

Of the pantomimes we have already spoken briefly. In addition to garnering the fare for these "harlequinades" from previous and present theatre, the producers of the increasingly popular pantomimes often made up their presentations from whole cloth. But since the pantomimes were primarily spectacle, and only very secondarily literary drama of any sort, we need not linger over them.

Playwrights of the eighteenth century, following popular taste, tended to stress the rewards of virtue, the demands of gentility, and the trials of character, with much emphasis on disguises, surprises, and unexpected wealth. Though many of the plays are quite lively, and certainly pleased contemporary audiences, their artificiality and superficial treatment of character have rendered the majority of them quite without interest to today's audiences. Many men of talent but few of genius wrote for that theatre.

Culminating developments in playhouses

The eighteenth century saw the development of the large, opera-type playhouse which has remained in use down to the present day. Drury Lane in London will illustrate this tendency. We have seen that the first, small house, built by Killigrew in 1663, was burned to the ground in 1672. The somewhat larger second building, on the same plot, was designed by Christopher Wren and opened in 1674. During most of the succeeding century, it underwent extensive remodeling and enlargement until it was condemned and completely torn down in 1792.

We have seen, also, that the first remodeling was done by the then-manager Christopher Rich, in 1696, when he provided for more seats by cropping the apron four feet and converting the downstage proscenium doors into boxes. But so firmly entrenched was the use of the double proscenium doors, that the loss of the lower pair was compensated for by adding a pair to the area above the proscenium arch, to either side of the stage.

Lacy and Garrick enlarged the seating capacity somewhat when they took over the patent in 1747. Then, in 1762, a major change occurred. Garrick had long been wanting to banish from the stage those spectators who, relying on the tradition of stage seating, had long spoiled performances. But stage seating was a good source of revenue, particularly on actors' benefit nights when patrons crowded the area, their total admission price going to the actor whose benefit it was. Often they formed a complete amphitheatre on the stage, effectively screening out the scenery and making entrances and stage movement difficult. Garrick knew that he could not deprive his company of the money represented by stage seating without compensating for it elsewhere. So he remodeled the interior of the theatre to provide more seating space, and the next year prohibited the public from behind the scenes, with little or no protest from his company.

Sheridan enlarged the house once more in 1781, increasing the capacity to two thousand. These successive enlargements were demanded by increasing attendance; average daily attendance swelled from about 650 in 1742 to almost twelve hundred by 1775, with the theatre capacity enlarging from about one thousand to about fourteen hundred.

This Drury Lane Theatre, which stood for a hundred years in constant use, was an intimate playhouse with three galleries opposite the stage, the lower two of which had been converted from boxes, and three rows of boxes along the sides. In this old house, as one of the critics of the New Drury Lane remarked,

> The moving brow and penetrating eye of that matchless actor [Garrick] came home to the spectator. As the passions shifted, and were by turns reflected from the mirror of his expressive countenance, nothing was lost (Richard Cumberland, *Memoirs*, London, 1807, Supplement, p. 58).

But the old house was replaced in 1794 with the largest theatre in all of Europe (figure 88). It had a capacity of over thirty-six hundred seated in an almost semicircular auditorium, with five rows of boxes along the sides and two opposite the stage, topped by two galleries, in addition to the pit. The portion of the proscenium arch over the stage apron was also fitted with boxes, but there was no stage door, nor the large columns usual to English theatres. The contemporary Richard Cumberland, complains that

> Upon the scale of the modern Drury many of the finest touches of his [Garrick's] art would of necessity fall short. The distant auditor might chance to catch the text, but would not see the comment, that was wont so exquisitely to elucidate the poet's meaning, and impress it on the hearer's heart (*Memoirs*, p. 58).

Many similar complaints were lodged against this cavernous house.

The stage was, likewise, of impressive proportions—forty-three feet wide by thirty-eight feet high at the proscenium opening,

266

extending to ninety-two feet in depth. The backstage area was eighty-five feet wide and more than a hundred feet high, so that none of the scenery from the old house could be used, and all had to be built anew. The house was equipped with water piped to every part in case of fire, and an iron curtain was hung at the proscenium to shut off the stage in such an emergency. Nevertheless, the theatre was completely destroyed by fire in 1809.

The other patent house of eighteenth-century London was the Covent Garden Theatre, built and opened by John Rich in 1732. At that time it was eighty-six feet long from the proscenium opening to the opposite wall, and fifty-six feet wide. This rectangular area had a row of boxes opposite the stage, with two galleries above and three rows of boxes along the sides. Its capacity was about two thousand. It was highly decorated with draperies, pilasters, and friezes, but the stage area was small.

The house underwent alterations in 1784, when the seating capacity was increased to just over three thousand by the addition of more seats in the same space, thus reducing the room for the individual spectator. Then again, in 1791, the interior was redecorated in such a way as to make the sightlines from the first gallery very difficult. The resultant hue and cry caused another remodeling in 1794 (figure 89), when all the seats were raised for better viewing, and a new ceiling was installed. The stage area was also enlarged. But the whole edifice burned to the ground on September 20, 1808.

Before moving to Covent Garden, Rich's company had been playing at Lincoln's Inn Fields, in the old, converted Lisle's Tennis Court of Restoration days. It continued in sporadic use through most of the century. Dorset Garden, the grandiose structure of the Restoration, was soon abandoned in the new century because of bad acoustics, and the Haymarket Theatre, built for Betterton by Vanbrugh in 1704, was turned over to opera for the same reason.

The Little Theatre in the Haymarket, opened in 1720, was in operation through most of the century, at one time under the brief management of Henry Fielding whose sharp satires are said to have instigated the Licensing Act of 1737 which restricted the production of legitimate drama to the two patent houses. Later in the century Samuel Foote obtained a license to operate it legitimately at seasons when the patent houses were not playing. It has an interesting proscenium arrangement, with a door to either side set on a slant, and a latticed window above each door. This theatre is still in use today.

The Goodman's Fields Theatre, opened in 1733, persisted after the Licensing Act by offering concerts; between the parts of the concert

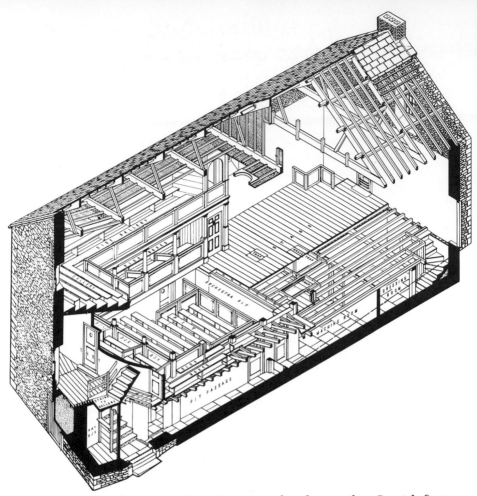

one or two plays were given. It was at this theatre that Garrick first
appeared in London, in the role of Richard III. And either here or at
Sadler's Wells, another unlicensed theatre, the brothers Hallam went
bankrupt in 1750, and planned to recoup their fortunes by sending an
acting company. to the Colonies.

Few of these unlicensed theatres were as large as the patent
houses, and those in the provinces were also small in comparison.
For instance, the New Theatre Royal, built in Edinburgh in 1768,
and in operation for ninety years, was a building only fifty by a hundred feet, built at a total cost of fifteen hundred pounds including
scenes, wardrobe, and decorations. It is supposed to have seated 630
and was, at the beginning of the next century, taken over by no less
a person than Sir Walter Scott.

Typical of these provincial stages is that of Richmond, in England, built in 1788 and still standing (figure 90). It is a rectangle,

268

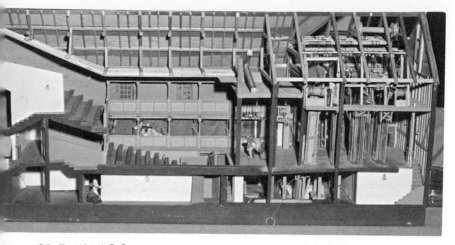

90 Provincial theatres
Left, the Georgian Theatre, Richmond, Yorkshire, 1788, measured
and drawn by Richard Leacroft, A.R.I.B.A. Above, a scale model of the
theatre built at Williamsburg, Virginia, in 1718. The similarities of
construction are plainly evident: the single pair of proscenium doors,
the orchestra pit, the side boxes, and the galleries. This plan was
to remain standard in theatre construction for a very long period of time.
(Richard Leacroft Theatre Collection; Colonial Williamsburg)

measuring twenty-four by fifty-four feet inside, and seating about
four hundred people. The sloped floor of the pit has eight rows of
benches, terminating in a row of boxes with a gallery above and a
single row of boxes along the sides. The stage is twenty-seven feet
deep, including a five-foot apron, and is raked. The proscenium arch
is seventeen feet high, about fifteen feet wide, and has a single set of
proscenium doors.

Dublin had had a theatre since 1635, and the Smock Alley Theatre, opened in 1662, was a fertile source of talent for the London
stage, as well as a rewarding stop for visiting actors. From 1758 to
1819 a second theatre, the Crow Street, also flourished there.

Theatres built in America

In America, the Hallam Company, arriving in 1752, played in a
series of temporary structures. In Williamsburg, their first stop, they
performed in a converted warehouse which had been in use sporadically for various amateur performances (figure 90). It had pit, boxes,
balconies, and a gallery. No doubt it was very small. They played
in other makeshift buildings in New York, Newport, Annapolis,
Charleston, and in Philadelphia, where the first permanent theatre
in America was built by David Douglass, who had taken over the

91 More eighteenth-century theatres
Left, the interior of the Park Theatre, New York, as painted by John Searle in 1822. This house, erected in 1820, replaced the original 1798 building which had been destroyed by fire. Note the three tiers of boxes with a gallery above, and the proscenium doors. Right, a riot at Covent Garden in 1763. This old print shows the lighting arrangements, the stage boxes, the orchestra pit, and the actors performing on the apron stage with the scenic background behind the proscenium. (New York Historical Society; Henry E. Huntington Library and Art Gallery)

company by reason of marrying Lewis Hallam's widow. The Southwark Theatre opened in November, 1766, and during its first season produced *The Prince of Parthia*, as we have mentioned above. It was a substantial structure of brick below and wood above, painted red, with interior pillars to support the roof. It was used continuously as a theatre for more than thirty years, and was used for other purposes for more than a century.

The other theatre of importance built in America in this period was also constructed by Douglass, and was called the John Street Theatre. It was opened in New York in 1767. William Dunlap (*History of the American Theatre*, 1833), our first historian of American theatre, says it had two rows of boxes, a pit, and a gallery, and was "an $800 house." It probably seated about a thousand people. During the Revolution, the British requisitioned the house for amateur theatricals, but it fell again to the American Company after the Revolution, when Lewis Hallam, Jr., returned with them from Jamaica. In the last decade of the eighteenth century, four theatres of importance were erected in America: the Federal Street and the Haymarket in Boston, the Chestnut Street in Philadelphia (modeled after the Royal Theatre at Bath in England), and the Park Theatre in New York (figure 91). Since each of the latter two cities already

at Covent Garden Theatre in 1763. in consequence of the Managers refusing to admit half-price in the Opera of Artaxerxes.

had one good theatre, these three centers of population could now boast six theatre buildings. All were of the accepted design, with sloped pit floor, two to three rows of boxes, one or two galleries, a raked stage, an apron, and usually a set of proscenium doors. It would be a long time before theatres broke this mold and branched out to new forms.

New departures in settings

As the playhouse increased in size, scenic investiture increased in complexity. The pantomimes and operas, which greatly relied on visual interest, eventually affected design for the legitimate theatre. For almost two-thirds of the century, however, the patent houses relied on the use of the stock sets developed in the preceding period, and they were put upon the stage time after time in many different plays. Tate Wilkinson, writing in the eighties, speaks of a particular set at Covent Garden which had been in use since 1747, and which he looked upon as "a very old acquaintance." The palace, garden, temple, and prison were in constant use, as a 1743 inventory of Covent Garden illustrates. These were, of course, painted on flats, backdrops or shutters, and borders. The flats were operated in grooves, as Inigo Jones had long ago prescribed. Interiors as well as exteriors

271

were handled in this way, the walls of a room being formed by a triangular arrangement of wing flats ending in a back flat, and exteriors using the same arrangement except that the flats were now trees or buildings of one sort and another.

It may have been the challenge of scenic effects in the pantomimes that induced Garrick, in 1771, to engage the Alsatian Philippe Jacques de Loutherbourg as scenic artist for Drury Lane. In any event, his work there was significant for he first introduced illusionistic, realistic scenery to England (figure 92). True, he rarely designed for legitimate drama, concentrating on the dramatic entertainments which were a part of the Drury Lane repertory, but his ideas and production methods were important for the future of scenic art. For the flat backdrop he sometimes used three-dimensional forms, giving the illusion of great distance. He achieved spectacular effects in outdoor settings, journeying to Derbyshire for on-the-spot sketches to be translated to the stage for *The Wonders of Derbyshire;* he started with authentic sketches in his recreation of a scene in the South Seas. He employed cloud effects and transparent scenery, and experimented successfully with new ways of using elemental effects. He tried stained glass and colored silks for lighting effects, and dispensed with the hot and smelly footlights in favor of side and top lighting on the stage itself. The influence of his work is apparent when we read of no less than a member of the Royal Academy designing stage scenery in 1780, by which time it had become the custom for the scene designer to be called in for consultation at the beginning of production on a play. And it is obvious from the record that "Loutherbourg pieces" were frequently given for the express purpose of displaying his unique faculties.

With William Capon, who came to Drury Lane when it moved into its new and greatly enlarged house in 1794, the old wing and border systems for the standard plays were almost completely discarded, and new sets, obviously intended to become standard, were designed. Capon was a Romanticist imbued with the artistic possibilities of the Gothic style, and this style he transposed to the stage with careful research and draftsmanship. His work marked the end of the temples and palaces which had dressed the theatre for so long, and ushered in a new era.

By this time, also, the use of forced perspective had practically disappeared, and all the grooves, when used, were of one height. The front curtain was still raised at the beginning of the show and lowered at the end, but there was an ever-increasing use of act drops, often specially prepared for particular performances.

92 *Eighteenth-century stage setting*
Wings and backdrop for *Omai*,
designed by Loutherbourg in 1785.
The flats are realistically painted, and
the edges cut out. The arrangement
for this photograph shows their
relative positions as they would
have been set on the stage.
(Victoria and Albert Museum)

We may be sure that the wonders of the new scenery were employed in the provinces as quickly as possible, though often the reincarnation was, of economic necessity, on a much less ambitious scale. When the Hallam Company came to America, it brought with it a complete set of cast-off scenery from London, including the green front curtain which was standard for a long time in both English and American theatres. But even here, as the century progressed, spectacular scenic effects were tried. There is an interesting and minute description of the stage effects for John Burk's *The Battle of Bunker's Hill*, produced in Boston in 1796, which tells of practical hills, houses on fire, and a quite realistic battle. Some of the effect was achieved by means of painted cannons and painted smoke borders and flats, but these were coupled with actual gunfire, real smoke, and flame. In Charleston, a production of *The Tempest* opened with an attempt at a real storm and shipwreck.

All during the century, theatres struggled with the problem of lighting, using oil lamps which gave better illumination but smelled and smoked, or candles, or a combination of the two. They would wait long for gas, and then electricity, to make spectacular developments in lighting possible.

273

93 *Eighteenth-century costuming*
Left, Garrick, in four roles, wears a basic contemporary costume adding
fur for Lear, slashed sleeves and a simulated cross-gartering for Richard
II. Hamlet and Macbeth have no historical touches. Right, Macklin
as Shylock, with curious long trousers over which he wears an
eighteenth-century waistcoat, and the long Jewish gabardine. (Henry
E. Huntington Library and Art Gallery)

Music was almost always a part of theatrical representation, even
in straight dramas, with a special section of the pit, that nearest the
stage, usually assigned to the musicians. The arrangement was much
like our present-day "orchestra pit."

Within the limits of economy and possibility, the visual aspect of
theatre received increasing attention.

Innovations, too, in costumes

Eighteenth century costuming followed the lines laid down by
Restoration theatre, which in turn derived much of its practice from
Elizabethan playhouses. But there were some interesting innovations
of significance also to be observed.

Study of various theatrical prints of the time, as well as of printed
records, seems to indicate that the men and the women performers
followed separate systems. The actors' costumes for tragedy were

274

of four types: contemporary, Roman, Eastern, and special. Garrick played Macbeth in knee breeches, a scarlet and gold coat, and a tie wig. Hamlet was played in the same contemporary dress, but all in black (figure 93). Woodward played Mercutio in colorful eighteenth-century costume and a tricorne hat; Romeo was similarly attired. In plays with Roman backgrounds, the actors retained the knee breeches, but often wore tunic-like tops and mantles, and sometimes breast-plates and plumed helmets. Quin played Coriolanus in the stiff ton-nelet (an umbrella-like skirt reaching to the knees) of the Paris Opera and the plumed headdress that was usual for heroes (figure 94). Many prints show lacings up the calf as if sandals were being simulated. In parts like Othello and Bajazet, the costume consisted of roomy, full trousers, a loose coat often trimmed with fur, and a turban, some-times with plumes (figure 95). Boots and a scimitar completed the outfit. The special costumes were traditional, and generally wigless. Such a one was Falstaff, who appeared in an Elizabethan collar, large buskins, and a cloak (figure 94). Shylock wore long, wide trousers, a long black gown, and a red tricorne. For comedy, contemporary dress was universally worn, whatever the period of the play. The richness of the actor's wardrobe was often enhanced by gifts from the nobility of cast-off garments. In the pastorals and pantomimes, individual and fantastic garments were worn.

It was the general rule, however, that no matter what the costume of the actor, the actress playing with him appeared in the most fash-ionable dress of the eighteenth century. The plumes were added for tragic heroines, but Cleopatra, Andromache, Merope, or Queen Eliza-beth were universally clothed in the highly decorated, hoop-skirt fashion of the times, with hair dressed high and usually powdered (figure 97). An occasional print will show a bow in the direc-tion of historical costuming, but even such hints are more of the eighteenth century than otherwise. Due largely to the influence of Mrs. Bellamy, the traditional black velvet gown of the previous pe-riod's tragedy queen was given up, and the richest possible dress substituted. She tells of preparing a costume for Cleopatra by adding many diamonds to the silver tissue gown once worn by the Princess of Wales. With the allowance made her by the manager for costum-ing herself, she sometimes had her gowns made in Paris, and, by her own account, sometimes changed costumes from night to night for the same character and play. The only governing principle apparent in the costuming of women (in this day when players largely cos-tumed themselves) was that the actress should look as bewitchingly fashionable and beautiful as possible. Chambermaids, country

94 *Quin in two Shakespearean roles*
Left, Quin as Coriolanus. He wears the stiff skirt, called a "tonnelet,"
which was popular on the French stage, and the head feathers which were
usual for heroic characters. Right, as Falstaff, he again has a
feathered hat, but wears a ruff and boots with his eighteenth-century
dress. These touches were sufficient, for his audiences, to make him
a noncontemporary, or "historical" character.
(Harvard Theatrical Collection)

wenches, and servants all appeared in hoops and powdered hair and
satin shoes, with no thought of authenticity, and this practice largely
continued throughout the century in spite of many criticisms of it.
Reform would require a stronger managerial hand as well as a concern by the ensemble for the total stage picture.

Almost the only exception to the uniform fashionable dress for
women was Sarah Kemble Siddons, who, even when she early appeared in the stays and hoop petticoats usual with the other actresses,
did not powder and curl her hair but wore it smooth and braided,
much to the delight of the great artist Sir Joshua Reynolds because
it truly showed the size and shape of her head. She later became
enamored of the Greek style, and gave up the stays and hoops for
tragedy, adopting the drapery of Greek statuary for these roles.

The men were more adaptable to change, perhaps because less
vain than the women. As early as 1721, Aaron Hill was urging costumes more nearly like the period the character was portraying, and

in 1734 he provided sketches "in the old Saxon dress" for a play of his own. Macklin caused a sensation in 1773, when he played Macbeth in "the old Scottish garb" even though his Lady appeared in the costume of contemporary fashion. Garrick followed with a *King Lear* in old English costume. Kemble dressed the witches in Macbeth as weird creatures, and attempted a reform in the Hamlet costume. Toward the end of the century, also, actors began to realize that when the script called for disheveled dress, it was right to wear it so, and not accede, as Garrick earlier did in his Macbeth, to wrong-headed demands for perfect grooming no matter what the circumstances in the play. By this time the stars at least made an attempt at correct costumes, although the rest of the cast might be in all sorts of contemporary dress. To the eighteenth-century mind, "historical" meant simply "not conventional or contemporary," and it remained for succeeding periods to develop a semblance of historical accuracy in costuming.

On the whole, eighteenth-century costuming would appear to be a hodgepodge, and no decent order was to come from this chaos for some time.

Makeup was more universally used by women than by men, and was basically a powder makeup. White, black, red, and pink were the prevalent colors, applied from papers or pads of carded wool. Men ordinarily did not use makeup except when playing parts of a much greater age than their own, or for disguises. In the former instance, lines were drawn on the face with ink; in the latter, the use of false noses, beards, and wigs predominated. Lampblack was sometimes used for traditionally Negro characters. Makeup was removed either with cocoa butter or with plain soap and water. Although Garrick has been pointed out as being proficient in makeup, the general practice must have been rather crude, the effects garish. Makeup was to improve in refinement and effectiveness as stage lighting improved.

The Age of Great Acting

It is sometimes said that the eighteenth century was the Age of Great Acting because there were no great playwrights; that if the critics and writers who began to proliferate in that period had had challenging dramatists to deal with we would not have heard so much about the actors. There may be some truth to this contention, for acting is surely one of the most ephemeral of all the arts, and of the art of this period we know only what we read. Yet the actors of the century did have Shakespeare, Congreve, and Jonson to deal with, and from all accounts met the challenge successfully.

95 Mr. and Mrs. Barry in two plays
Left, the Barrys as Jaffier and Belvidera in *Venice Preserved;* right,
as Bajazet and Selima in *Tamerlane*. Again feathers are the sign of
heroic characters. Mrs. Barry wears elaborate eighteenth-century English
dress with a train; the black gown of Belvidera is reminiscent of
Restoration stage practice. Mr. Barry's bow to the Orient, as Bajazet,
is evident in the full trousers and coat worn over his customary
small-clothes. (Henry E. Huntington Library and Art Gallery)

If we read the critiques judiciously, and study with care the various sketches, prints, and portraits of actors in various roles, we can only come to the conclusion that eighteenth-century acting was a powerfully developing art, and that it no doubt produced at least two of the greatest talents the English stage has ever seen—David Garrick and Sarah Kemble Siddons. Their methods form an interesting contrast.

Garrick's was the more comprehensive genius. In addition to being a consummate actor, he was director, manager, playwright, and adapter. In his person are summed up all that was best of theatre practice in his day. Coming from a completely nontheatrical family, and having had but little previous experience, he burst, as it were, a full-blown and finished artist upon the theatre world in 1741. It was on October 19 of that year that he startled theatregoers with his Richard III. His rise was meteoric. Taking over the management of the Drury Lane theatre in 1747, with James Lacy as his partner, he assumed responsibility for the artistic side of the productions, leaving the business details to his partner. During the almost thirty years of his association with that theatre, he set a standard of production and performance that was truly memorable. He acquired the best performers available for his company, whether or not he agreed with their artistic principles, and whether or not they were his rivals in popularity. He exacted "order, decency, and decorum" from them, set up a rehearsal schedule to which he demanded absolute adherence, expected his company to be letter perfect in their parts, and eventually provided them with the best that could be secured in the way of plays, costuming, and scenery. He even gave them a heretofore unheard of security by setting up his Actors Fund to take care of their old age and incapacitation. He was, withal, an astute businessman, who made a fortune for himself and a sizable income for his fellow-players. He was truly a protean genius.

His acting style had the appearance of being perfectly right, perfectly natural. Yet it was the result of careful calculation. In person of middle height, with no great beauty, he had his body under perfect control at all times, moved with great agility and grace, and displayed amazing versatility and vitality. He seems to have had that indefinable quality of all great actors which immediately and irrevocably engages an audience's attention and sympathy. In his long career in the theatre, he essayed fewer than a hundred parts, exhibiting great wisdom in their choice so that he always appeared to best advantage whether in tragedy or comedy. Though he paid some attention to the total stage picture and disciplined his entire company, it is said that he invariably demanded stage center whenever he appeared, and was constantly conscious of his effect upon the audience. He was the center of the orbit around which the other actors moved. Generally speaking, of course, his parts were central roles, and the emphases of the plays were not thus misplaced. His governing principle was by no means a complete emotional involvement in the part, for it is said that in his offstage moments during even the most trying of roles he could attend to bits of theatrical business with perfect ease and judgment.

Mrs. Siddons, on the other hand, achieved her success by a complete emotional capitulation to the part she was playing. It is said that she never spoke a line on the stage which she did not feel, and that often, after a performance of one of the tragic heroines for which she was famous, she reached home still dissolved in tears. She was an indifferent comedienne, but there has been no greater Lady Macbeth, to name but one of the many triumphant parts she played in her thirty-seven years at Drury Lane. She and Garrick belonged to different generations; she came to Drury Lane after his death and lived through the first quarter of the next century—but in the art of acting she was certainly his equal.

Another of the twelve children of the provincial actor Roger Kemble, was Mrs. Siddons' brother John Philip Kemble, whose ability

96 *Garrick in performance*
Left, the closet scene from *Hamlet*. See figure 82. The Ghost is still
dressed in armor; the background is now mid-eighteenth century;
the costumes belong also to the period of the production. Betterton's
full-bottomed wig has given way to the periwig. Right, the
tomb scene from *Romeo and Juliet,* with Mrs. Bellamy. Juliet happily
awakens in this version before Romeo kills himself. Again the
costumes are contemporary with the actors rather than with the period
and place of the play. (Harvard Theatrical Collection)

and fame were only a shade less than hers. He, too, managed Drury
Lane and later Covent Garden, but his genius was not so many-sided
as that of Garrick. He was a far better actor than manager, although
he did spend much time in the preparation of production books for
his performances, particularly the Shakespearean revivals. He is said
to have been a superb Hamlet, and played a distinguished Macbeth
to his sister's Lady. He, too, lived on into the next century.

Though Garrick is generally credited with reforming the acting
style of the times, his natural delivery was not the first to be seen on
the English stage. True, the accepted style of acting tragedy was, as
on the French stage, the sonorous line, the strutting effect. Chief
exponent of this customary style was James Quin (1693–1766), a
great hulk of an Irishman ideally suited to comedy parts (he made
a superb Falstaff, figure 94), who yet insisted on being a tragedian
and performed in a bellowing recitative with labored movement and

incongruous gesture. His comment on first seeing Garrick is famous: "If this young fellow is right, then we are all wrong." Yet Garrick had the aging Quin as a member of his Drury Lane company.

Contemporary with Quin and also a member of Drury Lane was another Irishman, Charles Macklin (ca., 1700–1797), who did a remarkable Shylock there before Garrick's advent as manager (figure 93). Quite independently (or perhaps we should say in the tradition of Betterton), he had developed his own style of natural acting, beginning first with the sense of the lines, delivered in perfectly normal tones and intonations, then heightened for stage projection. The interpretation traditionally assigned to Shylock was that of a comic character; Macklin, as a comedian, was assigned the part. But he completely changed the interpretation, over the protests of Fleetwood, then manager of Drury Lane. The applause with which he was greeted caused Fleetwood to say, "Macklin, you *was* right, at last," and Alexander Pope to remark, "This was the Jew that Shakespeare drew." Macklin, less artful than Garrick, less controlled, less gifted in other phases of theatrical activity, nevertheless taught a system of acting that is surprisingly modern in its concept.

Other notable names of the older generation are those of John Wilks (1665–1732), who was good in both tragedy and comedy, and was one of the managers of Drury Lane before the advent of Garrick; Barton Booth (1681–1733), who was reputedly unsurpassed in his attitudes, or poses assumed while listening to other performers; Colley Cibber (1661–1757), who was a versatile utility actor and became a significant theatre historian; and Anne Oldfield (1638–1730), whose career of unbroken triumph ended with a burial in Westminster Abbey which greatly impressed at least one of the onlookers, Voltaire. Contemporary with Garrick was Spranger Barry (1719–1777), whose very good looks and superior ability made him a rival to Garrick in the esteem of the public (figure 95), their playing of the same parts often being minutely compared; his wife Ann (1734–1801), who is said to have been unsurpassed in comedy, especially as Millamant; Kitty Clive (1711–1785), who frequently battled with Garrick over her desire to play tragic roles although, as Garrick insisted, she was far more suited to the comic roles in which she was eminently successful; and Peg Woffington (ca., 1714–1760), sometime mistress of Garrick who was greatly admired for the spirit and elegance of her performances, no less than for her natural ready wit and intelligence. Of less skill but of some importance were the actor-soldier-of-fortune Anthony Aston, who first came to America in 1703, and who wrote a play for his own performance; and the whole Hallam company, who

97 *Two Cleopatras*
The play is Dryden's *All for Love*. At the left, Mrs. Yates in a 1777
production. At the right, Mrs. Hartley in a production of 1776.
Eighteenth-century actresses generally wore the most elaborate possible
contemporary dress, whatever the part they were playing; these two
Cleopatras nicely illustrate the principle.
(Henry E. Huntington Library and Art Gallery)

later performed with such success in America. Though as in other
aspects of theatre the acting of the eighteenth century was a mixture·
of the old and the new, it presaged a development which eventually
revolutionized the art.

Though Garrick attempted to discipline rehearsals and performances, with no small degree of success, the usual practice was somewhat chaotic. These were repertory companies, with each actor
having at his command the roles of his "line," and being engaged for a
particular company because of his proficiency in these roles. Parts in
new plays were assigned by the company managers in conformance
with these established lines. Stage business in the traditional roles
was based on the performance of the actor who first created the part,
and the attempt was made to maintain this conception—hence the
furor over Macklin's reinterpretation of Shylock. Since so little in
the way of originality was expected or demanded of actors, rehearsals
were rather peremptory and lackadaisical affairs. A revival ordinarily
entailed one quick runthrough at ten in the morning on the day of

performance, and from many accounts actors were prone to miss even this. New plays were prepared in a week to ten days, the rehearsals being held in the same four-hour period in which the revivals were rehearsed. If, by reason of the particularity of the author or manager, a new play took as long as two weeks to prepare, the situation was considered quite unusual. No wonder there are many derogatory contemporary comments about the laxity of performers who were not in command of their lines, whose stage business faltered, or who had grown too old for effectiveness in particular parts. There was evidently a great need for a disciplinarian such as Garrick.

Benefit nights continued in full swing in this period, the end of each season being devoted to them, and seats on the stage being allowed for them, even after stage spectators had been generally abolished. Actors usually worked for the season on fixed salaries which varied from sixty-five dollars to one hundred dollars a week in our money. Sometimes stars were engaged for a flat sum per season, as was Peg Woffington, at a thousand pounds per season—a really immense sum considering that when Garrick first became the chief actor of Drury Lane his acting salary was exactly half that amount. Mrs. Oldfield is said to have earned six hundred pounds for sixty nights, and Quin eight hundred for a season. These salaries were augmented by the benefit nights (at which seventy-five to two hundred pounds were raised for the individual), by special gifts and subscriptions on the part of the public, and by teaching fees. Prominent actors took apprentices and also tutored members of the nobility.

Neophytes in the acting companies worked for a six-month probationary period with no salary at all, and then were paid from ten to thirty shillings a week, depending on their ability and the parts they played.

The eighteenth century marked the height of the provincial circuit system. Acting companies, in an earlier age known by the names of their patrons, now called themselves by the names of the towns which constituted their headquarters. From such a town the individual acting company journeyed to surrounding towns for varying periods of time, ranging from two to three or four months. There were many such provincial circuits throughout England; the most famous were at Bath, Norwich, York, Liverpool, Manchester, Bristol, and Newcastle, all of which operated under royal patent. Special licenses were issued by the Lord Chamberlain, who had replaced the Master of the Revels as an officer for this function, for Brighton, Windsor, Richmond, and Surrey, since these were places of royal residences. These and many other companies not only supplied the provinces with continuing dramatic fare, but served as training grounds for the London theatres. As in the London companies, benefit nights supplied a good share of the actors' incomes, which were otherwise fairly small.

The tradition of the author's third night (when he received all the profits) still persisted, but his payment for the play was now no longer a flat fee, but rather was tied in with production expenses. He could also realize something for publication rights, and this fact became increasingly important in an age of increasing printed materials.

Theatre workers in England in the eighteenth century enjoyed a better reputation than their predecessors generally, and better than their counterparts on the Continent. Garrick moved in the very best social, literary, and artistic circles of his time, and many other performers were held in high esteem. Perhaps their own preparation and performance had something to do with this, but the increasing democracy of their social milieu had more to do with it. Learned and worthy men and women had been in the theatre before, but not for a very long time had actors been accorded the honors given those of eighteenth-century England—and those honors were to increase in succeeding generations.

Summary

In the eighteenth century, England began that domination of world affairs which continued into the present century. Not only in politics, but also in literature, English ideas penetrated to other cultures and had lasting influences. America, too, though declaring its political independence from England, was in all other ways, and particularly in theatre, a reflection of the older society.

In the profusion of human concerns which characterized the eighteenth century, theatre was seldom of prime importance. With the notable exceptions of Goldsmith and Sheridan, writing for the theatre engaged the attentions of only second- or third-rate writers. Even Goldsmith owes a part of his fame to fields of writing other than drama, and Sheridan was vigorously concerned in other activities for a good part of his life. Some worthwhile plays were written by such theatre people as Garrick and the Colmans, but they are not of the first order of literary genius.

The old dependence of theatre on the aristocracy was being replaced by the patronage of less cultured members of society, with a consequent proliferation of nonliterary entertainment. Even in those theatrical presentations most closely approximating literature, there was a marked tendency to meet the tastes of the new audiences by an emphasis upon sentimentality and bourgeois drama. Not until the tastes of the public could be educated to demand the best would superior dramatic fare once more appear.

In the art of acting, however, the period reached great heights and contributed great acting talents which have become legendary. David Garrick, the greatest of these, is in many ways the most typical mirror of his age, developing a perfection of art by rule and precept, much as Pope did in the writing of poetry. The other great acting talent of the age, Sarah Kemble Siddons, is the harbinger of the new Romantic movement which was growing slowly through the neoclassic period, in that she represents the triumph of intuition and total involvement in presenting a character. Partly because acting dominated the arts of eighteenth-century theatre, we may lay to its door the rather dubious distinction of being the seedbed for the star system. But the prevailing practice of the day was that of permanent repertory companies performing continuously, mainly in revivals and adaptations.

On the production side we may lay to this period the development of very large theatre buildings and the establishment of the picture-frame stage as a preferred, if not exclusive, method of production. Both of these items were to dominate theatre practice for many years to come. In addition, the period introduced the use of act drops, and made some slight progress in authentic costuming, though only for actors and not for actresses. Staging grew increasingly complex, with a definite tendency to stress the spectacular and the extravagant. It was a turbulent and interesting time, the culmination of several trends which had preceded it, the harbinger of much that was to come.

CROSS-CURRENTS

IN CONTINENTAL THEATRE

The eighteenth century is often regarded as a sterile period in the history of theatre. How can its accomplishment compare, for instance, with Shakespeare's stage, with that of Lope de Vega, with the theatre of Molière? Obviously, it does not approach the greatness of any of these. Yet in its own way it was an exceedingly interesting and fertile period. It was a time of seeding rather than of harvest, a begetting rather than a consummation. It was a period of great ideas, great contradictions, great conflicts, and some few great emergences. Theatre to some measure reflected all of these, and if there was no really great theatre in the eighteenth century, it was simply that the climate for it did not exist.

France found tinsel in the tradition of the *Roi Soleil;* England learned to curb the incompetence of monarchy with parliamentary powers; Germany and Italy struggled for a recognizable national identity; Russia made her first tentative contacts with the Western world; and Spain had long since passed her glory. These were, as Thomas Paine observed in 1776, "the times that try men's souls."

The application of this phrase is wider than Paine believed, for in addition to political ferment, there was a like ferment in theology, in philosophy, in sociology, in aesthetics. This was the age of Lessing, Kant, Rousseau, Voltaire—pathmakers all. On the Continent, more than in England, the leaders of thought were often directly concerned with theatre. Diderot, longtime friend and associate of Rousseau, was extensively involved in theatre. Along with Voltaire, he considered that theatre was one of the greatest and most effective means for teaching and influencing opinion and action, for training the emotions and sympathies, for demonstrating, in an art form, the chain of cause and effect in nature. Diderot was greatly impressed by the bourgeois drama of George Lillo, believing that this genre of realistic domestic tragedy would have an immediate and powerful effect on its spectators. He was a realist in the theatre long before the term was invented, extending his attention not only to situation and character, but to stage settings, costume, and movement as well. He wrote plays as well as a large number of critical works to illustrate his theses, but being more conversationalist and moralist than dramatist, he was more effective in his precepts than in his practice. Voltaire, on the other hand, with his agile talent for trimming his bark to prevailing winds as well as his outstanding skill in literary expression, was much more successful and active in theatre. Lessing also, less flamboyant and more consistent than Voltaire and with just as patent a literary skill, did much to demonstrate the practicality of his theories through dramatic works of undoubted power.

98 *Elaborate staging*
Left, Louis Jean Desprez design for *Gustaf Vasa* in Stockholm, 1786.
Right, Giorgio Fuentes design for Mozart's *Titus* in Frankfort am Main, 1799. Not only elaborate sets, but also huge crowd scenes were popular on the Continent, as these two designs indicate.
(Stockholm Nationalmuseum; Theater-Museum, Munich)

99 The German Hanswurst
This ubiquitous character appeared in many guises and in all kinds of plays, as this print with its eulogy of his prowess testifies. He was by all odds the most popular character on the German stage for several decades of the century. (Harvard Theatre Collection)

Because the expiring classical drama was firmly entrenched in the most powerful producing agency of the period, the Comédie Française, the new ideas were forced to seek a home in the burgeoning playhouses of the boulevard. The many playwrights who wrote for these houses were, as the century progressed, influenced by their less cultivated audiences to an overemphasis upon incident, single-facet characters illustrating pure virtue and pure vice, tricks of staging, and spectacular presentations. These circumstances caused the development of escapist melodrama and extravagant and sentimental romance, rather than the realistic drama that Diderot envisioned. The emphasis put upon the individual as opposed to the social whole—implicit in Rousseau, Kant, and Diderot—encouraged a break with old forms and the generation of new ones. Thus, though the century began entrenched in neoclassical conventions, it ended in Romanticism. From a slavish adherence to generalization and rules, it changed to individualism and complete disregard of rules.

The progress is an interesting one, fraught with many crossfires, rallies, and retreats. In the turmoil, theatre was often uncertain of its direction, sometimes even of its existence. But the fabulous invalid never completely succumbed, and there are some interesting and significant symptoms to note on the way.

England and Spain influence the Continent

It seems to be true that the development of great theatre is concomitant with the rise of nationalism; Sophocles in Greece, Shakespeare in England, Lope de Vega in Spain, and Molière in France all flourished at periods of intense patriotism and national consciousness. Yet the nature of theatrical art is such that its influences, ideas, and practices transcend national boundaries, and largely disregarding politics, form a world community of their own.

Continental theatre in the eighteenth century graphically illustrates this statement. France, which had provided inspiration for the English Restoration theatre, now for the first time began to see the glories of "that inspired barbarian," as Voltaire called Shakespeare; in addition, the French developed a sentimental drama of their own from the example of English writers in this genre. Spain, too, had its influence on French theatre through the predilections of Beaumarchais; Spanish theatre in the eighteenth century, on the other hand, was almost completely "Frenchified." In Paris, with a most vigorous theatrical tradition behind it, there were five public theatres in operation in addition to numerous and varying court theatres. Foremost was the Comédie Française, charged with the production of legitimate drama, and leaning toward tragedy. A vigorous rival was the Comédie Italienne, no longer solely devoted to the *commedia dell'arte*, but producing most notably the plays of Marivaux, as well as several other French writers. In addition, there was the Opera and two houses devoted to spectacle, farce, and pantomime—Nicolet's and l'Ambigu-Comique. By 1784, there were ten theatres in Paris; in 1791 there were fifty-one.

For a considerable period the nascent drama of Germany aped that of France, performances themselves being given in French. Frederick the Great, for some time a patron and admirer of Voltaire, preferred French to German all his life, and Gottsched, the critic, forced the French mold upon German dramatic practice with singular persistence. The so-called *Aufklärung*, the Age of Enlightenment, in Germany, was the result of French-worship and the neoclassic spirit. Reaction against this arbitrary standard produced a style of theatre called *Sturm und Drang (Storm and Stress)*, and a shift to English models more compatible with the German national character. Ultimately a truly German style emerged.

100 *Famous German theatre personalities*
Left, Carolina Neuber as Elizabeth; right, Friedrich Schroeder as
Falstaff. Germany's most vigorous actress and most talented actor appear
here as Elizabethan characters, but there is little in the costume of
either to suggest that period, except perhaps the rudimentary
ruff on Falstaff. (Theater-Museum, Munich)

Russian theatre was first German and then French before it became Russian. In Italy there was war between Goldoni, whose leanings were French and who spent his last years in Paris, and Gozzi,
whose popularity was great in Germany.

Holberg develops Danish national theatre

In tiny Denmark the genius Ludvig Holberg ridiculed Frenchified
Danes as well as Germanic excesses to foster a vigorous and typical
national drama. It was for the national theatre in Copenhagen that
Holberg wrote, the only other national theatre to be established
since the Comédie Française in 1680. It had been opened by the
enterprising Frenchman, René Montaigu, in 1722, and Holberg was
immediately persuaded to write for it. Closed from 1728 to 1745
because of the assiduous religiosity of the then-reigning monarch,
it opened once more when the climate again turned auspicious.

The Royal Swedish Theatre opened its doors in 1737. A grandiose scheme for a German National Theatre lasted for two years (1767–1769) in Hamburg, expiring with an epitaph from Lessing: "What a naive idea to give the Germans a national theatre when we Germans are not yet a nation!" The Vienna Burgtheatre, dating from 1741, became a truly national theatre, like the Comédie Française, in 1776. The first state-supported, professional theatre in Russia began in 1757, and another National Theatre in Stockholm was opened in 1773. Theatre by then had become active all over the Continent.

Theatre employment respectable and admired—but not settled

This century marked the decline of the dilettante and the part-time worker in the theatre and the rise of theatre as a distinct art and employment. This development is particularly notable in acting, which took on stature as a respectable, even an admired employment in many areas.

In Germany, however, where the imported opera had achieved respectability and aristocratic sanction long before theatre did, there were no standing theatres until the last third of the century. Dramatic performances were given by companies of wandering players, much as had been the custom in pre-Shakespearean England and provincial France. Indeed, the first companies in Germany seem to have been English ones. The Elector of Saxony received a company of English players in 1586, and in 1592 a troupe under one Robert Brown was performing at Frankfort-on-Main. The companies of Reynolds, Roe, and Spencer continued the tradition through the Commonwealth period, first performing in English, then in a mixture of German and English with much and exaggerated pantomime, then finally in German entirely. The programs were mixtures of improvisation, low comedy, exaggerated tragedy, and farce. But in 1727, when the gifted actress Carolina Neuber (figure 100) met and was charmed by Johann Christoph Gottsched, an association of the two was formed to regularize German theatre according to the classical rules as received from the French. The theatrical public, however, was still so sparse that until the end of her life·(1760), Neuber was essentially a traveling player. The German companies differed from their earlier English predecessors chiefly in that many of the players were students who left their books either temporarily or permanently to join the strolling players.

In Italy, Goldoni began writing for the Teatro Sant'Angelo in Venice in 1734, where a capable company of *commedia* artists were in residence. He there attempted to substitute regular comedy, written rather than improvised, for the horseplay and buffoonery of the *commedia*. At the time there were seven playhouses in Venice, with resident companies who toured the peninsula in off-seasons. Here the tradition of aristocratic participation in theatrical activities, as a parallel to the professionalism of the *commedia* players, endured perhaps the longest. We find a member of the Arcadian Academy at Rome (Joseph Cooper Walker) writing in 1799 that Italian towns still abounded in private theatres, and that theatrical activities were yet the favorite amusement of the Italian nobility. Many of the nobles maintained private companies of actors and musicians, and in addition all the large cities had public theatres for both opera and drama.

In Russia as the century progressed the companies were either groups of free citizens—the "independent" companies—or troupes of serfs, trained and maintained by the landed nobility for their amusement and often bought and sold. When a noble acquired a freeman to augment his serf company, the newcomer was allowed the distinction of prefixing the equivalent of "mister" before his name on the programs. One of the most noted, and one of the first, private companies was that of Carl Knipper at the Petersburg Foundling Home; many of his pupils later became famous.

Leading players, and even whole companies sometimes traveled outside their national boundaries to perform in foreign cities; French companies played in London, German ones in St. Petersburg, and Italian ones in Paris. In the settled centers of theatrical activity, the ranks of metropolitan players were being constantly enlarged or changed by accessions from the provinces; Quin and Macklin, for instance, had come to London from Dublin. Not only plays traveled from country to country, but also players and production techniques.

Audiences set the pace

Whatever the origins of the stage presentations, the audiences everywhere were supreme and dictatorial. The German public defeated Gottsched's attempt at purification of their theatre fare, insisting on the *Nachspiel*, or farce, no matter how serious the occasion, and clinging to their love of native comic characters even to the extent of enjoying a Hanswurst (figure 99), or Pickleherring, in *The Merchant of Venice*. The Italian public's love of the riotous and irregular *commedia* temporarily defeated Goldoni's attempts at reform and led to his removal to Paris, where the sophisticated public often unmercifully derided an actor whose enunciation slipped, or whose gesture was not in the accepted mode. In Spain, the theatres were general meeting places, with admission to the house separate from that required for a seat; also, the bullfight was beginning to displace the theatre as the national amusement.

In the theatres of Paris, still the most brilliant on the Continent, there was seating on the stage for more than half the century. Voltaire, convinced that this practice spoiled the reality of the performances, as Diderot had previously maintained, succeeded in abolishing spectators from the Comédie stage in 1759 by soliciting a gift of sixty thousand francs from the Count de Lauraguais to compensate the actors for the decreased revenue they would thus suffer. The pit was still the resort of the quarrelsome element of the masculine public, and guards (Diderot complained that they "stifled his enjoyment") were assigned to keep order. Boxes were rented for the season by the noble and the wealthy, a practice which assured a basic income for the actors. But that very basic income, complained Mercier, tended to make them lazy.

In almost all areas, eighteenth-century Continental theatre was more sensitive to the demands of a changing audience than had been its immediate predecessors excepting only the theatre of Shakespeare, whose audience so largely determined the direction of its accomplishments.

Translations and adaptations

During the whole of the eighteenth century, there was a lively business in translated and adapted plays. Corneille, Racine, Molière, and the lesser French dramatists were translated or liberally adapted in Italy, Russia, Germany, and the Scandinavian countries, as well as in Spain. We have seen how George Lillo's *London Merchant* invaded the Continent, as did Cumberland's *The West Indian* and Addison's *Cato* which appeared in 1732 under J. C. Gottsched's aegis. For all its lack of appeal to us, this was one of the few English plays which Voltaire praised. Richardson's novel *Pamela* (1740), influenced a number of plays in a new type called the *drame,* and was at least once directly rendered into another language. Goldoni produced his *Pamela Unmarried,* taking the liberty to make Pamela's father an exiled Scotch count, because an Italian audience would not tolerate the marriage of a gentleman to a plebeian.

Shakespeare was increasingly influential in original playwriting, and was often translated into French and German. J. F. Ducis had a very great success with *Hamlet* in 1769 by rewriting it in alexandrine verse. He then did the same with *Macbeth.* The great German actor Schroeder made several of Shakespeare's plays popular with the German public, taking some interesting liberties with them:

293

101 *Eighteenth-century scene design*
Left, a production in Amsterdam, with the wing, backdrop, and
border system in perspective, and a curious relic of the Middle Ages in the
décor of Hell. This is a scene which could be shifted in full view of the
audience. Right, Guiseppe Galli-Bibiena designed this elaborate
proscenium and stationary set for an opera in Vienna as early as 1716.
(Harvard Theatre Collection; Theater-Museum, Munich)

Hamlet did not die in Schroeder's version, and there was no duel with
Laertes; Cordelia came to life again in *Lear,* and the old King did
not die (this was, of course, the standard happy ending that was also
played in England throughout the century); *Othello* also had a happy
ending. This sounds like what Hollywood does today in adapting
stories for the screen, and it was probably done for the same reason:
to suit the tastes of an audience who were sentimental enough to
want things to turn out well for the hero, whether or not there was
any dramatic justification.

A curious holdover from earlier times was still evident in the
writing and elaborate production of Church drama and religious
plays in Spain, Italy, and Russia. Some of these were adaptations of
Biblical stories, like the ten sacred dramas of Annibale Marchese;
some were of the morality type, like *About the Penance of a Sinful
Man,* written by the churchman Dimitry, Metropolitan of Moscow,
given in St. Petersburg in 1752. But most of the theatres of Europe had
long outlived this type of play, and turned to other things.

Original writings stale and slavish

There were still classical tragedies in abundance, poor and thin
though the strain had become. They were still on classic models as
interpreted by the French, who were the high priests of the cult. In
Italy, where many noblemen now wrote tragedies, an interesting

exception to French Classicism was Count Vittorio Alfieri of Asti (1749–1803), who knowing neither French nor Greek drama modeled himself on the Romans, and turned out a long list of typical plays— *Il Polinice, L'Antigone, L'Agamemnone, L'Oreste, La Merope, La Sophonisba,* to name only a few. Alfieri's is a name still remembered, as is that of Scipione Maffei (1675–1755), who has been called "the glory of the tragic muse of this age." His most noteworthy play is *Merope.* Perhaps the only other name which has interest for us today is that of Gasparo Gozzi (1713–1786), elder brother of the more famous Carlo, who admired Voltaire and wrote tragedies after him. Prizes were sometimes given by aristocrats, both in Italy and Spain, for the best tragedy, but the gesture brought forth no plays of merit.

Voltaire's influence extended to Russia, where Alexei Sumarokov (1718–1777) wrote a long list of plays with plots from Russian history, adhering to the unities and using the heroic style. Nikolev was another writer of tragedy, using materials chiefly from the classics. In Germany, Gottsched had begun the classical emphasis before Voltaire's eminence, and the earlier examples of tragedy in Germany follow Corneille and Racine: Behrmann's *Horace* (1733) from Corneille's play, *Timoleon* (1735), and Koch's *Titus Manlius* of the same period. But here as elsewhere Voltaire was soon translated and slavishly copied as well.

As for the master himself, though he was convinced, and able to convince others, that he was revitalizing classical tragedy, his result was to completely destroy its vitality. Voltaire's tragedies compare poorly with those of Corneille and Racine. Why, with his undoubted genius, should this be so? Voltaire was the ultimate spokesman of his age. Believing, with Diderot, that theatre was an admirable rostrum for the inculcation of moral truths he not only, as the modern critic Eleanor Jourdain says *(Dramatic Theory and Practice in France, 1690–1808,* 1921) implied a moral in the tone of his plays, but also made it explicit in the plot and in the words of his characters. His first play, *Oedipe,* presented at the Comédie Française in 1718, was a great success, but his next two in the same vein were failures for a variety of reasons. From that point on he largely abandoned the spirit of classical tragedy, injecting elements in which his contemporaries were interested: love stories, religious controversy, and the romance of strange times and places. His *Death of Caesar* (1743) shows the influence of Shakespeare's play, but the vitality of the original is here almost emasculated. His *Mahomet, or Fanaticism* (1742) has a religious thesis. In *Zaïre* (1732), love supplied the motive of the action. In *Sémiramis* (1748) he introduces a ghost, and

102 *Two plays by Schiller*
Above, a scene from *The Robber,* 1781. The costumes are presumably
sixteenth century but succeed only in not being eighteenth century.
Right, a scene from *The Bride of Messina,* 1803. Here the presumably
classical costumes include long tights for the men and some wreaths
of laurel leaves. (Nationale Forschungs-und Gedenkstätten, Weimar)

in *Tancred* (1760) he states in the preface that he wishes the appeal
of the play to be helped by the eye. With the exception of *Zaïre* and
Mérope, which deserve to be ranked with the best of French classical
tragedy, his tragedies have little to say to us today even though,
primarily through the long prefaces to each of his plays and his other
very facile and myriad writings, he was immensely influential in his
own day.

Other writers of some note in the field of classical tragedy were
Longepierre, L'Abbé Genest, La Noue, Campistron, and Crébillon,
the last of whom was a considerable rival of Voltaire's, primarily
because of the melodramatic and horrible nature of his subject matter, softened for his ultra refined audience by expository narrative
in the tradition of pseudoclassicism.

Voltaire, whose genius was primarily intellectual and critical,
should have been an expert writer of comedy. But he was too closely
attuned to the spirit of his age, and rejected the critical objectivity

of Molière in favor of the "man of feeling" who triumphed in the Romantic revolution. The closest to Molière in time and in character is J. F. Regnard (1656–1710), who drew on the humors of the provinces as did Molière. Another writer much like him is Dufresny (1648–1724). Marivaux (1688–1763), who wrote chiefly for the Comédie Italienne, was the best of the comedy writers of the early century, injecting psychological analysis of character into comedy as Molière had done. His best are two plays still popular, *The Surprises of Love* (1722) and *The Game of Love and Chance* (1730). The first significant writer of comedy in Russia, Fonvizin (1745–92), wrote realistic satires in the tradition of Molière such as *The Minor* and *The Brigadier*.

The eighteenth century insistence on opinions and social conditions increasingly deployed attention from character conflict, which had been the main concern of earlier comedy writers. Even Marivaux, albeit unwittingly, participated in the genesis of the sentimental comedy with such plays as *The Confident Mother* (1735), *The Faithful Wife* (1755), and *The False Confidences* (1737), the very first play of the French theatre ending in a marriage that cut across the boundaries of social class. Dancourt (1661–1725) and LeSage (1667–1747) both concerned themselves with middle-class manners; they used traditional names for their characters, but were realistic in that they worked out the plot to what seemed a logical conclusion rather than a manufactured dénouement. The latter's *Crispin, Rival of his Master* (1707) is one of his most delightful and successful plays. Toward the end of the century, Beaumarchais (1732–1799) produced a series of comedies in which he said he tried to combine the fun and intrigue of comedy with the emotional appeal of the *drame.* How successful he was is attested to by the continuing appeal of *The Barber of Seville* (1774) and *The Marriage of Figaro* (1784), the best of his many plays.

Goldoni—outstanding comedian

The changing tenor of the times was evident in other countries, too. There was no high comedy in Spain and Portugal, and none in Germany. The few comic plays in Russia, by Sumarokov and Knyazhnin, were true to type in using contemporary events and criticizing the foibles of society. *The Mother-Rival, The Querulous Woman, The Braggart, A Petty Quarrel* are the names of some of them. The chief inheritor of Molière's mantle was the Italian Carlo Goldoni (1707–1792), who ended his days in poverty in Paris. Writing more than a hundred plays in his lifetime, once at the rate of sixteen in a single year, he produced several that have lived to aftertimes. Justly his most famous are *The Mistress of the Inn* (1752) and *The Fan* (1765), although some critics consider *The Boors* (1759) to be his masterpiece. But even Goldoni said that he chose to picture virtue rather than to ridicule vice; thus he departed from the spirit of Molière and entered into the spirit of the new age. His rival Carlo Gozzi (1720–1806), beginning with the established *commedia,* injected fantastic elements, producing what he called "fairy dramas," and presaging the coming period of Romanticism. His best known play has been translated into English as *The Three Oranges* (1761). Holberg, in Copenhagen, the only other writer of the type in the eighteenth century, did not eschew ridicule, but reflected his age in his evident social consciousness. *Jeppe of the Hill* (1722) is his best play; in it he evidences his belief that changes in society should not take place too swiftly, and thus he allied himself with Diderot who preached the didactic mission of drama.

The drame—a popular catchall

The outstanding genre of the eighteenth century was the *drame* which may be said to include domestic tragedy, sentimental comedy, romanticized history, and possibly fantasy. All audiences everywhere were demanding it. Voltaire's *Nanine* (1749) was an attempt to satisfy this taste; in its preface he, like Lessing a few years later,

298

103 *Two famous plays, one famous player*
Left, Goethe as Orestes in his own *Iphigenia,* with the title character
in a voluminously draped pseudo-Greek robe. Right, a scene from
Schiller's *Wallenstein,* showing the Gothic influences on stage décor typical
of the late eighteenth century. The boots and the heroic feathers
are still in evidence for the men.
(Nationale Forschungs-und Gedenkstätten, Weimar)

justified the type by saying that true comedy may contain both
humorous and emotional scenes. Nivelle de la Chaussée, in *The False
Antipathy* (1733), produced a play primarily designed to arouse
tender emotions rather than to excite laughter. In this and in his
succeeding plays, the comic elements are merely episodic, becoming
less and less frequent in occurrence, until in *Mélinde* (1741) there is
no humorous line or role at all. One of his later plays, *The Governess*
(1747), was a precursor of *East Lynne.*

This drama of sensibility, which broke down the distinctions between comedy and tragedy, was often called by that paradoxical
name, *comédie larmoyante,* or tearful comedy. Diderot, primarily
a critic, found the type useful for didactic purposes and produced
three plays of the kind, notably *The Father of the Family* (1758).

104 *The Schouwberg, Amsterdam, 1772*
Above, an interior view toward the stage, showing the symmetrical
perspective scenery which was prevalent throughout the period and
the lighting of the stage apron by chandeliers in the proscenium arch.
Right, the floor plan of the house and stage, with sketches showing how
various machines are contrived and operated. The plan indicates
the use of several sets of wing flats, some set on an angle, and
three backdrops. (Harvard Theatre Collection)

Mercier was another practitioner. In Russia tearful comedy also flourished, with Lukin writing *Rewarded Constancy* and *The Spend-
thrift Reformed by Love.* In the same period, toward the end of the
century, Plavilshchikov produced *The Store Clerk* and *Wretched and
Solitary One,* whose very titles are typical of the genre.

It was in Germany that the new type had its chief impact. J. E.
Schlegel (1719–1749) anticipated it with his two comedies, *The
Triumph of the Good Woman* and *The Silent Beauty,* though these
were written in verse, and hence were not true to the genre in form
at least. (Diderot, in laying down rules for the *drame,* had said that
realistic drama must be in prose.) C. F. Gellert, with a play each in
1745, 1746, and 1747, truly established the type in Germany as La
Chaussée had in France.

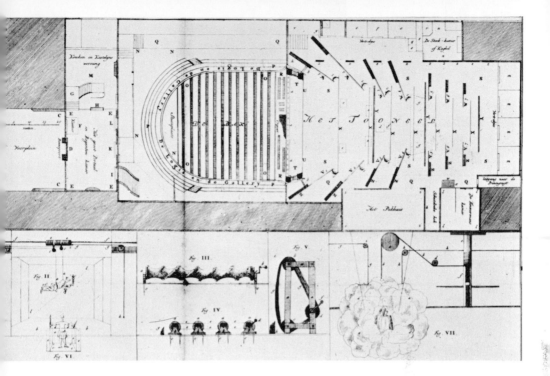

Lessing was perhaps its outstanding exponent. Under the influence of the English novelists and writers of domestic tragedy, he produced in 1755 *Miss Sara Sampson,* a play which was immensely influential with other writers. In Lessing's play the situation is real, the development logical. It does not depend, as do so many of La Chaussée's plays, upon mistaken identity and the long arm of chance. In it, of course, audiences of today find too much didacticism, too much sentimentality, and too many scenes designed to elicit tears. Nevertheless, as we have said, the fame of this play influenced a whole generation of German writers. Lessing had preceded it with *The Young Lady-Scholar* (1748), written for Carolina Neuber, and *The Jew* (1749), which included the first noble Jew in German literature.

Though Lessing was primarily a critic, and did immense service to German literature by successfully combatting the French pseudo-classicism of Gottsched, two others of his plays, *Minna von Barnhelm* (1772) and *Emilia Galotti* (1772) were of great significance. In the first, he created two memorable characters: Tellheim, a manly but sensitive soldier with a most punctilious sense of honor, and Minna, one of the most charming heroines in German drama. In the latter, he took the classic story of Virginia, killed by her father to save her

105 *Opera house at Stuttgart*

De la Guépierre's plan for the opera house at Stuttgart, with a
cutaway sketch of the interior, as published in Diderot's *Encyclopaedia*.
The floor plan shows more space allotted to the stage than to the
auditorium—a usual custom for a theatre which stressed spectacular
productions. Note the interesting seating arrangement in the plan, which
includes a special box in the center of the auditorium.

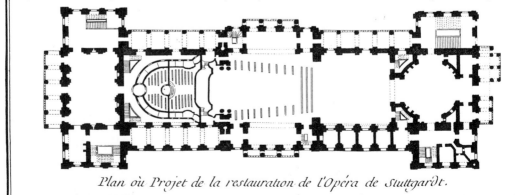

coupe du nouvel Opéra de Stuttgardt esquißé pour en voir l'effet sans aucunes regles de Perspectiv

Plan où Projet de la restauration de l'Opéra de Stuttgardt.

from the lascivious decumvir Appius, and translated it to a tragedy of common life. His chief disciples in the theatre were J. F. von Conegk, J. W. von Brawe, and C. F. Weisse, who was perhaps the most successful German playwright of his day.

The Age of Enlightenment was followed by the *Sturm und Drang* period in Germany, influenced by the Romanticism of Rousseau, Young, and Macpherson. It produced Goethe's *Goetz von Berlichingen* (1773), *Clavigo* (1774), and the first draft of *Faust* (1775). His imitators were F. M. von Klinger (one of whose plays gives the name to the period), J. M. R. Lenz, H. L. Wagner, J. A. Leisewitz, and Friedrich Mueller. The most typical and most widely known of the plays of this type were by J. F. von Schiller: *The Robber* (1781) (figure 102), *Fiesco* (1784), *Intrigue and Love* (1783), and *Don Carlos* (1787). *Sturm und Drang* was followed by a neoclassical period which had much of the romantic about it, to which Schiller contributed *Maria Stuart* (1800) and *Wilhelm Tell* (1804), and Goethe contributed *Iphigenia* (1779, figure 103) and *Tasso* (1780), as well as the final form of *Faust*.

German Romanticism preceded the similar flowering in France. In France, Romanticism was the culmination of developments like those noted here in Germany; it will be treated more extensively in a later chapter. From complete dependency at the beginning of the century, German dramatic literature had achieved by its end a complete independence and an undeniable vitality. The stream of dramatic literature in the eighteenth century is often muddied and contradictory, but eventually leads to new forms and new ideas.

Many playhouses, all alike

Proliferation in number, conformity in kind is the rule of eighteenth-century playhouses. We have mentioned that Paris, which began the century with three theatres in operation, had five in 1754, and fifty-one in 1791. In Italy, every city of any size had one or more theatres, and Venice had seven. The most celebrated public theatres were in Parma, Verona, Turin, Rome, Bologna, and Naples. Vienna had two famous playhouses, the Burgtheater and the Kärtnerthor. Though there was no subsidized national theatre in Spain, there were still many playhouses scattered throughout the provinces. Lisbon's theatre was burned by the Inquisition in 1745, however, and the drama languished. Peter the Great established a theatre in St. Petersburg, and built a playhouse in 1702. After his death theatre stagnated except for private amateur performances at the holidays. Anna Ioannovna opened a special theatre room in the Winter Palace in

106 *Two Bibiena designs*
The most influential scene designers of the eighteenth century were the
Bibienas, whose ideas found wide acceptance throughout the
Continent. These two designs illustrate a principle which they are
said to have discovered—the use of diagonal or asymmetrical
linear perspective. The intricacy and massiveness of the stage picture are
typical of the many designs from Bibiena hands. See figure 101.
(Harvard Theatrical Collection)

1734 to revive interest, but there were no regular theatrical performances in Moscow until 1756. In 1787 a ballroom was transformed into
a theatre in Kharkov, in honor of the Empress' visit, and about the
same time, Count Sheremetev, on his estate in Kuskovo, built a
theatre designed by Valli, a famous architect. The first issue of
Reichard's *Theater-kalender* in 1776 lists fourteen German theatres,
to which six more were added the next year. By the last decade of the
century, there were well over thirty. Notable among these were the
rejuvenated Hamburg Theatre under Schroeder's management, that
of Koch in Berlin, Seyler in Gotha, Döbbelin in Dresden, Marchand
in Frankfort, and Goethe in Weimar.

Almost without exception, whether the theatres were buildings
erected for the purpose, rebuilt from other structures, or installed in
large rooms previously having other uses, the theatre auditoriums of
the eighteenth century exhibited the same characteristics: pit, boxes,
galleries, and a stage with a proscenium arch.

The wooden structure built by Peter the Great near the Kremlin
in 1702 was 140 feet by 105 feet, and forty-nine feet high. It is
described as having a gallery, benches, doors, windows, and a lined
ceiling. That converted from a ballroom at Kharkov is described as
being lined throughout with red woolen cloth, as having armchairs

304

and benches in the orchestra, and large boxes seating twenty each, with a total seating capacity of four hundred.

Over most of the Continent, the horseshoe auditorium, taken from the original Italian design, was prevalent. Though the seventeenth-century structure at Parma, still in use, had no boxes, box seating was the preference of most eighteenth-century audiences. The Teatro S. Samuele at Venice is described as having seven rows of boxes, with theatres in general having from twenty-four to thirty boxes in a row. The Teatro S. Giovanni Crisostomo, chiefly devoted to opera, was typical of theatre design. It had five tiers of boxes, thirty-one in each tier, all highly embellished by sculptured ornaments, with four boxes on each side in the proscenium arch. The stage was eighty-five feet deep and sixty-three feet wide, and the auditorium was lighted by a great candelabra which could be withdrawn when the performance began.

This "chicken-coop" design for auditoriums, so prevalent in Italy and later throughout the Continent, may have been a development from the Italian Renaissance custom of setting up booths, sometimes one above the other, to accommodate the nobles and ladies at outdoor spectacles. In any event, it is a radical departure from the bank of seats which was incorporated into the Teatro Olimpico and other neoclassical structures.

Luigi Riccoboni, who marvelled at the size and splendor of the Venetian theatres, was disappointed when he visited the Comédie Française. He found the house cramped and crowded, and not splendid in appearance. The original house, which was replaced in 1782, had been built in 1689 (figure 69), at which time the company, hitherto playing in the Guénégaud, moved to the first house especially constructed for it. In the old house, there were only two tiers of boxes, with nineteen boxes to a tier. Atop these was the gallery, equipped with benches. The floor of the auditorium was divided into three parts: the orchestra pit, with benches for ladies to each side of a protracted center area used by the musicians; the standing pit, reserved for men; and the so-called amphitheatre, or sloping rear section of the floor, which was also equipped with benches. The apron of the stage extended twelve feet beyond the proscenium line, and until stage spectators were abolished in 1759, the area both before and behind the proscenium arch was equipped with benches behind a balustrade. The edge of the stage had footlights and a prompter's box. The stage itself was forty-one feet deep by fifty-four feet wide, but the spectators' benches used up a great deal of the acting area. The floor of the stage was slightly raked.

107 *Juvarra*
These two designs are in the nature
of working drawings, showing how the
effects are to be achieved. Left, the
elevation is accompanied
by a rough floor plan showing how
the painted flats are to be set; above,
numbers on the wings at the left and the
cloud borders show how these are
to be arranged. (Victoria and Albert
Museum, Museum of Modern Art)

When the new house was built in 1782, it conformed more nearly
to the design of which Riccoboni approved. The stage area was about
half the total length of the house, there was no extended stage apron,
no standing pit, no amphitheatre—and considerably more boxes. The
horseshoe-shaped auditorium had a floor completely equipped with
benches for spectators, much to the dramatist Mercier's disgust. The
new relationship between audience and stage was symbolized by the
proscenium arch, behind which the actors now played, and before
which Goethe, speaking of his own proscenium-arch theatre, warned
his actors they must never step. The picture-frame stage was firmly
established.

Settings keyed to variety

Just as the prevailing style in auditorium architecture was the
opera-type house, so the prevailing mode of stage setting was the

wing and groove system. Banishing the spectators from the stage of the Théâtre Français had made it possible to expand the use of scenery there, and the stage of the new Comédie Française had seven sets of side wings and a back curtain; that of La Scala at Milan had ten sets of grooves, with the possibility of using back-curtains at seven of these. In the poorer or less highly developed theatres, the settings were simple; the small ballroom theatre of Kharkov had but two stage settings, an interior and a forest, and a single front curtain. But often the stage appointments in Russia as elsewhere were sumptuous. Count Sheremetev's Valli-designed theatre is said to have had eight curtains, almost two hundred settings, fifty-two side sets, sixty-eight minor decorative accessories, seventeen large chests of wardrobe, and seventy-six chests of hand props.

The usual stage investiture of the smaller German theatres was the shutter arrangement of the Restoration stage, which they operated as "long and short scenes." At Weimar, Goethe's little theatre seated only five hundred people, though for the first time, the seats had arms and numbers, and the stage was but forty feet square, with a thirty-six foot proscenium opening. The stage machinery was simple, chiefly five sets of sliding wings, and the whole house was equipped with oil lamps which could be dimmed. Since Goethe conceived his mission to be that of raising the level of poetry in literature, he did not emphasize scenic investiture.

Elsewhere in Germany, however, the love for metamorphoses, machines, and disguises was evident from theatre handbills, and here as throughout most of Europe, elaborate stage effects wrought with pulleys and platforms and the various machines of the Renaissance came to enjoy high favor. Transformations, wherever they could be achieved, were tried. The fame of the Hall of Machines persisted as a model, and the relaxing of the classical rules of unity in time and place made changes of scene mandatory.

During the eighteenth century, the popularity of machines was to be effectively challenged, if not entirely displaced, by the magnificently conceived settings of the members of the Bibiena family and their followers (figure 106). This family, devoted to stage design, covered four generations, from the middle of the seventeenth century to the end of the eighteenth. The designs of the older members stressed the forced diminishing perspective in absolute symmetry which marked the theatre artists of the Renaissance. These were almost invariably highly ornamented in profuse baroque style, giving a feeling of immense space and magnificence. In the second and third generations, the designers tended to substitute for symmetrical

108 *Costumes and costume reform*
Above left, Dumesnil as Athalie in elaborate court dress with heroic
feathers; above right, Lekain and Vestris in Voltaire's *Sémiramis* in 1748.
The tonnelet of the men and the elaborate court dress of the women
were the admired and accepted costumes for eighteenth-century French
actors. On the facing page, left, Mme. Favart in *The Three Sultanas*, 1761,
for which costuming she was severely criticized. Right, costume
design "neither too Chinese nor too French" for Voltaire's *The Chinese
Orphan*, 1755. These illustrate the wind of change which was blowing
in the latter half of the century. Voltaire's reforms were moderate
and fairly well accepted; those of Mme. Favart, more extreme and less
well accepted. (Yale Theatrical Prints Collection, Harvard
Theatre Collection)

perspective the much more interesting angular perspective, keeping,
however, the same grandeur and ornamentation. Often stairways
and platforms, which may have been practical, were included as a
part of their designs. The Bibienas worked not only in Italy, but in
Russia and Germany as well.

One of their followers, Servandoni (1695–1766), brought the
principle of angular asymmetrical perspective to Paris, producing a
grandeur and spaciousness which Parisians had not seen before. The
Roman, Juvarra (1676–1736), working from the same artistic principle, produced designs which seem to provide for a permanent
architectural setting downstage, with changes of scene by means of

painted drops or flats behind (figure 107). The Venetian, Piranesi (1720–78), elaborated this idea by putting bold, dark architectural forms downstage, with lighter shapes beyond.

All of these effects would seem to have been achieved by the use of careful scene painting on flats and an appropriate arrangement of these on the stage, although a few of the forms might well have been partially sculptured.

Algarotti (1712–64), for nine years advisor to Frederick the Great on operatic problems, urged the addition of chiaroscuro lighting to the effects that these designers achieved by use of line and of dark and light areas, in order to underline the mood of the production. Thus, said he, the lights and darks of the scenic designer could be embellished by light rather than destroyed by it. Not only should lighting enhance the theatrical effect, he thought, but all illusion in scenery, costume, and acting, as well, should be aimed to this end. Algarotti has a very modern sound.

Thus, during the course of the century, variety in scenic investiture became the rule, with the type and kind dependent upon the species of play to be presented.

Attempts at costume reform

As in eighteenth-century England, so, too, on the Continent there were various attempts at costume reform, not all of them successful.

109 Watteau's "The French Comedians"
This famous painting, from the first quarter of the century, shows the
typically elaborate contemporary costume of the women, and for
the men, the fringed tonnelet, the high-heeled fringed boots, the feathered
hat, the intricate decoration. (The Metropolitan Museum of Art)

If anything, the traditional Continental costumes at the beginning
of the century were more formalized, and in many ways more ridiculous than those of the English. German actors of the early century
used a standard costume that was as curious, in its way, as that of
the French. All wore, universally, black velvet knickerbockers, which
each actor supplied himself. Atop this he wore a brown cloth coat
and a silk waistcoat given him by the manager. If he were to play
the part of a king, the waistcoat would be gold embroidered; he
would wear a full-bottomed wig, a hat with feathers, and would carry
a sceptre. Classic heroes were distinguished by a scarf tied across
the brown cloth coat, a helmet, and a sword. Sometimes a breastplate
of sham gold replaced the scarf for Greek heroes. For these characters, the hair was worn pigtail fashion, topped with a headgear
of feathers. In the poorer companies, lace was often cut from paper,
gold embroideries from gold paper. But whatever the period or the

character, the black velvet breeches were mandatory. Gottsched, to his credit, realized the ridiculousness of this outfit, and urged that his *Cato* be played in Greek robes. But when Carolina Neuber, quarreling with him in 1741, presented the play with authentic costumes, he was made as ridiculous in the eyes of the audience as she desired he should be. The departure was too radical. Five years later, the actor Ekhof was playing J. E. Schlegel's *Canut* in a red velvet coat instead of the brown cloth, a full-bottomed wig, and a cane hooked over his left arm. By 1773, German audiences were ready to accept Goethe's *Goetz von Berlichingen* at Hamburg in historically correct costumes, but such costume seems to have been the exception rather than the rule.

In France, too, there were reforms. Those which were not violent were well received; those which were too drastic were as ill-received as Gottsched's *Cato*. As in Germany, the early eighteenth-century French company had a standard method of costuming. The women were garbed in contemporary court dress, with large paniers, much fringe, lace, and bright ribbons on the dress, and diamonds and feathers in their elaborately dressed hair. The men had a hero's costume consisting of a large full-bottomed wig, three-cornered hat with many feathers, elaborately worked gilt armor, wide silk sleeves with lace cuffs, tonnelet, a sword belt with a small ornamental dagger, gilt-fringed gloves, silk stockings, and embroidered half boots trimmed with gold, with high red heels. In the hand was either a fan, a wand, a sceptre, or a cane, depending on the character. These were magnificent, expensive costumes, often costing from three to ten thousand francs. They were used even in the "antique" plays, with the sole exception that here the lover (an eighteenth-century innovation in the classics) wore the contemporary court dress without the tonnelet.

In 1751, the accomplished actress, Mlle. Clairon, discarded the panier to play Electra (figure 111), to Diderot's great delight; but the costume, even without the panier was far from Greek. Indeed, Mlle. Clairon felt that the true Greek costume belonged on statues, and that her representation of the style on stage need only follow the general outline.

The same sort of mild reform was effected by Voltaire four years later, when he asked the designer, Joseph Vernet, to create costumes "neither too Chinese or too French" for his production of *The Chinese Orphan* at the Comédie Française (figure 108). The result would seem hardly effective to us today—trousers showing below full skirts and elaborate headdresses marked by the usual feathers—but the

110 *Two costumes from Holland*
Left, Rosa Ritzler as an Indian princess; right, Charlotte Schirmer as
Elizabeth. These two figures from performances near the end of the
century illustrate once more the principle of using contemporary lines with
slight adaptations to give historical or geographic flavor. Ritzler
as an Indian is only a little more believable than Anne Bracegirdle
(figure 83) and Schirmer is hardly more convincing than Neuber
as Elizabeth. See figure 100. (Harvard Theatre Collection)

innovation was greeted with enthusiasm. When, the next year, Mme.
Favart at the Comédie Italienne appeared in *The Chinese* with
costumes actually made in China, she was received less enthusiastically. She had been severely criticized three years earlier, as well,
in *The Loves of Bastien and Bastienne*, for appearing in the title
role in a plain linen dress, simply dressed hair, and wooden shoes
such as village women wear. But she persisted in her search for
authenticity, and in 1761 appeared in *The Three Sultanas* in costumes
made in Constantinople (figure 108).

The ballet master, Noverre, had long inveighed against the panier
and the tonnelet, but so advanced were his recommendations concerning not only costume but movement, that he had little practical
effect. More telling was the appearance of the actor, Lekain, as
Ghengis Khan in *The Chinese Orphan*, minus tonnelet and dressed
in long Turkish trousers, fur-trimmed cloak, and turban with ostrich

plumes. He used an adaptation of the same costume when he appeared as Orosmon in *Zaïre*.

But as in England both actors and actresses were very fond of their sumptuous dress, the actresses particularly always wishing to appear at their most beautiful and magnificent, regardless of the part they were playing, and verisimilitude in costuming made headway very slowly, despite the urgings of Voltaire and Diderot.

The universal use of white makeup (powdered pearls or a starch-bismuth mixture applied with a wash) was slowly displaced by such a one as Mlle. Clairon, who said that it precluded all facial expression—so much a part of characterization—and urged that others use, as she did, nothing but an artistic heightening of the natural features, and a coiffure suited to the character.

Thus did a few practical visionaries point the way for things to come.

Reforms effected in acting

More reforms were effected in the department of acting than in theatre architecture and costumes, for this was the Age of Great Acting on the Continent, as well as in England.

Paris was the theatrical center of Europe and the Comédie Française, in all its aspects, had counterparts throughout the Continent. The accepted style of acting was bombastic and declamatory, and hedged about with conventions. For more than half the century, the acting area at the Théâtre Français was restricted to an open square about twelve feet on a side because of the audience seated on the stage. The players formed a semicircle on the stage, moving front and center as they spoke, declaiming their lines with a sonorous delivery in tragedy and a chanting singsong in comedy. Movement was graceful and studied, gesture restrained. Michel Baron caused a sensation in his younger days by letting his hands go above his head —a gesture scandalously against the rules. These practices were affected even by the most lowly of the German traveling companies.

The attempts at a more natural style which were tried throughout the century were the work of individual gifted actors and actresses, reinforced by precepts set down from time to time by critics, playwrights, and managers. In France, the final banishment of the audience from the stage of the Théâtre Français allowed more freedom of gesture, more attention to motivated action and to stage pictures, which contributed toward underlining and enhancing the emotional impact of given scenes. Voltaire and Diderot were exponents of a more natural style of acting; in Italy, Goldoni prefaced his sixteen

111 *Actors and costumes*
Above left, Champmeslé as Phèdre; above right, Lecouvreur as
Cornelie; below left, Talma as Nero; below right, Clairon as Electra.
In all of these, some approximation to historical accuracy is present, but
it is evident, in the print of Clairon, that the drapery was superimposed
over the eighteenth-century female silhouette. (Yale Theatrical
Prints Collection, Harvard Theatre Collection)

famous comedies with a set of rules for actors which included audible, clear enunciation; natural gestures; ensemble playing; and a decorous offstage life. The principles of Ekhof and Schroeder in Germany culminated in Goethe's famous *Rules for Actors,* stressing much the same standards as Goldoni had earlier enunciated.

These rules had been preceded by a number of experiments in the training of actors. The playwright Capacelli had founded a theatre at Bologna to institute a new style. Ekhof started his Academy for Actors in 1753, and Russian theatre might be said to have begun with an official decree in 1756 providing for the training of an acting company as a part of the royal Corps of Cadets. By 1779, a theatrical training and acting company had been established at the St. Petersburg Foundling Home under Carl Knipper.

As we have said, the major changes came through successful individual endeavors. Michel Baron (1653–1729), who began so auspiciously in Molière's theatre, retired from the stage at the peak of his career, leaving the boards to the howlers, like Pierre Beaubour (1662–1725) who took over his place at the Comédie. His feminine counterparts were Mlle. Champmeslé (1642–98) and Mme. Duclos (1668–1748). Encouraged by the success of Adrienne Lecouvreur (1692–1730), Baron returned to the stage in 1720, at the age of sixty-seven, after almost thirty years of retirement. Though Baron and Lecouvreur, who played together, acted with more seeming truth than their contemporaries, their performances were far from what we would call natural. Neither ever fell below a certain level of heroic grandeur, though gesture and movement were freer. Voltaire, admiring Lecouvreur after her death, called her "this incomparable actress," who spoke to the heart and showed feeling and truth where formerly had been artificiality and declamation (figure 111).

For all his lip service to naturalness in the art of acting, though, Voltaire really championed a speaking style which, while differing from formal declamation, still stressed the sound of the words over their content. When Mlle. Clairon (1723–1803), contrary to his coaching, acted his *Électre* speaking naturally, he was led to exclaim, "It is not I who wrote that, 'tis she; she has created the part!"

Clairon was one of the most talented actresses of the French theatre, pronounced by Garrick "a perfect actress," as indeed she was. Endowed with much physical beauty and a vivid imagination, she studied her parts in minute detail, planning every aspect of vocal inflection, gesture, and movement, so that the result was an artistic unity with a feeling of truth. Her rival, Mlle. Dumesnil (1713–1803), on the other hand, was a purely inspirational actress who scored in

112 Iffland and Schroeder
Right, the actor-playwright Iffland in Cumberland's *The Jew* (1794),
one of his most popular parts. Left, Schroeder as King Lear.
This magnificent actor possessed the rare quality of transforming himself
to the part he was playing, and essayed many Shakespearean roles
with great success. (Theater-Museum, Munich)

the passages of great emotional stress, but might otherwise be most
commonplace (figure 108). She depended upon inspiration rather
than studied art, but throughout her long career had many ardent
partisans. She, like Clairon, was more effective in tragedy than
comedy, but a popular contemporary, Mlle. Gaussin (1711–67), was
unique in being equally effective in both types.

Among the men, the two great names of French eighteenth-
century theatre are Lekain (1729–78) (figure 108) and Talma (1763–
1826) (figure 111), the one unprepossessing in appearance, the other
darkly handsome; the one to die a decade before the Revolution, the
other to become its darling and live beyond it. Both studied to produce a unified characterization which carried the sense of the scene
and the intention of the playwright in voice, costume, gesture, and
carriage. They are as close as we come to natural acting in this century—a movement which was greatly aided by the appearance of the
drame, a type of play mainly realistic, requiring natural movement
and conversation.

Perhaps because tradition was not as strong in Germany as elsewhere in Europe, and forms other than classical tragedy were more
popular, there was more scope for the development of new skills in
acting. In any event, one of the world's greatest actors developed in
Germany in this period—Friedrich Ludwig Schroeder (1744–1816).
Tall, handsome, graceful (he had been an acrobat and a dancer),

he was not only an inspired actor, but a talented director and manager as well. Born into a theatrical family, he lived all his life in the theatre, playing more than seven hundred parts. In his long management at Hamburg, beginning in 1771 and lasting, with two intermissions, until his retirement in 1798, he insisted upon company discipline and ensemble playing, requiring strict order and punctuality in rehearsals and performances. At the same time, he managed his own theatrical education. Having been inspired by the acting of the older Konrad Ekhof, he put himself under strict discipline, carefully progressing from light comedy to more complicated parts, then to the greatest. In his first presentation of *Hamlet* at Hamburg, he did not play the lead himself, but took the part of the Ghost, though he later scored in the title role. He also played Macbeth, Shylock, Falstaff, Richard II, Iago, the Miser, Arnolphe, Orgon, Angelo in *Emilia Galotti*, Werner in *Minna von Barnhelm*, and hundreds of other roles. Dissatisfied with his tenor voice, he finally achieved a full, rich baritone, and, by force of will power, curbed his passionate temperament to serve his clear intelligence. He was immensely successful, made a fortune, and retired to a large estate (figure 112).

Popular also during most of Schroeder's career was the older Ekhof (1720–78), first theorist of the German stage, who insisted that acting must come from within. Two other more erratic talents were those of Iffland (1759–1814) (figure 112) and Fleck (1757–1801). The first, like Mlle. Dumesnil, had brilliant moments but found difficulty in sustaining a long part; the second was so temperamental that it is said audiences never knew if they were to see "the great or the little Fleck."

There are no names among the women to compare with these, although one must admire Carolina Neuber (1697–1760), not so much as an actress, but as a devotee of theatre, who did much to establish the future greatness of the German stage. Schroeder's mother, Sophia (1714–92), and his sister, Dorothea (1752–1821), were both much admired in their day, as was Charlotte Ackerman (1757–74). But the bright star of German theatre was unquestionably Friedrich Schroeder.

Company organization changed little

The development of the art of acting tended to make actors more versatile, but companies were generally organized throughout the century to employ actors for special lines, as had been the case in the previous period. In Paris, male parts in tragedy included kings, tyrants, lovers, and the secondary roles; female parts were princesses, mothers, lovers, and the seconds. In comedy, the male parts were financiers (a type new to this age), *manteaux,* or old comic parts, lovers, valets, and peasants; for the women, *duègnes* or old comic parts, coquettes, lovers, and maidservants. Foremost in each part was the master of the line, and each had his double, or understudy. The actors were engaged by the First Gentlemen of the Chamber (the group of nobles charged by the King with overseeing theatrical affairs), who also issued regulations concerning the finances and discipline of the theatre. The company met weekly on Monday mornings to discuss affairs of the theatre, to hear new plays, and to distribute parts. The male members took weekly turns being business manager, and one of them was stage director, except when a playwright like Voltaire took over the directing of his own works. The freedom of the players to control their own company still existed to an extent, but was not so great as in the days of Molière.

In Germany, such a democratic organization would sometimes exist, as at Mannheim where committees chose the plays and cast them and everybody aired his opinions about everything. But more generally companies were under the supervision, more or less autocratic, of an appointed superior, like Iffland at Berlin, Schroeder at Hamburg, and Goethe at Weimar.

Russia had a system all its own. The players were classified and hired to these parts: leading tragic and comic lover, second tragic and comic lover, third tragic and comic lover, noble father, comic father, first domestic, second domestic, moralizer, clerk, and two confidants; women's parts were the same three lovers, two chambermaids, an old woman, and two confidantes. Companies were generally supervised by an aristocrat; members were not permitted to marry except with the supervisor's consent. Salaries were fixed by imperial budget; in the serf companies, owned and operated by wealthy landowners, there were, of course, no salaries. The serfs were whipped for bad performances, and often traded or sold. Sometimes they earned their freedom by good performances, and once, at least, a serf actress married into the nobility, after her master had duly elevated her, of course.

While the lot of Continental actors and actresses was not, on the whole, as salutary as that of the English players, it was constantly improving in many respects. Church opposition was still strong, particularly in Germany and Russia, but even in France the "infamous" stigma had not entirely evaporated. Evidenced chiefly by edicts against Christian burial for actors, the opposition, for instance, caused Carolina Neuber's coffin to be lifted over the churchyard wall rather than be carried through the gate, and her monument to be erected in a public crossroads. It constantly criticized actors' morals; members of the profession countered by urging decorum in private life and often insisted on it.

Summary

Just as the literary influence of England spread to the Continent in the eighteenth century, there were recurring mutual influences among the theatres of the various countries, with, toward the end of the century, the German theatre emerging as a significant national entity.

On the Continent, more men of literary persuasions were involved in theatre than in England and America. Both Voltaire and Diderot in France, with sizable reputations in other fields of writing, devoted a large part of their attention to theatre, both in playwriting and dramatic criticism. In Germany, Lessing and Goethe, with prodigious accomplishments in other fields, were also among the most significant of theatre workers. On the Continent, also, more time and attention were given to criticism and theory, all those mentioned above making important contributions to this field. As for the plays themselves, the Continental versions of the domestic tragedy turned out rather better than the English varieties, though, outside of Goldoni and Beaumarchais, no comedy touches that of Sheridan.

Acting, of all the arts of theatre, showed the greatest advances on the Continent, just as it did in England, with the great names of Schroeder, Talma, Lekain, Lecouvreur, Clairon to match those of Garrick and Siddons. All of these performers were members of permanent theatre companies, and developed within the framework of a constantly producing unit. Some of them were managers as well as actors, and all succeeded, to some extent, in developing new techniques in the art of acting.

The number of theatres increased greatly everywhere in the eighteenth century, with many national theatres being established on the Continent. The trend in theatre architecture was almost universally toward large and highly decorated houses, with audience accommodations in the opera-type, horseshoe auditoriums, and stages effectively pushed behind proscenium arches. Magnificent effects were popular in stage design, with the architectural emphasis of the Bibiena tradition the paramount style. A few designers and producers concerned themselves with the total stage picture, and this aspect of production was to receive increasingly effective emphasis in the next century.

ORIENTAL THEATRE

For many centuries, the Eastern Hemisphere was itself divided into two distinct parts—the world of Asia and the world of Europe. We have been dealing up to now with the theatre of Europe, and may seem to have implied that no other existed. Quite to the contrary, however, Asian lands developed, independently, unique and highly civilized cultures, including remarkably advanced theatre. A form of drama, roughly paralleling that of ancient Egypt, was evidently extant in China about 2000 B.C. It seems to have been a dance-drama commemorating religious festivals, military successes, and ancestors, and was confined to the nobles and the priests. The epic period of Hindu literature began about the same time as the institution by Pisistratus of the Great Festival of Dionysus at Athens. The greatest Hindu playwright, Kalidasa, flourished about 350 A.D. Chikamatsu, the Shakespeare of Japan, was born about thirty-five years after Shakespeare's death.

There were contacts, over many centuries, between these two worlds. India saw its first Aryan invasion from the north about the tenth century B.C., and Alexander the Great (356–323 B.C.) had conquered a large portion of that country before his death. In the eighth century A.D. the Arabs and Mohammedanism came to India. In the thirteenth century, it was threatened by the greatest conqueror of them all, Genghis Khan, who took his Mongol hordes even into Europe after consolidating his conquests throughout most of Asia.

In 1500 the Portuguese came, then a century later the Dutch and the English, to be followed by the French about 1670. The early Christian Church had arrived in India by the third century, and in China by the fifth, but was slowly strangled by the Moslems and the barbarians. Christian and Moslem contended over Indo-Asia for the next thousand years (indeed, the struggle still progresses, with various other less violent faiths also entering the field from time to time). In any event, from 1500 on, the Church was a significant factor in bringing elements of Western culture to all parts of the Far East. These evangelistic endeavors, coupled with various commercial and military operations culminating in the opening of Japan by Commodore Perry in 1854, brought East and West into ever-increasing contact. Despite westernizing influences the culture of these lands remained essentially indigenous, and markedly different from that of the Western world.

Eastern culture penetrated the Western world slowly. Everyone knows of the long sojourn of Marco Polo in the court of Kublai Khan toward the end of the thirteenth century, which had been preceded by an earlier voyage on the part of his father and two uncles. Both before and after that, the wonders of gunpowder, spices, silks, and the printed book were brought from Cathay to Europe. Columbus discovered America on a fruitless search for a western passage to those fabulous lands. In the sixteenth and seventeenth centuries, the Portuguese, Dutch, English, and French traders brought back from India, China, Japan, and the Malay Archipelago, spices, textiles, and precious gems, along with other less commercial evidences of Eastern

113 *Shadow puppets from Java*
These fantastic figures, made of pierced leather and mounted on sticks, are operated from below against an illuminated backdrop, while the lines are spoken and sung by offstage voices. The intricate lines of the figures are indicative of the highly decorative costume which is everywhere prevalent in oriental theatre.
(The American Museum of Natural History)

civilization. Willow-ware plates and other china pieces, Canton wall-papers, and furniture incorporating oriental motifs appeared in many well-to-do and noble houses during the late seventeenth and early eighteenth centuries.

In the middle of the eighteenth century, oriental influence reached into theatre. The fourteenth-century Chinese play, *The Romance of the Western Chamber* had been translated, and Voltaire, sails trimmed to the currents of his age, had taken his theme for *The Chinese Orphan* from *The Little Orphan of the House of Chao*. We have remarked about the oriental influence on eighteenth-century costuming, and the same period saw the introduction of the eastern shadow show to western audiences. Dominique Séraphin established a Shadow Theatre in Versailles in 1774, and the "Chinese Shadows" were taken to England by Ambroise the next year. In 1789, Sir William Jones translated Kalidasa's *Sakuntala* into English, and it earned high praise from many, including Goethe. Early nineteenth-century Romanticism quickened interest in the remote culture of the Orient, with several literary works deriving from the East, and more plays being translated. There is record of a company of Chinese actors playing for Napoleon III in Paris in 1860, having previously performed for thousands of Chinese in California soon after their immigration for the famous Gold Rush. In the 1880's, the Jackson Street Theatre in San Francisco was converted to oriental drama, and in 1930, the Chinese actor Mei Lan-fang was received with great acclaim in Europe and America, Stanislavski naming him one of the world's great actors. The twentieth century also saw western productions of Hindu and Chinese plays, as well as several instances of English-language dramas in the oriental manner. The high point of western investigation of oriental theatre was reached in the 1920's with several scholarly books on the subject being published in that period. After World War II, another upsurge of interest in things oriental resulted in several Broadway productions with eastern themes or characters. In the spring of 1960, Japan's Grand *Kabuki* theatre—actors, sets, and all—was playing in New York.

Oriental theatre, because of its major differences from our own, and because of its high degree of artistic competence, will always be of interest to the western mind.

Brahma begets theatre

As in the West, so in the East, theatre grew out of religious observance. The origin of theatre in India is traditionally ascribed to the supreme god Brahma, who ordered the sage Bharata (now one of

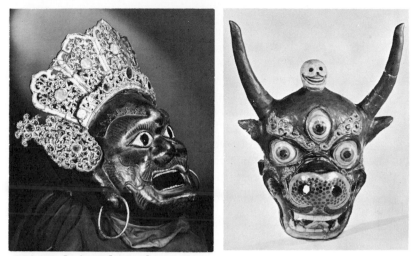

114 *Masks for Tibetan drama*
These two masks, of papièr mâché, are used in the religious drama of
Tibet. They are highly decorative even though fierce in appearance, and,
like the ancient Greek masks, fit entirely over the head of the wearer.
(The American Museum of Natural History)

the words for "actor" in India), to set up a playhouse, instructing him
in the four Vedas—dance, song, mime, and sentiment.

Whatever the legendary character of this creation, these elements
have remained constant in Hindu theatre. Developing from the dialogue form of the Vedic hymns which date back to 1500 B.C., real
theatre actually emerges from the great source books of Hindu drama,
the *Mahabharata* and the *Ramayana,* epics which appeared about
the fifth century B.C. The most important period of Hindu drama follows these in time, and takes inspiration almost wholly from them.
In the lands east of India—Burma, Thailand, Java, and the Malay
Peninsula—theatre sprang from the same sources and developed similar forms. Tibet, also, was influenced early by Buddhism and the
drama to be found there was and still is religious in origin and under
the direction of the Buddhist church. In China, where the beginnings
were rooted in religious observance, additional influences such as
the celebration of military victories, honoring ancestors, and observing harvests also crept in. The Chinese tradition spread to Korea and
thence to Japan.

Theatre for aristocrats

In all of these lands the drama was long and chiefly confined to
the nobility and the upper classes, since they were the only persons

thought capable of understanding and appreciating (and, incidentally, of paying for) theatrical productions. In both China and India, seedbeds of all oriental drama, the earliest serious theatre was under the direction of the priests and was performed for the nobility. The first treatise on theatre in India, dating from the third century B.C., tells us that theatrical performances would take place in connection with some festival or public celebration, upon which occasion the king, or some other rich patron, would call upon a group of actors to perform in either temple or palace.

Actors formed a distinct caste and were held in low repute, though some few of them might gain the friendship of influential patrons. A Chinese emperor of the third century B.C. is said to have employed many troupes of actors, whose chief duty it was to perform at court banquets. At the same time, in the Buddhist monasteries, the priests embellished for their humbler listeners the stories of which they were masters. These priestly performances were forbidden after the tenth century. The performers in the court plays were taken from the lower ranks of society, and for a very long time in China as in India actors were little regarded as persons. Theatre was a diversion for the leisure class, and the lower orders had largely to be content with puppets and shadow shows when, indeed, they had any time at all for diversions.

All during its great period, Hindu drama paid at least lip service to its religious origins, performances beginning invariably with a musical program, then an invocation or prayer, then proceeding to a dialogue between the director and the chief actress to let the audience know that, after all, this was merely entertainment. The ensuing plays were likely to be very long, with eight or ten acts of exceedingly varied content, and an inevitably happy ending. The increasing pressure of the Moslem invasions had, by the eleventh century, virtually destroyed this theatre, though some degenerate types of farce lived on. Various incursions of European cultures did no more than impose western forms, and there was no true revival of Hindu theatre until the advent, late in the nineteenth century, of the neoromantic Rabindranath Tagore.

Chinese theatre more literary, more literal

In China, on the other hand, the Mongol invasion under Kublai Khan in the thirteenth century paved the way for greater participation in theatre, because Chinese literary men, heretofore engaged in public office through the elaborate system of literary examinations, were debarred by the new conquerors from office; they turned to theatre as a means of livelihood.

115 *Manuscript of Kalidasa*
The illustrations on this ancient manuscript convey something of the
grace and emphasis of gesture which actors in the old classical drama of
India possessed. Differentiation of costume, particularly in color,
is also apparent. (Boston Museum of Fine Arts)

Their themes began to embrace all classes and ideas, and the plays
became, in time, an exceedingly popular entertainment, reaching a
peak in the nineteenth century. Plays were usually of four acts with
a prologue and prefatory poem and many diversions between the
acts. Often a theatrical performance consisted not just of a single play,
but of scenes from many plays arranged after some predetermined
plan and lasting from early morning to late afternoon or from early
afternoon to late evening. As can be imagined in such a theatre, there
was much eating and drinking, and coming and going, and we shall
see as we talk of the playhouses later, that they were designed to en-
compass these activities.

Japan—entertainment and theatre
The derivative theatre of Japan developed along class lines, with
the classical and traditional *Noh* drama reserved at first for the

emperor or the shogun who usurped his power, then, much later, becoming the diversion of aristocrats and wealthy commoners as well—but always playing to a highly restricted audience.

The popular theatre of Japan is the *Kabuki*, which incorporates some aspects of the *Noh* as well as of the *Bunraku*, or marionette theatre. Its presentations are far more variegated and spectacular than the more classic *Noh*, combining for popular appeal most of the elements which we have come to call entertainment as opposed to theatre. As in the Chinese theatre, a typical program might consist of scenes from well-known plays, interspersed with dance or pantomime, with perhaps a melodrama in addition, and a final dance number.

In the 1890's, there was a movement to bring occidental methods to the Japanese stage, and, in 1909, a Free Theatre was established after the pattern of the Moscow Art Theatre. Twentieth-century Japanese theatre has been marked by various repressions, as well as a second influx of occidental influences, so that *Noh, Kabuki,* and *Bunraku* have experienced some difficulty in maintaining themselves. But a quite recent resurgence of interest in the old forms has strengthened the hope that increasing westernization will not utterly destroy this "theatre theatrical."

Situation, sentiment, and a happy ending

The oriental theatre was, for long periods and in many places, almost completely unliterary. Many of the so-called playscripts are no more than a framework for the actors who are by all odds the most important element in the total theatrical picture. In Java, for instance, spoken parts were added to the traditional dance and pantomime only under western influence. In the shadow plays, the leader recites all the lines, often improvising on the well-known plot lines, and directs the orchestra which always accompanies the performance. In the plays using live actors, a similar convention is observed; the actors, in pantomime and dance, simply act out the lines spoken by someone else. In the few Tibetan scripts which have been translated it is obvious that they are but fragmentary guides, large portions being improvised during performance. In Burma and Cambodia the few extant texts are based on the *Mahabharata* and the *Ramayana;* theatre performance is, and always has been, a combination of dance and pantomime with an integral musical accompaniment.

In considering the plays of India, where there is a considerable body of literary drama, we must forget our accustomed designation of tragedy and comedy, for the Hindu plays cannot be made to conform to this pattern. Hindu criticism set up ten forms of the drama,

116 *Scene from a Chinese play*
In this scene from *Killing the Tiger General*, the male character wears
a long beard and stylized face makeup. The female characters wear the
"rippling water" sleeves. (Zung, *Secrets of the Chinese Drama*)

the divisions being determined by material, type of hero, and sentiment to be evoked. In no case was the tragic denouement to be allowed; no matter what the vicissitudes of the characters, the ending
must be a happy one.

The highest form of drama was the one in which the subject was
legendary, the hero royal or divine, and the sentiment heroic or erotic.
The best of the Hindu dramas, Kalidasa's *Sakuntala* is of this genre;
the hero is the legendary king Dushyanta, the heroine is the di-
vinely guarded Sakuntala, and the story is of the star-crossed love of
these two who are finally reunited. It was evidently written about
400 A.D., and besides seeing some performances on western stages, it
was made within recent memory into a beautifully evocative motion
picture. It is typical of all of Hindu drama in its long lyrical passages,
its emphasis upon situation and sentiment over character conflict,
and its inclusion of humorously playful characters as servants and
officials. In conformance with Hindu tradition, the noble characters
speak Sanskrit, the literary tongue, while the lower orders speak in
Prakrit, the popular tongue.

Kalidasa mentions as his predecessors other playwrights of some renown. The most notable of these is probably Bhasa, whose play *The Poor Charudatta* provided the basis for a later play, *The Little Clay Cart,* traditionally ascribed to King Shudraka, also a predecessor of Kalidasa. Though a play of great interest and charm, *The Little Clay Cart* differs in species from *Sakuntala,* for it takes its characters from ordinary life. It is again a love story, this time of a Brahman and a courtesan (not, indeed, a mistress in the occidental sense, but a socially approved, skilled, and intelligent companion, like the Japanese geisha). It was produced in the 1920's by the Neighborhood Playhouse in New York.

The first dramas of known authorship in India are fragments dating back to the first century. They are of two plays by the Buddhist Asvaghosa, and deal with religious conversion. Bhasa is somewhat tentatively credited with thirteen plays discovered as late as 1912. But the name of Kalidasa is supreme in India's golden age; his three plays (among other works of poetry) are generally conceded to be the finest flower of Hindu literature. *The Hero and the Nymph* is of the epic stamp; *Agnimitra and Malavika* of *The Little Clay Cart* type.

After Kalidasa, there are few names of importance. Harsa, a seventh-century king of northern India, is notable for his three plays about love triangles. Bhavabhuti, in the eighth century, has three outstanding plays, again on the theme of star-crossed lovers. Bhatta Narayana and Rajasekhara in the next century deserve mention, the latter for *The Camphor Cluster,* written entirely in Prakrit. Before the eleventh-century submersion by the Moslems, two other playwrights of note appeared: Vishakhadatta whose *Raksasa and the Seal* deals with political intrigue, and Krishnamisra whose *The Rise of the Moon of Knowledge* personalizes abstract qualities like Error and Reason, and their conflict in man's mind. There was no further native Hindu drama of any literary merit until Rabindranath Tagore in the nineteenth century. His *Chitra* and his *The King of the Dark Chamber* are both poetic romances. Since that time, there have been a few additional dramatists; perhaps the newly found nationalism of India will produce more.

China's dramatic output cannot be classified by western divisions, for in the main the plays include both tragic and comic events and justice is always done even though it means employing a quite obvious *deus ex machina,* such as bringing back the spirits of the dead to settle matters.

The evolution of the plays had much to do with their form. In addition to origins in religious observance, there were three other early

117 *Two* **Noh** *characters*
Left, a seventeenth-century painting of a character in the *Noh* drama.
The fan is an ubiquitous hand prop used to simulate many objects. Right,
a different type of fan is used by this fierce character who is masked
and wigged. (Boston Museum of Fine Arts)

influences. About the time of Confucius (*ca.*, 551–478 B.C.), there
were in the Emperor's court actors who gave heroic scenes in praise
of ancestors as well as a special company of dwarfs or fools who presented short sketches which pointed out in story form the faults of
the administration. That this was sometimes perilous is attested by
the fact that the great Confucius himself once felt impelled to order
the death of an actor who had carried his criticism too far. During
the T'ang Dynasty (720–907 A.D.) the populace was amused by professional story tellers who embellished their historical, heroic, melodramatic, or tragic tales with song and dance. In much the same
fashion, the Buddhist priests told stories from the scriptures, bringing large audiences to the temples to hear them. Often the songs incorporated in these stories were set to popular tunes, and dance was

329

118 Bunraku *theatre*
Two *Bunraku* marionettes and an operator. Some idea of the size of
these dolls may be gained from a comparison with the figure of the
puppeteer in the background. Chikamatsu wrote many of his
plays for the *Bunraku*. (Japan Tourist Association)

included wherever possible. By the Sung Dynasty (960–1127 A.D.),
these forms had been amalgamated into long performances of dancing, singing, and narrative; an early Chinese theatre historian reports
some 280 of these plays from the Sung Dynasty, and 690 from the
next, the Chin Dynasty.

When the Mongols came and literary men turned to writing for
theatre, the performances became more truly plays. Dialogue and
dramatic action were substituted for the long poetic and narrative
passages, even while song and dance were retained. Hundreds of
these plays were written during the rule of the Mongols (1280–1368),

and 116 still survive. Chinese scholars say the best of these is *The Sufferings of Tou-E,* but the first to be translated into English was *The Romance of the Western Chamber,* which, in a later version by S. I. Hsiung, was successfully performed in England in 1938. It was from this period that Voltaire was inspired for his *The Chinese Orphan;* and *The Chalk Circle,* in a translation by Klabund, received a beautiful German presentation in the 1920's.

The Ming Dynasty (1368–1644) produced more than six hundred plays, the most famous of which is *Romance of a Lute;* as *Lute Song,* this play had a fairly successful run on Broadway in the 1940's. In all of these plays, there is no thought for the unities of time, place, or action, and the subject matter is extremely varied, taken from all walks of life. The Chinese classify their plays by subject matter: historical, military, civil, romantic, criminal, ethical, fantastic, problem. Toward the end of the nineteenth century there developed a new form of play, without music, but it has never been as popular as the traditional form. The Sino–Japanese War in the 1890's brought a rash of patriotic plays, as did the Japanese invasion of 1937. The advent of Communism in 1950 brought the same kind of doctrinaire plays that have marked Soviet theatre production.

Korean drama, which began in the Buddhist temples, was secularized by historical epics and by ancestor worship; these morality performances are still popular. Literary influences came from the Chinese. In the tenth century, the persecution of Buddhist monks caused a wave of propaganda plays both for and against them. The most important Korean drama was written in the fifteenth and sixteenth centuries, but we know little of it because of the difficulty of translating the many puns and plays on words in which it is chiefly composed.

Kabuki *and* Noh

The drama of Japan, on the other hand, is fairly well known to us, consisting of two main divisions, the *Noh* and the *Kabuki.* The *Noh* dates from the fourteenth century, presumably having its origin in the Shinto-worship dance called the *Kagura.* This ancient worship was modified by the coming of Buddhism in the sixth century, and the Shinto dances were supplemented with dance-dramas written by Buddhist priests. The consolidation of the form is credited to one of these priests, Kwanami Kiyotsugu (1333–1384), fifteen of whose plays are still extant. More famous was his son, Seami Motokiyu; we still know more than one hundred of his plays. They are about the length of a one-act play, and deal with historical or religious events commemorating heroes or declaiming the virtues of the Buddhist philosophy. Four or five of these are given at a single performance, interspersed with specially developed short, comic interludes given without musical accompaniment.

The *Kabuki* had its origin about 1600 with the renegade temple dancer O'Kuni, who began dancing in a dry riverbed (thus lending the name "beggars of the riverbed" to actors). She soon gathered about herself a company of women, children, and then men, and her success generated numerous imitations. Charges of immorality eventually suppressed these performances, and in the final form of the *Kabuki,* only men performed.

Much of the early *Kabuki* was purely improvisational, but with the advent of Chikamatsu in the latter half of the seventeenth century, it acquired literary distinction. His first known play appeared in Tokyo in 1677, and was called *The Evil Spirit of Lady Wisteria.* He is supposed to have written more than a hundred plays, fully as long as those of Shakespeare or longer. They include history, comedy, tragedy, melodrama, realism, and romance. Violent action marks many of them. Chikamatsu is credited with initiating a highly influential genre in his *Shinju* plays, which revolve about the idea of double suicide for love. Current happenings, such as the scandal of the Ronins in 1701, were sources for *Kabuki* plays, as were the legendary and historical events of both China and Japan. Murder, torture, suicide, battles, frequent change of scene, long periods of elapsed time, characters from all walks of life—these are to be found in the *Kabuki* drama, with, of course, the integral song and dance which pervades oriental theatre.

Chikamatsu also wrote for the *Bunraku,* or doll theatre, which enjoyed popularity from its inception in the fifteenth century to its height in the eighteenth (figure 118). Though it is highly ingenious, it lacks one essential for good theatre—the actor; all the parts are spoken by a single seated person, while one or more operators manipulate the puppets.

Since the nineteenth century, when the Shakespearean scholar Tsubouchi began to bring decided western influences into Japanese drama, Japan has seen productions of Ibsen, Wilde, Shaw, Strindberg, Maeterlinck, and O'Neill, but its typical and indigenous drama remains the *Noh,* the *Bunraku,* the *Kabuki.*

Playhouse is the setting

In oriental theatre it is impossible to consider settings apart from the playhouses, since "setting" as we know it does not exist, except,

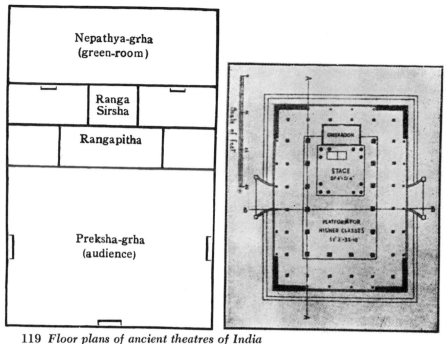

119 *Floor plans of ancient theatres of India*
Left, the final form of the classic Hindu theatre, rectangular in shape,
with equal space allotted to actors and to audience and the stage
divided into its traditional areas. Right, the plan of an old temple
theatre at Trichur, in the Kochin State, Kerala. The rectangular form is
maintained, as is the relationship of greenroom to stage area, but the stage
itself differs from the plan at the left. (*The Theatre of the Hindus*)

as we shall see, in the *Kabuki*. Theatre types range from a mere space
for acting to the elaborateness of the Japanese houses.

In Tibet, plays were, and still are, given in the open space before
temples, sometimes using the temple steps, while the audience sits or
stands about as it chooses. Performances in the lands east of India
were also generally outdoors, with a roof of matting supported by
pillars protecting audience and actors. Such even was the Dancing
Shed, which was the Royal Theatre of Cambodia as late as 1883—a
thatched-roof structure open on three sides, with space behind the
stage wall for dressingrooms. The Burmese theatre building is similarly rudimentary, with bamboo platforms on three sides to hold the
distinguished guests, the balance of the audience sitting or standing
on the ground around the stage, which is simply a floor of matting. A

tree is the only stage decoration, either stuck in the ground at stage center, or attached to one of the poles supporting the roof. Lighting, when necessary, is supplied by earthen pots of petroleum-soaked flares. The orchestra sits on the ground to either side of the stage. The playhouse of the Chinese traveling companies was a similar temporary and portable structure, with roofed bamboo platforms around three sides and standing room in the center on the ground. Here, however, the stage was a fourth platform, larger than the others, and roofed.

The courtly drama of India, China, and Japan might be given in specially built structures in gardens, or in the converted halls of palaces and temples. In the whole period of classic drama in India, there may not have been separate and permanent theatre buildings. Researches seem to indicate that the earliest arrangement of playing space was triangular in form, then square, and finally rectangular, although the three may have existed simultaneously. Each of these basic shapes could be of three sizes, the smallest for monologues (one of the divisions of playwriting), the largest for spectacles, and the middle size preferred for all other presentations. The space was about equally divided between players and audience.

In the rectangular theatre the stage had two equal major divisions, front and back, and two doors connected these; the back area was a greenroom for the actors. The playing area was again divided equally from side to side, with the central portion at the back elevated (figure 119). In the square theatre and the triangle the same division of stage areas prevailed, but in these was no elevated platform and but one door to the greenroom. The auditorium was richly decorated with woodwork, carved to represent creepers, birds, and animals. The walls were covered with beautiful paintings on a variety of subjects prescribed in one way only—they must be "pictures of pleasure." One ancient reference mentions a theatre at Ikkeri, built by King Venkatappa, which was worked in ivory and sandalwood and inlaid with precious stones, surrounded by a garden. Another refers to a circular theatre, but details are lacking.

In the Cochin State, Kerala in southern India, some old temple theatres are still extant, such as the one at Trichur (figure 119). This is a rectangle, with a floor about four feet above ground level, the intervening space being of intricately carved granite. There are two entrances, north and south. A raised platform in the center of the wooden superstructure runs east and west and is divided into three sections. The westernmost is the greenroom and is marked off by screens. Two doors lead to the central portion, which is slightly raised to form the stage. This is a square area with an ornately carved

120 *A Chinese court theatre*
Model of the traditional classical Court Theatre of China as it looked in
`1830. It has an apron stage, surrounded by pit and galleries, with
a formal background and no scene changes. (The Cleveland Museum of
Art, Collection of the Educational Department)

ceiling supported by ornamented pillars. The rest of the interior is
for seating the audience. A row of carved pillars around the entire
structure supports the roof. The modern scholar of South Indian
theatre, K. R. Pisharoti, says that the old Sanskrit dramas are still
occasionally performed in this theatre temple, but does not give the
date of its construction.

In the ancient theatres the audience was seated on stone or wooden
benches placed on a rising series of stepped platforms, with the down-
front-center space reserved for the patron or the guest of honor, and
the remaining seating space divided by pillars into sections for the
four castes.

Though stage walls and curtains were richly decorative, there was
no attempt to change or localize this decoration for individual plays.
Properties were sometimes used, such as the toy cart of which we
hear in *The Little Clay Cart* or the artificial elephant employed in the
story of the Udayana. Such properties, as well as arms and accessories, were said to have been made of stiffened cloth, wood, metal,

335

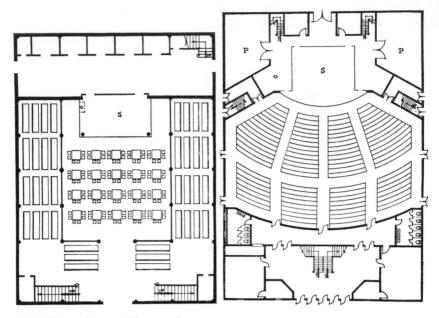

121 *Floor plans of Chinese theatres*
Left, the traditional Chinese teahouse theatre, with tables and chairs
for the gentry on the main floor and galleries for the women and
less affluent members of society. Right, a modern Chinese theatre, with
rows of seats substituted for the tables and chairs, but with stage
appointments still approximating those of older times.
(Zung, *Secrets of the Chinese Drama*)

mud, and wax. But for the most part, properties were indicated by
the gestures of the actors, gestures which became highly conventional and significant. British domination brought in an infusion of
western theatrical customs, and theatres on the European model
were built in the chief centers of population, incorporating, to some
degree at least, English theatrical traditions and practices.

In China, the early plays were performed in the halls of great
houses, or in pavilions in the gardens or orchards. The most famous
of the orchards was that of the Emperor Hsuan Hsung, or Ming
Huang (713–756), whose troupe performed in his Pear Garden where
he founded a school for actors. It was called, literally, Young Folks of
the Pear Garden. He thus became the patron saint of Chinese theatre, and even today before going on the stage Chinese actors burn
incense to his image which stands in all greenrooms.

When the first public theatres in the large cities were built they
were called tea houses, and the drinking of tea and the eating of

sweetmeats by the audience is still an accompaniment of Chinese performances. The typical structure was a squarish rectangle, with about one-fourth of the total area devoted to backstage space. The stage itself projected out into the auditorium and was raised. Tables and stools for the wealthier patrons filled the ground floor, with a railed gallery supplied with benches around three sides for the less wealthy. A second-floor gallery provided boxes and benches for the women spectators. The stage, whether indoors or out, was roofed over, being supported by two columns at the downstage corners. The wall at the back of the stage, beautifully painted or hung with an em-broidered curtain, terminated at either side in a curtained doorway to the backstage area. The door at stage left was for entrances, at the right for exits. The orchestra had a small balustraded section upstage right, where it remained throughout the performance. In the modern Chinese theatre the tables have disappeared, although tea drinking still remains a pastime of the audience. The seats are now arranged in curved rows with aisles, each row provided with a shelf for the ubiquitous teapots, and the stage has retreated to an almost pro-scenium-like form, with a wide, curving apron, to which a door opens on either side. The upstage right and left entrances have been re-tained, and the orchestra now sits backstage (figure 121).

There are no stage settings as such. Whatever things are necessary for the drama in hand are supplied from the property rooms by the two property men, clothed in black, who are supposed to be invisible to the audience. An ordinary table may be a wall, a mountain, an altar, a bridge, a battlement. Chairs placed on the left indicate the honor of the occupants. Two or more chairs covered with a cloth may be a bed. An actor carrying an oar is in a boat. City gates are a cloth banner supported by two sticks in the hands of the property men. Banners represent armies; four black flags flourished by the property men indicate a violent wind; four white ones painted with waves represent water; two yellow ones painted with wheels make a chariot. A red flag held before the face of an actor means that his head is cut off, and a red sack tossed on the stage represents the sev-ered head. Small bits of paper tossed on the stage make a snowstorm. A tassled horsewhip enables the actor to ride an invisible horse; if he falls then or at other times, the property man supplies him with a cushion upon which to land. Physical topography and architectural details are supplied by the actor's pantomime: if he is climbing a hill or a flight of steps, he raises his knees high to indicate it; an exagger-ated step over an imaginary doorsill indicates a door. Thus, the visual elements of Chinese theatre are highly conventionalized, placing

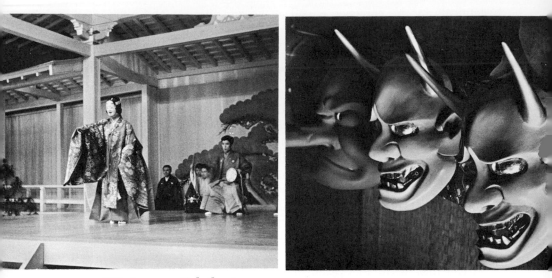

122 *Japanese* Noh *theatre*
Left, in this performance in a *Noh* theatre the masked leading actor
is portraying a woman. Visible at the left is the bridgeway for entrances
of the actors, with one of the three pine trees in view; at the right
is the formal pine tree painted on the back wall of the stage. The steps
leading to the pebbled path around the stage can be seen in the
lower left corner. Right, *Noh* masks ready for painting. The creation
of masks for this drama is a revered art form in Japan; this photograph
shows two types of masks. (The American Museum of Natural History)

primary emphasis upon the skill of the actor to supply all the necessary details.

In Japan, the acting area of the classic *Noh* play is adapted from
the ancient Shinto dancing platform, being of highly polished cypress
and hollow below so that the feet of the dancing actors will resound.
It is about three feet high, about eighteen feet square, and is covered
over by a pointed temple roof supported by four pillars which have
significance in the actors' movements. Downstage left, a short extension of the stage accommodates the singers; upstage left a short,
railed enclosure houses the musicians and stagehands. The flute
player sits at a pillar also upstage left. A door in the stage wall behind this pillar is for the musicians and chorus. Actors enter from
stage right over a long, roofed bridgeway running diagonally back
to a curtained doorway. The back wall of the stage is painted with
a formalized pine tree; three potted pine trees are spaced along the

338

actors' bridgeway to symbolize heaven, earth, and humanity. A few short steps lead from downstage center to the pebbled path surrounding the stage, but they are never used in performance. The audience sits or stands in the open area surrounding the stage. The properties are as rudimentary and symbolical as those of the Chinese theatre, and perhaps are even more austerely used. Four poles with a flimsy roof make a palace; if the roof is thatch, it is a cottage. A fan, in the use of which the Japanese are particularly adept, may be a dagger, a tray, a knife, or almost anything else. Again, the skill of the actor rounds out the visual scene.

In the *Kabuki,* however, both properties and setting are apt to be more literal. The *Kabuki* theatre naturally derived from that of the *Noh,* but the bridgeway for the actors early became a runway, generally extending from the down right corner of the stage out through the audience. The temple roof of the early stage was later reduced to a painted representation. The audience stood in walled-off pens on the auditorium floor, the walls being convenient runways for the purveyors of tea and sweetmeats. The more affluent spectators sat on cushions in the boxes surrounding the three sides of the roofed-in playhouse (figure 123). The stage was higher than that of the *Noh,* stage and runway being elevated to the heads of the standing spectators. As this theatre gained in popularity, the stage became wider and shallower, and was, after 1760, equipped with a revolving stage. Both this and the runway were adopted by western theatre, the latter being a feature of Max Reinhardt's production of *Sumurun* early in the twentieth century, and then being taken over by the burlesque houses. The revolving stage, also, was built into the Munich Theatre by Lautenschläger in 1896.

The oriental *Kabuki* stage and runway were frequently supplied with traps, and the revolving stage often moved with actors on it, while they walked, presumably from one location to another. A part of the stage was recessed, and was revealed by a curtain that rolled back to one side. The scenery and properties of the *Kabuki* are factual and elaborate (within the limits of Japanese artistic asceticism), and the traditional invisible stagehands are present to keep things moving. But even in this most literal of oriental theatres, the effect is far from the reality we expect and demand on occidental stages; it remains a stylized art, incorporating not only the spoken word but dance and music as well.

In the traditional oriental theatre, house lights are not extinguished during the performance, but merely dimmed. In consequence, stage lighting tends to greater brilliance than it does on occidental stages.

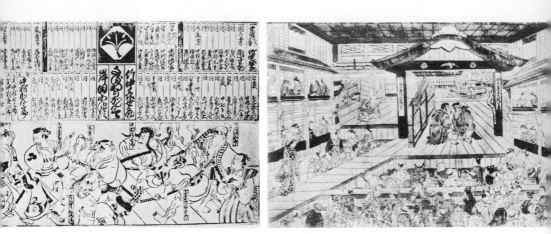

123 Kabuki *theatre*
Left, an early eighteenth-century playbill. In addition to the names of
plays and characters, this interesting advertisement shows sketches
of the performers, each with a title. Right, an eighteenth-century print of
a *Kabuki* theatre, clearly showing the elevated stage, the galleries,
the standing pit with its penlike subdivisions, the runway through the
audience over which an actor is making his entrance. The setting
is less austere than in the *Noh* theatre, with set pieces and backgrounds
in use. (Boston Museum of Fine Arts)

This greater brilliance, coupled with the gorgeous appearance of the
actors, makes for a rather dazzling effect.

Costume and makeup heighten stylized effects

If settings are largely nonexistent in the oriental theatre, costumes
and makeup are varied and elaborate, achieving an intricacy seldom
found on the western stage.

Costuming in the classic theatre of India was more realistic than
the later uniform gorgeousness of China and Japan. The dramas of
Kalidasa and his near-contemporaries were carefully costumed to
indicate the characters' differences in class, profession, and nationality. Gods and demigods appeared brightly arrayed like kings;
nobles wore elaborate and many-colored garments. But cowgirls wore
plain garments of dark blue; ascetics, garments of rags or bark; people engaged in religious services, plain, uncolored robes. Physical and
mental states were reflected in the costuming, dirty and ragged
clothes connoting misery or poverty. Faces were painted to reflect

340

the area from which the character derived, as well as his station in life. Brahmans and kings, as well as people from the north and west, wore reddish-yellow; persons from the Ganges valley and members of the two lower castes wore dark brown; those from the south of India, as well as members of primitive tribes, were painted black.

Masks were and still are used in the religious dramas of Tibet and the dance-dramas of Java, and were also used in the early Chinese theatre. In China, however, they were quickly replaced by face paint, which over the centuries has achieved a high degree of elaboration and significance. The patterns and combinations of colors are standard for specific character types: predominant white indicates treachery; black, bluntness and integrity; blue, stubbornness and ferocity; red, loyalty and courage; yellow, strength and cunning; pink and grey, advanced age. Outlaws and demons wear green; gods and immortals wear gold. The patterns are stylized, such as that of the Monkey God, who paints his face in a triangle of crimson, with golden circles around the eyes and nostrils; for Tou Erh-tun, the brigand chief, a blue face is lined with curves of black and white, a second pair of eyes is painted below the actor's own, and the forehead painted to represent many-colored gems. Types of beards also help to indicate age and character. They may be red or blue, black or brown, long or short, divided or straight—each quality signifying a definite attribute. Cunning characters generally wear long moustaches, good characters never. This fierceness and splendor are reserved for the male actors; female characters wear only heightened natural makeup.

Both men and women are gorgeously appareled. The styles are adaptations of the noble dress of the eighth to the sixteenth centuries, but there is little attempt to make them historically accurate. Again the symbolism of color is used, with emperors in yellow, officials in red, civilians in blue, old people in brown, and rough characters in black. They are splendidly decorated; the stage warrior, for instance, appears with embroidered tiger heads on his heavily padded shoulders and long, scalloped panels dropping from his waist. He also wears thick-soled shoes, reminiscent of the Greeks, to give him height. If he is a general he also wears four small, triangular flags across his back at the shoulders, and a magnificent headdress trailing two long pheasant feathers. Elaborate headdresses surmount the female characters, and on ceremonial occasions many of the characters wear long, full sleeves ending in a filmy, wide white silk cuff which covers the hands and waves gracefully through the various gestures of the pantomime. Both costuming and makeup are nonrealistic, but rather conventional and stylized, telegraphing to the audience the disposition, station, and function of the character as soon as he appears.

Masks are retained in the Japanese *Noh* theatre (figure 122). There are fifteen standard masks, beautifully carved of wood and painted, which are reserved for the use of the First Actor who may change masks many times in the course of a performance. Other actors in the *Noh*, as well as all of those in the *Kabuki*, wear face paint in brilliant designs and colors. The female characters, like those on the Chinese stage, wear natural makeup, slightly heightened and stylized. The costumes are magnificent in color and highly decorative. No less rich than the nobles are the garments of the commoners, being differentiated only by cut and color. High and elaborate headdresses are often featured, and there is much jewelry and ornamentation. Like the costuming of the Chinese theatre, that of Japan makes little pretense to reality, relies largely on symbolism and formalism, and gives an effect of very rich oriental splendor.

Stage belongs to actors

Theatre in the Orient is supremely the actor's theatre. It is his skill which commands the attention of the tea-sipping, morsel-eating audience, and which stirs their imaginations to set the stage with whatever intricate scenery and properties are called for. The oriental actor is a highly skilled practitioner.

In the classic theatre of India, and in the lands to the east which took their dramatic inspiration from India, the custom was generally to have the women's parts played by women. Indeed, in Cambodia, the entire responsibility for the training, rehearsing, and costuming of the royal company of actors falls to one of the principal ladies of the court, who has a corps of women to assist her. Here, women players predominate, men being used chiefly when the plays are from the *Ramayana*. In Tibet, on the other hand, women never participate. Male characters are acted by the priests, female characters by laymen.

Actors in classic India formed a special caste, and the various acting companies were each under the direction of a leader who was married to one of the actresses. The leader was called a *Sutradhara*, or "Stringholder," from the ancient puppet plays. He was an actor-manager-director, and on occasion supervised the construction of the temporary theatre buildings as well. He also, as we have mentioned above, addressed the audience directly at the beginning of the production, remarking on the play, its author, and the occasion, and complimenting the audience on their refinement and taste. His

342

124 *Chinese actors in costume*
Left, Mei Lan-Fang, the great female impersonator, shows the props
and gesture fitted to indicate starting on horseback in *The Rainbow Pass*.
Right, a female and a male character (with beard) are posed in the
traditional gesture which indicates they are on board ship in the play
The Valiant Fisherman and His Daughter.
(Zung, *Secrets of the Chinese Drama*)

wife ordinarily assisted him in this presentation. In the operation of
the company, he had two men to help him, and the other eight or ten
players worked under these men. The companies were mostly itinerant, seeking patronage for their repertory from city to city. Except
in unusual cases, the actors were generally despised as a caste, even
though their art was admired.

The characters they portrayed followed definite classifications.
There was the noble, handsome, and brave hero; the resourceful but
wicked enemy of the hero; his companion or confidant; the rake; the
manservant; the comic; the beautiful and accomplished heroine; her
confidante, and so forth. It is to be assumed that each actor specialized in a "line," for the demands on each were arduous. Series of conventionalized gestures indicated going on a journey, mounting a

125 *Japanese actors*

Costumed figures on a six-panel screen of the Ukiyoe period. A
comparison of these will show the variety of masks and costumes, the
vitality of the gestures, the grace of the postures common to these oriental
performers. (Boston Museum of Fine Arts)

chariot, climbing a mountain, groping in the dark, and so on. The
system seems to have had many parallels with the later *commedia*
companies of Italy.

In China and Japan, acting is traditionally a male vocation. It is
true that when Ming Huang established his College of the Pear
Garden in the eighth century, both men and women were among the
trainees. In fact, the original Japanese *Kabuki* was established by a
woman. But women were banned from the Chinese stage in the
eighteenth century, when, it is said, an emperor married an actress;
in Japan they were forbidden by imperial edict less than a hundred
years after they began. It is true that, in the twentieth century,
women again appear on Chinese and Japanese stages, more in Japan
than in China; there have even been all-girl companies in Japan. But
men have long been preferred, even in female roles; the greatest
actor to come out of China in recent times has been Mei Lan-fang, a
female impersonator.

The training is long and arduous, beginning in early youth. Each
actor is expected to master a hundred to two hundred roles, each
with its special characteristics, gestures, and movements. In China,
there are four large classifications of types: males in general, robust
males, females in general, and broad comedians. An actor generally
makes his reputation in one of these types. Within each type there
are numerous subsidiary types, each interpreted in a specific way.

344

Vocal characteristics are important. Robust males and broad comedians speak in a forced bass, other types in falsetto. They sing to the accompaniment of string, brass, and percussion instruments, and must master the art of making themselves heard above these piercing sounds. Each character has his own walk and set of gestures. There is a "language of the fan" and a "language of the sleeve," and every movement follows a strict convention. Actors enter and exit to a tempo set by the orchestra, and every movement is a studied rhythm. The female impersonators work to emphasize the difference between the sexes, with even the slightest crook of the little finger designed to emphasize the fragility and delicacy of the fair sex. It is a triumph of art over reality.

Since there is little or no opportunity for change of facial expression because of the painted faces and, in the Japanese *Noh*, the masks, performers must rely on other means to communicate emotional effects. In the *Noh*, this communication is aided by the construction

126 *Japanese theatre in Japanese art*
Above, in this screen, stage, actors, audience, and box-office are arranged in decorative fashion. Below, costumed actors in *The 47 Ronins* carry the props and assume the characters of the parts they play. (Boston Museum of Fine Arts)

of the stage, on which the dancing feet of the actors beat a rhythm that reveals emotional states. It is obvious that the oriental actor must be skilled in prose and verse, in song and dance, and pantomime; that he must have his voice and every muscle of his body under absolute control at all times. Continuing application and constant discipline are his lot. Yet with few exceptions, such as the general esteem for *Noh* performers, he has long been held in low repute. Occidental standards have changed this opinion in modern times, and the great success which Mei Lan-fang had in Europe and America did much to raise the status of his fellow-actors in Asia. And, of course, the motion pictures have created stars in the western tradition.

Summary

The oriental theatre has proved through many centuries that realism is not a necessary concomitant of theatre.

The dramatic literature of the Orient has little in common with that of the Western world. It makes no attempt to hold the mirror up to nature; it is in no wise realistic. Virtue is always rewarded, evil always punished; happy endings are universal. We might call it escapist drama, but it has an undeniable charm, a touch of fantasy that is genuinely and almost universally appealing.

Its manner of staging is well suited to its subject matter. In the Orient theatrical presentation has been almost without exception a highly refined and symbolic art form. The essence of human experience, not a representation of life, is the goal of drama, evident in themes, staging, costumes, and acting. Oriental abstractions are sometimes meaningless to western eyes, their prolixity often tedious. Yet the kernel of oriental theatre art has been an emphasis upon the skill of the artists, and in the timeless atmosphere of Asia this art has reached a great refinement. The splendor of the costumes and the skill of the actors have had some effect on western theatre, both in design and performance, and certainly two very practical contributions to western theatre technique have been the revolving stage and the runway through the audience.

346

EUROPEAN ROMANTICISM

We have been maintaining throughout that theatre is one of the most social of the arts, and must therefore be seen against the background of the times which produce it. Nineteenth-century Europe formed a somber setting, for almost the whole period was marked by violent political unrest. From the French Revolution in 1789 to the Franco–Prussian War in 1870, the whole continent was in turmoil. France, with violent paroxysms, saw the establishment of two empires, a monarchy with three successive kings, and three republics. Italy, in 1861, after many internal and external struggles, established a unified kingdom from the many city-states and principalities which had heretofore divided the peninsula. Germany, after violent internecine struggles, achieved unification ten years later. Even Spain had its first republic for a brief period of five years in the seventies, and Norway won separation from Denmark early in the century. Russia, where a kind of feudal organization endured longer than anywhere else in Europe, would wait for the new century to undergo its violent revolution.

By and large, the changing political map of Europe reflected the continuing realignment not only of governments but also of social classes. The rejection of the aristocracy and the emergence of the middle classes, begun quietly and slowly many years before as the mercantile bourgeoisie gained in power, erupted violently in the French Revolution, and proceeded with increased pace during the

347

various phases of the Industrial Revolution throughout the whole of the century. Not only was the divine right of kings challenged, but eventually the right of any human being to sovereignty over any other human being. The principle that all men are created equal was tested again and again, and during the course of the century most people in most countries of the West came to agree that most people *ought*, at least, to be equal. Practice often denied the principle, but at least the principle was upheld as an ideal.

Discovery and speculation in science (called natural philosophy, as distinguished from moral philosophy, until the middle of the century) brought forth many new ideas which troubled the intellectual atmosphere and had repercussions in all areas of human activity. The force of new ideas had been in operation in the preceding century, of course, in the continuing struggle between the entrenched Classicism and nascent Romanticism. The triumph of the latter in literature we call the Romantic Revolution, heralded in 1798 by the *Lyrical Ballads* of Wordsworth and Coleridge. It was paralleled in Germany by J. P. Richter, Herder, and Novalis, though the declared Classicism of Goethe had earlier shown many of the traits of Romanticism. The triumph of Victor Hugo in France marked the complete submergence of French classical literature.

The triumph of Romanticism, with its emphasis upon individual inspiration, proliferated variety in literary forms, for the form was the man. Earlier ideas of form and discipline in the arts gave way to the belief that each man was his own best judge of both methods and materials, that all he need do to create a masterpiece was to "look in [his] heart and write," as Sir Philip Sidney had said three centuries before. That highly personal form of literary art, the novel, came to full flower in this century, and in drama such a variety of expression was to be seen that order and form were hard to distinguish. The beginning given to new forms by the experimenters of the previous period now came full flood, and diversity is the mark of nineteenth-century drama.

Theatre under strict control in surging political turmoil

Diversity—and a lamentable divorce from literature—marks theatre through most of the nineteenth century. With few exceptions, plays of real literary merit did not emerge until the revolutionary inspiration, which had already wrought great changes in political, economic, and social fields, reached the theatre itself. Perhaps the very quantity of theatrical productions contributed to their poor quality. Certainly the unsettled and unsettling times tended to stress

348

127 *The Burgtheater in Vienna*
Left, the exterior view; right, the interior about 1840, with a romantic
scene as stage setting. The tiers of boxes are typical of Continental
theatre interiors throughout the century. The tiers extended around
three sides of the auditorium, in what has been called "the
hen-coop plan." The decorations were elaborate.

the escapist aspects of theatre rather than its possibilities as a profound art form. Certainly, also, the emergence of the predominantly
uncultivated middle and lower classes encouraged inconsequential
subject matter in the drama, and spectacular display in its production.
The Romantic impulse, originally dedicated to seeing beauty in common things, developed along lines which took it further and further
from actuality. The drama, particularly, became largely escapist and
crowd pleasing, devoid of ideas as well as of reality. Victorious in the
commercial sense, it rode triumphantly along until it became ridiculous and had to be replaced, near the end of the century, with something new.

This theatre was, as always, the result and the reflection of the
times in which it lived. It was harried, diverse, sometimes grand,
often foolish, and perennially interesting.

In the political turmoil of a large part of the nineteenth century in
Europe, the theatre was sometimes neglected, sometimes banned,
sometimes put to uses far from artistic. Caught up in the conflicting
loyalties of the French Revolution, the century-old Comédie Française was split into opposing factions; Talma became the darling of
the Republicans, and moved with his company, in 1791, to the new
theatre of Les Variétés Amusantes. (In this house, remodeled since,
the Comédie plays today.) The Loyalists, after a short interdiction

349

when there were no dramatic performances in Paris, continued at the old house. Talma called his company the Théâtre de la République, while the older company was known as the Théâtre de la Nation.

These companies were reunited in 1799, the year in which Napoleon became First Consul, though during the period of the Republic more than fifty theatres had sprung up all over Paris. It was then, as now, the center of French theatrical activity. Napoleon thought of himself as (among other things) a patron of the arts; in 1812 he signed the famous Decree of Moscow, which limited the number of Parisian theatres to eight, each with its sphere of activity defined, and reserved the production of classic plays, as heretofore, to the Comédie Française. The management as set up by this decree, with some modifications by decrees of 1850, 1859, and 1945, is still in force today. Thus has the continuity of French theatre descended in unbroken line from Molière to the present time, with an emphasis upon repertory and the production of classics both new and old, and a strict insistence upon training for membership in the company. The manager was and is appointed by the government, though the shareholders, as in Molière's day, have a voice in the affairs of the theatre, exercising it vigorously or weakly as the abilities of the incumbent manager permit.

The head of state in Russia also dictated and regulated theatrical activity there. Tsar Nicholas I, in his drastic reorganization of Russian life, brought the theatre under the regulation of the Third Department, or Secret Police, arrogating to himself as head of the Department all theatrical matters, including the selection of the repertory and the distribution of the parts. There were two theatres in St. Petersburg at this time, one devoted to ballet and opera and one to drama. Although under Nicholas' successor and through the rest of the century many theatres were built in many provinces, and theatre managers and owners frequently came from the merchant class, all theatres continued under the jurisdiction of the Secret Police. They exercised a strict censorship on the performance of plays, as well as on the number and kind of playhouses allowed. Thus, though there was a gradual transition from a theatre completely dominated by the aristocracy to one owned and managed by the middle class, government participation in theatrical activity was strong throughout.

Censorship was also strong in the theatres of Vienna, where other companies rivaled the government-patronized Burgtheater (figure 127). Censorship was also implicit, at least, in the court theatres of the German principalities and the Italian city-states. Though theatrical production in most places tended to pass from the hands of the aristocracy to those of middle-class entrepreneurs, the ruling classes were keenly aware of the potential use of theatre as a propaganda instrument. Just as the French theatres of the Revolution became the mouthpieces of the new sentiments, so Italian theatres saw a wave of patriotic and nationalistic plays, and the Russian theatre was organized in defense of the status quo through the Secret Police of the Third Department.

This widespread regulation had its reaction toward the close of the century in various "free" theatres set up as private producing agencies in various parts of the Continent. That is another story, and belongs to a later chapter. Another kind of freedom from government restriction—or rather, circumvention of it—was found by those producers who instituted in their playhouses various forms of bastard theatrical art like melodramas, vaudeville, pantomimes, *opéras comiques*, and so forth. Convention and reaction, the struggle of the new against the old, were as evident in theatrical activity as they were in other fields, though, until the last quarter of the century, no great or lasting changes were effected in theatre.

Further inroads on the tradition of actor-managers were made during this period, with more and more nonacting managers coming to the fore. The fortunes of actors were as unstable as ever, except in such permanent companies as the Comédie Française, though even there merit often suffered at the hands of influence, as in the case of an inferior actress being elected shareholder over the very able M. Worms because she had an influential friend in the imperial government. Criticism of the free lives of players was still current, being directed notably against such an eminent performer as Sarah Bernhardt. But the rise of acting as a respectable profession went steadily forward in the public regard, to the point where Brander Mathews could write in 1880 that he felt confident it would not be long before the Republic of France would award the Legion of Honor to actors no less than to novelists. And we will see that the English actor Henry Irving received in 1895 the first knighthood ever conferred upon an actor.

The relationship between actors and audience was still a close one, Parisian playgoers expressing their disapproval of play or player in quite definite terms, with frequent police intervention. Often the hisses of a dissatisfied audience were fought by the hired claques who sat, under the direction of a leader, in the seats just beyond the orchestra pit. They were an accepted institution in French theatres until 1878, when the Comédie dispensed with them. These claques often made or broke a performance.

351

128 *A contrast in Paris theatres*
Left, the grandiose Paris opera house, opened in 1874; the elaborate
design and spacious appointments of this theatre influenced many
subsequent theatre buildings. Right, an Honoré Daumier lithograph of
the interior of the Théâtre Ventadour, showing the cramped interior
and the dark little boxes that were typical of Paris theatres.
(Photo Cinemati, Paris; Boston Museum of Fine Arts)

Playgoers purchased their tickets from any one of half a dozen
ticket offices throughout the city, or at the theatre just before the
performance, paying then as now in New York an extra sum for the
convenience of the ticket office. Playbills cost extra, as did the foot-
stools which the old female ushers could supply. Advertising was
under government regulation, with each theatre being assigned a
particular color for its posters, with all printing in black, and the size
a uniform fifteen by thirty inches. These were displayed throughout
the city on posts and walls. It is said that when an enterprising American wished to display his large, colored circus posters in Paris in
1867, he had to obtain special permission to do so. By the last decades
of the century, performances in the theatres began at seven o'clock
and lasted until midnight or after. The chief offering was preceded by
one or more short pieces which often operated as proving grounds
for new writing and acting talent.

Throughout all these years, amid all manner of change, the French
audience maintained its love of and interest in theatre, and it constantly grew in size and range of interest. In Russia, theatrical interest and activity spread so rapidly that before the end of the century,
Russian dramatists had contributed some of the most significant plays
to be written in that era. Germany made rapid strides in theatrical
development, and there was a resurgence of theatrical interest in
Spain and Italy. In the smaller countries of Scandinavia and middle

and southern Europe, national theatres were founded and native playwrights sometimes rose, like Ibsen, to international stature.

Extravagance and escapism

As we have mentioned earlier, new plays of this period displayed some marked divergences from earlier types, and a wide diversity of subject matter and treatment. The long-cherished distinctions be-tween tragedy and comedy were completely broken down. Roman-ticism brought many changes in both matter and manner; but toward the end of the century tastes turned to "the light of common day" which marked the so-called Realistic school.

Translations and adaptations, unprotected by international copy-right, were produced on stages everywhere. The Shakespeare cult in Germany, begun by Schroeder, was carried on by an excellent series of translations under the editorship of Ludwig Tieck. Shakespeare was produced also in France, in Czechoslovakia, in Russia, and in Italy, with increasing reverence for the original texts. The other classic dramatists continued to hold the boards, with more or less success depending on their interpreters, as did the "copies of copies," as Schiller called them, of the more recent past.

But our chief concern is with the playwrights who were contem-porary with the theatre which produced their work. Napoleon, eager to have his own great tragic poet, as Louis XIV had his Racine, tried to elicit great tragic plays by edict and subsidy. But the effort was fruitless; the genre was dead. Napoleon had to content himself with criticisms of Talma's interpretations of the great classic parts, and with ordering the Comédie company to play, often at a moment's notice, in all the great capitals of Europe so that their admiring peoples might see the glory of France. He was slightly more success-ful in his patronage of comedy, for under his prompting, Louis Picard produced *The Small Town* (1801), which traveled to Germany and thence to England as *The Merry Widow.*

Of the few names which we could mention in tragedy and comedy as previous ages knew them, none would be significant today, except perhaps that of the Austrian Franz Grillparzer, who wrote on classic themes at one point in his career, and the Dane Adam Oehlen-schlaeger, among whose thirty-odd plays are numerous tragedies influenced by his study of the Greek drama.

Romanticism was the prevailing spirit of the first half of the nine-teenth century. The long-regarded rules of the neoclassicists were abandoned in favor of freedom of form and content. The domestic comedies and tragedies of the preceding period developed into

353

predominant genres, and many other types were added. As we have mentioned before, the Romantic movement had its first significant manifestations in Germany. Concomitant with Lessing's strictures against French neoclassicism and his own study of English criticism and playwriting, there arose tremendous interest in England's greatest playwright. Shakespeare was now explained not as being great in spite of his flouting of the Aristotelian rules but precisely because of it. His plays were considered vast pictures of life itself having no unity of time or place; the only unity the plays needed, or knew, was the unity of the hero. All one needed to do to produce great drama was to create many outstanding personalities and have them go through many events.

The young Goethe was caught up in this mistaken interpretation of Shakespeare's greatness, without giving due consideration to the fact that the Englishman wrote primarily for the theatre he used, his plays being fashioned for the Elizabethan playhouse and its spectators. Thus Goethe published, in 1773, his *Goetz von Berlichingen*, with fifty-four changes of scene and forty-one speaking characters, outdoing his master, whose *Antony and Cleopatra* (most lavish of the Shakespearean canon in change of scene) had but thirty-eight. Goethe's play was fashioned for the contemporary reader rather than for contemporary theatre in which each of these fifty-four scenes would require a shift in the stage decoration. Nevertheless the play was produced, and its success in book form as well as its production gave impetus to an increasing looseness of dramatic form—"the technique of the curiosity box," as Goethe called Shakespeare's plays —which completely disregarded the English master's logical plot development.

On this pattern F. M. von Klinger produced his *Storm and Stress* in 1776, from which the *Sturm und Drang* movement takes its name; J. M. R. Lenz, his *The Soldiers* (1776), which is a series of sensational events loosely related to a single character; and J. F. von Schiller, his *The Robber* (1781), concerning which he said that he was not interested in conforming to "the stringent rules of theatrical composition" but wrote frankly for the reader "without seeking the dubious advantage of stage adaptation." Almost all of his plays are prolix and complicated, *Wallenstein* (1799) being actually three plays in length, with two of them having five acts each. Only *Intrigue and Love* (1783) of his early plays, and *Maria Stuart* (1800) of his later ones, exhibit any discipline of form or regard for the exigencies of staging.

The fact that Schiller and Goethe were men of genius gave their work the power to put its stamp on many lesser plays of lesser men.

The excesses of their early Romanticism—perhaps their observation of what excess did to lesser men—caused both of them to declare for Classicism, to use poetry rather than prose, and to actually write on classic themes. But they were never really Classicists in spirit or in practice. Their influence on their followers and on the French Romantics was tremendous.

It was Schiller's study of Greek drama that led to the inclusion of the idea of Nemesis in his own plays, and thence to a whole series of fate-tragedies based upon the operation of a curse. Such were the widely popular plays of Werner, Müllner, Kleist, and Grabbe. Both the *Ritterdramen* (plays of chivalry) and the *Rührstücke* (sentimental melodramas) were outgrowths of the early Romantic movement in Germany. They proved more popular on the stage in their own day than did the plays of Schiller. Kotzebue's plays were *Rührstücke* in their most extravagant form, and were widely copied and translated in other parts of Europe, in England, and in America.

In France, the connecting link between the tearful comedy and Romantic tragedy was the melodrama. It developed in the boulevard theatres, which pleased the great popular taste in presenting plays of sensibility full of surprises, intrigue, disguises, and discoveries. Its chief practitioner was that odd and talented man René Pixerécourt who wrote or collaborated on more than one hundred plays, writing always, as he said, for those who could not read while himself being inordinately proud of his fine library. Strongly influenced by the work of the earlier German Romanticists, he concentrated on three-act plays with spectacular plots which strained credulity, with characters to suit: the virtuous and outraged heroine, the manly but misunderstood hero, and the diabolical villain. He was the first to use the word "melodrama" in the sense in which we understand it today, and wrote two papers setting forth his views on this genre. He made a fortune writing and producing for these secondary theatres of Paris, losing most of his money in 1835 in the disastrous fire of the Théâtre de la Gaîté.

While the commoners were thrilled and horrified by the melodrama, the aristocrats and the intellectuals were bored by the classical repertoire of the Comédie Française. Romantic drama tried to reconcile the two forms and please both audiences. Lemercier, though he did not call himself a Romanticist and felt it necessary to apologize for his lapse from the sacred rules in the Author's Note accompanying *Christophe Colomb* (1809), did nevertheless present a play at the Odéon which was not in the Classical tradition and which aroused considerable controversy.

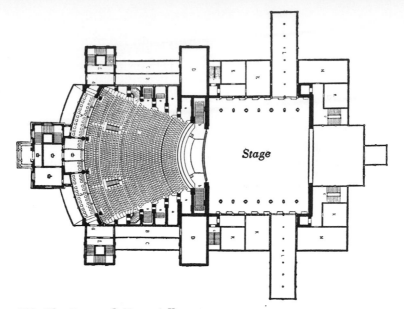

Stage

129 *The Bayreuth Festspielhaus*
This revolutionary theatre plan is a radical departure from the usual nineteenth-century idea. Conceived by Wagner, and opened in 1876, it features a fanshaped auditorium with rising rows of seats and no boxes whatsoever. The stage, however, was equipped for the elaborate transformations which were still popular.
(Sachs, *Modern Opera Houses and Theatres*)

But the heads that were cracked in that battle were as nothing compared to the storm that greeted the work of Victor Hugo two decades later. In the intervening years Mme. de Staël, Constant, Lebrun, and Stendhal took up the Romantic banner. Visits of Kemble and Macready were used as proof of the superiority of the free-ranging English system over the strictly disciplined French dramaturgy. Hugo raised a storm in the preface to his published six-hour play, *Cromwell*, in 1827, in which he argued eloquently for the new literature. By October, 1829, *Othello*, in a version by Alfred de Vigny, was being played at the Comédie, though not without vociferous opposition. Then, in February 1830, accompanied by hoots, catcalls, skirmishes, and open battles, *Hernani* was produced at the Comédie. When the dust of battle cleared, this five-act melodrama, written under the influence of Shakespeare by a man of genius, had won the day for Romantic drama. Hugo became a hero.

Alexandre Dumas (père) writing for the Théâtre de la Porte Saint Martin, produced many plays of the same type, notably *Antony* (1831) and *La Tour de Nesle* (1832), then turned to dramatizations of his own novels of which he had written more than one hundred; the formlessness of the typical Romantic play was well suited to the discursiveness of the novel form. Dumas (fils) is best known for the rendering of his novel, *The Lady of the Camellias* (1852) into a play. But the bulk of his dramatic writing, coming in the second half of the century, is devoted to social questions and belongs with a new genre.

Alfred de Musset, writer of exquisitely witty dialogue, had little influence on contemporary theatre, because after an initial failure on the boards he wrote solely for publication. But his skillful plays have more interest and genuine literary merit than those which were produced when written; they have since been widely played.

In Italy, Romanticism was channeled into the service of the nationalist cause, as in Niccolini's *Nabucco* (1819), which, paying lip service to the unities, is sometimes claimed by the Classicists. But his later plays, with their impassioned outcries against foreign powers and the absolutism of the Church mark him definitely as a Romantic. Manzoni's lyrical historical tragedy, *Il Conte di Carmagnola* (1820), and the early plays of Paolo Ferrari are other examples of this type.

In Spain, the earlier Romantic tradition of Lope de Vega and Calderón received new impetus in the work of Francisco Martinez, Juan Eugenio Hartzenbusch, and Antonio Gutierrez whose *El Trovador* (1836) served, some twenty years later, as the basis for Verdi's opera, *Il Trovatore*.

The extravagance of the Romantics, their prolixity and formlessness, soon found a critic in Eugene Scribe. Though he is now held in a contempt almost as great as his fame was in his own day because of the ultimate insignificance of his subject matter and the obvious mechanics of his technique, his influence was salutary. Scribe developed the "well-made" play which is neatness personified, though no less Romantic than the type of play he set out to reform. To its clearcut structure and easily identified character types could be tacked all kinds of improbabilities and theatrical effects. He wrote more than four hundred plays, often with a collaborator; none of them is remembered today, except, perhaps, his least typical: *Adrienne Lecouvreur* (1849) gave a spectacular acting part to Rachel, Bernhardt, Ristori, Modjeska, and others. His successor in the well-made play was Victorien Sardou, who like Scribe was immensely successful, widely copied and translated, and remembered today mainly because Bernard Shaw once epitomized his type of writing as "Sardoodle-dom."

Occasionally a well-made play rose to greatness. One of the earlier ones contains keen insight into human motivations, as well as a

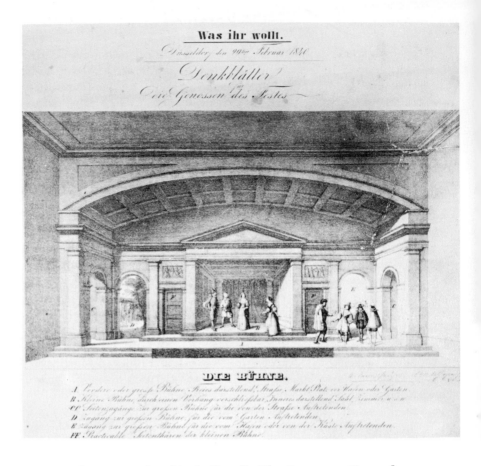

superior literary style; this is Gogol's *The Inspector General,* produced in 1836 at the Moscow Maly Theatre, and still very interesting and playable. Perhaps it was both the incipient realism and the folk quality of Gogol's play that interested the eminent Pushkin (1799–1837), who had spent his life in pursuit of these qualities, and whose powerful play, *Boris Godunov* (1825) was banned from the stage in Russia for many years. Pushkin was the first writer of eminence to insist that the vernacular, as opposed to French, German, or Church Slavonic, was the best medium for literary and dramatic expression in Russia; it is interesting to note how quickly after him Russian playwriting rose to greatness.

A wave of patriotic plays had been made to order for Tsar Nicholas I, who also encouraged melodrama and vaudeville as escapist theatre for the masses. But, in spite of political interdiction (or perhaps because of it), the mid-nineteenth century saw the emergence of the great national drama—and playwrights such as Gogol (1809–52),

130 *Simplified settings*
Left, Immerman's Shakespearean stage, Düsseldorf, 1840. This
structural stage setting was superimposed upon a regular proscenium
stage, and remained unchanged throughout the performance.
Above, the stage for the Passion Play at Oberammergau. This, too, is a
permanent structural setting, and is very similar to that at the left. It
is, however, built for an outdoor production. (Theater-Museum, Munich)

Turgcnev (1818–83), the two Tolstoys (Alexei, 1817–75, and Lev,
1828–1910), Chekhov (1860–1904), and Corki (1868–1936). Alexei
Tolstoy's historical trilogy, *The Death of Ivan the Terrible, Tsar
Feodor Ivanovich, Tsar Boris,* was written between 1866 and 1870,
but was banned by the Third Department, and not produced until
the opening of the Moscow Art Theatre in 1898. The reception accorded Gogol's *The Inspector General* caused his self-exile. Turgeniev's most famous play, *A Month in the Country* (1850), was not
staged until 1872 because of censorship. And Chekhov, perhaps the
greatest playwright of them all, would wait for the new theatre movement to give him adequate production.

The development, after the middle of the century, of Realism and
Naturalism had some roots in the Romantic's concern for common things and common people, for nature in its primitive state, and
thus parallels the continued production of the still popular Romantic
drama. Even Ibsen, who is the cornerstone of this "new theatre,"

progressed from Romanticism through historical drama incorporating psychological insights, to the powerful social and psychological studies which are the basis for his widespread fame and influence. Again, as in the preceding century, new forms grew slowly beneath the pattern of the established, breaking through in the last decades of the period to predominant triumph.

French playhouses typical of Continental theatre architecture

Though the First Empire attempted to limit the number of theatres in Paris, the proscription was of comparatively short duration; it was totally abolished in 1867, and by the third quarter of the century there were again upwards of fifty houses in the metropolitan area, including one in almost every outlying ward of the city proper. Of these, about twenty might be called leading houses, patronized chiefly by the upper classes; the rest were secondary houses, devoted to the entertainment of the middle and lower classes.

Among the leading theatres, the first was, of course, the Théâtre Français, housing the venerable Comédie. The house to which Talma and his insurgents moved in 1791, in the Rue de Richelieu, is the one still occupied today, although it has gone through various renovations and rebuildings, notably after a disastrous fire in 1900. A renovation in 1864 provided for a fine foyer, or public reception room, in which the audience gathered between scenes and before and after the performance. The building in the nineteenth century was a free-standing structure, seating fourteen hundred spectators, with a colonnade marking the front of the ground floor. In addition to the auditorium, it housed (as it still does) a valuable museum of portraits and statues, including Houdon's famous bust of Molière. Dramatists as well as players are included in the galleries, and the list of artists who are represented is an impressive one. The library on the fourth floor houses, in addition to the complete records of the long history of the Comédie, many precious manuscripts of plays first presented there. Here is the record of a theatrical organization older than any other in the Western world, housed in a building which is still an active theatre center.

Other theatres of the nineteenth century which offered Parisians the same fare as the Comédie were the Odéon or Second Théâtre Français, the Gymnase Dramatique, and the Vaudeville. The original Odéon had been built during the reign of Louis XVI and was occupied for a while by the Comédie Française. It was destroyed by fire in 1799, rebuilt, and for a time called the Théâtre de l'Impératrice. It burned again in 1818, but Louis XVIII ordered it rebuilt at once and gave it permission to act all the plays of the Classical repertory, which had hitherto been the exclusive right of the Comédie. It was at this time that the Odéon was called the Second Théâtre Français, but it never rose to the eminence of the first house, functioning somewhat as a "bush league" for aspiring players and playwrights. In 1959, it was officially designated Le Théâtre de France, under the directorship of the renowned Jean Louis Barrault. The Gymnase Dramatique began in 1820 as a sort of public practice room for students of the Conservatory, the government-supervised school of theatre. Its function became much like that of the Odéon in relation to the first theatre of France. The Vaudeville was founded in 1792 by two secessionists from the Opéra Comique, and devoted about fifty years of its existence to the production of the light, topical amusements set to music that were called vaudevilles at that time. Then, in 1852, it produced Dumas' *The Lady of the Camellias*, a straight play which met the requirements of the theatre's operation by including one song. So successful was this innovation that the Vaudeville continued in the new genre from that point on.

Another group of somewhat larger theatres devoted themselves to drama and spectacle. The most famous of these was the Thèâtre de la Porte Saint Martin, which housed most of the plays of the insurgent Romantics. It had been built in 1781 to house the opera, but closed in 1796 when the opera moved out. It reopened in 1802 with melodrama, and was closed again from 1807 to 1810. From then on it concentrated on spectacle and melodrama, and, as we have seen, housed the Romantics. It is interesting to note that the Porte Saint Martin housed the first dramatization of Jules Verne's *Around the World in Eighty Days*. At the Gaîté were offered "fairy pieces" and musical extravaganzas, enlightened now and then by the music of Offenbach and Gounod. The Châtelet was devoted to spectaculars of military or geographical persuasions, often having whole menageries parade across the stage. The Ambigu Comique, early in the century the scene of many of Pixerécourt's fabulously successful melodramas, eventually became the refuge of the Naturalists.

The *opéra bouffe* (comic opera), which rose to great popularity in the later nineteenth century, was housed chiefly in the Bouffes Parisiennes, the Renaissance, the Folies Dramatiques, and the Variétés—the last of which was the chief home of Offenbach. But all through the century, the Opéra Comique remained, as it had been previously, the chief house for light opera.

The most imposing of theatrical buildings in Paris was the new Opéra, or National Academy of Music, built at great expense, through

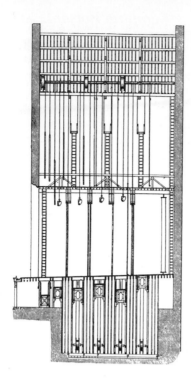

131 *Continental stage machinery*
This sketch shows the complications of stage machinery necessary in the large theatres. Much understage and overstage construction was demanded by the complicated scene changes. (Sachs, *Modern Opera Houses and Theatres*)

good times and bad over a period of twelve years, and finally opened in 1875. It is a grandiose structure, in an extravagantly decorated style, designed by Charles Garnier, and often copied throughout the Western world. Seating twenty-one hundred persons, it replaced the old opera house in the Rue Le Peletier with an opulence almost unbelievable, and a tremendous stage most intricately fitted out with machinery.

The general design of the theatres of Paris built or remodeled during the century was fairly standard. The wide proscenium arch contained three tiers of two boxes each, from which stretched three or more oval or horseshoe galleries, one built almost directly over the other. The first of these had two or three rows of chairs, backed by a row of boxes; the second was generally all small boxes; the third was furnished completely with benches. Where a fourth gallery was included, it, too, was given over to benches, inhabited by the "gallery gods." The floor of the orchestra was still divided into three parts: orchestra chairs nearest the stage, a pit with seating on benches, and, under the first gallery, a tier of dark little boxes. Brander Mathews complained, in 1880, that even the best of Parisian theatres were very uncomfortable, with narrow aisles often crowded with extra chairs, and very hard and narrow seats. Consideration for the comfort of the audience would wait for a future time.

This French model, inspired by the Italian opera house, was still, in the nineteenth century, the prevalent style of theatre interior just about everywhere. A notable exception and herald of a new era in theatre building was the Festspielhaus at Bayreuth (figure 129), sketched out by Wagner and built by Otto Brückwald in 1876. Asking that every spectator have a full view of the stage, Wagner demanded and got a house without galleries, the floor of the auditorium inclined, the rows of seats slightly curved. It was the first radical change in a style which had endured for about two hundred years, and it had significant influence on both the design of new theatres and the renovation of old ones. We can see how, though revolutionary for its day, it was no more than a return to the basic plan of the old Teatro Olimpico, and behind that, to the theatres of ancient Rome.

It will not profit us significantly to enumerate all the theatre buildings on the Continent. By and large, there were two sizes: the larger theatres housing opera and spectacle, and the somewhat smaller ones housing the drama. Indeed, in Moscow and St. Petersburg the two officially sanctioned theatres were named just that: Bolshoy, or Great; Maly, or Small, with the Moscow Maly, opened in 1824, developing into perhaps the most famous of Russian theatres. The tiny Maly in St. Petersburg was replaced by the Alexandrinsky, a larger house, in 1832, about the same time that a third house, the Youth Theatre, was opened for light comedy presented by the graduates of the Government Theatrical School. The removal of the ban on theatre construction in 1882 encouraged the opening of many private theatres, both in the capitals and in the provinces, chiefly modeled on the French style. The numerous theatres of middle Europe and Italy, many of them first built in the eighteenth century, also persisted in the opera-type house. Not without reason was the theatre called an auditorium, a place for hearing, rather than a spectatorium, or place for seeing. Even the popularity of spectacles did little to alter the design of theatres for a long time, and the revolution was accomplished only when theatre people realized that all those who have come to the plays should both *see* and *hear* them advantageously.

The Romantic imagination stops at set design

Through most of the nineteenth century, stages, their equipment and properties, were generally the direct inheritance of former times, subject to modifications caused by the new plays and the tastes of the theatregoing public. Stages were usually one or one-and-a-half times

363

the size of the auditoriums, and were equipped with the elaborate machinery made popular by Vigarani and Torelli in an earlier age (figure 131). Though much of the stage machinery stood idle in the more literary dramas (such as they were), full use of the elaborate systems for ascents, descents, discoveries, and reveals persisted in the nondramatic stage spectacles that were ever popular with a large portion of the public. In the quasiliterary melodrama, as popularized by Pixerécourt, elaborate effects were the rule, with that intrepid producer devoting much of his time and effort to intricate and unusual special effects. There are records of snow storms, floods, the uprooting of trees, earthquakes, and other like phenomena "so terribly lifelike," as one contemporary remarked, as to excite "cries of admiration mingled with fright."

The most popular means of dressing the stage, through most of the century, was still the flat-wing system. On the Continent the wings were generally attached to a carriage system below stage through slots in the stage floor, so that by turning a windlass a set of flats could be withdrawn into the wings while another moved into place. This change was accomplished in full view of the audience. With this system the backdrop was generally lowered through a long, thin slot, while another was raised by pulleys to take its place. The flats might have had irregular edges to simulate trees or buildings, and they might have been, in part, transparencies. They were usually painted in strong colors to compensate for the inadequate lighting that prevailed. Borders were universally used to dress the top of the stage, and these were controlled by ropes and pulleys attached to the gridiron. The predominant effect of the entire indoor and outdoor setting was still that of the earlier perspective scenery; for indoor scenes, furniture was usually painted on the flats. The angular perspective introduced by the Bibienas remained popular, as did the innovation of Piranesi in massing dark forms in the foreground with lighter forms upstage.

Theatre's Industrial Revolution

As time went on, the wing flats were sometimes hinged to provide a "return" on an oblique angle from the flat itself which paralleled the footlights, and this finally developed into the box set. The new scheme did not entirely replace the wing set, but simply became another means for dressing the stage. At first the overhead borders were retained with the box set, then, as better means of lighting were developed, the borders were replaced by a ceiling, and the box set reached its apogee.

132 *Elaborate stage settings*
Left, Joseph Quaglio's design for Schiller's *Wilhelm Tell*, given in
Munich in 1806. This Romantic setting is typical in its elaborate
picturesqueness. Right, Friedrich Beuther's Temple of Isis for Mozart's
The Magic Flute, given in Weimar in 1817 under Goethe's direction.
The massive structural forms and the diagonal linear perspective
show the Bibiena influence. (Theater-Museum, Munich)

Another development of the period was the use of multiple sets,
not like those of the medieval mysteries, with mansions stretched in
horizontal line across the stage but with rooms above rooms, as for
the plays of Nestroy in Vienna in the 1830's. Though each part of this
compound set comprised an acting area, stage properties and furniture were likely to be painted on the scene rather than to be practical.

In some theatres the preference for three-dimensional set pieces,
inaugurated by Loutherbourg at Drury Lane, required the use of
multiple stage traps of various sizes and shapes through which these
pieces could be changed from below. Many European theatres had
vast cellars under their stages to accommodate this type of scene
change. The system eventuated in the elaborate elevator stage which
Edwin Booth installed in his theatre in New York in 1869, wherein
whole sets could be changed in the basement and raised to the stage
floor.

During the nineteenth century the candle, which had lighted
theatres for many generations, and the oil lamp were replaced first
by gas and then by electricity. Gas was first patented for manufacture
in 1781, and was installed as a lighting system in 1816 in the Chestnut Street Theatre, Philadelphia. In 1817, the Lyceum in London
converted to gas, and finally, by 1830, it reached the Continent via
Berlin. Light sources for stage and auditorium were now controlled
by literally miles of flexible tubing attached to a gas table behind
scenes, where all or some of the lights could be dimmed or brightened

133 *More elaborate stage settings*
Left, Sanquirico's temple setting for a melodrama given in Milan in
1826. The dark forms downstage and lighter ones upstage are
reminiscent of Piranesi. Right, Simon Quaglio's Roman Hall for a
production in Munich in about 1850. The same characteristics, but not in
so marked a degree, are evident here as in the setting at the left.
(The Metropolitan Museum of Art; Theater-Museum, Munich)

as the production demanded. Concomitantly, theatre fires increased
in number.

The brilliance of stage lighting was enhanced by the development
of limelight (produced by heating a cylinder of lime to incandescence by the use of a gas mixture) as early as 1816, and in 1846 the
Paris Opéra was using an arc light formed by passing an electric
current between two rods of carbon. The same designer, M. J.
Dubosc, who perfected the arc light from the original experiments
of Sir Humphry Davy earlier in the century, also developed a lightning machine, a rainbow projector, and a luminous fountain—all
based on the arc-light principle. But adequate theatre lighting
awaited the invention of the incandescent lamp by Thomas Edison
in 1879; its first installation was made in 1880 and 1881 at the Paris
Opéra. Four theatres in Germany became completely electrified in
1883: the Landestheater in Stuttgart, the Residenztheater in Munich,
the Staatsoper in Vienna, and the Stadttheater in Brünn. Theatres in
London and New York quickly followed. Now a light source was
available capable of infinite variation, and for the first time in the
theatre's long history, lighting became an integral and sometimes all-
important feature of the total production.

Along with the changes in the mechanics of staging, went an
increasing attention to accuracy and authenticity. The reforms urged
by Diderot and Mlle. Clairon in the preceding century regarding

134 More Quaglio settings
These are by Angelo Quaglio, whose family worked as designers for
most of the century in Germany. Above, his setting for *Die Meistersinger*
at Munich in 1868, showing a vista in linear perspective; below, the
original model of a set for Schiller's *Maid of Orleans* at Munich in 1875.
(Theater-Museum, Munich)

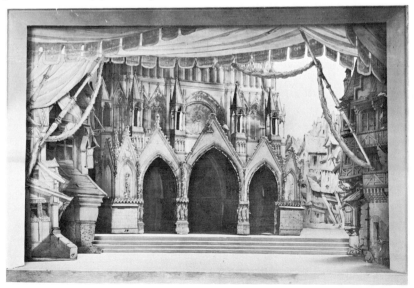

costumes, began to have some effect in settings as early as 1810, when Joseph Schreyvogel at the Burgtheater in Vienna strove for historical accuracy, and had his designer, Antonio de Pian, make suitable settings for Schiller's *Wallenstein* in 1814, and for Grillparzer's *The Ancestress* in 1824. His successor, Heinrich Laube, carried this idea forward. A similar interest was evidenced by Count von Bruehl in Berlin, who, in addition to stressing historical accuracy, seems to have been the first to utilize projections from a type of magic lantern as a part of the stage setting. Franz Dingelstedt, appointed director of the Munich Theatre in 1851, gave the minutest attention to his stage settings, and the climax was reached by Duke George II of Saxe-Meiningen, called "the theatre Duke." He expended much time and effort on research so that every detail of his productions would be most minutely accurate, even engaging an armorer to recreate outmoded ways of dress. From 1874 to 1890 he made theatre history, influencing theatre in all parts of the Western world and inspiring Stanislavski in Russia.

But the theatre Duke never solved the problem of quick set changes. The use of platforms to achieve different acting levels in different scenes, a worthy innovation in itself, often caused interminable waits at intermissions, particularly in multiple-scene plays like those of Shakespeare. Three other Germans—Gottfried Semper, Ludwig Tieck, and Karl Immerman—tried to simplify the Shakespearean performance by simulating what they thought to be Shakespeare's own stage. The first two collaborated on a design to create what they thought the Fortune must have been, and six years later, in 1840, Immerman designed for Düsseldorf a fluid stage with an architectural setting which was imposed on the standard proscenium-arch stage of the theatre. Thus the Germans led the Continent in the progress of theatre art (figure 130).

The innovations which came in stages and staging in the last few decades of the century really belong to the new movement in the theatre, and will be treated in a later chapter.

Historically accurate costumes

During the nineteenth century, costuming developed authenticity as we know it today—that is, an historical accuracy in line and detail adapted to the configuration of the contemporary actor or actress, and not necessarily presenting an exact duplicate of the original appearance. Ellen Terry's Portia, for instance, really looks quite different from that of Katharine Hepburn although each is authentic or true to the time and place of Shakespeare's original character.

135 *The Theatre Duke*
Sketch by the Duke of Saxe-Meiningen for the scene in which Joan is
captured in Schiller's *Maid of Orleans*. This is typical of the Duke's
practice in carefully working out the disposition of each individual in the
great crowd scenes for which his productions were famous.
(Collection of Duke George II, Meiningen Museum)

As we have seen, the mild costume reforms effected by Voltaire
and Mlle. Clairon in the 1750's were accepted by their audiences, but
the more truthful authenticity of Mme. Favart, at the same time,
evoked only opposition. In the last years of the eighteenth century
Talma, influenced by the painter David, made for himself an authentic Roman costume for his part (a minor one) in Voltaire's *Brutus*.
In those days, there were no dress rehearsals, and actors supplied
their own costumes. Imagine the shock of both players and audience
when Talma appeared in Roman tunic with bare arms and legs. Contrast his appearance with the hoop-skirted actresses and the be-
plumed and beribboned actors. He scandalized his older colleagues,
but evidently pleased the younger portion of his audience. As he
gained prestige as an actor he was able to win others to his costuming
principles, but not without protest from such a one as his father-in-
law, the actor Vanhove, who, when presented with his first correct
Roman costume, protested that it had no pocket for his handkerchief,
and how was he to play tragedy without that indispensable prop?
    In the very year of Talma's death, 1826, Ludwig Tieck was writing
in his collected *Dramatical Papers* from his experience as director of
the Dresden Court Theatre, that historically correct costumes were

not even desirable in the theatre, but that actors should use a "poetic and pictorial" costume, such as "had perhaps never been worn by anyone in real life." And he further maintained that Othello should not be dressed in oriental costume, for instance, because it "of necessity must always produce a disturbing and repellent effect."

But in Vienna, Schreyvogel and then later Laube, directors of the Burgtheater, carried on their battle for historically correct costuming, and Count von Bruehl, at the Royal Theatre in Berlin, is said to have done an historically correct *Henry IV* in 1817. When Koch did Goethe's *Goetz von Berlichingen* in medieval costume in 1774, it was more for reasons of avoiding censure for the political topicality of the play than for the sake of accuracy, but Goethe himself appeared as Orestes in something closely resembling classical garb only six years later (figure 103).

In France, Paul Lorimer, designer for the Paris Opéra, strove unceasingly for accuracy in costuming, but, in general, until near the end of the nineteenth century, historical costuming consisted merely of the addition of period details to dresses which followed the current mode in their main outlines.

A genuine and lasting reform was effected by the theatre Duke of Saxe-Meiningen, whose exhaustive researches and careful attention to detail made memorable stage pictures. He gave the minutest attention to details of every costume, and since his productions were usually plays demanding great crowd scenes, the number of costumes required was staggering. The pictorial effect of the crowds, arranged and moved to underline the emotional intent of the particular scene, was rendered outstanding not only by the costumes and sets, but by virtue of the fact that in this company the members of the crowd were not the usual supernumeraries, but polished actors who might in other plays of the repertoire play leading roles, and who were studiously coached in every movement and utterance. The carefully staged crowd scenes and the meticulous costuming made a deep impression wherever the Meiningen appeared in their various tours (figure 135). It was not until the fame of these players had spread throughout Europe that the propriety of truly accurate costuming was generally accepted.

Grease paint, at last

Modern theatrical makeup was a nineteenth-century development, too. For more than half the century, stage performers were dependent upon powders of various colors and composition for stage effects. The whites, generally made from lead, often proved poisonous to the

Du ungezogener Schlingel!
Act II. Scene IV.

136 Costumes and characters
Left, the great Romantic actor Devrient as Falstaff. Note the closer
approximation to Elizabethan dress evident in this sketch. Right, a sketch
by the Duke of Saxe-Meiningen for a character in *Don Giovanni*.
Here the authenticity is undoubted and the details carefully worked out.
(Theater-Museum, Munich; Theaterwissen schaftliches Institut
der Universität Köln, Sommlung Weissen)

users. Reds and yellows, derived from cochineal and umber, respectively, were more or less harmless. Blacks were generally burnt cork.
Lines were achieved by the use of india ink under the powders;
changes in shape of nose or cheeks by gumming on appropriate wads
of wool, or forming a piece of paste from powder and gumming it on.

In about 1865, the German Wagnerian singer Ludwig Leichner,
through study and experiment at the University of Würzburg, developed the formula which resulted in the first appearance of grease
paint. He developed and numbered a series of colors and liners in
stick form, recommending their use as a part of his sales technique.
By 1873, his manufacture of the new makeup had become a thriving
business enterprise. By 1895, a wide range of colors could be obtained, and their use had almost completely supplanted the older

371

powder-based makeup techniques. For removing the grease paint, Leichner recommended liberal applications of cocoa butter. A lanolin-based cream has now supplanted the cocoa butter, but in most other details, modern makeup is still as Leichner developed it.

Romantic spirit encourages individual eccentricities

By 1800, the great Schroeder had retired from the stage, Iffland was near death, and the only actor of magnitude on the Continental stage was the Frenchman, Talma. His star shone brightly for a few years beyond the First Empire, but in spite of his many reforms in acting and in costuming, he was essentially a classical actor in the tragic-hero line. It is true, of course, that he was restricted in his interpretations by the materials with which he worked (the classical tragedies), and that his methods might have been better suited to the newer romantic plays which came into recognition after his death. In any event, the rise of the Romantic drama brought in a whole new school of actors and acting styles.

Most typical of the newer type was Frédérick Lemaître (1800–76), whose career lay chiefly outside the Comédie Française. An increasing number of his contemporaries made careers outside that venerable house—another mark of the emphasis on individual freedom which the Romantics stressed. Lemaître was the first French actor to be equally at home, and equally successful, in comic as well as tragic parts, and he rose to great eminence. His training had been in the Conservatory, but much of his early experience was in playing melodrama, farce, and extravaganza, and he became equally adept in all styles. His most signal victory was the creation of the character of Robert Macaire in an otherwise insignificant melodrama called *The Inn of the Adrets,* which he played not straight as it was written, but as a comedy part. He played many of Victor Hugo's parts, and that great Frenchman, on Lemaître's death in 1876, put the actor in the proud line of Thespis, Roscius, and Talma as one of the great actors of all time.

If one were to choose a prototype for the nineteenth-century Romantic actor, however, the choice would without question be the German, Ludwig Devrient (1784–1832). He presented a grandly wild appearance, with long dark hair, pale face with melancholy eyes and a sorrowful smile, and a general remoteness from the world in which he moved. He was greatly admired in Romantic parts throughout Germany, especially at the Burgtheater in Vienna where he made an amazing success. In his later career he played a wide variety of character parts, particularly Falstaff (figure 136), in which

137 *Rachel in two costumes*
Left, the renowned French actress appears in her most famous role as
Phèdre, wearing classic drapery and a fillet; right, as Rosalind in *Bajazet*
she wears a richly decorated oriental costume fitted to her well-corseted
figure. (Henry E. Huntington Library and Art Gallery)

he was said to be outstanding. He has often been likened to the great
English Romantic actor, Edmund Kean (1787–1833).

The famous Russian tragedian, Pavel Mochalov (1800–48), was
of the same type—wildly romantic and relying entirely on intuition
and the inspiration of the moment. Laceration of personal feelings
to create stage characters, rather than studied technique and discipline in their realization, was the stock-in-trade of the Romantic
actor.

The greatest names in the nineteenth-century theatrical firma-
ment, however, are women: Ristori, Rachel, Bernhardt, Réjane, Duse
—two Italian and three French.

Rachel (1820–58), often called one of the greatest actresses the
world had ever seen, was a typical Romantic in her short, brilliant,
and recklessly intense career. But her great fame was made in classical tragedy, her greatest part generally conceded to be Phèdre
(figure 137). She was accepted by the Comédie Française in 1838,
and died twenty years later, at the age of thirty-eight, after a stormy

373

138 *Two more famous actresses*
Left, Duse as Marguerite Gautier in *The Lady of the Camellias*, typical
of the tragic roles for which the Italian actress was famous. Right,
Bernhardt as the Queen in *Ruy Blas*. Again the contemporary silhouette,
highly decorated, constitutes the costume. (Theatre Collection,
New York Public Library; Harvard Theatre Collection)

association which saw her playing as often outside the Comédie as
in it. She created the first Adrienne Lecouvreur in Scribe's play, and
triumphed as Marie Stuart in Lebrun's drama. She was fabulously
successful in the French provinces, in London, all over Europe including Russia, and in America. Her style was an intensely emotional
one, suffusing the old classical tragedy with new life.

Rachel, in her last years, saw the rise of a serious rival in Adelaide
Ristori (1822–1906), who came to Paris from her native Italy in 1855.
She, too, made her great reputation in tragic parts, her most noteworthy being that of Maria Stuart in Schiller's tragedy. She traveled
to London, Spain, and America, and in her later years was often compared most favorably to Sarah Bernhardt, who was the flaming star
of the last three decades of the century.

Bernhardt (1845–1923) became a byword quite as much for her
flamboyant personal life as for her undoubted skill on the stage

(figure 138). Painter, sculptor, poet, and playwright, she was also adept at self-advertisement, managing through her long career to keep her name ever before the public. Her star propensities caused her to break with the Comédie Française, into which she had been accepted in 1862. It was, and is, the policy of the Comédie to acknowledge no stars, but to list the members of the acting company in the order of their seniority. To this practice Rachel and Bernhardt both objected. After 1880, Bernhardt never acted there again, traveling through Europe, America, and even Egypt and Australia. At times she herself managed three various Paris theatres, to one of which she gave her own name. She did all the parts in which Rachel had become famous, and added the great romantic heroines, as well, particularly Marguerite Gautier in *The Lady of the Camellias*. She loved breeches parts, made a great success in Rostand's *L'Aiglon*, and, curiously enough, triumphed as Hamlet.

Preferred by many in comedy parts was another Frenchwoman, Réjane (1857–1920), who, realizing her potentialities and limitations, confined herself to light comedy. She became as famous in her line as Bernhardt in tragedy. She traveled to New York, London, and South Africa with immense success.

The final star among the actresses of the century was the Italian, Eleanora Duse (1859–1924), whom Bernard Shaw preferred to Bernhardt (figure 138). She, too, did best in the tragic line. Duse became a public personality by a technique the obverse of Bernhardt's. She professed to hate publicity, and built up a legend of an enigmatic personality, which was as effective a technique with the theatregoing public as was Bernhardt's flashier approach. The legend was heightened by her unhappy passion for the poet, Gabriel D'Annunzio, and her far-flung, highly successful tours.

Only slightly less famous was Tommaso Salvini (1829–1916), perhaps the greatest Othello ever to appear (figure 139). He played this famous part in his native Italian with companies who spoke in their own native tongues, all over Europe and America, and evidently played it with an intensity and ferocity that was sometimes frightening.

One other name must be mentioned—that of Constant Coquelin (1841–1909). An incomparable comedian of the French national theatre, he brilliantly played all of Molière's heroes and was legendary in Rostand's *Cyrano de Bergerac* (1898). He was one of the few actors of all time who set down something of the technique by which actors achieve their ends, saying that the good actor must be two people—the one who performs and the one who regulates and

375

139 *Salvini in two costumes*
Left, the great Italian actor as Othello, his most famous role, with
authentic oriental touches to the costume; right, as Macbeth, looking
somewhat like a Viking. See figure 93. (Harvard Theatre Collection)

criticizes the performance. Thus he argued for a disciplined art which
would not be solely a matter of inspiration, but also of technique.

Repertory framework still prevails

We are inclined to remember acting by the brilliance of its individual artists, but the advancement of theatrical art does not depend
solely upon these individuals. At least equally important is the work
of repertory companies, which develop the difficult technique of
ensemble playing, doing justice to the playwright, and, in the long
run, being more fully satisfying in the theatre. All of the great talents
mentioned here were developed in repertory companies, though each,
in some measure, flourished outside that system.

The great strength of Continental theatre through most of the
nineteenth century was still within the repertory framework. Schreyvogel and Laube in Vienna, Tieck at Dresden, von Bruehl in Berlin,
the theatre Duke at Saxe-Meiningen, though they produced no stars
of the magnitude of these mentioned, paved the way for the
twentieth-century conception of acting by their insistence upon the
actor as a member of a group with concomitant artistic responsibilities. This conception requires that even a star be a member of the

ensemble and not a solo performer aided by a mere obbligato of obliging colleagues. The star system never became as firmly entrenched on the Continent as it did in England, and, more particularly, in America. We shall, therefore, look to the next chapter for a fuller consideration of both its glories and its evils.

Summary

The nineteenth century was a period of great upheaval, with many significant changes taking place in governments and in social structures. Theatre reflected few of these and turned rather to an escapist drama which, perhaps, was demanded by the largely new audiences who chose not to think about the weighty matters engrossing the world outside.

The prevailing atmosphere of a good portion of the nineteenth-century theatre in Europe was the effulgent light of Romanticism. Extravagance was the watchword. Extravagant entertainment, extravagantly contrived plots and characters, extravagant displays in acting and personality traits took the new audiences to a never-never land of makebelieve. Plays ostensibly founded on historical fact bent those facts to a thesis or a point of view; plays ostensibly rooted in contemporary life generally carried both situation and character to the extremes of virtue and vice. Even the so-called well-made play was a Romantic effusion. Theatre architecture remained largely rooted in the past; stage decoration was intricate and often flamboyantly unrealistic.

Yet the period did develop some practices that were important to aftertimes. The audience was almost completely democratized, hitherto unreached segments of the population being brought into the theatre for the first time. Nonacting managers and producers were established as the rule rather than the exception. There was some experimentation in theatre architecture, notably at Bayreuth, with its rejection of boxes and galleries and incorporation of banked seats. Gas and then electricity initiated experimentation and advance in the separate area of lighting. Historical accuracy in costuming developed to the point of complete acceptance and, indeed, there was often an overemphasis upon antiquarianism. Modern methods of makeup came into existence. The cult of the individual star triumphed. It was an active, almost a hectic, period which brought us to the doorway of today.

COMMERCIAL THEATRE
IN ENGLAND AND AMERICA

The American Revolution was genteel in comparison with many revolutions in the Western world that followed it. Its architects and engineers were neoclassic rationalists, and its result—the creation of a new nation—was in many ways a political accident. There were many on both sides of the Atlantic who deplored the expedient which divorced the colonies from Mother England, and the population of the new country lost a great number of able men when the Loyalists moved out. Political independence had been gained, but a true national identity and a cultural independence would be a long time coming.

The Articles of Confederation bound together thirteen sovereign colonies in a loose union; but the colonies had little in common and not much interest in common goals. The struggle to establish an effective national government was long and hard, engaging the best minds of the day. When Washington was inaugurated President on April 30, 1789, under the new Constitution, there were still many who were actively opposed to the federal form of government which he administered. Though the framework of a democracy was present, the true democratic spirit was largely lacking. The successful War of 1812 gave the new nation more of a sense of national identity, and with the election of Andrew Jackson, a man of the people indeed, democracy became more of a reality. Then the Civil War, a revolution almost as far-reaching as the preceding one, finally established the sovereign power of the federal government. The struggle had taken almost a century.

Less violent but equally as revolutionary were the events taking place in the mother country. George III was so ardently disliked by his subjects that the wave of republican sentiment lasted through the reigns of George IV and William IV, and was not dissipated until well along in the reign of the circumspect Victoria who came to the throne in 1837. The long series of reforms which preceded her coronation and followed throughout her reign constituted, in essence, a far-reaching revolution broadening the base of suffrage, clearing up various political and economic inequities, and assuring the emergence of middle-class domination of the constitutional monarchy. By the time Victoria died in 1901, modern England had been born.

140 *A typical nineteenth-century theatre*
Reconstruction by Richard Leacroft of the Theatre Royal, Plymouth, 1811, after drawings by John Foulston, architect. This carefully detailed and accurate drawing shows the construction of the typical nineteenth-century theatre, with benches in the pit, boxes and galleries, proscenium doors, orchestra well, wing system on stage, overhead and below-stage machinery including grooves, traps, and a cloud machine, and other backstage arrangements. With minor changes in individual cases, it could stand for practically any English theatre in use during the nineteenth century. (Richard Leacroft Theatre Collection)

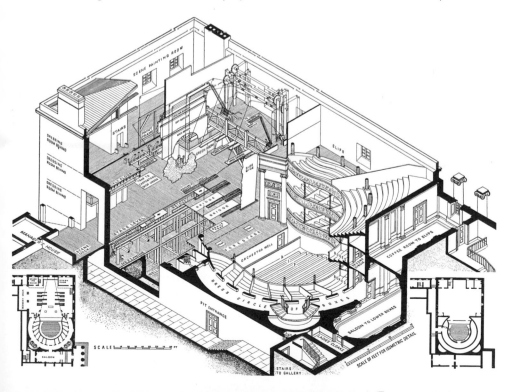

141 *Similar interiors regardless of size*
Left, the small Regency Theatre during a performance of *Othello*,
early in the century. Right, the much larger Olympic Theatre at
approximately the same time. Note the posts supporting the tiers, the
proscenium doors with boxes above them, and, in the Olympic,
the row of dark boxes on the first level.
(Henry E. Huntington Library and Art Gallery)

Both England and America were shaped by the revolution in
thought instigated by Darwin, and by the developments of the Industrial Revolution, just as Europe was. We shall see how these developments had definitive effects on theatre. Both England and America
had each its Romantic Revolution, America's coming somewhat after
that of England. Both countries were open to continuing influences
from the Continent. The world of-art is one world. Though it may be
temporarily influenced by political nationalism (we have seen examples of that from the earliest times to the present), it has more
similarities from one people to another than dissimilarities; it deals
not primarily with temporary political divergences, but with the
feelings, dreams, and aspirations of mankind, which are everywhere
more alike than different. Art has always overstepped national
boundaries, theatre no less than other forms.

As on the Continent, so in England and America, the drama
throughout most of the nineteenth century was largely divorced from
literature, and the memorable literary productions were in fields
other than playwriting. But here, again, there were some brilliant
exceptions, and as on the Continent the art of theatre itself made
revolutionary advances. Taken by and large, the nineteenth century
saw more changes wrought in more areas of human activity than any

other comparable period in the history of civilization. Theatre, as one very important area of human activity, reflected those changes.

Theatre develops as a commercial enterprise

For the greater part of the nineteenth century, English and American theatres were not only similar, but interchangeable. Players, plays, designers, and producers freely crossed the Atlantic in both directions in a more or less amicable commerce. Theatre entertainment grew to be completely universal in both countries, reaching upward and downward into every segment of society. The growth of railroad traffic led, in England, to the attrition of the hitherto prosperous provincial circuit system and the final substitution, by 1880, of an almost universal plan of touring London plays with either first or second companies.

In America, with its larger expanse of territory, the death of provincial repertory took a little longer. The thirst of the westward-moving pioneers for theatre was met, in part, by that uniquely American phenomenon of the showboat, which plied the great interior rivers through most of the century. Companies also traveled by stage and railroad throughout the interior of the continent. By 1806, there was a professional company of actors in Pittsburgh. By 1815, "Old Sam" Drake was playing in Lexington and Louisville, and Noah Miller Ludlow opened his St. Philippe Street Theatre in New Orleans just three years later. He removed to St. Louis in 1820, leaving New Orleans to James H. Caldwell. St. Louis remained the theatrical center of the west until 1837, when performances were first given in Chicago, whose phenomenal growth soon insured its supremacy. Sacramento had a theatre in 1849— a year memorable for other reasons, and San Francisco in 1850, the same year in which the Mormons opened a theatre at Salt Lake City. Seven years later there was a theatre at Omaha, and in 1859 one at Denver. This wave of theatre openings followed the movement of the western frontier, leaping from the Mississippi to the coast and then doubling back. It is estimated that whereas in 1800 there were but a handful of theatres and a mere 150 professional actors in the United States, by 1885 there were five thousand theatres in more than thirty-five hundred towns. The frontier theatres were rough affairs, and hazardous for ladies in the audience (of whom, fortunately, there were few) by reason of the eating, shouting, and roughhousing that characterized them. The showfolk were a hardy race, much put upon their mettle not only for mere survival but also to engage the attention of the rough audiences. Before the end of the century the western theatres were sending

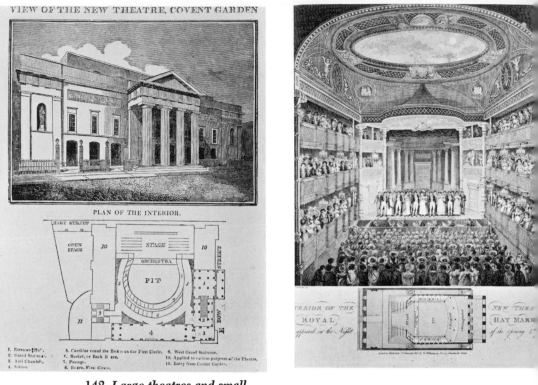

142 Large theatres and small
Left, the classical façade of Covent Garden with the Flaxman statues,
and a floor plan of the interior showing the horseshoe arrangement
of the boxes after the manner of the Italian opera house. Right, the little
Theatre Royal, Haymarket, 1821, and its floor plan which shows
a more rectangular arrangement, but still the persisting side boxes.
(Henry E. Huntington Library and Art Gallery)

back to the more refined east coast such capable people as David Belasco from San Francisco and Lotta Crabtree from the mining camps.

Philadelphia was the early theatrical capital of America, but from the thirties onward New York preempted its importance and became the center of theatrical activity in the United States, as London was in England. More than forty theatres were built in New York during the century, their construction following the movement of the population from the City Hall area to Fourteenth Street, to Herald Square, and thence to the present theatrical center between Forty-second Street and Fifty-ninth. Unhampered by prohibiting legislation, theatre proliferated in all the centers of population.

Commercial Theatre in England and America

The removal of restrictions on English theatres by the Theatre Act of 1843 might be supposed to have caused a similar growth in the number of theatres in the British capital and in the provinces. No longer would it be necessary for theatres to operate under the dodge of pantomimes or concerts; plays could be given freely, subject only to the censorship of the Lord Chamberlain's office. By this time, however, the variant forms of entertainment had become so popular that the already many British theatres simply continued to devote themselves to these rather than to the regular drama. But the patent houses, Drury Lane and Covent Garden, with the restrictions removed, did suffer from the competition of other now-open purveyors of legitimate drama.

The supervision of these various legitimate theatres was still largely in the hands of actor-managers, like Madame Vestris, Henry Irving, Charles Macready, Laura Keene, and Louisa Drew, but the ranks of the nonacting managers were continually swelling until by the end of the century they were more the rule than the exception, particularly in America.

It was in England and America—both without the established and subsidized national theatres possessed by most of the European countries—that the star system entrenched itself, and that theatre took on many of the aspects of a business rather than an art. Throughout most of the century, name actors visited or went on tour, generally appearing with local companies for stated performances without benefit of rehearsal, the local actors accommodating themselves to the visitor as best they could during the performance. Toward the end of the century, when the idea of ensemble playing was gaining ground, stars often began carrying with them at first a few supporting players and later whole companies. But to the very end of the period there were those theatre personalities who appeared in "foreign" theatres, relying on themselves alone to impress the local company and the audience.

A new audience with old habits

These audiences, as we have said, now embraced all segments of society, and they made their sentiments known most decidedly. The century began with the disgraceful "O-P" riots at Covent Garden in 1809, when for sixty-seven nights not a word of John Philip Kemble, Sarah Siddons, and their company could be heard above the shouting, stamping audience demanding a return to the old prices which had prevailed before the opening of the new and larger house. Kemble finally had to give in. A more serious happening was the infamous

143 Drury Lane and Covent Garden
Left, an interior view of the Drury Lane Theatre which opened in
1812; it was not quite so large as the immediately preceding house,
but still seated 2,800 people. The scene on stage is one from Macready's
production of *As You Like It* in 1842. Right, the interior of Covent
Garden, 1810. The lighting was thus arranged to permit a full
view of the occupants of the boxes, as well as to insure that the
occupants of the rear galleries would not have their view obstructed by
chandeliers suspended from the ceiling. (Henry E. Huntington
Library and Art Gallery)

Astor Place Riot in New York in 1849, when demonstrations against
Macready, initiated by Edwin Forrest's partisans, culminated in the
death of twenty-two people and the injury of thirty-six more. At the
London Haymarket there was another riot in 1880 when the Bancrofts substituted orchestra stalls for the old pit arrangement.

But whether violently, as in these cases, or by pressure of taste
and opinion at the box office, the audience dictated theatre fare. It
is the audience which is reflected in the bulk of nineteenth-century
theatre devoted to nonliterary entertainment. Plays of real merit were
few until the tastes of this largely new theatregoing public were educated or developed to receive them. For almost fifty years in England,
the educated and refined largely abandoned the theatre, and not until
the last quarter of the century did they return. It took just a little
longer for really good theatre to emerge in the United States. But as
always in both places there were some noteworthy exceptions.

This democratized audience also demanded its money's worth in
theatre fare. The programs were long, with opening time moving
from six to seven o'clock during the century, and half prices prevailing after eight thirty. The bill began with a "curtain-raiser,"

384

continued with the main fare, then often included one or more after-pieces. The audience moved in and out as it chose to see any or all of these. Parts of the house were retained as general admission, notably the rear of the pit and the galleries; but the practice of prebooking grew for the newly installed orchestra stalls and the remaining boxes. The distribution of playbills by hand and posting continued as a means of advertisement, and in the early part of the century, these also served as theatre programs, being increased in size to contain more information. The practice grew unwieldy, and about 1850 the separate theatre program made its appearance at the Olympic in London. Small and simple at first—and one of them sweetly perfumed by a manufacturer who took an ad on the back page—they, too, became elaborate books, and so remained until they were simplified again in modern times.

During this century, also, theatre criticism entered more widely into literature, with such people as William Hazlitt, Charles Lamb, Leigh Hunt, William Archer, Henry James, Brander Mathews, and James Huneker writing vividly and with great penetration about the art of theatre.

Through good times and bad, nineteenth-century theatre exhibited vigorous activity; it was for a time divorced from literature, then found its way back again.

No place for high-quality drama

The expanding population of the nineteenth century, the phenomenal growth of cities, the expansion of theatrical activities, and the inclusion of all types of society in theatre audiences created a demand for theatrical fare which, then as now, could not be filled by talented or even original writing. The theatres of England and America were glutted with translations and adaptations. Kotzebue, Scribe, Sardou, as well as numberless lesser writers, filled the stages of England and America. Sometimes the borrowed materials were transformed into pantomimes or musicals; sometimes burlesqued. Novels were dramatized as quickly as they were published, and were staged as extravagantly as the resources of a theatre would permit. Allardyce Nicoll (*History of Late Nineteenth Century Drama*, 1949) tells us that six different adaptations of Scott's *Ivanhoe* appeared in London in 1820 alone, and eight different versions of Dickens' *The Cricket on the Hearth* within a year of its publication in 1845. Shakespeare was set to music, given in pantomime, made into spectacle, and played straight. But what Charles Lamb called "the artificial comedy of the last century," which he greatly admired, was indeed extinct on the

144 Changing interiors
Above, John Scott's innovation at the San Pariel (1808), with no bottom
row of boxes, and the pit extending to the walls all around. A performance
of *Our American Cousin* is in progress. Right, Augustin Daly's
Fifth Avenue Theatre in New York, with no boxes at all except
those in the proscenium arch, two stepped-back galleries, and seats
with backs in every part of the house. This is the same construction
used by Edwin Booth in his theatre, and was an American development
eliminating side boxes. The horseshoe shape, however, persists.
Many American theatres of today have similar interiors.
(Henry E. Huntington Library and Art Gallery)

nineteenth-century stage. Restoration comedy required a special
audience largely lacking at that time. Political and social events had
helped to create an audience which, on the one hand, feasted on the
emotion of the melodrama and, on the other, escaped from a difficult and humdrum existence through the fantasy world of spectacle.
Cerebration was at a minimum in nineteenth-century theatre.

Original playwriting of the period reflects the tastes of its audiences, and the general divorce of literature from dramatic writing.
The best literary minds and talents were not employed in theatre
throughout most of the century.

The great Romantic poets sometimes tried theatre, but their
geniuses were too highly individualized to submit to its discipline.
Shelley, inspired by his reading of Greek literature, wrote *Prometheus Unbound* in 1819, but it is largely unplayable and has remained
a closet drama. In the same year, he submitted to Harris at Covent

386

Garden the script of *The Cenci,* which, however, remained unproduced until first acted by the Shelley Society in 1886. Wordsworth
and Coleridge wrote, respectively, *The Borderers* and *Remorse,* both
of which reflected the Gothic aspects of Romanticism, and *Remorse*
was actually produced at Drury Lane (1813). None of these men,
however, had any real affinity for theatre.

Byron, on the other hand, had at least served on the Drury Lane
Committee of Management from 1812 to 1816, and had written a
prologue spoken at the opening of the new house in the former year.
He wrote six dramas, two of which—*Manfred* and *Cain*—are not
really stage plays. The other four are more stageworthy: *Marino
Faliero, The Two Foscari, Sardanapulus,* and *Werner.* Macready suc-
cessfully produced the latter two in 1830 after Byron's death, and
Charles Kean subsequently revived *Sardanapulus* in 1834. Only one
had been produced during Byron's lifetime, *Marino Faliero* at Drury
Lane in 1821. *Manfred* and *The Two Foscari* were produced at
Covent Garden in 1834 and 1837, respectively.

Charles Lamb's second play, *Mr. H.* (1806), was an instant failure,
tradition having it that Lamb, in the gallery, hissed louder than anyone else. His first, *John Woodvil* (1802), was never produced.

Only two of Browning's plays were produced: *Strafford* (1837),
written at the request of Macready and produced by him; and *A Blot
on the 'Scutcheon* (1843). *King Victor and King Charles* remained
unproduced. Three decades later, Irving produced three plays by

145 *Charles Kean at the Princess*
In the 1850's Charles Kean produced a series of Shakespearean plays at
the Princess in London notable for their settings and costuming. Here
the usual wings and borders are carefully designed to simulate columns
and arches. Above is a model for his production of *Hamlet;* right, a scene
from his *Macbeth.* (The Cleveland Museum of Art, Collection of the
Educational Department; Victoria and Albert Museum; Crown Copyright)

Tennyson: *Queen Mary* (1876), *The Cup* (1881), and *Becket*
(1893). Also produced in other theatres were three more: *The
Falcon* (1879), *The Promise of May* (1882), and *The Foresters*
(1892). None of these plays has become a theatre piece for aftertimes, and would deserve no mention here except for the fame of
their authors.

Lesser men were writing for the theatre and reaping its rewards,
such as they were. The tradition of Classical tragedy died hard.
Joanna Baillie in her *Plays of the Passions* (3 vol., 1798–1812), James
Sheridan Knowles in *Virginius* (1820), and Sir Thomas Talfourd in
Ion (1836), *The Athenian Captive* (1838), and *Glencoe* (1840)
tried to keep it alive. So, too, did the American James Daly Burk in
Female Patriotism, or, The Death of Joan of Arc (1798), as did the
transplanted American, John Howard Payne in *Brutus* (1818). All
of these were produced, but none was successful except *Ion* and
Brutus, the first because of Macready's playing, the second because
of Kean's; it is true, though, that Payne's play, by its frequent revivals
through the century, proved itself the more durable.

Romance was the order of the day in England and America no
less than in Europe. Inspired by the interest of the Romantics in the
Gothic period, "Monk" Lewis had a great success with *The Castle
Spectre* in 1797, and established the fad for such extravagant melo-

388

drama on the English stage. Generous intermixtures of Pixerécourt were evident for many years on English and American stages. But Romanticism had other aspects. In America it was largely responsible for a widespread interest in Indian plays, beginning with James Nelson Barker's *Indian Princess* (1808), through *The Indian Prophecy* (1827) of George Washington Parke Custis, the *Metamora* (1829) with which John Augustus Stone won Edwin Forrest's prize for a full-length tragedy on an Indian theme, Penn Smith's *Pocahontas* (1830), the *Forest Princess* (1844) of Charlotte Barnes Conner, and myriads of others widely copied on both sides of the Atlantic. The vogue reached its end in 1855, when John Brougham laughed it off the stage with his burlesque *Pocahontas, or, The Gentle Savage.*

The extravagant characters and implausible situations of French melodrama were domesticated in such plays as Bulwer-Lytton's *Richelieu* (1839) and *The Lady of Lyons* (1838), both eminently successful in their day, and in the romantic plays of Robert Montgomery Bird in America, chiefly *The Gladiator* (1831) written for Edwin Forrest, and *The Broker of Bogota* (1834). These, with *Bianca Visconti* (1837) and *Tortesa the Usurer* (1839) by Nathaniel Parker Willis, *Leonor de Guzman* (1853) and *Francesca da Rimini* (1855) by George Henry Boker, represent the best of the type, largely written in verse, which enjoyed lavish success in both England and America. A resurgence of interest in romantic verse drama in the 1880's led to revivals of some of these, and to a few new representatives of the type by William Gorman Wills in England and Henry Guy Carleton in America. But by that time, the main interest of playgoers was in another field.

The "drama of common life," growing out of another facet of Romanticism, increased in popularity through the century. One of its manifestations was in national types, like the Irish of Dion Boucicault's *The Colleen Bawn* (1860), and the title character of *The Octoroon* (1859); in frontier types like James Kirke Paulding's *Lion of the West* (1830), and Joseph Stevens Jones' *The People's Lawyer* (1830), which fathered a whole line of Yankee characters; in German, Negro, and Italian types in the farces of Edward Harrigan; and in the somewhat different dramatization by George L. Aiken of Harriet Beecher Stowe's *Uncle Tom's Cabin* (1852), although this is more melodrama than anything else.

Another type of popular play was sentimental comedy, or domestic drama. In England, Tom Taylor and Charles Reade were its chief purveyors. Among the best of Taylor's seventy-odd plays are *Masks and Faces* (1852), *Still Waters Run Deep* (1855), *Our American Cousin* (1858), and *The Ticket-of-Leave Man* (1863). Reade's *Gold* (1853) and *The Courier of Lyons* (1854) were his most successful. And in America, the phenomenal success of *Rip Van Winkle* in various renderings throughout most of the century marked the triumph here of sentimental comedy.

A mild social comedy also had some popularity. Anna Cora Mowatt Ritchie's *Fashion* (1845) is often called the first American social comedy, and has some merit in the playing even today. Less well known, but equally good, are James K. Paulding's *The Bucktails* (1847) and William Henry Hurlbert's *Americans in Paris* (1858), the former placing his Americans against an English scene, the latter using France. Dion Boucicault's earlier *London Assurance* (1841) and Bulwer-Lytton's *Money* (1840) represent this genre in England. Social comment became more basic and implicit with the plays of T. W. Robertson: *Society* (1865), *Ours* (1866), *Caste* (1867), *Play* (1868) and *School* (1869) paved the way for the end-of-century Realism. In America, Bronson Howard produced *The Young Mrs. Winthrop* (1882), and James A. Herne *Margaret Fleming* (1890) and *Shore Acres* (1892), using American themes and declaring independence from foreign models.

Finally, J. R. Planché in England and John Brougham in America produced a whole series of burlesques on varied literary, political, and social topics which are not only interesting and often delightful in themselves, but are accurate mirrors of the ideas and issues which were engaging the attentions of their contemporaries. Certainly, too, the tuneful operettas of Gilbert and Sullivan, that marvelous culmination of musical theatre in the nineteenth century, ought to be at least

146 *The Keans*
Left, Edmund Kean as Richard III in 1824; right, his son Charles as
Hamlet in 1858. The elder Kean had a flashing brilliance which his
son never achieved, although the latter was far steadier and more
meticulous in his performances. The costuming in both portraits, while
not nineteenth century, is not historically accurate either, but more
nearly Elizabethan. See figure 93. (Henry E. Huntington
Library and Art Gallery)

noticed here. Sir William Schwenk Gilbert, librettist of that famous
series, had a considerable reputation as a playwright in his own day,
quite aside from his association with Sir Arthur Sullivan. It is one of
the ironies of theatrical history that neither the plays of Gilbert nor
the other music of Sullivan lived beyond the lifetimes of their cre-
ators, while the products of their collaboration are as alive and wonderful today as they have ever been. Finally, perhaps a passing word
should be given to the birth and heyday of that indigenous American
entertainment, the minstrel show.

By the 1890's in England, literary men of ability were again writing for the theatre; it took a little longer in America. But, as in Europe,
by the end of the century, dramatic writing had reassumed literary
respectability.

New theatres for old

Drury Lane and Covent Garden (figure 143), the traditional
strongholds of the drama in London, saw, during the nineteenth century, invasions of other forms of entertainment. The official removal
of their monopoly in 1843 soon caused Covent Garden to turn entirely

147 *William Charles Macready*
Left, Kean's great rival playing Iago in a costume which is neither
Elizabethan nor sixteenth-century Venetian, but a curious mixture of both;
right, playing Orestes in a costume more accurately Greek.
(Harvard Theatre Collection)

to·opera, while at Drury Lane pantomime and spectacle, as well as
visits of the Comédie Française in 1879 and the Meiningen Company
in 1881 helped to keep it going through the century. Other theatres,
more suitable for the drama, were displacing the venerable two.

The Covent Garden building, erected at great cost, and opened in
1808, burned down in 1856. It had been planned by Robert Smirke
and modeled on the Temple of Minerva on the Acropolis, with
statuary by Flaxman. The 1808 building was slightly smaller than the
one it replaced, but was still of cavernous proportions; there were
a pit, two galleries, and three tiers of boxes, one of which was private,
having its own entrance. The stage was sixty-eight feet deep and
forty-two feet wide at the proscenium. It was replaced in 1858 by the
present structure.

Drury Lane, opened in 1812, was designed by Benjamin Wyatt
after the universally admired theatre of Bordeaux. It, too, was slightly
smaller in dimensions than its predecessor but still seated about
twenty-eight hundred. The pit was approximately three-quarters
of a circle, with seven private boxes to each side and a front
lobby. This use of a front lobby as an entrance to the pit marked a
distinct departure from preceding designs in which the pit was
entered by side doors or long, narrow passages. Above the lobby and

the lower boxes was a circle of twenty-six "dress boxes" with a private entrance for select members of the audience. Then came the first tier, giving into the rotunda and grand salon at the front of the house, and having two private boxes at each end nearest the stage. Then came the second tier, above which were placed, at the sides of the house, fourteen boxes (seven on a side) with the lower gallery on the same level at the front of the house. Above the lower gallery rose the upper gallery, now on the sixth level. In the proscenium arch were four boxes, two to each side. The proscenium opening was thirty-three feet wide and nineteen-and-a-half feet high. The whole house was richly decorated, with crimson carpeting in the salon and coffee rooms. This is the house which, with many subsequent interior renovations, is still in use. Both Drury Lane and Covent Garden persisted in the opera-house tradition, with the pit enclosed by tiers of boxes.

A new kind of seating arrangement got its start in 1808, when John Scott, a color maker, built the little Sans Pareil, later the Adelphi, for his daughter and her one-woman entertainments. Here there was no bottom row of boxes, but the pit itself extended under the first tier to the walls all around (figure 144). The same plan was followed in the Coburg (later the Old Vic), built in 1818. By the 1830's and '40's the front part of the pit had been converted into orchestra stalls, and about the middle of the century these were furnished with comfortable individual seats called *fauteuils*. Thus was the Olympic built in 1850, and the Surrey in 1861.

By 1860, when Phipps built the Queen's, the first tier of boxes projected out so that there were two or three rows of seats free of supporting columns, backed by the usual boxes, above which rose the other tiers, still supported by columns. Progress in cantilever construction caused the removal of the supporting columns in the Gaiety (1868), the Vaudeville (1870), the Savoy (1881), the Prince's (1884), Terry's (1887), and the Garrick (1889). With the opening of the new Adelphi in 1858, the backless benches disappeared, and comfortable armchairs were installed. The modern theatre had been born.

Pillars to support the boxes had been omitted in the building of New York's first fine theatre, the Park, as early as 1798, and contemporary comment remarked on the unobstructed vision thus possible from every part of the two-thousand-seat house. There were but three rows of boxes, with the gallery rising from the top of the first row at the front of the house. In 1808 the English architect J. J. Holland brought the Park more into conformity with English houses by installing four rows of boxes, evidently with the columns then

393

148 *John Philip Kemble*
Left, Kemble as Hamlet
in the painting by Sir Joshua
Reynolds; right, as Macbeth
in a contemporary lithograph.
The tradition of feathers
for the tragic hero persists
in both of these costumes; the
difficulty of appropriate dress for
Macbeth is here fully illustrated.
Though he wears a kilt,
he also dons mailed gauntlets,
armor and classical sandals.
See figures 93 and 139.
(Henry E. Huntington
Library and Art Gallery)

usual in England. This building was destroyed by fire in 1820 and rebuilt the next year. The new house held twenty-five hundred (figure 91). A sloped pit extended under the first row of boxes and three tiers of boxes of fourteen each were supported by columns, with a gallery above. The stage was forty-five feet wide and seventy feet deep, and there was a single proscenium door to each side.

But the English pattern gave way to a more native design, and by the time Edwin Booth built his splendid theatre on Twenty-third Street in 1869, the only boxes remaining were three on each side in the deep proscenium arch, which no longer had the old proscenium doors. The pit was now the orchestra as we know it, sloping from a sunken orchestra pit to the front of the house. Three galleries, stepped back, sloped around front and sides of the house and over a portion of the orchestra. There were no supporting columns, and the rows of seats on every level were equipped with arms. This is the standard present-day American theatre, with some slight modifications of number and size of balconies, and the elimination of the stage boxes. Many of our theatres standing today, of course, were built in the latter part of the nineteenth century.

There would be little profit in naming all the theatres built in New York and London, and in other cities of America and England, for they almost invariably followed the plans of these we have described. It is interesting to note that boxes, often with private entrances, persisted longer in England than in America where the weight of aristocracy is not so heavy. But even theatres having these boxes with private access devoted most of their space to less specialized seating—an indication, perhaps, of the increasing democratization of the audiences.

The present Metropolitan Opera House in New York, opened in 1883 and still in use, is a grandiose example of nineteenth-century theatre architecture. It is soon to be replaced by a new house in the Lincoln Square development (or Lincoln Center for the Performing Arts, as it is formally called) which promises to be of interesting design.

Individual innovations in set design

It is highly likely that the wing-and-shutter system initiated by Inigo Jones in the court masques of James I had a life of almost three hundred years because it was a very practical and economical arrangement for theatres offering a constantly changing bill. The stock set, consisting of palace, garden, cottage, woods, cave—more or less, as the affluence of the particular theatre indicated—was standard throughout the eighteenth century and persisted through much of the nineteenth. It was a system capable of infinite refinement, particularly adaptable to theatres where set changes were done in full view of the audience. (Act drops to conceal changes of scenery were not usual in the theatre until the 1870's and '80's.)

In England the usual method of handling the wing-and-shutter system was different from that in Continental theatres. Here the wings and back shutters were arranged in grooves which consisted of shallow wooden troughs in groups of three to eight, fastened to the floor of the stage and to the underside of the fly-gallery above, into which the wings and shutters were slid from offstage. Sometimes there were ingenious arrangements of pulleys and ropes which allowed one set of pieces to be drawn off, revealing the set immediately behind, or, where the number of sets exceeded the number of grooves, for a new set to be drawn on. Sometimes these changes were individually operated by hand, but this method could not be as smooth and coordinated as the rope-and-pulley system. Many elaborations of the system were developed, whereby the centerstage portions of the upper and lower grooves were loose rather than fixed so that if a particular scene demanded a vista, the empty loose grooves, being hinged, could be drawn out of sight so as not to spoil the vista. Loose grooves were sometimes arranged on a pivot so that their scenes could be pushed to a diagonal position instead of remaining parallel to the footlights. The difficult movement of the larger and heavier back shutters was sometimes overcome by having the back scene painted on cloth backed by thin strips of wood which could be rolled much in the manner of the old rolltop desk.

149 *Stars of the early century*
Authentic costuming was not a concern of the theatre of the early
century, as the print on the left, of Mr. Wrench in the part of Benedick,
attests. Right, the great star, Sarah Siddons, as painted by Sir Joshua
Reynolds. The painting is called "The Tragic Muse"; it was in
tragedy that Mrs. Siddons made her great reputation.
(Henry E. Huntington Library and Art Gallery)

The Continental system of changing scenes by understage machinery through slots in the floor was never universal in England or
America, though Covent Garden, in 1857, and the Lyceum, in 1863,
did install it, and there is some mention of its earlier use at Drury
Lane and in Dublin. But by 1880, the grooves were back in use at the
Lyceum, for in that year Irving again removed them to install a system of scene support by braces, much in the modern manner. At the
same time he initiated the practice of dropping the curtain for scene
changes, which custom was no doubt necessitated by the now obvious
inability to change all the flats simultaneously.

Increasing attention was paid to the preparation of the stage flats,
scene painting becoming an important aspect of theatrical production. The nineteenth century gives us the name of the Grieve family,

who became as important to scene design in nineteenth-century English theatre as the Bibienas had been earlier on the Continent. The work of another scene painter, Charles Stanfield, became so popular that his name frequently appeared on the playbills in larger type than those of the principal actors. Ingenious effects were achieved by painting scenes on thin cloth in transparent colors, so that they could seem to disappear and reappear as the lights were changed before and behind them. Cut cloths became so intricate, particularly in the spectacles and the pantomimes, that the stage must often have appeared like a lace-paper valentine.

Madame Vestris and J. R. Planché, at the Lyceum, early introduced as much verisimilitude and historical accuracy as could be achieved with the groove system, and Madame Vestris is said to have established the success of the box set with the English public through a production of Boucicault's *London Assurance* at Covent Garden in 1841. Planché, a self-styled antiquarian, had designed an authentic *King John* for Charles Kemble at Covent Garden as early as 1824, and in 1838, the actor, William Charles Macready, played *Coriolanus* in a setting of the Republic, a distinct contrast to a contemporary production of Kemble's against the background of Imperial Rome. Samuel Phelps, at Sadler's Wells from 1844 to 1862, initiated a series of Shakespeare revivals which became noteworthy for their authenticity and Charles Kean carried this practice to an almost pedantic extreme in his productions at the Princess from 1850 to 1859 (figure 145). Elaborately pictorialized settings were continued by Henry Irving at the Lyceum in the last two decades of the century. These were generally magnificent, although founded on research into the supposed periods of the plays themselves, and firmly established the tendency to produce Shakespeare in highly elaborate settings. In some of these, painted crowds were augmented with live crowds to produce spectacular effects, and scenic vistas enlarged the stage pictures.

The elaboration of the wing system through the nineteenth century was accompanied by increasing complexity in stage effects, particularly in the use of various traps in the stage floor. The Corsican trap, invented for a production of *The Corsican Brothers* (1848), allowed figures to appear from below as if they were rising and gliding across the stage, by means of an ingenious slot which opened before the platform drawing the actor up an incline, and closed behind him. The Vamp Trap, developed for Planché's *The Vampire* in 1820, consisted of two spring leaves, in the stage floor or the scenery, which enabled the actor seemingly to pass through a solid. The

Star Trap, the Cauldron Trap, the Bristle Trap, and many others were developed to such an extent that the so-called trickwork of English nineteenth-century theatre became famous throughout the world. Various ascents, descents, and flyings were also continued and developed in this period, with overhead machinery to operate them, even to the extent of performers seeming to fly out over the heads of the audience and back again. The counterweight system for handling scenery was perfected, being used both below and above stage. These elaborate, and expensive, developments were made practicable by the growing institution of the long run as opposed to the hitherto prevailing repertory system. The long run was initiated in the spectacles and extravaganzas, but, gradually through the century, aided by the star system in acting, became likewise entrenched in the legitimate theatres, and theatre became a business rather than an art form.

It must not be supposed that any of these innovations received universal approval and widespread adoption at any one time; traditional, outmoded, and antiquated methods of stage presentation often existed side by side with the new. Indeed, the American producer W. B. Wood was bemoaning the practice, in 1852, of the use of stock sets, often glaringly incorrect, which was still general in American theatres. The opening of the Booth Theatre in 1869 was a signal event, for in addition to being a beautifully and comfortably appointed house, the stage was marvelously well equipped, with, as we have mentioned, an elevator arrangement that allowed whole scenes to be set in the basement and raised to stage level.

We have already remarked on the change in theatre lighting from candles and oil lamps to gas and then to electricity during this century. It is interesting to note that the Chestnut Street Theatre in Philadelphia was the first house to use gas for illumination. That was in 1816, and the next year, Drury Lane in London advertised itself as being entirely lighted by gas. The introduction of gas was the cause of controversy, the light being considered by some as too brilliant, by others as a great advance. Theatres installed, and then sometimes removed, the innovation. By the middle of the century, however, gas lighting was universally accepted, and was controlled by the prompter from behind the scenes. Gas lights were installed vertically inside the proscenium, and across the top of the stage on battens, with colored cloths to produce red, green, or white light from these or from other strategically located outlets in the stage area. Controls for the stage and the house were separate, and the first practice simply dimmed the house lights while the performance was in progress. Irving is credited with initiating the practice of blacking

398

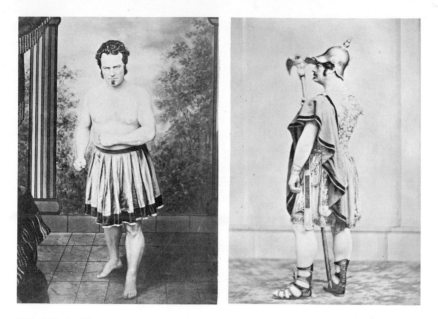

150 *Edwin Forrest*
Left, Forrest in one of his favorite roles, as Spartacus; right, as
Coriolanus. See Quin in the same role, figure 94. Something of the
force and fury that characterized Forrest as an actor is evident in the
portrait of Spartacus. The knee-length skirt was a favorite with
him, despite the fact that it was curiously unbecoming to his squarely
built figure, and hardly correct for the Roman slave.
(Harvard Theatre Collection)

out the house while the play was being performed, thus first using
a technique urged three centuries before by the Italian, Ingegneri.
Colored glass began to replace silk and paper as the medium for color
effects, and in the use of colored lights Irving again made great
contributions.

Electricity went through the same period of installations and re-
movals, disapprobation and approval, that had been the lot of gas.
As we have seen, limelight and arc light preceded the use of electric
bulbs, invented by Edison in 1879. Two years later, Covent Garden
installed stage lighting by the new bulbs, which was evidently
coupled with a dimmer system allowing variation in illumination
from a bright glare to total darkness. David Belasco says that the
first theatre to be lighted by electricity in America was the California,
in San Francisco, in 1879. By 1887 electricity had been installed in
most of the important theatres of Europe and America. The first

151 *Edwin Booth*
Left, Booth as Benedick in *Much Ado About Nothing;* right, as Hamlet.
This most renowned of American nineteenth-century actors wears,
for both of these characters, costumes whose elements are the same: tights
and a long-sleeved tunic. The decoration varies, but neither costume
observes strict historical authenticity. (Harvard Theatre Collection)

experiments in lighting the stage from the front of the house were performed by this same David Belasco at the Grand Opera in San Francisco in 1879, when he used an old bullseye lantern from a locomotive
as a light source. The advent of electricity meant a decrease in the
number of theatre fires, which had assumed alarming proportions
during the sixty-year reign of gas. During that time there had been
a total of three hundred and eighty-five disastrous fires in England,
France, and America.

Historical costuming gradually evolves

As we have said earlier, the nineteenth century is generally conceded to be the period in which costuming historically correct for the
period in which the play supposedly takes place became universal.
And, in the broad outlines of the statement, it is true. But the initiation
was by no means sudden or exact. We have seen that the French theatre in the eighteenth century made some indubitable progress in
accurate costuming, but that the reforms effected on the English stage
in the same period were comparatively meager.

During the first quarter of the nineteenth century, the same conditions prevailed. The popularity of the novels of Scott caused some interest in historical costuming, but the net results were simply the adding of Elizabethan details, for instance, to contemporary dress. The first attempt at historical accuracy for every character in the production was evidently that of J. R. Planché for Charles Kemble's production of *King John* late in 1824. Planché, after indefatigable research, dressed the cast in authentic thirteenth-century costumes, receiving for his effort the scorn of the actors who had to wear his "stew-pans" for hats, but receiving also, as he tells it, the unmitigated praise of the public.

In 1838 Macready did *Coriolanus* "with a true sense of antiquity," albeit the dress was no more than "an approximation to the toga," according to a contemporary report. That the majority of the so-called historical costumes of the period were just such approximations is evident from the fact that Macready as Macbeth is described by a German visitor as wearing a "fashionable flowered chintz dressing-gown" in the murder night scene. Another evidence is the fact that in the Shakespeare productions with which Charles Kean made the Princess Theatre famous from 1851 to 1859, Mrs. Kean, in *A Winter's Tale*, wore a perfectly correct Greek dress as Hermione, but wore it over a crinoline. And she was not alone in her adherence to this undergarment. For so long as it remained in style, all kinds of costumes were superimposed upon it. And, whatever the style of dress they were wearing, actresses persisted in having their coiffures the latest in attractive nineteenth-century styles.

The vogue for domestic dramas which were played, of course, in contemporary dress, and (notably at the Prince of Wales' Theatre under the Bancrofts in the third quarter of the century) with real furniture and box sets with practical doors and windows, furthered the demand for real properties and realism in dress in other types of drama. Thus the antiquarian fervor of Kean and Irving as applied to historical plays received additional impetus. The visits of the Meiningen players to London in 1881 brought an example of how effective truth to time and place could be, and spurred the efforts of English producers to this end. By the close of the century, accurate historical costume was the rule rather than the exception—quite the reverse of the century's beginning.

As on the Continent, the art of makeup was modernized in nineteenth-century England and America. The first description of the use of grease paint in English theatre occurs in 1877, some years after its introduction on the Continent. That these paints had been imported

401

from Germany is evident from the listing of colors given with the instructions for their use—the same numbers given by Leichner himself. Many actors still clung to the old powder makeup; as late as 1883 a writer on the art of makeup talks only in terms of powder and does not even mention grease paint. By 1890, however, powder was largely superseded by the more versatile and more durable grease paints. This somewhat slow adoption was no doubt aided by the advent of gas and then electricity, for the additional illumination required more care and more verisimilitude in the application of makeup.

Thus, care in the dressing of the actors paralleled care in the dressing of the stage, with realistic effects the ultimate goal.

Stars are born

Though the eighteenth century is generally called the Age of Great Acting, the term is no less applicable to the nineteenth. In England, the century opened with John Philip Kemble (figure 148) and Sarah Siddons (figure 149) as the outstanding pair, and closed with Henry Irving and Ellen Terry. America moved from dependence on imported English actors to the development of great native talents, notably Edwin Forrest (figure 150) and Edwin Booth (figure 151), both of whom had a European as well as an American reputation.

The nineteenth century was the age of great stars whose appearance generally assured the success of the pieces in which they were playing. They toured widely, in the early years traveling (as we have said) individually, then with a few supporting players, and finally with complete supporting casts. Acting was a family tradition, and there were many outstanding acting families: the Kembles, Keans, Tearles, and Trees in England; the Jeffersons, Booths, Drews, and Barrymores in America. Lacking the tradition of a great national theatre, such as that of France, both England and America witnessed the death of repertory companies during the nineteenth century, and the rise of long runs. Particularly in America, the uneconomical and in many ways inartistic method of assembling a cast for a particular show, playing it, and then disbanding the company, gained firm foothold.

As on the Continent, acting styles moved from the classical to the romantic. Just as Talma began the century in classical style in France, so in England John Philip Kemble (1757–1823) and his sister, Sarah Siddons (1755–1831), represented the acme of classical acting there. Dignity was the keyword of their performances. Though, like Talma, they were both interested in more truth in costuming and

152 *Two actresses*

Left, Mrs. Alsop as Rosalind in *As You Like It*, costumed in a rustic dress fashioned on the Empire silhouette then in vogue. Right, the American actress Charlotte Cushman as Lady Macbeth, in a costume curiously reminiscent of the midcentury female silhouette. The center-part coiffure was then the fashion, too. (Henry E. Huntington Library and Art Gallery)

stage presentation, their style of acting was measured and conventional, commanding and powerful. Each was best in the great tragic parts, working on a preconceived plan for a calculated effect, although Mrs. Siddons, as we have said, had some of the emotional drive in characterization that became the hallmark of the Romantics.

Deliberately opposed to the "cold" classical style, with what often descended to monotony of delivery, was William Charles Macready (1793–1873), who varied his delivery with calculated pauses to the extent that "the Macready pause" became famous in discussions of Victorian theatre (figure 147). Of an ungovernable temper, he made many enemies but also did much to advance the art which he professed to hate, insisting on stern rehearsal discipline, doing praiseworthy revivals of Shakespeare, and bringing Byron to the English stage. He traveled to France and to America, appearing here first in 1823, and last in May, 1849, when his rivalry with the American actor, Edwin Forrest, led to the infamous Astor Place Riot. The critic William Hazlitt said of Macready that this actor was the best tragedian he had known next to Edmund Kean.

Kean (1787–1833) was the true Romantic, and rival of Macready

153 *The Young Roscius*
William Henry West Betty, at the age of thirteen, took London by
storm in the 1804–05 season, ousting even Sarah Siddons and John Philip
Kemble in the public favor. This lithograph shows him in some of his
many parts. His triumph was shortlived, and he died in obscurity.
(Harvard Theatre Collection)

in tragic roles, doing best in those that required some madness or
frenzy. Coleridge's comment is still the best epitome of his style: to
watch Kean was "like reading Shakespeare by flashes of lightning."
He relied on gesture and facial expression more than on voice, and
excelled as Shylock, Richard III, and Iago (figure 146). He was of
the inspirational school of acting, as was George Frederick Cooke
(1756–1812), the first English star brought to America by William
Dunlap. Cooke's performances varied from brilliance to bathos, and
much of his inspiration is said to have come from the bottle.

The extravagant romantic drama demanded extravagant acting,
but there were always voices raised against it, such as those of
Charles Matthews (1776–1835), his son, Charles James (1803–78),
and Madame Vestris, whom the younger Matthews married. They
practiced and preached a more temperate style. It is true that the
newer, realistic play which the latter two chiefly produced was
more conducive to realistic acting—indeed demanded it. Thus, the
total effect was quite salutary.

The first home-grown American actor to appear on the English
stage was John Howard Payne (1791–1852), known chiefly today

because of the song, "Home, Sweet Home," which was originally a part of his light opera, *Clari* (1821). He was one of a vanishing breed of actor-playwrights. After some small success in New York, he went to England in 1813, where he appeared with greater success in London and the provinces, writing many plays and acquiring the friendship of Talma.

More flamboyant was Edwin Forrest (1806–72), whom William Winter once characterized as "a vast animal, bewildered by a grain of genius." He was a belligerent American, proud of his nationality, and the bitter rival of Macready. Large and imposing of figure, with a big voice, he excelled in bold and forceful roles such as Spartacus, Jaffier, Metamora, and Richelieu. He made many enemies, and was often accused of ranting. He had been one of the first native talents to score a success at the Bowery Theatre in New York, whose astute manager Thomas Hamblin devoted himself in the 1830's to enlarging the audience of his theatre. He capitalized on what he called native American talent in order to attract the new audiences who were not steeped in the tradition of English plays and players.

Quite the opposite of Forrest in personality and style was the greatest of nineteenth-century American actors, Edwin Booth (1833–93). Booth appeared not only in England, but in Australia and Germany as well, bringing honor both to himself and to his country. His career was temporarily halted when his brother, John Wilkes Booth, assassinated Lincoln, but he was well received on his return to the stage. Impressive in appearance, he was a careful theatre workman, studying his parts with great depth of understanding and projecting the characters sympathetically and fully rounded. He was a magnificent Hamlet, playing the part for a record run of one hundred consecutive performances in 1864.

As in the earlier days of American theatre, in the nineteenth century some English actors came to America and made it their home. Such were William Burton, John Brougham (another actor-playwright whose burlesques at the mid-century form an interesting chapter in theatre history), and the Wallacks, whose second generation Lester became one of the outstanding actors and managers of the latter part of the century. Laura Keene also came from England to establish an excellent repertory company in New York, and Louisa Drew to operate similarly in Philadelphia. One of Mrs. Drew's daughters married the English-turned-American actor, Maurice Barrymore, to found America's royal family of the theatre. The three Joseph Jeffersons were also of English origin, the first arriving in 1795, the last dying in 1905. There were also three generations of Davenports on

154 *Two more child actresses*
Kate and Ellen Bateman were popular child stars in both England and
America. They were the daughters of a theatrical couple, and after
various successes in America appeared first in London in 1851, when Kate
was eight and Ellen seven. Kate appeared as Richmond, Portia, and
Lady Macbeth to Ellen's Richard III, Shylock, and Macbeth. Ellen
retired from the stage in 1860, but Kate went on to success as
an adult actress. (Henry E. Huntington Library and Art Gallery)

the American stage in the nineteenth century. In the latter part of
the century the great names were James H. Hackett, E. H. Sothern,
Julia Marlowe, Mary Anderson, and Lotta Crabtree who began as a
child actress in the western mining camps and lived to great fame.
The American theatre also cheered a woman who, like Bernhardt,
was fond of playing men's parts, Charlotte Cushman (figure 152).
She appeared as Romeo in London in 1845 to her sister's Juliet. Ada
Rehan and Mrs. Leslie Carter also fluttered pulses toward the end of
the century, and Minnie Maddern Fiske, once also a child actress,
became famous for her realistic, natural acting in the plays of Ibsen.

Dominating the English stage in the latter half of the century were
Charles Kean (figure 146), not so erratic nor brilliant as his father; the
Bancrofts and John Hare, who, under Tom Robertson's direction at
the Prince of Wales's Theatre, brought natural acting to a degree of
perfection; and Henry Irving and Ellen Terry, whose names have
come down to aftertimes as the epitome of perfection. Irving, at least,

was not considered perfect in his own day, Henry James, for one, finding considerable fault with his art. But Ellen Terry, mother of the famous Gordon Craig, seems to have been the ideal artist—sensitive, warm, and in complete command of her craft. As we have said before, Irving was knighted in 1895 for his services to theatre, and was the first actor ever to be thus honored.

Squire Bancroft was knighted two years later, like Irving, for his services to theatre. His had been a lifelong endeavor to make theatre respectable, to achieve greater realism in stage production, and to raise the status of actors. He and his wife, in conjunction with Robertson, made material increases in actors' salaries, and early paid for the ladies' dresses—hitherto an almost unheard-of practice. They were also the first to institute a single play as the whole bill for their theatre, in the 1860's. They demanded long and careful rehearsals, much as did the nonacting manager Augustin Daly in the American theatre.

Actors' salaries varied greatly, as might be expected. A star commanded a truly fabulous sum, while lesser players got a mere subsistence. The star system worked great havoc in the old repertory system with its assured income. It was also instrumental in destroying potential talent by long runs and one-part players, as Eugene O'Neill's father, James—potentially perhaps a great actor—wasted his life playing a perpetual Count of Monte Cristo. For a good part of the century, actors' incomes were supplemented by benefit nights, that venerable institution which came in for much criticism. It was finally abolished by theatres like Wallack's in New York in 1868, who raised actors' salaries in order to do so.

Training was chiefly by family tradition, and the great vogue for child actors produced some competent persons as they matured. Otherwise, actors acquired skill by taking parts in whatever vehicle offered itself—mainly in the hinterlands—and through actual stage experience moved on to better parts with better companies in the more well-known theatre centers.

Extremes of affluence and poverty were perhaps more marked among the nineteenth-century actors than ever before, but their social status definitely improved. By the end of the century, only the die-hard puritanical element was still opposed to them.

Changes in the tastes of audiences, in types of plays, in methods of production, and in producing agents, all played a role in altering both actors and acting styles from the classical actor who played a line of parts throughout his lifetime, to the romantic, then the realistic actor who either played himself no matter what the part or created a variety of parts of varying kinds. With the production scheme in operation in the commercial theatres toward the close of the century, the actor was likely, in his lifetime, to play far fewer parts with far less variety than in previous ages of theatre. His training was likely to be haphazard, and his security—at least in England and America —practically nonexistent.

Summary

In England and America, no less than on the Continent, theatre of the nineteenth century was largely escapist. The bulk of dramatic writing was decidedly Romantic, with little reference to actuality or even plausibility. Since it was so far removed from the actual world and its problems, it produced little of lasting significance.

So far as the resources of theatres and producers allowed, the presentation of entertainments and plays was lavish and intricate. A special aura of glamor attached itself to theatre and theatre personnel, creating great stars and popularizing touring and one-part actors. The creation of a special "aristocracy" in the acting profession, particularly in democratic America, got its start in the nineteenth century. Great new audiences looked to the theatre as a relief from the difficulties of daily existence, as an escape from large and pressing problems. They would need to be educated to appreciate the true function of theatre before the largely fairy-tale atmosphere of the nineteenth century could be dissipated.

Repertory almost completely disappeared, and the long run became firmly established, thus making possible ever-increasing complexity of stage setting and elaborate production. The theatre grew to be as commercial as amusement parks, as much a big business as oil or railroads.

Both in England and America, more attention was paid to the comfort of the audience in the construction and appointments of theatre buildings, and the practice of a single play as an evening's entertainment was initiated. Though stages remained elaborate, the proscenium doors finally disappeared, and capitulation to the picture-frame stage was complete. Costuming developed true authenticity, and acting achieved such power as to engender extreme adulation in the treatment of theatre personalities. Finally, this period began the decided differentiation and specialization in production personnel which has reached a high point in the modern theatre. That is, the functions of producer, director, actor, and designer more frequently were performed by four different people rather than, as in many periods of theatre, by one or two.

THEATRE'S GREAT REVOLUTION

At the outbreak of World War I, Europe had enjoyed an unprecedented forty-three years of freedom from general conflict. Alignments and realignments of powers had flourished, but the constant shifts in diplomacy had succeeded in maintaining the so-called balance of power which insured a general, though fully armed peace. The predominant mood was one of optimism. Goods and people moved freely, without major tariff barriers or passports to check them. It was a time of colonialism and empire, and a time of general prosperity throughout Europe and America which brought a higher standard of living to more people than had hitherto been possible. Education, sanitation, road building, and the like became public responsibilities, and increasing attention was given to the welfare of larger and larger segments of the population. In America, particularly, urbanization spread rapidly, great fortunes were made, and the prowess of the American businessman—who might now be said to be the national hero—spread throughout the world. By the turn of the twentieth century, the United States had become a world power.

Tremendous strides had been made in science and invention. The years between 1870 and the First World War were (as indeed they still are) the age of coal, iron, steam, and electricity. Railroads, automobiles, telephones, typewriters, the motion picture, and even the airplane were among pre-World War I innovations which rapidly became an indispensable part of daily life. Regard for and interest in

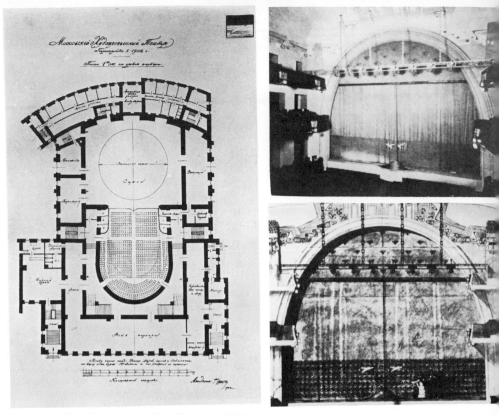

155 *The Moscow Art Theatre, 1902*
Stanislavski's famous theatre, showing (at left) a floor plan, with the
stage area larger than that allotted to seating, and at right, two views of
the stage. The upper one is the actual furnishing, the lower a redesign
to incorporate necessary functional units into an artistic whole.
In both, note the inclusion of the seagull which became a trademark
with this theatre. (Sayler, *Inside the Moscow Art Theatre*)

science grew apace, the scientific method was worshiped and applied
to even so unlikely an activity as the presentation of a character on
the stage. (For this is what Zola said he was doing in his early naturalistic dramas—analyzing man scientifically and with detached
observation, presenting him in a minutely realized background.)

The old *laissez-faire* policy was still the predominant philosophy
of politics and economics, though since the middle of the nineteenth
century a vociferous minority had been voicing socialist principles.
Marx's *Communist Manifesto* had appeared in 1848, and the first International Workingman's Association had been formed in London
in 1864. By 1874, however, it had been dissolved, and the *Manifesto*

itself was not translated into English until 1886. The plight of the exploited working classes, the slum conditions in great cities, the frequent corruption of local governments, were all lost sight of in the general prosperity and sense of wellbeing, which with minor recessions lasted through the last quarter of the nineteenth century until the outbreak of the war. Not many voices were raised in protest: the Fabian Society in England, Frank Norris and Lincoln Steffens in America, a few forward-looking writers on the Continent were voices crying in the wilderness. The twilight of Victorianism was suffused with the false glitter of material wellbeing, a prevailing optimism, and the panacea of a false internationalism which was to be swallowed up in the bitter rivalries of the First World War.

Glitter and tinsel

Theatre at the turn of the century was of a piece with its society. It was predominantly theatre of glitter and tinsel, with impossibly noble heroes, ideally sweet heroines, romantic love stories, happy endings, and lavish productions. It had only the remotest connection with real life and its unfaltering technique presented not a modicum of thought and certainly there was little desire for it. This escapist theatre was a big-business enterprise no less than oil or railroads, controlled by syndicates like that of the Frohmans and the Shuberts in America, the Cochrans, Butts, and Grossmiths in England. Even in countries like France, with a long tradition of national theatre, trust theatres prospered under such men as Franck, Trebórd, and Volterra, and the state-subsidized theatre languished in political intrigue and financial scandal, presenting approximately the same fare as its more commercial rivals. For the plays of the Realists and Naturalists there was certainly no market—not even a hearing.

An avant-garde of amateurs

So it happened that the rebirth of theatre fell once more largely to the hands of amateurs, to individuals and groups outside the established playhouses. Once the innovators had proved their worth by gathering a sizable audience to support them, the commercial houses were quick enough to adopt the changes.

André Antoine (1858–1943) was an amateur only by virtue of the fact that his theatrical training was more or less unacademic and that at the time he started his unique Théâtre Libre he was employed as a clerk in the Paris gas company. He had spent much time in study of the new literary movements of the 1870's and '80's. From the time that he took his first job as an errand boy at the age of twelve, his

411

reading had been avid and he continued it through a period as a bookseller's assistant. At this time he also enlarged his reading by attending lectures at the École des Beaux Arts and by frequenting museums and libraries. His evenings were spent in the theatres, as a claque at the Comédie Française, and as a supernumerary there, where he took part for years in the whole repertory and learned the actor's art by observation and imitation. He also joined an evening class in recitation and diction, and became the producer of classical plays for the group. After his rejection by the Conservatoire, in 1876, chiefly because he lacked private recommendation, he spent five years in military service after which he returned to the job at the gas company. Late in 1886, he joined the Cercle Gaulois, one of the many amateur dramatic clubs of Montmartre which gave conventional plays once a month. Encouraged by Arthur Byl, a budding playwright, he urged upon the group the production of unpublished plays, and collected a program of four short plays, including a dramatization of a short story by Zola. Against the alarmed opposition of Krauss, the retired army officer who shepherded the Cercle, Antoine produced his program and the Théâtre Libre, or Free Theatre, was launched.

The program appeared on March 30, 1887, to general critical approval, including that of Zola, who came and was impressed with both Antoine's acting and directing. Antoine was thirty at the time. One more program appeared that spring, to be followed by a season which included seven programs, at the beginning of which Antoine left the gas company to devote himself thenceforth to theatre. He much later divided his warfare against established theatre into three campaigns—the first from 1887 to 1895 at the Théâtre Libre against "the upholders of the theatre of the past"; the second from 1896 to 1906 at the Théâtre Antoine "for the conquest of the general public"; the third from 1906 to 1914 at the Odéon, his "last fight against official traditions and administrative routine." Antoine's primary *raison d'être* was to give a hearing to new playwrights of whatever dramatic genre; the course of events, however, made him the chief spokesman for Naturalism even though he always fought against such a narrowing emphasis.

The immediate and almost fantastic artistic success of Antoine (he faced financial disaster throughout his career) inspired the opening, in September, 1889, of the Freie Bühne (Free Stage) in Berlin. This institution, fostered and administered by nine young men of whom Otto Brahm, a critic, was chairman, aimed to found a stage free of the existing theatres, censorship, and financial preoccupations.

156 Setting at the Moscow Art Theatre
This is a model of the setting for Gorky's *The Lower Depths*. Both play
and production were triumphs of Naturalism. Setting, directing, acting,
and lighting were coordinated to give the impact of reality. (The
Cleveland Museum of Art, Collection of the Educational Department)

As did the Théâtre Libre, the Freie Bühne operated with a small
subscription audience drawn from the intelligensia, played each production only once or twice, and rose to great critical acclaim. These
two theatres inspired similar organizations in many parts of France
and Germany, the most notable of which was the Freie Volksbühne
(Free People's Stage), initiated by Bruno Wille, which produced
plays for the working classes, also on a subscription basis, at a very
nominal cost. The Volksbühne movement was to enjoy great popularity in Germany.

By 1891, London had its Independent Theatre, run upon the same
plan, and established by Jacob T. Grein, an immigrant Hollander.
It was for the Independent Theatre that George Bernard Shaw produced his first play. The organization lasted for seven years, and in
large measure inspired the founding of the Stage Society in 1899
and the Abbey Theatre at Dublin in 1901. All of these organizations
were devoted to the developing of new dramatic writers and of a
style of acting more suitable to the new materials.

Perhaps the most famous, and certainly one of the most enduring,
of these new theatres was that established by Constantin Stanislavski
and Nemirovich-Danchenko in 1898 as the Moscow Art Theatre. By
reason of his comparatively prolific writing, Stanislavski's is perhaps
the best-known name in modern theatre. He had early been involved

in amateur theatricals on his father's estate, continued these activities in Moscow with the Society of Literature and Art, which he helped to found even while he kept working in his father's business establishment, and finally attained fulfillment in the Moscow Art Theatre. He had long been disgusted with the formalism of conventional theatre fare, was inspired by the performances of the visiting Meiningen troupe, and eventually developed the so-called Stanislavski method which is devoted, as he says, to "the inner truth, the truth of feeling and experience." His theatre weathered the October Revolution of 1905 and the Bolshevik Revolution of 1917, and is still today one of the major theatrical establishments of Russia and the world.

In America, stronghold of the theatre as big business, the establishment of the new theatres lagged almost a generation behind Europe. Though James A. Herne had tried a nonillusionistic production of his realistic *Margaret Fleming* in Boston in 1891, there was no significant contribution by an established acting company presenting the new drama until 1915, when the Washington Square Players —later to develop into the powerful Theatre Guild—began producing for a subscription audience in the tiny Bandbox Theatre in New York. In the same year the Provincetown Players began activities in Massachusetts and the next year moved to Greenwich Village. This was the group which produced the first plays of Eugene O'Neill. Meanwhile, the little theatre movement spread across the country, from Baltimore to Chicago and the West Coast, taking its inspiration from the European free theatres and placing itself in opposition to the theatre trust of the commercial houses. Thus the attrition of professional theatre, caused by the death of repertory and the rise of the long run, was somewhat compensated for by a resurgence of amateur participation which some enthusiastic writers of the time compared to the great amateur participation of the Middle Ages. Universities also began to contribute to the new spirit in theatre with the establishment at Harvard of the famous 47 Workshop of George Pierce Baker, and the founding of the theatre school at the Carnegie Institute of Technology in Pittsburgh, under Thomas Wood Stevens.

Commercial acceptance alters emphasis

Almost universally, the first aim of the free theatres was to present new and untried plays such as the commercial houses would not accept. As the appeal of these productions was proved, and the playwrights accepted for the professional houses, the experimental impetus was directed to the reform of acting and stagecraft. Acting, indeed, had metamorphosed concomitantly with the new plays, since

414

they demanded a new and different histrionic embodiment, and the emphasis of both Antoine and Stanislavski, for instance, had been quite as much on acting as on playwriting. Stagecraft followed, and the period immediately preceding World War I in Europe was marked by the influences of Gordon Craig and Adolph Appia, and the application of their principles by such an energetic dreamer as Max Reinhardt. Though innovations in stagecraft and production were numerous in Europe prior to the First World War, they were almost nonexistent in America until after the war, in spite of the visits of various European troupes, and the urgings of such visionaries as Sheldon Cheney, Kenneth Macgowan, and Robert Edmond Jones. First America would have to have its new playwrights, as Europe had first had hers. America was not to succeed to theatrical preeminence until the postwar period.

The new movement in the theatre also gave importance to two specialized theatre workers—the director and the designer. Both Antoine and Stanislavski had been greatly influenced by their observations of the work of the Duke of Saxe-Meiningen, the nineteenth-century *régisseur* who brought to the theatre the idea of a single, overriding, and unifying force to theatrical production. The idea, in itself was not new; Pixerécourt, early in the century, had voiced and practiced the identical principles. But the theatre Duke applied them to far more significant materials, and hence had an influence which the earlier Frenchman lacked. David Belasco and Augustin Daly in America, and Granville-Barker in England became exemplars of the type. Then the infusion of Gordon Craig's ideas of symbolic design and simplified staging, with the actor no more than a super-marionette performing at the behest of the director-designer, added a new concept to the role of the director. But supermen are rare in any age, and the postwar generation witnessed the division of labor in theatre into the differentiated roles of director and designer, with both specializations gaining increasing importance.

The forty years preceding World War I saw the introduction of practically all of the elements of today's theatre. The revolution in playwriting, acting, and production which was effected in that period almost completely changed the end-product of theatres everywhere. It was a revolution as vast in import and effect as any that had hitherto taken place—its result was what we know as the modern theatre.

Naturalism and Realism provide the materials of the revolution

It is significant that a play made from one of Zola's short stories was on the opening bill of the Théâtre Libre, and that Ibsen's *Ghosts*

415

157 Realistic settings
Above, Belasco's *Rose of the Rancho;* below, Antoine's *The Weavers.*
Belasco insisted upon absolute fidelity to reality in his settings, but
the plays he provided were almost invariably highly romantic. Antoine,
on the other hand, insisted upon realism not only in settings, but in
scripts and acting as well. (Theatre Collection, New York Public Library)

was the first offering of both the Freie Bühne and the Independent Theatre. For the genius of these two men—Zola (1840–1902) and Ibsen (1828–1906)—brought to the drama the new elements of Realism which had triumphed in the novel and which would seriously challenge the Romantic outpourings of the hitherto accepted dramatists. As late as 1880 there were two literatures in France—the novel and the drama. Zola was the recognized leader of the naturalistic novel, but had made no impression on the theatre. All three of the plays which he had written prior to this date had been failures, although *Thérèse Raquin* (1873), dramatized from one of his novels, had shown elements of great tragedy. Zola, with his characteristic extravagance, declared that the French theatre was a void, that the Augier – Dumas – Scribe – Sardou school of playwrights were mere hacks, presenting completely unlifelike characters and events in meticulously realized settings. The literary Naturalist, he declared, must be as much of a scientist as a biologist or a chemist, restricting himself to stating facts exactly as he found them, exhibiting no sympathies, passing no judgments; the Naturalistic play would become a scientific study of man, with a minutely realized setting which would perform the same function as description in the novel. It would be true to life—a slice of life or *tranche de vie* (as the genre came to be called), with no more organization or artifice than life itself possesses. It was chiefly through his dramatic criticism, published between 1876 and 1880, that Zola influenced the new movement in the theatre and became master to a line of disciples that included Antoine, Becque, Hauptmann, and, to some extent, Ibsen himself.

Like Zola, Ibsen was greatly interested in the new scientific discoveries of his time. Darwin's *Origin of Species* (1859) was translated into Norwegian in the early 1870's; lectures and discussions of heredity and environment, of the survival of the fittest, ensued. In all this Ibsen was tremendously interested, as he also was in the series of Zola's novels which had begun in 1868. His earlier plays had been in the Romantic tradition, the best of them being *Peer Gynt* (1867), that marvelously bewildering study of universal man, written in a style full of grandeur and deep understanding. But with *Pillars of Society* (1877), he began the series of realistic social plays upon which his international fame chiefly rests. He became the darling of the Germans, among whom he was then living. There followed, at two-year intervals, *A Doll's House, Ghosts, An Enemy of the People, The Wild Duck, Rosmersholm, The Lady from the Sea, Hedda Gabler,* and *The Master Builder.* It was in his subject matter, particularly, that Ibsen partook of the new thought, for he by no means

158 The Prince Regent Theatre, Munich
Left, an exterior view; right, interior view. The Prince Regent
Theatre in Munich is typical of new theatre construction in Europe at the
turn of the century. It follows the Festspielhaus plan of a fanshaped
bank of widely spaced seats in continuous rows and many exits
in the side walls. (Theater-Museum, Munich)

illustrates the formless slice-of-life technique advocated by Zola. His
plays, like those of Sudermann in Germany, are well plotted and
meticulously structured. It is not difficult to see why some critics
have classed his dramas as the acme of the well-made play. Yet he
is more the herald of the new than the flower of the old; he is, in a
very understandable sense, what he has often been called—the father
of modern drama.

It was his subject matter that caused him to be banned and censored in the state and commercial theatres, and which caused the
free theatres to champion him. He did not regard his mission in the
same objective, amoral light as Zola did his; when compared with
Zola, he answered that he was similar, "Only with this difference,
that Zola descends into the cess-pool to take a bath, I to cleanse it."
Ibsen had an almost incalculable effect on dramatists everywhere,
even to the far reaches of Italy where the realistic dramas of Rovetta,
Praga, Traversi, Giacosa, Bertolazzi, and others took as their subject
matter the daily lives, problems, and idiosyncrasies of the people
they knew.

One of the most perfect examples of the slice-of-life play ever
written is Henri Becque's *La Parisienne* (1885), whose central character is a frivolous, extravagant, and coldly calculating society woman
who escapes being a monster by virtue of the playwright's skill.
Becque (1837–99) had previously written *The Crows* (1882) and

418

several other plays in the Naturalist genre, and found so much difficulty in getting them produced that in 1882 he rather cynically and
bitterly called for a new theatre which would give plays like his a
hearing. Antoine answered five years later, and the *pièces rosses* (literally, "nasty bits") became, in spite of Antoine's efforts, indelibly
linked with the Théâtre Libre. Antoine himself insisted that his theatre was open to all types and kinds of plays so long as they were new
and original, but the force of circumstances made *pièces rosses* predominate. François de Curel, Eugène Brieux, Georges Ancey, Porto-
Riche, Hennique, Méténier, are but a few of the native dramatists
whom Antoine brought to public attention, and the first three of
these, at least, achieved lasting reputations.

Antoine also first produced the great Tolstoy's *Power of Darkness*
on February 10, 1888, thus introducing a new foreign playwright,
and paving the way for subsequent productions of Ibsen, Hauptmann,
and Björnson.

Hauptmann's *Before Sunrise* (1889) had been the first native
German play presented by the Freie Bühne; it deals with the jilting
of his sweetheart by Alfred Loth, idealist and reformer, when he
finds that she is the daughter of an inveterate drunkard and sister of
a dipsomaniac, with the subsequent suicide of the jilted Helen.
Hauptmann (1862–1946) continued in the naturalistic vein with
Lonely Lives (1891), *The Weavers* (1892), *The Beaver Coat* (1893),
Drayman Henschel (1898), and *Gabriel Schilling's Flight* (1912).
His romantic tendencies, however, became apparent as early as 1893
in *The Assumption of Hannele,* and flowered in the symbolic fantasy
of *The Sunken Bell* (1896) and *And Pippa Dances* (1906). The total
body of his work makes him the foremost of modern German dramatists. His development reversed that of Björnson (1832–1910) who,
like his compatriot Ibsen, had turned from the Romantic drama to
Naturalism, producing *Leonarda* as early as 1879, and *The Gauntlet*
and *Beyond Our Powers* in 1883. He, too, was much admired by the
Germans, but turned to novel writing in disappointment over the
reception accorded his plays.

The third great Scandinavian, the Swedish Strindberg (1849–
1912), was also a novelist, although he never forsook one form for
the other. His commitment to Naturalism began with *Sir Bengt's
Wife* (1892), was most notable in his two most famous plays, *The
Father* (1887) and *Miss Julie* (1888), and appeared as well in *Easter*
(1901) and *The Dance of Death* (1901). Strindberg has been called
a misogynist for his strictures against marriage, apparent in these
plays. Like Hauptmann he also wrote a number of nonrealistic,

symbolic plays like *A Dream Play* (1902) and *The Ghost Sonata* (1907). The number and variety of his works have made him Sweden's greatest modern writer.

In addition to Tolstoy, the Realistic movement in Russia produced Maxim Gorki (1868–1936), whose *The Lower Depths* (1902) might stand as the perfect example of Naturalism (figure 156), and Anton Chekhov (1860–1904), one of the world's great dramatists. Prior to the founding of the Moscow Art Theatre in 1897, he had been poorly received. *Ivanov* (1887), the grimmest of all his plays, had been hissed at its first performance; *The Seagull* (1896) was greeted with unseemly laughter on its first presentation. Neither play was fully appreciated until given later by the Moscow Art Theatre. In 1899 the same group produced *Uncle Vanya*, in 1901 *The Three Sisters* and in 1904 *The Cherry Orchard*. In this last play, a "tragedy of life's trivialities," as Gorki called it, Chekhov reached the pinnacle of his career; Madame Ranevskaya, Trofimov, Lopakhin are memorable characters in the finest tradition of theatre, each drawn from the life around him as Chekhov had observed it.

Such observation and fidelity to reality were apparent also in the plays which sustained the Abbey Theatre in Dublin at its first inception in 1899, although the nature of its founders rendered the Irish movement far more poetic than those of other lands. William Butler Yeats (1865–1939) was first a poet, then a playwright, and in even one of the most famous of his plays, *Deirdre* (1906), dramatized from Irish heroic legend, he is more the lyric poet than anything else. One of his co-founders, Edward Martyn (1859–1924), was fired by both Ibsen and Irish nationalism, but never succeeded in mastering natural dialogue, while the third founder, Lady Augusta Gregory (1852–1932), was successful only in the short plays which displayed her strong feeling for the everyday problems of the Irish people. The greatest of Ireland's dramatists was John Millington Synge (1871–1909), who at Yeats' behest spent several years in close observation of the common people of Ireland and then produced a series of unparalleled plays, including *The Shadow of the Glen* (1903), *Riders to the Sea* (1904), *The Well of the Saints* (1905), *The Playboy of the Western World* (1907), *The Tinker's Wedding* (1909), and the unfinished *Deirdre of the Sorrows,* produced in 1910 after his death. To these outstanding names we should probably add those of Lord Dunsany, St. John Ervine, whose *John Ferguson* (1915) gave the Theatre Guild its first great success in 1920, and Lennox Robinson, whose most famous play is one of the best of Irish comedies— *The Whiteheaded Boy* (1916).

In England, the Realist movement had for precedent the genre pictures of Tom Robertson as presented by the Bancrofts. Influenced by Ibsen, Sir Arthur Wing Pinero (1855–1934) produced a series of social dramas which, though superficially of the new genre, basically were well-made plays in the tradition of Scribe, revealing little comprehension of the complexity of character or of original observation. *The Second Mrs. Tanqueray* (1893), *The Notorious Mrs. Ebbsmith* (1896), *Iris* (1903), and *Midchannel* (1909) are his most famous plays. Fresher observation and a keener appreciation of character are evident in the plays of Henry Arthur Jones (1851–1929): *Saints and Sinners* (1884), *The Middleman* (1889), *Wealth* (1889), *Michael and His Lost Angel* (1896) which Shaw considered to be his best play, and *Mrs. Dane's Defense* (1900). Galsworthy, Granville-Barker, and St. John Hankin also produced some plays in this period which showed an awareness of social problems.

But the true dramatic renascence of English theatre sprang from George Bernard Shaw (1856–1950), whose *Widowers' Houses* (1892) was the first native play produced by Grein's Independent Theatre. The following year he wrote *The Philanderer,* and *Mrs. Warren's Profession,* then, on the heels of the furor kicked up by these "unpleasant" plays, he turned to the far pleasanter *Arms and the Man* (1894). A mere listing of the plays he wrote between the opening of the Independent Theatre and the beginning of World War I will demonstrate his undisputed preeminence in British dramatic writing, if not, indeed, in world literature during that period: *The Man of Destiny, The Devil's Disciple, You Never Can Tell, Caesar and Cleopatra, Captain Brassbound's Conversion, Man and Superman, John Bull's Other Island, Major Barbara, The Doctor's Dilemma, Getting Married, Androcles and the Lion,* and *Pygmalion.* The vitality and variety of this impressive list show how Shaw was able to turn the new impulses in theatre to his own purposes, producing inimitable and great plays. Though he began as an Ibsenite, blaming Mrs. Warren's predicament on the capitalist society that forced her into an unsavory profession, he soon transcended both Realism and Naturalism and became purely Shavian, that blend of iconoclasm, intellectualism, restraint, revolution, and delight which made him a world figure.

In America only the most tentative of beginnings was made in the new drama prior to World War I. Bronson Howard (1842–1908) in 1882 treated the problem of divorce in *Young Mrs. Winthrop.* Then, influenced by William Dean Howells' championing of the European writers, James A. Herne (1839–1901) produced his *Margaret*

159 *The Vieux Colombier*
Two stage settings in the theatre of Jacques Copeau. Eschewing both
realism and pictorialism, Copeau developed a basic architectural
stage which could be changed by minor props and set pieces for various
scenes and plays. It was often called Elizabethan, and, in truth, it
does seem to have had its inspiration from the earlier period,
placing the emphasis upon the play and the players rather than upon
the setting. (Macgowan and Jones, *Continental Stagecraft*)

Fleming in 1892. It is a serious domestic drama, devoid of big scenes,
and relatively unconventional. It failed in New York. In 1906 and
1908 there appeared *The Great Divide* and *The Faith Healer*, both
by William Vaughn Moody (1869–1910), which, though somewhat
banal to present-day audiences, were fresh and new in subject and
treatment when they appeared. Eugene Walter (1874–1941) in *Paid
in Full* (1908) and *The Easiest Way* (1909) showed a desire to deal
frankly with social and economic problems. But none of these plays
had the intrinsic dramatic worth of their European counterparts, and
they were few indeed when compared with the bulk of American
prewar playwriting. Owen Davis with his melodramas, George Ade
with his gay satires, Charles Hale Hoyt with his rollicking farces,
Clyde Fitch with his social comedies, Augustus Thomas with his
local color plays, and David Belasco with his flagrant Romanticism
clothed in a deceptively realistic setting, were the most prolific and
the most highly successful dramatists of the new world.

There were non-Realistic plays in Europe, too. The artificial comedies of Oscar Wilde, the poetic dramas of John Masefield, the delightful fantasies of Sir James M. Barrie, were captivating audiences
in England, even as the famous plays of Edmond Rostand in France
and Gabriel D'Annunzio in Italy were delighting audiences with
their pure romance. We have seen, how as early as 1896, Hauptmann
had turned from Realism to write *The Sunken Bell*, and in 1908
Maurice Maeterlinck wrote his perennially popular *The Blue Bird*.

These are only the best of the avalanche of non-Realistic writing
which filled the theatres of the Western world. But the seeds of the
future were in Realistic theatre—the developments of the last forty

years have grown from it, either directly, or in conscious divergence. The great revolution that marked the change from nineteenth- to twentieth-century drama was in the plays of the free theatres and their successors.

Organized monotony in popular theatre

At the beginning of the present century, theatre everywhere was marked by an appalling standardization—playhouses, playwrights, producers, plays, players, decorators, and playgoers. The theatrical trusts which dominated show business operated on a mass-production basis. The Theatrical Syndicate (Klaw, Erlanger, Hayman, Nirdlinger, and Zimmerman) and the Shuberts between them controlled practically all of the five thousand legitimate playhouses in the United States, including thirty-eight in New York City, twenty-one in Chicago, fifteen in Philadelphia, and seven in Washington, D. C. Over two hundred and fifty traveling companies employed the services of twice as many railroad agents in arranging their tours. Charles Frohman organized a central booking system for the Syndicate, and those stars who wished to remain independent, like Richard Mansfield, William Faversham, Joseph Jefferson, and Sarah Bernhardt, were forced to play in tents and skating rinks. The expansion of railroad facilities and the clutch of the monopoly effectively strangled hundreds of local repertory companies throughout the land. The same conditions prevailed in England, where the London companies, or special road companies assembled in London, toured productions to the provinces while making money for the theatrical trusts in the capital.

Against such entrenched standardization the European free theatres took their stand; the little theatres spread across America; and such a hardy pioneer as Miss A. E. F. Horniman subsidized the Abbey Theatre in Dublin and established the Manchester Repertory Company in England. As we have noted, a protest and reform also began in the colleges and universities with the establishment of the 47 Workshop by George Pierce Baker at Harvard, the opening of the School of Drama at Carnegie Institute of Technology in Pittsburgh in 1914, under Thomas Wood Stevens, and the establishment of the Wisconsin Players by Thomas H. Dickinson in 1911. The full development of this type of theatre would come in the postwar period.

The many theatres built in Europe and America tended to follow one of two patterns—either the metamorphosed "hen coop" of the earlier nineteenth century, or the Bayreuth Festspielhaus plan. The former type appeared chiefly in England and France, the latter in

423

160 *Two settings*
for **The Valkyries**
Left, Max Bruckner's setting for a production at Bayreuth in 1896.
The emphasis here is upon a grand pictorial setting. Right, Adolphe
Appia's design for the same production. As Appia planned it, these
massive shapes do not come to life until properly lighted and until
actors move upon them. (Theater-Museum, Munich; Foundation
Adolphe Appia, Berne)

Germany and America, although the continuous rows of seats characteristic of the Bayreuth plan tended in America to be cut by wide
aisles, as dictated by the more stringent fire laws.

As early as 1875, two French architects designed a house with a
"dished" floor, the slant increasing sharply toward the back, thus
overcoming the disadvantages of the straight slant used in the Bayreuth plan. But this new idea did not become current in theatre
architecture until well into the twentieth century.

The orchestra pit was almost universally just below the stage,
between it and the first row of seats, although when Steele Mackaye
built his Madison Square Theatre in New York in 1880, he housed
the orchestra in an opening above the proscenium arch, in order not
to impose them between actor and audience. Outstanding practitioners of the new theatre architecture in Germany were Max Litt-
man and Oskar Kaufmann, with the Prince Regent Theatre in
Munich (figure 158) the outstanding example of the former's work,
and the Volksbühne in Berlin, with its immense space stage, of the
latter's.

In theatres of the basic Bayreuth design, the side walls were liberally supplied with exits, and the wider space between the continuous rows of seats allowed for quick movement of the audience in or out. H. C. Ingalls, in designing the 299-seat Little Theatre for Winthrop Ames in New York in 1912, used the continuous bank of seats, but cut it with two aisles, in conformance with American law, and had exits only at the front of the house. Other larger American theatres, built somewhat later, used a dished orchestra floor and a sharply sloped balcony. In America, too, stages tended to be more restricted in area than those of European houses, being neither so wide nor so deep. The average seating capacity of these houses tended to remain between fourteen hundred and seventeen hundred, although there were extremes in both directions. Theatre economics dictated a capacity large enough to cover mounting expenses and the heavy costs of elaborate productions.

The amateurs improvise

The amateur producing groups used whatever space was available. The Théâtre Libre opened in a little wooden building in the Passage de l'Élysée des Beaux Arts (now known as the Rue André Antoine), with a seating capacity of 343, then moved to an old eight hundred-seat house in the Rue de la Gaîté. Brahm gave the first productions of the Freie Bühne in the Lessingtheater. The English Independent Theatre, and its successors, the Stage Society and the Incorporated Stage Society, used whatever theatres were available for their sporadic performances. In America, the Provincetown Players began producing in a wharf building in Massachusetts, then moved to a converted stable (still standing and still in use as a playhouse) in Macdougall Street, New York. The Washington Square Players, which became the Theatre Guild, produced first in the Bandbox, then in the Comedy Theatre, and finally, after ten years, built their own Guild Theatre. Warehouses, storerooms, school halls were pressed into service by the various little theatre groups, transformations great or small being made in them as resources permitted. The English repertory companies in Manchester, Liverpool, and Birmingham used extant theatres, and both the Little and the Haymarket theatres in London struggled to establish repertory. The Vedrenne-Barker company, which performed with such distinction at the Court Theatre in London beginning in 1904, moved to other houses as exigencies demanded. A permanent home, however, had been built at Stratford on Avon for the Shakespeare Festival Company; it opened in 1879, incorporating, in a style peculiarly unfit for its material, the

425

traditional accoutrements of nineteenth-century theatre architecture. When this antique building burned down in 1926, Bernard Shaw sent a letter of congratulations to the manager.

The new movement which instigated major changes in playwriting and acting, and, to some extent in stagecraft, had very little influence in theatre architecture until the postwar period.

Realist settings—true to life and false to art

It is true that the Duke of Saxe-Meiningen deserves immeasurable credit for the care with which he prepared his *mise-en-scène*. Yet we must not forget that he worked within the limitations of the stage settings current in his day and age. Though he used platforms to vary the acting levels, he assumed that stages would continue to be set with scenery painted in perspective; he merely cautioned the stage director to so plan the actors' movements that probability would not be violated when the player was seen against the set. He assumed that roses, for instance, would continue to be painted on the set, then warns that great care must be taken so that the practical rose needed in the production would blend artistically with the painted ones. He did insist that objects on the set to be used by the actors—doorways, windows, benches, steps—should be plastic or three-dimensional and that the prevalent ozones, or strips of blue cloth in the flies to represent sky, should be replaced by arching foliage, rooftops, or, if necessary, by painted clouds.

The influx of the new Realism did nothing for stagecraft but intensify what Sheldon Cheney called "the perfect realization of a false ideal." We have seen how the box set developed during the nineteenth century; how actual furnishings were gradually substituted for painted properties. We are also aware that the literalness of many a stage set was at variance with the romantic and melodramatic properties of many of the plays themselves. It is interesting, and perhaps commendable, that David Belasco experimented for three months to find exactly the right color lights for a California sunset in *Girl of the Golden West*, and that for *The Easiest Way* he transferred to his stage, intact, wallpaper and all, the interior of a down-at-the-heel boardinghouse room. Indeed, Belasco was nothing if not a meticulous workman. Every scenic detail, down to the smallest of properties, was arduously sought out or carefully created so that, unpeopled by the players and devoid of the play, his sets were the marvels of his audiences for their literal truth.

When truth began to be conceived as necessary not only in setting, but in acting and writing as well, the realistic stage setting

161 *Two more Appia settings*
Above, design for *King Lear,* Act II; below, design for *Parsifal,* Act III.
These austere settings with many levels are typical of the revolutionary
designs of Adolphe Appia. With this type of setting, lighting and
costuming gained new importance. The emphasis was on the actor,
and the setting simply attempted to give him adequate space
through which to move. (Foundation Adolphe Appia, Berne;
Gabriel Jaques-Dalcroze, Geneva)

was even more admired. Antoine exalted the idea of the "fourth wall," saying that the ideal way to prepare a play was to set it completely, as if there were to be no audience, and then, when the décor and action were determined, decide which wall would be removed so that the audience could see what went on. Here is the application of Zola's principle of scientific observation, of the stage milieu replacing the passages of description in the novel. Nothing is to be left to the imagination of the audience—every detail is to be explicit.

The basic fallacy of this point of view is that it seems to exclude the audience from the production, that it makes them, as it were, eavesdroppers rather than participants. When Diderot was urging realism in stage settings more than a hundred years before, he had been careful to point out that the audience was included within the fourth wall—they were silent spectators to what went on within the room represented by the stage. The Realist movement ignored the audience almost entirely.

The new aesthetic—illusion via atmosphere

Yet at the very moment when this photographic realism was reaching its height in practice, insistent voices were heard saying that this surface truth was not a central truth, could not be truth to the spirit of drama, was indeed a denial of aesthetic truth. For the theatre is not life itself, but an art form, based on selectivity and aiming for unity of effect. Even the most realistic of stage settings cannot transfer the actual lath and plaster of a room, the literal stones of a wall into the theatre. The most that can be accomplished is to strive for the *illusion* of reality through the use of artificial substitutes in paint and canvas. Then we are faced with the paradox of real people and plastic properties seen against a manifestly unreal background—a painted backdrop, canvas trees.

Why not, said Adolph Appia (1862–1928), as early as 1895, put the emphasis where it belongs—not on the set, but on the actor. Instead of presenting a forest, for instance, with an actor moving about in it, show a scene which will give the *impression* of an actor *who is moving about in a forest*. Why not concentrate on the essential *feeling,* the essential communication between actor and audience? Now you can throw away all paint and canvas. By the proper combination of color and intensity of lights you can create whatever *mood* you need to enhance the performance of the actor. You can give him a neutral background of levels and space that does not come alive until it is lit and he is moving upon it. Thus the central truth of theatre is reached—the creation of atmosphere.

428

162 *Typical designs for the Russian Ballet*
Above, Leon Bakst's design for *Scheherezade*. Below, design for
Liturgy, by Natalie Gontcharovna. These richly decorative pictorial
settings are at the opposite pole from the Appia–Craig objective. They are
well suited to the visual appeal of the ballet, but overwhelming
when used in the production of plays, because they divert attention from
the spoken word which is the essence of drama. (Museum of Modern Art)

This is the essence of the new aesthetic movement in the theatre, conceived by Adolph Appia, preached by Gordon Craig (1872——), put actively to work by Max Reinhardt (1873–1943). The effect of space, of noble architectural settings, could be brought to the theatre only by leading the spectator to imagine them. A single column, a soaring arch lost above the proscenium, a lone candelabra could *give the effect* of a cathedral. A garden wall, a few pots of flowers, a conventionalized tree would make a garden setting. Interiors would use neutral hangings or screens with only the most essential of furnishings. Nothing would distract from the movement of the actor in the space provided for him. The set would be backed by a curving neutral dome (the Fortuny sky dome, at first made of silk, later of plaster) upon which the lights could play and which would put the emphasis on the forestage and the actor. There would, of course, be no footlights.

The extreme of this aesthetic ideal was the suggestion of Gordon Craig that the live actor be replaced by a super-marionette who could be counted on not to disturb with his personality the visual harmony created by the stage director, and various marionette theatres were actually established, chiefly in Germany. In Germany, also, Max Reinhardt took the live actor as far toward this ideal as possible in his wordless productions of *The Miracle* (1910) and *Sumurun* (1911), which toured Europe and America (figure 164). Even the Moscow Art Theatre, a stronghold of Realism, was touched by the new aesthetics. Gordon Craig designed a *Hamlet* (1912) for them, using a series of movable screens for the various scenes. On paper and in prospect the idea looked ideal; in practice it was a fiasco. Craig was a theorizer; he conceived designs often too grand to be realized on any theatre stage. Few of his plans were ever put to practical use. But through his basic ideas, he influenced a line of disciples who destroyed the false ideal of the imitation of reality, and who set the theatre back on the path where it belonged—theatricality.

The insistence of Appia and Craig on visual felicity in stage setting had another manifestation in the movement developed by the Russian Ballet under Diaghilev (1872–1929). To enhance the visual appeal of this form, painters were called in to the service of the théatre, and such ones as Leon Bakst and Alexander Benois produced infinitely varied and rich décor in which the dancers became part of an intricate and lush stage picture. Their *Scheherazade* (1910) was an unbelievably rich and sensuous oriental spectacle, for instance (figure 162). Some misguided theatrical managers, envious of these ballet performances, thought that they could titillate their audiences

163 *Two designs by Gordon Craig*
Left, a setting for *Macbeth;* right, a setting for the ideal theatre.
The generally perpendicular treatment of Craig is evident in these two
designs, and the massive proportions of many of his settings are
illustrated particularly in the *Macbeth* sketch. (Theatre Collection,
New York Public Library; Museum of Modern Art)

by splendid pictorial settings, not realizing that the drama, after all,
has a reliance on the spoken word which ballet has not. So they fell
into the same error that had engulfed the Realists—they produced
settings which overwhelmed both actor and play.

In the larger houses, huge turntables were installed, such as that
which Lautenschlager first built at Munich in 1896. Elevator stages,
like that of Steele Mackaye at his Madison Square Theatre, were
tried, as well as wagon stages with whole sets moving off into the
wings to either side. At the other extreme stage settings were reduced
to the barest minimum. When Jacques Copeau (1878–1949) opened
his Vieux Colombier in 1913, he dispensed with the proscenium arch
and footlights, as Antoine had dreamed of doing, but, contrary to
Antoine's minutely conceived realistic scene, he used a permanent

431

164 *Two Reinhardt productions*
Above, the setting for *Sumurun;* right, a design for *The Miracle* by
Norman Bel Geddes. The vast settings for these two massive productions
were typical of one phase of Reinhardt's work. That indefatigible
producer worked in many widely differing styles and types of plays,
playhouses, and productions. (Theatre Collection, New York
Public Library)

architectural setting, upon which he placed only the most essential
properties for the play in hand (figure 159). Granville-Barker (1877–
1946) ignored the proscenium arch when he took over Wallack's
Theatre in New York for an American season in 1915, building out
the stage to cover the orchestra pit and the first two rows of seats,
and playing Shaw, Ibsen, Galsworthy, and Shakespeare in a style
which completely ignored the picture-frame setting and the footlight
tradition. William Poel (1852–1934) in the 1890's gave Shakespeare
on a simplified architectural stage. Aided by the exigencies of war
scarcities the so-called simplified staging received great impetus during the war years. Lush décor was reserved largely for escapist
musicals and ballets; legitimate drama profited by a simpler production. The two divergent streams of the aesthetic movement, rich

pictorialism and tasteful sparseness, were to undergo further interesting development after the war.

Authenticity replaces beauty as costume standard

By the time that the new movement of Realistic drama was in full sway in theatre the principle of careful and accurate costuming had been universally accepted. Not only had the Duke of Saxe-Meiningen insisted upon historical accuracy in costuming, but on proper carrying of the costume by the actor. Helmets were to be worn straight over the brow; stances for persons wearing classical garb were to differ from those of eighteenth-century dandies. Costumes were to be worn as early as possible in the rehearsal period, so that the performers could grow into them.

David Belasco displayed the same zeal for correct costuming as he did for detailed settings. He tells of buying from a person met on the street the exact worn coat or pair of shoes that he needed for a character in a play, or of sending to France or Japan for costumes and materials for other productions. Antoine objected to the white hands and knees of the mountaineers in the Meiningen *Wilhelm Tell* which he saw in 1888, saying that it violated reality, and the Moscow Art production of Gorki's *The Lower Depths* spent much time and effort in achieving the requisite amount of filth and raggedness.

433

165 The Appia–Craig influence
Costume designs by Norman
Wilkinson for *Love's Labour's Lost*.
Austere settings with colorful and
lavish costumes were typical
of Wilkinson's work. (Museum
of Modern Art)

When Strindberg wrote his preface to *Miss Julie* (1888), he urged
that actresses cease insisting upon being beautiful, but be lifelike;
that they use little or no paint on their faces so that their emotions
may be clearly visible; and that actors do the same. Appia and Craig
both maintained that the director must have absolute control of all
the elements of production, including costuming and makeup, so
that a unified effect could be achieved.

In the pictorial settings of the Russian Ballet, the costumes were
designed and executed so that they became a part of the décor as
the dancers appeared on the stage. In the more austere Appia-Craig
settings, the costumes formed the chief decoration of the stage, standing out in brilliant contrast to the neutral backgrounds. When Granville-Barker produced *Twelfth Night* early in this century, Norman
Wilkinson and A. Rothenstein designed a plastic neutral background
and colorful costumes in a style Sheldon Cheney called "representative of the best staging being done in England."

Costuming now was conceived of not chiefly as a means of dressing the individual characters of a play to their individual advantage,
but as a contributing element to the whole mood and style of the play.
The long, flowing robe of crepe de chine in which Reinhardt dressed
the Lady Diana Manners for *The Miracle* was prophetic of the many

innovations in costuming which that wizard would introduce in the postwar years.

Costuming for women, of course, adapted itself to the full bosom, tiny waist and generous hips which was the ideal of feminine beauty in the days before World War I, and coiffures took into account the universally popular center part with the long hair drawn backwards in a slant over the forehead. Henrietta Crossman as Rosalind, Edith Wynne Mathison as Viola, Julia Marlowe as Juliet may have been correctly garbed from an historical and artistic point of view, but the style of their own day comes through in their photographs. This contemporaneity (perhaps anachronism) is more noticeable in women's costumes than in men's because, of course, the stylish female figure has changed so radically in the decades of this century. And stage costuming, however accurate and artistic, must always be affected by the people who wear it. Perhaps Gordon Craig was right in wanting to substitute super-marionettes for live actors!

New acting methods necessary in the new theatre

For the advent of the new Realism at the end of the nineteenth century, actors found themselves largely unprepared. In spite of the work of the two Matthews, of Madame Vestris, and of the Bancrofts, the predominant style—as exemplified by Sir Henry Irving and Ellen Terry—was dignified and more declamatory than intimate. Actors were still complimented on their points, much as singers were, just as if almost a century had not passed since the tirade was the true test of an actor's ability. Romanticism, also, had introduced a flamboyant manner to the stage, and the vestiges of it persisted.

But neither declamation nor flamboyance was convincing in the new theatre. Perhaps this is one reason why the earliest of the new theatres used amateur actors, training them in the new skills required. Antoine cautioned his players to disregard the admonition of Goethe and the theatre Duke about facing the audience when they spoke, and tried to orient them to the scene on the stage rather than to the house. Having been himself well trained in the prevalent style of the Comédie (it is said that he could give a perfect reproduction of the great favorite, Gôt), Antoine quickly realized its inadequacy for the plays he was presenting. It had no simplicity, no life, no naturalness. It was bound by conventions that insisted no actor speak while walking or sitting down, that lines be recited elegantly, that bodies appear statuesque and dignified. So he started with entirely new personnel, and taught them not to recite, but to live their parts. He taught them that movement is the actor's most intense means of expression, that the whole physical makeup must "speak" for the actor, that vocal expression must be natural, conversational. He taught them that each scene in a play has its own movement, which is a part of the total movement of the play; that no actor is more important than the play itself. He taught also by example, playing in such a way as to receive many critical plaudits for his truth to character. Wonderingly, one critic remarked that Antoine and his company played as if there were no stage, as if they were unconscious of being watched. Observing that the famed crowd scenes of the Meiningen were right pictorially but not vocally, in that the actors spoke in unison, he taught his crowds to speak as a real crowd would—now one, now another, over and under each other. So he produced a new kind of actor, and lost his players constantly to the commercial and state houses. He became, in effect, a training school for a new generation of actors in France. At the end of the first season, Mevisto went to the Porte Saint Martin, and Madame France to the Ambigu. By the end of the third season, ten of his amateurs had passed on to the professional stage, five of them to the Odéon alone. Lugné-Poë, who founded the Théâtre de l'Oeuvre in 1893, had been one of Antoine's actors, as had Firmin Gémier, assistant to Antoine at the Théâtre Antoine, and later director of the Odéon. The Théâtre Libre ceased to exist after about eight years, but its work had been sound; its principles were everywhere applauded, and Antoine went on to many more years of work at the Antoine and the Odéon.

The Moscow Art Theatre, too, began with amateurs, and Stanislavski constantly found it difficult to reteach professional actors in the new style. Early under the influence of the pictorial qualities of the Meiningen troupe, he soon found it difficult to accept their somewhat declamatory style of acting. As a result of the famous eighteen-hour conversation between himself and Nemirovich-Danchenko, the Moscow Art Theatre was founded in 1898, and he began the system which made his theatre the home of theatrical naturalism.

Stanislavski possessed that rare ability to analyze and systematize, and he set down his own development, plans, experiments and conclusions in a series of books which have become gospel to many twentieth-century actors. The essence of his so-called system is the careful training of the actor's perceptions and imagination, and the use of these abilities in the preparation of a role. This preparation must proceed over a long period of time, and concern itself not only with the outward manifestations or projection of character, but also with the inward feeling, or soul. Indeed, he stated, a complete realization of the "inner man" would lead to the projection of it, which

166 *More of the Appia–Craig influence*
Claude Bragdon's design of a setting for *The Glittering Gate,*
illustrating the use of line, with no decoration except for the focal gate.
(Museum of Modern Art)

must then become systematic through long and patient practice.
Some of his productions were in preparation for over a year before
they were seen in his theatre. The actor, according to him, needed to
perfect his art through a lifetime of study and playing. He insisted
that action or speech, merely for the sake of action or speech, was
bad; that every player must have a definite motivation for speaking
and acting, an objective in every scene toward which he played. This,
in itself, was nothing new, for the American director Augustine Daly
had insisted on the same discipline for his acting company a generation before; Belasco prided himself on the discussions and character
analysis that preceded every rehearsal period; Antoine had worked
on the same lines ten or fifteen years previously. Nor was Stanislavski's "inner emotion" new to the stage—many fine actors preceding
him had used just such a method, even including the meditative
preparation which he recommended before each performance. But
Stanislavski happened along at the right moment in theatre history,
and he had the talent, rare among performers, of codifying his ideas
and explaining his method. His system was to achieve worldwide
prominence, and the Moscow Art Theatre was to become the hallowed shrine of the postwar generation.

Another group which was to rise to prominence and influence got
its start in 1913 when Jacques Copeau, erstwhile critic and writer,
trained a group of amateurs and with Roger Martin du Gard and

167 *Two popular American stars*
John Drew and Ada Rehan as Petruchio and Kate in *The Taming of the Shrew*. While these very popular performers are dressed with a great deal of attention to authenticity, Mr. Drew still wears the mustache which was his invariable adornment, and Miss Rehan exhibits the hourglass figure which was so much admired before World War I. (Henry E. Huntington Library and Art Gallery)

Georges Duhamel opened the Vieux Colombier, as we have noted above. The French government sent this group to America in 1917–18, and the interior of the old Garrick Theatre was transformed to Copeau's neo-Elizabethan style. The players were received with great interest, and influenced both acting and production methods here. One of the players in that company was Louis Jouvet.

The Freie Bühne and the Independent Theatre did not have so great an influence upon acting. Their personnel was recruited chiefly from the ranks of the professional actors who were interested in the new materials and who lent their spare time to the new theatres. Otto Brahm sometimes despaired of the resultant intrusion of "Weimar classicism" into the performances, and with the hope of developing a true acting ensemble, accepted the directorship of the Deutches Theater in 1894. As we have seen, Grein's venture influ-

438

enced the establishment of several repertory companies where ensemble playing was the ideal.

The rise of the modern director

Before Antoine (if we except Pixerécourt), there had been no director in the modern sense of the term—a unifying intelligence that directs all aspects of a given production. After him hardly a play has been given without such direction. Both he and Brahm let the play develop through rehearsals, setting only the environment beforehand. Stanislavski, on the other hand, prepared elaborate production books covering every aspect of the play before it went into rehearsal. This was the method of Max Reinhardt as well. The Realist movement in the theatre, focused primarily on plays and actors, gave a new theatre worker to the world—the director in the modern sense. The aesthetic movement which received its impetus from Appia and Craig also stressed the importance of the director, but would also, in the years after the war, bring a final contribution in the development of the specialized work of the designer.

Summary

Theatre of the twentieth century began before the close of the nineteenth. Theatre's own revolution started outside of the commercial houses, but successfully transformed that protean creature by dispelling its false theatricality and bringing it closer to truth of materials and methods.

A whole new generation of playwrights, devoted to meticulous observation and objective presentation of situation and character, wrote many plays of significance. Literary men were once more involved in dramatic writing, developing new forms and new expression with skill—and often with genius. The new theatre produced the greatest English playwright since Shakespeare—George Bernard Shaw.

The new theatre also developed the intimate playhouse, exalted and then almost discarded the "fourth wall" of the stage. It brought photographic realism to an acme of perfection, then made beginnings in replacing it with a more disciplined theatricality. It made direction an art in itself, and not an adjunct as it had largely been for many years. And it gave a new significance to stage design.

Finally, and perhaps most significantly, the art of acting was transformed, finding new methods to produce a new end product, and codifying techniques which were to have inestimable influence in the years to come.

THEATRE TODAY

Future historians may well regard the first half of this century as a time of almost continuous war. We say that World War I was over in 1918, and World War II began in 1939. But in those years of so-called peace, there really was none nor has it truly existed in the years since 1946 when hostilities nominally ended. The harsh provisos of the Treaty of Versailles, the Russian Revolution, the failure of the League of Nations—all intensified national differences and conflicts of interest. War-impoverished peoples, desperate men everywhere, were rallied to seemingly great causes by Lenin, Mussolini, Hitler. The United States, basking in a false postwar prosperity, was rudely shocked by the stock-market crash of 1929 and the ensuing Depression, calling upon its own great man, Franklin D. Roosevelt, to see it out of trouble. Each nation and people became intensely concerned with its own affairs, looked with suspicion and hostility on peoples outside its national boundaries, built up high tariff walls, restricted immigration, often imposed harsh censorships—and inevitably fell into the holocaust of World War II.

Its aftermath has been a cold war, the world divided into two armed camps, with continuing and futile negotiations to reduce tensions and to further a one-world concept. New nations carved from old empires have proliferated, and the organization of the United Nations has attempted to mediate differences. The world has become an infinitely smaller place than ever before, with transportation and communication bringing even the remotest regions swiftly together.

440

The airplane and the telephone have encircled the world; man has begun to explore outer space. The atom as a source of energy has been put to both destructive and constructive uses, and man's technical competence has so far outrun his ethical judgment as to raise questions concerning the scientist's moral responsibilities.

The old Jeffersonian principle that that government governs best which governs least, has been superseded and here, as elsewhere, more and more responsibilities have been arrogated to itself by the central government. The New Deal and the Fair Deal attempted to assure security from the cradle to the grave; many of Great Britain's major industries have been nationalized, and the succeeding governments of France have taken over more and more social and economic functions. The totalitarian regimes of other countries have supervised every area of human activity.

Conflicts have not been limited to national groups, but special interest groups within specific political boundaries have also been at war. Minority groups, political parties, economic and social institutions have been belligerently self-assertive. Organization has multiplied upon organization until the citizen who does not belong to one or more of these multifarious groupings is a rarity indeed; there is hardly a segment of society which does not speak with some collective voice. Public education has become more and more widespread, with Americans even accepting the idea that every bright boy and girl who wishes it should be given a college education. Interest in the fine arts has gradually percolated to the less privileged members of society, with art galleries, museums, and symphony orchestras becoming a part of community life in many heretofore unreached areas. Suffrage has become more and more widespread, with limitations of sex, property, and education being diminished, and in many countries entirely removed.

Magazines and newspapers have proliferated, and book publishing has consolidated itself into a big business. Specialization by types of subject matter and by format has become widespread; paperbacks of all types of material, by the 1950's, accounted for a fairly large percentage of the total number of books published. The availability of printed materials has increased out of all proportion to population gains, and in spite of movies, radio, and television, more and more people seem to be reading a greater variety of things.

The multifarious bids for attention concomitant with the increasingly widespread and complex means of communication have generated a chaos and frustration that are typical of the present day. This atmosphere is reflected in literature in all its forms. Nihilism, despair,

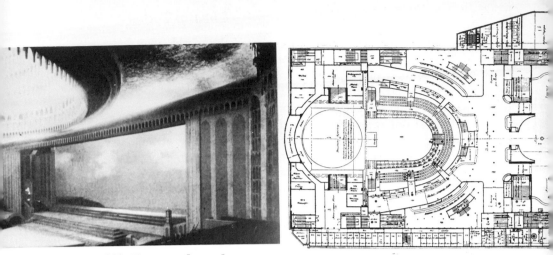

168 *Two very large theatres*
Above, interior and plan of the Grosse Schauspielhaus, Berlin. This
"theatre of the five thousand," conceived by Max Reinhardt,
combines the features of both the proscenium stage and the platform
stage; it has seats for thirty-five hundred people. The ceiling
treatment is interesting and unique. Right, exterior and plan of
the Red Army Theatre, Moscow. This large theatre seats over two
thousand people, and has a unique architectural plan, incorporating a
vast stage area in addition to the large number of seats. (Herold,
Das Grosse Schauspielhaus; Architecture de l'URSS, Moscow)

and conversely the search for a unifying principle, for a spirituality
beyond reality, have made their successive appearances. In contradistinction to the typical mid-Victorian, who thought himself living
in the best of all possible worlds, modern man has tended to think of
himself as living in the worst. Yet the faith seems to be growing that
times will be better. Men are finding dedications through which to
channel their energies; they are beginning to realize that "It is better
to light a candle than to curse the darkness." What the outcome of
it all will be is still very much an open question (to paraphrase a
great modern American playwright).

Theatrical production a popular community activity

Great diversity is the hallmark of twentieth-century theatre. All
kinds of playhouses and plays, all manner of producing and acting
groups, all varieties of settings, costumes, and lighting have been
tried and more or less accepted. Modifications of the old as well as
creations of the new have variously flourished. A few trends, however, seem to be emerging.

442

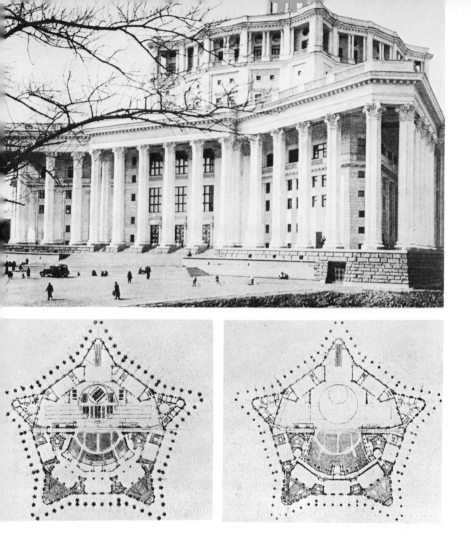

One of the most significant of these trends is the involvement of more and more people in theatrical activity. National theatres, supported wholly or in part by the government, have long been the European pattern as we have seen. France, Germany, and Russia led in this movement. Then followed the Low Countries, Denmark, Sweden, Hungary, Poland, Czechoslovakia. Finland founded its national theatre in the latter part of the nineteenth century, and in recent times, Ireland, Greece, Turkey, and Italy have seen government-supported theatres come into existence. The movement has also spread to Mexico and South America. In the United States, the impetus of the Depression gave a four-year life to the first, last, and only federally

443

subsidized theatre in this bulwark of individual enterprise—the Federal Theatre Project of the Works Progress Administration, which lasted from October, 1935, to July, 1939. At its peak, it employed ten thousand people, operated theatres in forty states, published a magazine, and sponsored a play and research bureau, serving not only itself, but school, church, and community theatres throughout the nation. It fostered Negro theatre, and developed the unique production technique of the Living Newspaper, which engendered so much criticism that a hostile Congress finally liquidated the whole program.

It took a war to bring government-subsidized theatre to England. The Council for the Encouragement of Music and the Arts was set up with private funds in 1940, then was taken over by the government in 1942. At the end of the war it was established on a permanent basis as the Arts Council of Great Britain.

Thus, at the beginning of 1959, the United States of America was the only major government in the world not assigning a part of its income to theatre. In January of that year, however, the Soviet government in Russia announced a new policy of the withdrawal of funds from the five hundred and thirteen professional repertory companies then in operation in the Soviet Union. They were voluntarily to remand their subsidies to the general treasury, depending thenceforth upon box office receipts for operating costs, wages, and royalties. The government, however, would continue to let them use the government-owned buildings and would aid with pension and health benefits. How this reversal of policy will affect the hitherto vigorous Russian theatre remains to be seen.

The growing popularity of the motion picture and the advent of talkies in 1927 took many legitimate theatres away from living drama and dedicated them to the new god. In the United States alone, the number of houses outside of New York available to stage plays shrank from fifteen hundred in 1920 to about five hundred in 1930. Then came radio, and, just before World War II, television. As each of these mechanical contrivances increased in popularity, the prophets of doom foretold the end of live theatre. But the record shows a situation far otherwise. This same period has been marked by diverse and unprecedented theatrical activity.

The free theatre movement, begun with such success at the turn of the century, continued to inspire the founding of myriads of working theatre groups everywhere in the Western world. From Madrid to Stockholm, from Provincetown to Pasadena, amateurs, semiprofessionals, and professionals created theatres with the basic idea of permanent acting companies giving plays in repertory. Often those

444

169 *Two double theatre plants*

Above, the theatre at Malmö, Sweden, opened in 1944. Below, the
theatre at Mannheim, Germany, completed in 1957. In both of these
houses a larger and a smaller theatre are included, with provisions for
changing both the area of space allotted to the audience, and the size,
shape, and location of the stage space. In the isometric drawing of the
Mannheim plant, the large house is on the right and the smaller house
on the left. (Swedish-American News Agency; National Theatre,
Mannheim)

which began on a purely amateur basis soon employed a professional, paid director, then became gradually professionalized, developing into true community theatres, often with training centers attached, like those at Pittsburgh, Cleveland, and Pasadena.

Some of these repertory companies, like the Group Theatre in the 1930's, made little attempt to organize support. But most of them, like the pioneer Antoine, sold subscriptions. Eva Le Gallienne, in New York in 1926, sold subscriptions for her Civic Repertory Company, which lasted six seasons. Margo Jones at Dallas, the Arena Stage in Washington, D.C., emphasized the subscription plan. The Theatre Guild, in its development from the Washington Square Players, became a huge producing organization dependent upon subscriptions on a widely organized basis. The producing organization at the Phoenix Theatre in New York has recently embarked on a wide subscription campaign. The various theatre clubs of Great Britain are subscription organizations, primarily developed as a means of giving a hearing to plays banned by the office of the censor. Travail et Culture (Work and Culture) in France took shows to various parts of the country on a subscription basis, and the whole "people's theatre" movement of Germany was based on the same operating plan. In recent years the commercial houses in New York City have attempted to bolster their support by preselling blocks of tickets or whole houses to theatre parties. Incoming shows frequently engage in just such widespread sales even before they have opened in New York, and a growing practice of "twofers," or the sale of two tickets for the price of one, has come in for much criticism as a means of prolonging the run of a play whose box-office receipts are faltering. Thus, assured support from audiences has been attempted, not only in countries with no government-supported theatre, but in those fortunate lands as well.

The total number of operating theatre groups is hard to estimate. In the United States alone the number runs into the thousands, exclusive of colleges and universities. In England there are about 150 repertory companies, and more in Scotland and Ireland. Russia has over five hundred companies, and West Germany more than one hundred.

The great cities, particularly London and New York, continue to be strongholds of commercial theatre, dedicated to making money. In New York the prevailing mode of production is first to gather funds by persons (not necessarily of the theatre) interested in presenting a particular script, then to collect a suitable cast from whatever source, then rehearsal in makeshift quarters while the sets and costumes are being designed and executed, then an out-of-town opening and a short period of playing followed by a New York opening and a long or short run (depending on the reception of critics and public), and finally the complete disbanding of the company and the dispersing of sets and costumes. More uneconomical and inartistic bases for real theatre could hardly be imagined, and the wonder is that integrated and outstanding productions are realized as frequently as they are.

But even in New York, where this pattern most universally prevails, recent years have seen tremendous activity in off-Broadway theatre. Private companies have produced all manner of plays—revivals as well as new scripts—and have tried out new production techniques wherever they could find quarters. However, with a few exceptions like the Circle in the Square, under José Quintero's direction, these units do not continue casts in play after play, and the presentations, like those on Broadway, last as long as they will draw. They do, however, provide a valuable training ground for new talent.

The summer-stock system in America has also served this function in presenting six- to ten-week seasons of plays, changing weekly, with resident companies. In the last few years, however, summer stock has been beset with a burgeoning star system and a growth of package shows which are gradually crowding the resident companies out of existence. Television and motion-picture stars, yearning for live theatre, have toured the summer circuits in vehicles designed to exhibit their talents.

Professional theatre assumes an international flavor

Following the pattern set by Reinhardt in Salzburg in the interwar period, many theatre festivals have developed in several countries. The most famous have been at Bayreuth, at Edinburgh, at Paris, and, devoting themselves to Shakespeare, at three various Stratfords—in England, in Canada, and in Connecticut. Other significant Shakespeare festivals have been held over a period of years in Ashland, Oregon, in Antioch, Ohio, and in New York's Central Park. Outdoor dramas have also flourished, both in England and America, where they have generally assumed the form of regional or historical pageants.

In spite of a nationalism intensified by two world wars, there has been in theatrical circles much exchange of information, personnel, and whole acting companies. The Moscow Art Theatre visited in New York in 1923, and since that time many other foreign theatre groups have appeared there, up to and including the 1959–60 season when

447

170 *A modern flexible theatre*
Left, the exterior of the Kalita Humphreys Theatre designed by Frank
Lloyd Wright for the Dallas Theatre Center. Right, the interior,
with a forty-foot revolving stage and concrete drum overhead to assist in
quick scene changes. Charles Laughton has called this "the most
beautiful theatre in the world." (Dallas Theatre Center)

the *Piccolo Teatro* of Milan was seen, and the 1960–61 season in
which both the Comédie Française and the Deutches Schauspielhaus
of Hamburg played in New York. Paris established a Théâtre des
Nations in 1954 which has brought many foreign productions from
all parts of the world, including Peiping. Since 1892, when the first
important International Music and Theatre Exposition was held in
Vienna, there have been many such meetings. In 1927 an International Theatre Congress was established. It was a war casualty, but
in 1949 came the International Theatre Institute, operating under a
UNESCO grant and having a continuing program of international
conferences and congresses.

Within national boundaries, various associations operate to foster
theatre activity—the British Drama League, the Scottish Community
Drama Association, the American National Theatre Conference, the
American Educational Theatre Association, the American National
Theatre and Academy, the latter founded by Congressional edict
though without federal funds.

Thus has theatre activity in this century become worldwide. We
are too close to the events to judge whether or not this widespread

participation will eventuate in truly great theatre, but there have been some remarkable signs along the way to indicate that this might be so.

American playwriting leads

Now that the twentieth century is more than half over, we might venture the prophecy that its greatest theatre belongs to America, particularly in playwriting. Since the First World War, the United States has produced a list of playwrights whose achievement seems destined to live to aftertimes, and has produced them in such quantity that they outnumber the significant playwrights of any other country. Of course, the number of new scripts in any given theatrical season is small when compared with the total production of that season— and the number of those with lasting values is even smaller. But a theatre which has produced Eugene O'Neill, Maxwell Anderson, Elmer Rice, Clifford Odets, Thornton Wilder, Tennessee Williams, Arthur Miller, William Inge—to name only a few of many—is bound to be significant in the annals of the future.

American playwriting came suddenly of age in the 1920's. Perhaps it was the nationalistic afterglow of World War I which caused this great creative activity, perhaps only the ripeness of time after a long development. But by the time of the stock-market crash of 1929, which ushered in the era of the Great Depression, American playwrights had won foremost attention in world theatre. Eugene O'Neill (1888–1953) climaxed his long series of one-act plays with *Beyond the Horizon*, his first full-length play commercially produced. It won the Pulitzer Prize in 1920, and critics hailed it as proof that America at last had a great naturalist talent of its own. But they were wrong; O'Neill was no Naturalist in the accepted sense of the term, as the incredible output of his next ten years would prove. This play was followed in quick succession by *Anna Christie*, *The Emperor Jones*, *The Hairy Ape*, *Desire Under the Elms*, *The Great God Brown*, *Marco Millions*, *Strange Interlude*, *Lazarus Laughed*, and *Dynamo*, in addition to an equally long list of less well-known and less highly regarded plays. These mark O'Neill's progress away from Naturalism into an exploration and highly successful conquest of varied dramatic forms. They put him in the forefront not only of American drama, but of world drama as well. His incredible activity was muted in the '30's, when only three of his plays were produced: *Mourning Becomes Electra*, itself a three-play unit; *Ah, Wilderness!*; and *Days Without End*. During the long years of his debilitating illness, which began in 1937, he continued to plan and write, hard at work on a nine-play

449

171 A flexible theatre on a college campus
Above, the exterior of the Student Art Center designed by Marcel
Breuer for Sarah Lawrence College. Right, the interior of the theatre,
and a floor plan. Alternate rows of seats are removable; an elevator stage
can be lowered for an orchestra pit or for parquet seating; the rear
stage wall can be converted to a proscenium for playing to an
audience seated outdoors. (Sarah Lawrence College)

cycle. Two more noncycle plays were produced before his death in
1953: *The Iceman Cometh,* in 1946, and *A Moon for the Misbegotten,*
in 1947. *A Long Day's Journey Into Night* appeared in 1956, and *A
Touch of the Poet,* the only cycle play with which he is said to have
been satisfied, in 1957. O'Neill began writing for an actively producing theatre group, and his plays are eminently theatrical. But he was
always passionately devoted to the expression of truth as he saw it,
regardless of any commercial, social, or ethical considerations. As
his health declined, he grew weary of the furor of actual production,
and retreated to his study; but his sense of theatre was always vividly
alive. Though he is said to have ordered the destruction of most of
his unfinished manuscripts, it yet remains to be seen if more will be
salvaged for a hungry public. O'Neill is America's contribution to the
select group of first-rank dramatists, and his work defies any easy
classification.

The 1920's also saw the first important plays of Maxwell Anderson,
Elmer Rice, Sydney Howard, George Kelly, Philip Barry, S. N.
Behrman, and Robert Sherwood. Anderson (1888–1959), after a solo
venture with *White Desert* (1923), made a resounding success, in
collaboration with Laurence Stallings, with the naturalistic anti-war
play, *What Price Glory?* in 1924. Amazingly fecund and versatile,
Anderson, until his death in 1959, dealt with a wide variety of subject

450

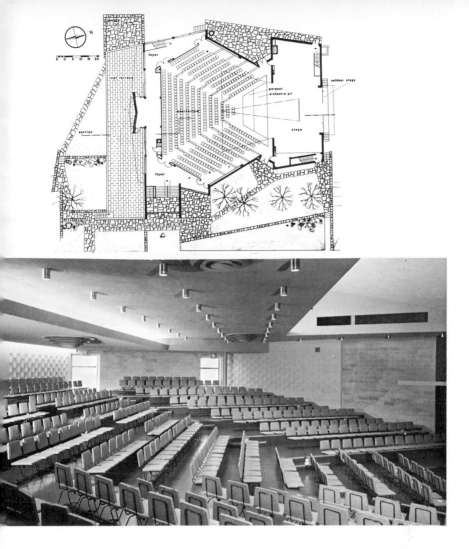

matter in varying theatrical forms. He wrote not only plays like
the modern realistic *Both Your Houses* (1933), but the riotous
satirical music drama *Knickerbocker Holiday* (1938), and a long list
of poetic plays on both historical and contemporary subjects, like
Elizabeth the Queen (1930), *Mary of Scotland* (1933), *Winterset*
(1935), *High Tor* (1937), and many others. Of the many plays which
Elmer Rice (1892—) has written (and still may write), at least
two have unquestionable permanent value. *The Adding Machine*
(1923) was one of the first, and remains perhaps the best of attempts
to present on the American stage, in American terms, the substance
of expressionist techniques originated in Germany. The chief character, Mr. Zero, is shown to be an ironically tragic product of our

451

regimented society—a theme which was to receive increasing attention after the Depression. His other great play is *Street Scene* (1929), the apotheosis of Naturalism in the American theatre. It was later musicalized by Marc Blitzstein, as was Sydney Howard's great play *They Knew What They Wanted* (1924), when *Most Happy Fella* appeared in 1956. Several other very good plays, including *Yellow Jack* (1934), were putting Howard into the front rank of American playwrights up to the time of his tragic death in 1939.

George Kelly (1877—), Philip Barry (1896–1949), and S. N. Behrman (1893—) are chiefly known for their peculiarly American comedies of manners, though Barry's *White Wings* (1926) is an unfairly neglected fantasy, and Behrman's later plays were affected by his preoccupation with world events. Affected similarly were the plays of Robert Sherwood (1896–1956), who began writing in the '20's, but had his first great success in 1931 with *Reunion in Vienna,* which, though a witty character comedy, basically deals with the contrast between a decaying society and new forces and ideas. *Abe Lincoln in Illinois* (1938) and *There Shall Be No Night* (1940) also successfully combined fundamental ideas with stageworthiness to produce memorable plays.

In addition to these outstanding dramatists whose start was in the '20's, that decade also produced a host of lesser names which compared favorably both with the playwrights of other countries and with those who had preceded them in American theatre itself. Many of these were concerned with the new forms of dramatic writing that were being tried in Europe. Howard Lawson, John Dos Passos, and Sophie Treadwell wrote plays with overtones of Expressionism and fantasy in free forms. There was a series of plays on Negro themes, climaxed in 1930 with the best of these, Marc Connelly's *The Green Pastures.* There was a series of folk plays, beginning with Hatcher Hughes' *Hell Bent Fer Heaven* (1924), and this type developed the great talents of Paul Green and Lynn Riggs. There were hosts of other plays as well, from mediocre long-run successes like Anne Nichols' *Abie's Irish Rose* (1922) to beautifully conceived but unsuccessful plays like Edwin Justus Mayer's *Children of Darkness* (1930). The output was enormous, and merely to chronicle the names of good plays and interesting playwrights would take pages of space.

To the group of practicing playwrights who began working in the '20's, the '30's added more distinguished names. Sam and Bella Spewack wrote a lively satire of Hollywood in *Boy Meets Girl* (1935), Paul Osborn a strange and bitter satire of human futility, *Morning's at Seven* (1939). The Group Theatre, the devoted band of which Harold Clurman writes in *The Fervent Years*, which existed for most of the period of the '30's, produced the first play of Sidney Kingsley, *Men in White* (1933), and nurtured Clifford Odets, whose long list of plays have become American classics. The '30's had their long-run champion in the Lindsay–Crouse comedy, *Life With Father* (1939), and saw the beginning of the careers of such disparate dramatists as Lillian Hellman, Robert Ardrey, Thornton Wilder, and William Saroyan. The two latter are almost unique among serious American dramatists in their fundamental conviction that man is admirable and that life is good. George S. Kaufman, whose early productions reach back to pre-Depression days, enjoyed a wide reputation in the '30's as collaborator with Morrie Ryskind and the Gershwins in what is surely the best of all musical satires ever written on American politics, *Of Thee I Sing* (1931), and with Moss Hart in a long series of comedies which includes *Merrily We Roll Along* (1934) and *The Man Who Came to Dinner* (1939).

The outstanding new playwrights of the '40's were Arthur Miller, Tennessee Williams, and William Inge, and these continued, in the '50's, to dominate the American stage. Other less forceful but still outstanding voices were also being heard: John van Druten, Carson McCullers, Garson Kanin, Mary Ellen Chase, Robert Anderson, to name only a few. There was a great rash of adaptations and dramatizations, and a series of complicated collaborations in the field of musicals. The last three decades saw the metamorphosis of the American musical into a distinctive dramatic form which has nowhere been equalled—a presentation in which music and story are closely integrated and which often (like *West Side Story*, 1957) deals with highly dramatic content and social criticism. In practically all genres of playwriting, American theatre has stood head and shoulders above its contemporaries in other lands.

English and French dramatic literature a good second

The English and French, however, have offered some effective challenges to American supremacy. Until his death in 1950, George Bernard Shaw was considered perhaps the greatest of living playwrights in Europe if not in the world. As we have seen, his first fame came in the closing years of the nineteenth century; his most active writing years were the 1910's and '20's, but he kept writing through the '40's. His plays are marked with a keen intellect and incisive dialogue, yet succeed in conveying, as well, a strong emotional impact. He is often accused of talkiness, yet his plays are everywhere

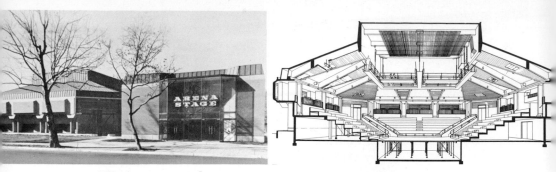

172 *A new arena theatre*
Above left, an exterior view of the theatre plant opened October 9, 1961,
showing the entrance to the building which houses offices, dressingrooms,
and workrooms, and the theatre building adjoining. Above right, a
cross-section perspective of the theatre building, showing the
arrangement of the seats with the tier at the left being movable, the boxes,
the light bridge and grid. Right, a photograph of the interior, with
set pieces at two of the entrances for actors. This plant, designed by
Harry Weese, is unique in arena theatre construction. (Arena Stage)

being performed on English-speaking stages and constantly being
translated into other languages. After World War I, he wrote notably:
*Heartbreak House, Back to Methusalah, St. Joan, The Apple Cart,
Too True to Be Good, The Millionairess, In Good King Charles's
Golden Days,* to add to the long and impressive list of outstanding
prewar plays. Shaw has, perhaps, been the only British playwright to
rival Shakespeare in the last three hundred years.

In a class by himself (though a very different class from that of
Shaw) was James M. Barrie (1860–1937), another of the older generation of playwrights; his most famous play, *Peter Pan* (1904), has
a subtitle, "The Boy Who Never Grew Up," which curiously epit-
omizes the dramatist. Something fey, something gentle, something
other-worldly seems to invest practically all of his plays; his *Dear
Brutus* (1917) and *The Admirable Crichton* (1903) are of permanent value.

The literary respectability which the drama achieved in the twentieth century is evidenced by the number of English literary men
who essayed the dramatic form. Poet Laureate John Masefield has
written several poetic dramas as well as some highly lyrical prose
tragedies. John Drinkwater (1882–1937), most famous for his truly
significant prose drama, *Abraham Lincoln* (1919), wrote poetic plays
as well. The novelists Somerset Maugham, J. B. Priestley, Clemence
Dane, and Graham Greene have also written for the theatre, as have
the poets A. A. Milne and W. H. Auden. But poetic drama as such

had no large success until the appearance in the theatre of T. S. Eliot and Christopher Fry. Eliot's first poetic drama concerned itself with Thomas à Becket, *Murder in the Cathedral* (1935); but his later plays, *The Cocktail Party* (1950) and *The Confidential Clerk* (1954), attempted to put poetry in the mouths of contemporary characters much in the way that Anderson had done in *Winterset*. Fry's greatest successes have been in costume plays like *A Phoenix Too Frequent* (1946) and *The Lady's Not for Burning* (1948), both highly original productions, but he has also made an enviable reputation in the translation of such French playwrights as Giraudoux.

The tradition of comedy has persisted on the English stage, with such notable practitioners as Noël Coward, Frederick Lonsdale, and Terence Rattigan. Clever, sophisticated, and beautifully urbane are the typical productions of each of these: *Blithe Spirit, The Last of Mrs. Cheyney,* and *O Mistress Mine.* Both Coward and Rattigan have written in other genres. There has been the equivalent of the American folk play in the works of the Scotsman, James Bridie, the English Dodie Smith, and, notably, the Irishman, Sean O'Casey, whose *Juno and the Paycock* (1924), *Purple Dust* (1940), and many other incisive dramas mark him as one of the most challenging of living playwrights.

Recent theatrical seasons have brought to the fore what seems to be a new generation of writers in the English theatre, like John Osborne, whose *Look Back in Anger* was the hit of the 1955–56

173 *A new theatre complex*
Model of the new Lincoln Center for the Performing Arts in New York City.
The building at the left will be the new Metropolitan Opera House;
to its right is the repertory theatre which is to be equipped with a flexible
stage. At the bottom is the ballet theatre which is to have a fixed
proscenium, a horseshoe-shaped auditorium and five shallow balconies.
The building in the center is the new concert hall for the Philharmonic
Orchestra; at the top, the new plant of the Juilliard School.
(Ezra Stoller, Lincoln Center for the Performing Arts)

season, and Peter Ustinov, whose multifarious activities as writer,
director, and actor have made his less energetic fellows admire and
wonder.

Besides O'Casey, who has lived most of his life in England, Ireland
has produced, notably, Lennox Robinson and Paul Vincent Carroll.
The latter's beautiful *Shadow and Substance* (1934) has had continuing success in both England and America. English drama has
been, in this century on the whole, witty and well mannered, restrained and artistic.

French drama, on the other hand, has been as tempestuous as the
political life of the country itself. Even the high tide of Antoine
Realism, whose vestiges may still be found in French theatre, was
marked by violent opposition in the symbolic and romantic dramas
of Maeterlinck and Rostand. The former initiated a theatrical form

and subject matter that greatly influenced playwrights like Lenormand, Pirandello, and Andreiev, and the latter created one of the greatest theatrical successes of all time in *Cyrano de Bergerac* (1897). Largely through the strength of the classical tradition and the influence of the Comédie Française, the past is always present in French drama. Modern critics are fond of dividing French playwriting into two distinct types: serious plays and entertainments, the former being noteworthy for a predominantly pessimistic view of life, the latter for a preoccupation with the "eternal triangle." It is possible, of course, to make such a division—in older days we might have called these simply tragedy and comedy. But modern developments in drama have wiped out these easy distinctions. The strain of comedy has survived in the popularity of the plays of Georges Feydeau and Sacha Guitry, of Louis Verneuil and Jacques Deval. But the more significant French drama has eschewed this Gallic cleverness and has concerned itself with the nature of man, with his relation to the universe, and his place in it. Swept by the succeeding winds of Impressionism, Surrealism, and Existentialism, French dramatists have exhibited a passionate religiosity as well as a passionate atheism. The intense involvement of Paul Claudel with religion bore fruit in such a play as *Division of Noon* (1906). The concern of Lenormand with the subconscious in such a play as *Time Is a Song* (1919) has subsequently led him to be dubbed the Eugene O'Neill of the French stage. In surrealist style, Jean Cocteau unshackled his drama and its characters from the laws of logic and nature, and produced, along with works in other literary fields, startling plays like *The Infernal Machine* (1934) and *The Terrible Parents* (1938), which have all the power and strangeness of a waking dream.

Perhaps the outstanding name among modern French dramatists is that of Jean Giraudoux, who, though he died in 1944, is still very much alive on the stages of the world. In his *Amphitryon 38* (1929), *The Trojan War Will Not Take Place* (1935), *Electre* (1937), *Paris Impromptu* (1937), and *Ondine* (1939), he displays amazing versatility, and a unique ability to find contemporary meanings in historical materials. Titled *Tiger at the Gates*, with Michael Redgrave as Hector, *The Trojan War, etc.* had a tremendous success in 1955, in both London and New York. A classical story forms the basis for Jean Anouilh's *Antigone* (1942), as well, but his *The Enchanted* (1948) is built of more contemporary stuff.

Philosophically an Existentialist and an atheist, Jean-Paul Sartre is constantly concerned with ethics in the conflicts of duties and rights, of classes and characters. His plays were the sensation of the decade of the '40's: *No Exit, The Flies, Dirty Hands,* and *The Respectful Prostitute.* Like the older Salacrou, Albert Camus concerns himself in such a play as *Caligula* (1938) with the absence of good and the epitome of evil, much as Sartre did in his *The Devil and the Good Lord* (1948). The futility of a godless world is explored in Beckett's controversial *Waiting for Godot* (1952), and the futility of human effort in the plays of Ionesco. Not without reason is the judgment that contemporary French drama is almost entirely pessimistic.

Italy, Spain, Germany, Russia

The nature of reality is the concern of Italy's one outstanding playwright of modern times, Luigi Pirandello. Though he died in 1936, he has had a continuing and immense influence on modern theatre. Turning from novel writing to theatre during the days of the First World War, he brought to the theatre a consideration of the same problem which he had been exploring in his novels—that of human personality conceived as an aggregate of conflicting and shifting selves. *Six Characters in Search of an Author* (1921), *As You Desire Me* (1930), *Right You Are If You Think You Are* (1918), and *Henry IV* (1922), are his best-known plays. Perhaps we should mention Alberto Casella for the great success enjoyed in America by his 1924 play, *Death Takes a Holiday* and the recent success (1959–60 season) of Diego Fabbri's *Between Two Thieves,* adapted by Werner LeRoy. This New York success marks him as an Italian playwright of current reputation. But, for the most part, as always, both the quantity and the quality of Italian playwriting has been inferior to that of other European countries.

Spain, likewise, has few names to contribute of any international stature, although in the present century there has been a renascence of drama unequalled since the time of Lope de Vega. Outstanding in this resurgence is Jacinto Benavente (1866–1954), who won the Nobel Prize in 1922, after having dominated the Spanish stage from 1907, when *The Bonds of Interest* appeared. He had been preceded by the somewhat older Echegaray, who wrote in the Ibsen style, and who also won a Nobel Prize in 1909. Joaquin and Alvarez Quintero collaborated on plays which reached the stages of other countries as well as their own, and the poetic drama, which had never really died in Spain, was taken to new heights by Federico Garcia Lorca, who was killed in the Spanish Civil War. *The House of Bernarda Alba* (1936), *Blood Wedding* (1933) and *Yerma* (1934) have made him famous in the theatres of the world. The religious motif has been accentuated by the plays of Martinez Sierra and his wife, whose *The Kingdom of God* in 1929 made an admirable vehicle for Ethel Barrymore in America. There have been other playwrights in Spain, of course, but these are the most important.

The playwrights of the new theatre in Germany were, as we have seen, chiefly Hauptmann and Sudermann, and the name of the former remains the greatest in twentieth-century drama in Germany, while that of the latter has declined in reputation because, while dealing with the new materials of Naturalism, he practiced the old and outmoded dramaturgy of the well-made play. As we have also seen, Hauptmann was not entirely devoted to Naturalism. His most outstanding contemporary, who belittled that form, was Frank Wedekind. His favorite theme was the narrowness of middle-class morality, his favorite dramatic form a loose construction of individual scenes. Wedekind died in 1918, but he was the chief inspiration of the Expressionist group who flourished immediately after World War I. Herworth Walden, one of the writers of this group, has defined Expressionism as "an attempt to give by means of concentration and intensity in word, sound, color, and movement a material abstraction of reality, and in a manner that violently excites the playgoer" (as paraphrased by Huntly Carter *The New Spirit in the European Theatre, 1914–1924,* p. 222). In other words, it is a movement which is at the opposite pole from Realism, extracting from a given situation and set of characters only the essential emotional content, and projecting this in deliberately theatrical and nonrealistic terms. The chief exponents of this style were Ernst Toller whose *Mass Man* (1919) is his most famous play (also performed in America), and George Kaiser, author of more than forty expressionist plays. Typical are his *Gas I* (1918) and *Gas II* (1920) which explore the problems of capitalist society, and *From Morn to Midnight* (1918) which deals with money madness in the individual. Also writing in this form were Walter Hasenclever, Fritz von Unruh, and many others. It was the most important dramatic movement of modern Germany, and produced, in altered form, the only dramatist who rivals the fame of Hauptmann in this century—Bertolt Brecht. His first play, *Drums in the Night* (1923), was expressionist in form, but he went on to develop the idea of what he has called "epic theatre," which substituted for the Aristotelian purging of emotions a deliberate attempt to encourage a certain detachment, a contemplative coolness on the part of both actor and audience, so that both may not be led astray by *identification* with the characters in the play, but may *understand* them intellectually. Being chiefly a poet, Brecht does not always

459

174 *A new theatre for Shakespeare*
Left, exterior construction, reminiscent of the tent in which productions
began, of the Stratford Shakespearean Festival in Ontario, Canada.
Center, interior view of the auditorium, showing the arrangement of the
2,190 seats around three sides of the thrust stage. Right, view
toward the stage designed by Tanya Moiseiwitsch. It is a permanent
setting, having eight acting levels and a trapdoor in the center.
(Stratford Shakespearean Festival)

succeed in this detachment, but his plays are interesting and chal-
lenging experiments. *The Three-Penny Opera* (1928) with music by
Kurt Weill, has achieved the spectacular success of a five-year run
in New York. His other most famous plays are: *Mother Courage and
Her Children* (1939), *The Good Woman of Setzuan* (1938), *The
Caucasian Chalk Circle* (1943), and *Terror and Misery of the Third
Reich* (1945), usually played in English as *The Private Life of the
Master Race*.

In Russia, the great names of the pre-Revolutionary theatre were
augmented by that of Andreiev, who, in such a play as *He Who Gets
Slapped* (1914), heralded the wave of nonrealistic plays which was
to accompany and follow the Revolution. That cataclysm was followed in the '20's by a period of wide experimentation in both playwriting and production. Since the Soviet hierarchy regarded the
theatre as a collectivist art they fostered its growth. The preserva-
tion of the traditional drama was accompanied by the creation of
new. The so-called Futurists, believing firmly in the Revolution,
called for a revolution in the art of theatre as well. Outstanding
among these was Mayakovski, who wrote the first important new play
of the Soviet regime, called *Mystery Bouffe* (1918), a mock-heroic

travesty subtitled "An Heroic, Epic, and Satiric Representation of Our Epoch." He went on to write *The Bedbug* (1929) and *The Bath* (1930), both praising the new regime. Anatol Lunacharsky, as People's Commissar of Education, not only encouraged a rereading of the past in the light of the present, but wrote several plays in this reinterpretive style: *Faust and the City, Oliver Cromwell, The Emancipated Don Quixote,* and *Napoleon Intervenes.* Glorification of the new regime appeared in the work of many other dramatists as well: Ivanov's *Armored Train 14–89* (1927), Kirshon's *Bread* (1931), Pogodin's *The Poem of the Ax* (1931), and many others. The early days were unique in tolerating such a play as Bulkagov's *In the Days of the Turbins* (1925), which showed some sympathy for the White Guard, and Katayev's comedy, *Squaring the Circle* (1928), which amusingly presented the individual's problems when confronted with Soviet rules and regulations. As Stalinism tightened its hold, however, the creed of the Soviet theatres was handed down to be New Socialist Realism. Mayakovski committed suicide, Meyerhold, the great innovator in staging, disappeared, and playwrights wrote to the prescription of the state, which outlawed romantic love and the inner conflicts of human beings, and glorified collectivism, the machine, and its own supremacy.

The machine, glorified in Italy and Russia and castigated in Germany, was the subject of one of the most telling of satires, the *R.U.R.* (1921) of the Czech Karel Capek as well as of his *The Insect Comedy* (1921), both of which had wide success on stages in all parts of the world.

Plays were being written everywhere, plays of all kinds in form and subject matter, and many of them would live to aftertimes. Those

461

which were written to prescription, with propaganda motives—the war plays of the West no less than the Socialist Realism of the Soviets—would disappear, unless, like R. C. Sheriff's *Journey's End* (1928) and Sherwood's *There Shall Be No Night* (1940), they spoke in universal terms of enduring human problems and values. The playwriting of the present century has been as varied and chaotic as the times themselves, but much has been added to the store of the world's great drama.

Theatres, theatres everywhere

As might be expected, the number of playhouses continued to increase in the twentieth century, although some decline was also evident occasionally. In 1900, there were forty-three theatres in New York City; by 1928 there were eighty. That was the high point; since that time many theatres have been demolished or turned to other uses. About forty-five serve the city at the present time, not counting the off-Broadway houses, or the cinemas, or television studios. The nearly five thousand houses of legitimate drama which we noted in America in 1885 had dwindled to about two hundred by the middle of the last decade. But this decline is somewhat offset by the construction, in the same period, of more than two thousand college and university theatres, plus untold hundreds of community or little theatres. What we may deduce is that commercial theatre has suffered attrition, while other forms of theatrical activity have expanded.

Theatre building in Russia spurted suddenly after the removal of the official ban in 1882, and by the beginning of World War II there were about one thousand theatres there, not counting children's theatres or amateur groups. Some of these, the best, had been in existence before the Revolution, and with some attention to repertory and management were allowed to continue. The Moscow Art Theatre, the Maly, and the three main houses in Leningrad are examples. But most of the post-Revolution theatres were founded and organized by the People's Commissar of Finance, and bore such names as Theatre of the Revolution, Realistic Theatre, Red Army Theatre, Trades Union Theatre—all very proletarian titles. Even today the Soviet is busy building theatres in the far reaches of Siberia, using the pattern of the Moscow houses.

Similar spurts and declines are traceable in other countries, with the most interest in theatre as a specialized type of architecture being evidenced in Germany. Western Germany alone has about two hundred professional theatres in a hundred cities, including eleven open-air theatres. Oslo, Norway, a city of 275,000, supports five theatres

175 *Another new theatre for Shakespeare*
Above, exterior view of the American Shakespeare Festival Theatre
at Stratford, Connecticut. It is octagonal in shape and of wood siding,
hence reminiscent of the theatres of Shakespeare's time. Below,
interior view of the stage with a scene from *The Taming of the Shrew* in
progress. The lattice hangings which form the stage set, designed
by Rouben Ter-Arutunian, can be arranged in various ways.
There is a generous forestage, set on a rake, and many entrances.
(American Shakespeare Festival)

176 *Arena stage*
The Penthouse Theatre, University of Washington. This was among
the first of the theatres designed specifically for arena staging and has an
elliptical shape. (Glenn Hughes)

and an opera house. There are ten endowed playhouses in Turkey.
Italy is currently experimenting with mobile theatres in tents as a
supplement to the standing theatres. Finland's thirty-two subsidized
professional repertory houses have an average yearly attendance of
more than 25 per cent of the total population of about four million.
This burgeoning of theatre establishments has been an outstanding
phenomenon of the twentieth century.

Needless to say, so large a number of playhouses indicates a wide
variety in their architecture, and reflects many divergent ideas as to
purposes. The majority of theatre buildings erected in this century
still house the traditional proscenium stage, with backstage areas
almost invariably being more spacious in European houses than in
American. Seating arrangements now almost universally follow the
fanshaped bank of seats on a sloping or dished floor, rather than the
old opera-house style, although loges—vestiges of the old rows of
boxes—persist in many English houses, and one or more balconies
are almost universal space savers in all but the smallest theatres.
The newer European houses tend to plan more space between rows
of seats than American houses, although an exception is the Russian
houses, where audiences are notoriously cramped by the narrow
seats and aisles. Russian theatres seem strange to American eyes
because they lack marquees and billboards; there are no names in
lights. The buildings tend to be severe and painted in dark colors.
They are generally rectangular in shape with sometimes one or two
shallow balconies in the traditional horseshoe shape. In Europe and
the Soviet Union, more theatres have been built as free-standing
structures than in America, where they are often incorporated in

464

structures dedicated to other purposes than theatre. While it is impossible to describe all the hundreds of theatre buildings erected in this century, a brief description of a few will illustrate the variety of types and kinds.

Outstanding among the very large theatres was the Grosses Schauspielhaus (figure 168), converted from the old Circus Schumann in Berlin by Max Reinhardt in 1919. A product of the period when people talked in terms of mass audiences and "the theatre of the five thousand," this auditorium seated thirty-five hundred people, and had a deep and wide forestage extending out into the audience. This stage was backed by a proscenium-arch stage with a sky dome and revolver. The banks of seats surrounded the forestage on all three sides. In a place so large, the feeling of intimacy presumably to be obtained by bringing the actors out into the audience by means of the forestage could not be successful; the building required spectacle rather than intimacy in the presentations.

Not quite so large but still considerably more capacious than most modern theatres, is the immense Red Army Theatre in Moscow (figure 168). The building, opened in 1940, has the exterior shape of a five-pointed star; its seating capacity is two thousand. It is this big theatre which housed the visiting American company of *My Fair Lady* in the spring of 1960. Almost as large as this Russian playhouse was the Ziegfeld Theatre in New York, opened in 1927, and seating seventeen hundred. It had a large orchestra pit, a wide and deep single balcony, and elaborate decoration by Joseph Urban.

Among the larger houses built in the 1950's is the uniquely designed Stratford Shakespearean Festival Theatre in Ontario, Canada (figure 174), which seats twenty-one hundred. Reminiscent of the Grosses Schauspielhaus is the jutting forestage, with seats on three sides. As designed by Tanya Moiseiwitsch, the fourth side forms a backdrop in which architectural units of columns, balconies, and steps can be adapted to the needs of varying plays. The outside of this free-standing building is curiously reminiscent of the circus tent in which performances on the spot first began in 1953. The American Shakespeare Festival Theatre at Stratford, Connecticut (figure 175), on the other hand, with its wooden siding and high stage house, has the flavor of Shakespeare's Globe in its octagonal form, but its interior sixteen hundred seats are arranged in the modern fanshaped manner with an overhanging balcony fronting a wide proscenium. Flexibility is obtained by a large forestage extending the entire width of the auditorium. The new repertory theatre planned as a unit in the Lincoln Center for the Performing Arts in New York City (figure

177 *Another arena stage*
A scene from *Playboy of the Western World* in the converted movie
house which was the first home of Arena Stage in Washington, D.C.
The acting area is rectangular, with four tiers of seats. This scene
demonstrates the importance of the floor in arena stage decoration.

173) calls for a twelve-hundred-seat house with the apron of the
stage extending well into the auditorium. The recently announced
plans for the ballet-opera theatre to be constructed in the same Center, however, curiously maintain the fixed proscenium and the horseshoe-shaped auditorium, with what is described as "five shallow
balconies" much like the old tiers of boxes.

Though theatre economics have continued to insist on a seating
capacity large enough to defray the costs of operation, many theatre
people have felt that these large houses are not suited to several kinds
of dramatic productions. In Europe some commercial houses have
solved the problem by incorporating two playhouses in the same
plant, as in the theatre at Mannheim, Germany (figure 169). This
magnificent new marble and glass building was opened in 1957, and
includes in one architectural unit, with mutual lobby and foyer space,
the Grosses Haus seating twelve hundred, and the Kleines Haus
seating six to eight hundred. The smaller house is designed so that
the stage can be moved to different positions for proscenium, arena,
or presentational staging.

Two stages are also incorporated into the startling new City Theatre opened in 1944 at Malmö, Sweden (figure 169). The smaller

house seats two hundred and four, but the larger one, by a cleverly arranged series of laminated maplewood screens hung from rails, can vary its capacity from four hundred to eight hundred, to twelve hundred, to a maximum of seventeen hundred. As planned by Sigurd Lewerentz and a group of associated architects, it incorporates a semicircular apron stage projecting thirty feet into the auditorium. This forestage can be lowered to form an orchestra pit, and the proscenium itself varied in size by raising up or sliding off the four sections into which it is divided. The building also houses extensive foyers and lounges, workshops, and a restaurant.

Buildings housing dual stages exist in America chiefly in colleges and universities, where some outstanding examples have been built, as at the State University of Iowa, the University of Wisconsin, Johns Hopkins University, and the University of Arkansas. The Cleveland Playhouse, a civic institution, is of similar design. As in Europe generally, these theatre buildings incorporate lobbies, workrooms, and ample backstage space in a specially designed, free-standing building with an interesting architectural façade. Among the more than two thousand university theatres built in the United States during this century, some have been planned, like that at Sarah Lawrence College (figure 171), to be adaptable, by moving seats and stage space, for more than one kind of dramatic presentation.

The predominant building trend, however, has been to a fixed-type house, either small and intimate like the art theatres of Paris, or large and spacious like many of those we have mentioned. Though the interior architecture still tends to a proscenium-arch stage and fanshaped auditorium, the stage is often no longer a standard picture frame, but so constructed as to be adaptable to varying forms of production.

The most radical departures have been in the construction of arena auditoriums, with the acting space in the midst of the audience. In 1924, Gilmore Brown and Ralph Freund built the Playbox at Pasadena, California, using this idea, although this type of staging had been previously experimented with by Azubah Latham at Teachers College, Columbia University as early as 1914. In 1932, the Russian director, Okhlopkov, used the same idea in his Realistic Theatre in Moscow, and in 1940, Glenn Hughes opened his Penthouse Theatre at the University of Washington in a building especially designed with an elliptical acting area and auditorium (figure 176). The idea was taken over by community theatres, Margo Jones opening her theatre-in-the-round in Dallas, Texas, later in the same decade; and, in 1950, Arena Stage opened in Washington, D.C., in a converted

467

movie (figure 177). The Washington company has recently moved into an especially designed house in the new civic center. As planned by the architect, Harry Weese, the building permits a degree of flexible staging and seating in the 750-seat capacity house. It is linked by a passageway-lounge to the working-area building, where offices, workshops, dressingrooms, and lobbies are housed. The auditorium unit contains the rectangular area of the stage itself surrounded by enclosing tiers eight rows deep, behind which is a circulation aisle. Above this aisle is a ring of boxes. The thirty by forty-foot stage area is trapped, and a lighting grid hung over it. One tier of seats is arranged for dismounting so that three-sided staging can be accomplished on occasion (figure 172).

Newest research into theatre form is being conducted by George C. Izenour at Yale University, who is currently developing an electronically controlled three-theatres-in-one, which may be built at some future time. Thus, while the majority of standing playhouses in the Western world still demonstrate the dominance of the proscenium arch and the fanshaped auditorium, many significant departures toward a more flexible arrangement of both actors and audiences are being tried.

Settings create only the Illusion of reality as design becomes an art

Even within the predominant proscenium style, many attempts have been made in particular productions to dispense with the idea of the fourth wall, which treated the production as if it were a peep show. This fourth wall was the natural concomitant of Realism and Naturalism. If we were to duplicate reality on the stage, then the setting must be solid and exact, the properties must be "real." Let us have tons of dirt for *Tobacco Road,* and real food for *Life With Father.* Let the actors ignore the audience and play their scenes as if only themselves were concerned. But what to do about that blank space between actors and audience? Pretend that it doesn't exist. Dress it with the logs of a fireplace, or call it the end of a dock, with the audience sitting in an ocean, as it were. In other words, ignore the fact that theatre is theatre, and let the spectators eavesdrop on a slice of life.

Needless to say, the excess of this practice could lead only to the excess of the ridiculous. The theatre is an art form, frankly depending on audience and the relationship of the play thereto. So, even though the squeaking screen door, the very solid staircase, and the sleazy interior could be welcomed in William Inge's *Dark at the Top of the*

178 *American designers for American plays*
Left, Jones's design for *Desire Under the Elms*. The siding of the
house can be removed in sections to reveal interior scenes. Right, Jo
Meilziner's design for *Winterset*. Both of these designs are excellent
examples of the principle that the play is interpreted by the décor no
less than by the actors. (Theatre Collection, New York Public Library)

Stairs in 1958, the idea became current in this century that the most
effective, perhaps even the most desirable, form of production was
not, of necessity, the minutely realistic. Indeed, the method suited
only particular types of plays, and even here the production profited
from a selection of details rather than a faithful reproduction of
reality. If a bench, a battered sideboard, a rough table and a stove
set on a groundcloth marked like flagstones, and topped with a piece
of overhead beam could create the illusion of reality for an Arena
Stage production of *Playboy of the Western World* (figure 177), of
what use would be further documentation? Arena staging is, ad-
mittedly, a thing apart, but even on the conventional stage the
reaction against a too-meticulous realism proceeded.

Inspired by the ideas of Appia and Craig, a whole generation of
scene designers came into being in both Europe and America, and
achieved an importance hitherto unprecedented—or perhaps we
should say unprecedented since the days of the Bibienas and Piranesi.

Typical of these new designers was Robert Edmond Jones, who,
perhaps more clearly than the others, set forth in precept and practice the guiding principle that the scene must enhance the play, not
from a pictorial basis primarily, but from the fundamental premise

469

that the play is interpreted and made meaningful by actor and décor. He once said that the obligation of the scenic artist was to "see the high original intention of the dramatist" and to work to "affirm and ennoble the art of the actor." He concerned himself with every detail of the visual aspect of the production—settings, lights, costumes, properties—working with a dedication and an intensity that inspired others and that produced many memorable designs.

For him, as for those who espoused the new principles everywhere, scene design was a creative act, imbued with high and artistic purposes. This creative act he performed for all types of plays from Shakespeare to *The Philadelphia Story* (1939), one of his most famous and effective designs being that for O'Neill's *Desire Under the Elms* (1924). With its brooding tree and clapboard house that opened to show various interiors at the times when action took place in each, it made this type of multiple setting (though not a new idea in itself) one of the popular styles (figure 178). It was seen again in such outstanding designs as those of Jo Mielziner for *Death of a Salesman* (1949) and of Stewart Cheney for *Voice of the Turtle* (1943).

Another type of setting adapted to multiple use was the so-called unit set, brought to significant development by designers like Donald Oenslager, Lee Simonson, Adolph Linnebach, Roger Furse, to mention only a few. This type stresses a basic arrangement of platforms, steps, columns, or other vertical masses, which can be changed for various scenes by curtains, screens, or other set pieces. It has, of course, a direct relationship to the permanent architectural stage setting of such theatres as Copeau's Vieux Colombier and Reinhardt's Redoutensaal, but is more directly concerned with the basic needs and shape of an individual play. Lee Simonson's design for O'Neill's *Marco Millions* (1927), those of Rouben Ter Arutunian for Shakespeare at Stratford, Connecticut, are examples of this type (figure 180). Sometimes these unit settings are enhanced by projections or painted backdrops, and sometimes the planes of the architectural forms are also painted.

These developments of recent years had their source, as we have seen, in the theories of Appia and Craig. Great practical impetus was given to these ideas in the work of Leopold Jessner (1878——) in Berlin, who became famous for his *Jessnertreppen,* which Macgowan and Jones have translated as "those crazy steps of Leopold Jessner." By breaking up the stage floor with a series of levels in steps of varying form and size, Jessner gave his actors another dimension through which to move. He further made wide use of colored planes and

179 American disciples of Appia and Craig
Above, design for *Macbeth* by Robert Edmond Jones; below, design
for *King Lear* by Norman Bel Geddes. These drawings, by two of the most
outstanding American designers, not only illustrate the importance of
design in the modern theatre but also emphasize the importance of
lighting to design. Sources and areas of light are shown in both.
(Museum of Modern Art; Barbara Bel Geddes)

surfaces and great variation in lighting. He developed the symbolism of color to a very high degree in settings, costumes, and lights, and, in the 1920's, staged many memorable productions.

This effort to "make the décor act" came to be called Expressionism in design, just as the attempt to give a material abstraction of reality in playwriting was called by the same name. Erwin Piscator, Theo Otto, P. Schillingowsky, and many others experimented along these lines. Often projections of signs or numbers, or moving pictures, became a part of the staged play, with the avowed purpose of having greater impact on the audience.

In Russia, these nonrealistic techniques reached an apotheosis in the constructivist settings which had their greatest vogue there. The movement was partly a revolt against painted settings, and stripped away, in essence, the paint and canvas, leaving only the basic forms of the constructed scenes for the actors to use. Partly also, it was a further development of the idea that setting should be conceived as an arrangement of forms to display the agility of the actor and to enable him to project various moods and emotions by large movements through space, and highly variable relationships in space with other actors. In many of the productions of Taïrov and Meyerhold, chief exponents of the form, the curtainless stage was filled with strange and unreal constructions of wood, glass, or metal, over, around, and on which the acrobatic actors could move. Often the action took place in the auditorium as well as on the stage, audience and play becoming one. Okhlopkov applied this technique by sometimes having several stages scattered through the audience, with the actors moving from one to another. But the fertile inventions of these Russians in the 1920's and early '30's came under official interdiction before 1940, and the stress on New Socialist Realism since that time has stifled experiment and tended to turn back the clock in Russia to an outmoded theatrical form, the literal Realism of the turn-of-the-century.

Expressionistic setting was seen in America as early as 1923, when Elmer Rice's *The Adding Machine* was produced, but the extremes of this and the constructivist forms have long since passed from theatrical popularity here. They have, however, in a most fundamental way brought about a realization of the validity of Meyerhold's "theatre theatrical"—not, to be sure, in the identical way he conceived it, but in a freeing of scenic conceptions, so that the designer today asks first what production method will best convey the essence of the dramatist's thought, and then creates his details to carry out this image. Thus, there is today a greater variation in types and kinds of

472

180 *Unit settings with changing elements*
Above, Lee Simonson's design for *Marco Millions*. The large architectural
forms remain constant throughout the play; the inserts change for
the various scenes. Below, René Fuerst's design for *The Oresteia*. This
set operates on the same principle as the above; here the changes
are made within the central arch only. (Theatre Collection,
New York Public Library; Mme. Fuerst)

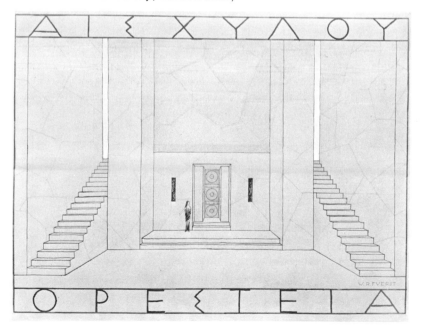

scenic investiture than ever before in the history of the theatre, varying all the way from minute fidelity to reality to the most unrealistic of abstractions. Scenic design, too, has come of age in the present century. As never before, lighting has come to play a fundamental role in theatrical interpretation, with lighting designers assuming importance as separate and significant entities. The development and perfection of lighting equipment has made this possible, and the newest of these developments is the electronically controlled switchboard as developed by George C. Izenour at Yale. Footlights, except in deliberately antiquarian performances, are never used, and light sources are often not confined to the stage itself, but emanate from all parts of the house.

Staging has utilized all devices from the simplest to the most complex. Revolvers, wagons, flies, platforms, flats, plastic set pieces, curtains, painted drops—all the resources of past and present find their place, depending on the play in hand. There has even been one resounding success, at least, which dispensed almost totally with any scenic investiture—the remarkable production of Thornton Wilder's *Our Town*, which opened in 1938 and gave proof that there is room for all kinds of visual techniques in theatre, but that, after all, the whole structure of scene design need not be a prerequisite for effective theatre.

Artistry gains in importance with authenticity in costuming

The various experiments and trends in scene designing in the twentieth century had their counterparts in costuming. As we have mentioned, the pictorial effects achieved by the painters working in theatre were aided by costumes designed in line and color to enhance the stage picture. Historical accuracy was taken for granted in noncontemporary plays, though even here the costume designer worked not so much in authentic materials and styles as in authentic effects, using whatever materials would lend themselves to this result. Canvas painted to look like brocade under the stage lights, silk jersey to drape like Egyptian cotton or Greek linen, bulky knit yarn silvered like coats of mail—these were the working materials of costumers. Sometimes noncontemporary plays were costumed in accordance with an overall production style, as was Max Reinhardt's famous production of *King Lear* in which he conceived the characters as statues cut from stone. The costumes here were made from rubber sheeting, carefully draped, folded, and painted in highlights. Sometimes, with a special interpretation in mind, noncontemporary plays were costumed out of period or in modern dress. Thus the Old Vic played

181 *Artists as theatre designers*
Left, setting by Salvador Dali for the ballet, *Labyrinth*, 1941. Right,
Marc Chagall design for *Congratulations, That's a Lie and the Police*,
1919. These highly individual and theatrical designs are typical of the
work of the many artists, particularly in France, who have designed
for the modern stage. (Museum of Modern Art; Marc Chagall)

Troilus and Cressida in Edwardian dress, and Orson Welles dressed
his actors in *Julius Caesar* in contemporary military uniforms.

Even where contemporary dress is demanded by the play, players
no longer wear whatever they think appropriate from their own wardrobes, but each detail is as carefully planned as if the setting were in
remote times. Costume design is now an art, its basic theory being
that each individual costume must bear a relationship not only to the
time and place of the play, but to the character's function in the play
structure and to his psychological orientation as well.

Costumes of the modern period then, are planned to harmonize
with the stage setting, to render the actor visible at all times when he
should be visible, and to make less conspicuous the less important
characters. Line and color are of paramount importance, with details
used only where they can enhance the total picture, and included
only if they are large enough to register with an audience. Lynn Fon-
tanne wears a floating evening gown in *O Mistress Mine* which probably would not appear at an actual party, but which is right for the
character in the play; Siobhan McKenna wears a shapeless sweater
and dress in *The Chalk Garden* which are exactly suited to her character.

In addition to their mission of projecting character and its relation
to the play, modern costumes must be wearable and durable, not

475

hampering the actor and lasting through many performances. So costumes today, whether contemporary in period or not, are designed with all these things in mind, as well as the necessity for taking into account the individual actor who will wear them. An additional hazard is posed by arena staging, where unsuitability of line or material is easily detected by the audience, and where a zipper on an eighteenth-century costume can be very distracting.

Costuming is, in many ways, even more important than scene design, for plays can be produced on a bare stage, with curtains, or with elaborate scenery, but there must always be actors, and they must always be dressed in some way. In plays with little or no scenic investiture, the costumes must be relied upon to convey time, place, and mood, so that the choice of dress for a play like *Our Town* is of great importance.

In the period following World War I, the excessive zeal of theatre people for the visual aspects of production almost drove drama out of the theatre. This was the period of great experimentation in line and color, the period when a "blue *Lear*," a "red *Hamlet*," a "grey *Resurrection*" were popular. It was the time when Jessner produced a *Richard III* with Gloucester in the coronation scene all dressed in flowing red, with his courtiers, likewise dressed, below him on a flight of red steps, with a red sky overhead. It was the time when in

182 *Unit settings*
Left, Gamrekelli's design for *The Robber;* right, Simonson's design
for *Hamlet*. The influence both of Constructivism and of the Appia–Craig
principles are evident in these two designs which provide many
acting levels and large, solid-looking structural forms which are interesting
in themselves. (Rustaveli Theatre Museum, Tiflis; Lee Simonson)

183 *Constructivist stage settings*
Left, Exter setting for *The Merchant of Venice*. Though there are few
painted flats in this set, the arrangement of the structural forms
gives a feeling of time and place, and offers many interesting
possibilities for the movement of the actors. Right, Kurt Soehnlein's
setting for *Orpheus in the Underworld*. The repetition of the curved line
with strong perpendiculars makes for a completely unrealistic, but
interesting, setting. (Kurt Soehnlein)

Masse-Mensch, a woman dressed in blue in a cage of scarlet bars was
surrounded by dark, formless figures. Expressionism in stage décor
made the individual less important than the mass effect. A similar
aim was evident in the use by Meyerhold of uniform blue denim
coveralls for both actors and actresses in his constructivist productions. Subsequent developments have tempered these extremes in
the West, and, of course, in Russia, official New Socialist Realism
has completely stifled them.

Nonrealistic theatre, generally, has given costume designers opportunity to let their imaginations flower, and romantic and fantastic
costuming often achieves startlingly artistic effects. In Europe, particularly, many easel painters have designed for the theatre: Derain,
Picasso, Matisse, Laurencin, Gris, Braque; from Russia have come
the richly oriental designs of Leon Bakst and Natalie Gontcharova.
The musical stage has been particularly fruitful of imaginative costuming, for here unusual design, sharp contrasts, and interesting line
can have freer play than in more conventional drama. A great number of costume designers, some of great talent, have grown up in
twentieth-century theatre. Sometimes, as was the case with Robert
Edmond Jones, and is currently with Cecil Beaton and Reuben Ter
Arutunian, the same designer plans both set and costumes. Sometimes, the costume designer is a separate entity from the scene designer, as are Dorothy Jeakins and the British firm of Motley.

184 *Two European designs*
Left, design of Nicolai Akimoff for the production of *Armored Train 14–69*, in Russia, 1927. Right, design of Vlastislav Hofman for *R.U.R.* in Prague. Both these settings are nonrealistic and exhibit some characteristics of Constructivism. (Museum of the State Dramatic Theatre, Leningrad; Museum of Modern Art)

Makeup, too, has reached great heights of refinement, with modern materials and methods able to make over the actor completely, as the thirty-four-year-old Hal Holbrook becomes the seventy-year-old Mark Twain for his *Mark Twain Tonight* (figure 187). Various types of grease, pancake, and panchromatic makeup now enable actors to enhance their good characteristics, subordinate the undesirable, or assume ages or stations in life not comparable to their own. The motion pictures have done a great deal to refine techniques, for the eye of the camera is not easily fooled, and much of this refinement has been absorbed and utilized in the theatre. Makeup has also been brought into line with the desire for unity of effect, fantastic face painting being in order with fantastic costuming and décor, and actresses, for the most part, no longer insisting upon being beautiful at the expense of the part they play. Wigs have reached a high state of perfection, too, with such an actor as Sir John Gielgud being able to portray a widely varied series of ages and character types by a judicious change of hairpiece—plus a consummate acting skill, of course! Even masks have been used to good effect in modern times. They are intrinsic to the production of such a play as O'Neill's *The Great God Brown,* and were used to good effect in the Brecht Berliner-Ensemble production of *The Caucasian Chalk Circle* at the Paris International Drama Festival in 1955.

The basic tenet of the early-century idealists and practitioners is still operating in all the production arts of theatre—that whatever is conceived and used must add to and enhance the total impact of the play.

Stanislavski Method *takes root in America*

In the period immediately following World War I, Russia was theatre's Mecca, and, for actors, Stanislavski was its saint. Americans, in particular, took up the Stanislavski cult with a fervor that was amazing. The Group Theatre, whose existence spanned the 1930's, was inspired by and dedicated to Stanislavski's principles. Organized and directed by Harold Clurman, Lee Strasberg, and Cheryl Crawford, it included the already experienced Stella and Luther Adler and Morris Carnovsky, and developed the talents of Franchot Tone, John Garfield, Lee J. Cobb, Elia Kazan, Sanford Meisner, Robert Lewis, Clifford Odets, Irwin Shaw, and John Howard Lawson. A glance at this list will show actors, directors, and playwrights still active, who have contributed many stellar moments to theatre in the last twenty-five years. Sanford Meisner and Lee Strasberg have continued the training aspect of the Group's activities, the former at the Neighborhood Playhouse School of the Theatre and the latter at the Actors Studio; a whole new generation of actors has been brought up in the Stanislavski tradition: Marlon Brando, Eli Wallach, Julie Harris, Kim Stanley, Maureen Stapleton, Uta Hagen—to name but a few. The Method, as the system is now reverently called, is still the subject of hot discussion and debate among actors. To discover how unsettled and virulent the arguments for and against The Method still are, you need only eavesdrop on any group of actors. Some will point out to you how the great John Barrymore—one of the most brilliant Hamlets who ever played—could be joking in the wings a moment before playing a stunning scene in tragedy—no Method actor, he. Another will point to the hour's preparation that Michael Redgrave needs before each performance of a tragic role. The truth of the matter, of course, is as it has always been that each actor must find his own best way of working.

The French method in England

Though Michael Chekhov, originally a member of Stanislavski's group, worked for a time in England, the chief influence there came from France and the principles of Jacques Copeau. Copeau voiced no allegiance to Stanislavski, though he worked essentially by the same methods toward the same results, placing perhaps a somewhat

479

185 *Two designs for* **The Emperor Jones**
The convict scene in the O'Neill play as designed by Cleon Throckmorton,
left, and Donald Oenslager, right. Both show the influence of
the Appia–Craig theories in the use of light and of shapes rather than
details. (Museum of Modern Art; Donald Oenslager)

more definite emphasis on developing vocal qualities and speaking
lines beautifully. Emphasis upon voice training and effective delivery has been characteristic of French theatre from first to last. The
immediate channel of Copeau's influence in England was Michael
Saint-Denis, who first founded his own London Theatre Studio in
1936 and then went on to the direction of the school at the Old Vic,
returning to France again in 1947 to become director of the Eastern
Center of the nationwide *Direction des Arts et Lettres.* From the
Old Vic came such actors as Sir John Gielgud, Laurence Olivier,
Michael Redgrave, Anthony Quayle, Peggy Ashcroft. In the late
1920's and early '30's, the leading actors of England were called
"leading" by virtue of their skill in light comedy and romance, like
Sir Gerald du Maurier. The style was easy and polished, natural and
realistic, and set a tone to which a whole generation of actors aspired.
Du Maurier had been for some years an actor in the company of Sir
Herbert Beerbohm-Tree, who had founded, in 1904, the Royal Academy of Dramatic Arts, which is still a major training center in England. The Continental influences, however, developed a new ideal
for leading players in England; they are now judged by their ability
to match the great classic—and, above all, the Shakespearean—roles.
Skill in comedy is not despised, however, for Sir John Gielgud is not
only a great classic actor, but also a most stylish comedian; Olivier
does a magnificent Richard, as well as an effective Archie in *The*

480

Entertainer; Peggy Ashcroft became famous in a wide variety of roles. So well-rounded have the English actors become that they are renowned for combining the best of all "schools" of acting, being especially proficient in submerging their own individualities to the part in hand and producing, like Alec Guinness, an amazing gallery of highly individual and highly differing portraits.

Versatility, flexibility on the Continent

Great versatility has also been the mark of French actors of repute, with Barrault, Jouvet, Jourdain, and, more recently, Gérard Philipe achieving success in a wide variety of roles. The ideal, at least, in both Germany and Russia is that the individual performer should be flexible in all dramatic types. The Brechtian epic theatre has injected an interesting new idea into the art of acting in its insistence that the actor must not be so involved in his part that he cannot stand aside and comment on it as well—a distinct departure from the prevalent practice of an actor living his part, of "being" and not "commenting." And in Russia, recent critiques have stated that the prevalent acting style seems to be that of a grand Classicism and turgid delivery which is reminiscent of the style of fifty or more years ago. In Italy, actors seem to fare best in comedy—perhaps an inheritance from the *commedia.*

Conditions of work and training have much to do with this situation. England, France, Germany, and Russia have many standing theatres with permanent acting companies attached. In Germany and Russia this has long been the pattern, with state and municipal funds being allotted as a matter of course to support staffs of one hundred or more in many towns and cities. Many of these standing theatres have academies or schools attached to them, and in Russia the system of training is as carefully worked out, under state supervision, as every other aspect of Soviet existence.

In the last fifteen or twenty years, there has been much progress in France toward decentralizing theatre, with the French Centres subsidized by both the central government and the local municipalities. In the School of Dramatic Art attached to the Eastern Centre, the ideal is the Copeau principle, to

> Recreate, by the forcefulness of their acting, their power of human observation, and their perfect mastery of body, a poetical climate arising from the dramatic transposition of reality (Michael Saint-Denis, "The French Dramatic Centers," *Theatre in Review*, Edinburgh, 1956, p. 43).

Voice culture is important—"the theatre lives by language," says

481

186 *Two ways of costuming Shakespeare*
Above, *Henry V* at the Stratford Shakespearean Festival in Ontario,
Canada, with authentic historical costumes.
Below, *Much Ado About Nothing* at the American Shakespeare
Festival Theatre in Stratford, Connecticut, with costumes and décor from
the Spanish-American southwest. So long as the total effect is a
unified one, modern designers feel free to depart from absolute
historical accuracy. But the milieu chosen must fit the play which
is being produced. (Herb Nott and Co., Ltd.; Friedman-Abeles)

Saint-Denis, the director. The students work with the professional company, now being recruited more and more not from Paris but from the provinces.

In Italy, there were no standing theatre companies until after World War II, when Paolo Grazzi established his *Piccolo Teatro di Milano*. Although a few additional theatres, on the Milan pattern, have begun to appear in other parts of Italy, the outstanding pattern in Italy is still, as it has always been, that of touring.companies performing from time to time in many and varied places. Comedy seems to travel best in Italy—hence that emphasis.

England, of course, has many standing theatre companies—more than 130 so-called repertory houses, each with its corps of actors and technicians. Outstanding among these are the Bristol Old Vic and the Birmingham Repertory Company. These, in themselves, form marvelous grounds for training in the short runs and variety of parts available for each performer. From such organizations have come most of the leading actors of the English stage, and many of them have become the darlings of the West End commercial theatre, which exists side-by-side with the repertories and the subsidized theatres.

Training and security
more accessible to European actors than to Americans

In America, however, with its emphasis upon Broadway success and long runs, and its almost complete lack of permanent theatre companies, there is little opportunity for "on-the-job" training, and no sort of security in the commercial theatre. Since the demise of the old stock companies, there have been attempts at establishing repertory here. Eva Le Gallienne attempted such an organization in 1926 with the Civic Repertory Theatre, and again later with the American Repertory Company. The Group Theatre was, of course, such an organization, and in the last few years Norris Houghton and Edward Hambleton got into operation a more or less permanent group at the Phoenix Theatre in New York. Arena Stage in Washington and the Margo Jones Theatre in Dallas, as well as a few others in various parts of the country, have worked on a year-to-year permanent company basis. Actual training has had various degrees of success in such ventures, the emphasis being normally more on production than on training. We might also point to the value of off-Broadway theatre as a training ground for young talent; but this, too, is a sporadic effort.

In the United States, the most significant training for theatre work has been in the colleges and universities where, during the last thirty

187 Makeup in modern theatre
Hal Holbrook as he appears in real life, and in his makeup for his
one-man entertainment, *Mark Twain Tonight*. So refined have makeup
techniques become in modern theatre that a complete change such
as this one is scarcely discernible even to the eye of the camera.
(Hal Holbrook)

years, many theatre departments have come into being. The first full
collegiate program in theatre arts was established in Pittsburgh at
the Carnegie Institute of Technology in 1914; Frederick Koch's Carolina Playmakers came into being at the University of North Carolina
in 1918; the Yale University School of the Theatre opened in 1926.
Since that time programs have been established at the Universities
of Iowa, Wisconsin, Michigan, Western Reserve, Northwestern, and
Stanford, along with innumerable other less extensive curricula elsewhere. According to a recent survey of the American Educational
Theatre Association, fifty-seven American schools are offering grad-
uate degrees in theatre arts, and many times that number have training on the undergraduate level. This is a peculiarly American
phenomenon, although Bristol University in England fairly recently
opened a theatre arts department, and quite recently, too, the Sor-
bonne in Paris instituted a similar program.

In most European countries, commercial theatres exist side-by-side
with the subsidized houses, and the actors are afforded a measure
of security that is not possible on the American scene. Salaries in
Europe are generally not so high as they are here, but they are

484

steadier. Leading actors of the Moscow Art Theatre receive the equivalent of from one hundred to four hundred dollars per month, the typical Italian star about fifty dollars a performance. German actors have a range similar to that in Russia, and the French and English are comparable. In America, the Broadway minimum is over a hundred dollars a week, though this figure may soar into the thousands for name players, who may also be assigned a percentage of the gross income of the show. Naturally everybody aims for the "big time," although the employment is as likely to terminate after a few performances as it is to last through a long run—more likely, if we are to trust the published statistics. Salaries, percentages, and many other provisos about working hours, traveling, and so forth, are controlled by the Actors' Equity Association, which has its counterpart in England.

Playwrights, too, have their protective associations. The first Dramatic Authors' Society was formed in England in 1832, but no regular royalties were paid until much later in the century. The Dramatists' Guild of the Authors' League of America was not founded until 1912, and did not become a significant force in theatre until 1926, when it negotiated a Minimum Basic Agreement with producers. Authors have been protected by International Copyright since 1887, supplementing the English Copyright Bill of 1832, and enlarged by the American Copyright Bill of 1891. In 1938, Robert Sherwood, Maxwell Anderson, Sidney Howard, S. N. Behrman and Elmer Rice formed the Playwrights' Company to produce their own plays, and in the 1950's the Dramatists' Guild organized its New Dramatists' Committee to foster new playwrights. One other organization, the American National Theatre and Academy, founded by Congressional action in 1935 but not implemented by funds, has fostered dramatic activities including playwriting through private donation; a few years ago ANTA publicized an interesting Forty Theatre Circuit Plan to supply professional theatre in all parts of the United States. Playwrights generally work on a royalty or percentage basis, and thus share the fortunes of their fellows.

A few outstanding actors have continued the old tradition of directing the plays in which they appear, notably Olivier, Ustinov, Gielgud, and Barrault. But by and large directing today has become a separate and distinct art. The individual practitioner—called in America "the director," in England "the producer," and on the Continent "the *régisseur*"—is the modern representative of the "guiding intelligence" of which Craig spoke and the modern counterpart of the Duke of Saxe-Meiningen, Reinhardt, Meyerhold, Copeau, and

Granville-Barker. He must have an intimate knowledge of acting, of stage design in all its applications, of costuming, of lighting, and, above all, of human nature. He oversees and guides all areas of a theatrical presentation except the financial one. Many modern directors were at one time actors, as were Tyrone Guthrie and Elia Kazan. Ideally, a competent director should have had experience in all phases of theatrical activity. He need not have been a specialist in any one phase, but he must have a working knowledge of all. More than anything else, he must have a creative imagination which enables him to visualize an effective end product, and the energy and understanding to use the various elements of theatre in bodying forth his vision. With the emphasis upon specialization which has been characteristic of modern theatre, fewer and fewer individuals have excelled in more than one theatrical activity, and directing has, as we have said, become largely a distinct function.

Acting today is generally considered a respectable profession, and outstanding members are accorded respect and honor. The Queen's List in England is sure to include one or more actors each year. Russian artists, held second in respect only to scientists, are often given top awards for unique achievement. The family tradition has to some extent been maintained in the present century, with the Barrymores,

188 *Masks in modern theatre*
Oedipus Rex at the Shakespearean Festival Theatre in Ontario, Canada. Here is a modern example of the use of masks: one of the theatre's oldest devices. They add to the cosmic emphasis of the plays in which they are used.
(Theatre Collection, New York Public Library)

189 *Two college productions*
Left, The Hunter College Theatre Workshop production of *The Prodigal*. For this production, a large forestage was erected beyond the conventional proscenium arch to cover the orchestra pit; particular attention was given to making all elements work to produce a unified whole. Right, a production at the Baylor University Theatre, where the stage is built with generous side aprons and the seats can swivel to face in different directions. (Baylor University)

the Skinners, the Chaplins, and the Perkins in America, and the descendants of Tom Robertson, Ellen Terry, and Beerbohm-Tree in England. Husband-and-wife teams have also been popular—the Lunts, the Harrisons, the Oliviers, the Cronyns. But individual talents have shown brightly as well—Barrault, Jouvet, Jourdain, Gielgud, Katherine Cornell, Helen Hayes, Judith Anderson, Laurette Taylor, Maude Adams, Jane Cowl, Margaret Rutherford, Dame Sybil Thorndike, and many, many more than we can possibly name here. Many theatre-trained actors have, from time to time, deserted to the moving pictures either temporarily or permanently, yet each new season brings its new star.

People who observe the uncertain and often frustrating careers of actors in the United States frequently voice a longing for the subsidized standing repertory companies which are typical of practically all other countries of the Western world. From the aspect of continuity of employment and job security, these subsidized houses are certainly desirable. Yet, in many such houses, assignment of parts goes chiefly by seniority with the choicest roles being played by the senior members. Thus there might often be seen an old, fat actress essaying Juliet to a Romeo long past his prime. In such a system it is hard for a young actor to be assigned the parts for which his age best suits him, or indeed of having any sizeable part until his years have made him less desirable for many of them. The very security of the subsidized actor's position may also tend to dull his energy and application to work. Actually, the best system is no doubt a dual one, a combination of the free enterprise that prevails in America, with a backbone of

487

tax-supported houses such as exist elsewhere. Such a system is, indeed, in operation in London, Paris, Munich, Milan, and other large cities of Europe, where state-supported and private enterprise houses exist side by side. The generally admired performances of actors from these places seem to bear out the effectiveness of the arrangement. But there will have to be a wonderful and widespread revolution in thought before such a system can become current in America.

Summary

Though theatre remained to a large extent a big business in the twentieth century, it did present some heartening innovations. Production became an art, with special fields for scene, costume, and lighting design, and practicing artists in each received due credit for their work. Acting profited by new impulses, and new methods of working were developed. Directing, too, rose to the level of an art, with separate, and sometimes overriding credit. Plays are now often said to be done by a particular director rather than, as for so long, by a particular star. Playwriting became highly diversified, with many outstanding names. For the first time in theatre history American dramatic writing dominated the world scene. New and interesting production styles were tried: Expressionism, Surrealism, Constructivism, epic theatre, arena staging, and a host of less well-defined techniques appeared. There were many reforms in theatre architecture, which effectively eliminated the old opera-type house in new construction, and stressed the development of flexibility in theatre interiors, coupled with adequate working space.

Most significant of all, however, was the increasingly widespread interest and participation in theatrical activity, even though motion pictures and television claimed the major share of public attention for varying periods. With the evident widespread activity in amateur and community theatres, it might be supposed that more people were participating behind the footlights, on the whole, than were sitting before them in the professional theatre. And though our interest here has been, perforce, chiefly in the professional theatre, an educated and appreciative audience is a fundamental for good theatre anywhere, anytime, and we can only hope that the current enthusiasm will further the health of that fabulous invalid—the professional stage.

18

SUMMING UP

So contemporary is the art of theatre that it must often seem a rootless phenomenon to the new audiences of the present day. But the present grows out of the past; "the past is prologue." Excepting poetry itself, the drama is man's oldest artistic statement. Acting, in one form or another, goes back to the very roots of civilization.

Theatre is an eclectic art form. It selects from literature, from music, from dance, from the spoken word, from architecture, from sculpture, and from painting elements which, when combined, make a new creation. In its long-lived and widespread manifestations, theatre has from time to time stressed one or the other of these elements. It has existed without literature, without the spoken word, without the graphic arts. Pantomime has flourished; pure declamation triumphed. But in its greatest periods and its finest productions, it has shown a judicious selection and artistic arrangement of most of these elements.

Whatever the selection and arrangement of theatre's artistic components, two literal and practical elements have been everywhere and at all times present in theatre—the actor and the audience. Theatre has always been the most social of all the arts and cannot exist without this actor-audience relationship and communication. The function of the actor may be circumscribed, enhanced, or supplemented by text, playhouse, setting, costuming—by any and all of the elements of theatre that have from time to time been borne in upon his art. The audience may be influenced by edicts, mores, customs, intellectual and emotional atmospheres. But the interaction of audience and actor is always present. Sometimes the actor gives the audience what he thinks it wants, sometimes what he thinks it should have. In the final analysis, however, the audience determines the theatre. Whether it be the wondering astonishment of the primitive at his campfire, the omnivorous curiosity of the virile Elizabethan, or the elegant detachment of a Louis XIV courtier, the composition, desires, and capacities of the spectators have always determined not only the performance of the actor, but practically all other aspects of theatre as well.

Neither the actor nor the audience can ever be eliminated from theatre. Gordon Craig tried to eliminate the former; various misinterpreters of Stanislavski the latter. Neither has been successful nor ever will be. All other attributes of theatre may bloom, decay, and die, but theatre itself will never die so long as there are people to act and people to watch and listen.

Theatre arts highly responsive to social context

Because theatre is so much "by the people, for the people," it is also very much "of the people." There is hardly any other cultural manifestation that so fully and accurately reflects the society in which it appears. Classic Greek theatre reflected the humanist society of ancient Athens, with its concern for the struggle of man against fate. Medieval theatre, as did medieval society, emphasized the anonymity of mankind and the supreme importance of the next world over this. Renaissance theatre, like Renaissance society, revived attention to the joys and sorrows of the present world and stressed the transcendent possibilities of the individual human being. Even the rationalism of the eighteenth century, the scientific interests of the nineteenth, and (shall we say?) the fragmentation of the twentieth, have been mirrored in theatre of each age.

Just as theatre exhibits the changes in prevalent ideas, so too does it exhibit more particular responses to smaller segments of society. Primitive drama everywhere deals with fundamental matters of life and death—insuring and increasing the food supply, and overcoming enemies, natural and human. It was often, also, a vital supplement to an inadequate spoken language.

The spoken language generally becomes a part of civilized theatre, but never displaces the need for action, except perhaps in the more highly intellectualized dramas of such a one as Bernard Shaw. The combination of word and action which we recognize as a performance, then, characterizes the society which produces it. The Greek concern for philosophical argument, the medieval interest in theology, the Renaissance emphasis on Humanism, Eastern detachment and abstraction are reflected in theatre in these times and places. More modern drama will illustrate the emotion and artistry of the Italians, the analysis, criticism, and turbulence of the Germans, the dark sensuality of the Russians, the rationalism and codification of the French, the social consciousness of the Scandinavians, the virility and maturity of the English, the assimilative faculty and the fierce individualism of the American. The student of world theatre will find specific illustrations for all of these.

The progress of theatre through the history of civilization has been interesting to observe. Primitive theatre involved all members of society because it had a serious and vital function to perform. In classic Greece and in medieval times, there was also wide participation because theatre served a religious purpose. As the religious purpose declined and died, theatre more and more operated on the pleasure principle. (We must talk here of the fundamental impetus, for it is obvious that theatre for pleasure is almost as old as theatre for worship, and religious drama has never wholly died.) With the ascendency of the idea of theatre as entertainment, audiences were fragmented along class lines, and the type of theatre predominant in a particular period depended upon the ascendency of a particular class. Molière's theatre was of the court of Louis XIV; Soviet Socialist Realism now dominates the Russian theatre. The predominantly nonliterary theatres of the eighteenth and nineteenth centuries catered to a rising but predominantly uncultivated middle class. In the great periods of English and Spanish drama, a virulent and proudly flamboyant nationalism replaced the religious zeal of earlier times, and so produced an interclass theatre of wide participation.

But the conflict of theatre as entertainment and theatre with a purpose has never been fully resolved and probably never will be. The succeeding waves of social-import plays, of propaganda productions, of heavily intellectualized drama, of various old and new subversions of theatre to sales techniques, illustrate the continuing struggle. Theatre is constantly being rescued from the marketplace, turned into a forum, subverted to didactic purposes, and then purified. It has been all things to all people in many times and places.

We have seen that the greatest periods of theatre arose in those times and places where individual societies were most conspicuously true to themselves, where the theatrical achievement was based not on copies or adaptations of foreign materials but upon indigenous cultural patterns and respect for the society's own cultural inheritance. The maintenance of an individual identity has always and everywhere been concomitant with great theatre. So in the present day, and for the future, we may hope that theatre in the various nations of the world will truly reflect their societies and will be an instrument whereby various cultures may come to know and to appreciate each other better and more fully. Just as in the past theatre at various times transcended national boundaries, so may we hope that it will do so in the present and in the future. Not that we would insist that such a phenomenon be the imposition of one culture upon another, as we have seen the Western world largely submerge the dramatic art of India for instance, but rather that theatre be a means for enlarging our understanding of the many excellent attributes of differing cultures each of which maintains its individuality. In the current enthusiasm for cultural exchange, theatre must play an ever larger part.

Only great plays afford great theatre

Western civilization has long been convinced of the power of the written word. This conviction has been evident in theatre by a too prevalent judgment that whatever is unliterary is poor theatre. The written word, by its very nature is more durable than people or things. So it is only natural that we come to judge the worth of past theatres by the literature (in its broadest meaning) that represents it. On what other basis *can* we judge? How can we resurrect the total theatrical production of ages gone? We can collect the fragments of ephemera that composed it; we can try to fit them together. But can we ever bring them to the life they once knew? It is a fascinating but often ill-starred venture.

The written words of theatre, the plays, either become literature after they have outlived the contemporaries to whom they originally spoke, or else nobody bothers to read them any more. They become literature when they have something to say which succeeding cultures will not willingly let die. But viewing the inundation of words which has passed over the world's stages since the beginning, one is forced to acknowledge that these enduring words are indeed a very small portion of the whole.

If our study of theatre has taught us anything, it must be that what is written down as playscript is not the only aspect of theatre worthy of attention. On the other hand, it is undoubtedly true that ideas are, and always have been, the most important things in the world. So we are not far wrong when we nominate as having great theatre those times and places where the play in its best and most universal statement was accorded a production worthy of it.

It is true that there have been more gaps in the writing of good dramatic literature than there have been lapses in good entertainment. A great play is the product of a single creative genius, while a great show may result from the amalgamation of many small talents. There have been far fewer great plays in the history of theatre than there have been great shows. But the greatest shows of them all, in the final analysis, have been those that began with a great play— *Oedipus Rex, Hamlet, The Sea Gull, Mourning Becomes Electra.*

As one surveys the wealth of dramatic literature which is the heritage of the Western world, one is struck with the fact that those accorded the highest degree of honor are the tragedies. Most people admire Molière tremendously, are charmed by the cleverness of Oscar Wilde, are fascinated by Bernard Shaw, but rarely admit that these are as great as Shakespeare, Sophocles, Chekhov, or O'Neill. The Orientals, of course, do not agree with us. For them, the refinement of sentiment is to be desired over the purging of emotions which we consider an essential part of tragedy. Western cultures have always been devoted to this idea. Even in that most rational of periods—the neoclassical—the great plays were motivated, like Racine's *Phèdre,* by emotion. Man is a rational being, of course, but he is far more greatly influenced by emotions than by reasoning. Hence the ascendency of tragedy in our esteem. Modern man is not alone in this estimation, for we have seen how in many periods of theatrical history the best comedy was second best to tragedy.

We have seen how analysis and criticism have both followed and led in the making of plays, how the clearcut and definite distinction between comedy and tragedy in the Classical era became blurred and inoperative in later periods. We have witnessed a proliferation of many types and kinds of plays. But we have also seen that the best plays, and the most enduring, have been those which were true to their purpose, which used the elements of dramatic writing (character, plot, scene) in such a manner that they were balanced and harmonious, and then had added to them that immeasurable and always mysterious quality of individual style and genius which set them apart from and above the bulk of writing with which they were surrounded.

Probably because it has been the most tangible and the most easily accessible of all the components of theatre, there has been no area of theatre history so thoroughly explored as its dramatic literature.

The greatness of the Greeks has been analyzed, and the effects of their subject matter and style traced down to the present day. The sources of Shakespeare have been rooted out, and the influence of his practices demonstrated in many lands and times. The applications of science in thought and technology have been pointed out in their effect upon the writing of drama. And the drama itself has been analyzed, by type, times without number. These type names are useful as a help in the understanding of individual plays, and critical theory does help in forming judgments on the ultimate worth of individual playwrights. The student of literature will be primarily interested in those plays which conform to Matthew Arnold's definition of literature as "the best that has been thought and said in all ages."

But more important to the student of theatre history is why these plays were written when they were, for what kind of audience, and for what kind of theatre. He will not then write off almost the whole of eighteenth- and nineteenth-century English and American theatre as being beneath notice, but will read with interest and understanding Bulwer-Lytton and Tom Robertson, Robert Montgomery Bird and Edward Sheldon as a part of the very interesting theatrical times in which they lived. And he will regard the rudimentary scenarios for the *commedia,* not as poor literature, but as the bases for one of the most interesting of all theatrical manifestations.

A place for actor and audience throughout history

In the wide history of theatre, the place for playing has been as varied as the types of drama. No more than an open space in the midst of the spectators was at first deemed necessary. The only thing essential was that these two constant elements in theatre—the actor and the audience—should each have their allotted space. The changes in the nature and relationship of these two spaces constitute the whole history of theatrical playhouses.

The problem has always been that all the spectators should see and hear what all the performers were doing and saying. The early Greeks had a natural solution to the problem. The hilly topography of the country allowed the playing space to be at the foot of a hill, and members of the audience could sit on the hill slope to watch in comfort. A standing audience was never characteristic of Greek theatre. When special edifices were constructed in early Greece the design followed that of the natural amphitheatre which had proved so eminently satisfactory.

In the lands to the west where the topography was different, the problem had to be solved in a different way. The Romans, with typ-

494

ical engineering ingenuity, built false hillsides for the spectators in their free-standing amphitheatres, though their raised stages were reminders of the pre-theatre-building era, when the sight and hearing problems were solved by having the actors perform on a platform raised in the midst of the spectators. For this was the universal solution to the actor-audience problem in all areas where the playing space could be found only in level country. Platform stages with standing audiences constituted a theatre in all places from England to Japan, at one period or another, except, as we have noted, in Greece. In India, and in the much-later and entirely derivative Russian theatre, where the first audiences were the nobility, seats were provided from the beginning.

As more or less permanent playing places were built, provisions for audiences began to be made along class lines. The honored and the wealthy were assigned to space especially arranged for their comfort and convenience, and were generally given seats. In the highly specialized court theatres, the monarch and his party had the central floor area to themselves, while the less favored members of the audience sat or stood about the perimeter; sometimes galleries were built for them. Thus did Louis XIII watch the Italian comedians at the Bourbon palace, and James I applaud the masques of Inigo Jones. Curiously enough, this is the essential arrangement of the Chinese teahouse theatre in its early form as well. For the wealthier and nobler members of the audience sat at tables on the ground floor, while the less respected members of society sat on benches in surrounding galleries. This is the essential arrangement of the modern playhouse, as well, for orchestra seats are the most expensive, and the less wealthy spectators are relegated to galleries where, however, they can observe not only the show on the stage, but also that in the audience space below them. With this arrangement, the stage is invariably elevated.

In the public playhouses, however, for a very long time, there were no seats at all on the ground floor, and the most desirable places were in the galleries. Such, of course, were Shakespeare's theatre, the Spanish corrals, the Italian opera house, and the successive homes of the Théâtre Français. Here, standees in the pit looked up to the raised stage, as well as to the seating spaces of the more affluent members of society. These surrounding galleries were, in time, compartmented into boxes for further distinguishing their occupants, and it is an interesting speculation, sometimes profered, that the lord's rooms of Shakespeare's playhouse developed into the proscenium boxes of a later era. The change to the present arrangement was a long time in coming. There was a standing pit in the Théâtre Français until 1782; there is still a special tier of boxes—a diamond horseshoe—in many an opera house and theatre today.

The shift in seating plan was influenced, to a large extent, by a growth in the size of theatres. In the immense edifices of Greece and Rome the choicest seats were those nearest the stage. As theatres in other parts of the world grew in size and complexity, the space nearest the stage began to be fitted out for the comfort of wealthier patrons, while the more ordinary citizens were relegated to the farther reaches of the house. So we have the introduction of various seating arrangements in the pit, and the improvement of sightlines for them by the sloping of the floor. This improvement, in turn, dispensed with the need for special boxes and they began to disappear.

The blurring of social-class lines was reflected in the playhouses by greater democratization of seating arrangements and the final discarding of the special box system in favor of a plan more like that of the Dionysian Theatre, but smaller. Since the introduction in 1876 by Wagner at his Festspielhaus of a boxless theatre, more and more theatre buildings have been constructed on this plan. It is interesting to note that this democratization generally took place in America earlier than it did in other Western countries. We know that there were only six boxes in Booth's 1869 theatre, while all other seating was "unspecialized."

Design in theatre interiors has also been influenced by the purpose for which the house was used. Was it to be an "auditorium" a place for *hearing*, or a "spectatorium," a place for *seeing*? The Italian opera-type house is primarily a place for hearing; the Roman-Greek-Festspielhaus-type, a place for seeing. Modern theatre architects feel that a playhouse must accommodate both functions; perhaps they will invent a new word to describe a place for both seeing and hearing. These two means of audience participation have concerned theatre builders from the start. Houses have been built large for spectacle, small for intimate drama; there have been platform stages, apron stages, and arena stages; and there have been all kinds of seating arrangements.

With the multiplication of types of drama and kinds of presentation since the Renaissance, theatre designers have been forced to ask of a particular theatre building what type of drama and what kind of presentation it was primarily to house, and plan accordingly. Today, when space and finances permit, the ideal theatre building includes a large house for the more spectacular presentations, and a smaller house for more intimate drama. This is the type of theatre

496

center built, for instance, for the Cleveland Playhouse, for the Hopkins Memorial Theatre, for the University of Iowa, and for the new theatre at Mannheim, Germany.

A solution to varying kinds of production problems in a single house has been proposed by such an architect as Walter Gropius, whose plan for a "total theatre" envisions a house in which arena, platform, and proscenium staging can alternate by shifting the seats and stage area in an elliptical edifice. It could, in addition, house opera, films, music, dance, sports, or meetings. A simpler flexible playing space was developed by Ralph Freund at the University of California in the 1940's by having movable seats and platforms to change seating and staging arrangements at will. This, of course, is a much smaller theater than that envisioned in the Gropius plan.

The ideal theatre building would allow for maximum flexibility in staging. It would provide that every member of the audience be given maximum opportunity to enjoy and to participate in the production. It would give the performers and technicians adequate and efficient working space. But it would not be so complicated that the machinery would overwhelm the production, with the play and the player being submerged by the mechanics. The ideal theatre has yet to be built.

Set design touches all the extremes

Just as the simple playing space of primitive drama became elaborated over the years to specialized and complicated theatre buildings, so, too, settings evolved. In the beginning, the only setting was the natural one provided by the playing space itself. Even the early plays of Aeschylus were without any planned scenic investiture. But the convenience of the actors dictated the necessity of providing space where they could retire when offstage and where costume changes could be made. The early Greek theatre put up its scene house, and the platform stages were equipped with a back curtain, or curtained space below the stage. The possibility of making the stage backing a part of the performance must early have been obvious, and stage decoration came into being.

The open-air performances of the Greek and Roman theatre dictated a convention of plays written to be performed as though in the streets, before palaces, or rows of houses. When dramatic exigencies demanded that the audience know what transpired indoors, machinery was invented for reveals. The architectural settings of the Renaissance, though built in roofed theatres, followed the conventions of the Classic age. The stage arrangements of Shakespeare's theatre

497

were a natural development from origins in the innyard productions, and also incorporated a convention for the revealing of supposedly indoor scenes. The simultaneous settings of the Middle Ages, demanded by the epic character of the plays produced, gave way in succeeding periods to the practice of changing scenes as the play progressed.

The problem of the multiscene play was solved in two ways: the stage décor remained static and conventionalized, with changes indicated by small properties, by the actors, and by the script, as in Elizabethan and oriental theatres; or ways were invented of shifting the whole stage décor from scene to scene. The latter method became increasingly complex, reaching its apogee in France's Hall of Machines and its copyists through succeeding generations. Many were the plays written to show off the machinery of a particular stage— from Versailles to Drury Lane to Radio City Music Hall. And many originally nonmachine plays were mutilated to the same end. Fortunately for theatre, the cost of these installations was prohibitive for all but the largest and wealthiest houses. Smaller theatres had to be content with less costly installations.

The roofing in of theatres carried with it a problem contrary to that which designers of open-air theatres had faced. Now the outdoors had to be simulated. The architectural settings of the Renaissance with their forced symmetrical and angular perspectives, and the various wing systems painted like houses, castles, gardens, or woods were the answers. A deplorable persistence in the literalness of the stage picture, fostered by the insistence of unimaginative audiences and given impetus by the Realists, developed the box set and all kinds of technical proficiencies in transposing to the stage a factual picture of real life. The stage retreated behind the proscenium arch, and the audience became a large, collective peeping Tom.

But the essence of theatre lies in the participation of audiences. Those who watch and listen are not mere eavesdroppers. They must have their minds challenged and their imaginations stretched by an artistic representation to which they can bring something of their own. The too-realistic stage setting is its own worst enemy, and besides, the motion picture can do this sort of thing much better than the stage can. By its very nature theatre must ask that its audience "piece out our imperfections with your thoughts." And lucky it is that this is so. For thus theatre is freed from literalness to artistic theatricality, and can take all times, places, and ideas for its province, evoking whatever thought or emotion it chooses by a judicious selection of stage décor, lighting, and music.

In earlier times, stage designers largely gained fame when their productions outshone the plays and the players. Thus we remember the names of the Bibienas, Piranesi, Servandoni, Torelli, and Loutherbourg. But today we expect of the stage designer that whatever he does will enhance the play and the players. This conception is only as old as the twentieth century, and leaves room for all kinds and types of settings. There may be none at all but the bare stage itself, as in *Our Town* and *The Cave Dwellers*. There may be simple three-dimensional forms that can serve for many times and places. There may be absolutely realistic interiors. There may be fantastic or symbolic representations. All depends on the play to be served, and the director's idea of the presentation. The same play may be presented in a variety of ways, as Shakespeare has been given down through the years. But only the best of plays can be thus varied. The less universal dramas often dictate a specific style of presentation and are rendered less effective if forced into another mold. It is the modern director's obligation to find the right style for the script at hand, or to find a script that fits the production method available. Ideas about this fitness of design to play will vary, of course, but the success of the individual production will continue to be measured by the judgment of the discriminating playgoer as to whether or not the various theatrical components have been unified into a satisfactory and satisfying whole. The perfect scenic investiture for any given production is always hard to find—and there is always room for experiment in a growing theatre—but the impact of that perfection, once found, unmistakably makes truly great theatre.

Costume—the actor's prerequisite

Costume is as old as the actor in theatre. Primitive dance-dramas may have done without settings or specialized playing areas, but the performers donned masks, or painted their faces, and wore upon their bodies various items that would aid their characterizations. The performer who represented the desired quarry in a hunting dance arrayed himself in the appropriate skin or feathers. The Duk-Duk of New Guinea put a huge wickerwork superstructure over his head and shoulders to give him the imposing stature called for. Costume has been everywhere and in all times an aid to impersonation without which the very art of acting does not exist.

The mask which certainly aided the spectators in identifying characters, must early have been of immeasurable use in helping the largely nonprofessional actor to submerge his own personality and assume that of the character whom he was to represent. It is easy to see why masks are universal in primitive theatre. Certainly the highly professional actors of Greece, of the Orient, or of the *commedia* did not need masks for this reason, but the function of the mask in quickly identifying person and mood to the audience was as valid as ever. Combined, in each of these instances, with a specialized costume, the mask constituted a shorthand which made it unnecessary for the dramatist to spend time in lengthy character revelation or mood evocation. The masks and costumes did this work for him.

Even in the more realistic theatre to which western audiences have become accustomed, makeup and costume are aids to the characterization the actor is seeking, and help the audience to size up the person and the situation quickly. So, in a sense, the tradition of the mask is still with us.

Though stage costume has always been, to some extent, specialized and different from that of ordinary life, the idea of historical accuracy in the costuming of noncontemporary plays is of comparatively recent origin. Theatricality of stage costuming has been in existence since the beginning, but not until the eighteenth century were the first attempts made toward any real accuracy, and not until late in the nineteenth did the practice become more or less universal. Even today, when the principle of historical accuracy is accepted without question, the costume designer does not really construct an antiquarian outfit for the actor, but adapts line and detail to a modern physique, striving chiefly for the general effect of the earlier age.

Through long periods of western theatre history, the individual actor costumed himself as he saw fit with only the broad outlines to guide him: the *costume à la Turque,* the *costume à la Roman.* He generally strove to make himself as striking a figure as possible. Only in the present century, really, has the costume designer become a highly specialized and arduously trained theatre worker, planning every detail of every costume with an eye to its suitability and correctness not only for the actor who will wear it, but for the character's position in the play and the play as a whole. We may say of costume what we have said of scene design: that its present aim is to interpret and enhance the play, in accordance with the master plan of production as conceived by the director. Costumes may be fanciful or real, ornate or utterly simple. But they must fit the person and the production.

We are apt to smile now at a seventeenth-century Caesar in a full-bottomed wig, at an eighteenth-century Macbeth in scarlet coat and small-clothes, at his Lady in powdered wig and full paniers. Yet if all the actors in a given performance wear comparable costume,

500

where is the disharmony? We accept a *Julius Caesar* in modern military uniforms, a *Troilus and Cressida* in Edwardian dress. Unity is all. The really deplorable stage pictures must have been presented when such a fiercely determined actor as Talma dressed himself in a real Roman tunic while his colleagues on the stage wore their own ornate and traditional powder, curls, and laces. It needed the strong hand of a *régisseur* to straighten out such chaos, and it was the famous Duke of Saxe-Meiningen in the latter part of the nineteenth century who finally and firmly established fitness, unity, and authenticity in costuming.

Richness and splendor have long been a tradition in stage costuming. The Greek tragic actor, the Renaissance nymphs and shepherds, the characters of Shakespeare's plays, were as richly adorned as the patron's purse or the individual actor's finances would allow. Even today the splendor of oriental costuming fills the eye of the beholder, shining from a very sparsely furnished stage. And though we now want our actors costumed as fits their characters for the most part, we are still pleased with the richness of the costuming in *Ondine*, with the riot of colors in *Oklahoma*, with the delightful but unrealistic dash of the ballet.

Let us have interest and originality, we say, but let us also have unity of effect. That is, after all, the true artistry.

Acting the most ephemeral of arts

Of all the arts of theatre, acting is the most ephemeral. We can read that the Greeks made "done like Nicostratus" a high compliment for actors. We can learn of the honors heaped upon Roscius. But we really have no idea at all of what these actors looked like and how they performed. We can look at a picture of Adrienne Lecouvrier with her eyes cast soulfully upward, and wonder if this rather wooden pose is what her contemporaries applauded as acting from the heart. We can see the carefully posed figure of little David Garrick as his Lady Macbeth towers over him, and we wonder at the grace and power his viewers constantly spoke of. We can see the mustachioed, squarely-built figure of Edwin Forrest, looking slightly ridiculous in a knee-length costume for Spartacus, and wonder at the adulation paid him. We are inclined to be suspicious, as one might be of the reputation of a former movie idol like Rudolf Valentino. But we need only see a rerun of one of those old films, say *The Four Horsemen of the Apocalypse*, to realize that the style of acting is different, certainly, but the inevitable magnetism of the actor reaches across the years and their many changes and is delightfully satisfying to watch.

For styles of acting change, but the essential quality of great acting never changes. It is that indefinable quality which singles out an individual from the mass of his fellow-actors, makes his performances a joy to watch, and his person the object of respect and adoration. All great actors everywhere, and at all times, have possessed this quality—Isabella Andreini, Thomas Betterton, Frederick Schroeder, David Garrick, Ellen Terry, Tommaso Salvini, Sarah Bernhardt, Laurence Olivier. It is the seal of greatness, and the mark of those whom contemporary comment eulogizes.

As for the rest, there are only two types: good actors and poor actors. The good actors are those who by natural talent and constant application and discipline meet the challenge of impersonation imposed upon them by the plays in which they act, and who satisfy the feeling of the audience for the fitness of the whole. It has always been so. Poor actors are those who by unsuitability of talent and lack of discipline do not meet the challenge of their parts. There have always been many more actors unremembered than those whose names have reached history.

It is very true that Talma might not please a modern audience, that even "the divine Sarah" might well seem too flamboyant for us. But both of these, and all their myriad predecessors and contemporaries, worked in different theatre from ours, with different demands in the way of scripts, stages, and the tastes of audiences. They worked for theatre that they knew—and many of them were great in it.

Demands on actors have varied from age to age. Greek theatre and the *commedia* demanded performers skilled in dance and song as well as impersonation. French classical theatre wanted, above all, a sonorous and flexible voice. They were good actors who met these needs, poor who did not. Every change in dramatic material has required a change in acting style. The dignified declamation of heroic tragedy gave way to the extravagances of Romanticism. This in turn bowed before the rage for Realism and "natural acting." Now, as the force of Realism becomes spent, we are being once more concerned with style in acting. These changes have taken place all through history, and always will.

What we want in an actor—what audiences have always wanted —is that he should impel us to that state which Coleridge called "the willing suspension of disbelief." We want to believe in what he is doing, and we want him to believe in it, too. Even the hypercritical audiences of eighteenth-century France, who would hiss an actor if he missed a syllable in the difficult alexandrine verses, were no doubt disturbed because his lack of proficiency disrupted the perfection of a highly polished art. Our emphases are different today. We even subject Shakespeare to The Method, and let the verse go hang. But the principle is the same.

In the critiques of acting down through the centuries, we are always meeting with praise for performers who acted from the heart. We cannot interpret this statement in the totality of its meaning for the present day, for obviously the conventions of movement and gesture and intonation were tremendously different in times past, and we must read what is said about actors in the light of the theatre in which they worked. But we can generalize to the extent of saying that these highly praised actors, no matter what the methods by which they worked, achieved that synthesis of technique and spirit which satisfied their spectators. Thomas Betterton, we know, was called a superlative actor, free from rant and exaggeration, yet the rules he laid down for actors were much concerned with precise bodily gestures to convey specific impressions. Discipline has always been a part of good art. There is no easy road to stardom. The only requisite is that the finished performance should have the simplicity and rightness and sense of ease that are always present in a good art product.

Today the acting profession is much embroiled in a heated argument as to the starting point for characterization. Should the inward image, or soul, come first, and the outward manifestation follow? Or is the reverse procedure the correct one? The argument is not new. When Stanislavski first set down his famous six steps—wanting, seeking, experiencing, impersonating, blending, and influencing— he was simply codifying the progress of a universally good acting job. The urge to create a character, the finding of ways to do it, the using of past experiences to build emotional reserve, the application of these to the character to be played, the unification of all the component parts, the projection of the character to the audience—all of these, though not necessarily in that order, have ever been the hallmarks of good acting. Whether theatre is centered on the actor, as Stanislavski felt it should be, or on the director, as Meyerhold insisted, it is the actor who meets the audiences and who carries the burden of the play. His task is to be convincing to a particular audience in a particular time and place. Whatever method he uses to achieve this end is good and right.

The actor is, in the final analysis, a protean creature. Even today, when the cult of personality is probably at its height, we incline to place in a lower order of greatness those performers who bend each character to their individual traits when we compare them to those who can transform themselves to the image of the character they are representing. There is still something of an inscrutable mystery in this achievement. Actors are not ordinary mortals. They were emissaries of the divine Dionysus in ancient Greece, emissaries of the devil to the early Church. They were a despised caste in early Hindu times; honored performers in the *Noh* drama of Japan. Their fortunes have risen and fallen and risen again. Though their "clouds of glory" may often have been considerably bedraggled, the glory somehow always attached to them, as it still does today.

With the audience, they are the only other absolute constant, from first to last, in theatre history. Reviled or glorified, they are one of the two elements that theatre can never be without. Their skill makes theatre, and without them there is no theatre.

Summary

Theatre has been always with us. As we look over what lies behind we may conclude that great theatre existed at different times in different places. The fifth century B.C. belonged to the Greeks, the fourth century A.D. to the Hindus, the thirteenth to the Chinese, the sixteenth to the English and the Spanish, the seventeenth to the French, the eighteenth to the Japanese, the nineteenth to the German and perhaps the Russian. The twentieth century seems to belong to the Americans, but it is yet early to tell. Great plays, great interpretations, and great audiences make great theatre. In all its long and varied history, theatre has had its rivals and its enemies. Yet it has never been totally eclipsed, and often it has been glorious. As an exceedingly demanding art form, it has always spoken for its age, and been an integral part of the society which produced it. Through a study of theatre in all its aspects one may learn, as in perhaps no other way, what the world of yesterday must have been. If we can use that study to help us understand the world of today, and to appreciate one of the most human and most social of all man's accomplishments—theatre itself —we will be adequately rewarded.

PLAY LIST

As basic material for the study of theatre, it is suggested that one or more plays in each of the groups below be read as the periods in which they were first produced are studied. For the plays which are more difficult to find, volumes including them are listed in the appropriate sections of the bibliography. For those which have been more universally printed, the sources are numerous enough to make a specific listing unnecessary.

Primitive and Classic Theatre
(chapters 1, 2, 3, 4)
Aeschylus: *Agamemnon*
Aristophanes: *The Birds, The Frogs*
Euripides: *Medea, Electra*
Menander: *The Girl from Samos*
Plautus: *Miles Gloriosus*
Sophocles: *Antigone, Oedipus Rex*
Terence: *Phormio*

The Middle Ages
(chapter 5)
The Brome Abraham and Isaac
The Chester Mystery Plays
Everyman
Heywood, John: *Johan, Johan*
Maistre Pierre Pathelin
Lyndsay, David: *Satire of the Three Estates*
The Second Shepherds Play (Wakefield Cycle)
The York Cycle of Mystery Plays

The Renaissance
(chapters 6, 7, 8)
Aretino: one of the dialogues in *Works*, vol. 1
Calderón: *Life is a Dream*
Dekker, Thomas: *The Shoemakers' Holiday*
Greene, Robert: *Friar Bacon and Friar Bungay*
Jonson, Ben: *The Alchemist, Volpone*
Kyd, Thomas: *The Spanish Tragedy*
Lope de Vega: *The Mayor of Zalamea, Madrid Steel*
Machiavelli, Niccolo: *Mandragola*
Massinger, Philip: *A New Way to Pay Old Debts*
Shakespeare, William: Any or all
Tasso: *Aminta*

The Seventeenth Century
(chapters 9, 10)
Congreve, William: *Love for Love, The Way of the World*
Corneille, Pierre: *Le Cid*
Dryden, John: *All for Love, or The World Well Lost*
Etherege, George: *The Man of Mode*
Farquhar, George: *The Beaux Stratgem*
Molière: *The Misanthrope, The Imaginary Invalid, Tartuffe*
Otway, Thomas: *Venice Preserved*
Racine, Jean: *Athalie, Esther, Phèdre*
Vanbrugh, John: *The Relapse*
Wycherley, William: *The Country Wife*

The Eighteenth Century
(chapters 11, 12)
Addison, Joseph: *Cato*
Beaumarchais: *The Barber of Seville, The Marriage of Figaro*
Cumberland, Richard: *The West Indian*
Goethe, Johann Wolfgang von: *Faust, Part I*
Goldoni, Carlo: *The Mistress of the Inn*
Goldsmith, Oliver: *She Stoops to Conquer*
Gozzi, Carlo: *The Three Oranges*
Lessing, G. E.: *Minna von Barnhelm*
Lillo, George: *The London Merchant, or, The History of George Barnwell*
Sheridan, Richard Brinsley: *School for Scandal*
Steele, Richard: *The Conscious Lovers*
Voltaire: *Zaïre*

Oriental Theatre
(chapter 13)
A *Bunraku* Play
A *Kabuki* Play
A *Noh* Play
Hsiung, H. I.: *Lady Precious Stream*
The Little Clay Cart
Sakuntala

The Nineteenth Century
(chapters 14, 15)
Bird, Robert Montgomery: *The Broker of Bogotá*
Boker, George Henry: *Francesca da Rimini*
Bulwer-Lytton, Edward: *Richelieu, The Lady of Lyons*
Dumas, Alexandre (fils): *The Lady of the Camelias*
Gogol, Nikolai: *The Inspector General*
Herne, James A.: *Margaret Fleming*

Hugo, Victor: *Hernani*
Rostand, Edmond: *Cyrano de Bergerac*
Schiller, J. F.: *Maria Stuart*
Stowe, Harriet Beecher: *Uncle Tom's Cabin*
Turgeniev, Ivan: *A Month in the Country*
Wilde, Oscar: *The Importance of Being Earnest, Lady Windermere's Fan*

Modern Theatre
(chapters 16, 17)

Benavente, Jacinto: *The Bonds of Interest*
Capek, Karel: *R. U. R.*
Chekhov, Anton: *The Seagull, Uncle Vanya*
Coward, Noël: *Tonight at 8:30*
Fry, Christopher: *The Lady's Not for Burning*
Garcia Lorca, Federico: *The House of Bernarda Alba, Yerma*
Giraudoux, Jean: *Tiger at the Gates*
Ibsen, Henrik: *A Doll's House, Hedda Gabler*
Inge, William: *Come Back, Little Sheba*
Katayev, Valentine: *Squaring the Circle*
O'Neill, Eugene: *Marco Millions, Mourning Becomes Electra*
Pinero, Sir Arthur Wing: *The Second Mrs. Tanqueray*
Pirandello, Luigi: *Six Characters in Search of an Author*
Rice, Elmer: *The Adding Machine*
Shaw, Bernard: *Pygmalion, Heartbreak House*
Wilder, Thornton: *Our Town, The Skin of Our Teeth*
Williams, Tennessee: *The Glass Menagerie, Summer and Smoke*

SUGGESTED STUDY PROBLEMS

The following are suggested as types of work problems which may help students to develop familiarity with the milieu of theatre in many times and places. At the same time they may, through such exercises, consolidate and put to use a mass of information which might not otherwise

come to life. It is also hoped that the problems may stimulate creative imagination. The individual instructor will no doubt think of many more.

Primitive and Classic Theatre
(chapters 1, 2, 3, 4)

1 Write a brief scenario for any one of the American Indian dance-dramas.
2 Pretend that you are I-kher-nefert writing of what you plan to do in your production of the Abydos Passion Play in the year 1868 B.C.
3 Draw up a "character plot" for the play you read, assigning the chief actors to roles, and indicating where supernumeraries appear on stage.
4 For the play you read, draw up a complete prop list for the production as given in its contemporary theatre.
5 Make a stage diagram for the first production of the play you read.
6 Discuss, giving examples, the changing functions of the chorus in three Greek plays.
7 Sketch the wardrobes of the chief actors in *Medea*, including masks.
8 Classify the characters by type in *Miles Gloriosus*, and briefly describe each type.

The Middle Ages
(chapter 5)

1 Imagine yourself an eyewitness to the production of an interlude in the Middle Ages. Give an account of it.
2 Describe the stage setting for a fifteenth century French mystery play.
3 Draw up a descriptive list of costumes for the play you read.
4 Draw a detailed sketch and plan of a pageant wagon for a particular mystery play production. Indicate the production.
5 Imagine yourself a participant in the Feast of Fools. Describe the event.
6 Write a plot outline for a morality, including a list of the characters and a brief description of each character.

The Renaissance
(chapters 6, 7, 8)

1 You are a *commedia* producer. Draw up a scenario for your company as a production for a large fair in a country town.
2 You are present at the opening of the Teatro Olimpico. Describe the event.

3 You are an Italian nobleman planning a pastoral for your garden theatre. Write a letter to the person you have chosen to produce it, explaining what you want.

4 You are a knowledgeable Spanish gentleman who has just seen a Lope de Vega play in a public theatre. Write a critique.

5 You are a contemporary of Calderón and think him superior to Lope de Vega. Write a defense of your point of view.

6 Draw up a seating chart and scale of prices for (a) a private theatre, and (b) a public playhouse, *circa* 1600 in England.

7 Suppose yourself the casting director for the play you read. Draw up a list of requirements—physical and histrionic—for persons you will audition for each role.

8 For each character in the play you read, draw up a list of costume items and hand props for production in their contemporary theatre. For this problem use either the Dekker or a Jonson play.

9 Explain, with diagrams, how the special effects are to be achieved in *Friar Bacon and Friar Bungay*.

10 Suppose yourself a contemporary. You have just seen a performance of the play you read, and you write a letter to a friend in Italy describing your experience.

The Seventeenth Century
(chapters 9, 10)

1 As a member of the Académie Française, write a paper condemning the performance of *The Cid*, which you have just seen.

2 As Madame de Maintenon, write a letter to Racine, requesting him to compose a play for St. Cyr. Detail exactly what you want.

3 For a court performance of *The Misanthrope*, draw up descriptive program notes, including the spectacular and ballet presentations between the acts.

4 As a contemporary of Dryden, point out his superiority over Shakespeare in his dramatization of the story of Antony and Cleopatra.

5 Draw up a cue sheet for scene shifting in Congreve's *Love for Love* or for *The Way of the World*, giving pieces to be moved and scenes to be set or revealed.

6 You are a member of the court party attending an English Restoration play at the first Drury Lane. Describe your impressions of play and playhouse.

7 Draw up three sample playbills. Include at least one French one.

8 Draw up descriptive costume lists, including hand props, for two plays you read.

The Eighteenth Century
(chapters 11, 12)

1 Write an imaginary dialogue between Quin and Garrick on the subject of acting.

2 Write a defense of the prevailing method of costuming actresses in the eighteenth century.

3 Write a letter to Garrick, as manager, urging the use of the front curtain and/or act and scene drops.

4 Write a protest to the management of the Comédie Française on the behavior of the audience—of which you are a member.

5 Protest to Goldoni over his attempt to regularize the *commedia*.

6 As Gottsched, admire Addison's *Cato*.

7 As Voltaire, write an explanation to your cast of your views on acting.

8 You have just seen one of Mme. Favart's "authentic" plays. Write your reaction as a typical viewer.

Oriental Theatre
(chapter 13)

1 Write an imaginary introductory speech for the manager of an acting company in classic India, to precede the performance your company is presenting.

2 Draw up an imaginary edict for the establishment of the College of the Pear Garden.

3 Sketch the face makeup for the characters in a Chinese play.

4 Sketch the setting for a Kabuki play, using the revolving stage.

5 Write a description of the presentation of a Noh play in the palace of the Emperor.

The Nineteenth Century
(chapters 14, 15)

1 Make up a cue sheet for the claques you hire for a presentation at the Comédie Française.

2 Write a letter to Gogol from Moscow, urging him to return from his self-exile.

3 Congratulate Ibsen on his change to social drama from his earlier styles.

4 As a newspaper correspondent, write a dispatch for an American paper on a French theatre production starring Sarah Bernhardt.

5 As Wagner, write a defense of your design for the Festspielhaus at Bayreuth.

6 Sketch a stage set for a wing-flat and back-shutter presentation of the play you read.

7 As a typical member of the audience, write your reaction to the installation of gas lighting in the Chestnut Street Theatre in Philadelphia in 1816.

8 Write a dispatch to your American newspaper employer on the visit of the Meiningen to London in 1881.

9 As a German actor, write a letter to an English colleague, urging his adoption of the new grease-paint makeup.

10 As a contemporary, demonstrate Goethe's Classicism as compared with English Romanticism.

Modern Theatre
(chapters 16, 17)

1 As a United States Congressman in 1939, write a speech urging the withdrawal of funds from the Federal Theatre Project.

2 Draw up a floor plan and stage plot for a free theatre you are opening in 1900.

3 Lay out the design for the ideal theatre plant as you see it.

4 Draw up a list of stage and hand props for the play you read.

5 Make up a prospectus for the establishment of a permanent repertory company; plan that it can be used to solicit funds for the company.

6 Write an explanation for your decision to open a theatre specializing in arena staging.

7 Explain the ideal production style, including sets, lights, and costumes, for the play you read.

8 As a director, lay out the requirements for a play of your choice, which can function as a working plan for your costume designer.

9 Write an imaginary dialogue between two actors, one of whom is a Method actor, the other not.

10 Make up a course of study for present-day training in theatre arts.

GLOSSARY OF TERMS

Act-drop. A late eighteenth century term applied to the painted cloth which closed the proscenium opening between the acts of a play.

Adventurer. A term applied in the Restoration to an essentially non-theatrical person buying shares in theatrical companies.

Afterpiece. A term which came into use in the eighteenth century to designate that portion of a theatrical entertainment which followed the main presentation; usually a one-act farce.

Agonothetes (Gr.). The official who produced the plays presented at the drama festivals.

Alcaldes (Sp.). Mayors or magistrates.

Anapesmata (Gr.). Traps (*q.v.*).

Angel. Modern word for a person who supplies money to finance the production of a play.

Antagonist. A word coming from the Greek which designates the character in a play who opposes the protagonist or hero.

Apariencias (Sp.). Stage devices which allowed for the sudden appearance of characters.

Aposentos (Sp.). The boxes of the *corral* theatres, the highest priced accommodations.

Apron. That part of the stage which extends beyond the proscenium arch and the front curtain; sometimes called the forestage.

Arc Light. An especially intense and concentrated light source formed by passing an electric current between two rods of carbon; used first at the Paris Opera by M. J. Duboseq in 1846.

Arch border. See Border.

Archon (Gr.). Public official in ancient Greece who chose the plays and the leading players for the drama festivals.

Artificios (Sp.). "Tricks" or stage devices which were intended to surprise the audience.

Atellanae (Lat.). Improvised comedy on topical themes.

Author's night. Performance of a play from which the author received all the profits; comparable to the actors' benefits.

Autor de comedias (Sp.). A company manager in Spain's Golden Age.

Auto sacremental (Sp.). A church play; comparable to the French *mystère* and the English saint and cycle play.

Aufklärung (Ger.). Eighteenth-century German literary movement which upheld French neoclassicism as the model for playwriting.

Backcloth. The flat, painted canvas used generally with a wing-flat (*q.v.*) set to cover the area at the back of the scene; usually hung from the grid (*q.v.*).

Backing flat. A canvas-covered frame which is painted and set behind openings in the stage set to conceal the area beyond it.

Backstage. All the areas behind the scene set on the stage, including wings, dressing rooms, and so on.

Balcony. Applied, particularly in America, to the seating area above the ground floor or orchestra.

Ballad opera. A burlesque form developed in the eighteenth century which is characterized by songs written to popular tunes.

Ballet. A dramatic presentation in dance and mime to the accompaniment of music.

Barrel system. A method of moving scenery from below the stage level.

Batten. A pipe or rod suspended from the grid (*q.v.*) upon which can be hung lights or scenery.

Benefit. Traditionally, a performance given so that the profits may be assigned to a particular performer; in modern American theatre, a performance for which tickets are inflated in price, the profits going to some organization or cause.

Blues. A nineteenth century term for sky borders. *See* Borders.

Boards. A term originating from the wooden stage floor; "to tread the boards" is to act, to be "on the boards" is to be an actor.

Bookholder. The prompter in the Elizabethan theatre, who not only "held the book" during the performance, but saw that actors were ready for their entrances and gave them their props (*q.v.*).

Book-keeper. The person in the Elizabethan theatre who kept the manuscript copies of the plays, as well as the individual parts of the actors.

Border. A narrow strip of painted canvas which is fastened at the top edge only to a batten (*q.v.*) to hide the top of the stage as seen from the auditorium; an "arch border" is cut on the lower edge like an arch and painted to blend with side wings which it meets; a "tree border" is cut and painted like a tree; a "sky border" like clouds or sky (sometimes called "blues" or "cloudings").

Box set. An arrangement of flats on the stage forming three walls, with a ceiling overhead.

Box office. That portion of the theatre where tickets are sold; probably originating in the slotted box into which Elizabethan theatregoers put their penny for general admission.

Boxiganga (Sp.). A traveling company of actors in the Spanish Golden Age, consisting of six or seven men, two women, and a boy.

Brace. An extensible wooden stick used in a diagonal position to support flats on stage.

Breeches parts. Roles meant to be assigned to men but often played by women.

Bululu (Sp.). A lone player traveling on foot.

Bunraku (Jap.). The Japanese doll theatre.

Burlesque. Originally an exaggeration of word, action, or both, to point out absurdities; now often applied to a type of variety show which lays stress on the female form.

Buskin. British word for the Greek *kothurnos* (*q.v.*).

Cambaleo (Sp.). Company of traveling performers comprising five men and a woman.

Cantores (Lat.). The specialized performer who did all the singing required in a specific performance; another performer delivered the spoken words.

Capa y estapa (Sp.). "Cloak and sword" play founded upon intrigues, mistaken identities, and so forth.

Carros (Sp.). The wagons on which religious plays were given.

510

Catwalk. A narrow bridge suspended from the grid (*q.v.*) to enable stage-hands to reach various parts of the scenery and lighting hung in the flies above the stage.

Cavea (Lat.). The curved rows of seats for spectators in the Roman theatre.

Cazuela (Sp.). Literally "stew-pan"—applied to the section of the theatre assigned to unaccompanied women spectators.

Ceiling. A canvas-covered frame usually hinged to fold in half, used to cover the top of a box set.

Cellar. The area below the stage area, usually housing machinery employed for changing sets.

Chef d'emploi (Fr.). The leading actor in any specified line of parts.

Chiusetti (Ital.). Those portions of a *commedia* performance consisting of lyrical outbursts on the part of the performers.

Choregus (Gr.). Citizen of ancient Greece who bore all expenses for festival performances of plays, except for the salary of the leading actor who was paid by the state.

Chorus. In ancient Greece, the performers who sang and danced in the *orchestra*; now more generally applied only to groups who sing, although a group of performers who dance in musical plays is also referred to as a chorus.

Choreuti (Gr.). A member of the classic chorus.

Choryphaeus (Gr.). The leader of the chorus in classic drama.

Chronicle play. Term applied, especially in England, to plays based on historical events, such as those of Shakespeare on the English kings.

Circuit. Term applied in England to a group of provincial theatres visited at regular intervals by a company of players specifically constituted to do so.

Claque. A group of persons hired to applaud at specified times during a performance; originated in the Roman theatre.

Cloudings. Borders (*q.v.*) cut and painted to represent clouds.

Cofradias (Sp.). Philanthropic organizations which profited from theatrical activity in Spain's Golden Age.

Comedias (Sp.). Three-act plays on secular subjects.

Comedias a fantasia (Sp.). Full-length plays with romantic subject matter.

Comedias a noticia (Sp.). Full-length plays using realistic subject matter.

Comedias de cuerpo (Sp.). Full-length plays using historical, mythological, and legendary materials.

Compañia (Sp.). The largest of the Spanish traveling companies, consisting of from sixteen to thirty persons.

Compañias de parte (Sp.). Acting companies organized on the shareholding principle, as distinct from those with a proprietor and fixed salaries.

Compagnies des fous (Fr.) Medieval societies generally devoted to the performance of short secular plays.

Comisario de comedias (Sp.). Official charged with the licensing of plays for performance.

Commedia dell'arte (Ital.). Comedy which originated in the Italian Renaissance, largely improvised, using stock characters and masks.

Comoedus (Lat.). An actor specializing in the performance of comedy.

Confrérie (Fr.). Medieval term for an organization formed to produce religious plays.

Constructivism. Post-World War I movement in stage design which eschewed realism and concentrated on an arrangement of basic forms in space, with a view to enlarging freedom of movement for the actors.

Copiste (Fr.). The prompter, archivist, and copyist of the seventeenth-century French acting company.

Corral (Sp.). Originally a theatre formed by using the open space within a block of houses; later applied to theatres in general.

Corpus Christi Day. Designated by Pope Clement V in 1311 as the Thursday after Trinity Sunday (two months after Easter); became the traditional time for presenting the cycle plays in England.

Counterweight. System of compensating for the weight of flown scenery to expedite its movement on and off the stage.

Curtain. Fabric hung in folds in the proscenium opening to hide the stage from the audience; also often used to indicate the end of a performance in phrases such as "at the final curtain."

Curtain raiser. Term originating in the nineteenth century to indicate a short play given before the chief offering of the evening.

Cut cloth. Variously shaped borders (*q.v.*) particularly in Victorian theatre.

Cycle play. A series of Biblical plays as given during the Middle Ages.

Cyclorama. A curved canvas drop around the sides and back of the stage which is painted to look like sky, and which allows for the use of flies (*q.v.*).

Dalmatic. An ecclesiastical vestment, sometimes used as a costume in the medieval religious plays.

Décorateur (Fr.). The seventeenth-century theatre artisan who designed not only the stage sets but the interior of the house as well.

Deus ex machina (Lat.). Literally "god from the machine" derived from the practice in classic Greek theatre of having supernatural beings lowered to the stage by the *mechane;* now applied to any agency that inorganically effects the resolution of a drama.

Dimmer. A mechanical device which allows for varying intensities of light to be used on stage.

Director. In America, the theatre worker who supervises the preparation of the actors in their parts and is responsible for the unity of the production through consultation with designers and other theatre workers.

Disguising. Popular diversion of the Tudor court; generally a masked ball.

Dithyramb. In Ancient Greece, a chant or choral song detailing the exploits of a god or hero.

Downstage. That portion of the stage area closest to the audience.

Dress circle. Generally the first tier of boxes in a theatre interior with several tiers.

Drolls. Short dramatic pieces, or skits; usually bits from longer plays, given during the Commonwealth and early Restoration.

Drop. A piece of scenery, usually of painted canvas, suspended from a batten and having no stiles at the side, but with a rail top and bottom.

Duègnes (Fr.). Eighteenth-century term for old comic women characters.

Eccyclema (Gr.). Stage device in ancient Greece for revealing scenes purportedly transpiring indoors; a type of wagon (*q.v.*).

Emmelia (Gr.). Name of the dance movement used in classic tragedy.

Entremeses (Sp.). Short pieces accompanying longer works.

Epilogue. A speech, usually in verse, given by one of the actors after the conclusion of a play.

Episkenion (Gr.). The second story of the Greek theatre stage house, particularly in Hellenistic times.

Existentialism. A modern philosophical movement, particularly popular in French literary circles, which stresses personal decision in the face of a purposeless universe.

Expressionism. A movement originating about the time of World War I, which aimed at the artistic expression of emotional reactions rather than the representation of reality.

Fabula palliata (Lat.). A form of Roman comedy using Greek materials as subject matter.

Fabula togata (Lat.). A form of Roman comedy using Roman materials as subject matter.

Farce. A type of comedy in which the emphasis is upon situation rather than upon character; the action of the play is usually broad.

Fate tragedy. A German nineteenth-century dramatic form in which the plot is concerned with the operation of a curse.

Fastnachtsspiel (Ger.). Shrovetide play, mingling religious and popular elements.

Fescennine verses. A type of verse, originating in Etruria, comprised chiefly of marriage songs of a rather wanton nature, which remained popular with the Romans to the time of the Empire.

Festaiolo (Ital.). Medieval leader of a company of players.

Festoon drape. Term applied to a front curtain which is raised by drawing it up at particular spots to different heights so that portions of it remain visible and form a frame for the stage.

Feu (Fr.). The sum allotted to actors for lighting and heating their dressing rooms in the seventeenth-century French theatre.

Fiestas de los carros (Sp.). Those occasions upon which the *autos sacramentales* (*q.v.*) were given.

Flat. A canvas-covered frame, usually rectangular in shape and painted, used in multiples for setting the scene on stage.

Flies. The area above the stage, out of the view of the audience, where scenery may be stored or lifted from the stage area.

Fleshings. A type of leg covering popular in the pastoral dramas of the Italian Renaissance to give better form and color to actors' legs; used occasionally for the same purpose today.

Folk play. Type of presentation popular in the Middle Ages; subject matter was largely drawn from legendary materials.

Follow spot. A concentrated beam light operated so that it will constantly frame a particular performer as he moves about the stage.

Footlights. Strips of lights in the floor at the edge of the stage apron, popular from the time of the Restoration but infrequently used in modern theatre.

Forestage. Another term for apron (*q.v.*).

Front of house. A term applied to all of the areas of a theatre ordinarily assigned to the audience, as distinguished from backstage (*q.v.*).

Frons scaena (Lat.). The elaborately decorated wall of the stage house in the Roman theatre.

Gallery. The name usually given to the seating area placed nearest the roof in a theatre and thus farthest from the stage, containing the least expensive seats.

Gangarilla (Sp.). Traveling company consisting of three men and a boy to play the women's parts.

Garnacha (Sp.). Type of traveling company consisting of five to six men, one woman, and a boy.

Gauze. A drop (*q.v.*) of scrim cloth or bobbinet which appears opaque when lit from in front, but practically transparent when lit from behind; it is used for special effects.

Gas table. The device behind the scenes by which a technician controlled the amount and intensity of the stage and house lights during the days when theatres were lit by gas.

Gestes. The songs sung by the minstrels of the Middle Ages.

Giggue. Sometimes *jig.* An impromptu closing given by one or more of the actors after the play in the days of Shakespeare.

Gleeman. The teller of tales and singer of songs in Anglo-Saxon England; usually itinerant.

Gods. A term dating from the eighteenth century applied to the occupants of the upper gallery probably because they were certainly nearest Heaven.

Goliard. A wandering scholar or clerk of the Middle Ages.

Gracioso (Sp.). Literally "farcical actor"; the name given to the comic servant character in the drama of the Golden Age.

Gradas (Sp.). The backless benches along the sides of the pit in the *corral* theatres of Spain.

Green room. The social room for performers behind the scenes; probably so called because it was usually hung or painted in green.

Grid. The open framework above the stage from which battens (*q.v.*) and so forth are suspended.

Grooves. The tracks, on the stage floor and overhead, upon which wing flats (*q.v.*) are moved; usually more than one in a given spot.

Ground row. A long, low piece of scenery used across the bottom of the stage at the back, usually hiding special lighting equipment.

Hand props. The small, necessary objects carried on or off the stage by the actors in the course of performance.

Hanswurst. Popular character on the German stage in the seventeenth and eighteenth centuries; a clown type.

Haupt-und-Staatsaktionen (Ger.). A type of seventeenth-century play dealing with events in high places, and usually including a Hanswurst as one of the characters.

Heroic drama. A term sometimes applied to English neoclassical tragedy of the late seventeenth century.

Heroic feathers. Feathers worn on the headdresses of actors and actresses to denote dignity and high station in life;

513

customary for almost a century from Restoration times on.

Hireling. An Elizabethan theatre worker who was paid a set fee, and was not a shareholder in the acting company.

Histriones (Lat.). Actors.

Housekeeper. A person in Elizabethan theatre who, singly or with others, owned and received the income from the theatre buildings themselves, as distinct from the sharers.

Humanism. The Renaissance movement which pursued and disseminated the study of Greek and Roman cultures.

Hyposcenium (Lat.). The front wall of the raised stage in the Roman theatre.

Hypokrites (Gr.). Actor.

Impressionism. An early twentieth-century movement in literature which emphasized the immediate effect of actions or objects with little attention to detail; also a movement in painting and in music.

Infami (Lat.). A term applied to actors to indicate that they were without civil rights in ancient Rome.

Ingénue. The stage role of a young woman, usually naive; the actress who plays such a role.

Inner stage. A portion of the area at the back of the stage which can be cut off from the rest by curtains or flats and can be revealed for a change of locale or specialized setting.

Inset. A small scene set behind an opening in a larger scene.

Interlude. The medieval and early Renaissance English name for a short dramatic sketch.

Intermezzi (Ital.) The fifteenth and sixteenth-century name for interpolations of a light character performed between the acts of serious drama or opera.

Invenciones (Sp.). Contrivances or trick work in stage presentations of the Golden Age.

Jácara (Sp.). A ballad set to music and used as a part of a theatrical entertainment in the seventeenth century.

Jig. *See* Giggue.

Jongleur (Fr.). Medieval word for a traveling juggler or trickster.

Juglares (Sp.). The same performer, in Spain.

Juvenile. A stage role for a youthful male; the actor who performs such a part.

Kabuki (Jap.) Popular type of Japanese theatre, usually emphasizing violent action and using more scenery than the classic Noh drama (*q.v.*).

King's box. Special seating area for the King and his party, particularly in Restoration theatre, immediately opposite center stage in the first tier of boxes.

Kiva. Special hut or house, erected in multiples by the Hopi Indians, for the drama of the Great Serpent.

Kordax (Gr.). The dance form associated with classic comedy.

Kothurnos (Gr.) The thick-soled boot of the actor in classic tragedy.

Kyogen (Jap.). Short sketches given as comic interludes in Noh theatre.

Lazzi (Ital.). Bits of comic business, or action, used by the performers in the *commedia dell'arte* (*q.v.*).

Liberties. In Elizabethan England, the sites of former church holdings, now the property of the Crown, not subject to municipal ordinances.

Libretto (*pl.*: libretti). The words or text of an extended musical composition; the book which contains such text.

Liencos (Sp.). The painted canvas set pieces of the stage in the Golden Age.

Limelight. An intense illumination produced by heating a cylinder of lime to incandescence with gas, developed in the nineteenth century; by extension, a position of prominence occupied by a performer, who is said to be "in the limelight."

Lines. The words assigned to a particular actor in a given performance.

Loa (Sp.). The prologue, or compliment to the audience, which preceded early Spanish theatrical productions.

Ludi Romani (Lat.). The Roman games, or festivals, which included dramatic performances.

Machiniste (Fr.). Seventeenth-century theatre worker who produced the scenery; now a scene shifter.

Maître des feyntes (Fr.). Medieval term for the artisan who designed and supervised stage effects, chiefly in the religious plays.

Manteaux (Fr..) Eighteenth-century word for the roles of old comic men.

Mastaba. Ancient Egyptian tomb with sloping sides and a flat roof.

Mask, masque. As an object, a face covering as varied and as old as theatre itself; as an entertainment, a presentation stressing spectacle and music.

Mechane (Gr.). A classic Greek stage device for lowering personages from above the stage.

Melodrama. A type of drama stressing a succession of improbable incidents, chiefly one-dimensional characters.

Method, The. An American term for a system of acting, based on the teachings of Stanislavski, stressing inner truth.

Mime. Type of theatrical entertainment in Roman times consisting of short dramatic sketches marked by buffoonery and jesting.

Minstrel. Traveling singer of gestes (*q.v.*) in medieval times.

Miracle play. Medieval plays concerned chiefly with the lives of the saints.

Moralité (Fr.). A didactic play, flourishing in the fourteenth and fifteenth centuries, which used allegorical characters.

Morality play. English term for the above.

Mosqueteros (Sp.). Literally, "musketeers"; applied generally to the men in the standing pit of seventeenth-century Spanish theatres.

Multiple setting. A type of stage setting where more than one locality is represented on the stage at the same time; sometimes called "simultaneous setting."

Musico (Sp.). In the Golden Age, that member of an acting company particularly hired to play a musical instrument.

Mystery play. Another name for the cycle plays with Biblical subject matter.

Nachspiel (Ger.). Eighteenth-century farce.

Naturalism. A literary movement of the late nineteenth century which stressed the presentation of persons and objects as nearly as possible in their ordinary, everyday forms.

Naumachia (Lat.). In Roman times, a simulated sea battle in a flooded colosseum or theatre orchestra; in Renaissance times, a water carnival.

Narr (Ger.). The medieval fool.

Neoclassic. Literary movement, chiefly of the seventeenth century, which stressed adherence to classical forms and materials.

Noh (Jap.). Classic Japanese drama dealing with historical or religious materials, played with masks on a particularly constructed stage.

Numberer. Theatre official of the Restoration charged with seeing that spectators paid the appropriate admission for whatever portions of the evening's entertainment they witnessed.

Nursery. School instituted for the training of actors in the Restoration.

Off stage. Towards or beyond the limits of the visible set on stage.

Ombres Chinoises (Fr.). A type of shadow show adapted from oriental practice, and popular in the eighteenth century.

Onkos (Gr.). The raised, dome-shaped top of the actor's mask.

Onnagata (Jap.). Female role, played by a male.

On stage. The term used to indicate a position in view of the audience.

Opèra bouffe (Fr.). Comic opera of a farcical nature.

Opèra comique (Fr.). Comic opera.

Orator. Manager of a seventeenth-century French acting company, who made a speech at the end of a performance announcing the next presentation.

Orchestra. Originally (Gr.), the dancing circle for the chorus in the classic theatre; by extension, the ground floor of present-day theatres.

Ozones. Strips of blue cloth hung from battens and used for sky in stage settings.

Pageant. In medieval England, the wagon on which the plays of the cycles were presented.

Palais a volontè (Fr.). An unlocalized stage setting of palace and temple in eighteenth-century theatre.

Pantomime. In Roman times, a type of theatrical presentation in which a chorus sang and actors mimed tragedies and love stories; in later times, a type of stage presentation with elaborate sets and music in which there is no speaking of lines.

Patent houses. Term applied to the theatres of the Restoration which operated by special license from the Crown.

Parados (Gr., *pl.: parudoi*). The passageway between the scene house and the rows of seats in the ancient Greek theatre used by both chorus and audience.

Paraskenia (Gr.). Projecting wings at either side of the stage in the ancient Greek theatre.

Paso (Sp.). One-act comedy of the seventeenth century.

Pastoral. Type of theatrical presentation, originating in the Italian Renaissance, giving an idyllic and artificial representation of country life.

Patio. The inner court of a house, open to the sky, early used in the south of Spain for theatrical performances.

Periaktos (Gr., *pl.: periaktoi*). Three-sided set pieces used at either side of the stage in the early Greek theatre; they could be rotated.

Pièces à machines (Fr.). Theatrical presentations of the seventeenth-century, written and produced primarily to show the wonders of stage machinery.

Pièces rosses (Fr.). In the late nineteenth century, plays dealing with unpleasant or ugly aspects of life.

Pinakes (Gr.). Painted screens used between the columns fronting the raised stage of the Hellenistic period.

Pit. The ground-floor standing room area of the Elizabethan theatre; now sometimes still used to designate comparable areas in modern theatres.

Platea (Lat.). The unlocalized acting area of the medieval multiple setting.

Platform stage. Generally, a stage arrangement whereby the acting area is not behind the proscenium arch, as in the Elizabethan theatre.

Portae minores (Lat.). The smaller doorways flanking the great central door in the Roman theatre; generally four in number.

Porta regis (Lat.). The great central doorway on the stage of the Roman theatre.

Praetextae (Lat.). Plays of the Roman theatre using history as subject matter.

Premier garçon du théâtre (Fr.). Seventeenth-century theatre functionary who performed the duties of stage manager.

Proagon (Gr.). In early Greek times, a presentation by the performers and playwright a few days before a festival performance, designed to arouse interest in the forthcoming production.

Producer. In England, generally, the person responsible for the staging of a play; in America, the individual who raises the money for production and oversees all details both artistic and financial.

Prologue. An introductory speech, often in verse, given at the beginning of a play, which generally calls attention to the theme of the play.

Prompt. To supply an actor with his cue or his line if he has forgotten it.

Prompter. One who holds the book of the play and prompts.

Prompt box, prompt corner. Positions from which prompting is done.

Property room. Storage space for stage props.

Props. All objects on stage exclusive of scenery. *See also* Hand props.

Proscenium. Literally, "before the scene"; the frame or arch which encloses the stage area behind which is hung the front curtain.

Protagonist. The leading character in a play; first used as a designation in classic Greek theatre.

Pulpitum (Lat.). A raised platform for actors in early Roman times.

Pundonor (Sp.). "Point of honor"; principal emphasis of the "cape and sword" plays of the Golden Age.

Puys (Fr.). Groups of secular performers in the Middle Ages whose leanings were literary and who presented both farces and religious plays.

Quick-change room. Arrangement on stage level for actors requiring a costume change when their time offstage is too short to permit their returning to their dressingrooms.

Rake. The slope of the stage floor upward from the audience.

Rail. The piece of wood forming the top or the bottom of a flat.

Realism. Literary and theatrical movement beginning in the late nineteenth century which attempted to treat subjects with fidelity to nature or to real life.

Régisseur (Fr.). Term applied since the Middle Ages, particularly on the Continent, to the stage director.

Rehearsal. The preparation and practice of an acting company for the ultimate performance before an audience in a given play.

Relieve. A set piece in three dimensions; first applied in the Restoration.

Repertorio (Ital.). A set speech of advice or tirade in the *commedia dell'arte*.

Reveal. A false-thickness piece used in the openings of a box set, such as doors or windows, to give the appearance of solidity.

Revolving stage. A large turntable in the center of the stage on which varying numbers of sets are placed; it is turned to show a single set to the audience.

Repertory. A type of theatrical organization which has several plays ready to perform, and produces them alternately.

Rhetorick. In Elizabethan times, the study of voice and gesture in systematised form.

Ritterdramen (Ger.). Nineteenth-century plays of chivalry.

Romancero (Sp.). Early Spanish heroic ballad.

Rührstücke (Ger.). Nineteenth-century sentimental melodrama.

Sacre rappresentazione (Ital.). The "holy drama" or Bible play of the Middle Ages and later.

Satire. A type of literary composition which holds up to scorn or ridicule various follies, vices, and abuses, often with the purpose of correcting these excesses.

Satura (Lat.). Literally, "medley"; a kind of variety show popular in early Roman times.

Satyr play. Type of classic Greek drama perpetuating the worship of Dionysus, in which the performers were dressed like satyrs; riotous and often lascivious.

Scabilla (Lat.). A kind of wooden tap on the shoes of the dancers in Roman pantomimes.

Scaena ductilis (Lat.). Moveable painted screens used between the columns on stages of the early Greek theatre.

Scene. The stage setting; also the division of a play or the act of a play; also the locale where the action supposedly takes place.

Scop. Traveling entertainer in Anglo-Saxon England.

Segundo galan (Sp.). The second leading man of a theatrical company.

Set. The scenery and properties for an act or scene (n.); also, the act of putting this scenery in place on the stage (v.).

Set piece. Any piece of scenery, usually rather small, standing by itself in the scene.

Sequentiae (Lat.). Wordless sequences of notes sung on the last syllable of the "Alleluia" in the Mass of the early medieval church; an early step in the development of the cycle plays.

Shadow show. Puppets lighted from behind which cast shadows on a screen or cloth hanging between them and the audience.

Sharer. Member of an Elizabethan acting company whose income was derived from the division of the profits.

Shares. Designated and predetermined portions of the profits of acting companies, particularly in seventeenth-century France and Restoration England; assigned whole or in part to various members.

Shite (Jap.). The leading actor in a Noh company.

Show boat. A river packet, fitted out with a theatre, which, in America, traveled from place to place on the great inland rivers, giving performances.

Shutters. Two flats which met to close off the scene at the back in Restoration theatre; they could be drawn off.

Siglo de Oro (Sp.). The Golden Age of Lope de Vega.

Sikinnis (Gr.). Bawdy dance characteristic of the classic satyr play.

Sill irons. Term used to describe flat metal pieces used across the bottom of openings in flats to add strength.

Simultaneous setting. *See* Multiple setting.

Skene (Gr.). Name for the scene house in ancient Greek theatres.

Skenography (Gr.). The art of decorating the stage in the classic theatre.

Sky border. *See* Border.

Sky dome. Curved plaster dome around the sides and back, and over the top of the stage, for the purpose of creating unusual lighting effects; now generally transplanted by the cyclorama (*q.v.*).

Slips. The late eighteenth and early nineteenth century designation for the ends of the upper tiers of seats nearest the stage.

Sociétés joyeuses (Fr.). Groups producing secular plays in the Middle Ages.

Sotie (Fr.). Short, farcical medieval play; topical and satirical in nature.

Soubrette. The role of a pert young maid servant or lady's maid in a play; the actress playing such a role.

Stage brace. *See* Brace.

Stage door. Entrance from the outside to the onstage areas, used by performers and technicians.

Stalls. In England, the individual seats in the orchestra between the front of the stage and the pit.

Stiles. The wooden strips which form the sides of a flat.

Stock company. A more or less permanent company of actors who prepare and present plays in sequence at stated intervals; in America, "summer stock" is applied to such a group functioning through the summer months.

Stock set. A standard stage setting of drawing room, garden, and so forth, used in more than one play.

Sturm und Drang (Ger.). Eighteenth-century literary movement, Romantic in nature.

Subplot. A secondary line of action in a play.

Super. Short for "supernumerary"; a performer who has a small part with no lines to speak.

Surrealism. A twentieth-century movement in literature and art, based on the uncontrolled exercise of imagination and, as influenced by psychoanalysis, seeking to suggest the activities of the subconscious mind.

Tablados (Sp.). Temporary stages of the Golden Age used in conjunction with *carros* (*q.v.*) in the presentation of elaborate religious plays.

Tableaux vivants (Fr.). Biblical, allegorical, historical or fanciful scenes, using the still and silent figures of live actors, mounted on platforms or wagons, and featured in the festivities welcoming personages of note throughout the period of the Renaissance.

Tail. The train of the tragedy queen during the Restoration and early eighteenth century.

Tarltonizing. The extemporaneous composition of witty verse, from Richard Tarleton, Elizabethan actor who excelled in this pursuit.

Théâtres de la foires (Fr.). Open-air stages and their productions at the great fairs of France and Italy during the late Renaissance and seventeenth century.

Theatrum (Lat.). Amphitheatre-like hall of the early Renaissance, usually small in size.

Theoric money. Term used for the sum of money considered the due right of every Athenian citizen to enable him to see the plays at the Great Festival of Dionysus.

Throwline. The cord used to tie flats together to form a wall, as in a box set.

Thymele (Gr.). The altar set in the center of the orchestra in the ancient Greek theatre.

Thyromata (Gr.). The openings in the stage-house wall on the second story of the Hellenistic theatre.

Tirade. Long, impassioned speech typically written for the leading characters of French neoclassic drama.

Tireman. Elizabethan theatre functionary roughly equivalent to the modern wardrobe master.

Toggle rail. The middle rail of a flat.

Tonnelet. Short, bell-like skirt formed of wickerwork covered with cloth and decorated with fringe; typically worn as stage costume by early eighteenth-century French heroes.

Tormenter. Curtains or flats at the sides of the stage behind the proscenium, forming an inner frame for the stage.

Tragic carpet. Green baize covering for the stage floor, put down when a tragedy was to be played, and in use from the late seventeenth to the early nineteenth century.

Tragoedus (Lat.). Roman performer specializing in tragedy.

Tramoyas (Sp.). Devices on the stage allowing for visual illusion and tricks.

Transparencies. Term used in the Restoration and after for what the modern theatre knows as a gauze cloth (*q.v.*).

Trap. Any opening in the stage floor or walls of the scene which can be closed when and if it is desirable. The grave trap is traditionally center stage in the floor, the corner trap in a corner of the stage; the Corsican trap allowed figures to rise from below stage and seem to glide across the stage while continuously rising; the vamp trap, in the stage floor or the walls of the scenery, allowed actors seemingly to pass through a solid since it consisted of two spring leaves which closed behind him; there are many other variations.

Tree border. *See* Border.

Tribunalia (Lat.). Special boxes, one to either side of the stage, in the Roman theatre.

Trilogy. Series of three plays, usually on a single theme or with a single story line.

Tropes. *Sequentiae* (*q.v.*) with words added—one syllable to each note of music.

Upstage. In a direction away from the audience.

Vaudeville. In the nineteenth century, light topical amusements set to music; more recently a variety show with many differing acts, or "turns."

Velum (Lat.). The linen roof sometimes stretched over the spectators in the Roman theatre.

Vestuario (Sp.). Name given the dressing-rooms of the actors in theatres of the Golden Age.

Vexillators. The medieval standard bearers who gave notice to the public that a cycle-play was ready for performance.

Vista. Nineteenth-century stage setting featuring a high scene in perspective.

Vomitoria (Lat.). The arched exit passageways in the Roman theatre.

Wagon stage. A number of low platforms mounted on rollers, each carrying a portion of the set, rolled on from the wings to form the complete set.

Well-made play. Term applied to the nineteenth-century dramas of Scribe and Sardou particularly, which were characterized by clear-cut plot structures and easily identifiable characters.

Wings. Offstage areas to either side of the stage; persons or objects there are said to be "in the wings."

Wing flat. A flat at the side of the stage parallel to the footlights or the edge of the stage; matching pairs of these set in perspective formed the standard stage set almost universally from the Renaissance to the nineteenth century.

Zanni (Ital.). Generic term applied to the male servant characters in the *commedia dell'arte*.

BIBLIOGRAPHY

This bibliography is not exhaustive. It lists significant and helpful books in the various periods of theatre, and will serve as a basis for further study and research.

General
Altman, George and others. *Theatre Pictorial. A History of World Theatre as Recorded in Drawings, Paintings, Engravings, and Photographs.* Berkeley: University of California Press, 1953.

Anderson, John. *The American Theatre.* New York: Dial, 1938.

Baker, Blanche. *Dramatic Bibliography.* New York: H. W. Wilson, 1933.

Baker, Henry Barton. *History of the London Stage, 1576–1903.* 2 vols. London: Routledge, 1904.

Barton, Lucy. *Historic Costume for the Stage.* Boston: Baker, 1935.

Bates, Alfred (ed.). *The Drama.* 22 vols. London: Athenian Society, 1903–9.

Cheney, Sheldon. *The Theatre, 3000 Years of Drama, Acting, and Stagecraft.* New York: Longmans, Green, 1929.

Clark, Barrett H. *European Theories of the Drama.* New York: Crown, 1947.

Cleaver, James. *The Theatre Through the Ages.* London: Harrup, 1946.

Coad, Oral S. and Mims, Edwin, Jr. *The American Stage.* "Pageant of America Series." New Haven: Yale University Press, 1929.

Cole, Toby and Chinoy, Helen Krich (eds.). *Actors on Acting, The Theories, Techniques, and Practices of the Great Actors of All Times as Told in Their Own Words.* New York: Crown, 1949.

Davenport, Millia. *The Book of Costume.* 2 vols. New York: Crown, 1948.

Freedley, George and Reeves, John A. *A History of the Theatre.* New York: Crown, 1941.

Fuller, Edmund. *A Pageant of the Theatre.* New York: Crowell, 1941.

Gassner, John. *Masters of the Drama.* New York: Crown, 1947.

Gilder, Rosamund and Freedley, George. *Theatre Collections in Libraries and Museums.* New York: Theatre Arts, 1936.

Granville, Wilfred. *Theatre Dictionary: British and American Terms in the Drama, Opera, and Ballet.* New York: Philosophical Library, 1952.

Hartnoll, Phyllis. *The Oxford Companion to the Theatre.* Oxford: Clarendon, 1957.

Hewitt, Barnard. *Theatre, U.S.A., 1668–1957.* New York: McGraw-Hill, 1959.

Hughes, Glenn. *A History of the American Theatre, 1700–1950.* New York: French, 1951.

————. *The Story of the Theatre.* New York: French, 1928.

Macgowan, Kenneth and Melnitz, William. *The Living Stage.* Englewood Cliffs, N.J.: Prentice-Hall, 1955.

Mantzius, Karl. *A History of Theatrical Art.* 6 vols. Translated by L. von Cassel. London: Duckworth, 1903–21.

Millet, Fred B. and Bentley, Gerald E. *The Art of the Drama.* New York: Appleton-Century-Crofts, 1952.

Moses, Montrose J. and Brown, John Mason. *The American Theatre as Seen by Its Critics.* New York: Norton, 1934.

Nagler, Alois M. *Sources of Theatrical History.* New York: Theatre Annual, 1952.

Nicoll, Allardyce. *The Development of the Theatre* (3rd ed., rev.). New York: Harcourt, Brace, 1948.

————. *The English Stage.* London: Nelson, 1936.

————. *World Drama: from Aeschylus to Anouilh.* New York: Harcourt, Brace, 1950.

Odell, G. C. D. *Annals of the New York Stage.* 15 vols. New York: Columbia University Press, 1927–49.

Oenslager, Donald. *Scenery Then and Now.* New York: Norton, 1936.

Quinn, Arthur Hobson. *A History of American Drama from the Beginnings to the Civil War.* New York: Crofts, 1946.

————. *A History of American Drama from the Civil War to the Present Day.* New York: Crofts, 1945.

Reinach, Salomon. *Orpheus, A History of Religions.* New York: Liveright, 1930.

Sachs, Curt. *World History of the Dance.* Translated by Bessie Schoenberg. New York: Norton, 1937.

Simonson, Lee. *The Stage Is Set.* New York: Harcourt, Brace, 1932.

Sobel, Bernard. *The Theatre Handbook and Digest.* New York: Crown, 1948.

Stevens, Thomas Wood. *The Theatre from Athens to Broadway.* New York: Appleton-Century, 1932.

Stuart, Donald Clive. *The Development of Dramatic Art.* New York: Appleton, 1928.

Thorpe, Evelyn. *Here We Go Round. The Story of the Dance.* New York: Morrow, 1926.

Van Loon, Henrik. *The Arts.* New York: Simon & Shuster, 1937.

Ward, Alfred Charles. *Specimens of English Dramatic Criticism, 17th–20th Centuries.* London: Milford, 1945.

Wells, H. G. *Outline of History.* New York: Garden City, 1925.

Who's Who in the Theatre. London: Pitman, published annually.

Primitive Theatre

Brown, Ivor. *First Player. The Origin of Drama.* New York: Morrow, 1928.

Budge, E. A. Wallis. *Osiris and the Egyptian Resurrection.* London: Warner, 1911.

Calverton, V. F. *The Making of Man. An Outline of Anthropology.* New York: Modern Library, 1931.

Fraser, James George. *The Golden Bough: A Study in Magic and Religion.* New York: Macmillan, 1922.

Harrison, Jane Ellen. *Ancient Art and Ritual.* New York: Holt, 1931.

————. *Mythology.* Boston: Marshall Jones, 1924.

Havemeyer, Loomis. *The Drama of Savage Peoples.* New Haven: Yale University Press, 1916.

Macgowan, Kenneth and Rosse, Herman. *Masks and Demons.* New York: Harcourt, Brace, 1923.

Malinowski, Bronislaw. *Myth in Primitive Psychology.* New York: Norton, 1926.

Ridgeway, William. *The Dramas and Dramatic Dances of Non-European*

Races. Cambridge: University Press, 1915.

Speck, Frank G. and Broom, Leonard. *Cherokee Dance and Drama.* In collaboration with Will West Long. Berkeley: University of California Press, 1951.

Greek and Roman Theatre

Allen, James Turney. *Stage Antiquities of the Greeks and Romans and Their Influence.* New York: Longmans, Green, 1927.

Bieber, Margarete. *The History of Greek and Roman Theatre* (rev. ed.). Princeton: University Press, 1960.

Cornford, Francis M. *The Origin of Attic Comedy.* New York: Macmillan, 1934.

Donaldson, John William. *The Theatre of the Greeks.* London: Bell, 1887.

Flickinger, Roy C. *The Greek Theatre and Its Drama* (4th ed.). Chicago: University of Chicago Press, 1960.

Fowler, Harold N. *History of Roman Literature.* New York: Macmillan, 1932.

Haigh, A. E. *The Attic Theatre.* Oxford: Clarendon, 1907.

Hamilton, Edith. *The Greek Way.* New York: Norton, 1930.

Harrison, Jane Ellen. *Prolegomena to the Study of Greek Religion.* Cambridge: University Press, 1908.

Kitto, H. D. F. *Greek Tragedy. A Literary Study* (rev. ed.). New York: Doubleday, 1950.

Lord, Louis B. *Aristophanes: His Plays and Influence.* Boston: Marshall Jones, 1925.

Pickard-Cambridge, A. W. *The Theatre of Dionysus in Athens.* Oxford: Clarendon, 1946.

———. *The Dramatic Festivals of Athens.* Oxford. Clarendon, 1953.

Saunders, Catharine. *Costume in Roman Comedy.* New York: Columbia University Press, 1909.

Vitruvius. *Ten Books on Architecture.* Translated by Morris Hicky Morgan. Cambridge: Harvard University Press, 1914.

Medieval Theatre

Chambers, E. K. *The Medieval Stage.* 2 vols. Oxford: Clarendon, 1903.

Cohen, Gustave. *Histoire de la Mise en Scène dans le Théâtre Religieus du Moyen Âge.* Paris: Champion, 1926.

Frank, Grace. *The Medieval French Drama.* Oxford: Clarendon, 1954.

Hussey, Maurice (ed.). *The Chester Mystery Plays.* London: Heinemann, 1957.

Jusserand, J. J. *English Wayfaring Life in the Middle Ages.* Translated by Lucy T. Smith. London: Unwin, 1897.

Mackenzie, W. Roy. *The English Moralities.* London: Gill, 1914.

Monmerque, L. J. *Théâtre Français au Moyen Âge.* Paris: Firmin Didot, 1929.

Nicoll, Allardyce. *Masks, Mimes, and Miracles.* New York: Harcourt, Brace, 1932.

Pollard, Alfred W. *English Miracle Plays, Moralities, and Interludes.* Oxford: Clarendon, 1927.

Purnis, J. O. (ed.). *The York Cycle of Mystery Plays.* New York: Macmillan, 1950.

Rudwin, M. J. *Historical and Bibliographical Survey of the German Religious Drama.* Pittsburgh: University of Pittsburgh Press, 1924.

Stuart, Donald Clive. *Stage Decoration in France in the Middle Ages.* New York: Columbia University Press, 1910.

Stratman, Carl J. *Bibliography of Medieval Drama.* Berkeley: University of California Press, 1954.

Young, Karl. *The Drama of the Medieval Church.* 2 vols. Oxford: Clarendon, 1933.

Early Renaissance and Elizabethan Theatre

Adams, John Cranford. *The Globe Playhouse, Its Design and Equipment.* Cambridge: University Press, 1942.

Adams, Joseph Quincy. *Shakespearean Playhouses.* Boston: Houghton Mifflin, 1917.

Albright, Victor E. *The Shakesperian Stage.* New York: Columbia University Press, 1909.

Baker, Henry B. *The London Stage, 1576–1888.* London: Hallen, 1889.

Baldwin, Thomas W. *Organization and Personnel of Shakespeare's Company.* Princeton: University Press, 1927.

Boas, F. S. *An Introduction to Tudor Drama.* Oxford: Clarendon, 1933.

———. *University Drama in the Tudor Age.* Oxford: Clarendon, 1914.

Bradbrook, M. C. *Elizabethan Stage Conditions.* Cambridge: University Press, 1932.

Brooke, C. F. Tucker. *The Tudor Drama*. Boston: Houghton Mifflin, 1911.

Campbell, Lily B. *Scenes and Machines on the English Stage During the Renaissance*. New York: Macmillan, 1923.

Chambers, E. K. *The Elizabethan Stage*. 4 vols. Oxford: Clarendon, 1923.

Crawford, J. P. W. *Spanish Drama Before Lope de Vega*. Philadelphia: Lippincott, 1937.

Cunliffe, J. W. *Influence of Seneca on Elizabethan Tragedy*. New York: Stechert, 1925.

Ducharte, Pierre Louis. *The Italian Comedy*. Translated by Randolph T. Weaver. London: Harrup, 1929.

Harbage, Alfred. *Shakespeare's Audience*. New York: Columbia University Press, 1941.

————. *Shakespeare and the Rival Traditions*. New York: Macmillan, 1952.

Hewitt, Barnard (ed.). *The Renaissance Stage. Documents of Serlio, Sabbattini and Furttenbach*. Coral Gables: University of Miami Press, 1958.

Hodges, C. Walter. *Shakespeare and the Players*. New York: Coward McCann, 1948.

Hotson, Leslie. *Shakespeare's Wooden O*. New York: Macmillan, 1960.

Kennard, James Spencer. *Masks and Marionettes*. New York: Macmillan, 1935.

Kernodle, George R. *From Art to Theatre*. Chicago: University of Chicago Press, 1944.

Knight, G. W. *Principles of Shakesperian Production*. London: Faber & Faber, 1936.

Lawrence, W. J. *Physical Conditions of Elizabethan Public Playhouses*. Cambridge: Harvard University Press, 1927.

————. *Pre-Restoration Stage Studies*. Cambridge: Harvard University Press, 1927.

Lea, Kathleen M. *The Italian Popular Comedy: A Study in the Commedia dell'Arte*. 2 vols. Oxford: Clarendon, 1934.

Linthicum, M. Channing. *Costume in the Drama of Shakespeare and His Contemporaries*. Oxford: Clarendon, 1936.

Manly, John M. *Specimens of Pre-Shakesperian Drama*. Boston: Ginn, 1897.

Nagler, Alois M. *Shakespeare's Stage*. New Haven: Yale University Press, 1959.

Nungezer, Edwin. *A Dictionary of Actors and Other Persons Associated with the Public Representation of Plays in England Before 1642*. New Haven: Yale University Press, 1929.

Poel, William. *Shakespeare in the Theatre*. London: Sidgewick & Jackson, 1913.

Reed, A. W. *Early Tudor Drama*. London: Methuen, 1926.

Rennert, Hugo Albert. *The Spanish Stage in the Time of Lope de Vega*. New York: Hispanic Society, 1909.

Reynolds, G. F. *The Staging of Elizabethan Plays at the Red Bull Theatre, 1605–1625*. New York: Modern Language Association, 1940.

Shoemaker, William H. *The Multiple Stage in Spain During the Fifteenth and Sixteenth Centuries*. Princeton: University Press, 1935.

Smith, Winifred. *The Commedia dell'Arte*. New York: Columbia University Press, 1912.

————. *Italian Actors of the Renaissance*. New York: Coward McCann, 1930.

Stopes, Charlotte C. *Burbage and Shakespeare's Stage*. London: Moring, 1918.

Sullivan, Mary. *The Court Masques of James I*. New York: Putnam, 1913.

Thorndike, Ashley H. *Shakespeare's Theatre*. New York: Macmillan, 1916.

Underhill, John Garret (ed.). *Four Plays by Lope de Vega*. New York: Scribner, 1936.

Venesky, Alice S. *Pageantry on the Shakespearian Stage*. New York: Crown, 1951.

Welsford, Enid. *The Court Masque*. New York: Macmillan, 1928.

Wiley, W. L. *The Early Public Theatre in France*. Cambridge: Harvard University Press, 1960.

The Seventeenth Century

Bentley, Gerald Eades. *Jacobean and Caroline Stage*. Oxford: Clarendon, 1941.

Boswell, Eleanore. *The Restoration Court Stage*. Cambridge: Harvard University Press, 1932.

Despois, E. Z. *Le Théâtre Français sous Louis XIV*. Paris: Hachette, 1894.

Elwin, Malcolm. *The Playgoers Handbook to Restoration Drama*. New York: Macmillan, 1928.

Fournel, François Victor. *Les Contemporaines de Molière*. Paris: Firmin Didot, 1863–75.

Harbage, Alfred. *Thomas Killigrew, Cavalier Dramatist.* Philadelphia: University of Pennsylvania Press, 1930.

Hawkins, Frederick. *Annals of the French Stage from Its Origins to the Death of Racine.* 2 vols. London: Chapman & Hall, 1884.

Hotson, Leslie. *The Commonwealth and Restoration Stage.* Cambridge: Harvard University Press, 1928.

Krutch, Joseph Wood. *Comedy and Conscience After the Restoration.* New York: Columbia University Press, 1949.

Lancaster, H. C. *French Dramatic Literature in the Seventeenth Century.* 5 vols. Baltimore: Johns Hopkins Press, 1929–36.

Lough, John. *Paris Theatre Audiences in the Seventeenth and Eighteenth Centuries.* Oxford: University Press, 1957.

Lynch, James, J. *Box, Pit, and Gallery, Stage and Society in Johnson's London.* Berkeley: University of California Press, 1953.

Miles, Dudley. *The Influence of Molière on the Restoration Comedy.* New York: Columbia University Press, 1910.

Nicoll, Allardyce. *History of Restoration Drama.* Cambridge: University Press, 1923.

———. *Stuart Masques and the Renaissance.* New York: Harcourt, Brace, 1938.

Odell, G. C. D. *Shakespeare from Betterton to Irving.* 2 vols. New York: Scribner, 1920.

Ordich, T. F. *Early London Theatres.* London: Stock, 1894.

Rosenfeld, Sybil. *Strolling Players and Drama in the Provinces, 1660-1765.* Cambridge: University Press, 1935.

Southern, Richard. *Changeable Scenery.* London: Faber & Faber, 1952.

Spencer, Hazelton. *Shakespeare Improved: Restoration Versions.* Cambridge: Harvard University Press, 1927.

Summers, Montague. *The Playhouse of Pepys.* New York: Macmillan, 1935.

———. *The Restoration Theatre.* New York: Macmillan, 1934.

Thaler, Alwin. *Shakespeare to Sheridan.* Cambridge: Harvard University Press, 1922.

Oriental Theatre

Arlington, L. C. *Chinese Drama from the Earliest Times to the Present Day.* Shanghai: Kelly & Walsh, 1930.

Avand, Muk Raj. *The Indian Theatre.* New York: Roy, 1951.

Bowers, Faubion. *Theatre in the East: A Survey of Asian Dance and Drama.* London: Nelson, 1951.

Buss, Kate. *Studies in the Chinese Drama.* New York: Cape and Smith, 1930.

Chu-Chia-Chien. *Chinese Theatre.* Translated by James A. Graham. London: Lane, 1922.

Edwards, Osman. *Japanese Plays and Playfellows.* London: Heinemann, 1901.

Ernst, Earle. *The Kabuki Theatre.* New York: Oxford University Press, 1957.

———. *Three Japanese Plays from the Traditional Theatre.* New York: Oxford University Press, 1959.

Fenollose, E. F. and Pound, Ezra. *Noh, or Accomplishment.* New York: Knopf, 1917.

Guhathkurta, P. G. *Bengali Drama.* London: Routledge, 1930.

Hamamura, Yonezo and others. *Kabuki.* Translated by Fumi Takano. Tokyo: Kenkyusha, 1956.

Haas, George C. O. *Dasarupa: A Treatise on Hindu Dramaturgy.* New York: Columbia University Press, 1912.

Horrwitz, E. P. *The Indian Theatre.* London: Blackie, 1912.

Kincaid, Zoe. *Kabuki: the Popular Stage of Japan.* New York: Macmillan, 1925.

Lombard, Frank Alanson. *An Outline History of the Japanese Drama.* London: Allen & Unwin, 1928.

Scott, A. C. *The Classical Theatre of China.* London: Allen & Unwin, 1957.

Waley, Arthur. *The Noh Plays of Japan.* New York: Knopf, 1922.

Wilson, H. H. and others. *The Theatre of the Hindus.* Calcutta: Susil Gupta, 1955.

Yajnik, R. K. *The Indian Theatre.* New York: Dutton, 1934.

Yohannan, John D. (ed.). *A Treasury of Asian Literature.* New York: Day, 1956.

Zucker, Adolph Edward. *Chinese Theatre.* Boston: Little, Brown, 1925.

The Eighteenth Century

Aghion, M. *Le Théâtre à Paris au XVIII Siècle.* Paris: Librarie de France, 1926.

Armstrong, Cecil. *The Century of Great Actors.* London: Mills & Boom, 1912.

Avery, E. L. *Congreve's Plays on the Eighteenth Century Stage*. New York: Modern Language Association, 1951.

Bateson, F. N. W. *English Comic Drama, 1700–1750*. Oxford: Clarendon, 1929.

Bernbaum, Ernest. *The Drama of Sensibility*. Boston: Ginn, 1915.

Boaden, James. *Memoirs of Mrs. Siddons*. London: Gibbings, 1893.

Bruford, W. H. *Theatre, Drama, and Audience in Goethe's Germany*. London: Routledge & Kegan Paul, 1950.

Cibber, Colley. *Apology for His Life*. 2 vols. London: Nimmo, 1888.

Diderot, Denis. *Paradox of Acting*. London: Chatto, 1883.

Dunlap, William. *History of the American Theatre*. New York: Scott, 1833.

Dryden, John. *Essays*. Oxford: Clarendon Press, 1900.

Fitzgerald, P. H. *Life of David Garrick*. London: Simpkin Marshall, 1899.

Fyvie, John. *Comedy Queens of the Georgian Era*. London: Simpkin Marshall, 1899.

Genest, John. *Some Account of the English Stage, 1660–1830*. 10 vols. London: Carrington, 1832.

Goldstein, Malcolm. *Pope and the Augustan Stage*. Stanford: University Press, 1958.

Green, Frederick Charles. *Eighteenth Century France*. New York: Appleton, 1931.

Gray, Charles Harold. *Theatrical Criticism in London to 1795*. New York: Columbia University Press, 1931.

Hawkins, Frederick W. *The French Stage in the Eighteenth Century*. 2 vols. London: Chapman, 1888.

Hedgecock, Frank. *David Garrick and His French Friends*. London: Stanley Paul, 1911.

Hyde-Smith, Naomi. *A Portrait of Mrs. Siddons*. New York: Viking, 1933.

Jourdain, Eleanor Frances. *Dramatic Theory and Practice in France, 1690–1808*. New York: Longmans, 1921.

Knight, Joseph. *David Garrick*. London: Kegan Paul, Trench, Truber, 1894.

Loftus, John. *Steele at Drury Lane*. Berkeley: University of California Press, 1952.

Melville, Lewis. *Stage Favorites of the Eighteenth Century*. London: Hutchinson, 1929.

————. *Life and Letters of John Gay.*

London: O'Conner, 1921.

Molloy, J. Fitzgerald. *Life and Adventures of Peg Woffington*. 2 vols. New York: Dodd Mead, 1892.

Nettleton, G. H. *English Drama of the Restoration and Eighteenth Century, 1642–1780*. New York: Macmillan, 1914.

Nicoll, Allardyce. *History of Early Eighteenth Century Drama*. Cambridge: University Press, 1925.

————. *History of Late Eighteenth Century Drama*. Cambridge: University Press, 1927.

Paget, Violet. *Studies of the Eighteenth Century in Italy*. New York: McClurg, 1907.

Scholz, Janos. *Baroque and Romantic Stage Design*. New York: Buckhurst, 1949.

Seilhamer, G. O. *History of the American Theatre*. Philadelphia: Globe, 1891.

Sherwin, Oscar. *Mr. Gay*. New York: Day, 1929.

Southern, Richard. *Changeable Scenery*. London: Faber & Faber, 1952.

Stein, Elizabeth. *David Garrick*. New York: Modern Language Association, 1938.

Sichel, W. *Sheridan*. 2 vols. New York: Houghton Mifflin, 1909.

Watson, E. B. *Sheridan to Robertson*. Cambridge: Harvard University Press, 1926.

The Nineteenth Century

Archer, William. *Eminent Actors*. London: Asperne, 1894.

————. *Masks or Faces?* New York: Longmans, 1888.

Arvin, Neil Cole. *Eugene Scribe and the French Theatre, 1815–1860*. Cambridge: Harvard University Press, 1924.

Brereton, Austin. *Life of Henry Irving*. 2 vols. New York: Longmans, Green, 1902.

Brown, Thomas Allston. *History of the New York Stage, 1836–1918*. New York: Dodd Mead, 1923.

Carson, William G. B. *The Theatre on the Frontier: The Early Years of the St. Louis Stage*. Chicago: University of Chicago Press, 1932.

Clarke, A. B. *The Elder and Younger Booth*. New York: Osgood, 1882.

524

Cole, J. W. *Life and Theatrical Times of Charles Kean.* London: Bentley, 1859.

Cost, March. *I, Rachel.* New York: Vanguard, 1958.

Doran, John. *"Their Majesties' Servants".* London: Nimmo, 1897.

Eaton, Walter Prichard. *At the New Theatre and Others.* Boston: Small Maynard, 1910.

Filon, P. M. A. *The English Stage.* New York: Dodd, 1897.

Frohman, Daniel. *Memories of a Manager.* New York: Doubleday Page, 1911.

Graham, Philip. *Showboats: The History of an American Institution.* Austin: University of Texas Press, 1951.

Grube, Max. *Geschichte du Meiningen.* Berlin: Hesse, 1926.

Hawkins, F. W. *The Life of Edmund Kean.* 2 vols. London: Tinsley, 1869.

Hornblow, Arthur. *History of the Theatre in America.* 2 vols. Philadelphia: Lippincott, 1919.

Hutton, Laurence. *Curiosities of the American Stage.* New York: Harpers, 1891.

Kennard, Joseph Spencer. *The Italian Theatre.* 2 vols. New York: Rudge, 1932.

Klenze, Camille von. *From Goethe to Hauptmann.* New York: Viking, 1926.

Lewes, George Henry. *On Actors and the Art of Acting.* New York: Brentano's, 1875.

Macqueen-Pope, W. *Nights of Gladness.* London: Hutchinson, 1956.

Mathews, Brander. *The Theatres of Paris.* London: Sampson, Low, Marston, Searle & Rivington, 1880.

Nicoll, Allardyce. *History of Early Nineteenth Century Drama.* Cambridge: University Press, 1930.

———. *History of Late Nineteenth Century Drama.* Cambridge: University Press, 1949.

Pearce, C. E. *Madame Vestris and Her Times.* London: Stanley Paul, 1923.

Rowell, George. *The Victorian Theatre: A Survey.* London: Oxford University Press, 1956.

Sherson, E. *London's Lost Theatres of the Nineteenth Century.* London: Lane, 1925.

Toynbee, William C. (ed.). *Diaries of William Charles Macready.* New York: Putnam, 1912.

Vardac, A. Nicholas. *Stage to Screen: Theatrical Method from Garrick to Griffith.* Cambridge: Harvard University Press, 1949.

Varneke, B. V. *History of the Russian Theatre.* New York: Macmillan, 1951.

Walkley, Arthur B. *Playhouse Impressions.* London: Unwin, 1892.

Wilson, Albert Edward. *Penny Plain, Two Pence Colored: A History of Juvenile Drama.* New York: Macmillan, 1932.

Witkowski, George. *German Drama of the Nineteenth Century.* New York: Holt, 1909.

Wood, William Burke. *Personal Recollections of the Stage.* Philadelphia: Baird, 1854.

The Twentieth Century

Andrews, John and Trilling, Ossia. *International Theatre.* London: Sampson Low, 1949.

Bakshy, Alexander. *The Path of the Modern Russian Stage.* Boston: Luce, 1918.

Blum, Daniel C. *A Pictorial History of the American Theatre, 1900–1956.* New York: Greenberg, 1956.

Bowers, Faubion. *Broadway U.S.S.R.: Ballet, Theatre and Entertainment in Russia Today.* New York: Nelson, 1959.

Boyd, Ernest A. *The Contemporary Drama of Ireland.* Boston: Little, Brown, 1928.

Boyle, Walden. *Central and Flexible Staging.* Berkeley: University of California Press, 1955.

Brown, John Mason. *Upstage.* New York: Norton, 1930.

Burris-Meyer, Harold and Cole, Edward C. *Theatres and Auditoriums.* New York: Reinhold, 1949.

Byrne, Dawson. *The Story of Ireland's National Theatre.* Dublin: Talbot, 1929.

Carter, Huntly. *The Theatre of Max Reinhardt.* London: Palmer, 1914.

———. *The New Spirit in the European Theatre, 1914–1924.* New York: Doran, 1925.

Chandler, Frank W. *The Contemporary Drama of France.* Boston: Little, Brown, 1925.

Cheney, Sheldon. *The Art Theatre.* New York: Knopf, 1925.

———. *New Movement in the Theatre.* New York: Kennerley, 1914.

———. *The Open Air Theatre.* New York: Kennerley, 1918.

————. *Stage Decoration.* New York: Day, 1928.

Clark, Barrett H. *The Continental Drama of Today.* New York: Holt, 1915.

———— and Freedley, George. *A History of Modern Drama.* New York: Appleton-Century, 1947.

Clurman, Harold. *The Fervent Years.* New York: Knopf, 1945.

Cook, G. C. and Shay, F. (eds.). *Provincetown Plays.* New York: Appleton, 1921.

Copeau, Jacques. *Souvenirs du Vieux-Columbier.* Paris: Nouvelles Editions Latines, 1931.

Craig, Gordon. *On the Art of the Theatre.* New York: Dodd Mead, 1925.

————. *The Theatre Advancing.* Boston: Little, Brown, 1910.

————. *Towards a New Theatre.* New York: Dutton, 1913.

————. *Scene.* New York: Oxford University Press, 1923.

Dickinson, Thomas H. *The Contemporary Drama of England.* Boston: Little, Brown, 1931.

———— (ed.). *The Theatre in a Changing Europe.* New York: Holt, 1937.

Esslin, Martin. *The Theatre of the Absurd.* New York: Doubleday, 1961.

Fay, Gerard. *The Abbey Theatre, Cradle of Genius.* Dublin: Claimore & Reynolds, 1958.

Flanagan, Hallie. *Arena.* New York: Duell Sloane & Pearce, 1940.

————. *Shifting Scenes of the Modern European Theatre.* New York: Coward-McCann, 1928.

Fuerst, W. L. and Hume, S. J. *Twentieth Century Stage Decoration.* London: Knopf, 1928.

Gagey, Edmond H. *Revolution in American Drama.* New York: Columbia University Press, 1947.

Gorchakov, Nikolai. *The Theatre in Soviet Russia.* Translated by Edgar Lehrman. New York: Columbia University Press, 1957.

Gorelik, Mordecai. *New Theatres for Old.* New York: French, 1940.

Gregor, Joseph and Fülop-Miller, Rene. *The Russian Theatre.* Philadelphia: Lippincott, 1930.

Gregory, Lady Isabella. *Our Irish Theatre.* New York: Putnam, 1913.

Guicharnaud, Jacques. *Modern French Theatre. From Giraudoux to Beckett.*

New Haven: Yale University Press, 1961.

Henderson, Archibald (ed.). *Pioneering a People's Theatre.* Chapel Hill: University of North Carolina Press, 1945.

Hewitt, Barnard (ed.). *Adolphe Appia's "The Work of Living Art" and "Man is the Measure of All Things".* Coral Gables: University of Miami Press, 1960.

Houghton, Norris. *Advance from Broadway: 19,000 Miles of American Theatre.* New York: Harcourt, Brace, 1941.

————. *Moscow Rehearsal.* New York: Harcourt, Brace, 1936.

Jones, Robert Edmond. *Drawings for the Theatre.* New York: Theatre Arts, 1925.

Jones, Margo. *Theatre-in-the-Round.* New York: Rinehart, 1951.

Komisarjevsky, Theodore. *The Costume of the Theatre.* London: Bles, 1931.

Krutch, Joseph Wood. *The American Drama Since 1918.* New York: Random House, 1939.

Langner, Lawrence. *The Magic Curtain.* New York: Dutton, 1951.

MacClintock, Lander. *The Contemporary Drama of Italy.* Boston: Little, Brown, 1920.

Macgowan, Kenneth. *Footlights Across America.* New York: Harcourt, Brace, 1929.

———— and Jones, Robert Edmond. *Continental Stagecraft.* New York: Harcourt, Brace, 1922.

Mackaye, Percy. *The Civic Theatre.* New York: Kennerley, 1912.

Miller, Anna Irene. *The Independent Theatre in Europe.* New York: Long & Smith, 1927.

Mitchell, Roy. *Creative Theatre.* New York: Day, 1929.

Moderwell, Hiram K. *The Theatre of Today.* New York: Dodd Mead, 1923.

Morris, Lloyd. *Curtain Time.* New York: Random House, 1958.

Nemirovitch-Danchenko. *My Life in the Russian Theatre.* Boston: Little, Brown, 1936.

Phelps, William Lyon. *Twentieth Century Theatre.* New York: Macmillan, 1918.

Pronko, Leonard Cabell. *The World of Jean Anouilh.* Berkeley: University of California Press, 1961.

Samuel, Richard and Thoms, R. Hinton. *Expressionism in German Life, Litera-*

ture and the Theatre. Cambridge: University Press, 1939.

Schlemmer, Oska. The Theatre of the Bauhaus. Middleton: Wesleyan University Press, 1961.

Sayler, Oliver M. Max Reinhardt and His Theatre. New York: Brentano's, 1924.

See, Edmond. Mouvement Dramatique. Paris: Les Editions de France, 1933.

Selden, Samuel. The Stage in Action. New York: Crofts, 1941.

Simonson, Lee. The Art of Scenic Design. A Pictorial Analysis of Stage Setting

and Its Relation to Theatrical Production. New York: Harper, 1950.

Stanislavsky, Constantine. My Life in Art. Translated by J. J. Robbins. Boston: Little, Brown, 1938.

Tynan, Kenneth. Curtains. New York: Atheneum, 1961.

Van Gyseghem, Andre. Theatre in Soviet Russia. London: Faber & Faber, 1935.

Waxman, Samuel M. Antoine and the Théâtre Libre. Cambridge: Harvard University Press, 1926.

Weiner, Leo. Contemporary Drama of Russia. Boston: Little, Brown, 1924.

INDEX

Index

529

530